ENCYCLOPEDIA OF AMERICAN HISTORY

Three Worlds Meet
Beginnings to 1607

VOLUME I

ENCYCLOPEDIA OF AMERICAN HISTORY

ENCYCLOPEDIA OF AMERICAN HISTORY

Three Worlds Meet
Beginnings to 1607

VOLUME I

Peter C. Mancall, Editor
Gary B. Nash, General Editor

Facts On File, Inc.

Encyclopedia of American History:
Three Worlds Meet (Beginnings to 1607)

Copyright © 2003 by Peter C. Mancall
Maps Copyright © 2003 by Facts On File, Inc.

Editorial Director: Laurie E. Likoff
Editor in Chief: Owen Lancer
Chief Copy Editor: Michael G. Laraque
Associate Editor: Dorothy Cummings
Production Director: Olivia McKean
Production Associates: Rachel L. Berlin and Theresa Montoya
Art Director: Cathy Rincon
Interior Designer: Joan M. Toro
Desktop Designers: Erika K. Arroyo and David C. Strelecky
Maps and Illustrations: Dale E. Williams and Jeremy Eagle

Facts On File, Inc.
132 West 31st Street
New York NY 10001

Library of Congress Cataloging-in-Publication Data

Encyclopedia of American history / Gary B. Nash, general editor.
p.   cm.
Includes bibliographical references and indexes.
Contents: v. 1. Three worlds meet — v. 2. Colonization and settlement —
v. 3. Revolution and new nation — v. 4. Expansion and reform — v. 5. Civil War
and Reconstruction — v. 6. The development of the industrial United States —
v. 7. The emergence of modern America — v. 8. The Great Depression and
World War II — v. 9. Postwar United States — v. 10. Contemporary
United States. — v. 11 Comprehensive index
ISBN 0-8160-4371-X (set)   ISBN 0-8160-4361-2 (v. 1)
1. United States—History—Encyclopedias. I. Nash, Gary B.
E174 .E53 2002
973′.03—dc21   2001051278

Contents

List of Entries

About the Editors

General Editor: Gary B. Nash received a Ph.D from Princeton University. He is currently director of the National Center for History in the Schools at the University of California, Los Angeles, where he teaches American history of the colonial and Revolutionary era. He is a published author of college and precollegiate history texts. Among his best-selling works is *The American People: Creating a Nation and Society* (Addison Wesley, Longman), now in its fifth edition.

Nash is an elected member of the Society of American Historians, American Academy of Arts and Sciences, and the American Philosophical Society. He has served as past president of the Organization of American Historians, 1994–95, and was a founding member of the National Council for History Education, 1990.

Volume Editor: Peter Mancall, University of Kansas, received his Ph.D. at Harvard University. He is a published author of several books, including *Envisioning America: English Plans for Colonization of North America, 1580-1640* (St. Martin's Press, 1995) and *American Encounters: Natives and Newcomers from European Contact to Indian Removal* (Routledge, 2000).

Foreword

★

The Encyclopedia of American History series is designed as a handy reference to the most important individuals, events, and topics in U.S. history. In 10 volumes, the encyclopedia covers the period from the 15th century, when European explorers first made their way across the Atlantic Ocean to the Americas, to the present day. The encyclopedia is written for precollegiate as well as college students, for parents of young learners in the schools, and for the general public. The volume editors are distinguished historians of American history. In writing individual entries, each editor has drawn upon the expertise of scores of specialists. This ensures the scholarly quality of the entire series. Articles contributed by the various volume editors are uncredited.

This 10-volume encyclopedia of "American history" is broadly conceived to include the historical experience of the various peoples of North America. Thus, in the first volume, many essays treat the history of a great range of indigenous people before contact with Europeans. In the same vein, readers will find essays in the first several volumes that sketch Spanish, Dutch, and French explorers and colonizers who opened up territories for European settlement that later would become part of the United States. The venues and cast of characters in the American historical drama are thus widened beyond traditional encyclopedias.

In creating the eras of American history that define the chronological limits of each volume, and in addressing major topics in each era, the encyclopedia follows the architecture of *The National Standards for United States History, Revised Edition* (Los Angeles: National Center for History in the Schools, 1996). Mandated by the U.S. Congress, the national standards for U.S. history have been widely used by states and school districts in organizing curricular frameworks and have been followed by many other curriculum-building efforts.

Entries are cross-referenced, when appropriate, with *See also* citations at the end of articles. At the end of most entries, a listing of articles and books allows readers to turn to specialized sources and historical accounts. In each volume, an array of maps provide geographical context, while numerous illustrations help vivify the material covered in the text. A time line is included to provide students with a chronological reference to major events occurring in the given era. The selection of historical documents in the back of each volume gives students experience with the raw documents that historians use when researching history. A comprehensive index to each volume also facilitates the reader's access to particular information.

In each volume, long entries are provided for major categories of American historical experience. These categories may include: African Americans, agriculture, art and architecture, business, economy, education, family life, foreign policy, immigration, labor, Native Americans, politics, population, religion, urbanization, and women. By following these essays from volume to volume, the reader can access what might be called a mini-history of each broad topic, for example, family life, immigration, or religion.

— Gary B. Nash
University of California, Los Angeles

Introduction

Three Worlds Meet covers the period from 1492, when Christopher Columbus made his historic voyage to the west, to 1607, the year of the founding of the English settlement at Jamestown, Virginia. It treats "American" history from what we can call its conception to its birth. Unlike the other volumes in this series, *Three Worlds Meet* does not focus on the territory that eventually became the United States. Instead, the entries here cover aspects of the history of the Atlantic world and the four continents on its periphery. Readers will find much on early modern Europe, Africa, and the Americas. Although some entries span the landmass of the modern-day United States, most focus on the peoples from different continents who encountered one another in the century following Columbus's expedition.

What follows in these pages will provide readers with the background necessary for understanding the development of the United States. Even as late as 1607 there was no guarantee that the English would establish successful colonies in North America. At that time the indigenous peoples in the Americas still believed that their lives and communities were secure. The noxious commerce in human beings known as the slave trade had only begun to bring Africans to the Western Hemisphere. Various Europeans envisioned colonies in North America, and books circulating across the Continent from printing presses (a new invention) offered abundant information about what could be found across the Atlantic. Much of the information turned out to be false, and many peoples' dreams never came to fulfillment, but the events from 1492 to 1607 nonetheless left a legacy that Americans continue to confront five centuries later.

— Peter C. Mancall
University of Southern California

ENTRIES
A TO Z

A

Aataentsic

The HURON believed that Aataentsic, although "the mother of mankind" in their creation story, was a deity who brought harm to human beings.

According to the Huron, Aataentsic had originally dwelled in the sky with her husband, where spirits lived in a forested land much like earth. One day she fell to earth through a hole in the sky. As she fell toward the ocean that covered the world, the tortoise saw her falling. He told the other water animals to dive and bring up earth. As they returned, they piled the earth on his back, forming the land. Aataentsic fell safely on this land. Soon after her fall, she gave birth to twin sons, Iouskeha and Tawiscaron. Iouskeha sought to help human beings. He brought good weather, made the lakes and rivers, and showed human beings how to hunt. He also taught people to use fire and grow corn. His brother Tawiscaron was not favorably disposed to humans, and when the brothers grew up they fought, and Iouskeha drove him away. His blood, which fell on the ground as he fled, turned into flint. After this time, Iouskeha and Aataentsic lived together in a bark house far from Huron country.

Aataentsic, who may be identified either as Iouskeha's mother or his maternal grandmother, tried to undo his good works and to harm human beings. She sent disease, made people die, and controlled the souls of the dead. If a traveling Huron found her cabin, she would try to harm him, but her son would try to help the unfortunate traveler. She appeared as an old woman, though she could make herself young again as she pleased. Iouskeha grew old like any human being, but when he became old could rejuvenate himself and become young again.

The anthropologist Bruce Trigger suggested that the story of Aataentsic and Iouskeha functioned to compensate both men and women for the limitations in their roles in daily life. Men, who killed animals in the hunt and other human beings in war, were aggressors in daily life. The male deity Iouskeha, on the other hand, was a life-bringer who gave human beings corn and fire and tried to help them. In Huron society, women raised crops and cared for children, but through the story of Aataentsic they were "flattered by being mythically endowed with dangerous and aggressive qualities." The idea that Aataentsic and her son, though very different in personality, lived together in a bark cabin may have emphasized the complementary roles men and women played in daily life.

Further reading: Elisabeth Tooker, *An Ethnography of the Huron Indians, 1615–1649* (Syracuse, N.Y.: Syracuse University Press, 1991); Bruce G. Trigger, *The Children of Aataentsic: A History of the Huron People to 1660,* vol. 1 (Montreal: McGill-Queen's University Press, 1976); ———, *The Huron: Farmers of the North* (New York: Holt, Rinehart & Winston, 1969).

— Martha K. Robinson

Abenaki

The Abenaki, whose name means "People of the Dawnland," lived in northern New England when Native Americans first met Europeans.

Before 1492 Abenaki territory extended from Lake Champlain on the west to the White Mountains on the east. From north to south it reached from southern Quebec to the Vermont–Massachusetts border. Soon after contact with Europeans the Abenaki suffered from devastating epidemics. The rate of depopulation from these epidemics, which struck before sustained contact with Europeans, is unknown but may have exceeded 75 percent. Because of these death rates and because the first European explorers to visit the Abenaki homeland left few accounts of their journeys, Abenaki history is difficult to reconstruct.

The Indians of New England shared many cultural traits. Many of the groups, including the eastern and western Abenaki, the Maliseet, the Micmac, and the PASSAMAQUODDY nation, referred to themselves collectively as the Wabanaki. The eastern Abenaki lived in Maine; the western Abenaki in New Hampshire and Vermont. The Abenaki did not have the kind of formal tribal structure that Europeans looked for among the peoples whom they met. Instead, they traveled in small bands made up of related families. These bands might come together for a common purpose, such as planting, preparing for war, or holding religious ceremonies, but the Abenaki did not recognize any central authority over all the bands. The Abenaki did have chiefs, some of whom were powerful. More commonly, chiefs had limited powers and could not coerce their followers.

Because the growing season in northern New England is short, the Abenaki did not rely on agriculture. They grew CORN, beans, TOBACCO, and squash, but the staples of their diet came from hunting, fishing, and gathering. Abenaki men hunted, while the women prepared food and clothing. The Abenaki lived in conical wigwams or longhouses. In either case, men constructed the frame, which the women then covered with sewn bark pieces.

The Abenaki believed that the world was full of spiritual forces, some of which were hostile to people. They believed that shamans, or *medeoulin*, could offer protection against dangerous forces. Such shamans might be dangerous themselves, since they could use their powers either to help or to harm the people.

The first known Europeans to visit the area arrived with GIOVANNI DA VERRAZANO in 1524, though the Abenaki did not participate in the fur trade until the 17th century. By the early 17th century the eastern Abenaki and the Micmac were fighting over access to European trade goods.

Further reading: Colin G. Calloway, *The Abenaki* (New York: Chelsea House Publishers, 1989; ———, *The Western Abenakis of Vermont, 1600–1800: War, Migration and the Survival of an Indian People* (Norman: University of Oklahoma Press, 1990); Gordon M. Day, "Western Abenaki," in *Handbook of North American Indians*, William C. Sturtevant, gen. ed, vol. 15, *Northeast*, ed. Bruce G. Trigger (Washington, D.C.: Smithsonian Institution, 1978), 148–159; Dean R. Snow, "Eastern Abenaki," in *Northeast*, ed. Trigger, 137–147.

— Martha K. Robinson

Abyssinia   See Ethiopia

Acadia

The original designation for parts of the North American eastern seaboard that once stretched from colonial New Jersey to the present-day Canadian maritime provinces of Nova Scotia, New Brunswick, and Prince Edward Island,

today Acadia refers only to the lands of present-day Maine and the Canadian maritime provinces.

The origins of the name *Acadia* are unclear. GIOVANNI DA VERRAZANO, an Italian navigator who explored for France, was the first known European to use the term. Verrazano possibly derived it from words used to describe the landscape such as *quoddy* or *cadie,* or more likely modified the word *Arcadia,* the term for a pastoral paradise commonly used in Greek and Roman literature.

Human life in Acadia dates back at least 10,000 years, but knowledge of this history is poor because of meager archaeological records. The circumstances of the first meeting between Europeans and the peoples native to Acadia also remains a matter of conjecture. By July, 1534, when the French explorer JACQUES CARTIER provided the first written account of the inhabitants of Acadia after trading with a group of Micmac, many Europeans had interacted with native peoples. Cartier described the Micmac and MALISEET peoples as enthusiastic traders; the ABENAKI, living along the Kennebec River in present-day Maine, impressed other writers with their bark-covered conical shelters and brilliantly engineered bark canoes.

Often the early interchanges between European settlers and Micmac and other native peoples were amiable, but eventually the relationships proved disastrous to the indigenous peoples. The Micmac taught settlers how to hunt the wildlife of Acadia and shared with them their knowledge of medicinal plants and herbs. In return, the French introduced alcohol and new diseases to the native peoples and helped instill a dependence on European goods that hastened the ruin of traditional ways of life.

Early settlement also proved difficult for the French. Many settlers succumbed to scurvy during the long winters of the early 1600s, while the politics of gaining commercial rights to the new territory, rather than concern for the health of settlers, dominated the French mainland. The majority of settlers, known as Acadians, depended upon the land for their livelihood. They developed a system of dikes that prevented marshes from being flooded by high saltwater tides, yet allowed rainwater and melting snow to flow out. This ingenious alteration of the landscape converted vast salt marshes into arable land. The tremendous amount of labor required to build and maintain the dike system bound neighbors together while the reliability of crop yields spared established communities the miseries of famine. Later, from 1680 to 1740—an epoch known as the golden age of Acadian history—Acadian birth rates were high and child mortality relatively low. Large families of many generations often lived under the same roof, held together by kinship ties and Catholicism.

Though smaller communities were relatively stable, larger political struggles continually interfered in Acadian life. The English claimed the region by rights of the 1497 and 1498 explorations of navigator JOHN CABOT, but sovereignty of the area switched several times during the long struggle for regional supremacy between the English and the French, who first colonized the area at the Bay of Fundy in 1604. Moreover, English settlers from as far away as Virginia resented the French intrusion into Acadia and in 1613 destroyed the French settlement of Saint-Sauveur on the coast of present-day Maine before making their way north and looting and burning the French town of Port Royal. These actions initiated the 150-year struggle for control of the Acadian regions, though most Acadians remained politically neutral. King James I of England granted the land to the Scottish statesman and poet Sir William Alexander in 1621, but control of the region remained unsettled until the English gained permanent, though contested, control of mainland Acadie, or Nova Scotia, through the 1713 Treaty of Utrecht. Yet under the terms of the treaty Île Royale (Cape Breton) and Île Saint-Jean (Prince Edward Island) remained French, provided that those who remained swore an oath of allegiance to the monarch of Great Britain.

Further reading: Sally Ross and Alphonse Deveau, *The Acadians of Nova Scotia: Past and Present* (Halifax, Nova Scotia: Nimbus, 1992); Bona Arsenault, *History of the Acadians,* trans. Brian M. Upton and John G. McLaughlin (Québec, Canada: Le Conseil de la vie française en Amérique, 1966).

— Kevin C. Armitage

Acosta, José de (1540–1600)

A Spanish Jesuit missionary, Acosta is best known for his missionary work in PERU from 1572 to 1586 and his books *De Procuranda Indorum Salute* (1576), in which he avowed that the indigenous peoples of the Americas could be saved according to the teachings of the Catholic Church, *Historia Natural y Moral de las Indias* (1590), a natural history of MEXICO and Peru and a general history of Aztecan and Incan cultures, and *Doctrina Cristiana y Catecismo para Instrucción de los Indios* (1585), the first book published in Peru, consisting of three catechisms printed in Spanish, Quechua, and Aymara.

Born to a wealthy merchant family in CASTILE, Spain, José de Acosta entered the Society of Jesus, or the Jesuit order, in 1552 and took his vows in 1554. As a Jesuit Acosta was trained according to the tenets of Renaissance humanism, an educational and cultural movement popular from the 14th to the 16th centuries in Europe, which focused on classical training in various fields such as philosophy, theology, medicine, and jurisprudence. Acosta taught at Jesuit schools in Spain and Portugal from 1557 to 1559, at which time he commenced university studies

in theology at Alcalá. Acosta was ordained a priest in 1567 and spent the next four years preaching in small towns in Spain. In February 1571, after many requests to be appointed to missionary work, Acosta was assigned to preach and teach theology in Peru. The 14 years Acosta spent in Peru coincided with a period of major reorganization by the political representatives of the Spanish throne, under whose jurisdiction Peru lay. Don Francisco de Toledo, the viceroy to the Kingdom of Peru, made sweeping changes to the political and economic structure of the colony, publicly executing INCAN leaders, confining indigenous peoples to segregated settlements, or REDUCCIONES, and establishing a tribute system, called the *mita,* requiring forced labor in mines. By the last decade of the 16th century, resistance to forced labor in the mines took many forms, including appeals to the justice system. Acosta was one of about 40 Jesuits in Peru and was active in ministering to the Spanish colonials as well as preaching and catechizing indigenous peoples and African slaves. From 1576 until 1581 Acosta served as the provincial (regional leader of the Society of Jesus) of Peru, during which time he actively opposed the severity of Toledo's treatment of the indigenous peoples. Acosta spent his final five years in Peru acting as scribe for the Third Provincial Council of LIMA, which consolidated secular power over the clergy and designed a standard catechism for use with the indigenous population (published in the *Doctrina Cristiana*). After one year in Mexico, Acosta returned home to Spain in 1588, where he became an adviser to King PHILIP II. Acosta died in Salamanca in 1600.

Further reading: Claudio M. Burgaleta, S.J., *José de Acosta, S.J. (1540–1600): His Life and Thought* (Chicago: Loyola Press, 1999); Jeffrey L. Klaiber, "The Posthumous Christianization of the Inca Empire in Colonial Peru," *Journal of the History of Ideas* 37 (1976): 507–520; Sabine MacCormack, "Pachacuti: Miracles, Punishments, and Last Judgment: Visionary Past and Prophetic Future in Early Colonial Peru," *American Historical Review* 93 (1988): 960–1006.

— Lisa M. Brady

adelantado

A prestigious military title that all Spanish CONQUISTADORES aspired to during the medieval period as well as during the conquest of the NEW WORLD.

The title comes from the verb *adelantar,* which means "to advance," and developed during the RECONQUISTA. Essentially, it signified a war hero who "advanced" into enemy territory and captured land for his king. *Adelantados* received instant patents of nobility as well as extensive lands in the areas they conquered. When the progress of the Reconquista slowed and came to an end with the fall of Granada in 1492, the title fell out of favor. It returned with the Spanish conquests in the Americas—indeed, it became one of the most highly sought titles in the New World. It provided poor soldiers of fortune one of the only ways to enter into the ranks of the nobility. In Spanish America the position of the *adelantado* was essentially that of a military governor. He possessed executive and judicial powers within the territories he conquered. Additionally, he had limited power to write legislation, particularly labor regulations for plantations and mines. The *adelantado* also held the right to appoint subordinate officials in his lands and to distribute land as a reward to his followers.

Because it was a position of great honor and power, the Spanish Crown granted it only to the greatest conquistadores. CHRISTOPHER COLUMBUS assumed the power to grant the title and bestowed it upon his brother BARTHOLOMEW COLUMBUS, essentially giving him the island of HISPANIOLA as his personal territory. VASCO NÚÑEZ DE BALBOA was the first explorer to receive the title directly from the Crown, although JUAN PONCE DE LEÓN was the first actually to exercise the powers of the office. Several of the important figures from the conquest era achieved *adelantado* status, but few of them passed the title on to their heirs. The Crown was deeply concerned about creating a powerful landed nobility in the New World. By 1600 the Crown had abolished the title, giving its powers to the office of the viceroy.

Further reading: C. H. Haring, *The Spanish Empire in America* (Oxford, U.K.: Oxford University Press, 1947); Lyle N. McAlister, *Spain and Portugal in the New World, 1495–1700* (Minneapolis: University of Minnesota Press, 1984).

— Scott Chamberlain

Africanus, Leo   See Leo Africanus

Aguilar, Francisco de (ca. 1469–1561)

One of the more intriguing CONQUISTADORES, Francisco de Aguilar was one of the lieutenants of HERNÁN CORTÉS who in his later years gave up his worldly possessions and entered the Dominican order.

Scholars know relatively little about Aguilar's early years in Spain, although it seems he was christened Alonso de Aguilar in 1469. By the early 1500s he had built a close relationship with several conquistadores, including Cortés and PEDRO DE ALVARADO. When Cortés left CUBA to explore the mainland in 1519, he selected Aguilar to be one of his officers. From the moment the expedition landed in the YUCATÁN PENINSULA, Aguilar displayed integrity, courage, and a quick intelligence. He was also contemplative and thoughtful—attributes that would eventually lead him away from a military career. During the course of the Aztec conquest, Cortés came to rely upon him as a steady, dependable officer who could shoulder enormous responsibility. After Cortés had seized and imprisoned the Aztec emperor MOCTEZUMA II, he assigned Aguilar with the important task of guarding him. Because Aguilar was more dependable than daring, he never distinguished himself in battle as did Alvarado. Still, Cortés valued his services highly and rewarded him handsomely after the conquest was complete.

As part of his payment Aguilar gained a series of ENCOMIENDAS, which were grants of native labor. According to colonial documents, his most important *encomiendas* were in Tlapa and Chilapa in central MEXICO. Aguilar also gained the right to establish a *venta*, or hostelry, between the principal port of VERACRUZ and the city of Puebla, located to the east of Mexico City. This was the principal highway of NEW SPAIN—the great thoroughfare by which the collected wealth of the colony traveled to the coast for shipment back to Europe. By virtue of these rewards, Aguilar became enormously wealthy and influential. Surprisingly, only a few years later, he abandoned his wealth, land, and property. In 1529, at the age of 50, Aguilar took the vows of a Dominican priest, taking the name Fray Francisco de Aguilar. While not entirely without precedent (BARTOLOMÉ DE LAS CASAS had a similar transformation), this abrupt career change shocked many. DIEGO DURÁN referred to it as a "curious episode" in his *History of the Indies,* but for Aguilar the choice seemed natural since he had an introspective disposition that fit well with life in the cloister; his writings show he had a probing intellect and was constantly concerned with the morality of the conquest. In later years he developed gout and lived in almost constant pain. He died in Mexico at age 92.

Aguilar is primarily remembered today for his brief account of the conquest of the AZTECS, which he began at age 80 with the encouragement of his brothers of the order. In his preface he apologized for his sparse, direct style, but these elements make his account appealing for modern audiences. Aguilar's short narrative still captures the dangers and raw terror of the conquest.

Further reading: Patricia de Fuentes, *The Conquistadors: First Person Accounts of the Conquest of Mexico* (Norman: University of Oklahoma Press, 1993); Peter Gerhard, *A Guide to the Historical Geography of New Spain* (Norman: University of Oklahoma Press, 1993).

— Scott Chamberlain

Aguilar, Gerónimo (Jerónimo) de (fl. 1519–1531)

A Spaniard who was shipwrecked on the coast of the YUCATÁN PENINSULA in 1511, Gerónimo de Aguilar learned the Mayan language, making him a crucial interpreter for HERNÁN CORTÉS when the latter rescued him in 1519.

Not much is known of Aguilar's early years, although it is clear that he came to the NEW WORLD with one of the first waves of CONQUISTADORES. He was not a ranking officer and hardly seemed destined for glory, although a series of accidents led him to play a prominent role in the conquest of the AZTECS.

During an early expedition to explore the Yucatán, which most Spaniards at the time considered to be another Caribbean island, his ship foundered, though many of the crew made it safely to shore. There they met with hostile MAYA, who captured them and sacrificed all but two men. Aguilar was sold as a slave, while the other, GONZALO GUERRERO, married a local woman and rose to become a prominent local war chief. In fact, Guerrero began to organize active resistance to Spanish incursion into the Maya area. While living among the Maya, Aguilar learned to speak Yucatec Mayan fluently, although he maintained his faith and European culture.

Subsequent explorers heard rumors of "white men" living somewhere in the Yucatán, although Cortés was the first to investigate these stories when he arrived at Cozumel Island in 1519. With persistence, Cortés was able to find Aguilar and to secure his freedom. Eyewitnesses reported that when Aguilar saw his countrymen he fell down weeping and praising God. His report that Guerrero had "gone native" deeply disturbed his compatriots, who could not believe that a man would willingly abandon his European culture to live among "inferior" heathens. Many conquistadores distrusted Aguilar, for he had lived long among the "Devil worshippers" and even learned their language. Many fully expected him to betray them as Guerrero had.

Yet in short order Aguilar took on a key role in the conquest. In TABASCO Cortés acquired the slave woman MALINCHE, who spoke the Aztec language of NAHUATL as well as her native Mayan. She translated the Aztecs' messages to Aguilar, who translated them from Mayan into Spanish. Through this system Cortés was able to communicate with the Aztecs as well as their disgruntled neighbors and enemies. Cortés used this intelligence to good effect, learning much about his enemies while keeping his own motives and plans secret.

Aguilar maintained his position of importance for only a short while. The shrewd Malinche quickly learned Spanish herself and became Cortés's mistress, making Aguilar's skills as an interpreter redundant. He continued to play an active role in the conquest of MEXICO but did not particularly distinguish himself in the fighting. In 1526, five years after the fall of the Aztecs, Cortés rewarded Aguilar with a small group of ENCOMIENDAS, specifically in Molango, Malia, and Sochicoatlan. He died in 1531 without an heir, and his *encomiendas* reverted to the Crown.

Further reading: Inga Clendinnen, *Ambivalent Conquests: Maya and Spaniard in Yucatan, 1517–1570* (Cambridge, U.K.: Cambridge University Press, 1987); Peter Gerhard, *A Guide to the Historical Geography of New Spain* (Norman: University of Oklahoma Press, 1993).

— Scott Chamberlain

Akan

The Akan, inhabitants of the forest regions of modern-day southern GHANA and Côte d'Ivoire, speak Twi (part of the Kwa language family) and today include the Akyem, Akwamu, ASANTE, Fante, and Guan, all in Ghana, and the Baule and Anyi of Côte d'Ivoire.

The Akan originated in the basin of the Pra and Ofin Rivers in modern-day Ghana. Oral traditions indicate that centralized government did not exist in Akan communities until after the 15th century, when the Akan were incorporated into northern trade networks. Small Akan communities bound by kinship, clans, and common religion gradually transformed into centralized states as the trans-SAHARAN trade routes that previously terminated in the savanna extended into the forest regions. The Akan traded GOLD and kola nuts in return for Turkish carpets, blankets, cotton cloth, leather, and brassware.

Economic and political transformations continued with the arrival of the Portuguese in 1471 on the Ghana coast. The booming Atlantic trade brought French, English, and Dutch merchants in the 16th century, followed by the Danes and Swedes in the 17th century. The Atlantic trade also brought maize (see CORN), sweet potatoes, and manioc from the Americas that strengthened Akan agriculture. The growing economic competition created political tensions that accelerated Akan state formation. A Dutch map printed in 1629 showed 38 states along what had become known as the GOLD COAST. The 100-year period from 1650 to 1750 marked the most active period of Akan state formation. It also coincided with the height of slave exports (see SLAVE TRADE) from the region.

Two of the earliest and most powerful Akan states were Denkyira and Akwamu, which rose to power through control of gold-producing areas, trade routes, and coastal towns. They maintained power by developing effective military strategy and incorporating villages into a dual arrangement of military and civilian administrative structures.

Further reading: T. C. McCaskie, *State and Society in Pre-Colonial Asante* (Cambridge, U.K., and New York: Cambridge University Press, 1995); Ivor Wilks, *Forests of Gold: Essays on the Akan and the Kingdom of Asante* (Athens: Ohio University Press, 1993).

— Tom Niermann

Alexander VI, Pope (1431–1503)

A member of the famous Borgia family, Pope Alexander VI, through the TREATY OF TORDESILLAS, divided the NEW WORLD between Spain and Portugal.

Alexander VI, born Rodrigo Borgia, came from a family with high church connections; his mother was the sister of Pope Callistus III. Borgia became a cardinal in 1456. With the help of his family's wealth and influence, he was elected pope in 1492, the same year CHRISTOPHER COLUMBUS made his historic voyage. Though ambitious and hard working, he was perhaps best known for his moral failings. He had a long-term mistress and may have had as many as nine children, two of whom he fathered after becoming pope. As pope, Alexander approved of the expulsion of JEWS from Spain in 1492 and promoted a crusade against the Turks. His contemporaries, while admiring his political abilities, were repelled by his sensuality and moral lapses.

Further reading: Margery A. Ganz, "Alexander VI," in *Encyclopedia of the Vatican and Papacy*, ed. Frank J. Coppa, (Westport, Conn: Greenwood Press, 1999); J. N. Hillgarth, *The Spanish Kingdoms, 1250–1516,* vol. 2 (Oxford, U.K.: Clarendon Press of Oxford University Press, 1978); J. H. Parry, *The Discovery of South America* (London: Paul Elek, 1979); Christine Shaw, "Alexander VI," in *The Oxford Encyclopedia of the Reformation*, vol. 1, ed. Hans J. Hillerbrand (New York: Oxford University Press, 1996), p. 19.

— Martha K. Robinson

Algonquian

The precontact language of groups of Native American peoples who lived along and near the east coast of North America in territory stretching from the modern-day Maritime Provinces of Canada to North Carolina, the term *Algonquian* also refers to specific groups of indigenous peoples.

Before Europeans crossed the Atlantic, numerous Algonquian languages were spoken in eastern North America. These languages included Maliseet, Micmac, Passamaquoddy, Massachusetts, Narragansett, Quiripi, Mahican, Munsee, Nanticoke, Powhatan, and Carolina. Of the 29 known and identifiable Algonquian languages, 21 are now extinct, and others have few speakers; the Penobscot version of Eastern Abenaki, for example, had only 10 speakers in 1970.

The term *Algonquian* also refers to specific groups normally identified by their location at the time of contact with Europeans. Thus, anthropologists and linguists refer to Eastern Long Island Algonquians and Virginia Algonquians. The peoples whom the English mathematician and ethnographer THOMAS HARRIOT met at ROANOKE in the 1580s are known as North Carolina Algonquians.

The term *Algonquian* should not be confused with *Algonquin,* which refers to a sub-Arctic indigenous nation whose original territory stretched westward from the St. Lawrence River toward the Great Lakes; their neighbors included the HURON, Nipissing, and St. Lawrence Iroquois.

Further reading: "Coastal Region" and "Eastern Algonquian Languages," in William Sturtevant, gen. ed., *Handbook of North American Indians,* vol. 15, *Northeast,* ed. Bruce G. Trigger (Washington, D.C.: Smithsonian Institution Press, 1978), 58–295.

Alvarado, Pedro de (ca. 1485–1541)

One of the most ruthless CONQUISTADORES, Pedro de Alvarado played an important role in the conquest of the AZTECS as a captain in the army of HERNÁN CORTÉS before leading his own conquests in southern MEXICO and Guatemala.

Alvarado was born in Spain in 1485. From an early age he became a restless soldier of fortune who traveled extensively. Lured by the promise of riches in the NEW WORLD, he sailed for HISPANIOLA in 1510. In the Caribbean he heard tales of wealthy kingdoms farther west and sailed with JUAN DE GRIJALVA in 1517 to explore the coast of the YUCATÁN PENINSULA. When Cortés set out with a larger force in 1519 to explore the mainland, he selected Alvarado as his principal captain. During initial forays around the Gulf Coast of Mexico, Alvarado displayed courage, arrogance, and a willingness to use excessive force that would be the hallmarks of his career. At least initially, the Aztecs seemed to believe that the Spaniards were gods returning from the east (see QUETZALCOATL), and because of his fiery red hair, the Aztecs assumed Alvarado was an incarnation of the sun god, Tonatiuh. Until his death, natives referred to him by this name.

As Cortés's most trusted captain, Alvarado was closely involved in all the major events of Aztec conquest. Along with Cortés, he entered the Aztec capital of TENOCHTITLÁN and set up a base camp from which to dominate the city. In 1520 DIEGO DE VELÁZQUEZ, the governor of Cuba, sent soldiers to arrest Cortés for overstepping his orders and authority. Cortés took a squad to the coast to deal with these soldiers, leaving Alvarado in charge of the Spanish base in Tenochtitlán. One evening, the Aztec nobles performed a ceremonial dance just outside the Spaniards' compound. For unknown reasons Alvarado sealed off the ceremonial precinct and slaughtered the unarmed dancers. This provoked a massive retaliation from the Aztecs, who besieged the compound. When Cortés returned the Aztecs allowed him to reenter the base, hoping to trap him in the city. Once Cortés realized his dangerous situation, he castigated Alvarado for his actions and planned a desperate escape from Tenochtitlán. This disastrous retreat was called the Noche Triste, or "Sad Night," in which the Spaniards suffered horrible losses. Because of his bravery during this and later battles, Alvarado regained Cortés's favor, which would be crucial in later years.

Once the Aztecs had finally been defeated, Alvarado struck out on his own to conquer kingdoms for himself. In 1523 he seized control of the wealthy Mixtec kingdom of Tututepec, along the Pacific coast, which had remained independent of the Aztec Empire. He moved farther south into Guatemala, where he successfully attacked the Quiché MAYA. With his soldiers he continued on to modern-day El Salvador before returning to Guatemala. In all his conquests, he followed Cortés's model of capitalizing on local discontent and using surprise attacks to overwhelm his foes. He treated his enemies brutally, at times shocking his own countrymen. In 1524, at the urging of Cortés, the Crown recognized his military achievements by naming him governor and captain-general of Guatemala, a position he retained until his death. Alvarado oversaw the founding of Santiago as the capital of Guatemala, but he was not comfortable being an administrator and soon left on other expeditions.

After the Guatemalan campaign, misfortune hounded Alvarado until the end of his life—and beyond. In 1534 he sailed to Ecuador, hoping to take part in the conquest of the INCA. His volatile temper quickly alienated his fellow conquistadores, and rather than face open hostilities with the men, Alvarado returned to Guatemala. In 1541 the viceroy ANTONIO DE MENDOZA persuaded him to explore

In Hernán Cortés's absence, Spanish soldiers under Pedro Alvarado begin a surprise attack on noblemen who, dressed in feathers, were dancing and making offerings to their gods. Aztec drawing *(The Granger Collection)*

Arizona and NEW MEXICO in search of the Seven Cities of Cíbola. Before he reached his destination he became involved in suppressing a native rebellion in northwestern Mexico. At the end of the battle he died accidentally when his horse collapsed on top of him. The subsequent power struggle in Guatemala is one of the more bizarre episodes of the colonial period. Upon hearing the news of her husband's death, Alvarado's widow, Doña Beatriz, appointed herself captain-general in her husband's place. Most of the colonial officials were shocked at her presumption, but they had little time to respond. Less than 24 hours later, heavy rains and an earthquake combined to unleash a massive mudslide that destroyed Santiago. Hundreds died, including Doña Beatriz. Survivors took this destruction as a sign of divine displeasure at having a woman as a military officer and governor. Abandoning the ruins, the townsfolk rebuilt Santiago some distance away under the direction of a new captain-general appointed by the Crown.

Today, Alvarado has a reputation for being bloodthirsty, if not psychotic. He often attacked without provocation and was ruthless both on and off the battlefield. Scholars frequently use his own writings to justify this reputation—and indeed, Alvarado describes his actions (including massacres and torture) with icy detachment. However, it is important to remember that these writings were intended specifically for the king, with an eye toward advancing his military career. Some scholars have suggested that if Alvarado had written his memoirs in his old age (as did BERNAL DÍAZ DEL CASTILLO and FRANCISCO DE AGUILAR), he might have been more concerned with his reputation and more diplomatic in his writings.

Further reading: Hernán Cortés, *Letters from Mexico* (New Haven, Conn.: Yale University Press, 1986); Patricia de Fuentes, *The Conquistadors: First Person Accounts of the Conquest of Mexico* (Norman: University of Oklahoma Press, 1993); Christopher H. Lutz, *Santiago de Guatemala, 1541–1773: City, Caste, and the Colonial Experience* (Norman: University of Oklahoma Press, 1994).

— Scott Chamberlain

Amazon River

The largest river system in the world, the Amazon and its tributaries form one of the most important geographical features in South America.

By any standard, the Amazon is enormous. The Amazon flows eastward nearly 3,900 miles from the foothills of the ANDES MOUNTAINS in western South America to the Atlantic Ocean. It possesses several hundred tributaries (many of which are still unexplored) that drain an area roughly 2.5 million square miles in size. At its mouth it is more than 50 miles wide, discharging 32 million gallons of water per second and depositing 3 million tons of sediment into the Atlantic daily. The water flow has a direct impact on currents and the salt content of the ocean for 200 miles. The lower courses of the Amazon experience tides; in certain phases of the moon, tidal surges up to 16 feet race up the river at speeds of 40 miles per hour. The area surrounding the river is one of the largest, wettest rain forests in the world, a haven to thousands of distinct species of plants and animals.

Before the European conquest the Amazon rain forest supported a number of native groups who had fairly well defined political and social systems. Most of the indigenous peoples practiced primitive farming techniques such as slash-and-burn agriculture, and manioc appears to have been their most important crop. Besides farming, many native peoples supplemented their diets by hunting for small game or fishing in nearby rivers. There were no great native cities in the Amazon, and the population of the entire region seems to have been no more than 5 million (compared to 25 million in central Mexico alone). Because the Amazon was remote from the centers of Spanish and Portuguese power, these native groups are not as well understood as are other South American cultures such as the INCA, Moche, and Tupí-Guaraní.

Exploration of the Amazon region proceeded in fits and starts. Spanish explorer Vicente Yáñez Pinzón probably reached the delta region in 1500. The first European to travel the length of the river was Francisco de Orellana, who entered the system at the Napo River in Ecuador in 1540. Orellana reported seeing native groups where women fought alongside the men. Recalling the Greek myth of the Amazons, he gave their name to the river. Later Spaniards, including the famous Lope de Aguirre, traveled into the Amazon area in search of EL DORADO, but finding neither kingdoms to conquer nor mineral resources to exploit, the Spanish government made little effort to claim the area. The Portuguese annexed the Amazon region in 1639, integrating it into their colony of BRAZIL.

Further reading: Susana Hecht and Alexander Cockburn, *The Fate of the Forest: Developers, Destroyers and Defenders of the Amazon* (New York: Harper, 1990); John Hemming, *Amazon Frontier: The Defeat of the Brazilian Indians* (Cambridge, Mass.: Harvard University Press, 1987); Alex Shoumatoff, *The Rivers Amazon* (San Francisco: Sierra Club Books, 1978).

— Scott Chamberlain

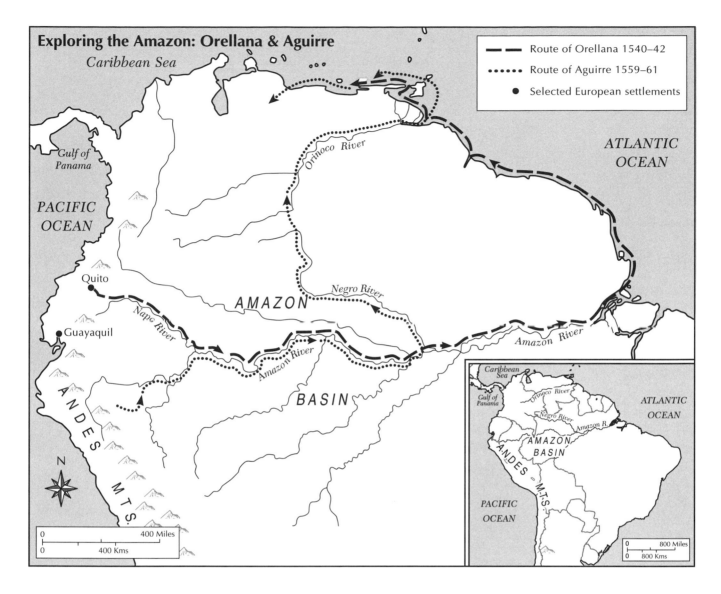

Exploring the Amazon: Orellana & Aguirre

Route of Orellana 1540–42
Route of Aguirre 1559–61
● Selected European settlements

Caribbean Sea

Gulf of Panama

PACIFIC OCEAN

Quito

Guayaquil

Napo River

ANDES MTS.

Orinoco River

AMAZON

Negro River

Amazon River

BASIN

Amazon River

ATLANTIC OCEAN

N

0   400 Miles
0   400 Kms

Caribbean Sea

Gulf of Panama

Orinoco River

Negro River

Amazon R.

AMAZON BASIN

ANDES MTS.

PACIFIC OCEAN

ATLANTIC OCEAN

0   800 Miles
0   800 Kms

ambergris

Europeans in the Middle Ages and the early modern period valued ambergris, a secretion of the sperm whale, as a fixative for perfumes.

Ambergris is a waxlike material produced in the intestines of sperm whales. Fresh, it has a strong, unpleasant odor. As it ages the odor dissipates and is replaced by a pleasant scent. By the ninth century, Europeans were using pieces of ambergris that washed ashore to make perfumes, medicines, and aphrodisiacs. By the 16th century Europeans realized that it was produced by whales.

Further reading: F. E. Beddard, *A Book of Whales* (New York: G. P. Putnam's Sons, 1900); Robert Burton, *The Life and Death of Whales*, 2nd. ed. (Totowa, N.J.: Rowman & Allanheld, 1980); Robert McNally, *So Remorseless a Havoc: Of Dolphins, Whales, and Men* (Boston: Little, Brown, 1981).

— Martha K. Robinson

Andes Mountains

An extensive mountain range running the length of South America that is one of the continent's most important geographical features.

The Andes form one of the largest mountain ranges in the world. They stretch nearly 4,000 miles in length, from the Panamanian Isthmus to Tierra del Fuego in the south.

The Andes cover an exceptionally large area and contain some of the highest peaks in the world, with many mountains reaching more than 20,000 feet. The range sits atop the confluence of two major tectonic plates, which has given rise to volcanism and frequent earthquakes. Throughout the colonial period these tectonic forces devastated European settlements, although much of the indigenous architecture evolved in such a way as to effectively resist earthquakes. Several smaller ranges make up the greater Andean system: the southern Andes, which run the length of modern Chile; the central Andes, from Ecuador to northern Argentina; and the northern Andes, in Colombia and Venezuela. Additionally, there is a large plateau region called the Altiplano in Bolivia that forms the largest flat area of the Andean system. Of these regions, only the central zone is densely populated. The Andes have an enormous impact on the climate of the region, creating an effective "rain shadow" that blocks the humid air of the AMAZON RIVER basin from reaching the Pacific coast. This means that the coastal zones of PERU and Chile are two of the driest places on earth, while eastern Peru is one of the wettest.

The Andean chain is a challenging area for human cultures to thrive. There is relatively little land for farming, and the high altitude means that oxygen levels are low. Still, several native empires flourished here, particularly the INCA. Spaniards under FRANCISCO PIZARRO entered the region in the 1530s and quickly subdued it. They set up the city of LIMA to rule the area, creating the viceroyalty of Peru that stretched the length of the Andes. The Spanish Crown quickly discovered that the Andes contained a great deal of mineral wealth, including the SILVER mines at POTOSÍ as well as deposits of mercury, copper, tin, and alluvial GOLD. These areas made the viceroyalty wealthy, attracting immigrants and capital. For most of the colonial period the Spaniards focused their attention on developing the Andean region while neglecting other areas such as the Amazon and the fertile pampas of Argentina.

Further reading: Karen Spalding, *Huarochirí: An Andean Society under Inca and Spanish Rule* (Stanford, Calif.: Stanford University Press, 1984); Werner Zeil, *The Andes: A Geological Review* (Stuttgart: Beiträge zur Regionalen Geologie der Erde, 1980).

— Scott Chamberlain

Anglo-Normans

A group composed of the Angles, the original inhabitants of southeast Britain, and the Normans of France, who wanted to gain control over territory that now consists of England, Scotland, Wales, and Ireland.

In 1066 the Normans invaded England and within a century gained control of the southeastern portion of the island. Over time they expanded their authority. They did so by organizing military forces to move into Wales that prevailed on the field of battle against the native Welsh. Although there had always been battles among competing groups, the invasion by the Anglo-Normans signalled something new in Wales: the rise to power of a foreign group. One annalist complained about "the tyranny, injustice, violence and oppression" wrought by the invaders, who seemed eager to force the local residents to flee from their ancestral lands. At the same time that they were imposing their will on the native Welsh, the Anglo-Normans moved north into Scotland, but the native Scots proved more resistant. Still, over time Scotland, too, became part of the political orbit of the Anglo-Normans, although resistance to their control continued for centuries.

In the mid-12th century the Anglo-Normans set their sites on Ireland. They did so with the blessings of Pope Hadrian IV (who, as it happened, was the only English-born pope ever), who in 1155 gave to King Henry II of England the title of king of Ireland. The pope ordered the king to "proclaim the truths of the Christian religion to a rude and ignorant people, and to root out the growth of vice from the field of the Lord." That mission must have seemed odd to the native Irish, who for centuries had inhabited "the isle of the saints" and were long known for their commitment to Christianity.

In the years after Hadrian's command the English organized an attempted seizure of Ireland. They benefited at first when one Irish king, Dermot MacMurrough (Diarmaid Mac Murchadha) invited Richard Strongbow (Strigul de Clare), one of Henry's knights, to come to Ireland to help him gain control over the entire island. Strongbow agreed, though the Anglo-Normans from the start believed that they crossed the Irish Sea not to help a native Irish lord claim control of the island but, instead, to gain possession of it for themselves. They also believed that the native Irish would welcome the invaders who possessed, so the Anglo-Normans thought, a superior culture that would attract any man or woman eager to escape the grasp of the primitive chiefs who claimed parts of Ireland before the invaders arrived.

The Anglo-Normans proceeded to cross the Irish Sea, but this mission proved more problematic than the conquest of Wales. In some places the invaders again destroyed local communities and did so with little concern for the human victims of their assault. In their attack on Waterford, along the southeast coast of Ireland, the Anglo-Normans catapulted Irish men and women—the living and the dead—over the city's walls.

The Anglo-Normans did not continue on their murderous assaults. In Ireland they found that local elites were willing to make alliances, some of which led to offers to marry into Irish families. Soon a new elite came into being in parts of Ireland, an aristocracy that could claim direct ties to Britain but that retained ties to Irish lands and, quite often, the peasants who rented farms on their estates. To solidify their position, they went on a torrid building campaign and erected strong castles across Ireland, many of which survive today. The castles often had stone walls three to four feet thick, with narrow windows and trap doors that those inside could use to launch arrows or pots of boiling water on any invaders who happened to get over the stone walls, which castle builders always constructed as their first line of defense against potential enemies. These castles dominated a landscape in which the vast majority of the rural Irish population continued to live in small wattle and daub huts with thatched roofs.

Over time the Anglo-Normans took on a new identity and became known to the natives as the "Old English." Rather than converting the native Irish to English ways, these people tended instead to live like the Irish themselves. They did so despite the fact that English policy makers tried, time and again, to figure out ways to bring Ireland under their control. In 1366 the English passed the so-called Kilkenny Statutes, a series of apartheid-like laws that attempted to prohibit the Old English from speaking Irish or marrying into Irish families, but the need for such laws suggested that the Anglo-Normans had, in fact, already failed; rather than trying to convert the native Irish to their ways, they instead resorted to trying to stop Britons from living like the Irish.

From the 12th century to the 16th century the English tried to build on the initial success of the Anglo-Normans in Ireland, but that original group's identity had become submerged over time, and so did their hopes of conquering Ireland with the same success they had found in Wales. In the mid-16th century the English Queen ELIZABETH I undertook a new campaign, characterized by large-scale transplantation of English colonists, murderous assault, and terrorism.

Historians study the experience of the Anglo-Normans in Wales and Ireland to better understand the deep background to the English colonization of North America and as a reminder that the indigenous peoples of the Western Hemisphere were not the first peoples whom the English (and their ancestors) had hoped to subdue.

Further reading: R. R. Davies, *Domination and Conquest: The Experience of Ireland, Scotland, and Wales, 1100–1300* (Cambridge, U.K.: Cambridge University Press, 1990); Liam De Paor, *The Peoples of Ireland: From Prehistory to Modern Times* (London: Hutchinson, 1986).

Apalachee

A native group in FLORIDA, the Apalachee encountered several of the early Spanish *entradas* into southeastern North America, and they eventually participated in the Spanish mission system established in Spanish La Florida.

The Apalachee inhabited the area between the Ochlockonee River and the Aucilla River in northwest Florida. They subsisted on a wide range of horticultural products, primarily CORN, and lived in organized villages headed by chiefs. These individual villages were incorporated into one large paramount chiefdom. The Apalachee often produced significant agricultural surpluses, and this economic vitality provided the basis for their military prowess through the development of a large population to supply ample numbers of warriors. As a result, their reputation extended far beyond their territory. The Apalachee fulfilled a significant role in the southeastern trade network that connected many of the paramount chiefdoms in the region. Most important, the Apalachee facilitated the trade of shells from the Gulf coast into the interior, where they were used for prestige display and in religious ceremonies. Controlling the shell trade gave the Apalachee access to exotic and sometimes sacred status symbols from the interior southeast that aided in the elite's control of the Apalachee paramount chiefdom.

The Apalachee first encountered the Spanish in 1528, when the expedition of Pánfilo de Narváez and Hernando de Soto encamped for the winter of 1539–40 among them. For the most part through their military capabilities, the Apalachee successfully protected their territory from these Spanish incursions, but eventually internal disruptions provided the Spanish with an opportunity to bring the Apalachee within the Spanish sphere of influence. In the early 17th century one of two rival factions invited the Spanish to develop missions within Apalachee territory in an effort to gain a political edge through an alliance with the Spanish and the unique items they could trade with the natives. FRANCISCANS began to establish missions among the Apalachee in 1633. Eventually many Apalachee succumbed to epidemic DISEASEs, and some later became slaves in the English colony of South Carolina.

Further reading: Mark F. Boyd, Hale G. Smith, and John W. Griffin, *Here They Once Stood: The Tragic End of the Apalachee Missions* (Gainesville: University of Florida Press, 1951); John H. Hann, *Apalachee: The Land Between the Rivers* (Gainesville: University of Florida Press, 1988); John F. Scarry, "The Apalachee Chiefdom: A Mississippian Society on the Fringe of the Mississippian World," in *The Forgotten Centuries: Indians and Europeans in the American South, 1521–1704*, eds. Charles Hudson and Carmen

Chaves Tesser (Athens: University of Georgia Press, 1994), 154–178.

— Dixie Ray Haggard

Arawak

The name of a specific native group (Lokono) that inhabited the Guianas and portions of Trinidad and of a family of languages originally spoken in portions of northeastern South America, the Greater and Lesser Antilles, and parts of Central America.

Linguistically related to Caribbean groups, Arawakan speakers lived in the Amazonian forests of South America and followed a hunting and gathering subsistence along the banks of the upper Amazon, the Rio Negro, and the headwaters of the Orinoco Rivers. They supplemented their food resources by sometimes raising turtles in pens and practicing slash-and-burn horticulture, but the limited fertility of these jungle areas forced groups located away from the major river systems to practice a seminomadic lifestyle. These South American Arawak often fought CARIB speakers who lived along the lower Amazon and the upper Orinoco Rivers and the Guiana highlands for control of the region.

The TAINO and Carib of the West Indies spoke Arawakan languages, and as a result scholars have often labeled them as "Arawak." Unfortunately, this implied close ethnic and cultural affinity with the South American groups, which was not the case. Island Carib culture and ethnicity probably resulted from the merger of Island Arawak speakers related to the Taino and Carib speakers in the Lesser Antilles. Although linguistically related to South American Arawak, the Taino represented an earlier migration to the Greater Antilles from South America and a separate cultural development that extended back centuries before contact with European Americans.

Further reading: Mary W. Helms, "The Indians of the Caribbean and Circum-Caribbean at the End of the Fifteenth Century," in *The Cambridge History of Latin America,* vol. 2, ed. Leslie Bethell (Cambridge, U.K.: Cambridge University Press, 1995), 501–545; Peter Hulme, *Colonial Encounters: Europe and the Native Caribbean, 1492–1797* (New York: Methuen, 1986); Irving Rouse, *The Tainos: Rise and Fall of the People Who Greeted Columbus* (New Haven, Conn.: Yale University Press, 1992); ——— *Migrations in Prehistory: Inferring Population Movement from Cultural Remains* (New Haven, Conn.: Yale University Press, 1986).

— Dixie Ray Haggard

Armada   See Spanish Armada

art and architecture

From the soaring spires of early modern European churches to elaborate buildings made from mud in western Africa to moveable longhouses found in the Eastern Woodlands of North America to cliff dwellings and adobe apartment houses in the southwest of the modern-day United States, the buildings that people inhabited—and the art that they used for decoration and prayer—reflected the ways that different communities organized their lives.

Of course, variation in art and architecture should hardly come as a surprise. As the distinguished art historian Vincent Scully wrote, "[t]he shape of architecture is the shape of the earth as it is modified by the structures of mankind. Out of that relationship, human beings fashion an environment for themselves, a space to live in, suggested by their patterns of life and constructed around whatever symbols of reality seem important to them." So it comes as no surprise that during the early modern period, art and architecture represented local cultures and tastes.

Consider, for a moment, the buildings that a visitor would encounter in different situations. In England the REFORMATION had led to the dissolution of monasteries but did not necessitate the destruction of church spires, such as that at St. Paul's in LONDON, which could be seen from far away. By contrast, the residents of an IROQUOIS village inhabited longhouses that could be taken apart and moved; situated in a clearing, they would have been visible to those who came near, but other than the smoke trailing from domestic fires, they could not have been seen by someone far away. The adobe apartments built by PUEBLO peoples in the Southwest often sat atop mesas and, as a result, were exposed to the eroding force of wind, but residents maintained them for generations despite the fact that they were in plain view of any potential enemies. The MAYA, AZTECS, and INCA built great cities, often hauling heavy stones through miles of dense forest to locations where they could build pyramids, ball courts, and public plazas; travelers today to TIKAL, CHICHÉN ITZÁ, PALENQUE, and MACHU PICCHU can find the remains of great ceremonial centers. Early modern travelers in Africa marveled at great buildings made out of mud, and those buildings also survived for generations because they were constantly maintained. Renaissance architects across Europe created memorable churches and residences, such as those inhabited by elite citizens of VENICE; their dwellings were situated not on roads but on canals, and the façade pointing toward the water was normally the most elaborate surface of the entire building. Architecture also reflected shifting political realities. In the west of Ireland, for example, the ANGLO-NORMANS had built fortified towers when they arrived in the 11th century; by the 16th century, although tensions remained between the Protestant English and the native Catholic Irish, the architects of Portumna Castle designed a fortified house, not a castle, that would become the residence of the local English lord.

Art, too, reflected regional differences. Many art history students today study the works of great Renaissance painters and sculptors such as MICHELANGELO and LEONARDO DA VINCI or the glittering gold-leaf mosaics to be found in medieval and early modern churches across Europe. But art existed everywhere and reflected local artists' and artisans' skills. Polychrome pottery styles developed by ZUNI and HOPI offered testimony to the designs favored in those communities. Enormous sculpted heads found in forested regions of MEXICO testify to the OLMECS' obsession with one form of artistic expression. The Aztecs, according to the Spanish who conquered them, created elaborate cities with ornate temples filled with precious icons that the invaders melted down in order to transport the GOLD more easily to Europe. Only in recent years have archaeologists cracked the code of much Mayan art; when they did so they discovered the ways that artistic depictions of self-mutilation reflected a monarch's way of divining how to govern.

In the wake of the 1492 voyage of CHRISTOPHER COLUMBUS and the long-distance journeys from western Europe around Africa and India to the SPICE ISLANDS, artistic styles traveled along with itinerants. When colonizers decided to establish settlements, they did not normally adopt the housing styles of the indigenous peoples they encountered. Instead, they imported styles they knew well. In places the juxtaposition could be jarring, as it still is at Acoma Pueblo, where an enormous Spanish mission-style church dominates the skyline, surrounded by one- to two-storey adobe houses. Europeans were so bent on maintaining their own styles of architecture that they did so even when adaptation to local building ideas would have made great sense. The English in the West Indies in the early 17th century, for example, suffered in houses with thick walls and glass windows when they could have lived more easily if they had built dwellings with shutters that let cooling breezes through in the evening. The rise of the PRINTING PRESS also facilitated the spread of artistic styles. SAMUEL PURCHAS could inform his readers about Mexico because he could show them pictures of that society preserved on a codex that traveled across the Atlantic.

Further reading: Fernand Braudel and Michel Mollat du Jourdin, eds., *Le Monde de Jacques Cartier* (Paris: Berger-Levrault, 1984); John S. Henderson, *The World of the Ancient Maya,* 2nd ed. (Ithaca, N.Y.: Cornell University Press, 1997); Peter Humfrey, *Painting in Renais-*sance Venice* (New Haven, Conn.: Yale University Press, 1995); Joy Kenseth, ed. *The Age of the Marvelous* (Hanover, N.H.: Hood Museum of Art/Dartmouth College, 1991); Jay A. Levenson, ed., *Circa 1492: Art in the Age of Exploration* (Washington, D.C., and New Haven, Conn.: National Gallery of Art/Yale University Press, 1991); Linda Schele and Mary Ellen Miller, *The Blood of Kings: Dynasty and Ritual in Maya Art* (New York: George Braziller, 1986); Vincent Scully, *Architecture: The Natural and the Manmade* (New York: St. Martin's Press, 1991); Eveyln Welch, *Art and Society in Italy, 1350–1500* (New York: Oxford University Press, 1997).

Asante

The homeland of the Asante, part of the AKAN cluster of ethnic groups, was in the territory of modern-day southern Ghana, Togo, and Côte d'Ivoire.

Asante spoke the Twi language, sometimes known as Akan, a part of the Kwa branch of the Niger–Congo language family. Today the Asante number around 2 million people and are the most influential ethnic group in modern Ghana. Because of the power and duration of the Asante Empire, the Asante of today are considered the guardians of traditional culture in Ghana.

The archeological record indicates that Asante ancestors lived in their homeland for more than 2,000 years. In the 14th and 15th centuries, as GOLD production and trade expanded, Akan kingships began to emerge. The development of powerful states emerged on the heels of European arrival along the coast and a further expansion of trade in the 16th and 17th centuries.

The first Asante king was Osei Tutu, who laid the foundation for the Asante Empire. He began to unite various clans and subgroups from about 1670–90. He established Kumasi as the Asante capital and legitimized his rule with the legend of the Golden Stool. According to the legend, the stool descended from the sky and gave those who sat upon it the authority to rule the Asante. Osei Tutu also initiated the celebration of Odwira as a festival symbolizing national unity. Osei Tutu succeeded in uniting neighboring city-states and organizing a bureaucratic system to ensure political and economic stability.

Further reading: Malcolm D. McLeod, *The Asante* (London, British Museum Publications, 1981); Edward T. Bowdich, *Mission from Cape Coast Castle to Ashantee* (London, J. Murray, 1819); T. C. McCaskie, *State and Society in Pre-Colonial Asante* (Cambridge, U.K., and New York, Cambridge University Press, 1995).

— Tom Niermann

Askia Muhammad I (Muhammad Turé [Askia al-Hajj Muhammad Ibn Ali Bakr Turé (Touré)]) (r. 1493–1528, d. 1538)

Ruler of the SONGHAI Empire at its zenith, Askia (King) Muhammad I greatly expanded the empire's territory and established ISLAM as its dominant religion.

In 1492 the founder of the Songhai Empire, Sonni Ali Ber, died, leaving his son as his successor (the cause of Sonni Ali's death was drowning, and there is some evidence to show that Muhammad I was behind his demise). Sonni Bakari Da'o renounced Islam, his father's religion, and tried to reestablish the traditional animistic Songhai religious system. An unpopular move, Sonni Bakari Da'o's perceived heresy inspired an attempted coup by Muhammad Turé early in 1493. Although he failed in this first attempt, Muhammad Turé succeeded later that year and established the Askia dynasty, which remained in power until 1591. Askia Muhammad I legitimated his coup d'etat by declaring it a jihad against the pagans Sonni Ali Ber and Sonni Bakari Da'o, and thus, as he perceived it, liberating the Muslim populace from pagan tyranny. Support for Askia Muhammad's coup by the cities TIMBUKTU and Djenne (see DJENNE-DJENO) solidified his position, and he rewarded the cities and their leading scholars with considerable autonomy.

Askia Muhammad ruthlessly eliminated all members of the two preceding dynasties, the Sonni and the Za, firmly establishing himself as the empire's ruler. He went on pilgrimage (hajj) to MECCA in 1496, returning to the Songhai capital city GAO in 1498; this pilgrimage served dual purposes, the first religious, the second political. By completing the hajj, Askia Muhammad demonstrated to his largely Muslim subjects his religious devotion. An additional outcome of Askia Muhammad's pilgrimage was to reinvigorate trade between Songhai and Egypt, through which he passed on his way to Mecca.

During his reign Askia Muhammad built up his military forces, with the river navy as the nucleus. His most significant achievements included military victories and advances in the administration of his state. By 1500 he had invaded several neighboring kingdoms, including MOSSI and MALI; 13 years later he attacked the HAUSA, capturing the most important TRADE ROUTES into Air. Askia Muhammad's empire stretched 1,600 kilometers along the NIGER RIVER, from Nioro in the northwest to the edge of Kebbi and Borgu in the southeast. He divided the empire into 10 provinces, each governed by a local administrator. He also created a type of cabinet with positions for finance, justice, and agricultural affairs. Each imperial city, including Timbuktu, Djenne, and Gao, had its own governor as well.

Askia Muhammad's administrative reforms went counter to Islamic teaching, causing Muslim scholars to question his piety. However, his pilgrimage to Mecca dispelled some of the concerns over his devotion to Islam. His journey to Mecca was as resplendent as that of MANSA MUSA I of Mali in 1324–25. When Askia Muhammad reached Cairo, one of the stops on his journey, the Abbasid Caliph made him khalifa over the lands of Takrur, increasing his aura of authority over his home and conquered lands. Under Askia Muhammad's rule, Timbuktu once again became a center of Islamic faith and education after a brief period of decline.

By 1528 Askia Muhammad was old, blind, and losing control of his empire. His son Musa deposed him that year but was assassinated in 1531. Muhammad Bounkan Kiria took the throne and exiled the elderly Askia Muhammad to an island in the Niger River but was deposed in 1537 by another of Askia Muhammad's sons, Ismail. Ismail ended his father's exile and brought Askia Muhammad to Gao, where he died in 1538.

Further reading: "Askia Mohammed," in *Historical Dictionary of Mali* 2nd ed., ed. Pascal James Imperato, (Metuchen, N.J.: Scarecrow Press, 1986), 87–88; "Askia Muhammad," in *Africana: The Encyclopedia of African and African American Experience,* eds. Kwame Anthony Appiah and Henry Louis Gates, Jr. (New York: Basic *Civitas* Books, 1999), 145; John Hunwick, "Songhay, Borno and the Hausa States, 1450–1600," in *History of West Africa,* vol. 1, 3rd ed., eds. J. F. Ade Ajiya and Michael Crowder, (London: Longman, 1985), 323–371, esp. 340–352; "Muhammad Ture" in *Dictionary of African Historical Biography,* 2nd ed., eds. Mark R. Lipschutz and R. Kent Rasmussen, (Berkeley: University of California Press, 1986), 160.

— Lisa M. Brady

Atahualpa (?–1533)

The ruler of the INCA empire at the time of the Spanish conquest, he was executed by FRANCISCO PIZARRO in 1533.

It is not entirely clear when Atahualpa was born, but Inca chronicles state that he was the favorite, although illegitimate, son of emperor Huayna Capac, who ruled in the late 15th century. Atahualpa had two important brothers—Manco Inca and Huascar, the legitimate heir to the throne. During their father's reign, Atahualpa was closely associated with the army and probably served as one of its commanders. In a devastating blow to the Inca empire, Huayna Capac died suddenly around 1525, most likely as the result of a SMALLPOX epidemic that spread ahead of the Spanish CONQUISTADORES. On his deathbed he ordered that Huascar would rule the majority of the realm from the holy capital of CUZCO, while Atahualpa would take control of the army and rule the northern portion of the empire from

The Inca emperor Atahualpa. Line engraving, French, 1584 *(Hulton/Archive)*

Quito. Not surprisingly, tensions between the brothers simmered for a while, erupting into a full-scale civil war by 1530. Huascar had the support of the elite and the city of Cuzco, while Atahualpa had the support of the army. Atahualpa swiftly defeated Huascar's forces and established a headquarters at the city of Cajamarca while he prepared to march on Cuzco in triumph. Despite Atahualpa's swift victory, the empire remained deeply divided.

The conquistador Francisco Pizarro entered into this unstable situation in 1532. Atahualpa, believing that he was the messenger of a distant king, agreed to meet with Pizarro at Cajamarca, and as a gesture of good faith had his army wait outside the city. Sensing an opportunity, Pizarro ambushed the ruler, slaughtering the emperor's unarmed, ceremonial bodyguard. With this swift stroke the Inca Empire essentially fell to the Spaniards. Commanders and nobles alike were not certain who to support at this stage and thus took no action. Atahualpa naively hoped to buy his freedom with one of the largest ransoms ever paid. He marked off a line as far up on his prison cell's wall as he could reach and offered to fill the room to that height once with GOLD and twice over with SILVER—measuring out to 11 tons of gold and nearly 25 of silver. He also plotted to maintain his power by ordering the assassi-

nation of Huascar. Unfortunately, his actions squandered precious time and resources that could have been better spent on organizing an effective resistance to the Spaniards. In the end, Pizarro felt that releasing Atahualpa was too dangerous and at the urging of his men ordered his execution. Faced with being burned alive as a heretic or converting to Christianity and receiving a quick death by strangulation, Atahualpa chose the latter, dying in 1533.

Shortly after Atahualpa's death, Pizarro crowned Atahualpa's other brother, Manco Inca, as a puppet emperor, but by 1535 Manco rebelled, retreated to the hidden fortress of Vilcabamba, and led a massive Inca uprising that endured until the 1570s.

Further reading: John Hemming, *The Conquest of the Incas* (New York: Harcourt Brace Jovanovich, 1970); Nathan Wachtel, *The Vision of the Vanquished: The Spanish Conquest of Peru Through Indian Eyes, 1530–1570* (New York: Barnes & Noble Press, 1977).

— Scott Chamberlain

audiencia

Audiencias were courts of appeal in Spanish America that possessed judicial and administrative authority that made them one of the most important governmental institutions in the Western Hemisphere.

Audiencias originated in Spain, but unlike their American counterparts, possessed only judicial authority. The first *audiencia* in Spanish America was founded in the city of Santo Domingo, on the island of HISPANIOLA, in 1511. Subsequently, the Spanish established *audiencias* throughout their American territory. Each viceroyalty, a territorial division of Spanish America governed by a viceroy, was divided into provinces. Each province had an *audiencia* located in its capital city. By 1787 there were a total of 13 *audiencias*. The judges who composed the *audiencias*, known as *oídores*, were among the best paid and most respected of the royal bureaucrats.

Audiencias were the highest judicial authority located in Spanish America. The courts heard appeals from lesser judicial authorities, such as the CORREGIDOR, the *consulado* (wholesale merchant's guild), and the miner's guild. In criminal cases the decision of the *audiencia* was final. In civil cases involving a substantial amount of money, the *audiencia*'s decision could be appealed to the COUNCIL OF THE INDIES or the king.

In certain circumstances the *audiencia* had original jurisdiction. For instance, the court handled all criminal cases that originated within the city where the *audiencia* was located. Likewise, the *audiencia* was the court of first instance for disputes among the religious orders (such as the JESUITS and FRANCISCANS) and for criminal cases in which a member of the clergy had been accused of breaking civil law. The *audiencia* also had original jurisdiction in all cases involving the interests of the Crown.

One function of the *audiencia* was to protect the legal rights of Native Americans. In the 16th century two days a week were usually reserved to hear cases involving Native Americans. Indians were entitled to a lawyer and did not have to pay legal fees. After 1600 a special court known as the Juzgado de Indios took over this function of the *audiencia.*

Audiencias possessed numerous administrative powers. They were authorized to enact local legislation with the approval of the Council of the Indies and the king. *Audiencias* also served as advisory councils to the viceroys and captain-generals on political issues. In addition, *audiencias* worked with their presidents to ensure that all royal orders were executed. If the position of viceroy or captain-general was vacant, the *audiencia* assumed the administrative duties of that office until a replacement arrived. The *audiencia* had the authority to review the conduct of all royal officials while they were in office, including the viceroys and captain-generals. Every three years the *audiencia* conducted a *visitación,* an inspection of its jurisdiction. The judge who performed the inspection had the authority to examine everything and everyone and to punish anyone who broke the law.

By allotting overlapping authority to the *audiencia* and the viceroy, the Crown ensured conflict between the two that would prevent either from gaining too much power and thus threatening the authority of the king in the Western Hemisphere.

Further reading: Mark A. Burkholder, "Bureaucrats," in *Cities and Society in Colonial Latin America,* ed. Louisa Scheel Hoberman and Susan Migden Socolow (Albuquerque: University of New Mexico Press, 1986); C.H. Haring, *The Spanish Empire in America* (New York: Oxford University Press, 1947).

— William Holliday

auto-da-fé

A term meaning "act of faith," the auto-da-fé was the public execution to which persons convicted by the INQUISITION were sometimes sentenced.

The auto-da-fé was a ceremonial public execution associated with the Inquisition in Spain. The original targets of this particular inquisition were *conversos*—Spanish JEWS and Muslims (see ISLAM) who had converted to Christianity—who had apostatized, reverting to the practices of their former faiths. The office of the Inquisition in Spain soon cast its net more broadly, seeking to root out any possible enemies of the Catholic Church. Once Protestant revolts broke out throughout Europe, inquisitors used their methods to keep unorthodox beliefs out of Spain and the Spanish Empire. More than 3,000 people were sentenced to the auto-da-fé between the beginning of the Spanish Inquisition in 1478 and its end around 1800.

Further reading: Henry Kamen, *The Spanish Inquisition: A Historical Revision* (New Haven, Conn.: Yale University Press, 1997); Edward Peters, *Inquisition* (New York: Free Press, 1988), 263–315.

— Marie A. Kelleher

Azores

An archipelago of nine Atlantic Ocean islands that lie at 39°43′ west longitude and 39°55′ north latitude and that became a crucial stop for European vessels heading to the Western Hemisphere.

The Azores sit atop a volcanic ocean chain in the eastern Atlantic. Centuries of geological action have given the islands remarkably fertile soil. In addition, a number of the islands have flat, well-watered coastal plains making them an excellent location for agriculture. Their more northerly location meant that the climate was cooler than other Atlantic islands such as Cape Verde.

The discovery of the Azores is shrouded in mystery. Although texts from as early as the 11th century refer to islands somewhere in the Atlantic west of the Iberian Peninsula, it is unclear whether such assertions were based on knowledge, speculation, or pure fantasy. What is clear is that the Azores lay within a Portuguese zone of navigation, a status that was formalized by the TREATY OF TORDESILLAS. Their importance to the Portuguese Crown can be gauged by reference to contemporary maps that portray the islands well out of proportion. Even given the imaginative nature of mapmaking at the time, such a representation illustrated the importance of the islands to the sailors of the day.

Despite their position well out into the Atlantic, Portuguese possession of the islands did not translate into using them as a springboard for western exploration. The Portuguese preferred instead to utilize some of the islands as mid-Atlantic refueling points for their West Africa trade routes. To this end they stocked them with cattle, sheep, and goats, knowing that the absence of a native population or indigenous carnivores would ensure the survival of the herds and flocks when the caravels returned from West Africa. The first permanent settlers arrived in the 1440s, and the islands initially proved an attractive destination. By the mid-17th century the population had grown so much that the islands became a significant recruiting ground for the Portuguese military. Despite this demographic success, the islanders never discovered an ideal crop to cultivate.

The climate was too cool for SUGAR, the crop that produced the most wealth for 16th-century Europeans. Although residents of the Azores did develop a credible export industry based on wheat and dye-plants, neither produced much capital. Most of the grain went to Portugal, while the dye was the objective of a hotly contested, if brief, competition between English and Dutch linen manufacturers. In addition to these modest export industries, the islanders also developed their own linen manufacturing as well as a moderately successful fishing industry.

Although the islands never produced the great wealth of colonies such as BRAZIL, their fertility made them self-sufficient while the continuation of their original role as a way station kept most of them within the flow of navigation. Certainly CHRISTOPHER COLUMBUS was aware of their existence, and the Azorean island of Santa Maria was his first landfall on his voyage back from the Americas in 1493, although his crew was arrested by the island's authorities when they made landfall and Columbus had to negotiate their release. The large numbers of bureaucrats, troops, and members of religious orders on the islands hampered the growth of prosperity on the Azores. The efforts of both Jesuit and Franciscan monasteries and colleges on the Azores added to the islands' prestige, but the inhabitants of these institutions constituted 10 percent of the population in some areas, thus putting a burden on the farmers and fishermen who had to support them.

Further reading: C. R. Boxer, *The Portuguese Seaborne Empire 1415–1825* (New York: Knopf, 1969); Alfred W. Crosby, *Ecological Imperialism: The Biological Expansion of Europe, 900–1900* (New York: Cambridge University Press, 1986); T. Bentley Duncan, *Atlantic Islands: Madeira, the Azores and the Cape Verde Islands in Seventeenth Century Commerce and Navigation* (Chicago: University of Chicago Press, 1972).

— John Grigg

Aztecs

One of many peoples of pre-Columbian central MEXICO, the Aztecs settled in the region of present-day Mexico City during the late 13th or early 14th century, and by the mid-15th century had risen to supremacy in the region, dominating most of their neighbors until their capital was destroyed by Spanish invaders in 1521.

It is difficult to chart the early history of the Aztecs with any certainty. Over many centuries Aztecs blended their history with origin mythology, rewriting their own story a number of times to reflect a belief in an Aztec manifest destiny as heirs of the TOLTECS and rightful rulers of central Mexico. According to most versions of the origin story, the god HUITZILOPOCHTLI led his people, originally known as the Mexica, from their home at AZTLÁN into the Puebla-Tlaxcala valley of central Mexico.

Legend aside, the exact date of the Aztecs' arrival in their eventual home is unclear, although they must have been there by the beginning of the 14th century. Groups already living in the region did little to make them welcome, partially because the newcomers had taken to raiding their neighbors for women, and the Aztecs soon found themselves at war. One of the indigenous groups, the Colhuacan, allowed the Aztecs to settle temporarily, living a degraded existence as serfs, but the Aztecs' intractable nature soon caused their reluctant hosts to expel them. The Aztecs recommenced their wandering until they finally found some swampy and thus uninhabited islands and founded the twin cities of TENOCHTITLÁN and Tlatelolco. Eventually the Aztecs drained the swamps for cultivation, making use of the "floating fields" known as CHINAMPAS.

In 1367 the Aztecs began to serve as mercenaries for the Tepanec kingdom of Azcapotzalco, probably the mightiest power on the mainland at that time. It was during this period that the leader of the Azcapotzalco, Tezozomoc, gave the Aztecs their first *tlatoani*, or "speaker," named Acamapichtli (r. 1375–95), replacing the system of tribal administrative heads that had ruled up to that time. The ruler, later called the *huei tlatoani* ("great speaker"), acceded to power over a series of days or weeks, beginning with his election or selection after his successor's death. The candidate had to prove himself in battle, leading captives for sacrifice back to the Aztec capital. He then would order new robes for all nobles who would be in attendance and issue invitations to neighboring nobles, including even traditional enemies. The populace marked the investiture of the new speaker with four to five days of feasting and dancing, culminating in a royal procession to five sacred sites in Tenochtitlán, where the new speaker offered sacrifices of incense and his own blood. Once finished, the speaker was considered semidivine (see MOCTEZUMA II).

During the reign of ITZCÓATL, beginning in 1427, the Aztecs became an independent nation, rebelling against the Tepanecs and destroying their capital. Itzcoatl was aided in this by TLACACLA, who served as his *cihuacoatl* ("woman snake"). Under their administration the Aztecs appropriated large tracts of land from nearby cities (many a part of the sphere of influence of the Aztecs' former Tepanec patrons). Aztec warfare took on a new dimension during the reign of Moctezuma I Ilhuicamina (1440–69), "the elder," with the introduction of the so-called FLOWERY WARS. These were battles staged not for killing or conquest, but in order that both sides might take captives for ritual sacrifice. In a related development, Tenochtitlán entered into an alliance with Texcoco and Tlacopan—this came to be known as the Triple Alliance—for the purpose of both mutual defense and for the waging of these sacrifice-oriented battles. CANNIBALISM may also have been a part of the religious observances, but only in ritual context: Aztecs commonly offered human hearts as sacrifices to their gods, but human flesh also served as a form of communion, or a means of consuming the essence of the divine.

With the help of their allies the Aztecs also launched an ambitious program of conquest. One of the greatest conquerors was the speaker Ahuitzotl (1486–1502) who, during his reign, expanded the Aztec domains to the present-day Guatemalan border, bringing most of central Mexico under Aztec rule, although large portions even within the very heart of the empire remained independent, including the enemy states of TLAXCALA, Huexotxingo, and CHOLULA. It should be noted that the Aztec Empire was not so much an empire of possessions in the sense of Western empires, but rather an economic empire based on the rendering of regular tribute payments. Still, the latter seems to have fostered no less resentment than the former would have—a situation that the CONQUISTADORES took full advantage of upon their arrival.

The program of conquest continued down to the reign of Moctezuma II (r. 1502–20). Part of the reason for the Aztecs' expansionist foreign policy lay in the sacrificial requirements of their gods, especially the cult of their patron god, Huitzilopochtli, but economic reasons also came into play. Tenochtitlán was unable to grow enough foodstuffs to feed its population, and, since it did not produce enough exports to pay for the foods in trade, the city's residents had to obtain what they needed either by force or by levying tribute. Conquest soon became part of a vicious cycle: Warfare provided the goods and captives necessary for elaborate ceremonials to overawe their neighbors and for the sacrifices needed to propitiate the gods who ensured the Aztecs' success in battle. But ceremony and sacrifice, as well as the ostentation that befitted the dominant power in the region, exhausted the treasury, necessitating further conquest.

Moctezuma II seems to have been the only ruler who attempted to move the Aztecs from a conquest-oriented military power into a stable, if autocratic, state. His efforts were largely dictated by the fact that the Aztecs had run out of territory into which they could profitably expand. Such a shift, however, would have required a restructuring of the Aztecs' economy and society. Moctezuma's attempts to do just that resulted in economic and social dislocations that seriously weakened the fabric of Aztec society and empire by the time Europeans first set foot upon the shores of Mexico in 1519.

Social Structure

The basic unit of Aztec social organization was the *altepetl*, roughly equivalent to a city-state. These were in turn divided into *calpulli,* which formed the fundamental

Aztec calendar stone   *(Hulton/Archive)*

administrative structure of the empire. (The *altepetl* of Tenochtitlán was composed of about 20 *calpulli*.) Each *calpulli* was a network that included many individual households but was not, strictly speaking, a clan or extended kinship network, as a *calpulli* could include not only extended family but also families related by close proximity over a long period of time. The *calpulli* also spanned class lines, and elite members traditionally provided commoner members with either agricultural land or nonagrarian employment, in return for which the latter owed the former services tribute. Each *calpulli* also had its own gods and maintained its own temples. The members elected the principal chief, the *calpullec*, for life. The *calpullec* served as the main link between the *calpulli* and the *altepetl*: They retained high local prestige and were firmly tied to kinship networks within the *calpulli*, but their official authority came from the central bureaucracy. The *calpulli* also served as a medium for larger state enterprises, from monumental building projects to military service. Warrior contingents fought in *calpulli* groups, and, while individual achievement was the main motivator, group tallies of casualties and captives were a point of pride.

Aztec society after the reign of Moctezuma I was also divided into a strict social hierarchy, all physically signalled by elaborate sumptuary laws that reserved certain types of dress, ornamentation, and even housing types to particular classes. At the top were the *teteuhctin,* or high nobility, who ruled the towns and cities of the empire. The *teteuhctin* exercised legal powers and monitored the flow of tribute payments. Members of this class, which included the great speaker, can often be identified in records by the addition of the honorific suffix *tzin* to their personal names, although their contemporaries could identify them on sight by certain types of rich clothing and ornamentation, which it was solely their privilege to wear.

The *pipiltin,* or lesser nobility, provided the imperial administrators and were generally descended from lords of one sort or another. This class also included members of non-noble descent, the so-called eagle nobles *(cuauh-pipiltin)* who had risen from the ranks of the commoners by distinguishing themselves on the battlefield. Members of this class as a whole differed widely in wealth: Records at the time of the conquest show that certain *pilli* had only seven *macehualtin* ("commoners") working under them,

while some of the latter might be wealthy enough to employ a number of workers of their own. Despite their status, nobles did not enjoy a life of leisure. Rather, they formed a part of the military hierarchy and could be shamed and even stripped of privilege if they shirked their martial obligations. As a result, male children of the nobility received special military training at the hands of seasoned warriors. This education was especially important because success on the battlefield was usually the gateway to higher, nonmilitary office for nobles—an option only rarely open to warriors of less august background.

Merchants, or *pochteca,* held a high position in Aztec society and functioned as ambassadors, spies, and warriors in addition to their official position. The important role that they played in the expansion and economic domination of the Aztec state merited them special honors. Moctezuma II treated merchants as a branch of the nobility, and if one died on a mission, he was honored as a fallen warrior both by the living and in the afterlife. Membership in the

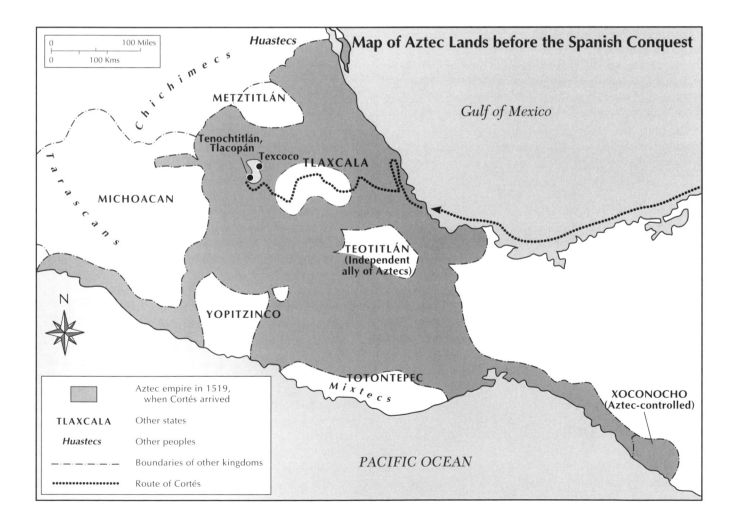

pochteca was hereditary, and all members belonged to one of the twelve merchant guilds. Members of this class often became so prosperous that Aztec law forbade ostentatious displays of wealth lest they arouse the rulers' jealousy. It should be noted that this was one of the few areas in which women were able to exercise semi-independent economic power. Although women were not permitted membership in any of the merchant guilds, they could and did trade by proxy and were agents of their male relatives' goods in the latters' absence.

The majority of the population, both in the city and in the countryside, were *macehualtin,* or commoners. Most of these worked lands belonging to wealthier members of their *calpulli,* although the families themselves maintained certain rights over the family plot provided that it did not lie uncultivated for two years or more.

At the bottom of the social hierarchy were the *mayeque,* semifree serfs who worked on the nobles' estates. According to one estimate, this group constituted about 30 percent of the population of the empire. About one-third of the produce of their labor went to their lord. Their low status did not mean that they were always the poorest members of Aztec society. A member of this class might, through inheritance, become wealthier than most *macehualtin* without any change in social status.

Slaves, or *tlacohtin,* are difficult to place in the socioeconomic hierarchy simply because their employment and consequent status depended on their skills. They might be purchased as agricultural labor, domestic servants, or even estate managers. Furthermore, because they could own property (including slaves of their own), some were able to become quite wealthy.

The Life Cycle

In all classes, birth was the point at which an Aztec's destiny began to be laid out. A woman's pregnancy was an affair for the whole community to celebrate, and birth was marked by family and neighborhood feasts and celebrations that could last for up to 15 days. The actual process of childbirth, by contrast, was a more private affair at which only women were present. After the midwife cut the umbilical cord, she recited a speech to the newborn, stressing the new arrival's obligations and place in society: Boys were instructed in their mission to provide sacrifices for the gods, while girls were admonished to keep a good home. Gender roles were emphasized again at a later ceremony, when baby boys were given miniature weapons, girls miniature brooms and weaving implements.

Children of both sexes received formal education beginning at about age 15 and lasting for five years, or until they were of marriageable age. Children of the nobility and sometimes *pochteca* children attended sex-segregated classes in the *calmecac,* in which priests instructed them in all aspects of Aztec religion and history. Education in one of these institutions was a prerequisite to holding any high administrative appointment or to going on to the *tlamacazcalli,* a kind of seminary for those who wished to enter the priesthood. Less well-heeled children attended the *tlepochcalli,* a military academy aimed at training male students to be warriors, while girls seem to have studied song, dance, and embroidery.

Families, rather than young couples, usually arranged marriages via matchmakers. Marriage seems to have occurred at age 20 for boys and slightly younger for girls, with the expectation that one would marry another member of one's own *calpulli.* Both the bride's family and the groom's schoolmasters had to give approval to the match. The ritual banquet took place in the home of the bride's family, after which she was borne to the groom's family home, where the couple would make their residence.

For women, at least, marriage marked a passage to adulthood. Book six of the Florentine Codex admonished the future bride to "regard one with respect, speak well, greet one well . . . Do not reject us, do not embarrass us as old men, do not reject thy mothers as old women." It should be noted that men could take as many secondary wives or concubines as they could afford to support. While in practical terms this meant that most commoners probably had only one wife, great lords had dozens or sometimes even hundreds.

For young men the passage into adulthood was marked not by marriage but by the taking of a first captive in battle, often a prerequisite to marriage. Boys' indoctrination into the warrior ethic of Aztec society began in earnest in the "House of Youth," a sort of youth auxiliary to the more formal academies they would attend when older. Beginning around age six or seven, they began to learn songs and dances telling of the glory of war in general and of their own *calpulli*'s warriors in particular. By the time they entered into formal weapons training around age 15, they had gained a firm sense of the importance of warfare both to the individual and the community. At about 18 years of age novice warriors ventured onto the field of battle for the first time, although only to observe a seasoned warrior with whom they had been paired. On their second foray they were expected to take a captive, although on this occasion they might make the capture a group effort of up to six novice warriors. Increased status marked this first capture, and additional privileges came with additional captures. Theoretically, at least, these privileges included the possibility of elevation to a branch of nobility distinct from the hereditary nobles, with the right to privileges and visible markers of status not allowed to commoners, but excluding the insignia and many of the privileges of those born nobles.

Aztecs, like most Mesoamerican cultures, believed that death and life existed in complementary opposition. For example, deceased ancestors could exert influence on the living, ranging from sending diseases to interceding with the gods. The Aztecs often held festivals to honor the dead, and the living could communicate with ancestors via offerings of food and flowers. (After the conquest, DIEGO DURÁN noted with some concern that certain aspects of these festivals persisted during the Catholic holidays of All Saints' and All Souls'.) Afterlife destination depended not on individual behavior but rather on social status and/or manner of death. Warriors who died on the battlefield and women who died in childbirth were the only ones guaranteed a happy afterlife. Most people had to undertake a more arduous journey before attaining their final rest. The underworld was made up of eight layers under the earth, each offering different hazards, such as clashing mountains, obsidian-edged winds, and sacrifice by arrow or by heart removal. The deepest of the nether regions was Mictlan, which the Spanish conquerors identified with the Christian hell. To aid their departed relatives in their arduous pilgrimages, families of the deceased provided them not only with provisions but also with valuables that might speed their journey, such as cacao beans, jade beads, and frothed hot chocolate.

Religion

Religion permeated all aspects of the Aztecs' existence, as it did for other peoples in the Atlantic world. In Central America indigenous peoples often shared certain religious ideals or deities. Most of the gods of the Aztec pantheon, for example, had adherents among the MAYA, OLMECS, and the civilization at TEOTIHUACÁN,

The cyclical nature of life was reflected in the cycle of the Aztec calendar: 20 day names and 13 day numbers, yielding a total of 260 combinations. Also, a solar calendar of 365 days was used, divided into 20 numbered-day months and ending in five "unlucky days." For all possible permutations of the combined calendars to exhaust themselves required 52 years, terminating in a dangerous five-day period in which the gods might choose to destroy the world, then in its fifth cycle, and begin a new cycle. Recognizing their good fortune at having escaped calamity, the Aztecs created the "new fire ceremony" dedicated to the god Xiutecuhtli.

The End of Empire

Only a few years after a new fire ceremony in Tenochtitlán the destruction of the Aztec empire actually occurred, but at the hands of the Spanish rather than the gods. After sending two exploratory missions to the coast of Mexico, the governor of Cuba, DIEGO DE VELÁZQUEZ, sent HERNÁN CORTÉS on a mission to trade and explore in Mexico as well as to make a settlement on the coast of Mexico that Velázquez could claim as his own. Cortés's 11 ships sailed from Cuba in February 1519 with a force of 600 fighting men, 200 native servants, 16 HORSES, 32 crossbows, 13 muskets, and 14 mobile cannon, landing in March on the coast of the TABASCO region. He defeated local natives in a quick skirmish, securing both an alliance and tribute that included the slave woman MALINCHE, who would later become invaluable as Cortés's interpreter and informant on local affairs. Soon thereafter, Cortés dropped any pretense that his mission was a peaceful one or that he was operating under the orders of Velázquez and embarked on a program of conquest.

Moctezuma II had by this time received word of the new arrivals and sent emissaries to greet them, possibly suspecting that Cortés or one of his entourage was the incarnation of the god QUETZALCOATL. It is likely that any such belief gave way as the invaders marched toward Tenochtitlán, conquering cities along the way, including Quetzalcoatl's cult center, Cholula, where they staged a mass slaughter of the resident nobles and warriors. After the now-intimidated Moctezuma failed in his attempts to deter them by gifts, blandishments, and even sorcery, the Spaniards entered Tenochtitlán, where Moctezuma allowed himself to be taken captive.

The tide was soon to turn in the Aztecs' favor, though only briefly. In the spring of 1520 Cortés received word that Diego Velázquez, angered that his deputy had exceeded his authority, had sent a detachment to bring Cortés back to Cuba. In his absence, he left PEDRO DE ALVARADO in charge. This temporary leader of the occupying forces, fearing an uprising at a religious observance incorporating several Aztec nobles and warriors, led the Spanish troops in what must have seemed to the inhabitants an unprovoked massacre of the city's civil and military leadership. Alvarado's action provoked an uprising that the occupying forces were hard-pressed to keep under control. By the time Cortés returned to the city with reinforcements won over from the troops sent to detain him, he faced a sullen population who refused to sell provisions to the Spaniards (much less provide them for free at Moctezuma's orders) and who continued to riot, now convinced of the necessity of expelling the invaders. The opposition even went so far as to elect another speaker in Moctezuma's place, CUITLÁHUAC, provided he could drive the Spaniards out of the city. A desperate Cortés prevailed upon Moctezuma to address his people and order them to resume trading with his troops, but the population of Tenochtitlán, now under the banner of Cuitláhuac, rejected their former leader's appeal and pelted him with stones, inflicting wounds from which he apparently later died.

The Aztecs' rebellion began in earnest on June 25, 1520. Cutting off the bridges within the causeways, they trapped the Spanish within the city. By June 29 Cortés and his men were trapped in the palace with no food and were losing men every time one of them tried to escape. On June 30, a night that Spanish chroniclers would remember as the Noche Triste ("Sad Night"), Cortés made portable bridges to traverse the eight spans of the TACUBA causeway and let his men help themselves to the GOLD, which they stuffed into their armor and helmets before making an attempt to escape the city, but only half had crossed the first gap before their Aztec pursuers destroyed their makeshift bridge, trapping most of the Spanish troops either in the city or only partway across the causeway. In the rest of the fighting that night, half the soldiers were killed or drowned, weighted down by plundered gold.

Cortés and his decimated forces were to have the final word (see Documents). About the time that the Aztecs were driving out the Spaniards, SMALLPOX, a DISEASE inadvertently brought by the invaders, began to rage through the densely populated city. Within months smallpox had claimed the lives of a large percentage of the population, including the new speaker, Cuitláhuac. Cortés later returned in April 1521 and laid siege to the city, now weakened and depopulated. By July the city's population, which stood at 200,000 before the Spanish arrived, had been reduced to 60,000 starved survivors who had no choice but to surrender to the conquistadores.

Further reading: Contemporary accounts of the Aztecs include Bernal Díaz del Castillo, *The True History of the Conquest of New Spain,* trans. A. P. Maudslay (orig. published in 1908–10; repr. New York: Farrar, Straus and Giroux, 1956); Diego Durán, *The History of the Indies of New Spain,* trans. Doris Heyden (Norman: University of Oklahoma Press, 1995); and Fray Bernardino de Sahagún, *General History of the Things of New Spain,* trans. Arthus J. O. Anderson and Charles E. Dibble, 13 vols. (Santa Fe: School of American Research and University of Utah, 1950–1982). For an account from the Aztec point of view, see Miguel León-Portilla, ed., *The Broken Spears: The Aztec Account of the Conquest of Mexico,* trans. Lysander Kemp (Boston: Beacon Press, 1961). General works on the subject include Michael Coe, *Mexico From the Olmecs to the Aztecs,* 4th ed. (London: Thames & Hudson, 1994) and Nigel Davies, *The Aztec Empire: The Toltec Resurgence* (Norman: University of Oklahoma Press, 1987). For an analysis of Aztec society and culture, see Inga Clendinnen, *Aztecs: An Interpretation* (Cambridge, U.K.: Cambridge University Press, 1991). For Aztec religion, see Kay Almere Read, *Time and Sacrifice in the Aztec Cosmos* (Bloomington: Indiana University Press, 1998), and Mary Miller and Karl Taube, *The Gods and Symbols of Ancient Mexico and the Maya: An Illustrated Dictionary of Mesoamerican Religion* (London: Thames & Hudson, 1993).

— Marie A. Kelleher

Aztlán

In Aztec history and mythology, Aztlán, supposedly an island in a lake in the west or northwest of MEXICO, was the place of origin for their people and the birthplace of their patron god, HUITZILOPOCHTLI.

NAHUATL for "place of whiteness" or "place of herons," Aztlán was the mythical point of departure for the AZTECS' peregrination to TENOCHTITLÁN. The Aztecs were seeking a replica of this original home when they finally arrived in Tenochtitlán. One tradition gives their date of departure as A.D. 1111. The name *Aztecs* literally means "people of Aztlán," although they and their neighbors referred to them as *Mexica.*

Historians differ as to how much of this origin myth to accept as historical fact. It cannot, however, be discounted merely as cynical self-aggrandizement on the part of the Aztecs, many of whom seem to have sincerely believed that their people originated in a place whose location became lost in the mists of time. Moctezuma I (r. 1440–69), for example, once sent forth about 60 magicians loaded down with the most precious gifts available to present them to the god or his emissaries, or to the less peripatetic descendants of their distant ancestors.

The vague and sometimes confused nature of the Aztec origin myth as well as the familiar motif of a people wandering in the desert in search of a new home led at least one contemporary European observer, Fray DIEGO DURÁN, to conclude that the Aztecs were one of the lost tribes of Israel. Quoting from the prophet Hosea, Durán pointed out that God had punished these tribes for their sins by condemning them to be perpetually cowardly and proposed this divine castigation as the reason for (and perhaps justification of) their defeat at the hands of decidedly inferior numbers of Spanish invaders.

Further reading: Michael Coe, *Mexico: From the Olmecs to the Aztecs,* 4th ed. (London: Thames & Hudson, 1994); Nigel Davies, *Aztecs: A History* (Norman: University of Oklahoma Press, 1980); Diego Durán, *The History of the Indies of New Spain,* trans. Doris Heyden (Norman: University of Oklahoma Press, 1995); Mary Miller and Karl Taube, *The Gods and Symbols of Ancient Mexico and the Maya: An Illustrated Dictionary of Mesoamerican Religion* (London: Thames & Hudson, 1993).

— Marie A. Kelleher

B

Baba, Ahmad (1556–1627)

Ahmad Baba, an Islamic scholar, writer, and jurist, wrote books and treatises on theology, jurisprudence, history, and Arabic grammar, some of which are still in use today.

Ahmad Baba was born on October 26, 1556, in Arawan, near the city of TIMBUKTU. At the time Timbuktu was part of the SONGHAI Empire, renowned for its dedication to Islamic scholarship. The city became a center of Islamic learning. Baba was a member of the influential Aqit family, who formed part of the ruling patriciate of Islamic scholars in Timbuktu. He studied Islamic theology and law, remaining an active part of the scholarly class in Timbuktu for most of his life. Ahmad Baba was a prolific writer, with a total of 56 works attributed to him, 32 of which still exist. Most of his works dealt with jurisprudence, but he also wrote on theological subjects, grammar, and historical biography. Ahmad Baba also wrote *Kifayat al-Muktaj*, a revision of the popular historical source *Nayl al-Ibthikaj* on Maliki Islam (see ISLAM). In addition to writing, Ahmad Baba was an avid collector, and his personal library contained thousands of volumes.

Although Baba lived most of his life in Timbuktu, he spent several years in exile in Marrakech, Morocco. In 1591 the sultan of Morocco invaded the Songhai Empire and took control of Timbuktu. The people of the city rebelled against the Moroccans in 1593 under the leadership of the local literati. In 1594 Mahmud ibn Zargun, the pasha of the region under the Moroccans, deported Ahmad Baba and other scholars to Marrakech. Despite his status as an exile, Ahmad Baba continued to teach and practice law with the permission of the Moroccan authorities, and it was here that he wrote *Kifayat al-Muktal*. After the death of the Moroccan sultan in 1607, Ahmad Baba returned to his native Timbuktu, where he died in 1627.

Further reading: Elizabeth Heath, "Ahmad Baba," in *Africana: The Encyclopedia of the African and African American Experience*, eds. Kwame Anthony Appiah and Henry Louis Gates, Jr. (New York: Basic *Civitas* Books, 1999), 53–54; "Ahmad Baba," in *Historical Dictionary of Mali* 2nd ed. Pascal James Imperato (Metuchen, N.J.: Scarecrow Press, 1986), 80–81.

— Lisa M. Brady

Bahía

One of the 15 regions (known as captaincies) into which the Portuguese Crown divided the colony of Brazil in the 1530s.

When a Portuguese fleet bound for India was blown across the Atlantic and discovered what became known as BRAZIL in the early 16th century, it appeared to offer little to the commerce-minded Europeans. Early Portuguese interest centered on the dyewood (or brazilwood) trees found there, and the first colonists set up a factory system similar to the one they used in Africa and Asia. Those who controlled the factories—better understood as trading posts—employed the natives of Brazil as tree harvesters. Because the isolated factories represented no threat to the natives, they willingly exchanged their labor for European goods. The shift in Portuguese policy from factories to settlement was precipitated by the French, who made significant inroads into the dyewood trade. Unable to prevent these French incursions by the use of naval power, the Portuguese decided that permanent settlement was the only solution.

Both unwilling and unable to expend the necessary funds to establish Crown-run settlements, the government divided the colony into 15 captaincies that ran from east to west across the country. The captaincy of Bahía lay in the middle of the country and was allocated to Francisco Pereira Coutinho. However, the viability of the settlements was threatened almost immediately when it became apparent that the Portuguese had miscalculated the cultural attitudes of the native population. The new settlers turned to SUGAR as a potential source of wealth and assumed that the native men would be as willing to work in the cane fields as they had been to harvest brazilwood trees. But while the natives considered tree-cutting to be men's work, they thought of field work as women's domain and resisted attempts to turn them into field hands. Furthermore, the establishment of permanent settlements constituted a real threat to the natives. In 1545, in response to the threat posed by newcomers, the Tupinamba Indians launched a series of attacks that virtually eliminated the Portuguese presence in Bahía.

The Portuguese did not return to Bahía until 1549, at which time they made the region a Crown colony and established the city of Salvador. Blessed with fertile soil and an appropriate amount of rainfall, Bahía (along with the captaincy of Pernambuco) became the center of Portuguese sugar production. By 1570 Bahía boasted 18 sugar mills, a number that had doubled by 1585. At that time Salvador's population of 14,000 made it the largest city in Brazil. Indeed, so rapid was the recovery of fortunes in Bahía that the Portuguese promoter, Pero de Magalhaes, wrote in 1576 that Bahía "is the part of Brazil most thickly populated by Portuguese."

But this economic growth came at a devastating price not only to the natives but to the newest arrivals in South America—African slaves (*see* SLAVERY). Following their return in 1549, the Portuguese used the natives as forced laborers, but in the 1560s the natives suffered from epidemics resulting from their exposure to Old World DISEASES. Further complicating the use of natives was the growing opposition of the Crown to enslaving the Indians, inspired in part by the JESUITS. Despite these twin problems, the transition to African slaves was slow in Bahía, and it was not until late in the 17th century that most plantations had completed the transition to a workforce composed entirely of Africans.

Through a combination of climate, geography, exploitation, economic management, and European demand, the sugar industry transformed Bahía (and other parts of Brazil) into a critical piece of the Portuguese colonial empire. Inspired by this success, the Dutch in the early 17th century formulated plans to mount a military assault on Brazil to bring it under their control.

Further reading: Leslie Bethell, ed., *Colonial Brazil* (Cambridge, U.K.: Cambridge University Press, 1987); C. R. Boxer, *The Portuguese Seaborne Empire, 1415–1825* (New York: Knopf, 1969).

— John Grigg

Balboa, Vasco Núñez de (1475–1517)

A Spanish CONQUISTADOR during the early period of exploration and conquest, Vasco Núñez de Balboa in 1513 was the first European to see the Pacific Ocean.

Following a childhood lived in poverty, Balboa first journeyed to the NEW WORLD in 1500 as part of the wave of Spaniards who sought the rich resources of mainland America or Tierra Firme. Tierre Firme, first discovered by CHRISTOPHER COLUMBUS during his third mission, included the northern coast of present-day Colombia and Venezuela.

Balboa spent several unremarkable years in unsuccessful farming and indebtedness on HISPANIOLA before, perhaps as a stowaway, he accompanied an expedition to the American mainland. In 1509, as part of a slave-raiding mission to the area, Balboa founded the settlement of Darién. Then, in search of the rumored golden kingdom of Birú vividly described by local natives, Balboa led a mission across the Isthmus of PANAMA. While he failed to locate this kingdom of gold, by 1513 Balboa succeeded in crossing the isthmus and thereby claimed the rights as the first European to reach the Pacific Ocean.

Balboa's accomplishment inspired jealousy in Pedrarias Dávila, the governor of the isthmus. Using a fabricated story of treason, Dávila and other seasoned conquistadores, including FRANCISCO PIZARRO, conspired in Balboa's arrest. In 1517 Dávila called for Balboa's execution.

In the aftermath of Balboa's journey across the isthmus, the Spanish used the knowledge of what he found to help them conquer the native peoples of present-day PERU and Chile. Knowledge of the Pacific also proved crucial to Spanish efforts to control the west coast of MEXICO and, eventually, CALIFORNIA.

Further reading: Charles Loftus Grant Anderson, *Life and Letters of Vasco Núñez de Balboa* (Westport, Conn.: Greenwood Press, 1970); John A. Crow, *The Epic of Latin America,* 4th ed. (Los Angeles: University of California Press, 1992); Kathleen Romoli, *Balboa of Darién: Discoverer of the Pacific* (Garden City, N.Y.: Doubleday, 1953); Edwin Williamson, *The Penguin History of Latin America* (New York and London: Penguin Press, 1992).

— Kimberly Sambol-Tosco

Bantu

The term *Bantu* refers to both peoples and languages south of a line from the southern Cameroon–Nigeria border in the west to the southern Somali border in the east.

Although the 600 Bantu languages share similarities in basic grammar and vocabulary, time and distance have made most of them mutually unintelligible. Similarly, Bantu cultures share basic similarities but immense variations remain. Cameroon marks the cradle of Bantu language and culture. A study of Bantu linguistic evolution revealed that Bantu migrations occurred in three great waves, or dispersals, labeled Original Bantu, West Bantu,

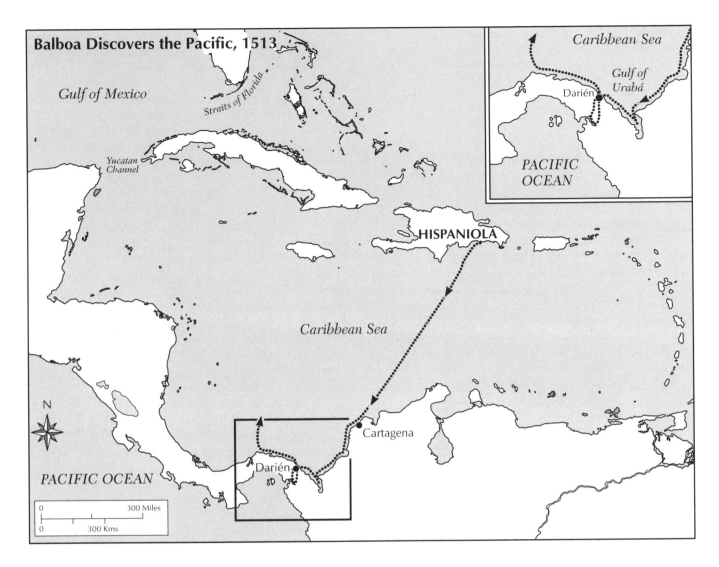

and East Bantu. The Original Bantu spread from what is now western Cameroon to the Great Lakes, then southward to the Ogowe Delta. West Bantu spread from what is now northern Gabon southward to northern Namibia, then eastward into the Zaire basin. The third dispersal, identified as East Bantu, spread from the Great Lakes eastward to the Indian Ocean, then turned south and spread to the southern tip of Africa.

The success of Bantu migration appears to be due to relatively stable village communities and a food production system that supplemented foraging. The villages were organized around several "houses" headed by leaders whose family members, friends, and servants made up each house. Usually about five villages banded together to form a district and helped one another in issues relating to economics, marriage, defense, and religion. Each house also created alliances with houses in other villages to form clans.

Consequently, Bantu communities became flexible social structures numbering about 500 people. These communities were more efficient than were the small social units of the neighboring foragers.

As the East Bantu migration evolved, its success depended not only on stable communities but also on the development of a farming complex that included grain cultivation and cattle herding. Slight differences in technology existed between Bantu peoples and non-Bantu peoples, but the success of Bantu migrations depended on stable communities and effective food production.

Further reading: Alfred T. Bryand, *Bantu Origins: The People and Their Language* (Cape Town: C. Struick, 1963); Muhammed el Fasi and Ivan Hrbek, eds. *The General History of Africa,* vol. 3, *Africa from the Seventh to the Eleventh Century* (London: Heinemann, 1988); David W.

Phillipson, *The Later Prehistory of Eastern and Southern Africa* (New York: Africana, 1977); Thurstan Shaw, et al., eds., *The Archaeology of Africa: Foods, Metals, and Towns* (London: Routledge, 1993).

— Tom Niermann

Barbados

Although the British did not pursue permanent colonization of Barbados until 1627, Spanish and Portuguese explorers landed on the island during the 16th century as part of European efforts to explore and eventually colonize the Western Hemisphere.

Before contact with European explorers, the inhabitants of Barbados lived in relative obscurity from the rest of the West Indies. Over the course of its history Barbados, a small island (430 square kilometers in area) with, at the time of European arrival, a substantial tropical rain forest, experienced various successive waves of migration of inhabitants from the South American mainland. Modern research suggests that, contrary to the assumptions of 16th-century Europeans, the four American Indian groups that migrated to Barbados from the seventh century until the arrival of the CARIB came from a similar ancestral background. During the mid-13th century one such group, termed *Carib* by the Spanish, replaced the Lokonos (ARAWAK) through conquest. The Carib maintained their stronghold on the island until at least the late 15th century.

As the Spanish and Portuguese explored the NEW WORLD during the late 15th and early 16th centuries, they learned that Barbados and much of the Lesser Antilles lacked significant quantities of gold. Thus, for some time they worked under the assumption that Barbados was of little value to their efforts in the West Indies. Then, in 1511, CHARLES V, responding to the need for mine laborers in CUBA, authorized various slaving expeditions to islands in the Caribbean. The Spanish extended their search for potential Indian slaves throughout the area, reaching Barbados during the early 1520s.

The arrival of Spanish CONQUISTADORES on Barbados coincided with the end of American Indian settlement on the island. Whereas European explorers recorded their experiences in other locations throughout the Caribbean, no such records exist for the first contact with inhabitants of Barbados. Thus, whether the depopulation of Barbados occurred before, during, and/or because of European activities has yet to be determined. While it is possible that the Spanish effectively removed the remaining inhabitants of Barbados to Cuba, it is also possible that the American Indian population relocated themselves on other islands, knowing beforehand of the impending arrival of the Spanish. What is certain is that during the first half of the 16th century, as Spaniards combed the Caribbean in search of laborers for their mines, they landed on Barbados and found it largely or entirely uninhabited.

Although the exact date of first contact between Europeans and American Indians on Barbados is unknown, scholars maintain that the first written reference to the island can be traced to a Spanish expedition in 1518. Then, in 1536, a Portuguese explorer, Pedro a Campus, landed on the island, describing it as deserted. The island remained uninhabited until the arrival of the British during the 17th century.

Further reading: Hilary Beckles, *A History of Barbados: From Amerindian Settlement to Nation-State* (Cambridge: U.K. Cambridge University Press, 1990); Peter L. Drewett, *Prehistoric Barbados* (London: University College London, 1991); F. A. Hoyos, *Barbados: A History from the Amerindians to Independence* (London: Macmillan, 1978); Lyle McAlister, *Spain and Portugal in the New World, 1492–1700* (Minneapolis: University of Minnesota Press, 1984); Jan Rogoziński, *A Brief History of the Caribbean: From the Arawak and the Carib to the Present*, rev. ed. (New York: Facts On File, 1999).

— Kimberly Sambol-Tosco

Barlowe, Arthur (fl. 1580s)

Arthur Barlowe's description of ROANOKE Island as an earthly paradise helped encourage SIR WALTER RALEGH to choose it as a site for the first English colony in North America.

In 1584 Ralegh sent two ships, commanded by Barlowe and Philip Amadas, to explore the coast of North America and recommend a site for a colony. Little is known about Barlowe's early life, although he had served under Ralegh in Ireland in 1580–81 and had, at some point, sailed to the eastern Mediterranean. Amadas and Barlowe reached the islands off the coast of North Carolina in July 1585. After exploring the vicinity they declared Roanoke Island a suitable site. Barlowe, in his report to Ralegh, compared the island to the Garden of Eden and described it as "full of deer, conies, hares, and fowl, even in the midst of summer, in incredible abundance," with trees "of excellent smell and quality." The two explorers also met and traded with some Indians in the area, reporting "[W]e were entertained with all love and kindness, and with as much bounty, after their manner, as they could possibly devise." The explorers returned to England, bringing two Indians, MANTEO and WANCHESE, both of whom learned to speak English and returned to Roanoke with a later voyage. Barlowe's glowing report on the potential of the land helped convince Ralegh, wrongly, that a colony could easily be built and sustained at Roanoke.

Further reading: Arthur Barlowe, "Discovery of Virginia, 1584" in *Hakluyt's Voyages: A Selection,* ed. Richard David (Boston: Houghton Mifflin, 1981), 445–453; Karen Ordahl Kupperman, *Indians and English: Facing Off in Early America* (Ithaca, N.Y.: Cornell University Press, 2000); ———, *Roanoke: The Abandoned Colony* (Totowa, N.J.: Rowman and Allanheld, 1984); David Beers; Quinn, *Set Fair for Roanoke: Voyages and Colonies, 1584–1606* (Chapel Hill: University of North Carolina Press, 1985).

— Martha K. Robinson

Battel, Andrew (fl. 1589–1614)

Author, prisoner, soldier, and trader, Andrew Battel was best known for his account of a journey that took him from LONDON in 1589 to BRAZIL and Angola before his return to England around 1610.

Little is known of the early life of Andrew Battel. He was probably born in Leigh, Essex, in the 1560s. Like many young men in Elizabethan England, he found his way to London, where he signed up for passage on a vessel that took him far from his native shores. He sailed from Plymouth on May 7, 1589, on one of four pinnaces under the command of Abraham Cocke bound for South America. Delayed by storms that forced them back to Plymouth, the ships traveled via the CANARY ISLANDS and the Guinea coast across the Atlantic. After 30 days at sea the ships docked at Ilhe Grande on the coast of Brazil. Seeking fresh supplies after surviving on seals for a month, Battel and some of the other sailors traveled to the island of Saint Sebastian, where he and four others fell captive to local Indians who left them with Portuguese authorities. Cocke left the captives behind and Battel never saw him again.

The Portuguese sent Battel to St. Paul-de-Loanda in Angola, where he spent four months as a prisoner. Battel gained his freedom, and after surviving an illness the Portuguese governor João Furtado de Mendonca hired him to lead a trading mission down the Congo River to acquire ivory, maize, and palm oil. Battel twice tried to escape but failed each time. After serving in battle with the Portuguese he eventually became a coastal trader once again, but the Portuguese left Battel among the Jagas, an interior nation, where Battel spent almost two years during which, he claimed, he learned that they practiced infanticide and sacrificed human beings. In 1610, under circumstances that remain unclear, Battel returned to London.

All knowledge of Battel's activities comes from SAMUEL PURCHAS, who published an account of Battel's voyages in 1613 and then a longer version in 1625. Like THOMAS HARRIOT, Battel provided an English-language ethnography for an audience eager to learn about the peoples who inhabited the far reaches of the Atlantic world.

His account included descriptions of various African groups, flora, and fauna, including descriptions of such exotic phenomena as zebras, chimpanzees, and the baobab tree. According to one 19th-century editor, Battel wandered along routes that were not traversed again by Europeans for at least 300 years.

Further reading: Peter C. Mancall, "Battel, Andrew," in *New Dictionary of National Biography* (Oxford: U.K. Oxford University Press, forthcoming); Samuel Purchas, *Purchas his Pilgrimes* (London, 1613), book 7. ch. 9; ———, *Haklaytus Posthumus* (London, 1625), part ii, book vii, ch. iii; E. G. Ravenstein, ed., *Strange Adventures of Andrew Battel of Leigh, in Angola and the Adjoining Regions*, Works Issued by the Hakluyt Society, 2nd ser., VI (London, 1901).

Behaim, Martin (1459–1507)

In 1492 Martin Behaim created a globe that depicted that world that Europeans knew before CHRISTOPHER COLUMBUS sailed.

Behaim was born in Nuremberg in 1459 but lived for some time as an adult in Portugal. In 1490 he returned to his home city, where the town council commissioned him to make a globe. The result, the oldest surviving globe in the world, depicted a small Atlantic Ocean, suggesting that ships that sailed west might quickly reach the riches of Asia.

Cartographic matters were much in dispute in the 15th century. Mapmakers disagreed about the size of the world, the possibility of finding new trade routes to Asia, and the existence of distant lands. Behaim's globe agreed in many respects with the geographical theories of Christopher Columbus. Both Behaim and Columbus believed that the world was much smaller than it is, for example, and that it might therefore be practical to sail west to reach Cipangu (Japan). There is, however, no evidence that the two men ever met or that Columbus was familiar with Behaim's work. Behaim's globe also showed a number of mythical lands, including the kingdom of PRESTER JOHN, the land of the Biblical Magi, and the islands of Antillia and St. Brendan.

Further reading: Anthony Grafton, *New Worlds, Ancient Texts: The Power of Tradition and the Shock of Discovery* (Cambridge, Mass.: Belknap, 1992); E. G. Ravenstein, *Martin Behaim, his Life and his Globe* (London: 1908); R.V. Tooley, *Maps and Map-Makers* (London: B.T. Batsford Ltd., 1987); Hans Wolff, ed., *America: Early Maps of the New World* (Munich: Prestel, 1992).

— Martha K. Robinson

Benin

For more than 3,000 years people speaking the Edo (Benin) language have lived in a 12,000-square-mile area just west of the Niger River in what is now Nigeria.

Over time small, relatively independent villages united into larger communities culminating in the ancient kingdom of Benin. This ancient kingdom is distinct from the present-day nation of the same name.

Tropical rain forests dominate much of the region. Consequently, early settlers survived by cultivating clearings and supplementing their agricultural production with hunting. Natural population growth, combined with the introduction of iron tools around A.D. 400 or 500, encouraged small communities to unite for defensive purposes and to more efficiently exploit natural resources. During the same period institutions developed within the growing communities that established a hierarchy of authority and division of power.

Archeological findings dating as far back as A.D. 400 provide evidence of the social and political changes occurring in this region. Village communities grew to towns, and local leaders expanded their role as regional rulers. By the year 1000 two centers of power had developed: Benin and Udo. These two power centers developed a model of government similar to the YORUBA, a neighboring people to the north. In fact, both the Yoruba and Benin traditions trace the lineage of their ruling dynasties to Ife, another city-state to the north. The Benin monarch was called the *oba,* who received his position through heredity and held spiritual and temporal authority, although his power was somewhat limited by a group of hereditary chiefs called the Uzama. The *oba's* power grew substantially around the 13th century, when Oba Ewedo dismantled the Uzama, built an impressive palace, and created a new court hierarchy made up of men who received nonhereditary positions. This consolidation of political power did not coincide with territorial expansion; Benin remained one of many Edo city-states.

Around 1480 an apparent conquest by an outside power provided the catalyst for enormous change within the Benin kingdom. Oba Ewuare was eventually able to drive the invading forces from Benin and rebuild the devastated city. Most important in the rebuilding process was the royal palace, which included quarters for skilled craftsmen dedicated to his service. These craftsmen formed guilds that produced the fine artwork for which Benin remains so well known. Ewuare also restructured Benin's political institutions. First, he created three bodies of courtiers: one responsible for his care, a second responsible for the care of his wives, and a third responsible for the care of the royal regalia. Each body contained three ranks, the lowest filled with free-born males who were required to fulfill mandatory service obligations to the *oba.* Ewuare

relied on three councils of chiefs for advice pertaining to matters of governing. Also, he applied primogeniture to the order of succession to the throne, and he introduced the *Ique,* an annual feast celebrating the *oba's* mystical powers.

For the next 30 years Ewuare expanded his territorial control by going to war with neighboring kingdoms. Much of Oba Ewuare's success stemmed from the centralized control he established, especially concerning the use of Benin's human and material resources. Tributes from more distant conquests flowed into Benin, while conquered regions closer to the capital submitted to direct rule.

Ewuare's authoritarian rule did not sit well with those he conquered, so Benin experienced a series of revolutions upon Ewuare's death. Despite the attempts of the citizens of Benin to limit royal power, the people had to embrace monarchical rule when insurgent provinces threatened the capital. Uniting under Ozolua, Ewuare's son, Benin suppressed the rebellions. Ozolua reaffirmed his father's authoritarianism and set out on a series of conquests consolidating power and expanding Benin's borders. Ozolua's son Esigie finally quelled all resistance to Benin's centralized, authoritarian system and reigned for almost 50 years. Esigie's reign marked the beginning of Benin's golden age as wealth from trade and tributary states flowed into the capital.

Benin reached the limits of territorial expansion around the middle of the 17th century. As the Atlantic trade developed, Portuguese merchants established trade relations with Benin that appeared to benefit both nations. In fact, Benin sent ambassadors to Portugal to learn more about Portuguese people and customs. Once based on ground pepper and agricultural products, Benin's economy became dominated by the SLAVE TRADE.

Further reading: Patrick Darling, "Emerging Towns in Benin and Ishan, AD 500–1500," in John Gledhill, et al., eds., *State and Society: The Emergence and Development of Social Hierarchy and Political Centralization* (London and Boston, Unwin Hyman 1988); Basil Davidson, *The Lost Cities of Africa* (Boston: Little, Brown, 1959); Jacob U. Egharevba, *A Short History of Benin,* 3rd ed. (Ibadan, Nigeria: Ibadan University Press, 1960).

— Tom Niermann

Bermuda

A series of islands off the eastern shore of North America on which Europeans landed in the 16th century but did not colonize until the Spanish decided to establish permanent settlements there during the 17th century.

The Bermuda Islands consist of a series of continuous islands, approximately 20 square miles in total surface area.

The island's formidable topography and mazelike appearance prevented European exploration until the 17th century; only then did newcomers push through the jagged waters and dangerous reefs to pursue settlement. Throughout much of the 16th century Spanish travelers referred to the difficult shores of the Bermudas as a "graveyard of ships." Mariners passing through the Bahamas Channel and up the Gulf Stream felt relieved when their ships passed the Bermudas, considered the last of their American obstacles on the route to the AZORES and home.

Although the date for first European discovery may have been as early as 1503, by 1511 the Spanish referred to the islands as "La Bermuda." In 1515, following his earlier, unrecorded landing on the islands, Juan Bermudez carried out a return mission. This time, Spanish courtier and official historian of the Indies GONZALO FERNÁNDEZ DE OVIEDO Y VALDÉS traveled with the expedition and chronicled his observations of the isolated islands. Unfortunately, Bermudez encountered challenging winds that prevented him from approaching the islands, and thus Oviedo's chronicles describe impressions of the Bermudas made from the surrounding waters.

During much of the 16th century the negative feelings toward the Bermudas stemmed from the fears of Spanish and Portuguese explorers who encountered the treacherous coast. According to Oviedo, in 1543 30 Portuguese men en route back to Europe from the West Indies found themselves victims of the rocky waters of the Bermudas and had to spend two months ashore in Bermuda while they worked to build a new boat to replace their lost ship. Upon their return home the men reported the abundance of food on the desolate islands. However, their stories of earlier shipwrecks further contributed to the dreaded image of the Bermudas held by an increasing number of Europeans. In 1544 the Venetian explorer SEBASTIAN CABOT referred to the Bermudas as the Islands of Devils on his *MAPPA MUNDI*.

During the second half of the 16th century, two separate French ships wrecked on the reefs of the Bermudas. In the latter case, the ship's captain, Barbotiere, thought himself safely past the rocky Bermudan waters when the ship unexpectedly hit a rock to the north of the islands on December 17, 1593. Twenty-six of Barbotiere's men rowed seven leagues to shore while more than half the crew drowned. During May 1594 the surviving men finally departed for France on a boat built from the scraps of their wrecked ship. The surviving chronicles of Barbotiere's experience on the islands come to us from the only Englishman aboard the ship, Henry May. May's account, later published by RICHARD HAKLUYT THE YOUNGER, represents the first real description of the islands and in part explains why historians typically refer to the experience of the French ship as "Henry May's shipwreck." During the 17th century the successful colonization efforts of England in the Bermudas ended the abominable image of the islands.

Further reading: Terry Tucker, *Bermuda: Today and Yesterday 1503–1980s* (London: Robert Hall Limited, 1983); Henry C. Wilkinson, *The Adventures of Bermuda: A History of the Island from Its Discovery until the Dissolution of the Somers Island Company in 1684* (London: Oxford University Press, 1958)

— Kimberly Sambol-Tosco

Bermuda Company

From 1615 to 1684 the Bermuda Company operated England's smallest and second-oldest colony, although not without a great deal of tension between London shareholders and BERMUDA colonists.

The Bermuda Company began as the result of a shipwreck. In 1609 Sir George Somers, admiral of the Virginia Company, led a relief fleet of eight ships bound to assist settlers in Jamestown, Virginia. A storm scattered his fleet, and later a hurricane struck the *Sea Venture*, Somers's flagship. Close to sinking, Somers's vessel wrecked upon one of Bermuda's coral reefs, and its passengers were not only able to gain the safety of land but found something of an earthly paradise. After a nine-month stay, Somers and his men built a new ship, the *Deliverance*, from the remains of the *Sea Venture* and crossed the Gulf Stream to Jamestown. Somers found the settlers at Jamestown ragged and starving, so he returned to Bermuda to procure food, particularly the turtles, wild hogs (introduced in the 1500s by Spanish sailors), and fish that populated the island. As tales of the natural abundance of Bermuda spread, the Virginia Company extended its charter to include the Bermuda Islands. However, running two companies under one charter proved to be an inefficient means of organization, so in June 1615 King JAMES I chartered an offshoot of the Virginia Company variously called the Bermuda Company or Somers Island Company.

The Somers Island Company supervised Bermuda from its offices in London for 69 years, choosing its governors, sending it ships loaded with supplies, and asking in return the export of pearls, whale oil, TOBACCO, silk, and AMBERGRIS, the intestinal by-product of sperm whales coveted by perfume manufacturers. The early Bermuda planters became strong PURITANS and created a legislative assembly. The chief source of company profit came from the export of tobacco. Slaves (see SLAVERY) performed much of the labor needed to procure salable goods. Most slaves in Bermuda were purchased from slave plantations in the West Indies, although American Indian slaves and some white slaves were among the 6,000 to 8,000 people who populated the island in the mid-1600s. Despite the natural abundance of the island, the economic potential of Bermuda proved to be limited. Bermuda tobacco could not compete in quality or quantity with tobacco grown in Virginia. The excessive harvesting of turtles led to their rapid decrease, so much so that in 1620 Bermuda's first parliament passed an act "against the killing of over young tortoises" due to the danger of "an utter destroyinge and losse of them." Likewise, the harvesting of cedar trees had to be forbidden, for the islands were practically denuded. Stockholders had to content themselves with a small, if safe, return on their investment.

As London stockholders realized the limited nature of Bermuda's economy, interest in the company declined. Although much stock in the company passed into the hands of the Bermuda colonists, the company charter fixed its headquarters in London, and a small group of stockholders controlled company policy. Company agents living and working in Bermuda retained a stubborn independence that troubled their London bosses. They chafed, for example, under the policy that demanded they trade solely with company ships, which gave the company a monopoly. On the other hand, stockholders in London became increasingly unsatisfied with the meager monetary returns from the Bermuda Company and the apparently arbitrary economic decisions made by company employees in Bermuda. The majority stockholder, a London merchant named Perient Trott, attempted to persuade his fellow stockholders to permanently reorganize the company. After those efforts failed, Trott petitioned the government to seize the Bermuda Company. Trott's efforts put into place a legal process that in 1684 resulted (years after Trott's death) in the forfeiture to the Crown under Charles II of the company's charter. It outlived the Virginia Company by 60 years.

Further reading: Richard S. Dunn "The Downfall of the Bermuda Company: A Restoration Farce" *The William and Mary Quarterly* vol. 20, no. 4 (October 1963): 487–512; Jean Kennedy, *Isle of Devils: Bermuda under the Somers Island Company, 1609–1685* (London: William Collins Sons & Co. Ltd., 1971); Terry Tucker, *Bermuda: Today and Yesterday 1503–1980s* (London: Robert Hale Limited, 1983).

— Kevin C. Armitage

black legend

La leyenda negra—"the black legend"—refers to an idea generated originally by Spanish historians to describe the ways the English characterized the Spanish conquest of the Americas in the century following the expedition of CHRISTOPHER COLUMBUS.

When the Spanish conquered much of the Western Hemisphere, some of their actions aroused attention by observers who believed that they used excessive force in their desire to take control of the indigenous peoples they encountered. The actions of CONQUISTADORES such as HERNÁN CORTÉS, whose soldiers terrorized the native peoples of MEXICO during their campaign against the AZTECS, aroused hostility not only from indigenous chroniclers but also from Spanish observers. Among those observers was BARTOLOMÉ DE LAS CASAS, who launched a stinging assault on the conquistadores' ways in his reports on Spanish actions in the West Indies and on the mainland. His accounts, most notably his *Brief Account of the Destruction of the Indies* (first published in 1552), painted a devastating portrait of the plundering ways of conquistadores who enslaved some indigenous peoples and murdered others. Las Casas did not suggest that the Spanish should withdraw from the Western Hemisphere. Instead, he hoped that his writings would force the Spanish Crown to place controls over the actions of military leaders. Las Casas also continued to believe that the Spanish had to remain in the Americas in order to accomplish what he thought was the most important objective of the colonial enterprise: to convert natives to Catholicism, a task that took on added urgency after Protestantism spread across much of northern Europe during the 16th century. In Las Casas's mind the elaboration of the grotesque excesses of the conquistadores would convince imperial bureaucrats that the conversion program would achieve its ends only if the ghastly abuses of human rights perpetrated by the conquistadores came to an end.

Although Las Casas intended his book to alter Spanish policy, in 16th-century Europe the diffusion of the technology that led to the PRINTING PRESS meant that publishers across the continent had the ability to spread the message of any text that came into their hands. Perhaps predictably, Las Casas's work soon appeared, in translation, in Protestant nations, including England, as did other works that described horrendous Spanish actions, including Girolamo Benzoni's *History of the New World* (first published in VENICE in 1565). When read by Protestant readers—English, Dutch, and Huguenot—such writings confirmed their worst fears about the Spanish. Here was proof, many thought, of the true nature of the Spanish. In the hands of skilled promoters of colonization like RICHARD HAKLUYT THE YOUNGER and SAMUEL PURCHAS, Las Casas's writings, which had once been conceived as a way to soften Spanish policy in the Atlantic, became an indictment of malevolent Catholics bent on killing any native peoples they could not otherwise control. In this context the black legend became a further goad to colonization efforts by the English themselves.

Even after the English had colonized eastern North America, they continued to hold onto the belief in the black legend. No matter how violent the English themselves were to native American Indians (or, for that matter, how violent the English had been to the native Catholic Irish during the military assaults launched by Queen ELIZABETH I during the mid- to late 16th century), they were, in their own minds, more humane than the Spanish had been. As the historian David Weber put it, "Anglo Americans had inherited the view that Spaniards were unusually cruel, avaricious, treacherous, fanatical, superstitious, cowardly, corrupt, decadent, indolent, and authoritarian," and many of them held to such prejudices for centuries. When the Flemish engraver THEODOR DEBRY created illustrations to accompany translations of Las Casas's work in the late 16th century, he managed to solidify, in the most graphic possible ways, the link between Spanish expansion and horrendous treatment of indigenous peoples. Such illustrations, like the text that inspired them, came to serve specific political ends. The black legend thus became entrenched in the ways that subsequent generations of observers understood the 16th century.

Further reading: Bartolomé de Las Casas, *A Short Account of the Destruction of the Indies*, ed. Anthony Pagden (London: Penguin Books, 1992); J. H. Elliott, *The Old World and the New, 1492–1650* (Cambridge U.K.: Cambridge University Press, 1970); David J. Weber, *The Spanish Frontier in North America* (New Haven, Conn.: Yale University Press, 1992), esp. 336–341.

Blaeu, Willem (1571–1638)

Willem Janszoon Blaeu and his son, Joan Blaeu, were among the most important cartographers of the 16th and 17th centuries.

Willem Blaeu produced globes, sea charts, and maps, including a map of Holland (1604), a map of Spain (1605), and a large world map (1605). His maps and those of his son were noted for their beauty and for the skill of their production. In 1608 he produced maps of Europe, Asia, Africa, and America, and in 1633–34 became mapmaker for the DUTCH EAST INDIA COMPANY. His map "Nova Belgica et Anglia Nova" (1635) was the first printed map to depict canoes and North American animals, including the beaver. The Blaeu family's most important works include two atlases: the *Appendix Theatri Ortelii et Atlantis Mercatoris*, published in 1631, and the *Theatrum Orbis Terrarum sive Novus Atlas*, first published in 1635. Their maps were reprinted in various editions and languages during the 17th century.

Further reading: Cornelis Koeman,"Atlas Cartography in the Low Countries in the Sixteenth, Seventeenth, and Eighteenth Centuries" in John A. Wolter and Ronald E. Grim, eds., *Images of the World: The Atlas Through History* (Washington, D.C.: Library of Congress, 1997) 73–107; Seymour I. Schwartz and Ralph E. Ehrenberg, *The Mapping of America* (New York: Harry N. Abrams, Inc., 1980); R. V. Tooley, *Maps and Map-Makers* (London: B.T. Batsford Ltd., 1987).

— Martha K. Robinson

Brazil

A large geographical region encompassing nearly half of South America that became Portugal's only colony in the NEW WORLD.

The AMAZON RIVER is Brazil's best-known and most important geographical feature. The river is one of the world's longest, and in terms of water volume is the largest river system on earth. A vast rain forest spreads out from its banks, sheltering thousands of species of plants and animals. The Amazon is not Brazil's only major river, however. In terms of its importance during the colonial period, the São Francisco River is perhaps more important. Flowing northward and running roughly parallel to the Atlantic coast, the river formed a crucial transportation link between northern Brazil and the central area of Minas Gerais. Geographers classify most of Brazil as being a tropical wet–dry climate, meaning that there are distinct rainy and dry seasons. The northeastern corner of Brazil, by contrast, is considerably drier and subject to frequent droughts.

Before the conquest, Brazil supported a substantial native population. Most of its inhabitants were farmers who had developed social, political, and economic systems to meet their needs. They were not, as myth often portrayed them, primitives who roamed the forest, lacking any particular culture. The largest ethnic group was the Tupí-Guaraní, who were divided into hundreds of localized tribes. They used slash-and-burn agriculture to produce manioc, the staple crop of the region. The Tupí-Guaraní were a highly spiritual people whose religion revolved primarily around nature spirits. Shamans provided an essential link between the people and the supernatural world by entering into spiritual trances and interpreting signs. The 16th-century French philosopher Michel de Montaigne immortalized these Brazilian natives in his famous essay "On Cannibals," which created the romantic image of the "noble savage" living in simple, direct communion with nature. For better or worse, this romantic image of Brazil's natives persists to this day.

The first Europeans to arrive in Brazil did so by accident. Under the TREATY OF TORDESILLAS with Spain in 1494, Portugal gained the right to explore and exploit the lands east of an imaginary north–south line lying 370 leagues

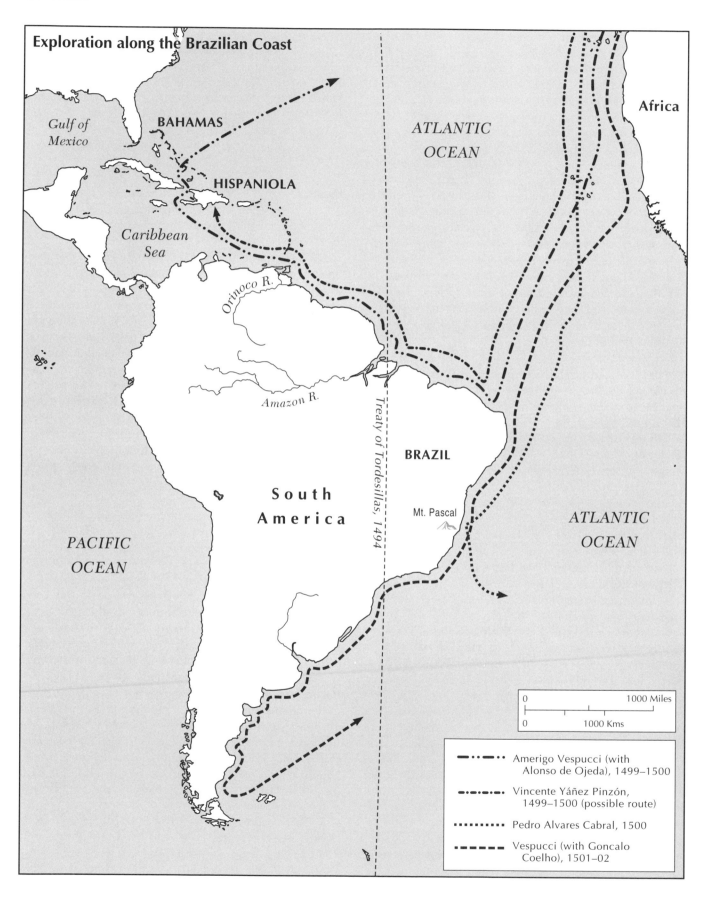

Exploration along the Brazilian Coast

Gulf of Mexico

BAHAMAS

ATLANTIC OCEAN

Africa

HISPANIOLA

Caribbean Sea

Orinoco R.

Amazon R.

South America

Treaty of Tordesillas, 1494

BRAZIL

Mt. Pascal

PACIFIC OCEAN

ATLANTIC OCEAN

0   1000 Miles

0   1000 Kms

–··–··– Amerigo Vespucci (with Alonso de Ojeda), 1499–1500

–·–·–· Vincente Yáñez Pinzón, 1499–1500 (possible route)

·········· Pedro Alvares Cabral, 1500

– – – Vespucci (with Goncalo Coelho), 1501–02

west of the Cape Verde Islands. The Portuguese were trying to keep Spain away from their holdings in Angola, the AZORES, and Goa, but unbeknownst to them this treaty gave them rights in the far eastern section of Brazil as well. In 1500 the Portuguese navigator PEDRO ALVAREZ CABRAL was trying to round the tip of Africa on his way to India. Encountering contrary winds, he was driven westward and ultimately reached the Brazilian coast near present-day Espírito Santo. The sailors were astonished by this "bountiful" region with such strikingly different flora and fauna, and Cabral promptly claimed the region for Portugal. The party stayed for only a few days before continuing their journey, but before leaving they dispatched a ship to inform the Crown of their discovery. Intrigued, the Crown commissioned AMERIGO VESPUCCI to explore the area in 1501. Vespucci charted the area between BAHÍA and Rio de Janeiro before returning to Portugal the next year. The exploration of the Amazon occurred much later; it was not until 1541 that Francisco de Orellana successfully navigated it.

Although the Portuguese arrived in Brazil in 1500, they neglected it for many years thereafter. There were two reasons for this neglect. Unlike the Spaniards, who attempted to conquer territory and control resources directly, the Portuguese were much more interested in establishing trading networks with existing kingdoms. The Portuguese "colony" was typically little more than a fortified trading center. Because no great kingdoms existed to trade with in Brazil, Portugal turned its attention elsewhere. Additionally, Portugal had already deeply invested in trade with Asia and Africa. Maintaining its far-flung outposts was proving to be an enormous drain on the small country's resources, and it could do little to develop Brazil. In theory and in practice, Brazil was a minor appendage to its growing empire in the East.

By the 1530s Portugal began to show signs of greater interest in Brazil, and imperial-minded bureaucrats took some preliminary steps to develop it as a colony. Explorers discovered a dyewood called brazilwood that grew in the coastal forests. (The name *Brazil* derives from these trees.) The pulp of the brazilwood tree produced a vivid, colorfast red dye that was highly valued in Europe. Concerned with reports that French interlopers were landing and cutting these trees, King João III established the Donatário (or captaincy) system both to reassert Portugal's control over the region and capitalize on the brazilwood trade. This system, implemented in 1533, sliced the territory of Brazil into 15 horizontal zones, assigning each zone to an individual who agreed to colonize, develop, and defend his territory at his own expense. In return, the donatary captain gained extensive estates, the right to assess taxes, and a monopoly on trade within his territory. Through this system the Crown hoped to gain a viable colony without having to pay for it itself.

With a few notable exceptions, the captaincy system was a dismal failure, and within a few years, the brazilwood trade collapsed. Desperate to find another export, some donatary captains attempted to cultivate SUGAR, but labor shortages and a general lack of resources hindered the development of the sugar trade. Further, French and native raiders began plundering the coasts, forcing the colonists to focus their attention on defense rather than on commercial enterprises. With its economy in shambles, its territory under attack, and the donatary captains nearing bankruptcy, Brazil's future appeared bleak.

In 1549 the Crown realized it would have to take a more active role in Brazil if it were to hold onto the territory. That year João III instituted a new political system called the Governo Geral with the clear goal of expelling the French, pacifying the natives, and developing the colony along planned, rational lines. Tomé de Sousa became governor general, and he arrived with 1,200 soldier–colonists and proceeded to create a strong, centralized government based in the city of Salvador (popularly called Bahía). The new administration was deliberately patterned after the governments of NEW SPAIN and PERU, with the *ouvidor* and the *relação* functioning as the CORREGIDOR and the AUDIENCIA, respectively. The most powerful colonial institution in Brazil was the *senado da câmara*, a town council similar in most regards to the Spanish CABILDO. Sousa took over the donatary captaincy of Bahía and made the others subordinate to the government of Salvador. The arrival of Portuguese troops and weapons turned the tide against the French, and by 1567 Portuguese commander Mem de Sá conquered the French settlement at Rio de Janeiro, effectively breaking French power in the area. Shortly thereafter he defeated the TUPINAMBA natives near Bahía, sharply curtailing native raids on Portuguese settlements. After 1580 the Dutch replaced the French as the greatest foreign threat to Brazil, although they did not become a real danger until the 1620s (see DUTCH EAST INDIA COMPANY).

As part of a program for economic development, the Crown promoted sugar cultivation, and soon the areas of Bahía and Pernambuco had become some of the most important sugar-producing areas in the world. In order to provide a stable workforce for this growing industry, the Portuguese encouraged the capture and enslavement of the indigenous people. The most famous slave hunters were the *bandeirantes,* based around São Paulo, who penetrated deep into the Brazilian interior in search of captives. DISEASE, overwork, and flight to the interior devastated the native population by 1600, forcing the sugar barons to turn to the African SLAVE TRADE to meet their labor needs. In time this steady influx of slaves gave Brazilian society an African element that set it apart from the neighboring Spanish territories.

Through these steps Portugal established a stable colony in the New World. By 1600 Brazil had 30,000 European colonists. Although it had a rough beginning, by 1620 Brazil had become Portugal's most valuable overseas territory.

Further reading: Leslie Bethell, *Colonial Brazil* (Cambridge, U.K.: Cambridge University Press, 1987); Charles R. Boxer, *The Portuguese Seaborne Empire: 1415–1825* (New York: Knopf, 1975); E. Bradford Burns, *A History of Brazil* (New York: Columbia University Press, 1980); Marshall Eakin, *Brazil: The Once and Future Country* (New York: St. Martin's Press, 1997); John Hemming, *Red Gold: The Conquest of the Brazilian Indians, 1500–1760* (Cambridge, Mass.: Harvard University Press, 1978).

— Scott Chamberlain

Brendan the Navigator, Saint (486?–575)

The *Navigatio* of Saint Brendan, dating probably from the late ninth or early 10th century, described the adventures of an Irish monk who sailed far to the west and allegedly discovered new lands.

The historic Saint Brendan was an abbot who founded a number of monasteries in western Ireland and possibly also in Scotland and Wales. It is not known if he made a long sea voyage, as his legend claimed, but some Irish monks may have sailed as far as Iceland. According to the *Navigatio*, Brendan and his companions went to sea in a coracle of ox hide carrying enough supplies to last for 40 days. They sought to discover the Island of the Blessed, an earthly paradise. The author of the *Navigatio* was probably a monk himself who embroidered the tale with miracles.

According to the legend, every year the monks found themselves at the same places for the major holy days of the Christian calendar. They spent the Thursday before Easter on an island of birds, where they stayed until Pentecost. They spent Christmas each year with the monks of Saint Ailbe, who never spoke except to sing hymns and psalms and whose food was given to them by God.

During their voyage the monks saw many strange things, including sea monsters, a massive, inexplicable column of crystal in the sea, and the entrance to hell. After seven years of traveling the monks found the Isle of the Saints, an earthly paradise. Delicious food and drink were always near to hand, and there was never darkness or night. They explored the island for 40 days and did not discover an end to it. When the monks came to a river they could not cross, a young man appeared and told them that it was time for them to return home. He promised that other Christians, in a time of persecution, would find a haven on the island and told the monks to fill their boat with precious stones and return home.

Scholars disagree about whether the *Navigatio* had its basis in a real journey. Cartographers in later centuries placed Brendan's island in various places to the west of Ireland, and explorers searched for it until the 18th century. The legend of Saint Brendan was widespread. About 120 copies of the story dating from the 10th to 15th centuries and written in various European languages have survived. Some writers have claimed that Brendan and his monks landed in America. If they did, they left no evidence of their accomplishment except in legend.

Further reading: Lisa M. Bitel, *Isle of the Saints: Monastic Settlement and Christian Community in Early Ireland* (Ithaca, N.Y.: Cornell University Press, 1990); David Hugh Farmer, ed., *The Age of Bede* (London: Penguin, 1983); ———, *Butler's Lives of the Saints* (Minneapolis: Liturgical Press, 1995); Felipe Fernandez-Armesto, *Columbus* (Oxford, U.K.: Oxford University Press, 1991); Valerie I.J. Flint, *The Imaginary Landscape of Christopher Columbus* (Princeton, N.J.: Princeton University Press, 1992); William D. Phillips, Jr., and Carla Rahn Phillips, *The Worlds of Christopher Columbus* (Cambridge, U.K.: Cambridge University Press, 1991).

— Martha K. Robinson

brigantine

A type of sailing ship featuring two masts, the brigantine derived its name because it was so popular among the "sea brigands" (pirates) of the Mediterranean.

The brigantine became popular as a pirate ship due to its speed, small size, and shallow draft. Its foremast carried square sails, and the main mast carried both square and fore-and-aft sails. After becoming popular in the Mediterranean, it became popular as a type of pirate ship throughout the Atlantic basin.

The origin and evolution of the brigantine as a ship type is obscure. The original brigantine, or *bergantin* in Spanish, was an extremely large boat (generally towed by a ship, as it was too large to be carried) powered by oars or sweeps but also featuring one or two masts. The design was advantageous for "brigandage" (piracy) because, with its combination of oars and sail, it could be used in very light or calm winds when larger cargo vessels would be unable to maneuver. As piracy spread through the Mediterranean in the 14th century the boats increased in size and began to feature an enclosed main deck and sturdier masts with lateen rigging, but they still more resembled a galley powered primarily by oars than a sailing ship.

With the European discovery of America, ship-bound trade rapidly increased throughout the Atlantic, and brigands of various nationalities brought their ships out to take advantage. To operate on the open ocean ship designers abandoned the lateen rig in favor of square sails on the foremast and square and fore-and-aft sails on the mainmast. They increased the size of the vessels as well, but the ships retained their single main deck and did not feature a fore or stern castle but sometimes had a slightly raised "quarter deck" over the stern.

The same handy qualities that recommended the brigantine design to pirates also impressed itself on those who had to defend against them. Various types of small scout, escort, and dispatch vessels of brigantine design and rig were incorporated into the navies of all the European powers. The exact dimensions, number and type of sails, and intended missions varied widely, and no true standardization ever took place. A variation of the brigantine, called simply a brig, featured the same two-masted, single-deck design but an all fore-and-aft rig on the mainmast.

Further reading: Romola Anderson and R. C. Anderson, *The Sailing-Ship: Six Thousand Years of History* (New York: Bonanza Books, 1963); Peter Kemp, ed., *The Oxford Companion to Ships and the Sea* (Oxford, U.K.: Oxford University Press, 1976); Roger C. Smith, *Vanguard of Empire: Ships of Exploration in the Age of Columbus* (Oxford, U.K.: Oxford University Press, 1993).

— Paul Dunscomb

Bristol

An English port city that played a key role in the expansion of English foreign trade and exploration.

Long before the seafaring ventures of JOHN CABOT and SEBASTIAN CABOT, British sailors looked westward, dreaming of discovering new lands and trade opportunities. By the early 16th century Bristol's merchants and sailors had developed three kinds of trade. First, they established and maintained commercial ties with the Iberian Peninsula. They exported iron, timber, sculptured alabaster, lead, tin, corn, barley, and malt and they imported exotic and highly profitable goods to be found in Spain and Portugal, including fruits, oils, leather, and Spanish iron. Second, they maintained and extended commercial links with Ireland. By the 15th century Bristol's vessels docked in Waterford, Cork, Limerick, Youghal, Galway, Burrishoole, Kinsale, and Sligo, many of them hauling peninsular wines. Before returning home the vessels would fill their holds with Irish goods destined for the Low Countries. Third, they moved beyond Ireland and established trade with residents of ICELAND. Although the Norwegians and Danes did their best to exclude foreigners from the Icelandic trade, Iceland's fisheries proved too alluring to English traders. Merchants out of Bristol sent vessels loaded with foods, cloths, wine, luxuries, ironware, and weapons—and just about anything else deemed necessary for sustaining life on Iceland. In return they brought back full cargoes of COD, pollack, salmon, and herring. The Icelandic market became so lucrative that the English made numerous attempts to establish permanent business settlements on the island, but however successful such commerce became, eventually the volume of trade fell off and the English who sailed west from Bristol had to find new targets for their entrepreneurial energies.

As early as 1497 John Cabot and his more famous son Sebastian Cabot left the port of Bristol en route to the English discovery of Newfoundland, identifying it as VINLAND of the legendary Norse sagas. The rediscovery deepened the Bristolians' interest in exploration. Much, however, remained a mystery, as sailors who arrived in the city told wild tales of seas populated by demons, strange animals, and still stranger humans. Nevertheless, Bristol's practical merchants remained undaunted. Still, despite their enthusiasm for trade, the death of King HENRY VII depressed English interest in exploration. Concentrating on the more familiar game of European politics, HENRY VIII turned his back on exploration while Spain, Portugal, and even France expanded their efforts in the Atlantic basin.

Within Bristol a small group, including the brothers Robert, William, and Thomas Thorne, Robert Thorne the Younger, Hugh Elyot, John Latimer, and Roger Barlow kept the spirit of transoceanic exploration alive during the first half of the 16th century. Robert Thorne, Latimer, and perhaps Barlow authored the *Declaration of the Indies*, while Barlow wrote his *Brief Summe of Geographie*. These tracts outlined the feasibility of finding a NORTHWEST PASSAGE via a north-polar approach. These Bristol visionaries served as precursors to later English promoters of exploration and colonization. It was of little surprise that RICHARD HAKLUYT THE ELDER and RICHARD HAKLUYT THE YOUNGER both found receptive audiences among the merchants of Bristol. The younger Hakluyt often visited the port city, urging the merchants to undertake new ventures. Bristol did not disappoint, continually bidding farewell to new expeditions throughout the 17th and 18th centuries.

Further reading: C. M. Macinnes, *Bristol: A Gateway of Empire* (New York: Augustus M. Kelly Publishers, 1968); David H. Sacks, *The Widening Gate: Bristol and the Atlantic Economy, 1450–1700* (Berkeley: University of California Press, 1991); J. A. Williamson, *Maritime Enterprise, 1485–1558* (Oxford: Clarendon Press 1913); ———, *A Short History of British Expansion* (London: Macmillan, 1922).

— Matthew Lindaman

C

Cabeza de Vaca, Álvar Núñez (ca. 1490–c. 1557)

A member of the ill-fated FLORIDA expedition of PÁN-FILO DE NARVÁEZ in 1527, Álvar Núñez Cabeza de Vaca survived shipwreck, hunger, and slavery before returning to Spain in 1536 and writing a report of his experiences that became one of the crucial European documents relating to North America during the first half of the 16th century.

Cabeza de Vaca was second in command when Narváez landed in Florida with an expedition of between 300 and 400 men on April 14, 1528. The expedition found itself in trouble from the beginning. They had left CUBA without enough supplies, and of the 180 HORSES they had brought, only 42 survived the trip to Florida. They spent two weeks exploring the area, hoping to find GOLD. They met Indians but found no gold and so moved on. Narváez, against the advice of Cabeza de Vaca, divided the party in two. A hundred men were to sail north along the coast of Florida, while the rest of the party traveled overland. The two parties soon lost contact with each other, and the sea party, after searching for a year, returned to NEW SPAIN. The land party, with Narváez in command, covered only about eight miles a day. They found almost nothing to eat, relying instead on bacon and biscuits that they had brought. For 15 days they saw neither Indians nor settlements. After crossing a large river they met a party of Indians who fed them maize (see CORN). Later in the journey they met another party of Indians, who brought them more maize and then followed them at a distance. By the time the expedition reached northern Florida, near present-day Tallahassee, relations with the Indians had deteriorated, and the Spaniards were exhausted and battling illness. Having discovered no gold, they decided to return to New Spain. They built five boats and set sail in September 1528, heading west. They drifted past the Mississippi River and toward Texas. The trip was very difficult; the survivors had very little food and did not have enough water to drink. By the time Cabeza de Vaca reached land, in November, three of the boats, including the one commanded by Narváez, had disappeared.

The other two boats, with Cabeza de Vaca and an unknown number of additional survivors, landed on a sandbar or island near Galveston Bay. In the years that followed, almost all the Spanish died. Some starved, died from exposure to the cold, or were killed by Indians; others traveled out of the area and were lost. Of the men who had landed in Florida, only four ever returned to Spain.

Soon after their shipwreck, Cabeza de Vaca and his companions encountered Karankawa Indians who indicated that they should heal the sick. When Cabeza de Vaca and his companions were unwilling, the Indians refused to feed them until they tried. The Spaniards prayed over the sick Indians, and Cabeza de Vaca reported that "all those for whom we prayed told the others that they were well and healthy." For a time the Indians treated them well, giving them food and hides. Because of linguistic and cultural barriers, Cabeza de Vaca and his companions did not understand the peoples they met, and for reasons that are unclear the Indians later enslaved them. Cabeza de Vaca remained in slavery for more than a year. He then resolved to escape, for, as he wrote,

> I could not bear the life I was leading. . .for among many other labors, I had to gather the roots they used for food, under water and among the reeds where they grew on the land; and my fingers were so lacerated from this that if a blade of straw touched them they bled, and the reeds tore me all over my body because many reeds were broken and I had to go into the middle of them with the little clothing that I wore.

Cabeza de Vaca escaped from the Karankawas and established himself as a healer and trader, traveling from one Indian group to another through what is now Texas and northern MEXICO. Along his journey he encountered three other survivors of the Narváez expedition: Alonso del

Castillo, Andrés Dorantes, and Estevanico, an African slave. Beginning in September 1534 the four of them traveled together. They learned to communicate with members of various Indian nations and presented themselves as holy men and healers. As they wandered they were accompanied by Indians who fed and protected them.

Cabeza de Vaca and his surviving companions encountered Indian groups about whom very little is known, and their relations with them are hard to interpret. His experience was unlike that of most Spaniards in the NEW WORLD: when he washed up on a Texas island, he had neither weapons, horses, nor European technology. He, rather than they, was powerless. As he traveled his opinion of the Indians improved, and he later sought to defend them against Spanish abuses. Like other Spaniards of his time, he believed that the Indians must convert to Catholicism and that the Spanish had a right to colonize Indian lands. When he met Spanish slave raiders in northern Mexico in 1536, they wanted to enslave the Indians with whom he had traveled. Cabeza de Vaca was angry at the thought and portrayed himself as a very different kind of Spaniard. According to his account, the Indians refused to believe that Cabeza de Vaca and the Spaniards were really of the same people. They said that "the Christians were lying, for we came from where the sun rises and they from where it sets; and that we cured the sick and they killed the healthy; and that we had come naked and barefoot and they well dressed and on horses and with lances; and that we did not covet anything, rather we returned everything that they gave us and were left with nothing, and the only aim of the others was to steal everything they found. . . ."

After eight years of travel, Cabeza de Vaca and his companions reached the village of Culiacan in April 1536. Cabeza de Vaca returned to Spain and stayed there for more than three years, during which he edited his account of his travels in America.

CHARLES V, the Holy Roman Emperor and king of Spain, appointed Cabeza de Vaca ADELANTADO (frontier governor) and governor over the region of the Rio de la Plata. When Cabeza de Vaca later returned to the New World, his authority extended over a vast area including southern Peru, Argentina, Uruguay, and Paraguay. This second expedition, however, was hardly more successful than the Florida expedition had been. His attempts to raise taxes and halt abuses of the Indians helped engender a revolt. In April 1544 rebels captured Cabeza de Vaca. They accused him of abandoning 13 of his men, committing crimes against both Spaniards and Indians, and substituting his personal coat of arms for the symbols of the Crown. They sent him back to Spain, where he lived in poverty. The lawsuits against him, begun in 1546, were eventually decided against him in 1551. As a result of these verdicts, he was stripped of his titles, forbidden to return to the Indies, and condemned to exile in Algiers. Near the end of his life the king granted him a small pension, but Cabeza de Vaca never regained the honors he had had earlier in life.

Cabeza de Vaca's words cannot be taken entirely at face value. As the literary scholar Rolena Adorno has observed, he was anxious to present himself as a providing a "saintly example," and his account of the events is the only one that has survived. Nonetheless, his experiences in Florida, Texas, and Mexico seem to have changed him from a typical CONQUISTADOR to one who, while still believing that the Spanish had a right to conquer, sought to do so in a humane way.

Further reading: Rolena Adorno and Patrick Charles Pautz, *Álvar Núñez Cabeza de Vaca: His Account, His Life, and the Expedition of Panfilo de Narvaez,* 3 vols. (Lincoln: University of Nebraska Press, 1999); David A. Howard, *Conquistador in Chains: Cabeza de Vaca and the Indians of the Americas* (Tuscaloosa: University of Alabama Press, 1997); Enrique Pupo-Walker, ed., *Castaways: The Narrative of Alvar Nunez Cabeza de Vaca,* trans. Frances M. Lopez-Morillas (Berkeley: University of California Press, 1993); David J. Weber, *The Spanish Frontier in North America* (New Haven, Conn.: Yale University Press, 1992).

— Martha K. Robinson

cabildo

The *cabildo* was a town council that formed the lowest level of the Spanish Empire's administrative structure.

Sometimes called the *ayuntamiento,* the *cabildo* played a vital role in the history of Spain and its colonies in the NEW WORLD. By the late 15th century the Spanish city had evolved into a new institution that had little to do with the cities of the earlier Roman, Visigoth, or Arabian periods. Born during the RECONQUISTA, Spanish cities were primarily fortresses of political and economic control designed to hold land taken from the Moors. Needing the towns' support, kings often granted them considerable rights and privileges. The town also was in charge of its own defense, organizing militias and seeing to the repairs of gates, towers, and city walls. As part of their centralizing reforms, FERDINAND AND ISABELLA—as well as the later Habsburgs—dissolved many of these concessions and sought to establish uniform royal control over their territory. The Crown followed a similar pattern in the Western Hemisphere. In an effort to pacify and settle the Americas, the Spanish government established a number of towns and gave them substantial rights and autonomy, although later the crown took steps to strip the towns of their privileges.

The *cabildo* was one of the defining features of Spanish towns. Each city, regardless of size, had a *cabildo,* whose job was to oversee the town's affairs and to provide for the town's defense. The *cabildo* contained two types of officials: *regidores* ("aldermen") and *alcaldes* ("magistrates"). The number of officials who sat on the *cabildo* ranged between five and 12 depending on the city's size and importance. In theory the *cabildo* was supposed to represent the townspeople, and the citizens elected these officials from members of the community. Besides these elected officials, the *cabildos* usually had a series of nonvoting bureaucrats who advised the council on various issues. These bureaucrats included notaries, the town lawyer, and a treasurer. In larger cities the head of the *cabildo* was often the local CO-RREGIDOR, a Crown official who usually oversaw a larger area (similar to a county in the United States). Unlike the other *cabildo* officials, the *corregidor* was an outsider appointed by the Crown. Over time this system led to considerable friction between the *cabildo*, which sought to protect the town's interests, and the *corregidor*, who sought to promote the Crown's interests.

Within the colonial system the *cabildo* had a wide variety of functions. In the political arena it had the power to set curfews and zoning ordinances. As the representatives of the people, *cabildos* often sent advisers to the AUDIEN-CIAS or viceroys and reserved the right to petition the king directly to resolve disputes or solve problems. Additionally, the *cabildo* held the right to assemble the citizens either for defense or to discuss issues of local importance. *Cabildos* also had wide-ranging social functions. They oversaw charity, health, and public education and organized festivals commemorating saints' days and other religious holidays. The *cabildo* also performed a variety of economic functions, including issuing land grants to individuals and maintaining common lands for livestock and firewood. Also, the council set prices on goods and services within the city. It regulated commerce among cities and collected taxes and tariffs such as the *alcabala* ("sales tax"). Finally, the city council commissioned public works projects, including the building and maintenance of streets, hospitals, slaughterhouses, and defensive works.

Initially, the *cabildo* held enormous power. At the beginning of the colonial period, it represented the only royal authority in the New World. CHRISTOPHER COLUM-BUS organized the cities of Navidad, Isabella, and finally Santo Domingo on HISPANIOLA to establish Spain's claim to the island. He immediately created a *cabildo* in each, which governed in the sovereigns' names. Until 1550 Spain's presence in the Western Hemisphere consisted of a few strategically placed towns surrounded by vast tracts of poorly explored, potentially hostile lands. Recognizing their limits, the Spanish government under CHARLES V was willing to give *cabildos* enormous leeway in governing their own affairs. As a result, *cabildos*, at least initially, controlled national and international commerce, served as royal

courts, and set colonial policy. At times the *cabildo* could trump the authority of Crown-appointed officials, an aspect of the council that HERNÁN CORTÉS used to his advantage in 1519. Commissioned by DIEGO DE VELÁZQUEZ, the royal governor of CUBA, to explore the coast of MEXICO, Cortés decided instead to conquer it on his own. In order to avoid the legal repercussions of disobeying orders, Cortés founded the town of VERACRUZ and established a *cabildo* as the voice of "the people." The *cabildo*, consisting entirely of his soldiers, duly commissioned Cortés to proceed with his plans, giving him legal protection from the governor's wrath.

Over time the Crown attempted to reign in the *cabildos'* powers. It set up a royal bureaucracy composed of Crown appointees who served as judges, administrators, and tax collectors, removing these tasks from the *cabildos'* lists of duties. The *cabildos* did retain some vestiges of these functions, but on a purely local level. Perhaps the biggest blow to the *cabildo* came during the reign of PHILIP II. As Philip's European wars drained away Spain's financial resources, Philip decided to sell royal offices—particularly the offices of the *cabildo*—to raise funds. In practical terms the sale of *cabildo* offices meant that the councils did not look after the well-being of the city as a whole but served the whims of those wealthy enough to buy their positions. Moreover, most of the offices went initially to wealthy families directly from Spain, who were not concerned with local issues. Finally, the officeholders were not necessarily competent, and since the offices were private property, they could pass down through generations of incompetent grandees. Across Spanish America residents of cities reacted to this change with horror. Some, such as the inhabitants of Santiago, took up a collection so that the town itself could buy the offices from the king and distribute them as it saw fit. Most cities were not so fortunate, and by 1600 the *cabildos* had become impotent organizations that argued over titles, individuals' honor, and procedural questions rather than issues of any substance.

Despite the decline of the *cabildo* by 1600, it remained a psychologically important institution. It was the only area of the colonial administration that represented a modicum of local rule and allowed direct participation by local citizens. Also, for most colonists, it was their main point of interaction with the colonial government. Whatever its flaws, the *cabildo* was the only institution that attempted to deal with the day-to-day concerns of the local population, and the colonists were grateful for it.

Further reading: C. H. Haring, *The Spanish Empire in America* (Oxford, U.K.: Oxford University Press, 1947); Lyle N. McAlister, *Spain and Portugal in the New World, 1495–1700* (Minneapolis: University of Minnesota Press, 1984); Preston Moore, *The Cabildo in Peru under the*

Hapsburgs, 1530–1700 (Durham, N. C.: Duke University Press, 1954).

— Scott Chamberlain

cabinet of curiosities

The predecessor of modern museums, cabinets of curiosities appeared throughout Europe during the 16th century, often to house exotic goods brought back to the Continent by explorers who traveled to the far reaches of the Atlantic basin and beyond.

Europe in the 16th century contained collectors of every sort. They were individuals who wanted to do more than just know about the wider world. They wanted to possess parts of it and to display their wares in a private museum, known as a *wunderkammer*—a "chamber of wonders." While the most elaborate cabinets could be found in Italy, such warehouses of the marvelous appeared across the Continent during the 16th century.

The desire to collect exotic goods was not new in the early modern period. Throughout medieval Europe men and women had been fascinated with the idea of gaining possession of part of a saint, and those fortunate enough to get a piece of bone would house it in a reliquary, many of which were studded with jewels. Many of the early cabinets resembled large reliquaries, and their owners were every bit as proud of their collections as were their predecessors who claimed to have a saintly relic. Judging from the pictures that proud owners had made of their cabinets, a 16th-century collection could include nearly anything that would elicit wonder. Some had beautiful shellfish attached to the walls alongside sea horses, large turtle shells, and the desiccated torsos of all sorts of marine creatures, birds, reptiles, and beasts that prowled the land. A prize specimen might be a crocodile, one of which Ferrante Imperato suspended from the ceiling of his cabinet in Naples, giving the monstrous oddity a place of pride in his collection. Imperato also displayed freaks of nature, such as a two-headed snake. Collectors might also gather items that reminded them of indigenous people whose material culture was unknown to most Europeans or even monstrous Europeans, who could be represented by portraits.

Over time cabinets of curiosities became larger and larger, and some eventually became the basis of modern museums, such as the Ashmolean Museum in Oxford, England, which had its origins in the cabinet kept by John Tradescant. Those who possessed these goods at times had catalogues prepared detailing their collections. In the process they advanced the study of natural history and provided a clear record of the range of species imported into Europe. Though cabinets typically contained things that were dead, their existence mirrored some Europeans' preoccupation with collecting anything rare. Such a desire lay behind Pope LEO X's desire to populate the Vatican with exotic denizens such as HANNO THE ELEPHANT. In 16th-century Europe (and well after), owning rare specimens demonstrated the possessor's obsession with the natural world and his or her desire to show off the wondrous entities that others brought into the cabinets. Cabinets also demonstrated some Europeans' obsession with the grotesque beings that inhabited their own world—the same kind of obsession that led to Ambroise Paré's writings about the MONSTERS and prodigies he claimed to have seen in France.

The European encounter with the Western Hemisphere proved a great boon to collectors. The Americas offered, as observers such as CHRISTOPHER COLUMBUS and JEAN DE LÉRY knew, a wide range of natural entities that no European had ever witnessed before. Printed books (see PRINTING PRESS) by such authors as the French royal cosmographer ANDRÉ THEVET, the Seville physician NICHOLAS MONARDES, and the naturalist Pierre Belon all included illustrations of new species and no doubt aroused the passion of those who had cabinets of curiosities. The first published catalogue of a cabinet appeared in Verona in 1584 describing the collection of an apothecary named Giovanni Battista Olivi, who hoped that the plants, flowers, and seeds in his holdings would help expand the *materia medica* of Europe. Imperato, owner of a famed cabinet, offered his thoughts about nature in his *Dell 'historia naturale*, published in Naples in 1599. Any artifact from a Western Hemisphere culture would be valued, from a feathered headdress or a mask to flutes carved from human legs consumed by cannibals in the collection of Bernhard Paladanus. In the great race to understand the meaning of the Americas, those who owned a *wunderkammer* had a great advantage. They could do more than speak knowledgeably about the discoveries of their age. They could also show them off in awe-inspiring rooms overflowing with the tangible proof of the wonders to be found in the NEW WORLD.

Further reading: Lorraine Daston and Katherine Park, *Wonders and the Order of Nature, 1150–1750* (New York: Zone Books, 1998), esp. 146–159; Paula Findlen, *Possessing Nature: Museums, Collecting, and Scientific Culture in Early Modern Italy* (Berkeley and Los Angeles: University of California Press, 1994); Oliver Impey and Arthur MacGregor, eds., *The Origins of Museums: The Cabinet of Curiosities in Sixteenth- and Seventeenth-Century Europe* (Oxford, U.K.: Clarendon Press of Oxford University Press, 1985); Joy Kenseth, "'A World of Wonders in One Closet Shut,'" in Kenseth, ed., *The Age of the Marvelous* (Hanover, N. H.: Hood Museum of Art/Dartmouth College, 1991), 81–101; Adalgisa Lugli, *Naturalia et Mirabilia: Il collezionismo enciclopedico nelle Wunderkammern d'Europa* (Milan: Gabriele Mazzotta, 1983).

Cabot, John (1453?–1498?)

A Venetian mariner who received a commission from King HENRY VII of England to seek a westward route to CATHAY (China) across the Atlantic in the late 1490s.

On his first voyage in the summer of 1497, Cabot and his men found and explored Newfoundland and marked the official European discovery of North America. On a second voyage in 1498, Cabot and his entire fleet of four ships was lost. No information about their fate has ever surfaced.

The historical record on John Cabot is sketchy. The later activities of his son, SEBASTIAN CABOT, who not only had considerable accomplishments to his credit but tried to steal his father's as well, have helped to push knowledge of the elder Cabot into the background. Exactly where or when John Cabot was born in Italy is uncertain, but it was no later than 1453, possibly in Genoa. It is certain that he became a citizen of VENICE in 1476, stating that he had lived there since 1461. He was a mariner; the name Cabot derived from his and his father's occupation as "coasters,"

or coastal sailors. His early training evidently came in the Mediterranean, and he was reputed to be a good sailor and excellent navigator.

It is very likely John Cabot was in Spain at the time CHRISTOPHER COLUMBUS returned from his first voyage in 1493. Finding no one interested in sponsoring a similar voyage in Spain or Portugal, he went to England, where, in January 1496, he proposed to make a similar voyage across the North Atlantic to find China and Cipangu (Japan). The king granted the commission on March 5, 1496.

Apparently there was little enthusiasm for the voyage in Cabot's hometown of BRISTOL. As a result, he was able to secure only a single small ship for his first voyage. The *Michael*, around 50 feet long, was smaller than Columbus's smallest ship, *Niña* (56 feet and 60 tons). Around May 20 Cabot set out for his westward voyage. He took his departure off Dursey Head, Ireland, and set course due west into the Atlantic. Although his voyage across the ocean was shorter than Columbus's, it took the same number of days (33) due to the less favorable winds of the North Atlantic.

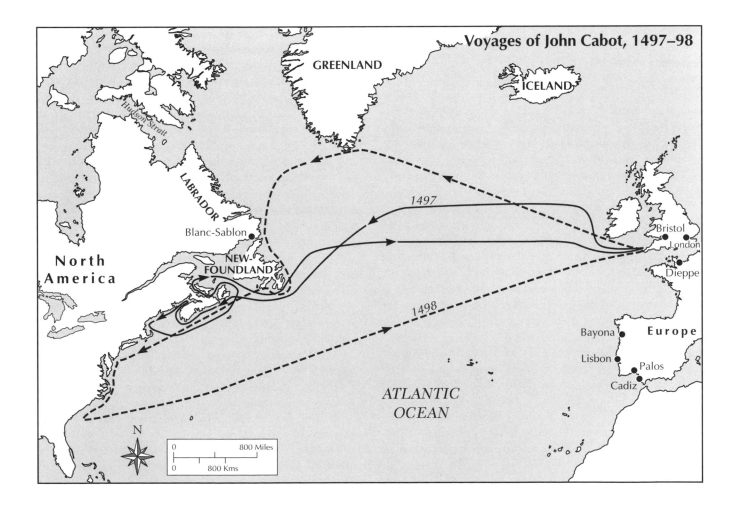

On June 24, 1497, the *Michael* made landfall off the North American coast. No one knows precisely where, but the best speculation is that he encountered Cape Degrat, the northernmost point of Newfoundland. Thus, John Cabot became the official discoverer of North America. Yet the odds are quite good that Leif Eriksson and other NORSE settlers had landed there almost 500 years earlier.

Cabot made only one brief landfall on the newly discovered territory to claim it for Henry VII and himself. He may have been discouraged from further exploration by fear of Indians or the vast swarms of mosquitoes that are still common there in the summer. Cabot spent about four weeks exploring the coast. Precisely where he went remains unknown, but the odds are he traced the eastern shores of Newfoundland and then retraced his course to take his departure from his original landing place. On July 20 he began his return voyage across the Atlantic, arriving in Bristol on August 6. Almost immediately after landing Cabot traveled to LONDON to inform the king of his discoveries and have him confirm Cabot's rights to the "New Found Land."

Cabot was convinced that he had found a northern promontory of the Asian continent. When put together with Columbus's alleged landfall in Southeast Asia, Cabot's claims suggested that the way to China and Japan lay somewhere in the middle. Cabot spent the winter of 1497–98 gathering vessels to join him on a second expedition. His success had a tonic effect on the traders of Bristol, because this time he was able to gather a fleet of five ships loaded with trade goods for the second voyage. Cabot's plan was to return to Newfoundland and make his way south along the coast in an effort to locate Japan. There he proposed to establish a "factory," or trading post.

The five ships left Bristol in early May 1498 (the exact date remains uncertain). It is not even known for sure who or how many men accompanied Cabot. One ship of the five dropped out relatively early in the voyage and landed in an Irish port. The other four sailed over the horizon and were never heard from again. What happened to them is unknown, but the North Atlantic is a treacherously stormy sea and the coast of Newfoundland, even in summer, is prone to ice, fogs, and gales, as later explorers such as SIR HUMPHREY GILBERT discovered too late.

Further reading: Samuel Eliot Morison, *The European Discovery of America; The Northern Voyages, A.D. 500–1600* (New York: Oxford University Press, 1971); Peter Edward Pope, *The Many Landfalls of John Cabot* (Toronto: University of Toronto Press, 1997); James Alexander Williamson, *The Cabot Voyages and Bristol Discovery Under Henry VII* (Cambridge, U.K.: Cambridge University Press, 1962).

— Paul Dunscomb

Cabot, Sebastian (1474?–1557)

Son of JOHN CABOT, Sebastian Cabot reputedly made several voyages of discovery under the sponsorship of the monarchs of Spain and England during the first half of the 16th century, but the only one we definitely know about (1526–1530) was a notable failure.

An accomplished courtier, schemer, and possibly a fraud, few of Sebastian Cabot's claims can be trusted. Still, as pilot major to the king of Spain (1512–48) and in a similar capacity to Edward VI of England (1548–57) he did much to promote exploration and systematize and distribute knowledge of new lands and improvements in navigation.

Some documents actually written by Sebastian still exist, but these accounts were written toward the end of his life, and in many ways his early years are even more obscure than his father's. The exact year and place of his birth are unknown, but he was mostly likely born in VENICE between 1471 and 1474. Although he eventually became an important authority on the science of navigation, it is unlikely he was a particularly good sailor. Whether he accompanied John Cabot on his voyage discovering Newfoundland in 1497 is uncertain; the documentary evidence is sketchy, contradictory, and mostly unreliable. Sebastian and some of his supporters claimed that he made voyages to North America in 1502 and 1508–09, but there is no hard evidence to support their boasts. When King HENRY VIII asked several LONDON merchants to provide ships for a proposed enterprise under Sebastian's command, the merchants bitterly objected, denouncing Sebastian as unqualified and a fraud. The proposed voyage never took place.

After several early voyages sponsored by King HENRY VII, interest in maritime exploration dried up in England for nearly 50 years. Therefore, it was not simply opportunism that compelled Sebastian Cabot to go to work for Ferdinand of Spain in 1512 (see FERDINAND AND ISABELLA). Originally he was taken on as a sort of nautical adviser for his reputed knowledge of the North Atlantic COD fisheries and the supposed NORTHWEST PASSAGE to China (see CATHAY). His knowledge of navigation, geography, and cartography soon got him appointed to the post of pilot major of Spain. His duties included the examination and licensing of all pilots, providing Spain with the latest in navigational devices and geographical knowledge, and keeping the official maps and charts up to date. Considering the remarkable voyages that Portuguese and Spanish captains were making during these years and the vast new lands they discovered, this was neither a small nor an insignificant undertaking.

But success often proved elusive for individuals such as Cabot, who had European monarchs supporting their ventures but who apparently lacked practical sense and experi-

Sebastian Cabot, from a painting (ca. 1903) by John Chapman after the original attributed to Hans Holbein the Younger *(Hulton/Archive)*

ence. When *Victoria,* the only survivor of FERDINAND MAGELLAN's fleet, completed the first circumnavigation of the globe in 1522, its return to Europe kicked off a dispute between Spain and Portugal about who could claim certain East Indian islands under the TREATY OF TORDESILLAS of 1494 (see Documents), under which the pope had divided the newly discovered lands of the Eastern Hemisphere into Portuguese and Spanish spheres. Cabot took command of five ships and sailed to the East Indies to prove they lay on the Spanish side of the line. He left Spain in 1526 but never made it farther than the South Atlantic. Hearing rumors of mineral wealth in the South American interior, he sailed into the Rio de la Plata in modern-day Uruguay and spent nearly three years searching for GOLD and SILVER mines. As a result, he abandoned the trip to the Pacific. In the end, Cabot quarreled with his fellow captains and presided over an escapade characterized by a failure to find mineral riches and the loss of ships and men. When the surviving ships returned to Spain on July 22, 1530, authorities placed Cabot under arrest.

Although not a good sailor, Cabot was an accomplished courtier who knew how to ingratiate himself with royalty. This skill never served him better than in 1531, when, after being convicted of dereliction of duty and having been sentenced to exile in Morocco, he managed to convince CHARLES V (Carlos V) to pardon him. He resumed his duties as pilot major and continued without any apparent difficulty until around 1547, when he and the king had a

falling out. He decided to head back to England and soon attached himself to the court of Edward VI as a sort of naval consultant.

The realization that England was being left behind in the race for exploration and trade was beginning to attract attention in London. Since the only two practical routes to the Pacific were controlled by rivals Spain and Portugal, some English policy makers believed that their nation needed to find either a NORTHWEST PASSAGE over the North American continent (or through the continent itself) or a NORTHEAST PASSAGE over the north coast of Russia. To promote this end a group of London merchants invested £25,000 in what they called "The Merchants Adventurers of England for the Discovery of Lands, Territories, Isles, Dominions and Seignories Unknown." Sebastian Cabot was elected to be the governor of this new company, fortunately shortened to just the Muscovy Company.

Under regulations written by Cabot—the only surviving documents written by him—various merchant adventurers of London began voyages seeking a Northeast Passage and to open trade with Russia. Sailing in the northern seas was extremely difficult, and the English soon abandoned the attempt to find a practical route to China. Although that venture failed, the company did set up a profitable trade with the Russians at the port of Arkhangelsk. The success of the company supplied practical training for numerous English mariners and provided a needed spur for English exploration. Cabot remained a consultant and adviser to English captains until his death in 1557.

Further reading: C. Raymond Beazley, *John and Sebastian Cabot: The Discovery of North America* (New York: B. Franklin, 1964); Samuel Eliot Morison, *The European Discovery of America, the Northern Voyages: 500–1600, the Southern Voyages: 1492–1616,* 2 vols. (New York: Oxford University Press, 1971); James Alexander Williamson, *The Cabot Voyages and Bristol Discovery Under Henry VII* (Cambridge, U.K. Cambridge University Press, 1962).

— Paul Dunscomb

Cabral, Pedro Álvares (ca.1467–ca.1519)

A Portuguese captain whose voyages in 1500 to Brazil, Africa, and India helped the Portuguese to redefine the lucrative spice trade and enhanced Portuguese claims to territory far from the Iberian Peninsula.

Born in the town of Belmonte near Covilhan around 1467, Cabral was the child of a noble family who traveled to the court of King John II to study. Over time he rose in status at the court, a perfect situation for a young son of an elite family. Accepted into the Order of Christ, an association of knights, he became an adviser to Dom Manuel (King Manuel I). He was serving in that capacity when VASCO DA GAMA returned to Portugal in 1499 after his historic journey to India.

In the aftermath of da Gama's success, the Portuguese were eager to establish control over the spice trade (see SPICE ISLANDS), a lucrative commerce that was then based in VENICE. The Venetians had risen to prominence in the trade because they stood at one of the crossroads of the ancient world: between Europe and the Middle East. Venice's dominance was based on the fact that spices did not, before 1500, tend to travel by sea from the Spice Islands to Europe. Instead, those hauling precious cargoes tended to bring their wares overland for long parts of the journey, a task that proved time-consuming and lengthy.

Because da Gama had shown that seaborne commerce between Portugal and the East was possible, the Portuguese came to believe that if they could establish a proper route and secure necessary stations along the way their fleets would be able to haul spices to the West more cheaply. For the task, the Portuguese turned to Cabral and in 1500 gave him command of a 13-ship fleet and orders to sail to the East. Thirty-two years old at the time, Cabral set out from Tagus, a port near Lisbon, on March 8, 1500, holding a letter from the king directed to the Zamorin of Calicut on a venture that quite literally and accidentally opened parts of the Atlantic world to the Portuguese.

To make his journey Cabral relied on the information he received from BARTHOLOMEU DIAS, an experienced explorer, and on Portuguese knowledge of wind currents in the Atlantic. According to reliable authorities, the best way to sail from western Europe to the East was to sail westward past the CANARY ISLANDS, to the Cape Verde Islands, and then turn south and east. Although Cabral planned such a route, when his ships passed the Cape Verde Islands the winds were not favorable, and so he decided to go southwest instead. By late April he had sailed so far east that lookouts on the ships saw land, but not Africa, as they had hoped. Instead, they saw Mount Pascal in Brazil. Cabral soon modified his plans and headed for the coast. When he landed he named this place Terra da Veracruz—the "Land of the True Cross" claimed for the king of Portugal. Since this territory was, in fact, in the part of the world that the pope had granted to the Portuguese in the TREATY OF TORDESILLAS in 1493, Cabral's discovery fulfilled what must have seemed to some the destiny of the Portuguese. But Cabral had no intention of remaining permanently in Brazil; after trading with the indigenous peoples he encountered there and restocking his ships' supplies, he headed east again, back toward Africa. By early May 1500 his fleet was back on its way.

Yet Cabral's journey continued to be unpredictable. When the fleet, now numbering 11 vessels, sailed near the Cape of Good Hope, they encountered a storm, and four of the remaining ships sank, including the one with Dias aboard. After stopping in Mozambique for a time and later spotting Madagascar (he may have been the first European to see it), Cabral continued on his journey to India. He finally reached Calicut on September 13, but troubles developed between the Portuguese and the Muslims (see ISLAM) who controlled commerce in the city. For reasons that Cabral and his associates apparently never understood, local residents one night stormed the post the Portuguese had established and killed or captured 50 of the Europeans, including three Franciscan missionaries. Cabral, seeking revenge, seized merchants' ships in the harbor, looted them, and killed most of the crews, but he wanted to punish his hosts even further, and so his ships bombarded Calicut, an event that poisoned relations between the residents of the city and the Portuguese.

In the aftermath of the violence, Cabral returned to Lisbon, another explorer who had expanded Europeans' knowledge of the Atlantic world (and beyond) and who had mixed relations with the peoples he had encountered. Two years later he married Dona Izabel de Castro, daughter of an elite family whose property enhanced Cabral's standing and finances. They had six children, three of whom—Guiomar de Castro, Izabel, and Leonor—joined the growing numbers of women religious who chose life in convents. Cabral died sometime before 1520 and was laid to rest, along with one of his children and his wife, in Santarem at the Convento de Graça (later the Asylo de São Antonio).

However obscure his final ending, still shrouded in mystery, Cabral remains a pivotal figure in the European expansion efforts of the 16th century. His story was well known in the 16th century, appearing (among other places) in the first volume of GIOVANNI BATTISTA RAMUSIO's *Navigationi e Viaggi* (Venice, 1550), one of the most important collections of travel accounts published during that age of overseas exploration.

Further reading: William B. Greenlee, ed. and trans., *The Voyages of Pedro Álvares Cabral to Brazil and India*, Publications of the Hakluyt Society, 2nd ser., LXXXI (London, Hakluyt Society, 1938); Angus Konstam, *Historical Atlas of Exploration, 1492–1600* (New York: Facts On File, 2000), 66–69.

Cacamatzin (Cacama) (1490–1520)

Cacamatzin, the nephew of the Aztec ruler MOCTEZUMA II and one of two rival rulers of Texcoco at the time of HERNÁN CORTÉS's arrival in MEXICO.

Cacamatzin was a member of the royal line of Texcoco, son of Nezahualpilli and grandson of Nezahualcóyotl. The reigning speaker of Texcoco, Nezahualpilli, had not named an heir from among his 145 children when he died in 1515, and his kingdom split in two. When the northern part of Texcoco went to Ixtlilxóchitl, enemy of the Aztec speaker Moctezuma II, the latter engineered the election of his nephew Cacamatzin to rule the remainder. At the time of his accession, he was only 25 years old but was already respected for his intelligence and bravery.

When Cortés landed at VERACRUZ, Cacamatzin advised Moctezuma to honor the newcomers with a lavish reception. He later became a leading member of the noble conspiracy to oust the invaders after they had imprisoned the Aztec great speaker. Betrayed by agents of Moctezuma himself, whom the conspirators sought to overthrow after having liberated him, Cacamatzin was kidnapped and brought as a prisoner to TENOCHTITLÁN, whereupon Cortés named Cacamatzin's adolescent brother Cuicuitzca as king of Texcoco. Cacamatzin and the other noble conspirators (including CUITLÁHUAC) were tortured and died during the Noche Triste (see AZTECS).

Further reading: Inga Clendinnen, *Aztecs: An Interpretation* (Cambridge, U.K.: Cambridge University Press, 1991); Michael Coe, *Mexico: From the Olmecs to the Aztecs,* 4th ed. (London: Thames & Hudson, 1994); Nigel Davies, *Aztecs: A History* (Norman: University of Oklahoma Press, 1980).

— Marie A. Kelleher

cacao

Beginning with the first Spanish transatlantic explorations during the 16th century, Europeans learned of the gastronomic and trading value of the cacao plant (commonly referred to as the "chocolate plant") and its centuries-old refinement process as conceived by the OLMECS and later practiced by the MAYA and AZTECS.

Records place the genesis of cacao cultivation with the Olmecs, possibly as early as 1000 B.C. The more modern term *cacao* is a derivative of the term *kakawa,* taken from the Mixe-Zoquean language spoken by the Olmecs. The term *cacao* refers to the domesticated tree or plant (*Theobroma cacao)* and its unprocessed products. Cacao grew well in the fertile, humid lowlands of the Mexican Gulf.

Although archaeologists know little of how the Olmecs used cacao, scholars believe that the Maya inherited the tradition of cacao cultivation from the Olmecs. Because the Maya inhabited relatively cool highlands, a climate not well-suited for cacao, they had to import the plant from other areas. Although some wild species of *Theobroma* probably grew in close proximity to the Maya homeland, they did not encounter cacao (domesticated *Theobroma*) until sometime after 400 B.C., possibly as late as 100 B.C. During this time the Maya probably adopted the term *cacao* from descendants of the Olmecs.

The term *cacao* appears in the *Popol Vuh,* the sacred book and epic of the early Maya transcribed into Spanish during the colonial era. The term has also been identified in hieroglyphic writing on pottery vessels used in the preparation of cacao for nobility and the ruling class. The Dresden and Madrid codices make reference to cacao as well, including a description of the symbolic association between chocolate and human blood and the use of cacao in spiritual rituals and feasts.

Sixteenth-century observers of the Maya wrote of the various customs surrounding cacao and the consumption of chocolate, including marriage proposals and festivals celebrated by those who owned cacao plantations. During the colonial period some Maya consumed chocolate during the baptismal ceremonies of children. Cacao held enormous religious and social esteem among the Maya, particularly a sacred version of a chocolate drink made from a mixture of cacao, maize, and other ingredients. While more common chocolate drinks certainly existed, scholars remain uncertain as to whether the middle and lower classes consumed chocolate in any significant way.

Among the Aztecs, only the elite—royalty, nobility, warriors, and some merchants—consumed chocolate. They considered chocolate an important alternative to the native agave-derived alcoholic beverage *octli.* In part because of the heavy penalty against public drunkenness, chocolate drinking flourished among the Aztecs on the eve of European conquest. In addition, the Aztecs, like the Maya, used cacao beans as currency.

Whereas the Maya consumed a warm chocolate beverage, the Aztecs prepared and drank it cold. Among the Aztecs the preparation of fine chocolate began with the grinding of the cacao beans followed by a steeping process. Next the person preparing the chocolate aerated, filtered, and strained the mixture until foam formed. Following the removal of the foam, the thickened, dried paste could be added to water to produce the final product. At times those who prepared chocolate added other substances, such as chili powder or dried flowers.

The first European encounter with cacao occurred in 1502 during CHRISTOPHER COLUMBUS's fourth voyage. During his last journey across the Atlantic, Columbus crossed the path of a Maya trading expedition that had cacao in its cargo. Columbus ordered the capture of the vessel and thereby took control of the cargo: root, grains, a maize-based drink, and "many of those almonds which in New Spain are used for money." While Columbus never actually tasted chocolate, the foreign substance the

Spaniards referred to as "almonds" would later be known to Europeans as the substance from which the Maya derived chocolate.

Although they initially turned away from the repelling taste they associated with chocolate, eventually Europeans in the Western Hemisphere began to consume chocolate. By the late 1530s at least some groups of Europeans consumed chocolate during public ceremonies. Over the course of the 16th century, a growing number of Europeans became consumers of chocolate. Many of them consumed the drink hot rather than in the cold form taken by the Aztecs. Europeans also added sugar to sweeten the otherwise bitter potion and added cinnamon, black pepper, and anise seed. Perhaps most significantly, they adapted the traditional froth-generating process used to prepare the drink by introducing a *molinillo* (a large, whisklike wooden stick) to whip the mixture. This change, Spaniards reasoned, represented an improvement on the indigenous method of pouring the liquid from one vessel to another in order to develop the liquid's foam.

During the century following Columbus's encounter with cacao, many Spaniards had a great deal of interest in Aztec knowledge and understanding of the properties and usefulness of hundreds of curative plants. In 1570 the royal physician and naturalist Francisco Hernández traveled to NEW SPAIN to research plants with medicinal value. From the Aztecs Hernández learned of the varieties of the cultivated cacao tree and came to believe that the plant had potential healing properties. In his report he categorized the cacao plant with other fever-reducing plants that possessed what he termed a "cold" nature. Others soon rendered opinions supporting the use of cacao in medicine, although some feared that consumption of chocolate could cause sexual arousal and thus feared its abuse, especially its consumption by women.

In 1591 Juan de Cárdenas put forth a treatise that convinced Spaniards of the value of cacao in digestion. Whereas "green" chocolate (unrefined cacao) would cause various digestive ailments and possibly melancholy and irregular heartbeats, Cárdenas concluded that when properly prepared, ground, and toasted cacao aided digestion and improved the disposition and physical strength of whoever consumed it.

By the 17th century chocolate had been incorporated into the diets and occasional materia medica of western Europeans. Over time its importance continued to grow, and cacao thus became, like TOBACCO, the potato, and the tomato, a part of the COLUMBIAN EXCHANGE that benefited Europeans.

Further reading: Daniel Alden, "The Significance of Cacao Production in the Amazon during the Late Colonial Period: An Essay in Comparative Economic History," *Proceedings of the American Philosophical Society* 120, 2 (Philadelphia, 1976); Sophie D. Coe, *America's First Cuisines* (Austin: University of Texas Press, 1994); Sophie D. Coe and Michael D. Coe, *The True History of Chocolate* (London: Thames & Hudson, 1996); Bernard R. Ortiz de Monellano, *Aztec Medicine, Health, and Nutrition* (New Brunswick, N.J.: Rutgers University Press, 1990); John D. Super, *Food, Conquest and Colonization in Sixteenth-Century Spanish America* (Albuquerque: University of New Mexico Press, 1988).

— Kimberly Sambol-Tosco

cacique

A term that initially meant chief, ruler, or leader of a TAINO chiefdom in the Greater Antilles at the time of contact with Europeans but eventually applied by the Spanish to all local indigenous leaders throughout the Americas.

Among the Taino caciques rose to power through their effectiveness as war leaders and traders and their ownership of seaworthy canoes. These leaders received their choice of food and trade items. They and their families usually lived in villages segregated from the rank and file that inhabited homes near the fields and rivers. These caciques ruled most of the Greater Antilles through organized chiefdoms. They generally established these chiefdoms along river basins extending from the interior mountains found on most of these islands to the ocean, thus allowing them to maintain control of a variety of resources needed for survival. Those that dominated the island of HISPANIOLA had reached a more complex level of organization than their neighbors. Those caciques who did not initially oppose Spanish expansion into the Caribbean became low-level administrators for the Spanish. Most eventually rebelled against colonial authorities and died in battle or were executed by the Spanish.

Upon expanding into North and South America from the Caribbean, the Spanish used local caciques to control native populations. Often these leaders and their lineages benefitted from the arrival of the Spanish because the Spanish needed them as informants for understanding native societies and as agents for implementing the Spanish system of government. By being freed from restrictions of higher imperial authority under the AZTECS, INCA, and other forms of complex, indigenous governments, many of these local caciques welcomed and prospered under Spanish imperial control.

Eventually the role of the caciques became obsolete when the Spanish created more traditional forms of town governments based upon CABILDOs (town councils) usually headed by appointed Spanish authorities. Still, some of these native aristocracies managed to remain in power at the head of the *cabildos* and often proved effective in limiting Spanish intervention in their societies. In general, the experience of local caciques and their lineages differed according to geography and historical context, with some suffering quick annihilation as others flourished under Spanish domination.

Further reading: Robert S. Haskett, *Indigenous Rulers: An Ethnohistory of Town Government in Colonial Cuernavaca* (Albuquerque: University of New Mexico Press, 1991); John Lynch, *Caudillos in Spanish America, 1800–1850* (New York: Oxford University Press, 1992); Murdo J. Macleod, "Cacique, Caciquismo," *Encyclopedia of Latin American History and Culture,* ed. Barbara A. Tenenbaum (New York: Scribner's, 1996); Irving Rouse, *The Tainos: Rise and Fall of the People Who Greeted Columbus* (New Haven, Conn.: Yale University Press, 1992); Samuel Wilson, *Hispaniola: Caribbean Chiefdoms in the Age of Columbus* (Tuscaloosa: University of Alabama Press, 1990).

— Dixie Ray Haggard

Cahokia

Cahokia, a city at the confluence of the Missouri and Mississippi Rivers, near modern-day St. Louis, had from 10,000 to 30,000 inhabitants in the 12th century A.D.

The Indian builders and inhabitants of Cahokia shared a cultural pattern that scholars have named Mississippian. Mississippian sites have been identified as far north as Wisconsin and as far south as Alabama. Although cultural traits varied from place to place, MISSISSIPPIANS lived in towns and practiced maize (CORN) agriculture. Important religious symbols included crosses with a circle in the center, sun symbols, human skulls, and birds. Some Mississippian peoples practiced human sacrifice.

Cahokia covered an area of roughly five square miles. The town included more than 100 earth mounds, the significance of which is not entirely clear. The largest of these, Monks Mound, was a pyramidal structure about 1,000 feet long and 775 feet wide covering an area of more than 17 acres. It was built in a series of terraces, with the top level about 100 feet above the ground. Until the arrival of Europeans, it was the largest man-made structure north of Mexico.

Burial evidence suggests that a distinct social hierarchy existed. Commoners were buried with few or no grave goods, while elites were buried with large quantities of exotic items and might be accompanied by sacrificed humans. In one of Cahokia's platform mounds, excavators discovered the remains of an elite male. His body was laid on a platform of about 20,000 shell beads. Other grave goods included a sheet of rolled copper, mica, hundreds of unused arrowheads, and other items. These grave goods suggest that Cahokians participated in a trade network that extended for thousands of miles. The copper in the grave apparently came from the area of Lake Superior, the mica

from North Carolina, and the stone for the arrowheads from as far away as Tennessee and Oklahoma. The grave also contained bundles of bones and the disarticulated remains of other individuals. Near the body were the remains of three men and three women, possibly sacrificed to accompany the dead man. In a nearby pit the remains of more than 50 young women placed side by side and stacked one on another suggest a mass sacrifice, as do the bodies of four men without heads or hands.

The structure of Cahokian society and the extent of its influence remain mysterious. Some scholars have theorized that Cahokia exercised direct political and military control over both nearby and distant populations. Later scholars have argued that Cahokia, though an important political, cultural, and religious center, did not have the resources to be a major military power or exercise direct control over distant peoples.

Cahokia was abandoned in the 15th century for reasons that remain obscure. The construction of defensive palisades suggests that the city was threatened by enemies. Environmental factors probably played a significant role. Some evidence suggests a period of especially hot, dry summers that may have hastened the exhaustion of the surrounding farmland. The Cahokians also may have depleted their supply of readily available firewood. The fate of the Cahokians is unknown. It is likely that they assimilated into various surrounding Indian populations rather than forming the direct ancestors of any particular Indian nation. Much about Cahokia remains mysterious. The inhabitants left behind no written language, and many of the mounds have been destroyed by erosion, quarrying, plowing, and urban development.

Further reading: Melvin Fowler, *The Cahokia Atlas: A Historical Atlas of Cahokia Archaeology* (Springfield: Illinois Historical Preservation Agency, 1989); Patricia Galloway, *Choctaw Genesis, 1500–1700* (Lincoln: University of Nebraska Press, 1995); George R. Milner, *The Cahokia Chiefdom: The Archaeology of a Mississippian Society* (Washington D.C.: Smithsonian Institution Press, 1998); Timothy R. Pauketat and Thomas E. Emerson, *Cahokia: Domination and Ideology in the Mississippian World* (Lincoln: University of Nebraska Press, 1997); Biloine Whiting Young and Melvin L. Fowler, *Cahokia: The Great Native American Metropolis* (Urbana: University of Illinois Press, 2000).

— Martha K. Robinson

Calabar

A region and a city in southwestern Nigeria, Calabar served as an important center for the SLAVE TRADE.

Located on the coast with navigable rivers and lagoons nearby, Calabar had an optimal setting for development as a trading center. Europeans established a port at Calabar as early as the 15th century to take advantage of its links to trans-Saharan trade routes and its potential as a major transatlantic trading center. Calabar was the closest European trade center to CAMEROON, which, by the 16th century, was a major source for slaves being shipped to the Americas. Although their time in Calabar was limited, slaves being shipped to the Americas integrated some of the region's cultural and social traditions into their own lives. The inspiration for Cuba's Abakuas—all-male secret societies—came from the leopard societies of Calabar. Organizations of accomplished, respected men who adopted the leopard as a symbol of their masculinity and based on a mystical tradition, the leopard societies created spiritual alliances among their members. In their American emanations these organizations helped maintain a vital link to the slaves' African heritage.

Further reading: "Abakuas," in *Africana: The Encyclopedia of the African and African American Experience* eds., Kwame Anthony Appiah and Henry Louis Gates, Jr. (New York: Basic *Civitas* Books, 1999), 2; Eric Young, "Cameroon," in Appiah and Gates, Jr., eds., *Africana*, 353–357; Ralph A. Austen and Jonathan Derrick, *Middlemen of the Cameroons Rivers: The Duala and their Hinterland c. 1600–c.1960* (Cambridge, U.K.: Cambridge University Press, 1999); T. Eyongetah and R. Brain, *A History of the Cameroon* (London: Longman Group, 1974).

— Lisa M. Brady

California

An area with an initially large and diverse indigenous population, California eventually became the often ignored northwest fringe of the Spanish Empire in North America.

Before contact with Europeans, California contained a diverse and large indigenous population that suffered significant losses after the Spanish moved into the region and divided California into the two mission territories of Baja (currently part of MEXICO consisting of the peninsula below modern-day California) and Alta California (the area presently encompassed by the modern-day state of California). Initially, the JESUITS controlled Baja California and the FRANCISCANS moved into Alta California, but the Spanish ruled both regions as a single administrative unit until 1804. The Spanish first explored California when an expedition led by Juan Rodríguez Cabrillo arrived on the coast in the summer of 1542. Cabrillo sailed up and down the coast of California making contact with various native groups until he died in an accident on San Miguel Island in January of 1543. Missionaries first moved into Baja California after 1697, and by 1840 they had developed 27 missions in the region. The Jesuit period of influence in Baja

California lasted from 1697 to 1768, when the Franciscans replaced them after the Spanish Crown expelled the Jesuits throughout the Spanish empire. During their time in Baja California, the Jesuits created a series of mission farms, villages, and ranches that covered the length of the peninsula. The Franciscans further developed the region from 1769 to 1773 until the DOMINICANS gained control of the missions from 1774 to 1840. The Spanish did not finally move into Alta California until 1769, and both Alta and Baja California remained outside the economic sphere of NEW SPAIN throughout the colonial era.

Before the arrival of the Spanish, the indigenous populations of Baja and Alta California combined exceeded 350,000 people speaking up to 80 different languages divided into several hundred dialects. The gentle climate of Alta California with its plentiful supplies of food created an environment in which large populations lived sedentary lifestyles linked together through networks of trade. They lived in small, autonomous communities of minitribes or bands that included either transient camps, semipermanent villages, or permanent villages of 50 to 500 people. The family formed the primary social unit, with groups of related families living in villages together. Several allied villages loosely organized themselves into egalitarian minitribes or bands that remained relatively isolated from other communities. Their subsistence consisted of fishing, hunting small game and birds, and the gathering of wild vegetables, fruits, and root plants. Those who lived on the coast or in northern Alta California benefitted from the most diverse subsistence in the region. Like their neighbors to the north in the Pacific Northwest, many of coastal Alta California's people became master seamen by building oceangoing plank canoes to harvest the rich supplies of fish, mollusks, and sea mammals. Those to the south in Baja California and to the east of the Sierra Nevadas survived in harsher, drier conditions that limited food options. Survival in this region depended upon an ability to remain mobile in order to collect seasonal food supplies quickly. Therefore, Baja California's aboriginal inhabitants lived in small bands rather than in large communities.

Most people in California lived in domed wickiups made of pole frames covered with brush, grass, or reeds with a smoke hole left at the top. Others lived in semisubterranean houses in which long poles supported earthen walls and ceilings. The only opening was a smoke hole that also served as the entryway. The most prominent groups in Baja California from south to north were the Pericu, Guaycura, Cochimi, Kaliwa, Paipai, and Nakipa, and those in Alta California from south to north were the Tipai, Mohave, Chumash, Salina, Yokuts, Costanoan, Miwok, Wappo, Pomo, Maidu, Wintu, Yuki, Yana, Yakima, Hupa, Wiyot, Yurok, Shasta, and Karok. Eventually, the situation of many California groups rapidly deteriorated as the Spanish forced many people to live and work in their missions.

After the establishment of the missions in Baja California, the Native American population in the region decreased from approximately 50 to 60 thousand in the 1690s to 2,000 by the 1840s. The introduction of European DISEASES into the region, a tragic component of the COLUMBIAN EXCHANGE, initiated this rapid decline in the indigenous population, and the reduction of natives into mission towns along with harsh labor requirements imposed by their Spanish rulers exacerbated the misery and death rate of the native people in Baja California. Few colonists ventured into Baja California because of its harsh climate and limited resources, but some did practice limited commercial farming. Additionally, after the mid-18th century, some Spaniards launched limited mining efforts, but for the most part the territory remained the domain of missionaries and their ever decreasing population of mission Indians during the period of Spanish rule.

The Spanish began to settle Alta California, the area encompassed by the current state of California, in 1769. They wanted to reinforce their claim to the western coast of North America, prevent the Russians moving in from Alaska, and stop British movement into the region from Canada and the Pacific Ocean. The Franciscans developed 21 missions in Alta California from 1769 to 1823. The Spanish government established four presidios (military fortifications) and three villages. Just as in Baja California, native people died from disease in alarming numbers wherever the Spanish established permanent residence. This was especially true for those indigenous people gathered into missions. From 1769 to 1832, 64,000 of 88,000 mission Indians died. Both Baja and Alta California remained part of the Spanish Empire until Mexico gained its independence in 1820. The two regions then became part of Mexico until the United States seized both Baja and Alta California during the Mexican-American War in 1846 and 1847. The United States returned Baja California to Mexico in the Treaty of Guadalupe Hidalgo in 1848.

Further reading: Sherburne F. Cook, *The Conflict Between the California Indians and White Civilization* (Berkeley: University of California Press, 1976); ———, *The Population of the California Indians, 1769–1970* (Berkeley: University of California Press, 1976); Joseph L. Chartkoff and Kerry Kona Chartkoff, *The Archeology of California* (Stanford: Stanford University Press, 1984); Robert H. Jackson, "The Formation of Frontier Indigenous Communities: Missions in California and Texas," *New Views of Borderlands History*, ed. Robert H. Jackson (Albuquerque: University of New Mexico Press, 1998), 131–156.

— Dixie Ray Haggard

Calusa

A nonagricultural chiefdom that occupied southwest present-day FLORIDA at the time of contact with Europeans, the Calusa effectively resisted Spanish attempts to missionize them until the mid-18th century.

Before contact with Europeans in the 16th century, the Calusa developed a stratified and highly organized society. This chiefdom built mounds and traded with the MISSISSIPPIANS to the north and some of the islands in the Bahamas and possibly CUBA, but they never developed agriculture. In reality, they had no need to grow crops because they could more than provide for themselves through systematic use of the abundant natural resources of southwest Florida. By controlling access to these subsistence assets and the trade with outside groups, chiefly elites gained control of Calusa society and maintained this control through their participation in and dominance of Calusa ceremonial life.

The Calusa first encountered the Spanish during JUAN PONCE DE LEÓN's first voyage to Florida in 1513. Pedro Menéndez de Avilés tried to establish missions among the Calusa and the Tequesta in the Miami area in 1566 with JESUITS, but they left in 1569. The FRANCISCANS also failed to create a mission among the Calusa in 1697. These missions failed primarily because these natives were not farmers, and therefore they did not accept living in small, sedentary missions under the control of the clerics. Additionally, Spanish authorities tended to treat them in a high-handed fashion without ever actually having successfully conquered them. DISEASE and raids by natives from the interior southeast decimated the Calusa population over the next several centuries until they ceased to exist as a political and cultural entity by the mid-18th century.

Further reading: John H. Hann, ed. and trans. *Missions to the Calusa* (Gainesville: University Presses of Florida, 1991); Clifford M. Lewis, "The Calusa," in *Tacachale: Essays on the Indians of Florida and Southeast Georgia during the Historic Period,* eds. Jerald Milanich and Samuel Proctor (Gainesville: University Presses of Florida, 1978); William H. Marquardt, ed., *Culture and Environment in the Domain of the Calusa*, Institute of Archaeology and Paleoenvironmental Studies Monograph no. 1 (Gainesville: University Presses of Florida, 1991); Randolph J. Widmer, *The Evolution of the Calusa: A Nonagricultural Chiefdom on the Southwest Florida Coast* (Tuscaloosa: University of Alabama Press, 1988).

— Dixie Ray Haggard

Calvin, John (Cauvin, Jean) (1509–1564)

John Calvin, born into a French Catholic family, would become one of the most important Protestant reformers of the 16th century.

Calvin earned a master's degree in liberal arts from the Collège de Montaigu in Paris in 1528. At his father's request he then turned to the study of law, earning a doctorate in civil law in 1532. The young Calvin was influenced by teachers who promoted the direct study of the Bible and the church fathers. Some of his teachers had been influenced by MARTIN LUTHER, and he and his friends read the works of Luther and the Catholic humanist Desiderius Erasmus. Calvin's interest in Protestantism threatened to draw the attention of the INQUISITION, and he fled Paris in 1533, moving to Basel. Between 1532 and 1534 Calvin seems to have experienced a gradual conversion from Catholicism to Protestantism, a process that he described as the work of God, who "subdued and made teachable a heart which, for my age, was far too hardened in such matters."

From Basel in 1536 he published the first edition of the *Institutes of the Christian Religion*, which ranks among the most important of REFORMATION texts. The first edition of the *Institutes* opened with an address to King Francis I of France, in which Calvin denied that French Protestants sought to destroy the church or attack royal authority. The remainder of the first edition included a discussion of the Ten Commandments and the Apostles' Creed as well as chapters on law, faith, prayer, the sacraments, the false sacraments, and Christian freedom. Calvin revised and expanded the *Institutes* several times during his life. By the time the final edition was published in 1559, the work had grown from the original six chapters to 80 chapters.

After the first publication of the *Institutes*, Calvin returned briefly to France. Taking advantage of a short amnesty for religious exiles, he settled some family business and then departed, heading for Protestant Strasbourg. Troop movements forced him to make a detour, and he stopped in Geneva, the city where he would spend much of the rest of his life.

In Geneva Calvin was pressed into service by Guillaume Farel, who had been preaching in the city for four years. Geneva, at the time an independent city-state, was already a Protestant city. Calvin soon became the leader of the Protestant movement in Geneva, where he sought to increase the power of the church over the behavior of the city's residents. His "Articles on the Organization of Church and Worship" (1537) included a catechism and profession of faith and required the celebration of the Lord's Supper at least once a month, with the exclusion of those deemed unworthy by the ministers. Calvin also hoped to institute a system by which "persons of good life . . . from among the faithful" would report the misdeeds of the citizenry to the ministers, who would then correct the wrongdoers. He insisted that if malefactors did not heed this correction, the ministers must have the power to excommunicate them. At this point the citizens of Geneva, who had only recently deposed their Catholic bishop, began to complain that Calvin was demanding too much power for the ministers. In April 1538 the elected city council expelled Calvin and Farel.

Calvin spent the next three years in Strasbourg, where he became the pastor of a French-speaking congregation, published a second, much expanded edition of the *Institutes*, and met with other reformers, including Philipp Melanchthon. In 1541, facing continuing religious unrest, the city council of Geneva asked Calvin to return.

Calvin remained convinced of the need for a well-disciplined and well-ordered church. Upon his return to Geneva, he proposed a church structure consisting of four offices: pastors, teachers, elders, and the consistory, which he intended to work together to strengthen and discipline the church. This system provided the basis for religious life in Geneva. Pastors preached, administered the sacraments, and met together in the Compagnie des Pasteurs, or "Company of Pastors." This body had no civil authority but met regularly to study the Bible, admit new members, and censure bad conduct. Teachers instructed children, catechumens, and theology students. The elders watched over the congregations to ensure that the faithful lived proper lives. The final office, the consistory, was perhaps the most controversial of Calvin's reforms. The consistory consisted of the Compagnie des Pasteurs and twelve lay elders chosen by the city magistrates. It was responsible for finding and disciplining both the religiously unorthodox and those whose behavior was morally suspect. The members of the consistory were first to exhort the offender to mend his or her ways, but could excommunicate him or her if necessary. Calvin believed that such discipline was necessary to ensure the purity of the church.

When those accused of religious offenses refused to recant, Calvin believed that more severe punishments were necessary to preserve the integrity of the Christian community. In 1544 Sébastien Castellion was forced to leave Geneva after rejecting the canonical status of the Song of Songs and criticizing some of Calvin's theological ideas. Similarly, Jérôme Bolsec was exiled when he repudiated the idea of predestination. Calvin's harshest action, one that permanently damaged his reputation, was the execution of the Spanish physician Michael Servetus, who was burned at the stake in 1553 for his rejection of the doctrine of the Trinity.

Geneva's fame as a center of Protestantism soon spread, and Calvin drew students from across Europe, including the Scottish reformer John Knox. Some 5,000 Protestant refugees from across Europe also settled in Geneva. Despite Calvin's fame and the respect paid to him by other Protestant leaders, he was never the unquestioned ruler of Geneva, and some Genevans opposed him throughout his residence in the city.

Calvin was not the greatest original theologian of the Reformation, but many of his ideas, including those on predestination and on the relation between church and state, influenced the development of Protestant churches. Like many other 16th-century theologians, Calvin believed in predestination, that is, that God had chosen some humans to be saved and the rest to be damned. For Calvin this belief was a necessary consequence of the absolute supremacy of God. If God is all-knowing, all-powerful, and the master of creation, then nothing can happen that he did not will to take place. Since the Scriptures suggest that some people will be saved and others damned, God must have predetermined who should receive the gift of salvation and who should not. No human works or efforts can change the decision of God, who acts according to his own unknowable will. No one can ever be certain, in this life, if he or she is among the saved. While some religious thinkers objected to predestination on the grounds that it suggested that God acted capriciously, Calvin suggested that the doctrine should be a source of comfort to believers. On a practical level the doctrine of predestination could serve as an explanation of why some people, upon hearing the Gospel, responded, while others did not. Although no one could ever be certain who was saved and who damned, Christians could hope that God had chosen to save those whom he had also chosen to listen attentively to his word.

Calvin was an active minister and took great interest in the question of the establishment of proper order and discipline within Geneva, but he did not want civil and religious authority to be united in a single power. In Geneva the clergy took an oath of allegiance to the secular authorities, and Calvin praised magistrates and princes as having "the most sacred and by far the most honorable of all callings in the whole life of mortal men." By maintaining order, he suggested, civil officials followed God's will, for order was necessary for Christian communities to thrive. Calvin himself generally favored republican forms of government. Nonetheless, he believed so strongly in the necessity of discipline that he argued that Christians should obey those in authority, even if their leaders were tyrannical. On the other hand, if civil leaders demanded actions contrary to the will of God, Christians had a responsibility to resist.

Although civil authority ultimately derived from God, Calvin also insisted on the power of the church to act freely in its own sphere. Individuals could not be allowed the freedom to worship as they chose, for such diversity of opinion and practice would lead to anarchy. Church officials should be active both in the fight against unorthodox beliefs and in enforcing church discipline."Of what use," Calvin asked "is a dead faith without good works? Of what importance is even truth itself, where a wicked life belies

it and actions make words blush? . . . Let the severity of the laws reign in the church. Reestablish there pure discipline." Church and state, for Calvin, should work together to maintain an orderly, doctrinally pure community.

Calvin died on May 27, 1564, at the age of 55. At his own request he was buried in an unmarked, common grave. His legacy survived in the Reformed churches and reached the Western Hemisphere with the PURITANS, who brought some of his ideas on predestination and government to North America.

Further reading: William J. Bouwsma, *John Calvin, A Sixteenth-Century Portrait* (New York: Oxford University Press, 1988); John Calvin, *Institutes of the Christian Religion,* trans. Ford Lewis Battles (Grand Rapids, Mich.: Eerdmans, 1975); *The Oxford Encyclopedia of the Reformation,* vol. 1, ed. Hans J. Hillerbrand (New York: Oxford University Press, 1996), 234–247; Alister E. McGrath, *A Life of John Calvin: A Study in the Shaping of Western Culture* (Oxford, U.K.: Blackwell, 1990); ———, *Reformation Thought: An Introduction,* 3rd ed.(Oxford, U.K.: Blackwell, 1999); Steven Ozment, *The Age of Reform, 1250–1550* (New Haven Conn.: Yale University Press, 1980).

— Martha K. Robinson

Camden, William (1551–1623)

An English historian during the late 16th and early 17th century, William Camden attempted to write a comprehensive history of his native land.

Camden, born in London in 1551, went to Oxford in 1566, where he eventually found a position at Christ Church (the college of RICHARD HAKLUYT THE YOUNGER, among others), although he apparently never received a degree. Like other scholars of his age, Camden had to find patrons who would support his work, first at Oxford and then from 1571 to 1575 when he traveled around England seeking materials for his historical writings. In 1575 he became a master at Westminster School, and he remained there until the mid-1590s. During that time he had an opportunity to meet other scholars, including the Flemish geographer Abraham Ortelius, who encouraged Camden to pursue his historical writing.

Unlike most antiquarians, whose pursuit of material goods was often an end in itself, Camden gathered artifacts with the goal of creating a grand history of Britain. Published first in Latin under the title *Britain, or a Chorographical Description of the Most Flourishing Kingdoms of England, Scotland, and Ireland, and the adjoining islands from the most profound antiquity* in 1586, his work aimed to put into a single volume the history of the British Isles since antiquity, a task so vast that few scholars would even think about attempting it, let alone completing it. In addition to *Britannia*, Camden also wrote *Annales The True and Royall History of the famous Empresse Elizabeth Queene of England France and Ireland &c. True faith's defendresse of Divine renowne and happy Memory. Wherein all such memorable things as happened during her blessed raigne, with such acts and Treaties as past betwixt her Majestie and Scotland, France, Spaine, Italy, Germany, Poland, Sweden, Denmark, Russia, and the Netherlands, are exactly described,* first published in London in 1625. In that work Camden often emphasized the efforts of English sailors and putative colonizers who during the 16th century struggled to expand the realm of Queen ELIZABETH I. Yet Camden also recognized that a nation's history included more than just the heroic moments, such as the dramatic victory over the SPANISH ARMADA in 1588. As a result, he included all sorts of information, such as details about earthquakes and other natural phenomena. By doing so his work of history served as both a chronicle of the past and a record of his own times, an achievement that gave his work a value that has lasted for centuries.

After Camden left Westminster in the mid-1590s, his patrons managed to secure other positions for him. In 1589, even while he was still at the school, he became a prebend at Salisbury Cathedral, a position that guaranteed him some income. Eight years later he became Carenceux king at arms at the College of Heralds, a ceremonial court position in which he, along with others, spent time granting coats of arms to families who sought them. Such duties might have been important in late Tudor England when individuals tried to secure the signs of royal privilege, but they were not time consuming and, as a result, Camden had time to continue revisions for his historical works. In 1609 he bought a house in Chislehurst in Kent, near London, and he spent much of his time during the last years of his life there.

After his death in 1623 his associates honored his achievement by burying him in Westminster Abbey and commissioning a suitable memorial: a marble effigy, still in place, with its hand resting on his *Britannia.*

Further reading: William Camden, *Britannia* (London, 1586); ———, *Annales The True and Royall History of the famous Empresse Elizabeth Queene of England France and Ireland &c* (London, 1625); ———, *The History of the Most Renowned and Victorious Princess Elizabeth, Late Queen of England,* ed. Wallace T. MacCaffrey (Chicago: University of Chicago Press, 1970); Hugh Trevor-Roper, *Queen Elizabeth's First Historian: William Camden and the Beginnings of English 'Civil History,'* The Second Neale Lecture in English History (London: Jonathan Cape, 1971).

Cameroon

Located on the Gulf of Guinea and bordered by the modern-day nations of Nigeria, Chad, the Central African Republic, the Republic of Congo, Gabon, and Equatorial Guinea, Cameroon is a nation of nearly 250 ethnic groups, with an early history that reflects its position as a geographical and sociocultural transition zone between West and central Africa.

Volcanic mountains run north from the gulf coast, with the largest, Mount Cameroon, forming part of the coastline. Numerous rivers run through the area, crossing savannah and grasslands in the north and west. Pygmies were the earliest inhabitants of Cameroon, but BANTU agriculturalists moved into the region, displacing the hunter-gatherer Pygmies. These agriculturalists, such as the Bakweri, Duala, and FANG peoples, settled in the forested region in the southern part of the area, establishing patrilineal villages.

Regional differences developed within Cameroon reflecting the economic and social developments of the larger regions it bordered. Influenced in the south by the Christian empires involved in the transatlantic SLAVE TRADE and in the north by the trans-Saharan slave trade, ISLAM, and the savannah empires, Cameroon became an integral link between west and central Africa. GOLD, salt and slaves formed the basis of trade north from Cameroon across the SAHARA to North Africa. An estimated 10,000 slaves crossed the desert each year, mostly from Cameroon. From the 10th to the 15th centuries, the Sao kingdom, located in Cameroon south of Lake Chad, became wealthy from the trans-Saharan slave trade. Despite its early introduction to the area (around the 10th century), Islam did not become an important force until the 1500s. The invasion of the Massa people and the rise of the KOTOKO kingdom, which replaced the Sao, brought wider acceptance of the religion.

With the coming of Europeans in 1472, the people of southern Cameroon began participating directly in the transatlantic trade in slaves. In that year Fernão do Po arrived at Mbini Island, just off the coast of the Cameroon mainland. The Portuguese presence in Cameroon not only gave the area its name (*Cameroon* comes from the Portuguese name for one of the region's rivers, Rio dos Camerões, which means "River of Prawns") but also resulted in important changes to the region's economy and sociopolitical structure. By the 16th century Cameroon became a major source of slaves for the Americas; coastal peoples including the Bimbia and Duala acted as middlemen, transporting captives from the interior to the Cameroonian coast. These captives were then shipped to CALABAR, the closest European settlement and a slave-trading center. In exchange for the slaves, the Bimbia and Duala middlemen received cloth, liquor, firearms, and other goods. Although the Portuguese initially dominated the trade from Cameroon, control of this lucrative business fell into hands of the Dutch, English, French, and finally Americans.

Further reading: Edwin Ardener, *Kingdom on Mount Cameroon: Studies in the History of the Cameroon Coast, 1500–1970* (Providence, R.I.: Berghahn Books, 1996); Ralph A. Austen and Jonathan Derrick, *Middlemen of the Cameroons Rivers: The Duala and their Hinterland c. 1600–c. 1960* (Cambridge, U.K.: Cambridge University Press, 1999); Tambi Eyongetah and Robert Brain, *A History of the Cameroon* (London: Longman, 1974); Eric Young, "Cameroon," in *Africana: The Encyclopedia of the African and African American Experience,* eds. Kwame Anthony Appiah and Henry Louis Gates, Jr. (New York: Basic *Civitas* Books, 1999), 353–357.

— Lisa M. Brady

Canary Islands

A group of seven islands off the coast of northwest Africa, the Canary Islands became an early testing ground for European expansion.

The Canary Islands consist of seven islands off the coast of modern-day Morocco. The closest to the African shoreline are Fuerteventura and Lanzarote, and the others, from east to west, are Gran Canaria, Tenerife, Gomera, Palma, and Hierro. Europeans had at least a dim knowledge of the islands from the time of Pliny, but sustained contact did not begin until the late 13th or early 14th century. The Italian navigator Lancelotto Malocello sailed in 1336 to the region and named Lanzarote after himself, an early example of the European tendency to rename any lands they discovered, even if they were, as in the case of the Canary Islands, already inhabited. In 1341 the Portuguese sent a military expedition that included Niccoloso da Recco, who left an account of the journey. When they arrived, de Recco wrote, they found a "mass of uncultivated stony land, but full of goats and other beasts, and inhabited by naked men and women" who looked like "savages." When four of the natives swam out to the ships, the Portuguese captured and enslaved them, an act, as the historian John Mercer put it, that constituted "the first recorded example of the trust and treachery henceforth to become commonplace in the Canaries."

During the 15th century the French and then the Spanish each colonized the Canaries. Claiming, as Europeans routinely did during this age of exploration, that they were motivated by the desire to spread Christianity to heathens, the newcomers attempted to justify their conquest of the islands and the indigenous peoples who already lived there. One European who witnessed the colonization of Fuerteventura wrote that it was "difficult to

catch [the natives] alive; and they are so built that, if one turns on his captors, they have no choice but to kill him." Because the islands offered abundant supplies of goats and salt, two useful commodities that became even more vital over time when the Canary Islands became an important destination for transatlantic voyages, Europeans did not back down in the face of any opposition they encountered. Thus the Spanish carried out a long and difficult campaign from 1478 to 1483 to conquer Gran Canaria despite the indigenous peoples' sustained resistance. The conquest was worth the cost to the Spanish, which recognized the value of the islands. They were not alone. The Portuguese Prince HENRY THE NAVIGATOR had great interest in the Canaries, and CHRISTOPHER COLUMBUS made them his first destination on his world-changing journey of 1492.

After the Spanish laid claim to the Canaries they engaged in a campaign of destruction that was almost unmatched. Their enslavement of the indigenous peoples, appropriation of their land, and attempts to eradicate native culture and substitute European ways and Christianity were sufficiently brutal to summon a response from BARTOLOMÉ DE LAS CASAS, who became a champion of the rights of indigenous peoples in NEW SPAIN. Yet despite protests, the Spanish nonetheless continued to plunder the islands. As early as 1480 they shipped captured islanders to SEVILLE as slaves, and the SLAVE TRADE in the Canaries increased dramatically in the following decades. Once SUGAR cultivation became the dominant form of enterprise, indigenous people from the Canaries arrived in MADEIRA and the AZORES as slaves, and African slaves landed on the shores of the Canary Islands. The population of the islands grew as a result, although it was mostly composed of slaves and masters; very few of the indigenous people survived the horrors of European expansion and colonization.

Further reading: John Mercer, *The Canary Islanders: Their Prehistory, Conquest, and Survival* (London: Rex Collings, 1980); Eduardo Aznar Vallejo, "The Conquests of the Canary Islands," in Stuart B. Schwartz, ed., *Implicit Understandings: Observing, Reporting, and Reflecting on the Encounters Between Europeans and Other Peoples in the Early Modern Era* (Cambridge U.K.: Cambridge University Press, 1994), 134–156.

cannibalism

The consumption of human flesh by foreign peoples terrified many Europeans during the 16th century, and they were convinced that many peoples in the NEW WORLD adored the practice of cannibalism (also known as anthropophagy).

The idea of cannibalism has perhaps always struck fear in the hearts of anyone who has heard about it. It is, after all, one thing to be killed in battle or die a natural death; it is quite another to harbor the thought that someone would consume one's flesh after death. As the historian Peter Hulme put it, "[n]o other word, except perhaps 'sex,' is so fraught with our fears and desires."

During the 16th century many Europeans were convinced that the native peoples of the Western Hemisphere practiced cannibalism. That Native Americans did so came as no great surprise to European observers, who tended to believe that the indigenous peoples they encountered were primitives who tended to indulge their vilest passions. Contrary to the notion that these Native Americans ate people for nourishment, Europeans came to understand that cannibalism, where it was practiced, was related to warfare and the need to vanquish enemies. Still, however much they might understand the custom, the idea of cannibalism continued to haunt Europeans' minds during the 16th century.

During his voyages to the west, CHRISTOPHER COLUMBUS heard that cannibalism might exist in the West Indies, and members of his expeditions believed that they had seen evidence. According to Diego Álvarez Chanca, a physician who accompanied Columbus's 1493 journey, residents of the islands confirmed that cannibals lived in the region. "We inquired of the women who were prisoners of the inhabitants what sort of people these islanders were and they answered, 'Caribs,'" he wrote to the city council of SEVILLE. "As soon as they learned that we abhor such kind of people because of their evil practice of eating human flesh, they felt delighted." Chanca then claimed that these island women feared CARIB men who ate captured men and also any of their children they did not want to take captive. Caribs took these women and kept them as concubines, and they also took boys but did not eat them quickly because, Chanca claimed he had heard, they did not taste very good. But the Carib, so Chanca's informants claimed, still captured boys; once in the Carib settlements, they would "remove their organs, fatten them until they grow up and then, when they wish to make a great feast, they kill and eat them[.]" Such reports circulated in Europe and convinced many that cannibalism was a deeply entrenched habit of at least some of the indigenous peoples—the Caribs—on the far shores of the Atlantic.

The definitive word on cannibalism in the 16th century came from the pen of the great French essayist Michel de Montaigne (1533–92), a courtier at the court of King Charles IX and later mayor of Bordeaux, whose *Essais*, first published in 1588, had an enormous influence in France and beyond. In the late 1570s Montaigne wrote the essay "Of Cannibals." In that piece he claimed to rely on the testimony of an unnamed man who had traveled to BRAZIL in 1557 and returned to France. Montaigne emphasized the fact that his informant was a "simple, crude fellow" who, as a result of his limitations, was bound to tell the truth of what he saw because, unlike a clever person who would exaggerate what he saw or invent things, less able observers did not have "the stuff to build up false inventions and give them plausibility." In other words, because the man was less intelligent he could be trusted to tell the truth about what he had seen.

According to Montaigne, his observer had watched the native peoples of coastal Brazil, quite possibly the TUPINAMBA described by such observers as JEAN DE LÉRY, consume human flesh. They did not do so indiscriminately. Instead, they did so only after they had taken captives in war and had brought them back to their settlements. Once there, Montaigne wrote, they "treated their prisoners well for a long time with all the hospitality they can think of," but eventually call others to gather together. Once together, the original captor "ties a rope to one of the prisoner's arms, by the end of which he holds him, a few steps away, for fear of being hurt, and gives his dearest friend the other arm to hold in the same way; and these two, in the presence of the whole assembly, kill him with their swords. This done, they roast him and eat him in common and send some pieces to their absent friends." But, Montaigne emphasized, these natives did not engage in such acts "for nourishment, as of old the Scythians used to do." Instead, the act was intended as a form of "extreme revenge" on an enemy.

What did Montaigne think of such an act? Unlike many Europeans, who harbored anxieties about the peoples of the Americas and feared that all of them would kill them in order to eat them, Montaigne asserted that such practices were no more barbaric than the ways that Europeans treated individuals they deemed threatening. "I think there is more barbarity in eating a man alive than in eating him dead," he wrote, "and in tearing by tortures and the rack a body still full of feeling, in roasting a man bit by bit, in having him bitten and mangled by dogs and swine (as we have not only read but seen with fresh memory, not among ancient enemies, but among neighbors and fellow citizens, and what is worse, on the pretext of piety and religion), than in roasting and eating him after he is dead." Europeans could call these native Brazilians "barbarians" if they so chose, but Europeans themselves "surpass them in every kind of barbarity."

Such a reasoned take on the consumption of human flesh did not, of course, convince all Europeans that cannibalism was no worse than death itself. HANS STADE, a German who traveled to Brazil on a Portuguese ship and became a captive, lived in terror that he would be eaten after he was killed. His account of his time in captivity emphasized the ubiquity of cannibalism and provided a graphic description for those who read his work. His views probably reflected Europeans' fears more closely than the more subtle views of Montaigne. And when the Flemish engraver THEODOR DEBRY redid Stade's rough illustrations for *America tertia pars,* first published in 1592, he provided Europeans with a grotesque and anatomically specific rendering of how at least one group of Native Americans engaged in cannibalism.

Given prevailing prejudices held by many Europeans who traveled to the Americas, it is difficult to know how widespread the practice of cannibalism might have been in the Western Hemisphere. There is no doubt that some people practiced it, nor is there any doubt that Europeans themselves consumed human flesh when they suffered hard times in the Americas.

Further reading: Felipe Fernández-Armesto, *Columbus* (Oxford, U.K.: Oxford University Press, 1991), esp. 102–103; Peter Hulme, *Colonial Encounters: Europe and the Native Caribbean, 1492–1797* (London: Methuen, 1986), esp. 78–87; Michel de Montaigne, "Of Cannibals," in *The Complete Essays of Michele de Montaigne,* ed. Donald M. Frame (Stanford, Calif.: Stanford University Press, 1958), 150–159; David Quint, "A Reconsideration of Montaigne's *Des cannibales,*" in *America in European Consciousness, 1493–1750,* ed. Karen Ordahl Kupperman (Chapel Hill: University of North Carolina Press, 1995), 166–191.

caravel

Small sailing vessels, originally developed by the Portuguese, that incorporated important advances in shipbuilding technology that made possible the great voyages of European exploration in the late 16th and 17th centuries and, more important, gave European (Portuguese, Spanish, English, Dutch, and French) sailors advantages in seaborne trade that allowed them to dominate the "carrying trade" of much of the world.

The original *caravela latina* first appeared in the Mediterranean in the 14th century as a large boat with two lateen-rigged masts that incorporated important advances in hull design. These included replacing the beakhead (the open section of the bow forward of the forecastle) with a simple curved stem (the timbers forming the bow where it meets the keel), as well as replacing the stern castle with a plain transom stern (timbers bolted athwart the stern post, from which the rudder was hung), giving the ship a flat stern and a platform for overhanging galleries. The result was a ship much stronger and able to sail closer to the wind (that is, more directly into it).

Christopher Columbus's caravels setting sail from Spain, 1492 *(The Granger Collection)*

The *caravela latina*'s lateen sails were too cumbersome and inefficient for long ocean voyages in the Atlantic Ocean and North Sea. The result was the creation of the *caravela redonda,* a three-masted vessel with square sails on the fore and main mast and fore-and-aft rigged sails on the mizzen. This proved to be an extremely "handy" (maneuverable) rig capable of impressive speed and responsiveness. The caravel quickly became the dominant ship type used in Europe. Although popular, the ships remained small, rarely more than 100 feet long (they averaged 75–80).

All of CHRISTOPHER COLUMBUS's ships on his voyage of 1492 were caravels; the *Santa María* (95 feet) and the *Pinta* (58 feet) were *caravela redonda* types, but the *Niña* (56 feet) began the voyage as a *caravela latina.* Its rigging was changed during a stop at the CANARY ISLANDS en route and afterwards, because of its shallow draft and good sailing qualities, became Columbus's favorite. The Portuguese explorations down the west coast of Africa were generally made in caravels, and the explorer BARTHOLOMEU DIAS became the first European to round Cape Horn in 1488 in one. The five vessels of FERDINAND MAGELLAN's fleet with which he attempted to circumnavigate the globe for Spain (1519–22) were all caravels, but only one, the *Victoria* under the command of Juan Sebastian de Elcano, finally returned.

Further reading: Roger Gardiner, ed., *Cogs, Caravels and Galleons: The Sailing Ship 1000–1650* (Annapolis, Md., Naval Institute Press, 1994); Peter Kemp, ed., *The Oxford Companion to Ships and the Sea* (London: Oxford University Press, 1976); Roger C. Smith, *Vanguard of Empire: Ships of Exploration in the Age of Columbus* (Oxford, U.K.: Oxford University Press, 1993).

— Paul Dunscomb

Carib

The term *Carib* has traditionally described the indigenous people of the Lesser Antilles, those tribes inhabiting the Orinoco and AMAZON River valleys in South America, and a language family.

The most accurate term to describe the people who inhabited the Lesser Antilles is *Island Carib*. The inhabitants of the Orinoco and Amazon River valleys should be referred to by their individual, tribal names, and Cariban is the proper name for the language family of these people.

Early colonizers constantly referred to the Island Carib as fierce and aggressive warriors because they resisted European expansion into the islands so fervently. Europeans contrasted the Island Carib with the TAINO by portraying the Taino as pacific. The assumed warlike nature of the Island Carib so captured the imagination of Europeans that they named the Caribbean Sea after these people. Additionally, the term *cannibal* is derived from the name *Carib*, even though evidence of this practice among the Island Carib is scanty at best.

Scholars debate the origins and actual identity of the Island Carib. Some believe they were simply another branch of the Taino, and others argue that these people were recent arrivals from mainland South America related to the Cariban-speaking people of the Orinoco and Amazon River basins. Most likely, the Island Carib represented a merger of Taino who occupied most of the West Indies with the late arriving Cariban speakers. Island Carib oral traditions maintained that they had recently arrived in the Lesser Antilles just before the arrival of CHRISTOPHER COLUMBUS in 1492 and married the wives of the men they had defeated and killed. The fact that Island Carib females and children spoke Taino (an Arawakan language) and adult males spoke a Cariban

pidgin gives credence to their oral traditions. The Island Carib perpetuated this situation by having the females and children live in residences separate from the adult males. The men obtained wives through raids on the Taino and practiced polygyny. In general, women were subservient to men and had to use the Carib pidgin language when addressing them. The Island Carib's close alliance with the Cariban-speaking Galibi on the islands of Grenada and Tobago and other Cariban speakers on the South American mainland also testifies to their probable late arrival in the islands of the West Indies.

The Island Carib subsisted by farming primarily manioc and sweet potatoes and supplementing these horticultural products with fish, shellfish, turtles, agouti, rice rats, and iguanas. The Island Carib also grew cotton, and they made beer that they consumed on social and ceremonial occasions. This last practice was not evident among the Taino. Island Carib villages consisted of circular huts for the women and children built around a rectangular men's structure. They maintained an egalitarian society that exhibited hierarchy only during warfare, when certain war leaders assumed command of expeditions based on their demonstrated abilities. The Island Carib practiced a shamanistic religion that did not have the organization or multiplicity of gods like that of the Taino.

The material culture of the Island Carib more closely resembled that of the Cariban South American tribes than that of the Taino, especially their ceramics. They made substantial canoes on which their livelihood in warfare and trade depended. In addition to basic ceramics, their home furnishings consisted of stools, baskets, and cotton hammocks. They usually wore only decorative garments, including crescent-shaped gold or copper pieces and green stone pendants, although on special occasions they also wore clothing woven from parrot feathers. In warfare they used a substantial longbow with poisoned arrows, war clubs, blowguns, and noxious gases made from the smoke of hot chili peppers.

In resisting European expansion into the West Indies, Island Carib raided plantations and often escaped with African slaves (see SLAVERY). Usually they adopted these captives into their society. Additionally, runaway slaves and African survivors of shipwrecks frequently fled to Island Carib–controlled areas. After two centuries of this syncretic process, a new ethnic identity emerged on some islands. Europeans called these new people "Black Carib" and feared them even more than the traditional Island Carib. Most of the substantial Island Carib populations that existed during the early years of European colonization of the Lesser Antilles disappeared as a result of the epidemic DISEASES introduced when Europeans arrived, slave raiding done primarily by the Spanish, and constant warfare with European colonists.

Further reading: Nancy L. Gonzalez, *Sojourners of the Caribbean: Ethnogenesis and Ethnohistory of the Garifuna* (Urbana: University of Illinois Press, 1988); Peter Hulme and Neil Lancelot Whitehead, eds, *Wild Majesty: Encounters with Caribs from Columbus to the Present Day: An Anthology* (New York: Oxford University Press, 1992); Irving Rouse, *The Tainos: Rise and Decline of the People Who Greeted Columbus* (New Haven, Conn.: Yale University Press, 1992); Samuel M. Wilson, ed. *The Indigenous People of the Caribbean*, (Gainesville: University Press of Florida, 1997).

— Dixie Ray Haggard

Caroline, Fort

Fort Caroline, an ill-planned and short-lived French colony on the east coast of FLORIDA, was captured by the Spanish in 1565.

The abortive colony originated in 1564 when French settlers, led by RENÉ DE LAUDONNIÈRE, settled near the mouth of the St. Johns River, where they built a triangular fort. The settlers, most of whom were French Protestants (see HUGUENOTS), included nobles, artisans, women, and children. Like other early colonies, Fort Caroline soon faced significant problems. Initial good relations with the nearby Indians soon soured, for the colonists had arrived too late in the year to plant crops and so relied on the Indians to feed them. The colony also suffered from internal divisions: Laudonnière was not a popular leader, and when the colonists' dreams of finding wealth were frustrated, they grew angry.

Laudonnière also forbade the settlers to use Fort Caroline as a base from which to attack the Spanish. As food ran short, some settlers deserted while others planned a rebellion against Laudonnière. In December 1564, 70 colonists forced Laudonnière to allow them to leave in two ships. After leaving Fort Caroline some of these rebels were captured by the Spanish and revealed the location of the colony.

Because Spanish treasure ships sailed near the coast of Florida, the Spanish were unwilling to allow any European rival to gain a foothold in such a strategic area. King PHILIP II of Spain sent Pedro Menéndez de Avilés at the head of a force of some 500 soldiers and 200 sailors to rout the French. At about the same time French reinforcements under Jean Ribault sailed from Europe to aid the colony. Ribault's seven ships, carrying some 800 men, arrived first, with Menéndez's fleet only a few days behind. Ribault attempted to defeat the Spanish in a sea battle, but his fleet was largely destroyed by a hurricane.

Menéndez then marched overland from Saint Augustine to Fort Caroline, where he attacked. Laudonnière, in the fort, commanded a force of perhaps 25 healthy soldiers and about 150 sick or wounded ones. The French mounted little defense, and Menéndez took the fort almost without resistance. A few of the French, including Laudonnière, escaped and eventually returned to France. The Spanish killed the 142 men they found in the fort but spared the women and children.

Menéndez renamed the fort San Mateo and then returned south to Saint Augustine. In two separate incidents his forces found groups of shipwrecked Frenchmen, survivors of Ribault's fleet. He convinced both groups (one made up of about 140 men, the other of about 70) to surrender unconditionally and then executed all the prisoners. These mass executions infuriated the French, and when San Mateo was recaptured by the French in 1568 the French commander hanged the entire garrison.

Further reading: Eugene Lyon, "Settlement and Survival," in *The New History of Florida* ed. Michael Gannon (Gainesville: University Press of Florida, 1996), 40–61; Lyle N. McAlister, *Spain and Portugal in the New World, 1492–1700* (Minneapolis: University of Minnesota Press, 1984); Jerald T. Milanich and Charles Hudson, *Hernando de Soto and the Indians of Florida* (Gainesville: University Press of Florida, 1993); David B. Quinn, *Explorers and Colonies: America, 1500–1625* (London: Hambledon Press, 1990).

— Martha K. Robinson

Cartier, Jacques (1491–1557)

The French explorer Jacques Cartier made three unsuccessful voyages to the St. Lawrence region of northeastern North America in the hopes of finding GOLD, other riches, or the NORTHWEST PASSAGE.

After the Spanish found remarkable treasures of gold and SILVER in Central and South America, other Europeans hoped to find mineral wealth in other regions of the Americas. They also sought the Northwest Passage, a sea route that would allow European ships to pass through the Americas on their way to China (see CATHAY) and the East.

In 1534 the French king Francis I sent Cartier, a native of St. Malo, to discover new lands in America. On his voyage he narrowly missed finding the St. Lawrence River and explored the west coast of Newfoundland and several islands. He sailed up the coast of New Brunswick as far as Chaleur Bay. At the entrance to the bay, Cartier and his men were greeted by Micmac Indians holding up furs on sticks to indicate that they wished to trade. The French were frightened and fired their cannons to repel the Indians. The Micmac returned the next day and this time traded furs for European goods such as kettles and knives. The Indians' desire to trade their furs for foreign goods suggests that Cartier was not the first European to

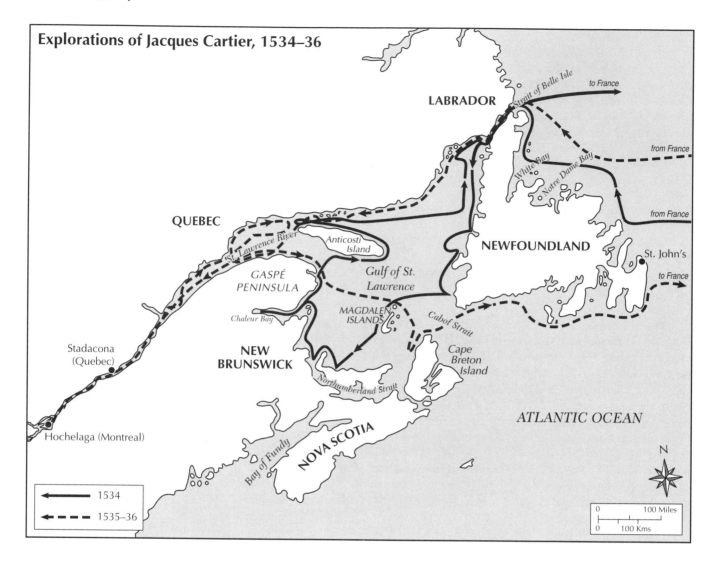

Explorations of Jacques Cartier, 1534–36

visit the region. Contact with European fishermen may have first taken place as long as 50 years before Cartier sailed.

Cartier and his men next met and traded with members of two Iroquoian tribes, the Stadacona and the HOCHELAGA, known collectively as the St. Lawrence IRO-QUOIS. Before leaving their territory in Gaspé Harbor, Cartier set up a 30-foot wooden cross and attached a sign that read "vive Le Roi De France." Donnacona, the Stadaconan headman, objected to this French attempt to leave a signal on his people's land. Cartier, having already offended the Indians, then seized two of Donnacona's sons (or nephews) and returned to France. Cartier seems to have hoped that the two young men would learn French and serve as interpreters on a later expedition.

In 1535 Cartier returned to Canada. On this second expedition he returned with Donnacona's two sons, Taig-

noagny and Domagaya, who had learned at least some French in their nine months in France. Despite the presence of two people who were at least partially bilingual, misunderstandings and missteps led to greater tension between the French and the Stadacona. The Stadacona were pleased to see the young men again but objected to Cartier's plan to sail farther inland on the St. Lawrence. Cartier had heard of the existence of an Indian town named Hochelaga, on the site of modern-day Montreal. Still searching for the Northwest Passage, he hoped to visit it to determine how far the St. Lawrence was navigable. It is impossible to know why Donnacona objected to Cartier's attempt to go inland, but the anthropologist Bruce Trigger suggested that Donnacona hoped that the Stadacona would make an alliance with the French that would allow them to act as middlemen, trading both with the French and with Indians who lived farther inland.

When Cartier reached Hochelaga, the residents greeted him warmly. Both the Indians and the French performed actions that must have seemed incomprehensible to those on each side. The Indians brought sick people to Cartier and indicated that he should lay his hands on them. Cartier, for his part, read to the Indians from the Bible and then climbed a mountain that he named Mount Royal. From this perch he saw rapids that convinced him that the river was not further navigable. With this discovery he had no further interest in Hochelaga and returned to Stadacona. This departure probably surprised and offended the Indians, who had prepared a feast for their guests.

Cartier and his men spent the winter of 1535–36 with the Stadacona. During the winter Cartier heard stories of a fabulous "Kingdom of the Saguenay," which lay somewhere in the interior of the continent. According to Donnacona, it was a land rich in gold and rubies, where white men dressed in wool lived. Relations between the French and the Indians deteriorated over the course of the winter. Both the Stadacona and the French were stricken by illness (see DISEASE). Cartier reported that more than 50 Indians died, and later 25 of the French died of scurvy. Even when the Indians showed Cartier how to brew a drink that cured the French of scurvy, he continued to distrust them. He believed that Donnacona and his sons, Taignoagny and Domagaya, were plotting against him. He also believed, possibly mistakenly, that Donnacona's authority was challenged by a rival, Agona. Because he no longer trusted Donnacona or his family, Cartier hoped to see Agona replace Donnacona as headman.

Cartier decided he could solve both problems at once. If Donnacona went to France, his absence would allow Agona to seize power. At the same time, if Donnacona told the king of France about the Kingdom of Saguenay, the king would surely support more voyages. Cartier seized Donnacona, his two sons, and seven other Indians. He promised that they would return to Canada the next year. Misunderstandings between the French and the Stadacona had already been common, and the kidnapping of Donnacona and his companions made the Indians angry. None of these 10 captives would ever return to Canada. A war between France and Spain delayed Cartier's return, and by the time he got permission for a third voyage in 1541, all but one of the captives had died of European diseases. Cartier did not bring the survivor, a young girl, on the voyage, fearing that she would tell the Stadacona that the others had all died. When Cartier reached the Stadacona, he told them that "Donacona was dead in France, and that his body rested in the earth, and that the rest stayed there as great Lords, and were married, and would not returne backe into their Countrey." The Indians were angry that Cartier had not returned Donnacona and the others, as he had promised.

Relations deteriorated even further when Cartier selected a site nine miles upstream and began building a colony. He brought settlers with him on this voyage, and they began planting crops and erecting buildings, including a fort. This clear intent to settle there infuriated the Indians, who determined to drive the French out of their land. During the winter they killed some 35 French settlers who ventured outside the fort. At the end of the winter, Cartier, having loaded his ships with minerals and stones that he mistakenly believed to be gold and diamonds, planned to return to Europe. He met Jean-François de la Rocque, sieur de Roberval, the lieutenant-general of Canada, in St. John's Harbor, Newfoundland. Roberval ordered him to return to the colony, but Cartier instead fled back to France. His "diamonds" and "gold" proved worthless, and he never returned to Canada. The colony that he founded was short-lived. Roberval and his men had more cordial but distant relations with the Indians. After a single winter in Canada, they returned to France in 1543.

Cartier returned to St. Malo, where he wrote an account of his voyages. He died on September 1, 1557.

Further reading: James Axtell, *The Invasion Within: The Contest of Cultures in Colonial North America* (Oxford, U.K.: Oxford University Press, 1985); Fernand Braudel, ed., *Le Monde de Jacques Cartier: L'aventure au XVIe siècle* (Paris: Berger-Levrault, 1984); Ramsay Cook, "Donnacona Discovers Europe: Rereading Jacques Cartier's *Voyages*" in *The Voyages of Jacques Cartier* (Toronto: University of Toronto Press, 1993); W. J. Eccles, *France in America* (East Lansing: Michigan State University Press, 1990); Bruce G. Trigger, *The Children of Aataentsic: A History of the Huron People to 1660*, vol. I (Montreal: McGill-Queen's University Press, 1976).

— Martha K. Robinson

Casa de Contratación

The main agency of the Spanish government that oversaw trade and commerce with the empire's American colonies.

The Casa de Contratación was one of the earliest colonial institutions established by the Spanish Crown. The discovery of GOLD on the island of HISPANIOLA in 1500 sparked a trading boom between Spain and the colonies, and the Crown became concerned that it would be unable to regulate the commerce or to collect all the taxes owed to it. The Crown also wanted to ensure that it received its share of profits from the mines; by law it was entitled to one-fifth of all precious metals discovered in the NEW WORLD. With these concerns in mind, the Crown established the Casa de Contratación at SEVILLE in 1503. As originally conceived, the Casa functioned solely to monitor and regulate maritime trade. By law, every ship departing to or arriving from the New World had to meet with officials of the Casa, register its cargo, submit to inspections, and pay any taxes or duties owed to the Crown. The Casa consisted of three important officials—a *contador* (comptroller), treasurer, and a factor—all of whom were royal appointees. In addition, there was a small number of clerks, notaries, and lawyers who assisted the main officers. To consolidate the Casa's control over shipping, the Crown decreed that all trade with the New World had to pass through the port of Seville under the Casa's watchful eye. As a result of this policy, Seville became the most important port in the Spanish Empire, a position it maintained throughout the 16th century.

As Spain's American trade boomed, the Casa took on more responsibilities. It moved from registering cargo and collecting taxes to trying maritime civil suits, supervising ship construction, and training navigators. By the 1520s it

began to advise the Crown on all matters related to the economy of the New World, becoming in effect a ministry of commerce. The Casa gained new powers and responsibilities in 1522, when the Crown instituted the flotilla system. Over the years pirates and foreign enemies had begun preying on Spanish ships. To protect and further control its commerce, the Crown decreed that there would be a single large fleet that would leave Spain, and another that would return from the New World. In both cases a group of heavily armed warships accompanied the fleet. On the one hand, this new regulation made it easier for the Casa to monitor cargos and eliminate contraband. On the other hand, it created a heavy burden for the Casa, which had the responsibility of outfitting, arming, and stocking the warships used to protect the treasure fleets.

Realizing that the Casa was too small to handle its new responsibilities, PHILIP II reorganized it several times between 1540 and 1590. First, he greatly increased the

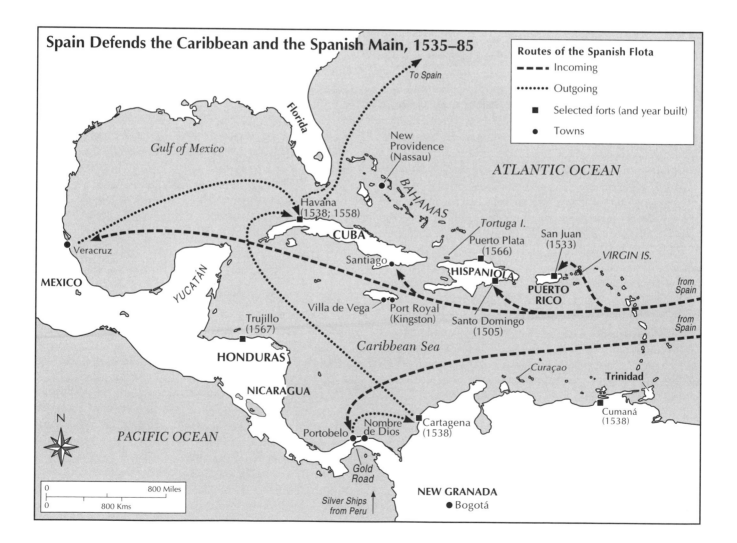

Spain Defends the Caribbean and the Spanish Main, 1535–85

support staff and selected a president to oversee its operations. In 1543 Philip tried to streamline its operations by removing its judicial powers to try civil suits. In 1580 he made the Casa responsible for trying maritime criminal cases. That year he also removed the burden of having the Casa provision warships to protect the treasure fleets, and by 1607 the Crown decreed that the Casa no longer had to arm the fleets, either. In an attempt to alleviate the pressures of sending out only one fleet, Philip also chose to send out two fleets to the New World, leaving at different times. While this strategy did not diminish the Casa's workload, it did spread it out over the course of a year.

The greatest period of the Casa lasted until the 1590s, and thereafter it began a long, slow decline. Philip's attempts to aid the Casa by assigning it more staff had the unfortunate side effect of creating massive bureaucratic delays. Often officials worked at cross purposes to one another. Also, there were not always clear lines of authority, causing bickering that delayed work for months at a time. Worse still, in an effort to raise money the Crown sold the positions at the Casa to the highest bidder, which meant that many of the officials were wealthy but not necessarily competent.

A cumbersome bureaucracy was not the Casa's only problem. Spain's commercial policies also hampered the Casa's ability to function effectively. Following the bullionist ideas of the time, Spain imported massive amounts of SILVER, to the exclusion of other products. This practice caused rampant inflation in Spain and priced Spanish goods out of the market. Spanish industries, such as the manufacture of textiles, collapsed. Increasingly, the Spanish colonists turned to smuggling to supply their basic needs, which devastated the official trading channels passing through the Casa. With fewer goods passing through the Casa, it could collect fewer and fewer taxes for the Crown.

Ultimately, the highly regulated commercial system controlled by the Casa was not flexible enough to meet the needs of the growing colonies. Goods arrived infrequently, and any attempt to ship merchandise across the Atlantic was needlessly expensive and required ridiculous amounts of paperwork. Nevertheless, the Casa continued to control maritime trade until the 1700s.

Further reading: C. H. Haring, *The Spanish Empire in America* (Oxford, U.K.: Oxford University Press, 1947); Lyle N. McAlister, *Spain and Portugal in the New World, 1495–1700* (Minneapolis: University of Minnesota Press, 1984).

— Scott Chamberlain

castas

The term used to describe persons of racially mixed background in colonial Latin America and who often had distinct legal, social, and economic status within the colonial system.

Originally, there were three broad ethnic groups present in colonial Latin America: Europeans, Africans, and indigenous peoples. In the name of "good order," the royal governments of Spain, Portugal, and the church encouraged people to marry members "of their own kind." They hoped to promote the ideal of equality within a marriage, in which both spouses had similar social, political, and economic standing. In reality, the conquest and settlement of the Americas made this ideal difficult to achieve. In the first place, at the beginning of the colonial period the overwhelming majority of European colonists were male. Lacking potential European wives, many chose to have more casual sexual unions with local women, creating a new generation of children with mixed ancestry. This process, known as MESTIZAJE, accelerated throughout the colonial period.

The largest *castas* group was the MESTIZOS, who had a European-indigenous ancestry. Unions between these groups began early in the colonial period. Many of the CONQUISTADORES took concubines over the course of the conquest, including HERNÁN CORTÉS, who had a son by his mistress MALINCHE before marrying her off to one of his lieutenants. Others settled down in the aftermath of the conquest with one or more native concubines from their ENCOMIENDAS. At times Europeans married indigenous noblewomen to gain land and social standing among the local population, and children of these unions had a relatively high social status within the colonial system, yet within a generation of the conquest the practice died out. In later years Spanish fathers did not always legitimize their mestizo children, leaving their legal status somewhat nebulous. As a result many colonists associated mestizos with illegitimacy and dishonor, even if the mestizo was a legitimate child. Crown officials from NEW SPAIN to PERU complained that mestizos were naturally inclined toward crime and public disorder. Still, many mestizos held important positions within colonial society. A substantial number earned a respectable living as artisans, while those with better connections secured low-level jobs in the Church or royal bureaucracy.

The second important *castas* group was the mulattoes, the children of African-European unions. By the 1550s Europeans began bringing African slaves to the New World in substantial numbers; by 1560 the African population was larger than the European population of New Spain. Over time many slave owners entered into sexual unions with their female slaves, at times elevating them to a quasiofficial status as a mistress. Out of a sense of obligation, many slave owners freed the children of these unions, giving them a somewhat elevated status relative to the slaves, although like the mestizos the mulattoes frequently carried a social stigma of illegitimacy that blocked their social mobility. Mulattoes often played a vital role in the colonial economy. They frequently accepted menial jobs as transporters, street cleaners, and in food production vital to feed the residents of cities. Many mulattoes were able to earn a substantial living by performing these vital, if sometimes unpleasant, tasks. In BRAZIL, for example, mulatto mule drivers were critical in moving goods to and from the highland city of São Paulo. By capitalizing on this economic power, they were able to become wealthy and influential in the region.

The third important *castas* group was the ZAMBOS, who were of African and native descent. This was the smallest group within Latin America, as well as the group with the lowest social status. Many Europeans thought of such a union as being unspeakable, creating a child of two "inferior" races that combined the worst elements of each. In much of Latin America, there were relatively few opportunities for Africans and natives to produce offspring, but ample chances existed for such unions on larger plantations where the landowner possessed both African and indigenous slaves (or servants). Most unions between these two groups occurred when African slaves escaped and formed runaway communities in remote areas such as northern MEXICO or the Amazon, where substantial numbers of natives continued to live.

In theory, the *castas* formed a distinct subgroup of colonial society that had its own set of legal rights and responsibilities. Royal officials developed a complex nomenclature to distinguish the exact composition of a person's ethnic background. For example, a mestizo who married a European would not produce a mestizo, but a *castizo.* Paintings depicting ethnically mixed families (with helpful labels provided) became popular in many areas of Latin America, particularly New Spain. In practice, the *castas* were highly fluid categories that defied easy definition. For the most part, a person's status as a mestizo, *zambo,* or mulatto was not based on ethnicity but on appearance, language, customs, and even dress. In this way, the categories were *social* categories rather than racial ones. For example, the cash-starved royal government was usually happy to sell certificates proclaiming "purity of blood" to those *castas* who could afford them. With such a certificate a mestizo could legally become "European" and thus gain access to better jobs or receive a reduction of taxes. Also, many indigenous people successfully avoided paying native tribute to the Crown by moving to a new location, dressing as Europeans, and proclaiming themselves to be "mestizos." As long as they could provide witnesses to testify on their behalf, royal officials would usually accept these arguments. Although many colonists associated *castas* with illegitimacy and dishonor, the *castas* played an important role in the New World, often functioning as a vigorous middle class that produced vital goods and services for their colonies.

Further reading: Mark A. Burkholder and Lyman L. Johnson, *Colonial Latin America,* 2nd ed. (Oxford, U.K.: Oxford University Press, 1994); Lyle N. McAlister, *Spain and Portugal in the New World, 1492–1700* (Minneapolis: University of Minnesota, 1984); Magnus Mörner, *Race Mixture in the History of Latin America* (Boston: Little, Brown, 1967).

— Scott Chamberlain

Castile

One of several Iberian kingdoms born in the wake of the RECONQUISTA, Castile grew to dominate the peninsula and much of the Atlantic world during the 15th and 16th centuries.

For many modern observers, the roots of most (if not all) of Castile's historical and cultural landscape may be found in the Reconquista, the centuries-long struggle to transform the Iberian Peninsula into a Christian land. Muslim (see ISLAM) forces had crossed into Spain from present-day Morocco in 711 and were only stopped between Tours and Poitiers in 732 in a confrontation with Frankish forces under the command of Charles Martel. The next several centuries of Iberian history were forged in the context of a program to reconquer this territory for Christendom. The turning point came in the period 1010–31, beginning with the Christian victory over and sack of the Muslim capital of Córdoba and ending with the collapse of the entire caliphate into fragmented *taifa* kingdoms. In the wake of this fall Christian kingdoms were able to become major territorial powers in the Iberian Peninsula, and Castile was to become the largest of these Christian successor states.

The Reconquista left its mark on both secular and religious aspects of Castilian society. The Castilian church, conceived in militant terms, was a crusading church whose professional members, from monks to members of Spain's many military orders, saw themselves as soldiers of the faith. Secular Castilians responded to the Reconquista with the development of *hidalguía,* an aristocratic ideal of a man who lived for war and honor and whose riches were gained through force of arms rather than through manual labor or commerce. In contrast with the neighboring Crown of Aragón, with its commercial and mercantile economy, Castile tended to be oriented toward war, a legacy of the long Reconquista, and to disdain trade in favor of agricultural, pastoral, and military endeavor.

While military activity was the focus of what it meant to be Castilian in the Middle Ages and early modern era, war was by no means the only type of activity in the kingdom. The greater part of the Castilian *meseta* was unsuited to agriculture, so sheep herding became the dominant method of land exploitation. The Castilian wool trade was given a boost by the introduction of North African merino sheep around 1300, coinciding with (or perhaps causing) a sharp increase in the demand for Castilian wool. This late medieval economic expansion had at least one broad-reaching consequence: it brought the inward-looking Castilians into closer contact with the rest of Europe, especially Flanders, whose textile industry came to forge close ties with Castile, eventually resulting in the former becoming one of the domains of the latter.

Prosperity from the wool trade was to some degree offset by the calamities that followed in the wake of the famines and plague of the 14th century. The demographic crisis that resulted from these misfortunes provoked a short-term manpower shortage and a long-term social conflict in which the aristocracy began to gain both political and economic ground on the Crown. Because Castile had very few cities, Castilian kings, unlike their counterparts in other kingdoms, did not have the bourgeoisie to use as a bulwark against the ascendant magnates. Nevertheless, a political crisis in the Crown of Aragón in the early 15th century allowed Castile to take the lead in the new joint monarchy established with the marriage of FERDINAND AND ISABELLA. By the time of their marriage, the once-powerful Crown of Aragón had been economically crippled and had little to contribute in the way of material resources. Castile was able to benefit from the administrative expertise of its longtime rivals, and the infusion of new ideas helped to propel Castile to the status of world power, laying the foundations for the Habsburg Empire (see CHARLES V and PHILIP II).

Despite the unification of the Aragonese and Castilian crowns, 16th-century Spain was in no way a unified state. Castile, Navarre, and Aragón each had separate languages, institutions, and customs, and kings of Spain had to govern each kingdom separately. Most early modern kings of Spain tended to focus on Castile, which was the largest, wealthiest, and most prosperous of the three peninsular kingdoms. Castile was also easier to govern through the Castilian nobles, who, despite their wealth, were politically insignificant, especially compared to the Catalan and Aragonese nobility, who had used the Cortes—the Catalan-Aragonese legislative body—as a tool to wrest concessions from the monarch in return for funding. Castilian nobles, on the other hand, refrained from contesting the Crown's authority so long as they were allowed to keep their tax exemptions. Only 18 towns sent representatives to the weak Castilian Cortes, and neither the nobility nor the clergy had the ability to participate.

Thus, 16th-century Spain, although a composite monarchy, had a distinctive Castilian flavor. Castilians under Charles V saw themselves and their empire as suc-cessor to Rome, but with a Catholic Christian overlay: Their mission was to uphold the faith in Christian lands (see INQUISITION) and to expand it to others. This philosophy led to an idea of Castilian exceptionalism in relation not only to non-Christians, but also to other Europeans. A Catalan observer in the 1550s remarked that Castilians wanted to be "so absolute, and put so high a value on their own achievements and so low a value on everybody else's, that they give the impression that they alone descended from Heaven, and the rest of mankind are mud."

The Castilian ascendancy and sense of superiority was almost certainly due in part to the kingdom's growing wealth resulting from trade with the NEW WORLD. Charles V presided over the first period of large-scale expansion in the Americas from 1504 to 1550, when the volume of trade increased by some 800 percent. Castilians were the primary beneficiaries of the expansion into the Americas. In 1524 Charles opened colonization of the Indies to any inhabitant of his empire, but his successor, Philip II, reversed this policy, limiting it to Castilians. The Crown of Castile got rich along with its subjects, partially from taxes and grants of monopolies, but most directly from the *quinta*, or "royal fifth"—the Crown's 20-percent share of all precious metals mined in Castilian possessions in the Americas.

Even so, the positive economic impact of the influx of precious metals should not be exaggerated. By 1554 contributions from the Americas accounted for only 11 percent of the Crown's total income. Although this level was to rise to 25 percent during the reign of Philip II, such funds proved insufficient to overcome Castilian Spain's inherent economic weaknesses. The Castilian ethic of Christian military expansionism, based on the centuries-long Reconquista, meant that Castilians generally valued military activity over mercantile ventures and that the latter were not highly developed among Castilians. Not even the Castilian-monopolized Indies trade was truly Spanish; its European exports generally originated outside of Castile, rendering Castilian merchants little more than extraordinarily well-positioned middlemen. The inherent economic deficiencies of the Castilian economy meant that very little of the GOLD and SILVER that arrived from the Americas actually stayed in Castile and was instead spent on importing manufactured goods the Castilians purchased from other countries.

Castile's economic difficulties in the 16th century were made worse by the economic disparities among the kingdom's population. Great magnates numbering 300 owned half the land in Castile, and the combined rents of the 26 Castilian dukes and marquises were equal to Philip's annual gold and silver shipments from the Indies. But this wealth could not be reckoned to contribute to the economic health of the Spanish Crown because nobles were exempt from taxation. Neither were the merchants and artisans a good source of tax revenue because their numbers in Castile were too small to constitute a significant contribution. The only source of tax revenue left was the peasantry. However, although the Castilian Crown taxed peasants heavily, their inherent poverty meant that their tax revenues could make very little difference to Castile's underlying economic problems.

The late 16th century saw the decline of Castilian Spain as a world power. Spurred on by political and military successes in Portugal and against the Turks as well as a self-perception as defender of the Catholic faith, King Philip II attempted to curb the spread of Protestantism in Western Europe. His planned venture had three complementary goals: the suppression of Calvinism in the Spanish Netherlands, the resolution of the French Wars of Religion in favor of the Catholic Church, and the conquest of England, whose privateers had been raiding the Spanish Indies and whose queen, ELIZABETH I, continued her father HENRY VIII's policy of declaring herself head of the English church, thereby flouting papal authority. Yet despite favorable circumstances, Philip failed in all three of these ventures. In 1593 Henry of Navarre converted to Catholicism as a part of the agreement by which he was crowned HENRY IV of France. This move both frustrated Philip's plans to place a Spanish princess on the throne and constituted a further roadblock to his vision of a unified Catholic Europe when Henry promised toleration of French HUGUENOTS. In the Netherlands Dutch Protestants rebelled, fled, or resisted but refused to be unified under a Spanish king and, more important, a Roman church. Most disastrous of all, Philip's invasion of England, finally provoked by Elizabethan assistance to the Dutch rebels, ended in utter failure in 1588, when the SPANISH ARMADA met defeat due to a combination of the skill of the English navy, the inexperienced leadership of the Spanish forces, and a chance storm that scattered the remnants of the Spanish fleet into the North Sea. The defeat of the Armada, combined with Castile's other failures, marked the end of Spain's dominance of Europe.

Further reading: Richard S. Dunn, *The Age of Religious Wars, 1559–1715*, 2nd ed. (New York: Norton, 1979); John Elliott, *Imperial Spain, 1469–1716* (New York: St. Martin's Press, 1977); J. H. Elliott, *Spain and its World, 1500–1700* (New Haven, Conn: Yale University Press, 1989); Henry Kamen, *Philip II of Spain* (New Haven, Conn.: Yale University Press, 1997); A. W. Lovett, *Early Habsburg Spain, 1517–1598* (Oxford, U.K.: Oxford University Press, 1986); John Lynch, *Spain 1516–1598: From Nation State to World Empire* (Cambridge, Mass. and Oxford, U.K.: Blackwell, 1992);

— Marie A. Kelleher

Cathay (China)

Popularized by MARCO POLO's book, Cathay was the name used by Europeans to describe China and Chinese lands until the 17th century.

Although Marco Polo was not the only European to travel to China in the 13th and early 14th century, his account of his travels was the only one that was widely circulated or well known. Through the knowledge gained during his 17 years there (1275–92), he was able to provide a remarkably detailed view of China and its geography in the early years of the Mongol, or Yuan, dynasty (1273–1368). However, because of his position as a servant of the Mongols, he also absorbed certain biases that colored his account. He neither wrote nor spoke Chinese but most likely used Persian or Mongolian as his official language. Consequently, all the Chinese place names he recorded were in Persian or Mongolian (Canbalu for Beijing, Quinsai for Hangzhou [Hankow], Censcalan for Guangzhou [Canton]). Because the emperor Khubilai had only recently conquered the Southern Sung Dynasty, Marco probably never traveled extensively there. He thus spent much of his time in northern China and rarely saw much of the south. Northern China tends to be open, arid plain lands; wheat was the principal crop and noodles the dietary staple. Southern China, far more mountainous, tropical, urban, wealthy, and populous, had an economy based on intensive wet rice agriculture. Marco's book provided detailed descriptions on conditions in northern China but was comparatively weak in describing conditions in the south.

This gap in his descriptions would not have mattered terribly except for the fact that the overland route to China was closed during the 14th century. Despite their fearsome reputation, the various Mongol khans provided a relatively safe and hospitable route for merchants and missionaries to travel without passports or other serious restrictions. Once the khans of Central Asia converted to ISLAM and the Black Death (bubonic PLAGUE) spread out of Asia and began to devastate much of Europe, contact between Europe and China ended. Far from the prying glimpses of Europeans, China and Chinese culture continued to grow and evolve. In Europe Marco Polo's Cathay did not and soon became more legend than fact. In fact, when Portuguese and Spanish explorers reestablished contact in the 15th century, they initially did not recognize China as Marco Polo's Cathay for some time, and explorers spent many years seeking a legendary land (sometimes city) of Cathay until as late as the early 17th century. The extent to which European conceptions of China were colored by Marco Polo's account is shown by the first voyage of CHRISTOPHER COLUMBUS (August 1492–March 1493). Although Columbus probably did not read Marco's book prior to his voyage, he was profoundly influenced by it second-hand through a summary made by Paolo dal Pozzo Toscanelli. It was Toscanelli's idea that one could reach Cathay by sailing west across the Atlantic more quickly and easily than the long eastward route around Africa. With this idea in mind Columbus secured a commission from FERDINAND AND ISABELLA of Spain to seek contact with the "Great Khan" of Cathay and find the island of Cipangu (Japan).

Columbus set out on his first voyage armed with letters from the king and queen of Spain for the great khan and an interpreter who, it was thought, could communicate with the Chinese. When in October 1492 he encountered islands at roughly the longitude that Toscanelli had predicted (unfortunately, Toscanelli had grossly underestimated the circumference of the earth), he was hopeful that he had actually reached Japan. When he landed in the West Indies, he thought he might have reached the Chinese coast. All of his subsequent voyages pushed deeper into the Caribbean in an attempt to reach Asia.

Once word of Columbus's discovery reached Europe it was not long before other explorers began to seek Cathay across the Atlantic. JOHN CABOT sailed from BRIS-TOL, England, on his first voyage to find Cathay (May–August 1497) but found Newfoundland blocking the path. Only slowly did it sink in with European explorers that a vast new territory stood in the way of the route to Asia. FERDINAND MAGELLAN found a strait into the Pacific near the end of South America in 1520. The English kept seeking a NORTHWEST PASSAGE through North America well into the 19th century.

The Portuguese were the first Europeans to renew contact with China. After first rounding the Cape of Good Hope in 1488, successive fleets of Portuguese ships carried explorers, traders, and adventurers who established forts and trading "factories" along the east coast of Africa, India, and the islands of the "East Indies" (modern-day Indonesia and Malaysia). Finally, in 1513–14 a ship under the command of Rafael Perestrello sailed up the Pearl River into Guangzhou (Canton). In the next seven years came two other fleets of Portuguese ships that did some trading but served mostly, through the arrogance of their commanders and their bent for casual piracy, to break contact with China for another 30 years.

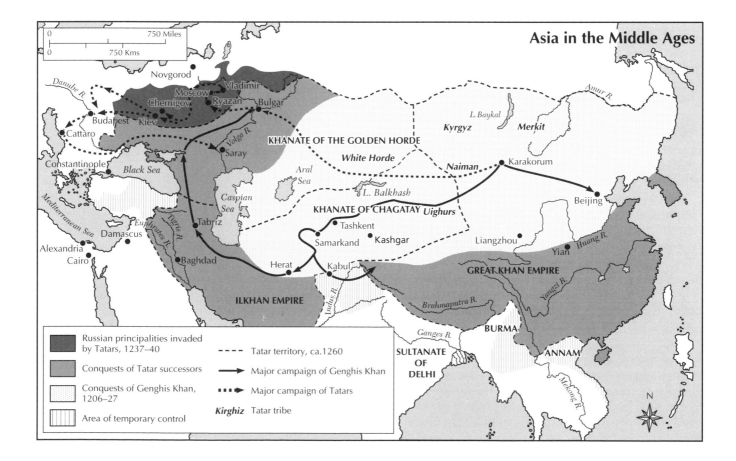

When Europeans reestablished regular links with east Asia in the 15th century, they only slowly began to appreciate that the China they were discovering was not Marco Polo's Cathay. The Yuan dynasty had been overthrown in 1368, and the native Chinese emperors of the Ming dynasty (1368–1644) had replaced the foreign, Mongol great khans. The Ming (despite the fact that they had dispatched large fleets throughout the Indian Ocean and as far as the African coast in the 15th century) were inward looking, passionately antiforeign, and thoroughly convinced of China's cultural superiority.

Yet in spite of their seemingly myopic views, around 1555 the Ming finally allowed the Portuguese to take over the isolated peninsula of Macao on the Pearl River delta well south of Guangzhou. (Macao was not returned to China until 1999.) From there a profitable but very limited trade grew and flourished, at least until the late 16th and early 17th century, when the xenophobia of the Ming led them to impose heavy restrictions on Europeans arriving there. As a result of these fears on the part of their hosts, the number of Europeans remained small, and few ventured beyond Macao or small factories in Canton. Among the Europeans were some Jesuit missionaries, including MATTEO RICCI, who were able to travel and reside in the Chinese interior and, later, in the capital.

The difficulties of matching Marco's outdated, Mongol-centric description of Cathay with the China Europeans were rediscovering led many to conclude that Marco's real Cathay had not yet been found. As a result, many 16th- and some 17th-century maps show Chinese lands discovered by the Portuguese but place the lands of Mangi and Cathay to the north. (Mangi was the Mongol name for the recently conquered provinces of southern China.) As greater knowledge of Chinese geography came in, some European geographers concluded that Cathay was not an undiscovered country but must be a city instead.

As the history of China became more widely known the truth of Marco's book was generally accepted. Western contact with China continued to be quite limited until the mid-19th century. Use of the word Cathay to describe China continued well into the 20th century, but this was much less a geographic description than a way to evoke a romanticized and far more hospitable land—a land like Marco Polo's China—than the more complex and unwelcoming territory Westerners frequently encountered.

Further reading: Ernest S. Dodge, *Islands and Empires: Western Impact on the Pacific and East Asia* (Minneapolis: University of Minnesota Press, 1976); John King Fairbank and Merle Goldman, *China: A New History* (Cambridge, Mass.: Harvard University Press, 1998); John Larner, *Marco Polo and the Discovery of the World* (New Haven, Conn.: Yale University Press, 1999); Denis Twitchey and John King Fairbank, eds., *The Cambridge History of China,* 8 vols. (Cambridge, U.K.: Cambridge University Press, 1978).

— Paul Dunscomb

Cayor

One of five Wolof kingdoms to separate from the larger Djolof (Jolof) state in the late 16th century, Cayor (also Kayor or Kajor) derived its power from trade with French and Portuguese merchants based in the coastal cities Gorée and Saint-Louis.

Located in what is today Senegal, Cayor rose to power through its participation in the transatlantic SLAVE TRADE. Previously a tribute state within the larger Djolof Empire, Cayor's connections with French traders, and therefore easier access to such goods as muskets, gunpowder, and iron, made its bid for independence in the mid- to late 16th century successful. Frequent warring with neighboring kingdoms such as the KAABU and internal slave raids provoked numerous revolts and caused famine within the new kingdom. In the late 17th century MARABOUTS, or Muslim clerics, led an antislavery revolt in attempts to oust slave-based states from the SENEGAMBIA region. Although the marabouts did not succeed in ending the slave trade, they were successful in spreading ISLAM to the area, especially among the peasants, who made up the majority of those taken as slaves. While attempting to suppress internal resistance, the kingdom of Cayor was also fighting external pressures. The French maintained a significant amount of power in Cayor, causing resentment among the kingdom's aristocracy. As late as 1871 the Cayor fought against the French for control of the region.

Further reading: Jean Boulegue and Jean Suret-Canale, "The Western Atlantic Coast," in *History of West Africa* vol. 1, 3rd ed., eds. J. F. Ade Ajayi and Michael Crowder (London: Longman, 1985), 503–530; "Early Senegambia," in *West Africa Before the Colonial Era: A History to 1850,* ed. Basil Davidson, (London: Longman, 1998), 93–103; "Senegal," in *Africana: The Encyclopedia of the African and African American Experience,* eds. Kwame Anthony Appiah and Henry Louis Gates, Jr., (New York: Basic *Civitas* Books, 1999), 1686–1690; "Wolof," in *Africana,* eds. Appiah and Gates, Jr., 2005–2006.

— Lisa M. Brady

Cayuga

One of the two "Younger Brothers" (along with the ONEIDA) in the IROQUOIS Confederacy, the Cayuga had 10 sachems (chiefs who represented them) in the league's grand council.

Originally located in what is now New York's Cayuga and Seneca Counties, the Cayuga maintained three principal villages in an area to the west of the ONONDAGA and just east of the SENECA. When Europeans first encountered them, the Cayuga population was probably comparable to that of the MOHAWK, including 300 or more warriors.

Subsisting on an economy that mixed horticulture and hunting (like the other Five Nations), the Cayuga increasingly came to rely on warfare and the fur trade to generate wealth in their society by the end of the 16th century. Nevertheless, all of the Iroquois tribes by and large remained fiercely independent, retaining their social and political structures despite the influx and influence of new goods and DISEASES from Europe. Even religious instruction from JESUITS, in which the Cayuga expressed some interest, exhibited adaptation to older forms of belief rather than simply outright adoption and did not result in widespread conversions or the complete abandonment of traditional ideologies.

Further reading: Frank G. Speck, in collaboration with Alexander General, *Midwinter Rites of the Cayuga Longhouse* (1949; rprt., Lincoln: University of Nebraska Press, 1995); Elisabeth Tooker, *An Iroquois Source Book*, 3 vols. (New York and London: Garland Publishing, Inc., 1985); Marian E. White, William E. Engelbrecht, and Elisabeth Tooker, "Cayuga," in William Sturtevant, ed., *Handbook of North American Indians*, vol. 15, *Northeast*, vol. ed. Bruce G. Trigger (Washington, D.C.: Smithsonian Institution Press, 1978), 500–504.

— Eric P. Anderson

Charles V, king of Spain and Holy Roman Emperor (Carlos) (1500–1558)

King of CASTILE and Aragón (as Charles I), duke of Burgundy, and later Holy Roman Emperor, Charles (Carlos) V was the most powerful European monarch of his era and presided over Spain's largest and most profitable phase of expansion into the Americas.

Charles—first ruler of Castile by that name and fifth of the Holy Roman Empire—was born in Ghent on February 24, 1500, with the blood of enough royal and noble lines to make him heir presumptive to half of Europe. His maternal grandparents were FERDINAND AND ISABELLA, whose territories had included the kingdoms of Castile and Aragón along with their substantial Mediterranean possessions; on his father's side he was grandson of the Holy Roman Emperor Maximilian I, who had married Mary of Burgundy, heiress to Franche-Comté

and the Low Countries. His territories included Burgundy, the Low Countries, Castile, Aragón, Naples, Sicily, Sardinia, the Spanish possessions in the NEW WORLD, and the Austrian territories of the Habsburg archdukes. The Habsburg connection also made him leading contender for Holy Roman Emperor.

Charles inherited the throne of Castile and Aragón in 1516. Although he was to become the ruler of diverse territories, Spain was in many ways Charles's hardest prize to claim. Charles was raised in the Burgundian court of his father, and his education and political training were Burgundian, including the Burgundian ideal of royal absolutism. Charles's Castilian subjects voiced an open preference for his younger brother, the Castilian-raised Ferdinand. When Charles finally did ascend the Castilian throne, he alienated the already restless aristocracy by setting up an essentially Burgundian court: Charles spoke no Spanish, and he installed Burgundians in important court offices, snubbing Castilian courtiers. The Cortes (the Castilian representative assembly) was barely able to force Charles to respect the laws of Castile, and his eventual agreement cost the Cortes a 600,000-ducat subsidy for Charles's foreign ventures.

After securing the rule of the combined territories of Burgundy, Castile, and Aragón, the 16-year-old Charles set his sights on the HOLY ROMAN EMPIRE. While Charles's Habsburg ancestry made him a leading candidate for the imperial dignity, his succession to that elective monarchy was never inevitable, and so Charles, like most other candidates for emperor, was forced to spend large sums to bribe the imperial electors.

Despite his successes, it is not possible to portray Charles, who spent only 16 years of his 40-year reign in Spain, as a particularly "Spanish" monarch. Neither can his rule be characterized as "imperial." Charles governed a composite empire made up of autonomous regions with no common administrative structure or type of rule. He held different titles and powers in each of his lands and was bound by each area's unique political situation at the time he stepped in. In the German imperial territories Charles was nominal overlord of a confederation of independent principalities. In Castile he was ruler of a territorially compact sovereign state enriched by GOLD and SILVER from New World conquests and thus freed from financial dependence on the Cortes. In the turbulent kingdom of Sicily, the Spanish viceroy shared authority with the local magnates, who monopolized financial and judicial administration in their own territories and maintained private armies. The Low Countries were a federation of nearly autonomous provinces controlled locally by the nobility, who also ran the central administration. Disunity evolved into a gradual proliferation of smaller states within Charles's empire, which did not survive his reign

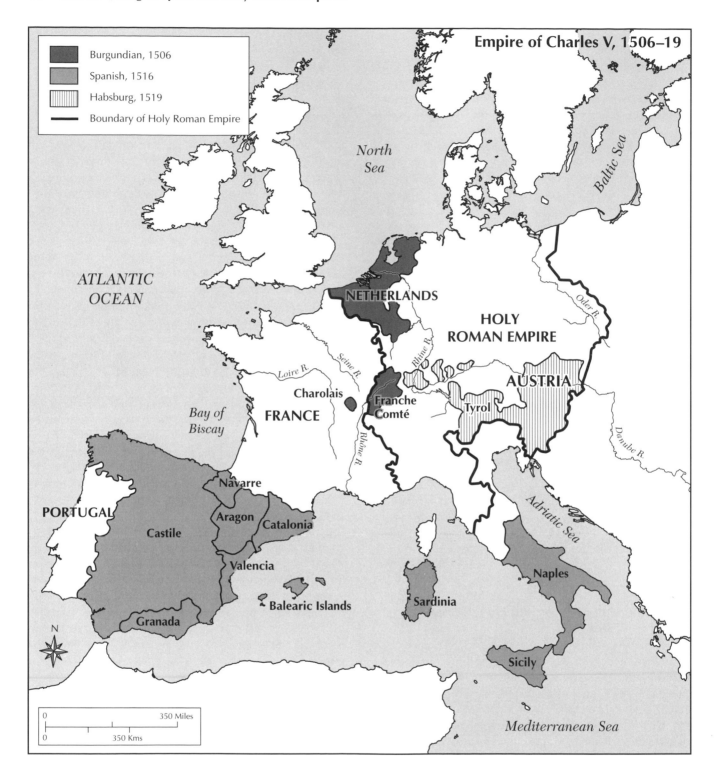

Empire of Charles V, 1506–19

Burgundian, 1506
Spanish, 1516
Habsburg, 1519
Boundary of Holy Roman Empire

intact. At his abdication he divided his territories between his brother Ferdinand and his son, the future Philip II.

Upon his accession as Holy Roman Emperor, Charles immediately faced a religious crisis in his German territo-ries. MARTIN LUTHER had expressed hope that the young emperor would promote reform, but contrary to Luther's expectations, Charles demanded that Luther recant his beliefs. Luther refused, and Charles, determined to proceed against Luther "as a notorious heretic," put him under the imperial ban, effectively making him an outlaw. The result was a religious split between Charles and the German princes, some of whom favored Lutheran reform doctrines.

Charles's campaigns throughout his empire to quash religious and political turmoil required a large amount of money. Although much of his funding came from "ordinary revenues," notably the sales tax levied on towns and villages in his domains, he eventually came to finance his ventures by using profits generated in the lucrative Indies trade.

Charles's involvement in the Indies dated back to 1517, when the 17-year-old king was approached by BARTOLOMÉ DE LAS CASAS, a friar whose mission it was to put an end to abuses of the natives of the Indies. Shortly thereafter, Spanish CONQUISTADORES conquered the empires of the AZTECS and INCA. Building on the Spanish conquests of the Indies, these new conquests enriched Spanish coffers with portions of the proceeds of silver mines in MEXICO and PERU. The continuing expansion of Spanish explorers and the high mortality experienced by the natives of HISPANIOLA required Charles to deal with the issues of Indian welfare raised by Las Casas. In May 1520 Charles issued an order to eliminate the ENCOMIENDA, a system for the exploitation of labor and land that many Spaniards believed was the source of the Indians' misery. This law was to apply to the new conquests on the mainland, as was Charles's subsequent order forbidding the conversion of the natives either by force or intimidation. But protests from the colonists caused HERNÁN CORTÉS to withhold publication of the orders, and Charles eventually withdrew them. On August 1, 1524, Charles issued a decree establishing the COUNCIL OF THE INDIES for the administration of imperial affairs in the Western Hemisphere, but he vacillated for years about how to protect Native Americans, and as a result the indigenous peoples continued to suffer at the hands of conquistadores.

Charles presided over the first period of large-scale expansion in the Americas from 1504 to 1550, when the volume of Spanish trade increased by some 800 percent. His subjects in the Americas were enthusiastic agents of expansion for a number of reasons. According to the chronicler BERNAL DÍAZ DEL CASTILLO, participants in Cortés's expeditions went to the New World "to serve God and His Majesty, to give light to those in darkness, and to get rich." Castilians were the primary beneficiaries of the expansion into the Americas. In 1524 Charles opened colonization of the Indies to any inhabitant of his empire, but his successor, Philip II, reversed this policy, limiting such ventures to Castilians. The Crown of Castile got rich along with its subjects, partially from taxes and grants of monopolies, but most directly from the "royal fifth"—the Crown's 20 percent share of all precious metals mined in Castilian possessions in the Americas.

In the early 1550s, faced with the combination of looming political and economic disaster in his empire along with with his own old age and general weariness, Charles began the process of gradually divesting himself of his political responsibilities. In October 1555 he abdicated control of the Low Countries to his son Philip II; three months later he granted his heir all Spanish possessions on both sides of the Atlantic. He relinquished control of Franche-Comté to Philip the following year and renounced the Imperial possessions to his brother Ferdinand. His abdication managed to forestall the political chaos that an improvised succession after his death might have brought but did little to remedy Spain's economic problems, leaving Philip a debt of 20 million ducats at a time when the Crown's ordinary revenue was only 2 million ducats per year. Charles retired to a monastery in Extremadura in September 1556. He continued to keep up on international affairs and to advise his son until his death on September 21, 1558.

Further reading: C. H. Haring, *The Spanish Empire in America* (New York: Harcourt, Brace and World, 1963); A. W. Lovett, *Early Habsburg Spain, 1517–1598* (Oxford, U.K.: Oxford University Press, 1986); John Lynch, *Spain 1516–1598: From Nation State to World Empire* (Cambridge, Mass. and Oxford: Blackwell, 1992); Eugene F. Rice, Jr., and Anthony Grafton, *The Foundations of Early Modern Europe, 1460–1559*, 2nd ed. (New York and London: Norton, 1994).

— Marie A. Kelleher

Chichén Itzá

The large, well-built MAYA city of Chichén Itzá was one of the most famous pilgrimage centers of the YUCATÁN PENINSULA, but although it has been known and visited for centuries, it paradoxically remains one of the least understood of the major Maya sites.

Chichén Itzá is located in north central Yucatán. One of the most important features of the site is a large sinkhole filled with water (called a *cenote*). The northern Yucatán is quite dry and contains no rivers or streams. Water did, however, collect in underground caverns. In some cases the roofs of these caverns collapsed, exposing these underground reservoirs. These cenotes, therefore, were crucial to the Maya and often took on deep religious significance as well. It is clear that the cenote at Chichén Itzá was the most hallowed spot in the region, and the Maya believed it was a doorway to the watery realm of the netherworld. For centuries pilgrims journeyed to the city to cast offerings into the cenote, including sacrificial victims.

Scholars have had great difficulty establishing a history of the site. Despite its size and known importance, relatively few archaeological excavations have been carried out at Chichén Itzá. Nonetheless, scholars have reconstructed a broad historical outline of the city. Chichén Itzá began its rise to power during the waning days of Mesoamerica's classic period (A.D. 200–800), after such prominent Maya sites as TIKAL, PALENQUE, and COPÁN had begun to decline. As the great cities to the south faded into obscurity, a number of cities from the Yucatán rose to prominence, including Chichén Itzá. A number of public buildings in Chichén Itzá date to around A.D. 800. According to legends that survived into the colonial period, Chichén Itzá was founded by three brothers who ruled jointly and built great buildings there.

Sometime around 987 a number of sources tell that a new group of invaders arrived by sea, invaded the Yucatán, and captured Chichén Itzá itself. These warriors were led by Kukulcán (Feathered Serpent), who in most respects is identical to the central Mexican god QUETZALCOATL (also meaning "feathered serpent"). Based on iconography, architecture, and linguistics, scholars have determined that the new invaders were, in fact, TOLTECS. The Toltecs quickly set up a kingdom in exile with Chichén Itzá as their capital and soon came to dominate the Yucatán.

During this time the city reached its peak of prosperity and influence, displaying a remarkable mixture of Maya and Toltec styles. Scholars once thought that the visible ruins of Chichén Itzá derived from two distinct

The Temple of Kukulcán, the Mayan god of rain, Chichén Itzá, Yucatán   *(Hulton/Archive)*

phases: an older section with mostly Maya art and architecture and a newer zone with Toltec features. Further study suggests that they were almost contemporaneous with each other and simply reflect different building traditions.

Along with artistic styles, Toltec and Maya societies mingled at Chichén Itzá as well. Maya and Toltecs apparently intermarried, and most of the ruling lineages in the Yucatán had some degree of Toltec blood. The fact that so many nobles had Toltec ancestors may explain the positive image of these invaders in the Maya histories. The murals at Chichén Itzá suggest that the Toltecs' invasion was terribly violent, but the chronicles speak of the Toltecs as great men who brought "good government." As a small minority, the Toltecs' language was all but lost within a few generations—they learned Maya and used it exclusively. But a number of words from the Toltecs' language (NAHUATL) did survive in Yucatec Mayan, including words for "shield" and "rule." Warfare was another area in which the two cultures intermingled. The armies of Chichén Itzá used the long thrusting spears typical of the Maya augmented with Toltec atlatls (spearthrowers), cotton armor, and curved, obsidian-bladed "short swords." Finally, the Toltec and Maya religions merged at Chichén Itzá. Those who built temples adopted a sacrificial stone called a *chac-mool*, which consisted of a man reclining with a drum-shaped stone on his chest. Carvings illustrate Toltecs taking part in traditional Maya ceremonies that reflect the fact that some Toltec rulers used established Maya rituals to deify their dead ancestors.

Chichén Itzá remained wealthy and strong until around 1150, when its power began to wane. It is unclear what sparked the city's decline, although with the collapse of the Maya to the south, Chichén Itzá lost several important trading networks. Perhaps more devastating was the decline and fall of the Toltec kingdom after 1100, which not only disrupted trade throughout MEXICO but sent waves of refugees fleeing across the region, destabilizing many of the surviving states. By 1224 the city's residents had mostly fled. At this time a wandering band of Maya speakers called the Itzá arrived and occupied the city. They maintained it and its great cenote as a holy shrine, in time giving their name to the city (which means "Mouth of the Well of the Itzá"). Between 1263 and 1283 another group of Itzá founded the rival city of Mayapan to the west and built it up as their political capital, while Chichén Itzá remained their religious capital. The situation was unstable, and the two cities soon developed a strong rivalry. By 1441 the rulers of both cities had become powerful enemies. Within 20 years these cities' residents were at war, and the Itzá, unable to conquer their foes, had to flee from the Yucatán. Despite these hostilities, Chichén Itzá remained a sacred site well into the colonial period; a small community remained there, capitalizing on the steady influx of pilgrims to the area.

Further reading: Michael Coe, *The Maya*, 6th ed. (London: Thames & Hudson, 1999); Clemency Chase Coggins and Orrin C. Shane III, eds. *Cenote of Sacrifice: Maya Treasures from the Sacred Well at Chichén Itzá* (Austin: University of Texas Press, 1984).

— Scott Chamberlain

Chimalpahin, Domingo Francisco de San Antón Muñón (1579–1660)

Born in Amecameca, MEXICO, Chimalpahin created volumes of material in NAHUATL on the history of the indigenous peoples of Mexico during the precontact and early Spanish imperial periods.

Born of humble birth and originally known as Domingo Francisco de Antón Chimalpahin Quauhtlehuanitzin, he later moved to Mexico City and replaced *Antón* with *Muñón* and made some claims to indigenous nobility. He wrote in Nahuatl and provided detailed accounts of the precontact and colonial history of Mexico. Chimalpahin's work provided the world with important information concerning Nahuatl observations, philosophy, and worldview. He produced most of his writing in the early 17th century while living in Mexico City. Most of his historical narratives took the form of annals listing events that occurred year by year, with little other organization. Chimalpahin filled most of these annals with significant ethnohistoric details he garnered from interviews with Nahuatl elders, the use of pictorial codices, the study of indigenous and town records, and other books detailing native history. His histories cover about a thousand years and focus mainly on his hometown of Amaquemaecan and the larger Chalco region. His most famous works include *Relaciones* and *Diario*, and for the most part they describe Chalco and its dynastic lineages. Chimalpahin produced a multitude of other writings, and periodically through the centuries scholars have found a host of other manuscripts attributed to him. Only the histories of fray BERNARDINO DE SAHAGÚN rival Chimalpahin's collections for information on this time period. Chimalpahin's work has proven more valuable because it provides the indigenous view.

Further reading: James Lockhart, "Chimalpahin," *Encyclopedia of Latin American History and Culture*, vol. 2, ed. Barbara A. Tenenbaum (New York: Scribner's, 1996), 138; Susan Schroeder, *Chimalpahin and the Kingdom of Chalco* (Tucson: University of Arizona Press, 1991).

— Dixie Ray Haggard

chinampas

Chinampas, or floating garden plots of dredged silt and compost from lake weeds, bordered the southern edges of TENOCHTITLÁN and supplied the city with most of its flowers and fruits.

Chinampas seem to have provided the means for the construction of the great Aztec capital of Tenochtitlán. The first Aztec settlers dug canals in the swampy ground, piling up vegetation to form their farming plots. They then spread mud from the canal bottoms onto the reed mats to form a fertile soil and anchored the whole complex with willows planted around the perimeter. Eventually, the roots of the plants used in the *chinampas* construction worked their way downward to take root in the lake floor.

Chinampas supported construction as well as agriculture. When HERNÁN CORTÉS arrived, he observed that half of the houses were "on the lake." These houses were not the masonry structures that so impressed BERNAL DÍAZ DEL CASTILLO and his companions; rather, they were constructions of light cane and thatch, while heavier building materials were confined to drier parts of the island. Frequent floods of the lake could inundate the *chinampas,* leaving their crops ruined by salty water. The AZTECS remedied this situation by constructing a 10 mile-long dike that sealed off a freshwater spring source.

Tenochtitlán was not the only city to use this technology; among other so-called *chinampa* cities were Culhuacán, Míquic, and Xochimilco. *Chinampa* technology may even date back to as early as 500 B.C. *Chinampas* were widely used because they were a reasonable response to the often swampy terrain and also because they were an especially productive means of agriculture because the fertile soil was able to support two or sometimes three crops per year.

Further reading: Pedro Armillas, "Gardens on Swamps," in John Graham, ed., *Ancient Mesoamerica* (Palo Alto, Calif.: Peek Publications, 1981), 117–130; Michael Coe, *Mexico: From the Olmecs to the Aztecs,* 4th ed. (London: Thames & Hudson, 1994); Nigel Davies, *The Aztec Empire: The Toltec Resurgence* (Norman: University of Oklahoma Press, 1987).

— Marie A. Kelleher

Cholula (Cholollan)

One of the largest, most important cities of ancient MEX-ICO, Cholula was a holy city dedicated to the god QUET-ZALCOATL and was the location of the largest pyramid ever constructed.

Located to the east of Mexico's central valley, Cholula has been inhabited continually since ca. 400 B.C.. It first rose to power, however, in the classic era (A.D. 200–800),

along with such cities as TEOTIHUACÁN, COPÁN and TIKAL. It was during this time that construction began on the Great Pyramid (Pyramid of Tepanapa). The original pyramid bears strong resemblance to the architecture of Teotihuacán, but as that great center declined, the Cholulans developed their own style. Between 600 and 800 the pyramid took on its final, massive form. The base of the pyramid was roughly 1,400 feet on each side and rose to a height of 210 feet, making it larger in volume than the Great Pyramid of Cheops in Egypt. Cholula and its pyramid became one of Mexico's most important religious and pilgrimage centers. During this time the city reached a population of perhaps 100,000 people and established extensive trading networks with other ancient Mexican cultures.

After 800 the city's political position waned, although its status as a holy city steadily grew. With the collapse of the old, classic-era powers, trade dwindled and foreign groups began to invade. A group of Putún MAYA (sometimes called the Olmeca-Xicallanca) from the TABASCO area invaded and seized the city, making it the capital of their kingdom. The invaders built up a new city, centered on the newer temple of Quetzalcoatl, to the west of the Great Pyramid. Over time the old city with its massive pyramid fell into ruins, and by the time of the European conquest, the Great Pyramid appeared to be nothing more than a natural hill. The cult of Quetzalcoatl gained strength throughout this time, with many myths claiming that the god briefly resided here before leaving for the east. Around 1292 the city was captured again by TOLTECS fleeing from the fall of their capital, Tula. In 1359 it fell under the dominion of TLAXCALA, and after 1450 it was overshadowed by the AZTECS. The city retained a precarious independence from the powerful neighbors around it due to its status as Quetzalcoatl's holy city.

During the Spanish conquest of Mexico, Cholula was the scene of a bloody massacre. Spanish sources state that HERNÁN CORTÉS discovered that the Cholulans had welcomed him into the city only to ambush him. Cortés decided to strike first and made a surprise attack against the city. Native sources argue that MALINCHE and the Tlaxcallans wanted to take vengeance on Cholula for siding with the Aztecs and convinced Cortés to slaughter the Cholulans. Whatever the reason, roughly 6,000 Cholulans died in the attack, and the city surrendered to Cortés.

Cholula declined rapidly after the conquest. Within a few months, the Spaniards destroyed most of the city's holy shrines. A PLAGUE in 1540 devastated the population, and thereafter the city was eclipsed by the new Spanish settlement at Puebla.

Further reading: Michael D. Coe, *Mexico: From the Olmecs to the Aztecs,* 4th ed. (London: Thames & Hudson, 1994); William M. Ferguson and Arthur H. Rohn, *Mesoamerica's Ancient Cities* (Niwot: University of Colorado Press, 1990).

— Scott Chamberlain

Church of England

The Church of the England dates from the REFORMATION of the 16th century, but its theology has come to represent a via media between Catholicism and Protestantism.

When MARTIN LUTHER tacked his 95 theses onto the door of his church in Wittenberg in 1517, he began a theological revolution within Christianity, but he provoked the anger of England's King HENRY VII. Henry wrote a treatise sharply critical of Luther and his scriptural emphasis. Entitled *Assertio Septum Sacramentorum,* Henry's tract included vivid vitriol aimed at Luther for the German's condemnation of the pope. Henry called Luther "the most venomous serpent who had ever crept into the church." The English king's loyalty to Rome in the early days of the Reformation earned him the title "Defender of the Faith."

Circumstances changed for Henry and Rome by 1530. Henry wanted to divorce his wife, Catherine of Aragón, in favor of the courtier Anne Boleyn. Catherine had not provided Henry with a male heir to the throne. Henry and his chancellor, Thomas Wolsey, a cardinal of the Roman Church and papal legate in England, petitioned the pope for an annulment of the marriage. But the Vatican refused, largely because of the presence in Rome of Catherine's nephew, CHARLES V, and the soldiers of the Holy Roman Empire. Wolsey never recovered from his failure to secure the annulment.

Infuriated by the pope's refusal, Henry pushed for an English solution to his predicament. His inner circle contended that the English had long been hostile to the papacy and that since medieval times the church in England had questioned the authority of the pope's jurisdiction over it. By Henry's time it had become possible for the king to convince the English episcopacy and the faithful that he had the right to rule in secular and religious affairs. Eventually he initiated a series of steps that severed the church in England from the church in Rome and established the English monarch at the head of the then-independent Church of England.

The English cleric Thomas Cranmer was essential to the process of separation from Rome and establishment of the new Church of England. Sir Thomas More had succeeded Wolsey as chancellor. More was an ardent and pious Catholic and refused to participate in the king's matrimonial chicanery. As a result, More was executed and later made a saint of the Roman Church. Cranmer became archbishop of Canterbury and Henry's most trusted adviser. He initiated legislation in PARLIAMENT that attempted to create and define the Church of England, a legislative process that stretched over the next half century.

The most significant of the early acts of state orchestrated by Cranmer was the Act in Restraint of Appeals in 1533. This act's preamble created the split with the Roman Church. It declared that England was at that moment, and always had been, a sovereign empire. The spiritual component of that sovereignty was the English Church. Thus, as one part of that empire, the church had the right to govern itself. Further, ecclesiastical complaints could no longer be appealed to Rome; they had to go through Henry.

The Ten Articles of Faith defined by the Church of England's fathers during the 1536 Convocation, intended to define the new church's theology, established doctrine and ritual remarkably similar to the Roman Church's. But the acts reduced the number of sacraments that bishops deemed necessary for salvation from seven to three (baptism, penance, and the Eucharist), and they wrote the article about the Eucharist so as to allow for both Roman and Lutheran interpretation.

Such ambiguity reflected Henry's own doubts. Privately, he continued to practice his faith in orthodox Roman fashion, insisting upon crosses, altars, vestments, and the sacrament of the Eucharist that included transubstantiation. Publicly he worked for the independence of the Church of England, promoting the new doctrines accordingly.

Monasteries provided the primary centers of opposition to Henry's publicly reforming acts. The monks owned approximately 7 million acres of land in England, a fact that raised more than a few eyebrows among the reformers. Henry assigned the archdeacon of Buckingham and others to visit the monasteries, account for their behavior, inventory their wealth, and report back. Although some scholars have deemed these reports specious, the results revealed enormous corruption in the monasteries and massive irregularities in worship. Henry used this information to confiscate their property. In the process he gained great wealth for the Crown. He also expelled many monks and nuns from England in 1536. Following the dissolution Henry's government in 1539 issued the Act of the Six Articles. The act allowed the priests, monks, and nuns who remained in England to marry, and it eliminated the sacrament of confession from English ecclesiology. The dissolution of the monasteries and the Act of Six Articles proved important steps in the transformation of the English Church. They guaranteed that Catholicism would have difficulty reestablishing jurisdiction in England, no matter what might happen theologically.

The promulgation of the Book of Common Prayer was the last among the Church of England's founding legislative activities. Created by Cranmer and issued in 1549, the text provided the church with a liturgy so important to Cranmer and the king that it became a criminal offense to use any other in England. The Book of Common Prayer, based on the rites and sacraments of the Roman Church but incorporating elements of theology made popular by the Reformation, gave to the church a coherent theology, although traditional minded clerics and laymen often practiced the older rites of the ancient church.

Over time the Church of England evolved in the face of serious challenges. In the early 1550s King Edward VI, Henry VIII's son by Jane Seymour, working with some of his Protestant relatives, reworked elements of the church's practices. Their efforts led to the promulgation of a second prayer book, and priests were no longer able to wear ornate vestments. Through such moves the Church of England moved ever further away from Catholicism.

When Edward died in 1553, Queen MARY, the daughter of Catherine of Aragón (Henry VIII's first wife) ascended to the throne of England. A devout and public Catholic, Mary attempted to reestablish Catholicism in England by returning England to the pope. She packed the Parliament with her supporters and had them repeal every ecclesiastical act that her predecessors had promulgated. Married clergy disappeared, as did the Book of Common Prayer. Even vernacular Bibles were outlawed. Mary revived heresy laws and burned 300 people at the stake, earning her the title of "Bloody Mary." The executions horrified people throughout England, and the death of the queen in 1558 signaled the end to any serious efforts to repudiate the English Reformation.

In the aftermath of Mary's attempt to wed the English church to Rome, Queen ELIZABETH I recognized that she needed to end any lingering doctrinal confusion. Despite the fact that she was personally torn between tradition and reform, she encouraged Parliament to pass acts that became known as the Elizabeth Settlement. These acts made Elizabeth supreme governor of the church, a phrase in contrast to her father's title of supreme head of the church. This was an attempt to appease radical Protestants who had gained power during Edward's reign. A third prayer book was issued based on Edward's second one, rather than the original. The new book included 39 Articles of Religion that would came to define religious policy in England for centuries. The Act of Supremacy and Uniformity of 1559 demanded that clergy adhere to the Elizabethan acts and to Elizabeth's role as the church's governor. Although Elizabeth's actions did not enthrall everyone in England—some traditionalists wanted to return to Catholic ways, while others had adopted ideas promulgated by radical continental theologians and became dissidents known as PURITANS—the Church of England remained the dominant religious institution in the realm.

After Elizabeth's death in 1603, the Church of England struggled for decades with its ecclesiology, theology, and finances. The Jacobean kings continued reforms, including the creation and publication of the King James version of the Bible.

Further reading: G. R. Balleine and Colliss Davies, *A Popular History of the Church of England* (London: Vine Books, 1976); Andrew Foster, *The Church of England, 1570–1640* (London: Longman, 1994); Sheridan Gilley and W. J. Sheils, eds. *A History Religion in Britain: Practice and Belief from Pre-Roman Times to the Present* (Oxford, U.K.: Blackwell, 1994); Aidan Nicholas, *The Panther and the Hind: A Theological History of Anglicanism* (Edinburgh: T&T Clark, 1993).

— David P. Dewar

cod

A fish native to much of the North Atlantic that became a major food supply for Europeans, especially after Basque fisherman perfected preservation techniques involving salt.

The Atlantic cod are descendants of a species of fish that began to evolve perhaps 120 million years ago. By the early modern period the descendants of these ancient fish lived in great schools that preferred relatively shallow waters, such as those to be found in the Grand Banks off modern-day Newfoundland and Labrador. The best areas for catching cod then stretched from the Grand Banks southward, near the coast of modern-day New England as far south as Georges Bank off the coast of Massachusetts. Cod were also remarkably fertile fish: A fifty-inch long female could lay 9 million eggs; although most eggs never produced a fish, enough matured so that the schools of cod off the North American coast were the greatest supply of cod in the world at the time. For the population of cod to remain constant, each female had to have two of the eggs become full-grown fish. Whatever the difficulties faced by these tiny eggs, which were perfect food for other fish, the odds were good that the schools would remain abundant, at least until there were serious pressures applied to cod from some external source.

During the early modern age cod was for humans perhaps the most important denizen of the oceans. NORSE sailors had relied on cod during their voyages to the Western Hemisphere, and by the time CHRISTOPHER COLUMBUS spread news about his findings, Basque fishermen had quite likely been sailing in American waters for years hauling cod. Cod became a major industry for the Basques, in large part because the Mediterranean had salt deposits and a warm sun, two ingredients necessary for extracting sufficient salt to preserve fish. (The Norse, by contrast, had to develop other preservation methods, none of them as effective as salting). Basques also profited from injunctions of the Catholic Church that required the faithful to avoid meat on certain days but allowed them to eat "cold" foods, including seafood. Anyone who could sell inexpensive fish thus had an opportunity for great profits.

When SEBASTIAN CABOT arrived in northeastern North America in the late 15th century, he found out firsthand about the great stocks of cod to be had. By then such knowledge was already known to merchants in BRISTOL, who had been sending ships for years deep into the Atlantic in the hope they would return with cod. As cod's modern-day "biographer" put it, this was "the fish that changed the world."

Further reading: Mark Kurlansky, *Cod: A Biography of the Fish that Changed the World* (New York: Walker, 1997).

coffee

First discovered in Ethiopia, coffee became one of the world's most popular drinks after people in the Middle East and Europe discovered that its consumption made its drinkers more alert and active.

It is impossible to know exactly when humans began to drink coffee. As the French historian Fernand Braudel commented, the plant's history "may lead us astray. The anecdotal, the picturesque and the unreliable play an enormous part in it." Stories about coffee's origins support Braudel's contention. According to legend humans recognized that coffee could be consumed after an Ethiopian goatherd named Kaldi watched his animals eating the leaves and berries of a mysterious tree and then become frisky. Curious, Kaldi himself then chewed on the leaves and ate the berries. Although the taste was bitter, Kaldi soon had enormous energy, and so he joined the goats in their frolics. He then went home, told others about what he had eaten, and the word soon spread. When Ethiopians during the sixth century crossed into Yemen, they apparently brought coffee with them. Local Arabs began to consume what they called *qahwa* (or *Qahwah*). Among those who became enamored of coffee's potential was the prophet Mohammed, who recognized that drinking coffee could help him stay awake and thus pray much longer.

The known history of coffee is much briefer. Few reliable references to coffee consumption exist from before 1470, when people were drinking coffee in Aden. Quite possibly the roasting of beans had begun as early as the year 1000, and by 1300 production was substantial in Yemen, where those who drank it appreciated it for the stimulant provided by the caffeine that is naturally provided by the coffee plant. Coffee reached Cairo by 1510 and Mecca by 1511, the year it was first banned there by clerical officials who decried the behavior of those who drank it. Turks in Istanbul were drinking coffee by 1517, and it spread outward into Turkish regions. By 1600 coffee consumption was widespread within territory controlled by Muslims (see ISLAM).

Europeans witnessed Arabs and Turks consuming coffee in the late 16th century. As the Augsburg physician Leonhard Rauwolf wrote in a book published in 1582, "they have a good drink which they greatly esteem. They call it 'chaube': it is nearly as black as ink and helpful against stomach complaints." Rauwolf described the way that locals consumed coffee in public, often in the morning, and that it was "common among them, so that one finds quite a few who serve it in the bazaar, as well as shopkeepers who sell the berries there." The Italian traveler Pietro delle Valle also witnessed coffee consumption when he was in Constantinople in 1615. According to him, local Turks drank coffee "in long draughts, not during the meal but afterwards, as a sort of delicacy and to converse in comfort in the company of friends. One hardly sees a gathering where it is not drunk." He described the mores of coffee drinking itself and the porcelain cups that drinkers used. Drinking coffee could lead to endless discussion, he concluded, "sometimes for a period of seven or eight hours."

During the early 17th century coffee consumption spread throughout Europe. Pope Clement VIII allegedly tasted coffee after some clerics believed it should be banned, but rather than halting its spread he instead purportedly said that "it would be a pity to let the infidels (Muslims) have exclusive use of it. We shall fool Satan by baptizing it and making it a truly Christian beverage." Coffee reached VENICE in 1615, Paris in 1643, Marseilles in 1644, Oxford by 1650, London by 1651, and Vienna in 1683. In Paris, where coffee had been provided by the Turkish ambassador Soliman Mutapha Raca, those who drank it soon believed that coffee had medicinal benefits; a medical treatise published in Lyon in 1671 enumerated its properties and thereby gave coffee an additional boost. Over time residents of Paris and other European capitals became hooked on coffee and opened establishments that existed solely for drinking it. These coffeehouses became fixtures of the metropolitan landscape across Europe, and the discussions that began in such businesses became, over time, a vital part of the public life of each city. In London, for example, the coffeehouse run by Edward Lloyd attracted merchants and sailors and, as a result, individuals who arranged insurance for voyages; over time the business in the coffeehouse became more important than the coffee itself, and the establishment became Lloyd's of London, one of the world's most prominent insurance firms. Coffee's alleged medicinal benefits increased its popularity. By the end of the 17th century, London alone had more than 2,000 coffeehouses.

When Europeans moved beyond the boundaries of their continent in the 17th century, they soon recognized that the climate in other parts of the world was ideal for the production of coffee. Thus the Dutch took coffee to Ceylon in 1658 and to Java in 1699. During the 18th century Europeans planted coffee in the Western Hemisphere. Coffee appeared in Martinique in 1723 and from there spread outward; eventually coffee plantations could be found in the islands of the Caribbean and on the mainland, from MEXICO to BRAZIL. Although coffee is still produced in its original territory, far more comes from the plant's new homelands, where Europeans brought it to satisfy their desire for what one Vatican official once called "Satan's latest trap to catch Christian souls."

Further reading: Fernand Braudel, *The Structures of Everyday Life: Civilization and Capitalism, 15th–18th Century,* 3 vols. (New York: Harper & Row, 1981); Alan Davidson, *The Oxford Companion to Food* (New York: Oxford University Press, 1999), 201–202; Mark Prendergrast, *Uncommon Grounds: The History of Coffee and How It Transformed Our World* (New York: Basic Books, 1999); Wolfgang Schivelbusch, *Tastes of Paradise: A Social History of Spices, Stimulants, and Intoxicants* (New York: Pantheon, 1992).

Cofitachequi

A MISSISSIPPIAN chiefdom that occupied the South Carolina piedmont and coastal plain at the time of contact with Europeans in the 16th century, Cofitachequi survived several invasions by Spanish *entradas* (newcomers) into their territory only eventually to disintegrate under the pressure of demographic collapse caused by the introduction of DISEASES from the Old World.

At its height the chiefdom of Cofitachequi possibly controlled a territory that extended from the coast of modern-day South Carolina to the foothills of the Appalachian Mountains in modern-day North and South Carolina. Primarily a Muskhogean-speaking people, the Cofitachequi may have first encountered Europeans in 1526, when they met a Spanish contingent headed by Lucas Vázquez de Ayllón, who called them the Duhare. HERNANDO DE SOTO's expedition provided the first detailed description of Cofitachequi after he led the invasion of the chiefdom in 1536. Soto forced the Cofitachequi to provide food, shelter, and porters to support his campaign and looted their temples for animal furs and freshwater pearls. After resting and finding no evidence of GOLD or SILVER wealth in the Cofitachequi chiefdom, the Soto campaign then proceeded to move into the Appalachian Mountains in search of the heralded COOSA chiefdom. Juan Pardo's *entrada* next made contact with Cofitachequi in 1566. Pardo attempted to establish a permanent post there, but the Cofitachequi eventually forced its abandonment. From 1562 to 1564, the French tried to establish a post in South Carolina and encountered a powerful Indian nation known to them as the Chiquola, almost certainly the Cofitachequi chiefdom. Cofitachequi last appears in the historical record in 1672, when its chief visited the newly established English colony at Charles Towne, and later when the chiefdom was briefly mentioned in Carolina records of 1681. By 1701 the Cofitachequi no longer inhabited the South Carolina region.

Further reading: David G. Anderson, *The Savannah River Chiefdoms: Political Change in the Late Prehistoric Southeast* (Tuscaloosa: University of Alabama Press, 1997); ———, *Knights of Spain, Warriors of the Sun* (Athens: University of Georgia Press, 1997); Chester B. DePratter, "The Chiefdom of Cofitachequi," in *The Forgotten Centuries: Indians and Europeans in the American South, 1521–1704,* eds. Charles Hudson and Carmen Chaves Tesser (Athens: University of Georgia Press, 1994), 197–226; Charles Hudson, *The Juan Pardo Expeditions: Exploration of the Carolinas and Tennessee, 1566–68* (Washington, D.C.: Smithsonian Institution Press, 1990).

—Dixie Ray Haggard

Columbian Exchange

The Columbian Exchange was the process of transferring various biota—livestock, germs, and plants—between the Old World and the New, setting in motion massive ecological and demographic changes in both hemispheres, particularly in the Americas.

Historians have only recently begun to unravel the story of what the scholar Alfred Crosby labeled the "Columbian Exchange," a stage in what he later described as "ecological imperialism." This story replaces an older version, which explained Europe's successful invasion of the Americas as the result of supposedly more advanced cultures and superior technologies. The idea of the Columbian Exchange, however, takes into account how the age of exploration remade the environment of the planet, particularly in exposing the Americas to new plants, livestock, and DISEASE. For example, on the second voyage of CHRISTOPHER COLUMBUS to HISPANIOLA in 1493, the shipping records list the variety of plants, animals, and colonists that he brought with him: "seventeen ships, 1200 men; seeds, cuttings, and stones for wheat, chickpeas, melons, onions, radishes, salad greens, grapevines, sugarcane, and fruit trees; and horses, dogs, pigs, cattle, chickens, sheep, and goats." Unintentionally, the expedition also brought weeds, rats, and germs. The story of the Columbian Exchange explores how these biological factors—many unintended and their consequences often ignored—were significant, even pivotal, in Europe's success in the NEW WORLD.

And while the Columbian Exchange refers primarily to exchanges between Old World and New, this global interaction also had important consequences for Africa as well, especially for its burgeoning Atlantic SLAVE TRADE.

One important component of the Columbian Exchange was the transfer of plants between the global hemispheres, both food crops and weeds. Root vegetables from the Americas were especially significant for agriculture: The potato, from South America, spread through northern Europe; the cassava, also from South America, spread through Africa and Asia; and sweet potatoes from the Americas became important crops in Africa as well. This exchange also involved grains. Maize (see CORN) from the New World continues to be a vital crop grown all over the world today. Europeans also introduced wheat and other grains of African and Eurasian origins. In addition, Europeans brought peach, pear, orange, and lemon trees as well as chick peas, grapevines, melons, onions, radishes, and various other fruits and vegetables. One unintentional consequence of this exchange of plants was the introduction of new weeds. On the whole, European weeds and grasses invaded the Americas, rather than vice versa. Only a few American weeds, such as horseweed and burnweed, have managed to survive in Europe, and not in great numbers. In contrast, in the Americas aggressive European weeds, including clover, plantain, and the dandelion spread rapidly, outcompeting the native plants and modifying many ecosystems.

One reason that weeds and nonnative grasses spread so widely in the Americas was the simultaneous introduction of livestock, another important component of the Columbian Exchange. Cattle, HORSES, and pigs adapted very quickly to New World grasslands and soon experienced population explosions. Upon arriving on islands in the Caribbean and South America, the Spaniards, for example, simply set the livestock loose to multiply and to provide protein and labor resources for their further invasions into the northern Americas. This intensive overgrazing destroyed native ground covers, making it possible for imported European grasses and weeds to establish themselves in place of native plants. European weeds and grasses quickly gained strong footholds in these endangered ecosystems. The omnivorous tusked European swine, especially, ate everything in sight, not just the plants, and quickly adapted to almost every ecological niche in the Americas. In the Antilles the swine devoured the local Indians crops of manioc roots, sweet potato, and fruit. They also decimated the populations of lizards and various small wildlife. Eventually, from BRAZIL to Virginia to New England, wild pigs ranged everywhere, creating havoc among local flora, fauna, and indigenous peoples' crops as they went.

Not only did Europeans introduce domestic livestock to the New World, they brought rats from Old World seaports as well. Rats devoured many of the grains and other stores on board ships on the passage across the Atlantic. Upon landing these rats came ashore with the remaining supplies and then swarmed through the New World. Rats fed on and competed with various small animal populations and also spread disease, such as the bubonic PLAGUE, a devastating parasite carried through the bite of the rats' accompanying fleas. Cats, dogs, and European rabbits went wild in the Americas as well as all sorts of insects, including the honeybee.

By far, the most devastating result of the Columbian Exchange was a dramatic reduction in the Native American population throughout the Americas. When the first humans crossed the Bering land bridge into North America, probably between 12,000 and 14,000 years ago, the freezing temperatures destroyed many Old World microorganisms that had traveled with them. This "cold funnel" removed diseases such as measles, smallpox, and influenza from the human population that migrated into North and South America. In addition, Europeans living in close contact with domesticated animals evolved new diseases. These processes turned out to be a mixed blessing; while precontact Native Americans never had to experience anything like the 14th-century bubonic plague epidemic that killed between 60 and 90 percent of the population in some areas of Europe, they also did not develop the natural immunities to Old World diseases. Frequent exposure to disease microorganisms serves to boost the immune systems of the humans who survive epidemics, offering at least some protection from future outbreaks of the same illness. Without a history of exposures, Native Americans were left biologically defenseless when Europeans arrived and, usually unintentionally, began spreading disease. Many scholars have argued that the disease exchange was to some extent two-sided, with the New World sending syphilis to the Old World. There is no clear consensus as to the origin of syphilis, however, and more research needs to be completed before we can determine whether this venereal disease existed in Europe before the first sailors began returning from the Americas.

While estimates on the precise population decline are still hotly debated, it is clear that the impact of European diseases was a crucial component in the success of early colonization efforts. Studies of archaeological remains suggest that there was a total indigenous population of at least 40 million or 50 million people in the Americas before contact. Whatever the precise numbers, the interloping Europeans were vastly outnumbered as they began their conquest of the New World. But shortly after Columbus arrived, diseases devastated the most populous regions of the Americas, allowing hundreds of Europeans to defeat millions of Indians. HERNÁN CORTÉS was able to conquer the city of Tenochtitlán in 1521 in large part due to an epidemic that decimated the Aztec capital. In Virginia, the Algonquian Indians expressed their fear of the "invisible bullets" that seemed to strike down the native population while the

English visitors were mysteriously unaffected. The physical destruction was matched by an immeasurable psychological toll as Native Americans struggled to explain the debilitating diseases that had suddenly appeared. Some fragmented Native American groups sought new alliances with the Europeans, who appeared to be able to control the deadly diseases. For their part, the English were convinced that the epidemics were a sign from God that the lands were intended for their use. The population decline in many areas was enormous—those that did not die from disease often fled their native lands in a desperate attempt to avoid the illnesses. Unfortunately, these efforts at escape only served to spread disease microorganisms into regions the Europeans had yet to visit. In Mexico alone, the population declined from approximately 30 million in 1519 to 3 million by 1568.

In addition to the transfer of plants, livestock, and diseases, the Columbian Exchange also set the foundations for a new global market. Europeans extracted raw materials from the Americas and then used the New World to expand their markets for manufactured goods. This new pattern of business had global effects. Europeans took GOLD and SILVER from mines in the Western Hemisphere that boosted their economies and increased Europeans' trade with Asia. The specific effects of this cycle are not yet totally clear, but at the least it seems likely that this transfer of raw materials eventually influenced the rise of certain families and classes in Europe's economic and social structures. These manufactured goods were also important in European exchanges for African slaves, forming the roots of the Atlantic slave trade that would flourish especially in the late 17th and 18th centuries. This increased trade and exchange of wealth particularly worked to the benefit of Europe, even providing the basis for the later Industrial Revolution.

This story of the Columbian Exchange, then, revises much of our previous understandings of the interactions between Europe, Africa, and the Americas during the 16th century. Without question, the transfer of plants, livestock, and especially diseases facilitated the European conquest and colonization of the Western Hemisphere. Yet while the biological and demographic consequences of the Columbian Exchange devastated Native Americans, Europe's population grew as a result of the cultivation of American foods, especially the potato, the tomato, and maize. Scholars are continuing their efforts to understand how the transfer of these nonhuman entities shaped the history of the Atlantic basin during the early modern age.

Further reading: Alfred W. Crosby, *Ecological Imperialism: The Biological Expansion of Europe, 900–1900* (New York: Cambridge University Press, 1986); Kenneth F. Kiple and Stephen V. Beck, eds., *Biological Consequences of the European Expansion, 1450–1800, An Expanding World,* vol. 6 (Aldershot, U.K.: Ashgate Publishing, 1997); John W. Verano and Douglas H. Ubelaker, eds., *Disease and Demography in the Americas* (Washington, D.C.: Smithsonian Institution Press, 1992); Herman J. Viola and Carolyn Margolis, eds., *Seeds of Change: Five Hundred Years Since Columbus* (Washington, D.C.: Smithsonian Institution Press, 1991); Sheldon Watts, *Epidemics and History: Disease, Power, and Imperialism* (New Haven, Conn.; Yale University Press, 1997).

— Maril Hazlett
—Melanie Perreault

Columbus, Bartholomew (Colón Bartolomé)
(ca. 1454–1514)

Bartholomew Columbus was a mapmaker and navigator who worked in support of his famous brother, CHRISTOPHER COLUMBUS, both in Europe and in the Western Hemisphere.

Columbus grew up in Genoa, where he worked as a wool carder. Like his brother, he moved to LISBON as an adult, although it is unclear which of the brothers moved there first. He supported his brother's efforts to gain support for an Atlantic voyage. At one point he may have traveled to England in an unsuccessful effort to gain support for a voyage from King HENRY VII. He also visited France, where he met the king's sister, Anne de Beaujeu. While Bartholomew was traveling, Christopher obtained the support of FERDINAND AND ISABELLA for his first voyage. By the time Bartholomew returned to Spain in 1493, Christopher had already returned from the Caribbean and had set sail on his second voyage.

The Spanish monarchs gave Bartholomew command of three CARAVELS. He sailed to HISPANIOLA, landing while his brother was exploring CUBA. Upon his arrival he found the colony in turmoil. The colonists abused the Indians and complained that Christopher Columbus had misled them about the nature of the NEW WORLD, taking them to a place of sickness and death rather than a fertile land where they would grow rich. Bartholomew served as captain-general of Hispaniola from 1494 to 1496, where he founded a new settlement, Santo Domingo.

By 1494 complaints about Christopher Columbus's administration of the colony had reached Ferdinand and Isabella, and they sent an investigator, Juan Aguado, to look into the complaints. In response to the complaints, Christopher returned to Spain, appointing Bartholomew ADELANTADO (military governor) and leaving him as governor, a position he would hold until 1498, but Bartholomew proved unable to halt the disorder on the island. His brother had instituted a policy by which Indians were required to pay a tribute in GOLD, cotton, or spices. As Bartholomew tried to build his new settlement of Santo Domingo, he stripped the earlier settlement of Isabella of supplies. The move angered the settlers and made it more difficult to collect the tribute. In 1497 Francisco Roldan led a rebellion against the Columbus brothers. He even gained Indian allies by promising an end to the tribute system. Bartholomew could not halt the rebellion, although he captured two important CACIQUEs and sent other Indians to Europe as slaves.

When Christopher Columbus returned from Europe on his third voyage he found the rebellion on Hispaniola continuing. With great difficulty Columbus pacified Roldan and his supporters by allowing them to form their own communities and granting them the right to use Indian labor, a system that would develop into the ENCOMIENDA. This solution was contrary to the orders of the queen, who wanted settlers to build houses and farm the land. Although Christopher Columbus managed to end the rebellion, complaints against him and his brothers continued. In 1500 Ferdinand and Isabella sent a royal agent, Francisco de Bobadilla, to investigate. When Bobadilla arrived at the harbor of Santo Domingo, Christopher and Bartholomew Columbus were out in the countryside putting down other rebellions, leaving their brother Diego (Diego Colón) in charge at Santo Domingo. Before stepping onto the land, Bobadilla saw the corpses of seven rebels hanging from the gallows and soon learned that five more were to be hanged. Bobadilla considered the continuing rebellions as evidence of the Columbus brothers' incompetence. He took control of the town, confiscated Christopher Columbus's goods, and sent all three brothers back to Spain in chains.

Ferdinand and Isabella freed the brothers, and Bartholomew accompanied Christopher on his fourth voyage to the West. He explored Veragua (modern-day PANAMA), where the explorers found some gold but were driven away by Indians. After taking part in this voyage, Bartholomew returned to Spain. In 1509 he and his nephew Diego sailed to Hispaniola, where he remained until his death in 1514.

Further reading: Miles H. Davidson, *Columbus Then and Now: A Life Reexamined* (Norman: University of Oklahoma Press, 1997); William D. Phillips, Jr., and Carla Rahn Phillips, *The Worlds of Christopher Columbus* (Cambridge, U.K.: Cambridge University Press, 1991); William L. Sherman,"Columbus, Bartholomew" in *Encyclopedia of Latin American History and Culture,* vol. 2, ed. Barbara A. Tenenbaum (New York: Scribner's, 1996).

— Martha K. Robinson

Columbus, Christopher (Colón, Cristobal)
(1451–1506)

Christopher Columbus's landfall in the Caribbean in October 1492, possibly on the island now known as San Salvador, marked the beginning of large-scale contact between Europe, Africa, and the Americas.

Columbus was born in the Italian republic of Genoa. His father was a wool weaver and merchant, although not a wealthy one. Columbus's formal education was limited, but he probably studied religion, geography, and arithmetic at the wool merchants' guild school. As an adult Columbus read widely and placed great faith in what he found in books.

The Genoese were known for their sailing ability, and Columbus went to sea at a young age. He sailed the Mediterranean for several years and settled in Portugal in the mid-1470s, where he lived for about a decade. While in Portugal he married Felipa Moniz in 1478 or 1479. They had one child, a son born in 1480 whom they named Diego. The extent of Columbus's sea voyages in these years is unknown. He probably traveled to England and Ireland and perhaps to Iceland. He traveled as far south as the Portuguese fortress of Sao Jorge da Mina, on the GOLD COAST of Africa, and was also familiar with MADEIRA and the CANARY ISLANDS. Columbus probably first tried to secure backing for a voyage into the unknown reaches of the Atlantic in 1485, when he approached King Joaõ II of Portugal. Little is known about this episode, but later traditions held that a committee appointed to look into the matter recommended against him.

Columbus lived in a world of explorers and discoveries. For centuries Europeans had known of and traded for the riches of the East. The overland routes to Asia were long and difficult, but the GOLD, gems, and spices (see SPICE ISLANDS) that merchants brought back were so valuable that Europeans continued to travel eastward, always looking for quicker and less expensive routes to the lucrative markets. Columbus proposed to reach the riches of the Indies by sailing west and going around the world. He was not the first to argue that the world was round; this fact was well known and commonly accepted by educated Europeans of his day. But although Europeans knew the world was round, they were not sure how large it was. The best estimate, originally made by Eratosthenes of Alexandria in the third century B.C., was accurate to within at least 5 percent, but no one in the 16th century knew if it was the right appraisal. Others calculated that the world was smaller, and Columbus's estimate was among the smallest. Not only did Columbus think the world was modest in size, he also believed that Asia extended farther to the east than it did. Furthermore, he accepted MARCO POLO's claim that the rich island of Cipangu (Japan) was 1,500 miles off the coast of China (see CATHAY). If these claims were true, then the Atlantic was narrow, and a ship that crossed it would find a quick route to the riches of the East. Columbus believed that the distance from the Canary Islands to Japan was a mere 2,400 nautical miles rather than the correct 10,600 miles. Europeans did not know what, if anything, could be found in the uncharted regions of the Atlantic. Maps from the time included both known places, like the Canary

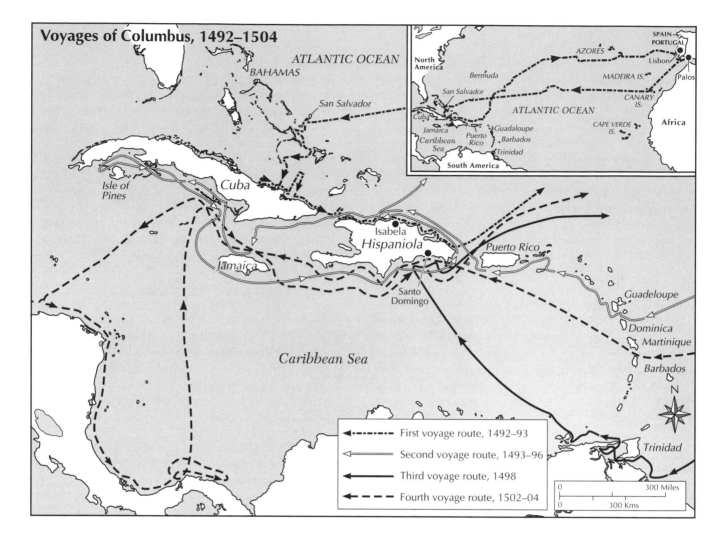

Voyages of Columbus, 1492–1504

First voyage route, 1492–93
Second voyage route, 1493–96
Third voyage route, 1498
Fourth voyage route, 1502–04

Islands and the AZORES, and unknown or even imaginary locales such as Antillia and the isle of Saint BRENDAN THE NAVIGATOR. Most scholars believed that, aside from islands, the vast ocean was empty. Some theorized that an unknown land, the Antipodes, might exist on the other side of the world. The idea of the Antipodes, although appealing to the medieval and Renaissance taste for order and symmetry, was controversial. If the Antipodes were inhabited, their peoples might not be descended from Adam and Eve, a horrifying idea. Furthermore, Europeans believed that the apostles had preached "throughout the world," which seemed to rule out the existence of an unknown continent.

In 1485 Columbus left Portugal for Spain. In 1486 he met with King Ferdinand II of Aragón and Queen Isabella I of CASTILE to try to interest them in his plans. FERDINAND AND ISABELLA appointed a commission to investigate his proposal, which rejected it on the grounds that Columbus had underestimated the size of the world. The

monarchs refused, at this point, to support a voyage, but they paid Columbus subsidies and indicated that they might support a later voyage, once they had conquered the Muslim kingdom of Granada. Columbus had to wait a few years for permission from the monarchs. While he waited in Spain, his brother BARTHOLOMEW COLUMBUS (Bartolomé Colón) traveled across the continent seeking sponsors for the venture. During these years in Spain, Christopher Columbus met a woman named Beatriz Enriquez de Arana, and in 1488 she gave birth to their son Hernando. Columbus never married her, probably because she was the daughter of peasants, but he provided for her throughout his life. He also legitimized their son, who would later write a biography of his father. In 1492, during the final siege of Granada, the monarchs agreed to sponsor a voyage. They granted Columbus noble status and promised to make him admiral, viceroy, and governor general over any lands that he claimed for Castile, as well as giving him one-tenth of the profits from his venture. The offices and Columbus's noble status were to be hereditary.

Columbus hoped to find a route to Asia when he began his first journey across the Atlantic, but he may also have been influenced by apocalyptic and millenarian religious ideas. During the Middle Ages and the Renaissance, prophecies about the end of the world circulated widely. Believers in prophecy expected that the end of the world would come at some point after Christians reconquered Jerusalem and converted unbelievers in other parts of the world. Events like the RECONQUISTA seemed to promise that Christianity would overcome other religions. After Spain conquered Granada in 1492 and expelled Muslims (see ISLAM) and JEWS, some Christians argued that Christian armies should next conquer Jerusalem.

The development of Columbus's religious ideas is unclear, but his interest in religion and prophecy increased as he aged. As early as the 1480s he was interested in the possible date of the millennium and may have known of prophecies that promised that the Spanish monarchs would play a significant role in its coming. The historian Felipe Fernandez-Armesto has argued that Columbus's religious ideas changed and intensified after his first voyage. According to Fernandez-Armesto, Columbus's "notion of reality and grasp of the limits of the possible [were] deeply shaken by his contact with the New World." While lost on the way home from his first New World voyage, he believed that he heard a celestial voice reassure him, and he had similar experiences at least twice more in his life. By 1498 he suggested that he had found the earthly Paradise. Around 1500 he began to suggest that his discoveries had been ordained by God to help bring about the millennium.

The First Voyage (1492–1493)

Columbus set sail with three ships on August 3, 1492. He reached the Canaries, claimed by Castile, and from there set sail due west. The voyage was relatively uneventful, and the ships benefited from a calm sea and favorable winds. The winds were so favorable that after about a month the sailors began to worry that there would be no winds to take them back to Spain. In the early morning of October 12, 1492, a lookout spotted a light on the shore. In the morning the ships reached an island that Columbus named San Salvador but which its native inhabitants called Guanahani. His landing place may have been the island now known as San Salvador but may also have been almost any of the islands of the Bahamas.

Columbus believed that he had landed in Asia and began exploring. He reported that the land was fertile and the native peoples were agreeable, but he found little trace of wealth. Columbus's initial relations with the islands' inhabitants were peaceful, and he described them as natu-

rally good and inoffensive. He did not believe that they had legitimate political institutions of their own and therefore claimed their land for Castile. Even at the beginning, his attitude toward the native people was paradoxical. In an early letter he wrote that he gave the Indians gifts to "win good friendship, because I knew that they were a people who could better be freed and converted to our Holy Faith by love than by force" and described them as handsome and intelligent. Yet in the same letter he observed that the native people "ought to be good servants and of good skill" and announced his intention to kidnap six of them and bring them to Castile.

For three months Columbus traveled to various islands of the Caribbean hoping to find a way to China or Japan. His greatest discovery on the first voyage was the island of HISPANIOLA, whose inhabitants possessed gold. He founded a settlement on the north coast of the island, which he named Villa de la Navidad. Because his largest ship, the *Santa María,* had run aground, he left 39 men in the settlement when he returned to Spain. Upon his return to Europe, Columbus claimed that he had found a west-

Christopher Columbus in a portrait by Sebastiano del Piombo, 1485–1547 *(Hulton/Archive)*

ward route to Asia. Others were skeptical, thinking that he had found new Canary Islands, the Antipodes, or the mythical land of Antillia. In general, scholars still believed that the world was too large for Columbus to have traveled to Asia. Whatever Columbus had found, the gold of Hispaniola seemed to promise wealth.

The Second Voyage (1493–1496)

Isabella and Ferdinand agreed to sponsor a second, larger voyage. On this voyage Columbus commanded more than 17 ships and 1,300 men, including his youngest brother, Diego. This expedition included several friars, whose instructions ordered them to Christianize the ARAWAK of Hispaniola. Columbus apparently planned to start a trading colony that would rely on exports of gold, cotton, and slaves (see SLAVERY and SLAVE TRADE). On this voyage he mapped several new islands, including PUERTO RICO, which he named San Juan Bautista. When Columbus returned to Hispaniola, he found that the 39 men he had left behind were all dead, mostly killed by the islanders. The natives said that the Spanish had quarrelled among themselves, kidnapped native women, and stolen gold. Columbus was becoming disillusioned both with the climate of the island and with its native inhabitants. Because the native peoples had fought the Spanish, he took their resistance as an excuse to enslave them. He and his men marched through the island trying to trade for gold and taking Indian captives.

Columbus built a new settlement, which he called Isabella, but chose a poor site for it. He had promised riches to the colonists who came with him, and when these riches did not appear, the colonists began to complain. They also mistreated the Indians. Columbus began exporting Indians to Spain as slaves. Although he claimed that the Indians, by fighting the colonists, had made themselves subject to slavery, his action angered Ferdinand and Isabella. The monarchs wanted the Indians to be Christianized and to be direct subjects of the Crown. If the Indians were harshly treated, Ferdinand and Isabella reasoned, they would not become Christians. Furthermore, if they were enslaved, they would be under the authority of their masters rather than subject to the Crown. In any case, the slave trade seemed pointless because the Indians frequently died on the voyage or soon after arriving in Europe.

In April 1494 Columbus left his brother Diego (Diego Colón) in charge of Hispaniola and went to explore CUBA, which he believed to be a part of the mainland. While Columbus was in Cuba, his brother Bartholomew arrived in Hispaniola and found the colony in disarray. Colonists returning to Spain from Hispaniola in 1494 were already reporting that Columbus and his brothers were incompetent. The major complaint against Columbus was that he had misled the settlers about the nature of Hispaniola and

thereby caused colonists to die. In response to the complaints, Ferdinand and Isabella sent an investigator, Juan Aguado, to report on the state of the colony. Aguado reported high rates of DISEASE among both Spaniards and Indians and added that many colonists had deserted. Columbus left his brother Bartholomew in charge and left for Spain to defend his administration of the colony.

The Third Voyage (1498–1500)

Despite suspicions about the abilities of the "Admiral of the Ocean Seas," Ferdinand and Isabella allowed Columbus to make a third voyage in 1498. The monarchs' declining trust in Columbus is indicated by the smaller size of this expedition. Columbus sent five ships directly to Hispaniola while he explored farther south. On this voyage he reached the mainland of South America, finding the Orinoco River, which flows from modern-day Venezuela. The size of the Orinoco convinced him that he had found a large landmass, and he wrote in his journal "I believe this is a very large continent which until now has remained unknown." When he finally reached Hispaniola, he found the colony in rebellion. A rival camp had emerged in the south of the island led by Francisco Roldán. They complained that the new site of the colony, Santo Domingo, was poorly chosen, that there was not enough food to feed the Spanish, and that Columbus and his brothers had too much power. In response to these complaints, Ferdinand and Isabella again sent an investigator, Francisco de Bobadilla, who arrived in August 1500 and found the colony in chaos. He deemed the charges against Columbus and his brothers serious enough that he had them put in chains and sent to Spain to face trial. Ferdinand and Isabella freed Columbus and allowed him to keep some of his titles, but they found the charges against him sufficiently disturbing to restrict his real authority.

The Fourth Voyage (1502–1504)

Columbus's final voyage was a disaster. His fleet consisted of only four CARAVELs, and the monarchs forbade him to set foot in Hispaniola. As Columbus drew near to Hispaniola, he recognized the signs of a coming hurricane. Fearing for the safety of his ships, he disobeyed the monarchs' order and landed there. He tried to warn the colony's governor, Nicolás de Ovando, about the storm, but Ovando ignored his advice and sent a fleet bound for Spain into the hurricane. Twenty-five of the ships sank, leaving only three or four to make it back to Europe. Columbus weathered the hurricane and spent much of the rest of his voyage exploring the coast of Central America. He landed in PANAMA, searching for a strait through the continent. Failing to find one, he established a settlement he called Río Belén, but the local Indians did not welcome the Spanish and succeeded in driving them away. At this point Columbus decided to return to Hispaniola. He had already lost two ships, and the remaining two were so worm-eaten that they nearly sank. The ships were so damaged that Columbus found it impossible to reach Hispaniola and put in at JAMAICA. There the survivors beached their ships and used them for shelter. They were marooned for nearly a year before being rescued.

After this misadventure Columbus returned to Spain. His voyages had made him rich, but he was unhappy. He spent his remaining years struggling with the Crown to try to retain his titles and claims to the islands. Unable to accept his own failures as an administrator, he felt betrayed by Ferdinand and Isabella, who had limited his privileges and removed him as governor of Hispaniola.

Columbus died in 1506, but not before his exploits had changed the world. During 1892, the four hundredth anniversary of his first crossing, scholars and the general public in many countries celebrated his achievements. A century later, during the 1992 quincentennial, another Columbus took center stage. Unlike the hero of 1892, the Columbus of 1992 was more often reviled than feted. Many individuals, including descendants of the indigenous peoples of the Americas, believed that he bore direct responsibility for the horrors that beset Native Americans in the generations after 1492. While most individuals who lived during the early modern age have faded into obscurity, it seems certain that Columbus will remain a figure of world-historic significance.

Further reading: Ida Altman and Reginald D. Butler, "The Contact of Cultures: Perspectives on the Quincentenary" *American Historical Review* 99 (April 1994): 478–503; Silvio A. Bedini, ed., *The Christopher Columbus Encyclopedia*, 2 vols. (London: Macmillan, 1992); Miles H. Davidson, *Columbus Then and Now: A Life Reexamined* (Norman: University of Oklahoma Press, 1997); Felipe Fernandez-Armesto, *Columbus* (Oxford, U.K.: Oxford University Press, 1991); Benjamin Keen, trans., *The Life of the Admiral Christopher Columbus by His son Ferdinand* (New Brunswick, N.J.: Rutgers University Press, 1959); William D. Phillips and Carla Rahn Phillips, *The Worlds of Christopher Columbus* (Cambridge, U.K.: Cambridge University Press, 1991).

— Martha K. Robinson

Company of Cathay (1577–1583)

A joint stock company chartered in London in 1577 under control of the English explorer MARTIN FROBISHER and several other prominent investors to seek the NORTHWEST PASSAGE to CATHAY (China) and to mine for GOLD ore allegedly found on Baffin Island during Frobisher's first voyage to the NEW WORLD (June–October 1576).

The original "right" to seek either a NORTHEAST PASSAGE (along the north Russian coast) or a Northwest Passage (along the North American coast) was granted by English kings to the Muscovy Company in 1553 and 1555. Frobisher and several influential friends succeeded in securing the right to the Northwest Passage from the Muscovy Company before his first voyage. He discovered Frobisher Bay (which he took to be a strait) on Baffin Island, just missing the entrance to Hudson Strait by a few miles. Hunting for minerals along the shore yielded a small amount of iron pyrite and marcasite that looked like gold-bearing ore—and was declared to be such by assayers in London—but was in fact worthless.

The Company of Cathay received a charter from Queen ELIZABETH I as well as a £1000 investment on March 17, 1577, with Frobisher named "General of the whole Company." He led a three-ship fleet back to his supposed strait on July 17. Because the company was a money-making enterprise, the efforts of Frobisher and his men were almost entirely dedicated to mining supposedly gold-bearing ore while they expended only a modest effort trying to discover the Northwest Passage to Cathay. They never discovered that Frobisher Bay was a dead end. The fleet returned to England in late September, the entire voyage having cost the company more than £6000. Although none of the 200 tons of ore yielded any gold, the company's German assayers predicted a sufficient yield to make a profit. As a result, the company planned a third voyage for the following year.

Frobisher returned to the bay at the head of a fleet of 15 ships and 120 men (including 40 "miners") in late July 1578. He made a brief wrong turn into Hudson Strait but turned back because the need for gold ore outweighed any interest in a Northwest Passage. The summer was unusually cold, and ice was a constant menace (sinking one of his ships). Despite the hardships, Frobisher's men gathered 1,350 tons of ore from points around the bay. After discussing the possibility of leaving two ships and several men to continue the work through the winter, those at the bay eventually decided that everyone should return to England. The fleet returned safely by October 1, 1578, but they had spent more than £9000 on this voyage with a result as disappointing as the earlier venture. Despite five years' labor, the stones yielded no treasure and eventually ended up paving English highways. The company finally declared bankruptcy in 1583.

Further reading: Pierre Berton, *Arctic Grail: The Quest for the Northwest Passage and the North Pole, 1818–1909* (New York: Lyons Press, 2000); Samuel Eliot Morison, *The European Discovery of America: The Northern Voyages, AD 500–1600* (New York: Oxford University Press, 1971).

— Paul Dunscomb

Aztec defending island against conquistador; priest baptizing an infant. Mexican Indian painting *(The Granger Collection)*

conquistador(es)

Bands of men who explored the Western Hemisphere during the first half of the 16th century, conquistadores opened up new lands, peoples, and resources to Spanish influence and thereby formed the leading front of Spanish conquest and colonization.

From as early as the 13th century CASTILE sought overseas expansion. Partly because of potential commercial gain but largely because of adventurism, the Castilians led expeditions to Africa and the CANARY ISLANDS during the 15th century. Then, during the late 15th and early 16th centuries, their focus shifted to the Indies. Some historians point to a warrior tradition honed during centuries of fighting when the Spanish worked to expel the Moors (see ISLAM) from the Iberian Peninsula. For these scholars it seems natural that Spain, finally free of Moorish domination, would then translate its crusading fervor and sharp military abilities to the pursuit of conquest in the NEW WORLD discovered by CHRISTOPHER COLUMBUS.

Following the death of Columbus in 1506, the age of the conquistadores began in earnest. Although the spirit of discovery and conquest can be traced back several centuries, the distinguishing features of the conquistadores included their tendency to function as part of warrior bands organized for conquest and also, at least during the early conquistadorial era, to search for treasure, land, and slave laborers as opposed to the pursuit of permanent settlement.

Using HISPANIOLA as the base from which they launched conquests of other lands, the conquistadores were originally those men who did not receive ENCOMIENDAS during the early settlement of Hispaniola. Over time the conquistadores consisted of a motley selection of members, ranging from poor or obscure settlers lacking substantial land holdings such as HERNÁN CORTÉS to those such as FRANCISCO PIZARRO, who possessed considerable standing and connections within the growing sphere of Spanish domination in the West Indies. In addition, not all conquistadores were motivated by the thrill and rewards of discovery alone. Some envisioned a more long-term role for themselves in lands newly claimed for Spain. They remained in the lands they subjugated even after the distribution of booty. Although diversity prevailed among the conquistadores, all who joined expeditions understood that they typically did so at their own expense and risk.

Beginning with Columbus, *capitulaciones* (legal agreements) between the Crown and explorers stipulated the conditions, including the time frame and group leader for a given enterprise and the distribution of profits, for any newly discovered or conquered lands. During the first half of the 16th century, the *capitulación* represented an inducement for would-be discoverers of new lands in the Indies. Further motivation came from the Crown and its desire to use the West Indies to set up intermediary centers for the trading of GOLD. Generally, however, the booty from an expedition proved far from impressive. Dependent on royal recognition for their accomplishments, conquistadores resorted to description of their alleged heroic deeds through rhetoric laced with nationalistic and religious sentiment.

The Castillian nobility tended to view conquistadores as fraudulent, self-promoting opportunists who advanced themselves through the bloodshed of indigenous peoples. Very few conquistadores received designations of nobility upon their return to Spain. More frequently, the Crown bestowed them positions of limited authority as bureaucrats in the territories they conquered.

Following Columbus's first voyage, the Spanish conquistadores engaged in more than 20 years of rather unproductive discovery and exploration. Yet even in this period, some conquistadores achieved lasting success. In 1509 VASCO NÚÑEZ DE BALBOA founded Darién; in 1513 JUAN PONCE DE LEÓN discovered Florida; and in 1520 Cortés led the conquest of the Aztec Empire. The founding of Hispaniola and CUBA also represented valuable early additions to the Spanish Empire. Then, during the 1530s and 1540s, in the wake of the long-fought but successful conquest of PERU, the number of conquistadores in search of fame and riches, instead of new lands, increased significantly.

Somewhat surprisingly, many of the expeditions led by conquistadores lacked superior military equipment and technology in comparison with indigenous groups. For example, during the conquest of the Aztec Empire, Cortés relied on but 15 cannons, 13 guns, and 16 HORSES. Although such equipment certainly placed them at an advantage, two factors proved more critical in the Spanish success: the ability of the conquistadores to exploit rivalries between and among indigenous peoples, and the devastating blow of epidemic disease, part of the COLUMBIAN EXCHANGE that accompanied their arrival.

Although overwhelmed and in many cases surprised by their conquerors, not all indigenous populations quietly accepted Spanish domination. As a result, the Spaniards did not enjoy universal ascent in every segment of the New World. A number of indigenous groups, including the Araucanian Indians in present-day Chile, adopted some of the conquistadores' strategies and weaponry and effectively used them to avoid domination by the conquistadores and subsequent groups of Europeans through the 19th century.

By the middle of the 1570s, the era of the conquistadores moved toward its end. During the late conquistadorial period explorers increasingly found themselves settling in significant numbers in the lands they conquered. Although such a pattern can be detected from the earliest Spanish voyages, as fewer and fewer undiscovered lands remained during the 1560s and 1570s, conquistadores began to realize that lasting wealth and status came typically not with the raiding and abandonment of an area but from its full settlement and exploitation.

Further reading: Guillermon Cespedes, *Latin America: The Early Years* (New York: Knopf, 1974); Patricia de Feuentes, ed. and trans., *The Conquistadors: First-Person Accounts of the Conquest of Mexico* (Norman and London: University of Oklahoma Press, 1993); Mario Gongora, *Studies in the Colonial History of Spanish America*, trans. Richard Southern (Cambridge, U.K.: Cambridge University Press, 1975); Edwin Williamson, *The Penguin History of Latin America* (New York and London: Penguin, 1992).

— Kimberly Sambol-Tosco

Coosa

A major MISSISSIPPIAN chiefdom centered in northwest present-day Georgia in the 16th century, Coosa dominated several ethnic communities that occupied the areas of eastern Tennessee, northwest Georgia, and northeast Alabama, and it survived the HERNANDO DE SOTO, Tristán de Luna, and Juan Pardo expeditions into the region only to suffer tremendous population losses caused by the introduction of European epidemic DISEASES.

The name *Coosa* referred to a chiefdom in the areas of eastern Tennessee, northwest Georgia, and northeast Alabama and the capital town of that chiefdom situated along the banks of the Coosawattee River in Georgia. In 1540 the Soto campaign entered this province in the Tennessee River Valley after crossing the Appalachian Mountains from the Carolinas. Soto proceeded to force the local inhabitants to serve as porters and provide his army with food and other supplies. After seizing the paramount chief of the province in the town of Coosa, Soto made additional demands on the population to replenish his forces, and he eventually marched toward central Alabama to invade the territory of the chiefdom of Mabila.

A detachment from Luna's expedition next made contact with Coosa in 1560. They found the chiefdom to have declined in size, especially in the immediate vicinity of the capital town of Coosa. After helping the chief of Coosa put down a challenge to his authority by the Napochies along the Tennessee River, these Spaniards left the region to report their findings to Luna himself. The Spanish made their last contact with Coosa in 1567 with the Pardo *entrada*. Pardo entered the Coosa province from the Appalachian Mountains following the path Soto took several decades before this expedition. Pardo met open resistance by allied native forces under the leadership of the chief of Coosa and finally returned over the mountains. The Coosa chiefdom seems to have declined after this point. It probably suffered severe population loss due to the accidental introduction of Old World epidemic DISEASES by the Spanish *entradas* and trade with coastal groups.

The demographic collapse, just one of the consequences of the COLUMBIAN EXCHANGE, led to Coosa being driven from northwest Georgia by the Cherokees. Eventually survivors from the chiefdom arrived in east-central Alabama as part of the Muscogee alliance system often called the Creek Confederacy.

Further reading: David J. Hally, "The Chiefdom of Coosa," in *The Forgotten Centuries: Indians and Europeans in the American South, 1521–1704*, eds., Charles Hudson and Carmen Chaves Tesser (Athens: University of Georgia Press, 1988), 227–253; Charles Hudson, Marvin Smith, David J. Hally, Richard Polhemus, and Chester B. Depratter, "Coosa: A Chiefdom in the Sixteenth-Century Southeastern United States," *American Antiquity* 50 (1985): 723–737; Charles Hudson, Marvin T. Smith, Chester Depratter, and Emilia Kelley, "The Tristan de Luna Expedition, 1559–1561," *Southeastern Archaeology* 8 (1989): 31–45; Marvin T. Smith, *Coosa: The Rise and Fall* *of a Southeastern Mississippian Chiefdom* (Gainesville: University Press of Florida, 2000).

— Dixie Ray Haggard

Copán

One of the most important classic MAYA cities and home of some of the most sophisticated stone carvings in Mesoamerica.

Copán lies in the Copán River valley, a tributary of the much larger Motagua River system in modern-day Honduras. It was at the eastern frontier of the Maya zone, well away from the other great cities of the area. The valley was fertile, and the river provided trade routes that allowed merchants from Copán to trade with cities in such distant regions as the YUCATÁN PENINSULA and TABASCO. Settlers lived in the region beginning around 900 B.C., but the city did not become important until the classic era (beginning in roughly A.D. 200). In A.D. 426, the ruler Yax-K'uk'-Mo' ("Green [or First] Quetzal-Macaw") founded a dynasty that lasted for almost 400 years, ending in 820. There is the distinct possibility that this man was a warlord from TEOTIHUACÁN who seized control over the city. During this time Copán reached its greatest height, its residents establishing political control over the immediate region and forming long-lasting political alliances with the residents of the great city of TIKAL and those of the more distant Teotihuacán.

Under this great dynasty the arts flourished, particularly stone carving. Nowhere else in the Maya world did artists develop such a refined, intricate style. A number of rulers from the great dynasty erected enormous statues of themselves in full ritual regalia. This "forest of kings" remains one of Copán's defining features. More impressive is the Hieroglyphic Stairs, one of the many buildings built by the great ruler Waxaklahun-Ubah-K'awil (695–738). Each of the 63 stairs remains covered with elaborate glyphs, numbering almost 2,500 in all, making it one of the longest historical texts in Mesoamerica. Unfortunately, the early archaeologists who restored the ruins could not read the glyphs and reassembled the stairs out of order, making any attempt to read them difficult in the extreme. Architecture also flourished at Copán, and the main Acropolis contained a number of beautiful, well-built structures. The great ball court is one of the best surviving examples from the Maya area.

After 700 Copán's fortunes began to wane, although the city did not vanish overnight. In 738 Waxaklahun-Ubah-K'awil was captured by enemies from the rival city of Quiriguá. Copán recovered quickly but did not regain its position of political dominance in the region. Yax Pasah (763–ca. 820) was an ineffectual ruler and was apparently dominated by the local nobility, but Copán's difficulties were not confined to politics. As the city increased in size, dwellings spread outward into the floodplain, leading to a reduction in the amount of land for farming. Ultimately, this sprawl became so extensive that residents of the city could no longer produce enough food to sustain themselves. The last known ruler at Copán faded from the historical record after 822, although the city retained its sizable population for almost another hundred years. After 900 the city's residents slowly abandoned their locale. Over the centuries the Copán River shifted its course, running through the ancient urban core and damaging many of the crumbling buildings.

Copán's remains played a vital role in the "rediscovery" of the classic Maya civilization. Between 1839 and 1840 the explorer John L. Stephens and the artist Frederick Catherwood visited the ruins, and Stephens was so impressed that he bought the site for $50. Stephens's account of the visit, *Incidents of Travel in Central America, Chiapas, and Yucatan,* became an international bestseller and gave most people their first knowledge of the Maya. Archaeologists began working on the site in the 1890s, making it one of the most thoroughly studied sites of the Maya area.

Further reading: Michael Coe, *The Maya,* 6th ed. (London: Thames & Hudson, 1999); William L. Fash, *Scribes, Warriors, and Kings: The City of Copán and the Ancient Maya* (London: Thames & Hudson, 1991); John Lloyd Stephens, *Incidents of Travel in Central America, Chiapas, and Yucatan,* 2 vols. (New York: Dover Publications, 1969).

— Scott Chamberlain

Córdoba, Francisco Hernández de (fl. 1517)

The leader of one of the first Spanish expeditions to the mainland of MEXICO, Córdoba helped pave the way for subsequent explorations under JUAN DE GRIJALVA and HERNÁN CORTÉS.

Córdoba was a man of some substance who left for the NEW WORLD to find his fortune and earn honor. By 1517 he made his way to CUBA, the base for numerous expeditions. Hoping to discover wealthy new islands, Córdoba and several soldiers (including BERNAL DÍAZ DEL CASTILLO) decided to strike out on their own. They pooled their resources and bought two CARAVELs, a brigantine, bread, salt pork, and other supplies on credit from Governor DIEGO DE VELÁZQUEZ. As the wealthiest, highest-ranking man among them, Córdoba became the expedition's leader. Despite minor difficulties, the Córdoba expedition reached the YUCATÁN PENINSULA in three weeks and discovered a large, well-built city—the first true city the Spaniards had yet encountered in the Americas. Excited by the great potential of this discovery, the Spaniards sent messengers to the local MAYA. Fatefully, the Spaniards understood the Mayas' sign language as greetings and invitations to enter the city and landed on the shore expecting hospitality. Unfortunately for them, the shipwrecked sailor GONZALO GUERRERO had turned against the Spaniards after living among the Maya and convinced the natives to attack the Spaniards on sight. The Maya ambushed the Spaniards, who had to fight their way back to the ships, but by then the CONQUISTADORES had seen enough GOLD in the town and on their adversaries to excite their greed.

Unfortunately for the Spaniards, conditions on the Córdoba expedition deteriorated from that moment on. The ships hugged the coast, seeing evidence of civilized peoples, but their crews' attempts to land and replenish their stores of water met with constant hostility. They sailed west and south until they reached the city of Campeche, where desperation drove them to try to parley with the local CACIQUE. They obtained water but sensed that an attack was imminent. Fearful for their lives, they beat a hasty retreat to the ships. Only days later they had to land again, and this time they met with a full squadron of Maya warriors. After a short, desperate battle, the Spaniards reached their ships but had lost more than half their party. Most of the survivors were wounded, including Córdoba himself. After this final disaster the expedition had no choice but to return to friendly territory. Lacking enough crew to man all three ships, they abandoned the brigantine and limped back to Cuba. Upon arriving Córdoba gave a flowery account of the Yucatán that sparked great interest among the conquistadores. He died of his wounds shortly thereafter, but not before inspiring Governor Velázquez to send other expeditions to explore the region.

Further reading: Inga Clendinnen, *Ambivalent Conquests: Maya and Spaniard in Yucatan, 1517–1570* (Cambridge, U.K.: Cambridge University Press, 1987); Bernal Díaz del Castillo, *The Discovery and Conquest of Mexico* (New York: Da Capo Press, 1996).

— Scott Chamberlain

corn

Corn was the basis for most of North and South America's advanced civilizations before European contact, and it immediately spread to Eurasia and Africa thereafter.

The species known to scientists as *Zea mays* has gone by many names. *Corn* in Old English meant generally a small particle or grain, but in particular the seeds of domesticated annuals such as wheat and by extension the whole plant. The members of CHRISTOPHER COLUMBUS's first voyage who discovered this new kind of corn recorded its name as *mahiz,* and *maize* in some form has always been its clearest name. The British took to calling it *Indian corn,* as opposed to *British corn.* Confusion over corn's origins led to further names; for centuries Europeans referred to it as *Turkish wheat.*

Corn is native to the Americas. Like all cereals it is a grass, although almost unrecognizable as such after many centuries of domestication. There was and is no wild corn, only scattered tame escapees. American Indians changed corn by artificial selection, setting aside the most desirable ears for later planting. Sometimes they made hybrids by planting different varieties near each other, but usually they sought inbreeding. Single families sometimes even maintained their own pure strains of corn. By 1492 Indians had developed thousands of varieties in all the main types we recognize today, including flour corn, sweet corn, and popcorn. European Americans did not consciously try to improve corn until the late 1700s.

Corn was entirely reliant on people for reproduction. It was planted across most of North and South America except in present-day Canada and the thousand-mile tip of South America. It was densest from present-day PERU to central MEXICO. The central grasslands of the modern-day United States, later famous for corn, were then a tough

The oldest printed picture of an ear of maize. Woodcut from Oviedo's *Historia Natural,* Seville, 1535   *(The Granger Collection)*

barrier of thick native sod, with only the riverbanks worth planting. American Indians had no hard metal tools or draft animals, so they planted corn by hand in untilled ground. Usually they prepared a field by killing the trees, hoeing the other vegetation, and forming small mounds about a yard apart. Fields resembled dot grids rather than rows. A planter poked a hole with a stick, counted a few seeds into the hole, and covered the seeds by foot to protect them from animals. Beans, squash, and potatoes were commonly planted between the mounds. Corn could be harvested very green or long-dead and dry because the husks protected the seeds. Some Indians maintained fields continuously through irrigation, terracing, and fertilizing, while others abandoned fields to forest and returned years later to reclear them once they had recovered.

Most Indians were almost as reliant on corn as it was on them. They worried and prayed over when and where to plant it, how to protect it from rats, birds, thieves, and wind, and how to store their harvested wealth. Native Americans ate corn parched, boiled, and roasted or ground into flour and baked into cakes. Sometimes the stalks of giant varieties were even used as building material. Corn played a religious role for many American peoples, varying in content but often deep in import, associated with blood, fertility, motherhood, and deities.

Corn amazed Europeans. Columbus returned with descriptions of it, and by at least his second voyage with samples of it that were propagated rapidly across Europe, first as curiosities but soon as agricultural goods. It spread from there along trading routes to northern and sub-Saharan Africa and by 1516 via Portuguese sailors to Asia. GIO-VANNI BATTISTA RAMUSIO included a picture of corn in his *Navigationi E Viaggi*, published in Venice in the mid-16th century, an image so durable that it was still being reprinted hundreds of years later. Corn's adaptability made it only a minor trade good but got it adopted as a "native" of many countries (hence "Turkish wheat"), so much so that many would later claim credit for its origin.

Further reading: Betty Fussell, *The Story of Corn* (New York: Knopf, 1992); R. Douglas Hurt, *Indian Agriculture in America: Prehistory to the Present* (Lawrence: University Press of Kansas, 1987); Paul Weatherwax, *Indian Corn in Old America* (New York: Macmillan, 1954).

— Robb Campbell

Coronado, Francisco (1510–1554)

In 1540 Francisco Vásquez de Coronado led a large, unsuccessful expedition into the American Southwest in the hopes of finding cities of GOLD.

In the 16th century Spanish CONQUISTADORES had found vast treasures of gold and SILVER in MEXICO and PERU. Later explorers hoped to find similar riches in northern Mexico and in the area that is now the southwestern United States. Rumors of fabulous cities in the Southwest began to spread when ÁLVAR NÚÑEZ CABEZA DE VACA and three companions returned from their eight-year sojourn among the Indians of Texas and New Mexico. Cabeza de Vaca had not found wealth in his travels, but he reported that he had heard stories of prosperous towns farther north. In 1539 a preliminary expedition set out under Fray Marcos de Niza. It was guided by one of Cabeza de Vaca's companions, the slave Estevanico. Estevanico traveled ahead of the main party, erecting crosses at various sites to indicate that he had found riches. At Hawikuh, a ZUNI pueblo, Estevanico demanded turquoise and women. The Zunis, angry and suspecting that he was a spy, killed him. Fray Marcos de Niza, hearing of Estevanico's death, did not approach the pueblo. Viewing it from a distance, he reported that it was a rich city and even larger than Mexico City. He returned to Nueva Galicia and reported that he had seen Cíbola, the smallest of the legendary Seven Cities of Gold.

Upon Fray Marcos's return Viceroy Antonio de Mendoza appointed Coronado to lead an expedition back to Cíbola. In the spring of 1540, Coronado headed north leading an expedition that included 336 Spanish soldiers, hundreds of Indian allies, and six FRANCISCANS. Some of the men brought their wives, children, and slaves with them. To transport and feed this army, Coronado brought herds of horses, mules, cattle, and sheep.

In July 1540 Coronado reached Hawikuh. The small pueblo of stone and brick did not fulfill the Spaniards' dreams of wealth, and Coronado had to prevent his disappointed men from attacking Fray Marcos de Niza, whose story was now revealed as false. Coronado sent the friar back to Mexico City (see TENOCHTITLÁN) and reported "He has not told the truth in a single thing that he said, but everything is the opposite of what he related, except the name of the cities and the large stone houses."

The Zuni of Hawikuh did not welcome the Spanish invaders. Zuni men laid down lines of sacred cornmeal at the entrance to their pueblo to indicate to the Spanish that they were not welcome. The Spanish, for their part, read the REQUERIMIENTO to the Zunis, declaring that the Indians must submit to the Pope and the Spanish Crown or face conquest by the Spanish. The Zuni attacked, but the battle ended quickly and the Spanish overran the pueblo. Despite this poor start, relations between Coronado's expedition and the Indians temporarily improved. Coronado visited other Zuni pueblos and met their leaders, who presented him with turquoise, deer and buffalo skins, and yucca fiber blankets. Two leaders from Pecos pueblo, whom the Spanish called Cacique and Bigotes, allied themselves with the Spanish.

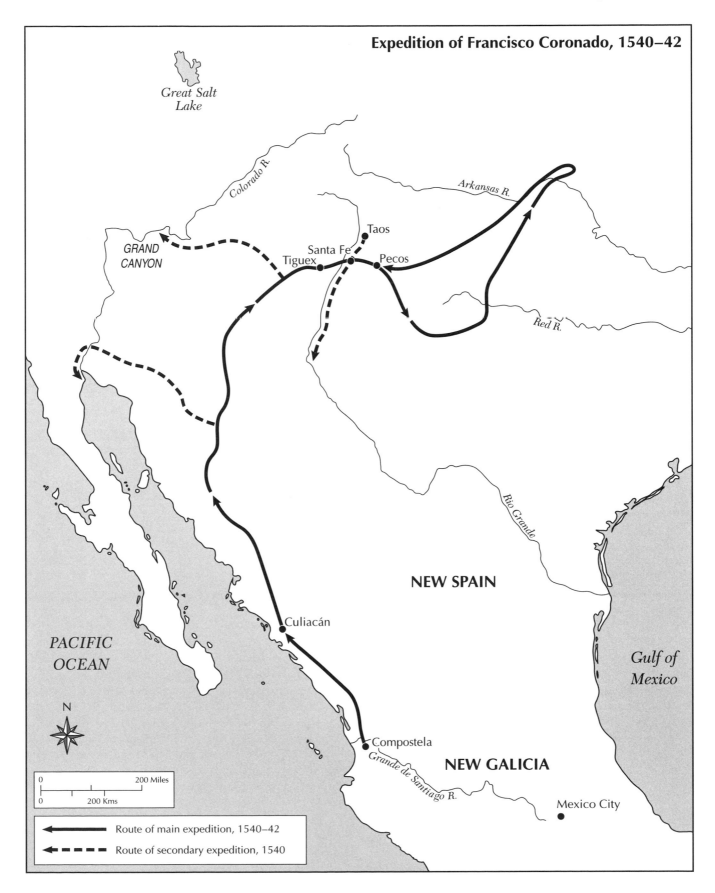

Expedition of Francisco Coronado, 1540–42

Great Salt Lake

Colorado R.

Arkansas R.

Taos

GRAND CANYON

Santa Fe

Tiguex

Pecos

Red R.

Rio Grande

NEW SPAIN

PACIFIC OCEAN

N

Culiacán

Gulf of Mexico

Compostela

Grande de Santiago R.

NEW GALICIA

Mexico City

0   200 Miles
0   200 Kms

Route of main expedition, 1540–42

Route of secondary expedition, 1540

Coronado still hoped to find rich cities. He sent Pedro de Tovar northward, into the HOPI villages. Tovar and the Hopi fought, and the Hopi surrendered. They told Tovar that a great river (the Colorado) existed farther west. Coronado sent approximately 25 men under the command of García López de Cárdenas to find the river. He hoped that they would meet up with Hernando de Alarcón, who had sailed from Mexico with supplies for the expedition. Cárdenas found the Grand Canyon but could not find a way down to the Colorado and so did not meet up with Alarcón.

Winter was approaching, and without the supplies carried by Alarcón, the Spanish faced a difficult time. The Pecos leaders, Cacique and Bigotes, told Coronado that there were vast herds of cattle in the east, and Coronado sent another expedition, this one headed by Hernando de Alvarado, to explore farther east. Alvarado and Bigotes were welcomed by the men of 12 pueblos north of present-day Albuquerque. The Spanish named the area Tiguex, and because the area seemed richer than Zuni, Alvarado suggested that the entire expedition spend the winter there. The Spanish also visited Taos and Pecos pueblos.

Because Alvarado wanted to explore the plains, Bigotes lent him two slaves from eastern tribes, a boy named Ysopete, who came from Quivira, and a man whom the Spanish called "the Turk." The Turk assured the Spanish that the land of Quivira held fabulous riches and claimed that Bigotes had a golden bracelet from Quivira. Alvarado decided to return to Pecos and ask Bigotes about the bracelet. Both Bigotes and Cacique denied having any such bracelet, whereupon Alvarado seized them and took them back to meet Coronado. According to the historian Elizabeth John, this "shocking violation of hospitality brought the Pecos warriors out fighting" and sowed "hostility and distrust where there had been valuable friendship."

The Spaniards' relations with the Indians continued to deteriorate. When Alvarado reached Tiguex he found Coronado planning to spend the winter there. The presence of the Spanish and their Mexican Indian allies placed great strain on the resources of the pueblos. The Spanish made the Indians vacate an entire pueblo so that they could move in and also imposed levies of food and clothing on each of the twelve pueblos of Tiguex. Tensions between the Spanish and the Indians increased, and when some Indians killed Spanish HORSES, Coronado struck back brutally. He destroyed the pueblo that he thought was leading the resistance and burned its survivors to death. The Spanish forced Bigotes, Cacique, Ysopete, and the Turk, in chains, to watch the destruction of the town and its people.

In the spring of 1541, Coronado and his men left Tiguex to cross the plains in search of Quivira. By the end of May, they believed that the Turk, who had told them so much about the wonders of the city, was a liar. Coronado sent most of his force back to Tiguex, while he and a group of about 30 Spaniards led by Ysopete continued on to Quivira. In July 1541 Ysopete led them to Quivira, but it, like Hawikuh, was a disappointment to the Spanish. Quivira was not a fabulous city of gold, but a Wichita Indian village. The Spanish killed the Turk and in mid-August turned around and headed back to Tiguex. The golden cities of Cíbola and Quivira had proved imaginary, and the Spanish could think of no reason to stay. They spent another winter in Tiguex, again levying supplies from the Indians, and returned to Mexico in the spring of 1542.

Coronado never fully recovered from his travels. In the winter of 1541–42, before returning to Mexico, he had suffered a severe head injury in a fall from his horse. He had also lost much of his wife's fortune, which he had invested in the expedition. Upon his return to Mexico, he was charged with misconduct in his behavior toward the Indians and spent several years in litigation. He was never convicted, although García López de Cárdenas, his lieutenant, was convicted of offenses against the Indians and died in prison. Coronado died in Mexico City in 1554.

Further reading: Elizabeth A. H. John, *Storms Brewed in Other Men's Worlds: The Confrontation of Indians, Spanish, and French in the Southwest, 1540–1795* (College Station: Texas A&M University Press, 1975); Edward H. Spicer, *Cycles of Conquest: The Impact of Spain, Mexico, and the United States on the Indians of the Southwest, 1533–1960* (Tucson: University of Arizona Press, 1962); David J. Weber, *The Spanish Frontier in North America* (New Haven, Conn.: Yale University Press, 1992); Richard White, *"It's Your Misfortune and None of My Own": A New History of the American West* (Norman: University of Oklahoma Press, 1991).

— Martha K. Robinson

corregidor

Infamous for their frequent abuse of power, the *corregidores* were the provincial administrators of *corregimientos* (territories within the jurisdiction of an AUDIENCIA) and were endowed with both judicial and political authority.

The office of *corregidor* originated in Spain. *Corregidores* were first appointed in CASTILE during the 14th century as part of an attempt by the Crown to check the growing power of municipal governments. Initially appointed to only a limited number of urban centers, Queen Isabella appointed *corregidores* to all significant towns in Castile in 1480. This bureaucratic expansion was part of FERDINAND AND ISABELLA's strategy to centralize authority in Spain.

In Spanish America the Crown appointed *corregidores* in the 16th century as a direct response to the flaws in the ENCOMIENDA. In particular, the crown wanted the *corregidores* to increase royal revenue, tend to the needs of the non-*encomendero* population, and check the political and economic power of the *encomenderos,* whom the Crown considered a threat to its authority. Broadly, then, *corregidores* in Spanish America served the same function they did in Spain: their task was to expand royal authority in the Western Hemisphere.

There were two types of *corregidores* in Spanish America, *corregidores de españoles* and *corregidores de indios.* Both possessed political and judicial powers, were barred from engaging in commerce or accepting gifts and/or personal services, and usually served a term of five years or less in office. In addition, upon leaving office both types of *corregidores* were subject to a review of their conduct, called a *residencia.*

The differences between the *corregidores de españoles* and *corregidores de indios* relate to jurisdiction. The *corregidor de españoles* was assigned to a Spanish urban center and its surrounding territory. He presided over the *CABILDO* and had the authority to intervene when the public or royal interest was at stake. In contrast, the *corregidor de indios* held jurisdiction over Native American municipalities and had responsibility for defending the lives and property of the Indian population. In practice, *corregidores de indios* were notorious for their corruption and in many cases were the worst abusers of the Native American populations they were supposed to defend.

The small salaries paid to the *corregidores* provided an incentive to engage in illegal activities, and their substantial local power made it possible for them to do so. They coerced Indians to perform unpaid labor, to sell their goods below market value, and through a system known as the *repartimiento* of merchandise, forced them to purchase unwanted goods at exorbitant prices. Such illegal activity provided ample opportunity for profit, making the office of *corregidor* a sought-after position. Over time such abuse of power led to numerous Native American revolts and contributed to a gradual phasing out of the office beginning in 1764.

Further reading: Mark A. Burkholder, "Bureaucrats," in *Cities and Society in Colonial Latin America,* ed. Louisa Schell Hoberman and Susan Migden Socolow (Albuquerque: University of New Mexico Press, 1986); J. H. Elliot, *Imperial Spain, 1469–1716* (New York: New American Library, 1964); C. H. Haring, *The Spanish Empire in America* (New York: Oxford University Press, 1947); Karen Spalding, *Huarochirí: An Andean Society Under Inca and Spanish Rule* (Stanford, Calif.: Stanford University Press, 1984).

— William Holliday

Cortés, Hernán (Fernando, Fernan) (1485–1547)

Most notorious for his exploits as a Spanish CONQUISTADOR in the NEW WORLD, Hernán Cortés, beginning with his arrival in COZUMEL in 1519, executed plans of conquering the Indian population and establishing a permanent Spanish settlement in NEW SPAIN and in the process provided a model for later European forays across North and South America.

Born in 1485 in the Spanish town of Medellín, Cortés experienced an unexceptional childhood as part of a family with a low income but good connections. Cortés was nine years old in 1492, when two crucial events occurred: FERDINAND AND ISABELLA triumphantly ended Moorish domination in Spain and CHRISTOPHER COLUMBUS arrived in the New World. After two years of studying law at the university in Salamanca, Cortés spent several years near his family's home before buying passage to the Indies at the age of 19.

Upon arrival on the island of HISPANIOLA, Governor Ovando, an acquaintance of his parents, granted Cortés an ENCOMIENDA. Cortés spent nearly six years on the island in relative obscurity as a farmer and trader. Then, in his mid-20s, he accompanied the contingent led by his friend Don Diego Velázquez de Cuéllar (see DIEGO DE VELÁZQUEZ) in a planned invasion of CUBA. Cortés benefited greatly from the largely uncontested Spanish occupation of Cuba, acquiring a tract of land much larger than what he previously owned on Hispaniola. Like other Spaniards, Cortés forced the Indians he inherited as part of his land parcel to work the mines on his property. On Cuba he pursued efficient and sustainable agriculture and mining and, according to some accounts, resisted the temptation to overwork his Indian laborers. Also while there, a disgraceful act of seduction nearly brought about Cortés's execution, after which he married a poor girl, Catalina Xuarez.

Following two earlier unsuccessful efforts by the Spanish to establish a sustainable presence in MEXICO, Cortés convinced Diego de Velázquez to appoint him captain-general of the fleet that would sail to Mexico. He also diligently recruited and prepared an impressive crew. Cortés's crew consisted of more than 500 men, and the presence of several HORSES and cannon aboard the ships made some suspicious that Cortés intended only to trade with the Indian groups he encountered.

Despite a last-minute effort by Velázquez to revoke Cortés's captaincy because of fears and rumors circulated by Cortés's fellow conquistadores that Cortés planned to take command of the project, Cortés and his enthusiastic crew departed for New Spain in February of 1519. In his haste to depart from Cuba before Velázquez, his immediate superior, had a chance to officially cancel the expedition, Cortés, in effect, declared himself answerable only to the Spanish Crown, and thus, upon returning with fabulous riches and newly obtained fame, Cortés assumed that he and his crew would ultimately be held blameless by the king.

After a somewhat discouraging voyage, Cortés and his 11-ship fleet arrived at Cozumel, where they repaired their vessels and probed the Indians of the island for information

The first meeting between Cortés and Moctezuma. Page from a map and historical record of the people of Tlaxcala that was painted in early colonial times. Standing at the right is Cortés's interpreter-mistress, Doña Marina *(The Granger Collection)*

about the Mexico mainland (see YUCATÁN PENINSULA). From Cozumel Cortés sent a small mission to the mainland in search of white men purportedly kept as slaves by the Indians of Yucatán. In the meanwhile, Cortés made small steps toward introducing the natives of Cozumel to Christianity. Although the mainland mission returned without any news to report, Cortés soon found encouragement in the arrival via canoe of GERÓNIMO DE AGUILAR, a Spaniard who had been shipwrecked during a 1511 expedition to Hispaniola. With the Mayan-fluent Aguilar as part of his group, Cortés had an important link to the Mexica people.

Finally, Cortés and his fleet left Cozumel for the mainland in early March 1519. The ships first landed at Champoton, where the Spaniards encountered Tabascan Indians prepared to fight. Adhering to accepted Spanish practice, Cortés ordered that the required message (see REQUERIMIENTO) be delivered to the Indians, declaring the right of Spain to assert sovereignty over all persons and groups considered vassals of the king. Partly because of the noise and chaos that emanated from the scene of confrontation and also because the Indians were unfamiliar with the Spanish and their customs, the Tabascans seemed not to comprehend the Requerimiento and a battle ensued. In the end, 800 Indians died; the Spanish suffered many injuries but only two casualties. As a peace offering, the Tabascan Indian chiefs presented Cortés and his men with gold gifts and 20 women to be kept as slaves. One of the maidens, MALINCHE, spoke fluent NAHUATL, an invaluable skill in the coming months as the Spaniards pushed farther inward toward Nahuatl-speaking Indians. She later became Cortés's wife and the mother of his child.

From Champotón the fleet journeyed westward to San Juan de Ulúa, continuing their pursuit of gold and fame. At San Juan de Ulúa Cortés received a peaceful welcome from the local Indians. As the Spanish rested at San Juan de Ulúa, Cortés, representing himself as an ambassador to the king of Spain, sent the local chief, Tendile, as a messenger to MOCTEZUMA, the king of Mexico. Twice Cortés sent Tendile to the mountains to call on Moctezuma, and with each return Tendile brought peace-offering gifts and relayed the message that Cortés should not visit Moctezuma.

At that time, because he held a precarious footing at San Juan de Ulúa, Cortés decided to move still farther northward. He also continued to hear fabulous tales of Moctezuma's kingdom. Discouraged by Moctezuma's refusal to see him, Cortés had also to contend with diminishing supplies and a new landing that offered less protection than San Juan de Ulúa. Perhaps most significantly, Cortés risked the possibility of personal demise if at that point he returned to Cuba without enough gold and other wares to cover the enormous expense outlaid for the expedition. Then, in a moment of absolute cunning, desperation, and legalistic maneuvering, Cortés effectively usurped Velázquez's control of the mission and officially turned focus away from the initial purpose of the expedition, trading and bartering with Indians, to permanent settlement. Through this scheme Cortés managed to keep his crew, although not entirely singing his favor, at least convinced that the mission ought to continue in pursuit of Moctezuma's empire.

Soon thereafter Cortés founded La Villa Rica de la Vera Cruz (VERACRUZ) in the name of the king of Spain before pushing on to Cempoala, where he received an amiable reception from local Indians who were part of the Aztec Empire. While in Cempoala, learning that the Totonacs considered themselves oppressed by the amount of tribute they had to pay to Moctezuma as their leader, Cortés used the situation to his advantage. Cortés also remained among the Totonac long enough to receive reinforcements from Cuba and to send two representatives to Spain requesting additional financial assistance from the king, justifying the purpose of the expedition and pledging his absolute devotion to the Crown.

Determined to push inland to the highlands without the option of ever turning back, Cortés, declaring their alleged unseaworthiness, had the remaining ships stripped of their supplies and destroyed. This act incensed his men, particularly those whom he had managed thus far only to keep on his side by intimidation and bribery, but despite internal conflict, Cortés and his men focused on conquest of the AZTECS.

In August 1519 Cortés left 150 of his men behind at Veracruz and departed for the Aztec capital. Along the difficult trek Cortés acquired assistance from certain Indian groups while encountering difficulty from others. At CHOLULA, a point reached by the Spaniards in late September, Cortés, by some accounts, met resistance from allies of the Aztecs planning to attack the Spaniards. By other accounts the battle that ensued resulted from Spanish bloodlust and Cortés's manipulation of rivalries that beset the Aztec Empire. News of 6,000 Cholulan casualties and the burning of the holy city spread quickly to an increasingly distressed Moctezuma.

After a number of exchanges via messengers, Moctezuma finally sent word that Cortés and his men might present themselves at the Aztec capital, TENOCHTITLÁN. Rumors circulated that rather than mere mortals, Cortés and the Spaniards were representatives of the feathered serpent QUETZALCOATL, the great god whose return to its domicile the Aztecs believed imminent. If indeed the Spaniards were divine emissaries, Moctezuma desired not to offend them or engage in warfare.

Then, as Cortés stalled at Tenochtitlán, a large Spanish expedition arrived with orders from Diego Velázquez to pursue and arrest Cortés. In a skillfully executed preemptive strike, Cortés marched back toward Cempoala, where he managed to outmaneuver and defeat the Spanish newcomers. With these men now on his side, Cortés returned to Tenochtitlán to confront the Aztecs. There, the Aztecs besieged Cortés and his men, and after a brutal battle the Spaniards retreated from the city.

After the battle, as the Spanish regrouped and acquired new Indian allies, inside Tenochtitlán the Aztecs enthroned a new emperor, CUITLÁHUAC, a replacement for the recently fallen Moctezuma. After months of preparation, in late December 1520 Cortés renewed his plans to retake the Aztec capital. On August 13, 1521, Cortés realized success as the desolated city of Tenochtitlán fell and the Aztecs surrendered. The ferocity of the Spanish assault stunned local Indians, who described its horrors in depth to Spanish missionaries who later arrived in Mexico (see Documents).

Following the conquest of Mexico, Cortés worked quickly and smoothly to impose Catholic ritual and Spanish law. Also, the Spanish immediately took steps to reclaim the booty of GOLD, SILVER, and jewels that had been lost when the Indians temporarily regained control of the capital. Cortés and his men took control of most of Moctezuma's empire and soon conquered bordering peoples who had not previously been under Moctezuma's dominion. Despite their efforts, in the end Cortés found no huge treasure, and

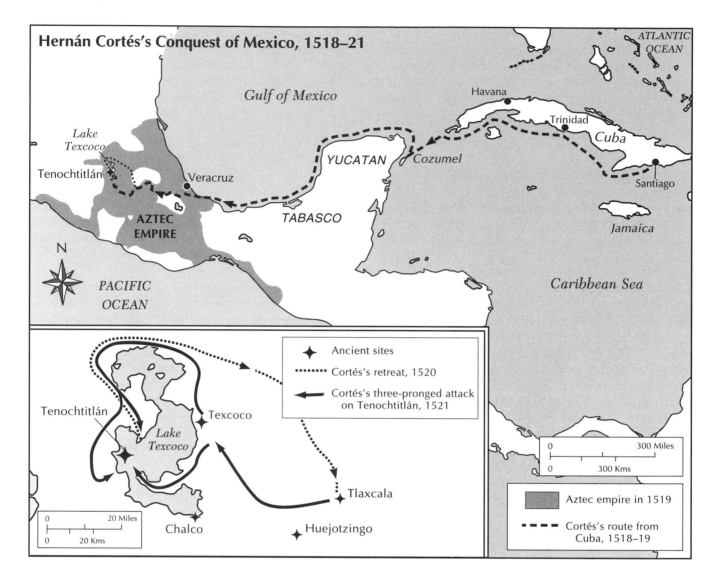

Hernán Cortés's Conquest of Mexico, 1518–21

so he directed attention toward the land grants that each Spaniard would receive as a reward for his efforts.

In early 1522 Cortés, optimistic about his new son with Malinche and with the opportunities offered him in New Spain, initiated plans to rebuild Tenochtitlán. During that time Cortés increasingly encountered competition from other Spaniards wishing to control New Spain, including Velázquez, his long-term rival and once-friend. During the first half of the year Cortés wrote a letter to the king discussing plans to send more treasure to Spain. Uncertain of affairs in Spain, he waited until the end of the year to send three ships with his letter, treasures, and other news intended to convince the king of the legitimacy of his activities and claims in New Spain. In the meantime Cortés behaved as if he already possessed the king's approval.

During the summer of 1523 Cortés finally received the belated decrees from the king that declared the conquistador the governor and captain-general of New Spain. Now endowed with legitimacy, Cortés continued to pursue long-term development in New Spain. He granted *encomiendas* with the requirement that each grantee remain on his land for at least eight years; if married, each grantee had to bring his wife to Mexico within 18 months. All unmarried settlers were encouraged to marry.

Cortés battled with other conquistadores who wished to lay claim to territory that he considered part of his domain. Increasingly weary and insecure about his position in New Spain, in 1524 he led a haphazard expedition into the Honduran forests seeking to suppress a revolt and to punish one of his men who dared to establish his own sphere of influence in Las Hibueras, present-day Honduras. This trip resulted in an illness from which Cortés never fully recovered. While in the rain forest, Cortés ordered the controversial execution of CUAUHTÉMOC and another native leader.

Believed dead by those in Mexico, Cortés returned from the journey to a huge welcome, but he soon had to deal with civil conflict and charges against him handed down from the Spanish Crown. In the autumn of 1528 he set sail for Spain, where he received the king's courtesy and a triumphant welcome from the Spanish people. Although the king acknowledged most of Cortés's accomplishments in New Spain, he did not grant him another chance to govern Mexico. Cortés then spent the next two years in Spain, during which the period of the conquistador came to an end in most of Mexico.

In 1530 Cortés returned to New Spain with his new wife and lived there in relative obscurity for 10 years. In 1547 he died in Spain. At his request, his remains were buried in Mexico.

Further reading: T. R. Fehrenbach, *Fire & Blood: A History of Mexico,* 2nd ed. (New York: Da Capo, 1995); Miguel Léon-Portillo, *The Broken Spears: An Aztec Account of the Conquest of Mexico* (Boston: Beacon Press,); Richard Lee Mark, *Cortés: The Great Adventurer and the Fall of Aztec Mexico* (New York: Knopf, 1993); Anthony Pagden, ed., *Hernan Cortés: Letters from Mexico* (New Haven, Conn., and London: Yale University Press, 1986).

— Kimberly Sambol-Tosco

Council of the Indies

Established by Charles I (CHARLES V) in 1524, the Consejo de Indias (Council of the Indies) acted as a colonial council and clearinghouse for the appointment of viceroys and all issues related to their function as head of a civil government in the NEW WORLD.

Following a period of exploration and conquest in a region, the Spanish Crown required the establishment of a civil government. Such a government effectively replaced the martial law of the CONQUISTADORES. Following the 1521 conquest of MEXICO, Charles formed the Council of the Indies in response to Spain's growing colonial empire.

Beginning in NEW SPAIN in 1535 and PERU in 1551, the viceroy system represented the top political institution in the colonies. The viceroy functioned as an administrator, fulfilled judicial and fiscal duties, and, as a personal representative of the king, held the highest position in each colonial bureaucracy. While in theory the king personally appointed all viceroys, the establishment of the Council of the Indies in 1524 introduced a system of checks and balances in regard to the viceroy's role. As a body of specialists based in SEVILLE, the council kept the king advised of colonial matters, reviewed reports from the viceroys in the Western Hemisphere, recommended policies and procedures, and wielded considerable control in enforcing initiatives related to overseas possessions. In addition, the council legislated proper behavior for viceroys and in many ways circumscribed their private lives while they served the territories under their protection.

A director of judicial, military, and political affairs related to the colonies, the Council of the Indies also acted as an advisory board in ecclesiastical and civil matters. More specifically, the council heard cases appealed from the AUDIENCIAS and the House of Trade, issued laws, and approved major colonial expenditures. Throughout the 16th century the council worked in conjunction with the CASA DE CONTRATACIÓN (House of Trade), which directed all colonial commerce.

Following the creation of the Council of the Indies, many conquistadores continued to enjoy extended periods in command of the lands they subdued without government officials or agencies obstructing their actions. In many cases, like judges and viceroys, the Council of the Indies had to operate within the structures and relationships established by the settlers of a region. Further limitations on the council's effectiveness stemmed from slow or absent communication with officials in the colonies and the inexperience of its members. Composed largely of men with university-based legal training and veterans from lower courts, the council included few men possessing familiarity with the Western Hemisphere. Thus, the council, which remained in existence through the early 18th century and ranked second only to the Council of Castile or the Royal Council, had to cope with some notable obstacles in its management of New Spain.

Further reading: John A. Crow, *The Epic of Latin America,* 4th ed. (Los Angeles: University of California Press, 1992); Edwin Williamson, *The Penguin History of Latin America* (New York and London: Penguin Press, 1992).

— Kimberly Sambol-Tosco

Counterreformation

The Roman Catholic response to the REFORMATION, which consisted both of efforts to halt the spread of Protestantism and to reform the Catholic Church from within, is known as the Counterreformation or Catholic Reformation.

The term *Counterreformation* has inspired scholarly controversy. Some modern scholars use it, but others draw a distinction between the "Counterreformation," which consisted of efforts to halt the spread of Protestantism and to regain lands for the Catholic faith, and the "Catholic Reformation," a movement for reform within the church.

Efforts at reform and renewal within the church pre-dated the Reformation by at least a century. Reformers often presented their goals as being conservative: They did not seek to introduce innovations into the church but instead to return to the simpler, more heartfelt religion of an earlier day. Those who sought renewal, on the other hand, were more likely to expect great changes in the church.

One important (but abortive) attempt at reform in the church before MARTIN LUTHER was the Fifth Lateran Council, which met in Rome from 1512 to 1517. At the Fifth Lateran Council, two monks, Vincenzo (or Pietro) Querini and Tommaso (or Paolo) Giustiniani, proposed that the church immediately make plans to send missionaries to the entire world, including the Americas. Many of their proposals seem to foreshadow the Reformation, because the monks sought to make the church more effective by mandating better training for clerics, eliminating most of the religious orders and reorganizing the rest, reforming the liturgy of the Mass, translating the Bible into vernacular languages, and making greater efforts to fight witchcraft (see WITCHES) and magic. In the end, however, the Fifth Lateran Council did little.

Such dramatic proposals seldom appeared from within the Catholic Church after the Reformation began. As the historian Steven Ozment has observed, "the Reformation's success made internal Catholic criticism and reform more difficult than ever. To censure even the most flagrant church abuses after 1517 was to be suspected of Lutheran sympa-thies." Proposals for change in the church or the develop-ment of new kinds of piety, depending on the time period and region, might be welcomed as healthy reforms or criti-cized as heresies—or both. The Jesuit order (see JESUITS), for example, was condemned by the Faculty of Theology of Paris as "a disturber of the peace of the church," and the Catholic mystic Saint Teresa of Ávila faced criticism from her ecclesiastical superiors as she tried to reform her order.

At the Colloquy of Regensburg (1541), Catholic and Protestant delegations sought to find points of agreement in hopes of ending the ever-widening division between the churches. Although the delegates compromised on the issue of justification, the Catholic and Protestant parties could not agree on papal authority or the sacraments. The COUNCIL OF TRENT, which met in three sessions from 1545 to 1563, showed less interest in the fading hope that the Christian churches could reunite. Instead, it focused on reforming and revitalizing the Catholic Church. It strengthened the powers of bishops, required the building of seminaries to train new priests, and forbade the accu-mulation of benefices. On doctrinal matters, the council rejected the Protestant doctrine of justification by faith, reaffirmed traditional Catholic beliefs and practices related to the saints and the sacraments, and strengthened papal authority.

In the decades after the Council of Trent, reforms ended or minimized some of the practices that Reformation thinkers had criticized. Church administration became more efficient, and the church focused more on pastoral care than it had in the past. In this effort the church sometimes demonstrated a "siege mentality" that made it less open to new ideas, as by the publication of the *Index of Forbidden Books* in 1559, which sought primarily to keep Catholics from reading Protestant works. The Counterreformation affected the Americas as well, where both new and restruc-tured religious orders (see FRANCISCANS and DOMINICANS) sent missionaries to convert the native peoples.

Further reading: John Bossy, *Christianity in the West, 1400–1700* (Oxford, U.K.: Oxford University Press, 1985); John M. Headley and John B. Tomaro, eds., *San Carlo Bor-romeo: Catholic Reform and Ecclesiastical Politics in the Second Half of the Sixteenth Century* (Washington: Folger Books, 1988); John C. Olin, *Catholic Reform: From Cardi-nal Ximenes to the Council of Trent, 1495–1563* (New York: Fordham University Press, 1990); Hans J. Hillerbrand, eds. *The Oxford Encyclopedia of the Reformation*, vol. 4 (New York: Oxford University Press, 1996) Steven Ozment, *The Age of Reform, 1250–1550* (New Haven, Conn.: Yale Uni-versity Press, 1980).

— Martha K. Robinson

Cozumel

Located 15 miles off the coast of the YUCATÁN PENINSULA, during the 16th century Spanish explorers relied on the island of Cozumel as an important and well-known stop-ping point during expeditions from CUBA to the Mexican mainland.

At its broadest point, Cozumel is 30 miles by 12 miles long. Modern estimates place the island's indigenous pop-ulation between 2,000 and 3,000 persons at the time of first contact with Europeans. The name *Cozumel* is derived from the Mayan expression for a shallow island, *Ah-Cuza-mil-Pet en.*

In May 1518, one week after departing from Cuba, JUAN DE GRIJALVA and his men, caught by a current, reached Cozumel during the second expedition by the Spanish to explore the Mexican coastline. Because they reached the island on the third of May, Grijalva named the island Santa Cruz in recognition of the holy day. Upon sight of the Spaniards, the Mayan-speaking natives ran away from their villages and took shelter in the nearby woods.

Grijalva saw stone houses, elaborate pyramids, and tow-ers constructed by the natives. Men from Grijavlva's expedi-tion wrote of impressive paved streets, a guttering system, strange crosses, and a white pyramid with a circumference in excess of 140 square feet. Religious rituals performed by the

Indians, including human sacrifices and other offerings presented to the goddess of the rainbow, Ix Chel, also astounded the Spanish. While at Cozumel Grijavlva met and exchanged gifts with the chief and learned that news of Spanish activities in the Caribbean had preceded their arrival on the island. There were supposedly two white men living on the island, but Grijalva failed to encounter either of them.

Although Grijavlva departed Cozumel not long after his arrival, the next Spanish expedition, led by HERNÁN CORTÉS in 1519, remained on the island considerably longer. As bad weather created difficulty for him, Cortés used the favorable harbor of Cozumel as a meeting point for his ships. Like Grijalva before him, Cortés, too, encountered things he considered quite surprising, including foods of unanticipated complexity, cotton hammocks, and beautiful picture books.

Via a translator, Cortés immediately began to spread the word of Christianity to the island's Indians, condemning indigenous ceremonies, idols, and human sacrifices. Although awed with the sophistication of Cozumel society, Cortés ordered his men to remove native idols from the temples and to replace them with Christian ornaments, including an altar with the Virgin Mary. The Indians were astonished by his actions but did not stop him. Cortés and his men remained on the island long enough to repair their vessels and to be joined by a white man, GERÓNIMO DE AGUILAR, who had been shipwrecked in Yucatán.

After Cortés's departure the Spanish continued to use Cozumel as a natural stopping point during their explorations and settlement of NEW SPAIN. Beginning with Cortés's efforts, the Spanish presence in Cozumel suggested the permanent influence of Spain among the Mexica people, particularly in the spread of Spanish law and religious practices. Although it later changed the location to TLAXCALA, in 1519 the Crown created a bishopric for Cozumel. Also, during the early 1520s the natives of Cozumel, like other indigenous peoples, experienced the debilitating effects of new DISEASE when Spaniards unwittingly introduced SMALLPOX to the island.

Further reading: Anthony Pagden, ed., *Hernan Cortés: Letters from Mexico* (New Haven, Conn., and London: Yale University Press, 1986); Hugh Thomas, *Conquest: Montezuma, Cortés, and the Fall of Old Mexico* (New York: Simon & Schuster, 1993); J. Eric S. Thompson, *Maya History and Religion,* The Civilization of the American Indian Series, vol. 99 (Norman: University of Oklahoma Press, 1970).

— Kimberly Sambol-Tosco

Cuauhtémoc (ca. 1496–1525)

One of the many nobles who opposed welcoming Spanish CONQUISTADORES, Cuauhtémoc was the AZTECS' last elected great speaker and eventually was executed by HERNÁN CORTÉS in 1525.

Born in TENOCHTITLÁN around 1496, Cuauhtémoc was raised by his mother after his father, Ahuízotl, died in 1502. At age 15 he entered the *calmecac,* the institution of higher education where the sons of warriors and priests learned the secrets of religion and astronomy and were trained to be fierce warriors. By dint of participation in numerous battles, he advanced to the rank of *tlacatecuhtli,* or supreme general, and it was during this time that he must have accompanied the Aztec army in its incursions to the south, especially in the FLOWERY WARS with TLAXCALA.

When Hernán Cortés landed at VERACRUZ in 1519, Cuauhtémoc, along with CUITLÁHUAC, was one of the only leaders to argue against the invaders' supposed divinity. (MOCTEZUMA II's advisers had identified Cortés as the incarnation of QUETZALCOATL.)

In late May 1520, when the residents of Tenochtitlán rose up against the resident Spaniards, provoked by an attack led by PEDRO DE ALVARADO on their nobles, Cuauhtémoc marched out at the head of an army to attack Cortés's troops, which were then just returning to the Aztec capital after a trip to the coast to quell the threat posed by PÁNFILO DE NARVÁEZ. When Moctezuma, at Cortés's request, ordered the indigenous forces to stand down, Cuauhtémoc proclaimed himself and his followers to be in rebellion against a king whom many felt had betrayed them.

The Spanish fled the city in the face of organized armed resistance and rebellion against their royal ally, and many died in the Noche Triste (the Sad Night; June 30, 1520), seeking refuge in the kingdom of Tlaxcala. Moctezuma died in or shortly after the attack, and the population elected Cuitláhuac as their new great speaker, but he also died in late November of that same year, a victim of SMALLPOX. Cuauhtémoc then took over the government of the region and was speaker when Cortés began his siege of Tenochtitlán in May 1521. In August he was captured and brought to Cortés, whose prisoner he remained until 1525, when Cortés, having heard rumors of sedition, ordered him executed.

Further reading: Michael Coe, *Mexico: From the Olmecs to the Aztecs,* 4th ed. (London: Thames & Hudson, 1994); Nigel Davies, *Aztecs: A History* (Norman: University of Oklahoma Press, 1980).

— Marie Kelleher

Cuba

The largest island in the West Indies, Cuba supported one of the largest indigenous populations in the region until it came under the control during the 16th century of the Spanish, who used the island to assist their forays into MEXICO and North America and to supply ocean-going Spanish ships.

At the time of contact with Europeans, two distinct indigenous groups occupied Cuba, the Guanahatabey and the TAINO. The western end of Cuba was occupied by the Guanahatabey. Speaking a different language from the Taino, who inhabited the other three-fourths of Cuba, the ancestors of the Guanahatabey traveled to the island from the YUCATÁN PENINSULA following a countercurrent that flows eastward from the Yucatán along the southern side of the Greater Antilles. These people did not produce pottery and made tools from stone, bone, and shell. The Guanahatabey subsisted on shellfish, fish, game, and wild vegetables and fruits. They lived in nomadic, small bands that migrated from the interior to the coast and back depending upon the season. They probably inhabited most of Cuba before the arrival of the Taino, but over time the Guanahatabey retreated to the western corner of Cuba, and they were living there by the time CHRISTOPHER COLUMBUS arrived in the West Indies in 1492. It is possible that the Guanahatabey had limited contact with the peoples who inhabited the southern tip of FLORIDA, who shared some similar material culture traits.

The Taino arrived in Cuba from HISPANIOLA. The Cuban Taino society developed along similar lines with other Taino societies in the Greater Antilles. They organized their societies into chiefdoms focused primarily on trade and lived in sedentary villages. They cultivated plants and went to sea for fish, shellfish, turtles, and birds. They harvested peanuts, sweet potatoes, manioc, a wide range of root crops, TOBACCO, and cotton. They used the slash and burn technique of cultivation and created artificial ponds to husband fish and turtles. They had a more extensive material culture than did the Guanahatabey, wearing GOLD and copper ornaments, sleeping in cotton hammocks, and crafting ceramics.

Although Columbus encountered Cuba on his first voyage in 1492, he did not pay much attention to it. In 1494, when he reached Cuba on his second voyage, he believed that it was part of the Asian continent. The governor of Hispaniola, Diego Columbus, sent DIEGO DE VELÁZQUEZ to conquer Cuba in 1510. After landing on the southern coast near Guantánamo, Velázquez engaged the Taino of the region and burned their leader at the stake. Velázquez established a *CABILDO* (town council) for the natives in Baracoa. Eventually, Velázquez's lieutenant, PÁNFILO DE NARVÁEZ, finished the conquest of the island by 1512. In 1513 Velázquez implemented the *ENCOMIENDA* system, in which the indigenous inhabitants of the island performed all the labor required by the Spanish under cruel and inhumane conditions. The earliest Spanish residents became quite wealthy exploiting the natives in the *encomiendas*. Primarily, this was achieved through gold mining and agriculture. By the middle of the 16th century, much of the indigenous population of Cuba had disap-

peared because of overwork and DISEASES introduced by the Spanish. Eventually, thanks to the work of BARTOLOMÉ DE LAS CASAS, the Spanish implemented new laws that made natives free subjects of the Crown.

After the conquest of Mexico and the discovery of great wealth there, Cuba began to lose its Spanish population and its importance in the Spanish colonial system. The process increased as the gold mines drained the ore deposits on the island. After the collapse of the mining industry and the establishment of the annual fleet system in 1561, the primary purpose for Cuba became the housing of crews and passengers as well as the repair, maintenance, and supply of the Spanish gold and colonial supply fleets. Beginning in 1553 Havana became the capital of Cuba, and the Spanish fortified this port, developing it into the gathering and arrival point for the annual fleets that crossed the Atlantic Ocean.

In the second half of the 16th century, the Spanish began importing African slaves to Cuba (see SLAVE TRADE). Used in a wide variety of activities, most slaves worked on HACIENDAS. Three types of haciendas developed on the island during this period. The first raised livestock—cows, horses, mules, and oxen; the second kind tended swine; the third type had residents who grew crops to support Cuba's population. Industry associated with harboring the annual fleets and the products of the haciendas dominated Cuba's economy until the Spanish developed SUGAR plantations in the 18th century.

Further reading: Mary W. Helms, "The Indians of the Caribbean and Circum-Caribbean at the End of the Fifteenth Century," in *Cambridge History of Latin America*, vol. 1, ed. Leslie Bethell (Cambridge: Cambridge University Press, 1984), 37–57; Irving Rouse, *The Tainos: Rise and Decline of the People Who Greeted Columbus* (New Haven, Conn.: Yale University Press, 1992); ———, *Migrations in Prehistory: Inferring Population Movement from Cultural Remains* (New Haven, Conn.: Yale University Press, 1986), esp. 106–156; Carl O. Sauer, *The Early Spanish Main* (Berkeley: University of California Press, 1966); David Watts, *The West Indies: Patterns of Development, Culture and Environmental Change Since 1492* (Cambridge, U.K.: Cambridge University Press, 1987).

— Dixie Ray Haggard

Cuitláhuac (d. 1520)

A member of the Tenocha royal line who became the 10th great speaker of the AZTECS upon the death of MOCTEZUMA II, Cuitláhuac led the expulsion of the Spanish invaders from TENOCHTITLÁN only to die 80 days after his ascension, a victim of the SMALLPOX epidemic that ravaged the city.

Cuitláhuac, brother of Moctezuma II, began his political career as lord of Ixtapalapa. Before the arrival of the Spanish, his best-known martial accomplishment was his leadership of the expedition to subjugate the Mixtecs in 1506. He, like his contemporary XICOTÉNCATL THE YOUNGER, opposed admitting the Spaniards into the heart of the empire, a stance for which the invaders imprisoned him along with several other nobles of the region. He was liberated in June 1520 in the revolt that followed the massacre at the Great Temple organized by PEDRO DE ALVARADO, whereupon a council of nobles and military leaders elected him great speaker, replacing the captive Moctezuma, who died in the rioting shortly thereafter. Cuitláhuac moved to organize the residents of Tenochtitlán for war, ordering ambassadors to solicit aid from potential allies, but could bring few of his plans to fruition, as his reign ended abruptly, only 80 days after it began, when he succumbed to smallpox on November 25, 1520. The works for the defense of the city that he initiated were continued by CUAUHTÉMOC.

Further reading: Michael Coe, *Mexico: From the Olmecs to the Aztecs,* 4th ed. (London: Thames & Hudson, 1994); Nigel Davies, *Aztecs: A History* (Norman: University of Oklahoma Press, 1980).

— Marie Kelleher

Cuzco

Laid out in the shape of a puma, Cuzco served as the religious and political capital of the INCA Empire from its founding by Manco Capac in approximately 1200 until the conquest of the city by FRANCISCO PIZARRO in 1543.

According to oral tradition, Manco Capac, the first Incan emperor, founded the city as the capital to his empire in approximately A.D. 1200. From Cuzco, beginning with the emperor Pachacuti, the Inca expanded their empire and influence primarily to the north and south along the ANDES MOUNTAINS, but they also expanded west to the Pacific Coast and to the east down into the tropical rain forest of the Amazon River basin. Cuzco's importance lay in its strategic location along the junction of major trading routes between the north and south as well as the highlands and lowlands to the west and east. Pachacuti rebuilt Cuzco and canalized the Tullumayo and Huatanay Rivers in stone beds to prevent flooding of the city.

Throughout the existence of the Inca Empire, rulers added to the size and prestige of Cuzco. Cuzco eventually contained more than 4,000 residences, granaries, storage sheds, religious temples, and imperial structures. Before the arrival of the Spanish, activity in Cuzco centered on the Palace of the Sun, a temple to the primary Incan deity, and the palaces of the former and current Inca. The Palace of the Sun occupied the central location within Cuzco, and outside the city the fortress Sacsahuaman overlooked the city. Built of stones that weighed up to 300 tons, Sacsahuaman along with the Palace of the Sun and the residences of the Inca testified to the high level of craftsmanship developed during the reign of the Incan emperors.

Francisco Pizarro arrived in Cuzco in 1533, and by 1543 the Spanish controlled Cuzco and the surrounding territory. The Spanish then proceeded to tear down the Incan buildings and replace them with new Spanish structures often built from the same stones used in the Incan structures. The Spanish used indigenous labor to rebuild the city and develop the city's and region's economy along Spanish lines. The Plaza de Armas eventually became the center of the city, and over time the Spanish built cathedrals and churches on Incan holy sites in an attempt to obliterate the old religion. Despite their intentions, many Incans tended to blend Catholicism with their traditional religion in a syncretic fashion similar to that of other natives throughout the Spanish American Empire.

Further reading: Burr Cartwright Brundage, *Lords of Cuzco* (Norman: University of Oklahoma Press, 1967); John Hemming, *The Conquest of the Incas* (London: Macmillan, 1970); John H. Rowe, *An Introduction to the Archaeology of Cuzco* (Cambridge, Mass.: Peabody Museum of Archaeology and Ethnology, 1944); John C. Super, "Cuzco," in *Encyclopedia of Latin American History and Culture,* vol. 2, Barbara A. Tenenbaum, ed. (New York: Scribner's, 1996), 348–350.

— Dixie Ray Haggard

D

Dagomba

Today an ethnic group in northeastern GHANA and Togo, the Dagomba established a kingdom in the 14th century.

Observers have explained the origins of the Dagomba, both as an ethnic group and as a people, in several ways. One tradition tells of the noble warrior Nyagse, who made the Dagomba into a nation through the conquest of villages and the massacre of local priests. Nyagse then created a hierarchical state in which the sons of the *ya-na*, or top chief, acceded to power. Another tradition connects the Dagomba to the MOSSI kingdoms, situating it as a "junior brother" in the Mossi hierarchy. According to this tradition, Sitobu, a second son of Na Gbewa, the founder of the Mossi people, left his father's kingdom to found his own. He slaughtered the local priests in his effort to gain political domination of the area. Succession to the throne in this tradition was determined by direct lineage to previous rulers, whose authority came from three "gate skins." Limiting the lines of succession in this way was intended to diminish the internal power struggles plaguing the kingdom by the end of the 17th century.

According to anthropological evidence, the Dagomba amalgamated into a distinct ethnic group around the 14th century, when migrant horsemen conquered the indigenous Gur speakers in the region who cultivated grains, raised cattle, and worked with iron. The spiritual leaders of these agriculturalists were the *tindamba* ("earth priests"). Although the conquerors assimilated linguistically, they imposed their social structure and cultural mores onto the indigenous peoples. The kingdom, known as Dagbon, was hierarchical, ruled by the top chief, or *ya-na*, but administered by the *tindamba*, who allocated land, appointed chiefs, and were the spiritual leaders.

The Dagomba kingdom prospered due to its policy of taxing the trade goods that passed through its territory. The HAUSA kingdom traded cola nuts, GOLD, slaves (see SLAVERY), salt, and cloth with the Dagbon and were instrumental in introducing ISLAM to the Dagomba kingdom.

Although Islam took a firm hold on the nobles of the kingdom, inspiring one king, Na Luro (d. 1660), to invite the Muslim scholar Shaykh Sulayman to establish a school in the kingdom, the indigenous religion endured among the commoners. The GONJA kingdom expelled the Dagomba from its western territories in the 16th century, forcing the Dagomba eastward. The Dagomba conquered the Konkomba people in the east, founded a new capital for their kingdom at Yendi, and ruled over the Konkomba as overlords.

Further reading: Ivor Wilks, "The Mossi and the Akan States, 1400–1800," in *History of West Africa*, vol. 1, 3rd ed., eds. J. F. Ade Ajiya and Michael Crowder (London: Longman, 1985), 465–502; David P. Johnson, Jr., "Dagomba," in *Africana: The Encyclopedia of the African and African American Experience*, eds. Kwame Anthony Appiah and Henry Louis Gates, Jr. (New York: Basic *Civitas* Books, 1999), 550.

— Lisa M. Brady

Dahomey

Located in present-day southern Benin, the early kingdom of Dahomey was a powerful partner in the SLAVE TRADE for much of its history, with the height of its power coinciding with the apex of the transatlantic slave trade.

Originally subjects of the Adja kingdom, which developed in response to European trading activity on the coast and to pressures from the YORUBA state of OYO to the north, the FON established their own kingdom at Allada early in the 17th century under the leadership of Agasu (see FON for the legend of Agasu). Succession disputes ensued after Agasu's death, forcing his son Dogbari to flee to the city of Abomey in 1620, which became the capital of the new kingdom of Dahomey. By midcentury Dahomey was a powerful kingdom controlled by a strong monarch compelled by law to increase the kingdom's territory and supported by a large, sophisticated army, which included 2,000 female warriors (known as Amazons). Much of the kingdom's power rested on its control of the region's slave trade from the main port city of Whydah, from which more than 2 million slaves were shipped to the Americas. Dahomey's economy went into decline after the closing of the slave trade in 1804 and increasingly relied on the less lucrative trade in palm oil.

Further reading: "Dahomey, Early Kingdom of," in *Africana: The Encyclopedia of the African and African American Experience*, eds. Kwame Anthony Appiah and Henry Louis Gates, Jr. (New York: Basic *Civitas* Books, 1999), 550–551; "Dahomey Kingdom, rulers of," in *Dictionary of African Historical Biography*, eds. Mark R. Lipschutz and R. Kent Rasmussen, 2nd ed. (Berkeley: University of California Press, 1986), 52.

— Lisa M. Brady

Darfur

The kingdom of Darfur, located on the dry grasslands of the SUDAN approximately midway between the Middle Nile and the NIGER RIVER, played an important role in the transcontinental trade routes that carried various commodities such as GOLD, salt, ivory, and slaves from the Atlantic to the Indian Oceans throughout the 16th century.

The name means "house of the Fur" in Arabic and refers to the agricultural Fur peoples ruled by the Tunjur, who had built a non-Muslim kingdom perhaps as early as the fourth century. According to traditional lore, the Tunjur replaced the earlier Daju kingdom. Archaeological excavation of the ruins in the ancient cities in the Darfur region suggests that the earliest kingdoms were Christian, probably descended from the exiled Meroe kingdoms of the Middle Nile. This is significant in several ways: Not only does it suggest that Christianity spread farther into the African continent from the east than was previously believed, but also that ISLAM came to dominate the region much later than had been assumed. Indeed, the Muslim faith most likely came to Darfur in the 14th or 15th century, gaining a certain foothold only with the conquering Kanem-Bornu king Mai Idris Alooma (r. 1571–1603) as late as the 17th century.

After the death of Mai ("king") Idris, Sulayman established the Keira dynasty of the independent Fur kingdom of Darfur. The Keira Sultanate reigned until 1916, when the Darfur kingdom became part of the British Empire.

Further reading: Robert Fay, "Darfur," in *Africana: The Encyclopedia of the African and African American Experience*, eds. Kwame Anthony Appiah and Henry Louis Gates, Jr. (New York: Basic *Civitas* Books, 1999), 562–563; "Kingdoms of the Old Sudan," in Basil Davidson, *The Lost Cities of Africa* (Boston: Little, Brown, 1987), esp. 51–124;

"Kanem-Bornu and the Hausa States," *West Africa before the Colonial Era: A History to 1850*, Basil Davidson (London: Longman, 1998), esp. 63–90.

— Lisa M. Brady

da Vinci, Leonardo   See Leonardo da Vinci

DeBry, Theodor (1528–1598)

A Flemish engraver who understood the power of the PRINTING PRESS to disseminate information widely, Theodor DeBry produced for European audiences the most accurate renderings of the Western Hemisphere and its peoples during the late 16th century.

DeBry was born in Liege in 1528, when that city was under the control of Spanish Catholics, an unfortunate circumstance for Protestants (including his family), who often found they could not live as they had hoped. Like many other early modern Europeans, such as the Hungarian scholar STEPHEN PARMENIUS, DeBry believed that he had to leave his homeland in order to pursue his career as a goldsmith and engraver. In 1570 he fled Strasbourg and traveled westward, eventually making his way to LONDON. There he took whatever work he could find, including the preparation of a series of engravings based on drawings of Sir Philip Sidney's funeral procession. While in the city DeBry met the English promoter of colonization RICHARD HAKLUYT THE YOUNGER. They soon began to work together to illustrate travelers' accounts of their experiences across the Atlantic.

DeBry always had an interest in engraving American scenes. Unable to do a series of illustrations based on JACQUES LE MOYNE's drawings and paintings relating to FLORIDA, the Flemish engraver, working with Hakluyt, began to transform the images he received from travelers such as JOHN WHITE, the English governor of the failed settlement at ROANOKE. Using White's illustrations, originally done in watercolor, DeBry prepared the copper-plate engravings that created the illustrations for THOMAS HARRIOT's *Briefe and True Report of the New Found Land of Virginia*, which appeared in four languages (Latin, English, French, and German) in 1590. After Le Moyne's death DeBry began to work on the Florida illustrations, but Hakluyt convinced him to publish the Roanoke materials first. Upon completing the pictures for Harriot's book, DeBry then set out to do more than engrave Le Moyne's images. He took it upon himself to engrave a massive series of scenes that was published over the course of the 1590s in various languages. These volumes are known now as the *Grands Voyages*, which depicted American peoples and places, and the *Petits Voyages*, which portrayed sights from Africa and the East Indies.

An engraving by Theodor DeBry after a watercolor by Jacques Le Moyne   *(Hulton/Getty)*

By the time of his death in 1598, DeBry had managed to create a series of precise images of the world beyond Europe's borders. Those pictures proved to have lasting worth and remain the most striking set of visual evidence that survives from what historians often call the "age of discovery."

Further reading: Michael Alexander, ed., *Discovering the New World Based on the Works of Theodore De Bry* (New York: Harper & Row, 1976); Bernadette Bucher, *Icon and Conquest: A Structural Analysis of the Illustrations of deBry's Great Voyages*, trans. Basia Miller Gulati (Chicago: University of Chicago Press, 1981).

De La Warr, Lord (1577–1618)

Thomas West, 12th baron De La Warr, was an important early figure in the development of English colonial America, particularly in Jamestown, Virginia, following its early difficulties.

De La Warr attended the University of Oxford but never received a degree. He enjoyed travel and adventure, participating in both as a private citizen and an army officer. His military career was notable and earned him a knighthood in 1599. His superior officer and mentor was the earl of Essex, one of Queen ELIZABETH I's favorites and a man who was executed for a plot against the government. De La Warr became implicated in the rebellion because of his close association to the leader of the plot. Before he died Essex wrote to the queen and absolved De La Warr of complicity. She must have listened, because after attaining peerage at his father's death De La Warr became a member of Elizabeth's PRIVY COUNCIL.

De La Warr became a member of the Council of Virginia in 1609 as the Virginia Company of London reorganized. The company recognized that Jamestown colony was failing, and the reorganization sought to change its course.

In 1610 De La Warr was appointed lord governor and captain general of the Virginia colony. His appointment was for life, and he joined the struggling settlement in the early summer. He had learned strict discipline in the army, and once he arrived in Jamestown he implemented rigorous new demands upon the colony's residents. He appointed a council from among Jamestown's prominent residents and organized the colony's work. Many of Jamestown's early settlers had died of starvation during the first few winters, so some of De La Warr's work units were sent into the wilderness to look for food. Among his legal and social reforms was the death penalty, instituted for a variety of offenses, including laziness. In addition, because DISEASE had contributed to Jamestown's early problems, colonists were whipped if they relieved themselves within a quarter mile of the colony's fort. The result was that formerly indolent Virginians began working in fort and field, and the colony's prospects improved. While some saw his measures as draconian, they worked. The Virginia colony stabilized.

Returning to England in 1611, De La Warr reported that the colony could succeed. He also recommended choosing future colonists with care to avoid the perils of lethargy and fecklessness exhibited by many of the first settlers. De La Warr spent seven years in England while retaining his colonial titles and responsibilities. Jamestown prospered during this period, although TOBACCO, rather than Lord De La Warr, can be credited for the success.

In early 1618 De La Warr set sail for Virginia once again, but he never arrived. He died at sea; the cause, date, and place are unknown. While De La Warr's involvement with the Virginia colony was brief and interrupted by a long visit to England, historians credit him with saving Jamestown, thus making it the first permanent English settlement in North America. His accomplishments were not forgotten by succeeding generations of colonists. The Delaware River, Delaware Bay, the colony and state of Delaware, as well as the Delaware Indian Nation all commemorate Lord De La Warr's contributions to England's first empire.

Further reading: Warren M. Billings, John E. Selby, and Thad W. Tate, *Colonial Virginia: A History* (White Plains, N.Y.: KTO Press, 1986); Richard L. Morton, *Colonial Virginia, Vol. 1: The Tidewater Period, 1607–1710* (Chapel Hill: University of North Carolina Press, 1960); John A. Munroe, *Colonial Delaware: A History* (White Plains, N.Y.: KTO Press, 1978); "De La Warr, Lord," in *Dictionary of National Biography*.

— David P. Dewar

Dengel, Lebna (Dauti [David] II) (ca. 1496–1540)

Emperor of the Christian kingdom of Abyssinia (see ETHIOPIA) from 1508 to 1540, Lebna Dengel successfully defended his kingdom from Muslim invaders in 1516 but could not repel the invaders in 1527.

Born in 1496, Lebna Dengel acceded to the Abyssinian throne upon the death of his father, Naod, in 1508. Because Dengel was only 12 years old at the time, his mother, Helena, served as regent. Muslim unrest and invasion characterized the early years of Dengel's rule, and as regent Helena requested the help of the Portuguese to defend the ancient kingdom from the Muslims. Dengel came into power in his own right before the Portuguese delegation arrived and suppressed a Muslim rebellion by the Adal sultanate at Zelia, a city on the Red Sea, in 1516. A Portuguese embassy arrived in Abyssinia in 1520 but left in 1527 after receiving a cool reception by Dengel. That same year Muslims under Ahmad Ibn Ibrahim assaulted Dengel's kingdom. The Adalite Muslims succeeded this time, destroyed monasteries for several years, and forced the largely Christian population in Abyssinia to convert to ISLAM. Dengel once again turned to Portugal for assistance, suggesting in 1535 that the Ethiopian Church be attached to the Roman See. Unsuccessful in ousting the Muslim invaders, Dengel fled to a monastery in Debra Damo (Ethiopia), where he died on September 2, 1540, before the Portuguese returned.

Further reading: "Lebna Dengel," in *Africana: The Encyclopedia of the African and African American Experience* eds. Kwame Anthony Appiah and Henry Louis Gates, Jr. (New York: Basic *Civitas* Books, 1999), 1142; "Lebna Dengel," in *Dictionary of African Historical Biography*, 2nd ed., eds. Mark R. Lipschutz and R. Kent Rasmussen (Berkeley: University of California Press, 1986), 119–120.

— Lisa M. Brady

Dias, Bartholomeu (1450?–1500)

A Portuguese navigator of the 15th century, Dias discovered the Cape of Good Hope on the southern tip of Africa.

Little is known of Dias's early life, although several Portuguese historians claim he was a relative or descendent of Joao Dias, who sailed around Cape Bojador in 1434, and of Diniz Dias. In 1481 Dias gained valuable seafaring knowledge when he accompanied Diogo d'Azambuja on an expedition to the GOLD COAST. In addition to this early expedition, Dias served as a cavalier of the royal court, superintendent of the royal warehouses, and as sailing master of the man-of-war *San Christovao* before October 10, 1486, when King JOHN (JOÃO) II commissioned him to lead an expedition aimed at sailing around the southern tip of the African continent in search of the Christian African king known as PRESTER JOHN.

Following 10 months of preparation, Dias departed from LISBON in late July or early August 1487. He was equipped with two armed CARAVELs, each weighing 50 tons, and one supply ship, commanded by his brother Pero. After sailing first to the mouth of the Congo, Dias followed the African coast before entering Walfisch Bay, where he probably erected stone columns near the present-day Angra Pequena. Stopping for a few days to take in water and supplies, he met a number of native Africans, who were intermittently hostile and friendly. Dias's crew included a few Africans whom the Portuguese had hoped would serve as interpreters, but the natives they encountered spoke different languages.

At approximately 29 degrees south latitude a violent storm lasting 13 days drove Dias and his crew far beyond the cape to the south. Vision impaired, Dias did not sight the cape when his ship rounded it. When calm weather resumed, he sailed eastward. Failing to immediately sight land, he turned in a northerly direction, landing in Mossel Bay. Following the coastline, Dias reached Algoa Bay, the northern-most point of the expedition. On the return voyage Dias sighted the cape, naming it Cabo Tormentoso ("Cape of Storms"), although the name was later changed to the Cape of Good Hope.

Dias returned to Lisbon 16 months after setting sail. There is no extant logbook, chronicle, or diary of his voyage, although João de Barros recorded the event some 60 years later. In addition, there is little extant evidence relating to the reception Dias received upon his return, although it appears as though John I gave him only lukewarm congratulations. The Portuguese monarch failed to follow up promptly on Dias's expedition. Only nine years later did he commission a similar voyage, this time with VASCO DA GAMA in charge and Dias along in a subordinate

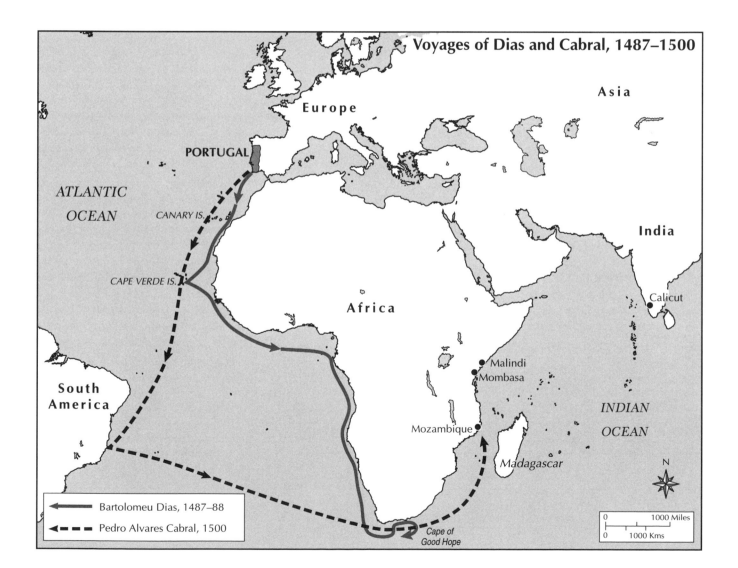

position. In 1500 Dias was involved in yet another expedition, this one led by Pedro Álvares Cabral, but Dias perished when his ship wrecked near the Cape of Good Hope, the landmark he had discovered 13 years earlier.

Further reading: Eric Axelson, *South-East Africa, 1488–1699* (Cape Town: 1973); Bailey W. Diffie and George D. Winius, *Foundations of the Portuguese Empire, 1415–1580* (Minneapolis: University of Minnesota Press, 1977); Edgar Prestage, *The Portuguese Pioneers* (London: A&C Black, 1933); E. G. Ravenstein, "The Voyages of Diego Cao and Bartholomew Dias," *The Geographical Journal* XVI (1900), 625–655.

— Matthew Lindaman

Díaz del Castillo, Bernal (1492–1584)

A foot soldier, Díaz accompanied HERNAN CORTÉS on his conquest of MEXICO and later recorded the events in the novel-like *True History of the Conquest of Mexico.*

Bernal Díaz del Castillo was born in the noble town of Medina del Campo in 1492. By the time Bernal reached his early 20s, he followed the example of many Spanish youths, leaving in 1514 for the NEW WORLD in search of fame and wealth. Altogether, Díaz participated in three exploratory ventures to Mexico, all launched from Spanish strongholds in CUBA. The third venture, piqued by the knowledge and allure of Mexican GOLD, was launched in 1521. Directed by Hernan Cortés, it possessed just more than 500 soldiers. Marching inland, the expedition met many CACIQUES and chieftains coming in advance of MOCTEZUMA II. Vacillating between diplomacy and a declaration of war, the Aztec sovereign kept to the former until the Spaniards made him a prisoner in his own palace. Collecting an immense treasure, Cortés and his party proceeded with an 85-day siege of the Aztec capital.

Following the conquest of the AZTECS, the Spaniards fanned out across Mexico looking for Moctezuma's mines. Seeking rewards of his own, Díaz returned briefly to Spain in 1539, making his case for a share of the riches. For his efforts he was granted a claim in Guatemala, where he settled permanently, serving as a magistrate of his community. During the 1560s the aging ex-soldier of Cortés assembled a manuscript that chronicled the conquest of Mexico. It is generally assumed that he undertook the project to correct a work entitled *The History of the Conquest of Mexico* published in 1552 by a former chaplain of Cortés's named Francisco López de Gómara. Never having set foot in the New World, the chaplain's account exalted the figure of Cortés at the expense of his soldiers. Díaz sought balance in his novel-like account, describing the merits of all participants in the venture, including the native Aztecs.

From his chronicle readers learned of explorations along the coast, the inland march, the luxury of Moctezuma's palace, the capture of the monarch, the siege and destruction of the Aztec capital, and the division of the spoils. The chronicle contains numerous colorful anecdotes to go along with invented speeches and dialogues. At the same time, it represents history as told by a common foot-soldier, a private who slogged through mud, endured hunger, and narrowly escaped with his life on numerous occasions—all taking place in a foreign and uncharted land. Díaz's writing style was no doubt influenced by the "romances of chivalry" that, beginning around 1500, influenced and captivated readers in all the literate classes throughout the 16th century. Highlighting the concept of life in which virtue, strength, and passion were all transcendent, this genre brought to readers accounts of fantastic places, riches, MONSTERS, and wonders. In the process, authors like Díaz promulgated myths including EL DORADO, Fountains of Youth, Amazons, the Seven Enchanted Cities, and other will-o'-the-wisps.

Further reading: Bernal Díaz del Castillo, *The Conquest of New Spain,* trans. J. M. Cohen (London: Folio Society, 1963); Bernal Díaz del Castillo, *The Discovery and Conquest of Mexico, 1517–1521,* ed. Genaro Garcia, trans. A. P. Maudslay (New York: Farrar, Strauss, Cudahy, 1958).

— Matthew Lindaman

disease

The epoch that historians have called the Age of Discovery—from roughly the time that CHRISTOPHER COLUMBUS first sailed across the Atlantic to the founding of the English colony of Jamestown in 1607—witnessed a wide range of epidemic and infectious diseases that devastated natives and newcomers across the Atlantic basin.

Before 1492 the peoples on either side of the Atlantic world had no contact with one another, at least not since the time when the land bridge across the Bering Strait had provided a route for Old World peoples to travel to the NEW WORLD. Still, diseases existed. Inhabitants of the Eurasian landmass had to deal with periodic epidemics of the PLAGUE, a disease that ravaged populations wherever it appeared. Plague could be spread by various vectors, although bubonic plague tended to spread from fleas to rats to humans. The scale of epidemics could be massive. The so-called Black Death of the 14th century broke out in Italy in 1347. By the time it ran its course, as much as one-third of the population of Europe had succumbed, and in some areas, notably in northern climates where livestock perished from neglect (due to the decline in the farming population), the death rate could be much higher because famine at sometimes followed the pestilence. Records from antiquity report epidemics of plague, although it is impossible to know for certain that each of these epidemics was caused by the same disease.

Plague killed men, women, and children, but other Old World diseases tended to be less virulent. The most important of these other illnesses was SMALLPOX, a disease that always existed somewhere in Europe, sustained in large population centers by traveling from one individual or group to the next. Such endemic diseases tended to afflict children, most of whom, so records suggest, survived because their immune systems were able to respond to the threat. Those who survived developed immunities to the disease, so that only rarely would an individual become sickened by the same virus twice. While smallpox was the most serious of these kinds of diseases, Old World peoples also coped with regular visits from chicken pox, measles, and influenza, among other ailments. An individual might bear scars from some diseases for the rest of his or her life—smallpox left particularly disfiguring marks—but the disease itself tended to leave few permanent complications.

Some Old World diseases had particular environmental causes. The most significant of these illnesses during the 16th century were malaria and yellow fever, both spread by mosquitoes. In parts of Africa and Sicily where these insects and their diseases were common, groups of people had developed genetic immunity that helped them withstand the dangers these afflictions could cause. Poor water, particularly common in European cities, could also be ideal breeding grounds for various kinds of bacteria that had the potential to assault the human body. Early modern Europeans complained about the "agues" and fevers that such infections caused, as well as the bloody stools that an infection could cause if the microorganism invaded the wall of the bowel. Dietary deficiencies also caused problems. The lack of a regular supply of vitamin C, for example, led to scurvy, a disease that particularly afflicted sailors on long ocean voyages.

In the Western Hemisphere individuals suffered from diseases as well, although these diseases tended to be less devastating than those that periodically circulated in the Old World. Paleopathological analysis of the skeletal remains of peoples who lived in the Americas before 1492 reveal that individuals suffered from various dietary deficiencies. Reliance on CORN (maize), for example, might have deprived various peoples of necessary vitamins and made them potential victims of an epidemic. Lesions on skeletons also suggest that Native Americans were periodically exposed to tuberculosis and various kinds of treponematosis (the family of diseases that includes syphilis and yaws). Although venereal syphilis could have an effect on an individual's fertility, there is little evidence that any dis-

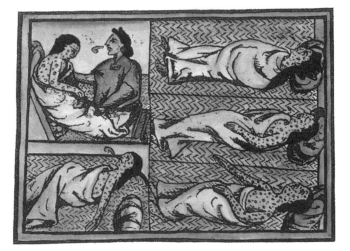

Aztec Indians, with smallpox contracted from the Spaniards, ministered to by a medicine man. Illustration from Father Bernardino de Sahagun's 16th-century treatise, *General History of the Things of New Spain*   (The Granger Collection)

ease played a significant role in limiting the size of indigenous families or communities.

However devastating disease might have been before 1492, however tragic it must have been for parents to tend to dying children or for children to grow up without parents, diseases tended to have limited effects on populations unless there was a major epidemic. However, when Europeans and Africans began to travel to the Western Hemisphere, their actions brought Old World diseases into populations that had never encountered them before. As a result, the spread of infectious disease became the most devastating aspect of what the historian Alfred Crosby has labelled the COLUMBIAN EXCHANGE.

Of these diseases, none proved so virulent or deadly as smallpox. Native communities across the Americas suffered heavily from this scourge. Unlike Europeans, who tended to survive an infection, smallpox routinely killed the indigenous peoples of the Americas, who had lacked prior exposure to the ailment and thus had never developed immunities to it. Thus, when smallpox entered a community, it afflicted adults as well as children, and many adults did not have the recuperative power that children tend to possess. Some indigenous healing rituals, such as jumping into a cold river to purge the body of an illness, exacerbated the consequences of smallpox because victims were often too weakened from the disease to swim to shore, and many apparently drowned. When smallpox hit a community, many victims eventually died because there were not enough healthy family or neighbors to provide them with care. Other diseases that tended to be endemic illnesses in Europe, such as influenza and chicken pox, quickly became raging epidemics once they were unleashed among peoples with no prior exposure (and thus no immunities). Such devastating contagions are sometimes called "virgin soil epidemics." Although scholars continue to disagree about the size of the population of the Western Hemisphere before 1492, there is a virtual consensus that native populations declined by approximately 90 percent from 1492 to 1800 and that most of the decline was due to the spread of epidemic diseases. Because Europeans often took advantage of epidemics by acquiring natives' land, survivors had diminished resources that could have helped their populations recover from smallpox or some other pathogen.

Of course, residents of the Old World who traveled to the Western Hemisphere also succumbed to diseases. In addition to dietary deficiencies caused by extended transatlantic voyages, Europeans often did not understand the new environments they inhabited. Thus, the nascent English colony of Jamestown had enormous difficulty during its formative years because its organizers believed that residents should be clustered together for defensive purposes at a site along the James River (in modern-day Virginia). They did not initially pay sufficient attention to the fact that colonists there dumped their waste (human and other) into the river, where they got their drinking water, nor did they understand that the lower elevation of the James River during the summer and autumn made it a prime breeding ground for two pathogens—*endamoeba histolytica,* which caused the "bloudie flixe" (bloody stools) associated with dysentery, and *salmonella typhosa,* which caused the "burning fevers" associated with typhoid fever. Together with other local environmental problems, such as the backwash of saltwater from the Atlantic that caused salt poisoning and its characteristic symptoms of irritability and lassitude, it is little wonder that early English colonists died at a horrific rate. Over time the increase in ships traveling back and forth between the Americas and Africa also provided ideal opportunities for disease-bearing mosquitoes to hitch a ride, thereby causing a health problem for Europeans who had arrived in the Western Hemisphere with no prior contact with malaria or yellow fever, diseases that eventually had an enormous impact on various communities (such as Philadelphia, which suffered a devastating yellow fever epidemic in 1793).

Of course, diseases do not simply appear and disappear. Some illnesses, such as smallpox, were highly contagious and tended to spread from group to group. That meant that smallpox, an unwanted visitor from the Old World, appeared in indigenous communities in the Americas long before anyone had actually seen a European man or woman. Indigenous trade centers and cities became ideal sites for the transmission of disease between native peoples. Further, since early modern peoples tended to see

illnesses as a sign of divine judgment, witnesses tried to make sense of the fact that epidemics tended to afflict natives more than newcomers. Scholars have speculated that the spread of disease made some indigenous Americans hostile to their traditional ways of thought and thus more open to the message of opportunistic missionaries, although such interpretations have not been embraced by everyone who has studied the spread of diseases in the Western Hemisphere. Whatever the number of individuals who succumbed to a particular disease, there is no question that the spread of epidemics became a defining feature of life in the Atlantic basin during the 16th century. Nor is there any debate about the fact that the indigenous peoples of the Americas tended to suffer far worse than the uninvited migrants who took up residence in the Western Hemisphere.

Further reading: Noble David Cook, *Born to Die: Disease and New World Conquest, 1492–1650* (Cambridge, U.K.: Cambridge University Press, 1998); Alfred W. Crosby, Jr., *The Columbian Exchange: Biological Consequences of 1492* (Westport, Conn: Greenwood, 1972); ———, *Ecological Imperialism: The Biological Expansion of Europe, 900–1900* (Cambridge, U.K.: Cambridge University Press, 1986); Jared Diamond, *Guns, Germs, and Steel: The Fates of Human Societies* (New York: Norton, 1998); David Herlihy, *The Black Death and the Transformation of the West,* ed. Samuel K. Cohn, Jr. (Cambridge, Mass.: Harvard University Press, 1997); Paul Slack, *The Impact of Plague in Tudor and Stuart England* (Oxford, U.K.: Oxford University Press, 1985); John W. Verano and Douglas H. Ubelaker, eds., *Disease and Demography in the Americas* (Washington, D.C.: Smithsonian Institution Press, 1992); Sheldon Watts, *Epidemics and History: Disease, Power and Imperialism* (New Haven, Conn.: Yale University Press, 1997).

Djenne-Djeno (Jenne-Jeno)

Replaced in the 12th century by the nearby city of Djenne, Djenne-Djeno was a major trading center in the central Niger Valley from the eighth to the 11th century.

The ancient city of Djenne-Djeno was located about 220 miles (354 km) south of TIMBUKTU. Before its decline after the 11th century, Djenne-Djeno served as an important commercial center in the NIGER RIVER Valley. Its ruins are still accessible, and archeological evidence shows that approximately 10,000 persons lived in Djenne-Djeno at its peak. The same evidence also suggests that residents of Djenne-Djeno enjoyed a relatively egalitarian society, as the dominant elite present in most European cities in the same period was absent in this desert urban center. By the 14th century residents deserted the city in favor of the more prosperous Djenne, only 2 miles (3 km) distant, which became an important intellectual and commercial center for the region.

The Bozo people originally founded the town of Djenne in the 13th century as a fishing village. In that century, after the decline of Djenne-Djeno, the Soninke established Djenne as a trading center, providing the desert city of Timbuktu with food, cotton, GOLD, cola nuts, and slaves (see SLAVERY) in exchange for salt and North African trade goods. Salt brought to Djenne was most likely bound for the gold fields in the AKAN forest. Trade between Djenne and Timbuktu, described at length by the chronicler LEO AFRICANUS in 1512–13, centered on the Niger and Bani Rivers. Djenne remained an independent city (outside the jurisdiction of the various empires rising and falling around it), and one seemingly without imperial aspirations, until Sunni Ali Ber conquered it in the 1470s. Djenne's location provided some security for traders, as it was surrounded by the two rivers for nearly half of each year. However, the protection of the rivers did not prevent more powerful invaders such as the MALI in the 14th century, the MOSSI in the mid-15th century, and the SONGHAI under Sunni Ali Ber in 1491 from laying siege to the city, nor from Moroccan invaders in the 1500s.

Further reading: Elizabeth Heath, "Djenne-Djeno, Mali" and "Djenne, Mali" in *Africana: The Encyclopedia of the African and African American Experience* eds. Kwame Anthony Appiah and Henry Louis Gates, Jr. (New York: Basic *Civitas* Books, 1999), 607; ———, "The Kingdoms of the Old Sudan," in *The Lost Cities of Africa,* Basil Davidson (Boston: Little, Brown, 1987), 51–124; ———, "Songhay Achievement," in *West Africa before the Colonial Era: A History to 1850,* Basil Davidson (London: Longman, 1998), 57–58; Nehemia Levtzion, "The Early State of the Western Sudan," in *History of West Africa,* vol. 1, 3rd ed., eds. J. F. Ade Ajiya and Michael Crowder (London: Longman, 1985), 129–166, esp. 146–149.

— Lisa M. Brady

Djibouti

Located on the Horn of Africa, Djibouti, a country bordered today by Eritrea, Ethiopia, and Somalia, was a vital link in the spread of ISLAM in Africa, with only the 14-mile (23 km) Strait of Mandeb separating the African continent from the Arabian Peninsula.

The walled seaport of Zeila mainly consisted of Arab and Persian traders, but its population also incorporated a minority of the Danakil or Afar peoples who typically lived in the rural areas surrounding the city. Trade in slaves (see SLAVERY) and SILVER supported the growth of the seaport and eventually led to the rise of the Adal kingdom, with Zeila as its center and capital. Zeila was one of the principal points of entry for Islam into the Horn of Africa. By the eighth or ninth century, Islam was the dominant religion on the coast of Djibouti. Its spread to the rural areas was a longer process, and Islam only established itself in Zeila's hinterland in the 10th and 11th centuries.

Djibouti's connection to Islam and the Middle East gave the Adal and other Islamic kingdoms on the Horn power to assert their independence from the Christian empire of Abyssinia. Throughout the 13th century and continuing as late as the 16th, power struggles frequently disrupted the region. Djibouti remained predominantly Muslim in this period, even after Western invaders defeated the Adal in the late 16th century.

Further reading: Basil Davidson, *The Lost Cities of Africa* (Boston: Little, Brown, 1987); Ari Nave, "Djibouti," in *Africana: The Encyclopedia of the African and African American Experience,* eds. Kwame Anthony Appiah and Henry Louis Gates, Jr. (New York: Basic *Civitas* Books, 1999), 607.

— Lisa M. Brady

Dominicans

The Dominican order, founded in the 13th century, played an important role in the Catholic response to the REFORMATION.

By the beginning of the 16th century, the Dominicans, like the FRANCISCANS, were divided into more- and less-observant wings. Some Dominicans earned a reputation for greed and laxity in the observance of their vows, while others became famous as teachers and preachers.

The Dominican order did not react in a unified way to the challenges of the Reformation. Some Dominicans supported reform goals and left the order to join Protestant churches. However, the Dominicans also supplied important critics of the Reformation, and Dominicans played important roles in the INQUISITION and at the COUNCIL OF TRENT. The order as a whole was known for its scholarship and produced some of the most notable Catholic thinkers of the 16th century, including Tommaso de Vio (Cajetan) and the theologian FRANCISCO DE VITORIA.

In the religious debates of the Reformation, one of the major questions concerned the role of grace and the nature of human beings. Some Catholics and most, if not all, reformers maintained that through the gift of grace God overcame a human nature that was entirely broken by sin and incapable of goodness (see MARTIN LUTHER). Against this Augustinian view, the Dominicans generally defended the view of the 13th-century Dominican theologian Thomas Aquinas, who held that grace perfected a human nature that was already created in the image of God.

Like the Franciscans and JESUITS, the Dominicans founded missions around the world. Dominican missionaries traveled to eastern Europe, the Philippines, Africa, India, Mesopotamia, and the Western Hemisphere. In the Americas Dominican preachers sometimes criticized colonial abuses of the Indians. In 1511, for example, Fray Anton de Montesinos preached a sermon in which he warned the colonists of HISPANIOLA that their mistreatment of the Indians merited punishment in hell. The most famous defender of the Indians, BARTOLOMÉ DE LAS CASAS, was also a Dominican.

Further reading: Jean Delumeau, *Catholicism between Luther and Voltaire: A New View of the Counter-Reformation* (London: Burns and Oates, 1977); Hans J. Hillerbrand, ed., *The Oxford Encyclopedia of the Reformation* (New York: Oxford University Press, 1996); W. A. Hinnebusch, "Dominicans" in the *New Catholic Encyclopedia,* vol. 4, ed. William J. McDonald, et al. (New York: McGraw-Hill, 1967): 974–982; Lyle N. McAlister, *Spain and Portugal in the New World, 1492–1700* (Minneapolis: University of Minnesota Press, 1984).

— Martha K. Robinson

Drake, Sir Francis (1540?–1596)

A prominent maritime admiral from England whose circumnavigation of the globe and exploits against Spain captured the imagination of Protestant Europe during the latter half of the 16th century.

The exact date and place of Drake's birth, as well as details surrounding his childhood years, remain subject to debate. A number of chroniclers list Tavistock as his place of birth, while others contend he was born in Plymouth. Most accounts state that by the age of 10, Drake served as an apprentice to the master of a small vessel, working as both a pilot and a coaster. By the age of 19, he owned his own small craft, more than likely an inheritance from his master. In 1565–66 he accompanied Captain John Lovell on a journey to the Spanish Main and Guinea. Shortly after he enlisted into the service of the Hawkins's family firm at Plymouth. Kin to Drake, the Hawkins family already ranked among England's richest and most famous merchant adventurers of the day. It was a common practice for 16th-century parents to send their children to serve or apprentice in houses of prosperous friends or relatives for their education. Like the Drake family, the Hawkins family did not come from noble stock, yet by the end of the 16th century both families enjoyed an elevated status.

In 1567 Drake commanded the ship *Judith* on one of SIR JOHN HAWKINS's slaving expeditions to the New World. In September of the following year, the Spaniards attacked the Hawkins party at San Juan de Lua. Of the expedition's four ships, only two returned to England. Drake's involvement in the failed venture kindled an intense hatred of the Spanish, which he carried with him the rest of his days. He set out the next year seeking to obtain compensation for the losses in the San Juan de Lua setback.

Over the next decade Drake raided numerous Spanish ships and colonial ports, exacting vast amounts of treasure while becoming a constant thorn in the side of the Spanish Crown. To the Spanish he became the infamous "Dragon" of the seas. Older English historical accounts referred to Drake's activities as privateering, a gentle description for what was, in reality, open piracy. Although not officially sanctioned by Queen ELIZABETH I, Drake's activities proved to be an international boon for the growing English interests in maritime ventures. As a result, Drake's activities gained him respect within England. Born into a provincial society racked by social, economic, religious, and diplomatic change, Drake used his skill in piracy as a stepping-stone for social advancement.

The West Indies became a favorite target for Drake's raids. In 1572, following one of his many successful raids in the West Indies, Drake led a party to PANAMA, where, with the help of thirty Cimaroons, he marched across the Isthmus of Panama. Although severely wounded in the thigh during the adventure, Drake returned from Panama with "more treasures than the pinnaces could carry." Restless and continually looking over the next horizon, Drake sought larger ventures and riches.

In December 1577 Drake led a squadron of four well-stored and well-provisioned ships—the *Pelican*, the *Swan*, the *Marigold*, and the *Christopher*—out of Plymouth. Along with English authorities, he concealed the object of the voyage so that the Spaniards would not be forewarned. In fact, they went out of their way to speak of the Mediterranean as their destination, with many of the squadron's crew not even knowing the true intentions of the venture. The Spaniards believed the English were headed to the West Indies, the Nombre de Dios, and the Treasure of the World that Drake had in his sights. Upon passing Cape Verde, the crew learned that they were bound to the coast of Brazil. By August 1578 Drake, reduced to a single ship, passed through the Strait of Magellan, well on his way to circumnavigating the globe. He celebrated the passing by changing the name of his ship, the *Pelican*, to the *Golden Hind.*

After passing through the strait, a furious storm pushed the ship as far to the south as 57 degrees. In uncharted territory, the crew discovered a number of new islands. The new route of passage would eventually bear Drake's name. Realizing that a return route via the Atlantic would be too long and dangerous, Drake opted to go farther into the Pacific, but not before raiding Spanish territory and ships along the western coasts of South, Central

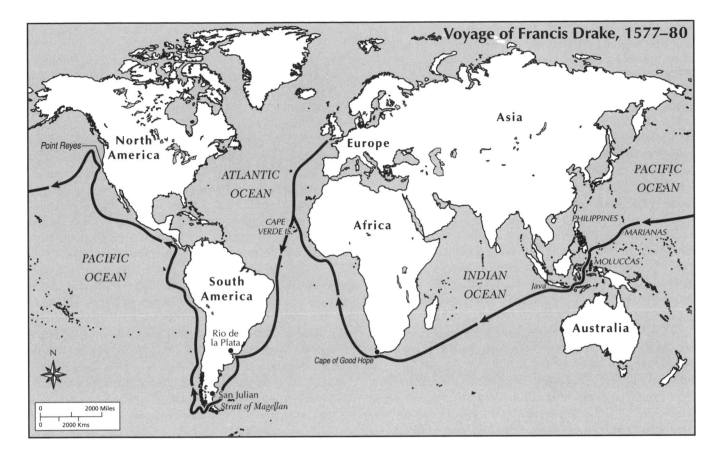

Voyage of Francis Drake, 1577–80

and North America. According to some sources, Drake and his party found respite in a small bay where, in the name of Queen Elizabeth, they carried out cordial exchanges with the native population. The geographical identification of this bay is a matter of some dispute. Many observers have argued that it was the site of the future city of San Francisco.

Upon Drake's return to England, Queen Elizabeth, under pressure by some to punish Drake for his raids on Spanish property, instead visited him on board his ship, knighting him on April 4, 1581, for becoming the first man of any nation to circumnavigate the globe. FERDI-NAND MAGELLAN's voyage was the only previous circum-navigation, but he had not lived to see its completion. The *Golden Hind* quickly became a sacred relic and source of national pride. One enthusiast went so far as to suggest placing it bodily upon the stump of the steeple of St. Paul's in lieu of the cathedral's spires. Without carrying through such extreme measures of veneration, the ship was docked and preserved at Deptford as a monument to the accomplishment.

While the *Golden Hind* basked in adulation, Drake briefly turned to politics, serving as mayor of Plymouth in

1581—he is credited with initiating the works to supply water to the town—and sitting in the 1584 PARLIAMENT as a representative of Bossiney in North Cornwall. In addi-tion, he continued as a key player in the growing tensions between England and Spain. Following the Parliament of 1584–85, the government commissioned Drake to carry out another raid upon the West Indies. Accompanied by vice admiral MARTIN FROBISHER, rear admiral Francis Knollys, and lieutenant governor of ground forces Christo-pher Carleill, Drake's maneuvers and raids in the Caribbean heightened the enmity between an already volatile Protestant England and Catholic Spain. Heartened by Drake's exploits, many in England welcomed a poten-tial war. Although England increased efforts in maritime enterprises in the 1580s, the nation lacked an overall strat-egy or plan. On the Spanish side, PHILLIP II stepped up his efforts to build the SPANISH ARMADA following Drake's lat-est strike.

Before returning to England, Drake's fleet sailed up the coast of FLORIDA, stopping at SIR WALTER RALEGH's Virginia colony. Per instruction, Drake was to supply the colonists with stores. Disheartened, RALPH LANE, governor of Virginia, convinced Drake to take all of the men back to

England, thus abandoning the colonization effort. Drake and the Virginia colonists arrived in England on July 26, 1586. It is possible that TOBACCO and potatoes first came to England at this time; both quickly became daily necessities in English life. Whether Drake, Lane, and their companions should be credited for the introduction remains uncertain to scholars.

When the English discovered a plot to murder Elizabeth I, a plot in which both Spain and Mary, Queen of Scots, were implicated, tensions between Spain and England grew. Mary's subsequent trial and execution in 1587 and Philip's increased efforts at building up the armada combined to bring war nearer. Regarding attack as the best form of defense, Drake left Plymouth on April 2, 1587, for the coast of Portugal, where he "singed the King of Spain's beard." He struck decisively at the great harbor of Cádíz, burning, sinking, or capturing more than 30 Spanish ships, thus temporarily delaying Philip's "Enterprise of England" until the following year.

Drake's actions in the war against the Spanish Armada are unclear. A popular story, adding to the lore of his reputation, had him playing a game of bowls when the armada entered the English Channel, stating to his fellow shipmates that they had plenty of time both to finish the game and to defeat the Spanish fleet. Although Drake made a strong claim to the position of supreme commander of sea operations, he was passed over because of his non-noble family lineage. Lord Howard of Effingham, hereditary Lord High Admiral of England, was granted the position. All accounts indicate that Drake, in charge of one of Hawkins's fighting galleons, cooperated loyally with Howard's orders. By August 8, writing to the queen from the decks of the galleon *Revenge*, he reported, "On Friday last upon good consideration we left the army of Spain so far to the northwards as they could neither recover England nor Scotland."

After the English defeated the armada and thus thwarted an invasion of their nation, the government commissioned a counter armada, with Drake and Sir John Norris (or Norreys) placed in joint command. The first expedition was to be powerful in both appearance and scope. Elizabeth's strongly worded orders stated that Drake and Norris were first to destroy the Spanish warships off the coast of Portugal, but she and her advisers added a second objective to the mission: an assault on LISBON, a plan aimed to punish the Spanish even further. Since Philip's annexation of Portugal in 1580, Don Antonio, a Portuguese prince, had laid claim to the throne, promising that his people would rise up against Spain if military support ever came from France or England. Drake, dreaming of the success and riches that an alliance with a liberated Portugal would bring, bought into the plan to attack Lisbon, but in the process he ignored the first objective, leaving the Spanish warships unscathed in Santander and other ports and thus missing a unique opportunity to cripple the Spaniards on their own coastline. Already irate, Elizabeth's anger rose even higher as the attack on Lisbon turned into a disgraceful and unsuccessful debacle. Drake and Norris returned to England discredited.

Between 1590 and 1594 Drake, minus the opportunity of further commissions, busied himself once again in politics, serving in his familiar roles as mayor of Plymouth and as a member of Parliament. In 1590 Drake and Hawkins founded the Chest of Chatham, a relief fund for disabled seamen. The chest, organized as a contributory pension scheme, led to the foundation of Greenwich Hospital. Two years later Drake dedicated an account of his 1572–73 raid on the Isthmus of Panama to Elizabeth, thus possibly smoothing relations between them. His nephew eventually published the account in 1626 under the title *Sir Francis Drake Revived*. In 1594 the queen decided to grant Drake another maritime opportunity, pairing him on an expedition with Hawkins with the objective to plunder, capture, and defend Panama.

Neither Hawkins nor Drake returned from the Panama excursion. Learning from the lessons and losses incurred by numerous Hawkins and Drake raids, the two aged mariners found the Spanish well prepared with their defenses. Following Hawkins's death en route to Panama, Drake, wracked by dysentery, found only further vexation and disappointment. He died on January 28, 1595, off the coast of Porto Bello. His men cast his body to the sea the following day. Despite the less than heroic last voyage, Drake's name was not lost in the annals of history, with legend and lore often intertwining with historical accuracy. Among the chroniclers of Drake's efforts was WILLIAM

Sir Francis Drake encounters the Indians of California
(Library of Congress)

CAMDEN, who celebrated Drake in his history of England. Spanish observers and historians have painted less positive portraits, depicting Drake as the most detestable figure of the period—the "Dragon"—whose acts of piracy could not be soon forgotten.

Further reading: Kenneth R. Andrews, *The Last Voyage of Drake and Hawkins* (Cambridge, U.K.: Hakluyt Society, 1972); Harry Kelsey, *Sir Francis Drake: The Queen's Pirate* (New Haven, Conn.: Yale University Press, 1998); *Sir Francis Drake Revived, Being a Summary and True Relation of Four Seasoned Voyages Made by Sir Francis Drake to the West Indies* (London: Nicholas Bourne, 1653); David Beers Quinn, *Sir Francis Drake as Seen by His Contemporaries* (New Providence, R. I.: John Carter Brown Library, 1996); John Sugden, *Sir Francis Drake* (London: Barrie & Jenkins, 1990)

— Matt Lindaman

Durán, Diego (ca. 1537–1588)

A sixteenth-century Dominican friar, Diego Durán learned NAHUATL, studied precontact indigenous manuscripts, and interviewed AZTECS to write his three books: the *Book of the Gods and Rites*, the *Ancient Calendar*, and the *History of the Indies of New Spain*.

Durán was born in SEVILLE but moved with his family to Tezcoco, near Mexico City, while still a child. He grew up speaking both Spanish and Nahuatl and joined the DOMINICANS in his late teens. Durán's knowledge of the Nahuatl language and the people who spoke it helped him research his chronicles of Indian life, which were often sympathetic toward the Indians. While Durán, like other Spaniards, was appalled by the Aztec practice of human sacrifice, he admired other aspects of ancient Aztec life. He also criticized priests and friars who worked with the Aztecs without understanding their language.

Durán believed that the Indians must convert to Catholicism to save their souls. His works were intended, at least in part, to guide missionaries and priests to a better understanding of Indian beliefs and practices in order to make the task of conversion easier. He recognized, for example, that the Indians celebrated some Catholic feasts with great enthusiasm because these feasts coincided with feasts in the old Aztec calendar. Durán distrusted such religious survivals but doubted that they could be eliminated. Like other European writers, he also suspected that the Aztecs were descended from one of the lost tribes of Israel. "I would not commit a great error if I were to state this as fact," he wrote, "considering their way of life, their ceremonies, their rites and superstitions, their omens and hypocrisies, [are] so akin to and characteristic of those of the Jews; in no way do they seem to differ." He also sug-

gested that the Apostle Thomas may have preached to the Aztecs, being remembered in their histories as QUETZAL-COATL.

Further reading: Fray Diego Durán, *The History of the Indies of New Spain,* ed. and trans. Doris Heyden (Norman: University of Oklahoma Press, 1994); Anthony Grafton, *New Worlds, Ancient Texts: The Power of Tradition and the Shock of Discovery* (Cambridge, Mass.: Belknap Press, 1992); Michael E. Smith, *The Aztecs* (Oxford: Blackwell, 1996); Stephanie Wood, "Durán, Diego" in *Encyclopedia of Latin American History and Culture*, vol. 2, ed. Barbara A. Tenenbaum (New York: Scribner's, 1996).

— Martha K. Robinson

Dürer, Albrecht (1471–1528)

Among the most important artists in northern Europe in the 15th and 16th centuries, Dürer was a master printer who found inspiration in German artistic traditions and in the Italian Renaissance.

Dürer received his initial training from his father, a goldsmith, and from the Nuremberg artist Michael Wolgemut. As an adult Dürer traveled to Italy and the Lowlands, where he learned new artistic styles and techniques. He soon became well known, and his patrons included the elector of Saxony, Frederick III, and the Holy Roman Emperor, Maximilian I.

Dürer produced woodcuts, engravings, paintings, and drawings. He also wrote treatises on art theory. His most famous works included portraits of prominent Europeans, including Desiderius Erasmus and Philipp Melanchthon. His work frequently drew on religious and allegorical themes, depicting scenes from classical mythology and from the Bible.

Although he was influenced primarily by European artistic traditions, Dürer also appreciated art from the Far East and the Americas. When a collection of Mexican art and artifacts, including gold and silverwork, weapons, and feathered clothing, was displayed in Antwerp, he was fascinated. "All the days of my life I have never seen anything that rejoiced my heart so much as these things," he wrote in his journal, "for I saw among them wonderful works of art, and I marveled at the subtle ingenuity of men in faraway lands. I cannot express the feeling that I had."

Dürer's travels and his interest in humanism also exposed him to new religious ideas. He corresponded with various Reformation thinkers, including Melanchthon. Although Dürer expressed interest in the reformers' ideas, he died before the publication of the first Lutheran confession of faith, the Augsburg Confession (1530). Since there remained, at his death, hope of reconciliation between the Catholic Church and the reformers, Dürer did not make a clear choice between Catholicism and Lutheranism (see MARTIN LUTHER and REFORMATION).

Further reading: Dagmar Eichberger and Charles Zika, eds., *Dürer and His Culture* (Cambridge, UK: Cambridge University Press, 1998); Colin Eisler, *Dürer's Animals* (Washington, D.C.: Smithsonian Institution Press, 1991); Jane Campbell Hutchison, *Albrecht Dürer: A Biography* (Princeton, N.J.: Princeton University Press, 1990); Mary Em Kirn, "Dürer, Albrecht" in *The Oxford Encyclopedia of the Reformation,* vol. 2, ed. Hans J. Hillerbrand (New York: Oxford University Press, 1996), 13; Erwin Panofsky, *The Life and Art of Albrecht Dürer* (Princeton:, N.J.: Princeton University Press, 1955).

— Martha K. Robinson

Dutch East India Company

Formed in 1602 to combat Portuguese and Spanish dominance in eastern trade, the Dutch East India Company emerged as one of the more powerful companies involved in trade between Europe and east Asia during the 17th century.

The East India companies were private endeavors but received charters and special trading rights granted by their respective governments. In addition to the Dutch East India Company, the English company was formed in 1600, the Danish company in 1616, and the French company in 1664. The Netherlands had long enjoyed a connection to products from the Far East, but the Hollanders were engaged in the role of intermediaries. As products from the Far and Near East filtered into Europe, the Dutch vessels sailed to LISBON, where they would exchange the grain, fish, and wood of northern Europe for the wine, fruits, and oil of southern Europe in addition to products entering Europe form the Far East. Accordingly, the Dutch used ships that were small and did not allow the crews to carry enough food or supplies for trips beyond Lisbon.

Beginning in 1594, a number of Dutch merchants began to set their sights beyond the coast of Portugal. They formed the Company of Far East Regions, a precursor to the Dutch East India Company. Theirs was the goal of reaching the Malay Archipelago, where they looked to establish commercial relations with the region and hoped to tap into the great emporium of the spice trade. The initial venture brought little profit, but it served to pique the interest of Dutch merchants and government officials alike. In 1598 no fewer than 22 ships equipped by five Holland and Zeeland companies sailed to profit in the East. Their combined successes came at the expense of declining Portuguese power on the open seas. The Spanish takeover of Portugal in the late 1500s further complicated matters.

The Portuguese and Spanish did not cede their Far East interests without a fight. Instead, the Netherlands and Spain entered the 17th century in a state of war. Countering the formidable Portuguese and Spanish navies, the Dutch combined a number of disparate and competing companies into the Dutch East India Company. The government granted the newly amalgamated national company a monopoly of the trade between the Cape of Good Hope and the Strait of Magellan. The initial charter was good for 21 years with the possibility of renewal. The company would be permitted to declare war and maintain armed forces in the regions under the charter's consideration.

In 1603 the Dutch East India company sent a fleet of 12 ships to the Malay Archipelago, where, two years later, the admiral of the Dutch fleet seized an important Portuguese port and established the first Dutch factory in the area. Yet another vessel from the fleet "discovered" the north coast of Australia and the south coast of New Guinea. As the Dutch East India company attempted to expand their base of operation, they met with opposition from the Spanish and Portuguese. The former controlled the Philippines along with the islands of Borneo and Java during the 16th century. Interested in tapping into the regional spice trade (see SPICE ISLANDS), the Dutch countered using both naval warfare and international law. The former was conventional while the latter challenged the medieval principle of monopoly and exclusive rights maintained by the Spanish government.

The distinguished Dutch scholar Hugo Grotius assumed an interest in the cause, writing a treatise under the title *Mare Liberum,* or *Of the Freedom of the Sea,* published in 1609. Grotius argued that the Spanish and Portuguese had no right to exclude other Europeans from the lucrative spice trade of the Far East. Widely read and translated into a number of languages during the 17th century, Grotius's treatise contributed to the foundation of the field of international law. On the more immediate horizon, the Spanish king refused Grotius's arguments, citing religious and absolute rights. With the rising threats from the French and English governments, the Dutch and Spanish negotiated for peace on April 9, 1609.

While the Dutch attempted to gain a foothold in the Far East trade networks, they simultaneously explored the possibility of discovering a NORTHEAST PASSAGE to the East. As early as 1594, JAN HUYGEN VAN LINSCHOTEN and Willem Barents attempted to sail around the north coast of Asia. Although failing to meet the principal objective, Barents later sailed to Nova Zembla, discovering and claiming Spitzbergen, a site of future whaling interests, along the way. In 1609 the Dutch East India Company sponsored one final expedition aimed at discovering a quick water route to the East. Under the direction of English sailing veteran Henry Hudson, temporarily hired away from the

English, the expedition sailed west instead of north and east. In the process Hudson explored the coast of North America from Chesapeake Bay to Penobscot Bay. As a result, Dutch merchants began dreaming of riches in North America in the form of the enormous quantities of furs they could buy and sell again in Europe at a handsome profit. The merchants of Amsterdam wasted little time in dispatching another ship to North America, this time under the auspices of a newly formed company of their own known as the Company of New Netherland.

Dutch interests in the Western Hemisphere consolidated under the Dutch West India Company in 1621. As the name implies, its purpose expanded beyond the colony of New Netherland to encompass operations in the tropical regions of America. Despite the foundation of the Dutch West India Company, the Far East continued to receive the bulk of Dutch merchants' interests. The Dutch East India Company continued to purchase spices, cotton goods, and silks in India, the Malay Archipelago, China, and Japan, leaving a lasting legacy from South Africa to the Far East well beyond the company's existence.

Further reading: Albert Hyma, *The Dutch in the Far East: A History of the Dutch Commercial and Colonial Empire* (Ann Arbor, Mich.: G. Wahr, 1942); George Masselman, *The Cradle of Colonialism* (New Haven, Conn: Yale University Press, 1963); Henry C. Murphy, *Henry Hudson in Holland* (The Hague: M. Nijhoff, 1909); T. Volker, *Porcelain and the Dutch East India Company, as recorded in the Dagh-registers of Batavia Castle, 1602–1682* (Leiden, Netherlands: E. J. Brill, 1954).

— Matthew Lindaman

E

East India Company (English)

The company used diplomatic and military means to expand English power into the East Indies and in the process helped to lay the groundwork for the later emergence of the British Empire.

Founded in 1600, the East India Company, formally titled the Governor and Merchants of London Trading into the East Indies (a name that lasted until 1708), began as little more than a small, speculative financial venture. Taking advantage of commercial opportunity brought about by the 1588 defeat of the SPANISH ARMADA, the lord mayor of LONDON joined several hundred other leading citizens to form and subscribe to a company for trade in the East Indies, the territory then dominated by the Portuguese (and later the Dutch). On December 31, 1600, Queen ELIZABETH I granted the company a 15-year charter that provided the subscribing merchants with the necessary monopoly. The first governor of the company, Sir Thomas Smythe, brought to the venture previous mercantile experience from similar positions he held in the Muscovy Company and the LEVANT COMPANY. The East India Company's first fleet sailed in February 1601 and returned laded with pepper from Amboina (modern-day Ambon, Indonesia). A second expedition in 1604 and a third in 1607 followed.

The company faced opposition from the Portuguese and the Dutch in the Dutch East Indies (modern-day Indonesia), yet backed by sufficient combat power the company broke into markets through either diplomatic or military means. In one notable advance two English ships in December 1612 defeated a Portuguese fleet consisting of four galleons and 26 frigates. The victory brought the company the privilege of establishing a factory at Saurat and trading concessions from the Mughal Empire. The company used this base to extend its commercial ties; soon its ships returned from the East with cotton, silk, indigo, saltpeter, and spices.

In later years the company continued to evolve. It proved crucial to the expansion of the British Empire and, further, it became a precursor for modern-day multinational business conglomerates.

Further reading: K. N. Chadhuri, *The English East India Company: The Study of an Early Joint-Stock Company, 1600–1640* (London: Frank Cass, 1965); John Keay, *The Honorable Company: A History of the English East India Company* (New York: Macmillan, 1994); Philip Lawson, *The East India Company: A History* (London: Longman, 1993).

— Kevin C. Armitage

Eden, Richard (1521?–1576)

A translator and cosmographer interested in topics ranging from science to navigation and exploration, Eden is best known for translating into English the first three books on the subject of America.

Born in Herefordshire about 1521, Eden studied at Queens' College, Cambridge, from 1535 to 1544. Following graduation he worked in a governmental position within the office of the treasury. Around 1552 he left governmental service to work as the private secretary of Sir William Cecil, Lord Burlegh. One year later he published a translated version of Sebastien Muenster's *Cosmography*. In 1555 Eden issued a compilation of translated works from the writings and maps of Muenster, PETER MARTYR, and SEBASTIAN CABOT. It also included a translation of *The Travels of Lewes Vertomannus, 1503*, later reprinted in RICHARD HAKLUYT THE YOUNGER's *Divers Voyages Touching the Discovery of America . . .* published in London in 1582.

Otherwise known as *The Decades of the New Worlde, or West India,* the compilation ranked as Eden's greatest literary feat. For more than 20 years it found no imitators. In 1576 Eden assumed the task of editing a revised edition but died before completing the task. Richard Willes finished the project, issuing it in 1577 under the title *The History of Trauaile in the West and East Indies.* Five years later Hakluyt published his first collection, *Divers Voyages.* Combined, these works helped to make oceanic literature a distinct genre in English letters. Eden, the pioneer of English geographic research, thus may also be considered a pioneer of English oceanic literature, leading a chain of writers such as the Hakluyts, THOMAS HARRIOT, and later SAMUEL PURCHAS.

Eden's translations came at a time when the earth held numerous geographical mysteries for Europeans. Although his subject matter derived from the explorations and conquests of the Spanish and the Portuguese, the texts proved valuable to the English gentry and merchants, who could now read of the world of oceanic exploration in their native tongue. Explorers profited as well. For example, before his oceanic ventures in the NEW WORLD, SIR FRANCIS DRAKE gleaned information on the West Indies and Spanish Main from Eden's translation of Pietro Martire's *Decades.* The translated version of the *Decades* influenced the poet and playwright WILLIAM SHAKESPEARE, as well, who based the character of Caliban in his *Tempest* on Pietro Martire's description of the Patagonian giants.

In 1559 Eden edited a revised version of Geminus's *Anatomy.* Two years later he devised woodcuts for an edited version of Martin Cortes's *Arte de Navigae.* The Muscovy Company sponsored the project, much as Hakluyt would later benefit from the patronage of the West Indies Company. In addition to containing a number of intricate woodcuts depicting mathematical instruments, the translated version of *Arte de Navigae* included a small outline map of the North Atlantic basin. Believed to be the earliest printed map of America to appear in England, Eden more than likely copied it from an original in Cortés's *Compendio.* After spending much of the 1560s and early 1570s traveling on the European continent, including a narrow escape from the massacre of St. Bartholomew, Eden returned permanently to England in 1573. He died three years later with a firm reputation as both a scholar and a man of science.

Further reading: Edward Arber, *The First Three English Books on America. [?1511]–1555 A.D. Being Chiefly Translations, Compilations, &c., by Richard Eden, from the writings, maps, &c., of Pietro Martire, of Anghiera (1455–1526) Sebastian Muenster, the Cosmography (1489–1552) Sebastian Cabot, of Bristol (1474–1557) with extracts, &c., from the Works of Other Spanish, Italian, and German Writers of the time* (Westminster, U.K.: A. Constable and Company, 1985); Lodovico de Varthema, *The Navigation and Voyages of Lewis Wertomannus, in the Yeere of Our Lorde 1503,* trans. Richard Eden (Edinburgh: Private printing for the Aungervyle Society, 1884).

— Matthew Lindaman

El Dorado

During the 16th century, with hopes that they would find a mythic gilded man ("El Dorado") and his golden kingdom, various European states pursued numerous failed expeditions into New Granada (present-day Colombia), New Andalucía (present-day Venezuela), and Guiana.

The myth of El Dorado grew in part from a religious ritual practiced by an Indian tribe that lived in the Bogotá highlands during the late 15th century. Annually the tribe gathered to witness the tribal chief plunge himself into the center of Lake Guatavita as part of a symbolic cleansing process. The act made for a spectacular image as the lake washed away the coat of GOLD powder that the chief's attendants ritualistically applied to his nude body. Sometime before the arrival of CHRISTOPHER COLUMBUS in the NEW WORLD, another tribe invaded and overpowered the group of Indians who practiced this ritual. Nevertheless, years later, long after the last ceremony at Lake Guatavita, the story of the gilded man ("El Dorado") and his city, also called "El Dorado," survived as folklore. Indians and Europeans exaggerated details and added embellishments over time. Before long rumors transformed the original ritual into a spectacular tale of a golden city whose palaces, streets, and nobility all demonstrated the mark of gold and wealth.

During the first half of the 16th century, the Spanish solidified their sphere of influence in the Western Hemisphere and looked in particular toward the lands of the Caribbean as a tropical paradise, rich in mines and a source of slave labor (see SLAVERY). Then, in 1533, when FRANCISCO PIZARRO led men into PERU, the native legend of El Dorado became known to Europeans for the first time. Pizarro's invasion of their homeland forced many INCA to retreat into the jungle. The Spanish, believing rumors that the dissidents carried with them much treasure, opted to pursue them. Ultimately, the Spanish thought they would follow the runaway Indians east until reaching the magnificent, ancestral home of the Inca, Paytiti. By then, the Spanish had also heard from an Indian messenger of another impressive kingdom in the east. For his Spanish listeners, the messenger, arriving in Peru just after the fall of the Incan empire, described the mythical empire of El Dorado.

In the beginning, one expedition after another set out for the fabled kingdom to the east of Bogotá. Over the course of five years, from 1536 to 1541, six major Spanish expeditions, along with many other smaller efforts, set out for the interior from Venezuela. Hopeful and lusting for gold and instant wealth, each mission set out in search of the gilded man and his city. In turn, each met failure, either through absolute exhaustion of resources and men or through death. DISEASE, exposure to severe elements, starvation, and aggressive Indian groups were but some of the obstacles encountered. The men that formed one expedition, for example, encountered such grave difficulties that they reverted to CANNIBALISM and other desperate measures. This mission, led by Francisco Pizarro's half brother, Gonzalo Pizarro, suffered from a greedy leader who abandoned his main force of men, opting to seek out and claim El Dorado as his own.

The most notorious El Dorado hunt occurred in 1561, when a band of ruffians found themselves in a desperate position in the jungles of Venezuela. Not long after the expedition began, the commander and his mistress met their ends as part of a bloody mutiny. Lope de Aguirre, the new leader of the troops, suffered from mental instability. After killing many of his own men, Aguirre ordered an unprovoked attack on the Spanish settlement on Margarita Island. The atrocities at Margarita motivated Spanish authorities to order the capture of Aguirre. Neither Aguirre nor his men realized their hopes of reaching El Dorado as another force of Spaniards brought about their demise in a brutal struggle.

In time, optimism sank, and although Spanish expeditions in search of El Dorado continued throughout the 16th century, dogged determination to find the city of gold replaced jovial anticipation. With each mission new rumors surfaced that further contributed to the allure of El Dorado. Along the way Spaniards encountered various groups of Indians who eagerly assisted the gold seekers by clarifying the supposed route to the city of gold. In addition, the viceroy of Peru provided encouragement for quests to El Dorado, particularly for those persons with a criminal or otherwise questionable background.

Eventually, vast numbers of unsuccessful missions suggested to many Spaniards that the actual location of El Dorado lay deeper within the unexplored territory of the interior. Then, in 1580, the CONQUISTADOR Don Antonio de Berrio inherited the estates of his wife's wealthy uncle, Gonzalo Ximénez de Quesada. Ximénez had stipulated in his will that Berrio, as the heir, must use a portion of the estate's income to finance the search for El Dorado. In 1592 Berrio established the first Spanish colony in Trinidad. From this base he pursued the hunt for the fabled city of gold for 15 years, moving farther into the interior mainland than any previous expedition. Along the way he experienced great losses due to disease, hostile Indians, and other chance difficulties.

Just before his death, Berrio succeeded in locating a lake, boxed in by seemingly impassable mountains, that he believed to be the golden lake so central to the legend of El Dorado. Berrio was even more intrigued to learn that a powerful group of Indians had settled on the lake 20 years earlier. Unfortunately, Berrio did not live to realize that CARIB lived on the lake, not the Inca who fled Peru two decades before, and that there was no gilded man and no golden empire.

In 1595 the English joined the hunt for El Dorado with SIR WALTER RALEGH leading the way. Raleigh used the fabled gilded man and his golden city as a tactic to acquire the necessary men and financial backing to support his interests in the Caribbean. Whether Raleigh initially believed in the existence of El Dorado is unknown, but he felt that the English had to usurp Spanish hegemony in the so-called Golden Antilles. Once in the Caribbean, Ralegh attacked and crushed Berrio's expedition, taking Berrio as hostage as the English continued their own search for gold.

During the late 16th and early 17th centuries, Ralegh searched for gold in Guiana and elsewhere in the New World. Although he initially refused to give in to the exaggerations and fantastic stories, at various times he fell victim to the myth of El Dorado, believing in the possibility of finding the elusive city. After Ralegh the English made other attempts to locate El Dorado. During the late 17th century the Scots, too, searched for the city of gold. Until its existence was finally disproved two centuries later, maps included references to the fabled city.

Further reading: Jan Rozoziński, *A Brief History of the Caribbean: From the Arawak and the Carib to the Present,* rev. ed. (New York: Facts On File, 1999); Timothy Severin, *The Golden Antilles* (New York: Knopf, 1970).

— Kimberly Sambol-Tosco

Elizabeth I, queen of England (1533–1603; r. 1558–1603)

The queen of England during the decisive half century during which her realm renewed its conquest of Ireland, attempted to consolidate the power of the Protestant REFORMATION, and began to establish settlements in the Western Hemisphere.

The daughter (and only child) of King HENRY VIII and Anne Boleyn, Elizabeth early in life received a first-class education in literature. Over the course of her life she wrote in English, French, and Latin and was a prodigious translator. She also received an unwanted education into the nature of factional politics in England, having had PARLIAMENT question the legitimacy of her birth and having served time in prison in the Tower of London and at Woodstock for her views. While at Woodstock, the well-educated princess wrote poetry, some of it found later on a window frame and even on a window itself, cut by a diamond. "Much suspected by me, Nothing proved can be," wrote "Elizabeth the prisoner." While in the Tower of London she prayed for salvation. "Help me now, O God, for I have none other friends but Thee alone," she wrote. "And suffer me not (I beseech Thee) to build my foundation upon the sands, but upon the rock"—a reference to the Book of Matthew—"whereby all blasts of blustering weather may have no power against me, amen."

Elizabeth I   *(Hulton/Getty)*

When MARY I died in 1558, Elizabeth acceded to the throne. Twenty-five years old at the time, no one could have anticipated that she would become, over the course of her long reign, one of the most important monarchs in 16th-century Europe. In 1559 the bishop of Carlisle made her head of the CHURCH OF ENGLAND, although few other high-ranking clerics were willing to participate. She immediately began to set church policy and almost as quickly began to support other Protestants in Europe, including some in France, Scotland, and the Low Countries, who were battling for their liberty. Her 1559 Act of Supremacy and Uniformity demanded that all clerics in England swear an oath recognizing her as "the only supreme governor of this realm and of all other her highness's dominions and countries, as well in all spiritual or ecclesiastical things or causes as temporal, and that no foreign prince, person, prelate, state, or potentate hath or ought to have any jurisdiction, power, superiority, pre-eminence, or authority, ecclesiastical or spiritual, within this realm." In 1563 she put forth the Thirty-Nine Articles, further assuring that her brand of Protestantism would remain the national church in the realm. Such actions only reaffirmed her status as an enemy to Catholics. In 1570 Pope Pius V declared that she

was a heretic and thus no longer deserved the allegiance of Catholics in England.

Elizabeth's desire to promote Protestantism also caused her to renew the centuries-long English effort to subdue Ireland and its native Catholic inhabitants. Long before, the ANGLO-NORMANS had tried to bring the Irish into the English realm, but their efforts languished. During the 1560s Elizabeth decided that the time had come to mount an armed assault against Ireland. She thus unleashed military officers to use whatever means necessary to force the native Irish to abandon their religion and adopt Protestantism. One of those officers was SIR HUMPHREY GILBERT, a West Country aristocrat who decided that the indigenous Irish would succumb only if he terrorized them. According to one of his English companions, Gilbert ordered his men to slice the heads off the bodies of the dead Irish who lay on the ground after a battle and to mount their heads on posts that lined the way into his tent, creating a "lane of heddes" meant to strike terror into the local people who needed to pass through this ghastly spectacle if they wanted to talk to him. He also thought it expedient to kill noncombatants because they provided the food needed for the Irish who battled the English. Combined with a program to send English men and women to establish new settlements in Ireland, Elizabeth's tactics constituted the most serious assault on Ireland in its history. Unlike the Anglo-Normans, who eventually blended into the Irish population, the new invaders did all in their power to force the natives to abandon all aspects of their ancient culture. The Elizabethan conquest, in the end, paid military and economic advantages for the English state, although the expansion of the realm into Ireland also meant the English had a larger territory to defend and a hostile and potentially violent population within its midst. A rebellion at the end of the century demonstrated that the Irish had not abandoned the hope of removing at least the most odious elements of the English presence from their homeland.

Elizabeth's zeal to promote the Protestant cause did not end with her efforts across the Irish Sea. She also persecuted Catholics closer to home, including Mary Stuart, Queen of Scots, whom Elizabeth imprisoned. When the imprisonment aroused sympathy for Mary, Elizabeth heeded the advice of her close advisers and agreed to have Mary executed in 1587. Although Elizabeth hoped that Catholics would give up their ways and join the Church of England—which, to some visitors from the Continent, resembled the Catholic Church in many ways—Catholics continued to practice their religion, and young English men trained for the priesthood on the Continent and then returned to provide for Catholics, often in secret. Catholics were not the only dissenters Elizabeth wanted to quash: She and her church also persecuted Protestants such as

PURITANS who did not share her views on crucial clerical matters.

In this age of religious ferment and conflict, Elizabeth's actions aroused emotions across Europe. Among those who believed the English needed to be punished for their actions was the Spanish King PHILIP II. In the spring of 1588, Philip sent Elizabeth a poem in Latin in which he asked her to offer no defense of Belgians, return Spanish treasure that SIR FRANCIS DRAKE had stolen from them, reestablish the monasteries that her father had dissolved, and "Restore the Pope's religion perfectly." She responded with a brief poem of her own. "When Greeks do measure months by the moon/ Then, Spanish Philip, thy will shall be done."

Understanding well her meaning, Philip responded by ordering a great fleet, the SPANISH ARMADA, to attack England. The fleet encountered a fierce storm that scattered the ships, and the English, although possessing an inferior navy at the time, prevailed in the conflict. Observers recognized the significance of the Spanish loss. The historian WILLIAM CAMDEN celebrated the defeat of the armada. In his *Annales The True and Royall History of the Famous Empresse Elizabeth Queen of England France and Ireland & c*, published in London in 1625, he realized that the defeat of the Spanish, who had "prepared a most invincible Navy against *England,*" was an event that could be explained only by divine intervention. That interpretation followed Elizabeth's own understanding of the victory over the armada. According to Camden, the queen "commanded publique prayers and thanks-giving to be made in all the Churches in *England,* and went her selfe in triumph amongst the Companies and societies of *London,* which marched on both sides of her Majestie, with their Banners, and [rode through] the Streetes (which were richly hung with blue hangings) in a Chariot drawne . . . with two Horses. . . . to Saint *Pauls* Church, where shee gave God humble thanks" and listened to a sermon praising God for sacred assistance. The queen herself offered prayers to the "Most powerful and largest-giving God" for having "protected our army from foes' prey and from sea's danger."

In the years following the armada defeat, Elizabeth began to give more sustained attention to the establishment of English colonies in North America. She had earlier granted to SIR WALTER RALEGH a patent to establish a colony along the mid-Atlantic coast, a patent that led to the founding of the short-lived settlement at ROANOKE, and another to Gilbert to lay claim to territory in modern-day Newfoundland, but before 1588 the threat of the Spanish navy had kept any transatlantic imperial ambitions in check. By the time the armada had been defeated and the English were praying to God for their deliverance from the Catholic menace, Elizabeth already possessed elaborate plans testifying to the benefits to be had from the establishment of colonies. According to RICHARD HAKLUYT THE YOUNGER, who in 1584 had presented her court with a secret document now known as the "Discourse of Western Planting," the English should colonize North America because they would reap great profits, find employment for otherwise unemployed or underemployed English men, and halt the spread of Catholicism in the Western Hemisphere. Elizabeth responded by supporting the ill-fated venture of SIR JOHN HAWKINS and Francis Drake to the West Indies in 1595 and of Walter Ralegh to Guiana, a venture that eventually led to his execution after Elizabeth's own death.

During the 1590s she also maintained her hostility toward Catholics, evident in her Act Against Papists of 1593, in which she tried to eliminate any threats from "popish recusants." The act aimed at "the better discovering and avoiding of all such traitorous and most dangerous conspiracies as are daily devised and practised against our most gracious sovereign lady, the queen's majesty, and the happy estate of this commonweal by sundry wicked and seditious persons, who, terming themselves Catholics and being indeed spies and intelligencers, not only for her majesty's foreign enemies, but also for rebellious and traitorous subjects born within her highness's realms and dominions, and hiding their most detestable and devilish purposes under a false pretext of religion and conscience, do secretly wander and shift from place to place within this realm to corrupt and seduce her majesty's subjects and to stir them to sedition and rebellion[.]" In order to reduce the danger of these unrepentant Catholics, the queen forced them to remain close to their homes and, if they persisted in their practice, to leave any English territory.

Over the course of her long reign, Elizabeth's courtiers crafted a number of different images of their queen. She was, at one point or another, depicted as Diana, the Rose of Beauty, the Vestal Virgin, the Saviour of the Protestant Church, and the Virgin Mary. Portraits reflected different elements of her character and career. The so-called Armada Portrait of 1588, for example, showed her with her hand on a globe and ships sailing by across an open window behind her, reflecting her belief that her navy would provide the means whereby the English could expand their realm across the Atlantic Ocean.

Further reading: Nicholas Canny, *The Elizabethan Conquest of Ireland: A Pattern Established, 1565–76* (Sussex, U.K.: Harvester, 1976); Susan Doran, *Elizabeth I and Religion, 1558–1603* (London: Routledge, 1994); Christopher Haigh, *Elizabeth I,* 2nd ed. (London: Longman, 1998); Wallace MacCaffery, *Elizabeth I* (London: E. Arnold, 1993); ———, *Elizabeth I: War and Politics, 1588–1603* (Princeton, N.J.: Princeton University Press, 1992); ———, *Queen Elizabeth and the Making of Policy, 1572–1588* (Princeton, N.J.: Princeton University Press, 1981); Leah S. Marcus, Janel Mueller, and Mary Beth Rose, eds., *Elizabeth I: Collected Works* (Chicago: University of Chicago Press, 2000).

encomienda

An *encomienda* from the Spanish Crown granted the recipient the ability to control labor and collect tribute from an indigenous community in Spanish America as a reward for service, but as it came to be practiced in the colonies it amounted to little more than institutionalized SLAVERY for native people.

Spanish colonists received *encomiendas* ("grants") of indigenous labor and control of land for service to the Spanish Crown in return for the promise to teach Christianity and European life ways to the indigenous people entrusted to the recipient *(encomendero)*. Most of the early *encomenderos* were CONQUISTADORES, and they tended to view the *encomiendas* as their own private little kingdoms. Additionally, many *encomenderos* illegally coopted the right to administer justice within the domain of their *encomiendas.*

Unfortunately for the region's indigenous inhabitants, the Spanish first firmly established this institution in the West Indies. From the Caribbean it spread to MEXICO and then PERU, with *encomiendas* of the 16th century ranging in size from thousands to only a few hundred natives. The *encomienda* proved to be a valuable tool in the Spanish conquest of Latin America. The institution expedited Spanish control of territory and facilitated the rapid introduction of Spanish culture and Catholicism to newly subjugated native peoples. Although the system had many positive attributes for the Spanish government in the early years, over time many Spanish colonists abused native workers and *encomenderos* often failed to educate the indigenous people under their control in the tenets of Spanish culture and/or Catholicism.

In most places *encomenderos* employed their indigenous workers to build the infrastructure for Spanish towns, raise livestock, grow crops for the Spanish and native populations, and work in mines. The *encomenderos* used Indian labor to lay the foundation for their accumulation of fortunes and political power. Many of the early *encomiendas* dominated the Spanish American economy and the political scene locally through the manipulation of town councils (CABILDOs). Some of these *encomiendas* developed into the large HACIENDAs that influenced Spanish America throughout and beyond the colonial era. The early *encomenderos* used their positions of power and wealth to take advantage of later-arriving Spanish settlers.

In an effort to curb the growing power of the first *encomenderos* and eliminate the abuse that native people suffered at their hands, the Spanish Crown issued the Laws of Burgos in 1512 and the New Laws in 1542. These laws limited the amount of personal tribute that could be collected, abolished personal servitude by natives, and reorganized local and territorial governmental structures. These measures attacked the heart of the *encomenderos'* power by limiting their access to wealth and their ability to control local government. Administrators appointed by the royal government finally gained the ability to collect tribute for the Spanish Crown, thereby depriving the *encomenderos* of one route to power. The government also encouraged the development of independent farmers, merchants, and mine owners, who eventually rose in power and prestige to challenge the *encomenderos.* Over time indigenous leaders took control of their *cabildos,* which limited *encomendero* political clout and ended some of the abuses that natives suffered under the *encomienda* system.

Further reading: Mark A. Burkholder and Lyman L. Johnson, *Colonial Latin America,* 3rd ed. (New York: Oxford University Press, 1998); J. H. Elliott, *Imperial Spain, 1469–1716* (London: Edward Arnold, 1963); Charles Gibson, *Spain in America* (New York: New American Library, 1977); C. H. Haring, *The Spanish Empire in America,* 3rd ed. (New York: Harcourt, Brace, and World, 1963); James Lockhart, "Encomienda and Hacienda: The Evolution of the Great Estate in the Spanish Indies," *Hispanic American Historical Review* 49 (1969): 411–429; Lesley B. Simpson, *The Encomienda in New Spain: The Beginning of Spanish Mexico* (Berkeley: University of California Press, 1966).

— Dixie Ray Haggard

entail

Entail, also known as fee tail, was a legal concept derived from feudal law that bound land inalienably to the grantee and then forever to the grantee's direct descendants.

The most extensive property tenure allowed under feudal legal systems, entail not only bound land to a lineal descendant of the tenant, but in cases where property lacked an heir the land reverted to the lord. Entails thus supported a landed aristocracy because they served to prevent the disintegration of estates through inheritance or lack of heirs. Often entails were restricted to males, granting preference to the eldest. Entail became popular in parts of the English North American colonies in the 17th century, but by the 18th century the system had collapsed.

Spanish colonists in the Americas used a system of entail (*mayorazgo* in Spanish), a popular feature of Iberian society. An equivalent institution called mortmain (dead hand, *mano muerta* in Spanish) existed for church estates. Attitudes toward race affected how people used their claims to aristocratic status. The upper class was the beneficiary of special privileges given to the nobility, clergy, merchants, mine owners, and universities, yet as attitudes toward race and social location intertwined, elite nonwhites sometimes adopted legal measures to protect their privileges. A small number of nonwhites thus acquired entails to protect their estates—sometimes huge rural properties—from fragmentation.

Further reading: Robert Jones Shafer, *A History of Latin America* (Lexington, Mass.: D.C. Heath, 1978); Carole Shammas, Marylynn Salmon, and Michel Dahlin, *Inheritance in America From Colonial Times to the Present* (New Brunswick, N.J., and London: Rutgers University Press, 1987).

— Kevin C. Armitage

Escalante, Juan de (?–1519)

A trusted friend and lieutenant to the Spanish CONQUISTA-DOR HERNÁN CORTÉS, in 1519 Escalante left the town of Villa Rica de la Vera Cruz, where he was chief constable, and attacked Aztec soldiers north of the city, decisively altering the course of Spanish conquest.

After arriving on the Gulf coast of MEXICO, Cortés and his men, including Juan de Escalante, established Villa Rica de la Vera Cruz (Rich Villa of the True Cross) adjacent to a small natural port. The settlement allowed Cortés and his followers to escape jurisdiction of the governor of CUBA, DIEGO DE VELÁZQUEZ, who originally sanctioned their exploratory expedition but forbade any settlement. Yet Cortés committed his men to conquest when he burned his ships after establishing his party on the mainland. The determined Cortés quickly made plans for an *entrada* (literally an entrance or expedition into a new area) to the city of TENOCHTITLÁN in the Mexican interior. Before leaving VERACRUZ, Cortés made formal and legal arrangements for the conquest of Mexico, including the provision that those left behind who protected the base area would receive bounty equal to the majority who were to march with Cortés. The important defense of Veracruz was entrusted to Cortés's friend and reliable lieutenant, Juan de Escalante. Cortés left Escalante with approximately 150 men, mostly the infirm and sailors from ruined ships, as well as two HORSES.

In late October Escalante embarked on an *entrada* of his own. After receiving reports that Aztec soldiers were extracting tribute from Totonac villages ostensibly loyal to the Spanish, Escalante marched northward and engaged Aztec soldiers with about 50 of his remnant Spanish troops, seven of whom carried primitive firearms, and some 2,000 to 10,000 Totonac Indians. The reasons for Escalante's decision remain unclear. Perhaps he considered the AZTECS an immediate threat to Veracruz; perhaps he sought to satisfy a personal need to engage in conquest. Whatever Escalante's motivations, the attack proved disastrous. The disciplined and professional Aztec soldiers routed Escalante's ragtag troops; many of the Totonac fled or perished, as did Escalante's horse. Aztec soldiers captured one Spaniard before Escalante and his wounded and disorganized forces beat a hasty retreat. Within days Escalante and seven other Spaniards died. Aztec soldiers, meanwhile, presented the severed head of the captured Spaniard to the Aztec leader MOCTEZUMA II.

Word of this disaster, the first of the Spanish conquest of Mexico, reached Cortés as he met with Moctezuma. Not only had Cortés lost his valued ally and friend Escalante, but Veracruz, his only base, remained exposed and vulnerable. Demanding retribution for the incident from Aztec leaders, Cortés imprisoned Moctezuma, killed several Aztec officers, and burned the contents of an armory.

Further reading: Hugh Thomas, *Conquest: Montezuma, Cortés, and the Fall of Old Mexico* (New York: Simon & Schuster, 1993); S. Jeffrey K. Wilkerson "Escalante's Entrada," *Research & Exploration* 9:1 (Winter 1993): 12.

— Kevin C. Armitage

Ethiopia (Abyssinia)

Today a land-locked nation bounded on the west by the nation state of Sudan, on the south by Kenya and Somalia, and on the east by Somalia, Eritrea, and DJIBOUTI, the 16th-century Christian kingdom of Ethiopia dominated the Horn of Africa, controlled important trade routes from the African interior to the Red Sea, claimed royal descent from King Solomon of Jerusalem, and was the alleged dominion of the mythical prince PRESTER JOHN.

The royal rulers of the early Ethiopian kingdom traced their descent to Maqeda, queen of Sheba, and King Solomon of Jerusalem. According to the *Kebre Nagast* ("The Glory of Kings," a chronicle compiled in the 14th century from local and regional oral histories, Jewish and Islamic writings, the Old and New Testaments, and apocryphal texts) Maqeda traveled to Jerusalem, where she and Solomon conceived a son, Menilek. Maqeda returned to Ethiopia with Menilek, founding the kingdom's Solomonic dynasty that ruled for nearly 20 centuries. In the fourth century the Solomonic rulers adopted Christianity as the official state religion and supported the building of many monasteries and other church structures, including the famous monastery at Debra Damo, which would provide sanctuary in the 16th century for the defeated Ethiopian king LEBNA DENGEL. After a four-century interruption of the dynasty's rule between the ninth and 13th centuries, the Solomonic line once again controlled Ethiopia's throne beginning in 1270 with the reign of Yekuno Amlak (r. 1270–85).

The restoration of the Solomonic line, legitimized by the *Kebre Nagast,* brought with it the expansion of the Christian kingdom against neighboring Muslim states, which developed beginning in the mid-seventh century with the spread of ISLAM from MECCA and the Arabian Peninsula onto the African continent. Ethiopia's Christian tradition solidified under Amda Siyon (r. 1314–44), who, in addition to expanding Ethiopia's territory, also increased the kingdom's involvement in the region's GOLD, ivory, and SLAVE TRADE. Amda Siyon was a powerful and savvy leader who incorporated Muslim merchants and communities into his realm, providing protection from raiders and royal reprisals in return for agreeing to pay the king taxes, recognize his authority, and accept his administration of the region. By the end of his reign, Amda Siyon controlled a large territory composed of Christian, traditional, and Muslim peoples, governed locally by *gult* holders (small, fieflike administrative lands controlled by a landlord loyal to the Ethiopian Crown). Amda Siyon's expansionism did not go unchallenged; in 1332 Sabradin, from the Muslim province of Ifat (Yifat), declared a holy war (*jihad*) against the Ethiopian king, destroying churches and forcing the peoples in the conquered areas to convert to Islam. Sabradin's revolt was, in the end, defeated, but it signaled the mounting tension between Ethiopia's Christian kings and its Muslim subjects. Religious conflict in Ethiopia was not drawn simply between Muslims and Christians but occurred within the Christian community itself. In 1400 Dawit I (r. 1380–1412) arrested the leader of the Sabbatarian movement, Abba Filipos, but released him after much public outcry.

Zar'a Ya'qob (r. 1434–68) unified the Ethiopian Church and used the Christian religion as the kingdom's main defense against Muslim attacks. Throughout his early reign Zar'a Ya'qob attempted to break Muslim control over the eastern regions of the kingdom in the hope of creating better connections with the West and with other Christian kingdoms. As it would be in the 16th century, the main obstacle to Ethiopia's expansionism was the kingdom of Adal, which gained its independence in the 14th century and dominated trade routes to Zeila from the interior. Adal's charismatic leader, Ahmad Badlay, led many forays into Ethiopia's Muslim regions, creating instability and dissent within the larger kingdom. However, Ahmad Badlay died in battle at Dewaro in 1445, which demoralized his army and brought defeat to the Adalite incursion. Zar'a Ya'qob exacted heavy tribute from the Adalites but allowed the region to maintain its own administration. With the defeat of Ahmad Badlay, Ethiopia enjoyed relative peace for the remainder of Zar'a Ya'qob's reign and witnessed a growth in its arts and literature, although much of it was lost in the subsequent disorder brought by recurring Muslim invasions. With the instability and infighting brought by Zar'a Ya'qob's death (the Ethiopian kingdom had no firm rule of royal succession), Christian control of the region began to fracture, and Muslim power and influence increased.

Once again, the kingdom of Adal represented the main opposition to Christian Ethiopian rule. Under the leadership of Mahfuz, emir of Adal in the 1490s, Adalite forces frequently raided Ethiopian border towns during Lent (a period of fasting), killing some and capturing others to send as slaves to Mecca. The Ethiopian king, Noad (r. 1494–1508), defeated Mahfuz, only to be killed by Adalite forces in 1508, leaving his wife, Helene, to serve as regent until his young son and successor, Lebna Dengel (r. 1508–40), reached majority. In 1517 Mahfuz and his Muslim forces faced Lebna Dengel's Christian army in a decisive confrontation. Before a battle between armies could ensue, Mahfuz issued a challenge to Lebna Dengel's men, asking if any would fight a duel to the death with him. A monk named Gabra Endreyas accepted the challenge, killed Mahfuz, and beheaded him. According to an Ethiopian chronicle of the event, Mahfuz's army fled after his death but were pursued and defeated by Lebna Dengel's army, ensuring an important victory over Adal for the young emperor.

Yet Mahfuz's death did not end the struggles between Adal and Ethiopia; internal conflict raged within Adal's Muslim community between secular pragmatists, who argued for independent but tributary status within the Ethiopian empire, and those who wanted Adal to be an independent Muslim state led by Ahmad ibn Ibrahim al-Ghazi, imam of Harer (1506–43). A self-proclaimed imam, Ahmad ibn Ibrahim al-Ghazi, known as Ahmad Grañ ("Ahmad the Left Handed"), inspired a devout following and gained substantial support for his *jihad* against both the secular government of Adal in the city of Harer and Christian Ethiopia. Once he gained control over Adal, Ahmad Grañ refused to pay tribute to the Ethiopian government, who then invaded the kingdom in 1527. The next year Adalite forces defeated the Ethiopians at Shimbra Kure. Ahmad Grañ continued his expansion into Ethiopian territory; by 1535 his forces controlled a large territory from the Red Sea to the interior. That year Lebna Dengel attempted to secure help from Portugal, but he died at the Debra Damo monastery in 1540 before assistance could arrive. In 1541 a Portuguese military expedition arrived, led by Christovão da Gama (son of VASCO DA GAMA). The combined forces of Portuguese and Ethiopian soldiers armed with modern weapons, including firearms, defeated the Muslim Adalites, but da Gama and half the Portuguese forces were killed. That same year Ahmad Grañ enlisted the help of Turkey, another

Muslim state, to defeat the Ethiopians and won a decisive battle in 1542. Ahmad Grañ occupied Ethiopia until 1543, when the Portuguese and Ethiopian forces under their new king Galawedos (r. 1540–59) defeated him. Ahmad Grañ was killed near Lake Tana while retreating to Harer in 1543, but his wife, Bati Del Wenbera, reached the city and married his nephew Nur, exacting from him a promise to continue the campaign against Ethiopia. Nur followed through on his promise in 1545, 1550, 1554, and in 1559 killed Galadewos and defeated his armies. Harer's threat to Christian Ethiopia lasted until 1577, and the Turkish threat in the north continued until 1589, when the Ethiopian king Sarsa Dengel (r. 1563–97) ousted the Turks.

After this final defeat of Muslim forces, many Ethiopians who had been forced by the invaders to convert to Islam renounced the Muslim faith and returned to the Ethiopian Church. Before his death in 1559, Galawedos wrote *Confession of Faith*, demonstrating his allegiance to the Ethiopian Church and warning his Portuguese allies against continued proselytizing for the Catholic Church. The tension between Ethiopian Christians and the Catholic Portuguese in the 16th century had its origins in 1493, when the first Portuguese envoy, Pero da Covilhaõ, arrived in Ethiopia looking for Prester John. More Portuguese arrived in 1508, and by 1520 a Portuguese embassy had arrived. Francisco Alvares, a member of this later party, wrote the first (and the only still extant) detailed description of Ethiopia before the Muslim invasion.

Despite early acceptance of Portuguese missionaries, Ethiopians were deeply mistrustful of them, resisting conversion to Catholicism. JESUITS arrived in 1557 but were expelled from Ethiopia by the emperor Fasiladas in 1630. By that time the Ethiopian kingdom, invaded by Cushitic Oromo herdsmen, had lost much of its authority. The kingdom went into a period of isolation and imperial decline lasting throughout the 17th century.

Further reading: Mordechai Abir, *Ethiopia and the Red Sea: The Rise and Decline of the Solomonic Dynasty and Muslim–European Rivalry in the Region* (London: Frank Cass & Co., 1980); Roderick Grierson and Stuart Munro-Hay, "Ethiopia," in *Africana: The Encyclopedia of the African and African American Experience* eds. Kwame Anthony Appiah and Henry Louis Gates, Jr. (New York: Basic *Civitas* Books, 1999), 693–700; Harold G. Marcus, *A History of Ethiopia* (Berkeley: University of California Press, 1994); Taddesse Tamrat, *Church and State in Ethiopia, 1270–1527* (Oxford, U.K.: Clarenden Press, 1972).

— Lisa M. Brady

Ewe

Living today in southeastern GHANA, southern Togo, and BENIN, the Ewe's early history is little known.

Although the Ewe's beginnings are somewhat obscure, archaeological evidence suggests that the Ewe, a subset of the larger Aja ethnic group, migrated westward from the OYO Empire in the YORUBA region of Nigeria sometime before the 16th century but maintained a longer period of occupation in Togo, beginning perhaps as early as the 13th century. The Ewe, a broad ethnic group consisting of numerous clans and other ethnicities, are closely related to the FON in Benin. Despite the close ethnic ties to the Fon, the Ewe opposed the early Fon kingdom of DAHOMEY as well as other strong monarchies such as the ASANTE. This resistance to strong central political structures may have hindered Ewe state formation. Instead of placing a single king at the head of their political system, the Ewe developed small, localized forms of governance. A system of checks and balances prevented hereditary chiefs from gaining too much power in relation to both family patriarchs and the local assemblies of female and male elders.

Lack of a centralized state may also have precluded the Ewe from forming a strong sense of group identity. Because of their decentralized political system, the Ewe homeland served as a refuge for other peoples fleeing increasingly strong kingdoms such as Dahomey and Asante. This policy of abiding displaced peoples resulted in the melding of the new and established ethnic groups in the area, and the Ewe culture continuously adapted to the pressures and influences of the region's new inhabitants. Furthermore, the Ewe's lack of a central authority left them vulnerable to slave raiding from the 17th to the 19th century. However, the Ewe maintained cohesion in other ways, mainly through language and historical experience, as well as through trade. Women played an important role in this commerce, bearing primary responsibility for trading fish and European goods for agricultural products at the markets.

Further reading: "From the Volta to the Niger, c. 1600–1800," in *A History of West Africa*, vol. 1, 3rd ed., eds. F. J. Ade Ajiya and Michael Crowder (London: Longman, 1985), 412–464; Mark O'Malley, "Ewe," in *Africana: The Encyclopedia of the African and African American Experience*, eds. Kwame Anthony Appiah and Henry Louis Gates, Jr. (New York: Basic *Civitas* Books, 1999), 721–722; "The Peoples," in *Cambridge Encyclopedia of Africa*, eds. Roland Oliver and Michael Crowder (Cambridge, U.K.: Cambridge University Press, 1981), 57–86.

— Lisa M. Brady

F

Fang

A Bantu-speaking ethnic group in what are present-day CAMEROON, Gabon, and Equatorial Guinea, the Fang, also known as the Fan or Pahouin, made up a large percentage of the slaves in the transatlantic and trans-Saharan SLAVE TRADE.

The Fang migrated to northern Cameroon in the seventh or eighth century, then moved farther south as pressures from the HAUSA kingdom and the trans-Saharan slave trade expanded. Skilled hunters and warriors, the Fang pushed other groups, including the Ndowe, farther toward the coast. The Ndowe later acted as middlemen in the slave trade, and the Fang became a primary target for slave raiders. Raiders captured thousands of Fang between the 16th and 19th centuries for sale at the slave markets.

Hearing stories from the Ndowe about the Fang's CANNIBALISM and finding human skulls in Fang households, European missionaries sought to convert the Fang to Christianity. However, the Fang were not cannibals; the skulls were part of the Fang's form of ancestor worship, in which individuals ate part of a deceased person in order to gain qualities of that person's character. The Fang were accomplished ironworkers and wood carvers, and aspects of these spiritual beliefs influenced their artisanal pursuits.

Further reading: "The Peoples," in *Cambridge Encyclopedia of Africa,* eds. Roland Oliver and Michael Crowder (Cambridge, U.K.: Cambridge University Press, 1981), 57–86; Eric Young, "Fang," in *Africana: The Encyclopedia of the African and African American Experience,* eds. Kwame Anthony Appiah and Henry Louis Gates, Jr. (New York: Basic *Civitas* Books, 1999), 729–730.

— Lisa M. Brady

Ferdinand and Isabella (Ferdinand: 1452–1516; Isabella: 1451–1504)

Queen Isabella I of CASTILE and her husband, Ferdinand II of Aragón, centralized royal authority in Spain, expelled JEWS and Muslims (see ISLAM) from their lands, and sponsored the voyages of CHRISTOPHER COLUMBUS.

In the 15th century Spain was not a united country. The two most important kingdoms were Castile and Aragón, and even after the marriage of Ferdinand and Isabella they remained politically and administratively distinct, although the monarchs made many decisions jointly. When explorers claimed new lands in the Americas, they claimed them for Castile, not for Spain. The monarchs themselves insisted on the separateness of their kingdoms and refused to use the title "king of Spain." In royal documents their kingdoms were always listed separately.

Isabella's claim to the throne of Castile initially was in dispute. The previous king of Castile was her half brother, Henry IV. He recognized Isabella as his heir on the condition that she marry Alfonso V, king of Portugal. In defiance of his wishes, she married Ferdinand, king of Sicily and heir to the throne of Aragón, in 1469. Henry then disowned her in favor of his daughter Juana. When he died in 1474, he left the succession in dispute. His death was followed by a civil war between Isabella's supporters and Juana's. Ferdinand played an important role in the conflict, during which he assumed control of Isabella's troops and brought military experts from Aragón to help her. The war ended with a peace treaty in 1479 that recognized Isabella's claim to the throne. Juana retired to a convent, although she maintained her claim to the throne of Castile until her death in 1530.

Ferdinand and Isabella paid little attention to Aragón, devoting their attention to the larger and more populous kingdom of Castile. Their marriage treaty required Ferdinand to live in Castile and stated that he and Isabella would

127

Ferdinand and Isabella seen bidding Columbus farewell on his first voyage   *(The Granger Collection)*

cosign all public decisions. During Isabella's life Ferdinand had considerable authority in Castile, although his expertise lay in foreign policy. When Isabella died in 1504, Ferdinand lost the title king of Castile and became regent for his daughter, Queen Juana.

Within Castile Ferdinand and Isabella sought to curb the power of the nobles and the towns. Isabella strengthened her authority by reorganizing various political and judicial systems. She governed with the aid of a royal council called the Council of Castile and created new courts, the *AUDIENCIA*s, in major cities. She also asserted greater control over government officials. She limited their tenure in office and revived two institutions, the *residencia* and the *pesquisa,* to investigate their performance. In order to prevent officials from transferring their loyalties to the areas they served, she also forbade them to acquire property or marry within their jurisdictions. In foreign affairs Ferdinand encouraged closer relations with Portugal. He also sought to contain French expansion and tried to ensure that Castile would dominate the western Mediterranean.

Ferdinand and Isabella regained land in Spain that was held by the Muslims. Their armies conquered the Muslim kingdom of Granada in 1492, achieving an impor-

tant goal of the RECONQUISTA. Isabella was known as "the Catholic," and while friendly writers praised her piety, she had no tolerance for other religions. The situation of Jews and Muslims had been worsening in Spain for a century, as the older tradition of *convivencia,* in which Christians, Jews, and Muslims generally tolerated one another, gave way to a renewed emphasis on Catholicism. In 1478 Ferdinand and Isabella introduced the INQUISITION to root out heresy. They were particularly suspicious of the *conversos,* Jews who had converted or had been forced to convert to Christianity. In 1492 they decreed that all Jews must leave Spain. The decree of expulsion gave the Jews three months to leave and forbade them to take GOLD, SILVER, weapons, or HORSES with them. Some 150,000 Jews were forced to leave the country, along with more than 300,000 Muslims.

Isabella and Ferdinand are perhaps most famous as the sponsors of Christopher Columbus. They were initially disinclined to support his voyage when their advisers correctly advised them that Columbus's estimate of the size of the world was too small, but during the final siege of Granada, they agreed to sponsor an Atlantic voyage. The expedition was a risk, but if Columbus did find a way to Asia, it was a risk that would pay off handsomely. The gold of the NEW WORLD would eventually show it to have been a worthwhile undertaking for the monarchs, but Columbus himself proved troublesome when he could not maintain peace in HISPANIOLA and overstepped the bounds of his authority. According to BARTOLOMÉ DE LAS CASAS, when Isabella heard that Columbus had given each of 300 colonists an Indian slave, she exclaimed "What power of mine has the Admiral to give anyone my vassals?" Still, Isabella and Ferdinand did sanction some forms of slavery in the New World and permitted the extension of the *ENCOMIENDA* in order to ensure Indian subordination.

Isabella died in 1504. Ferdinand retired to Aragón in 1506 but resumed the administration of Castile in 1510, when Juana, his daughter and queen of Castile, went insane. He died in 1516 and was buried with Isabella in the cathedral of Granada.

Further reading: Robert Chazan, "Expulsion of Jews" in *Dictionary of the Middle Ages,* vol. 4, ed. Joseph R. Strayer (New York: Scribner's, 1984); J. N. Hillgarth, *The Spanish Kingdoms 1250–1516,* vol. 2 (Oxford: Clarendon Press, 1978); Peggy K. Liss, *Isabel the Queen* (New York: Oxford University Press, 1992); Teofilo F. Ruiz, "Castile" in *Dictionary of the Middle Ages,* vol. 3, ed. Joseph R. Strayer (New York: Scribner's, 1984); Barbara A. Tenenbaum, ed. *Encyclopedia of Latin American History and Culture* (New York: Scribner's, 1996).

— Martha K. Robinson

Fernando Po

One of a chain of islands off the western coast of Africa, Fernando Po was claimed by Portuguese explorers in the late 15th century but never attained the same economic importance as the neighboring islands in the archipelago, SÃO TOMÉ and PRÍNCIPE.

The first Europeans to encounter the equatorial island located 20 miles off the west African coast were a group of Portuguese explorers led by captain Fernão do Po, who originally named the island Formosa ("beautiful") but whose own name became attached to the island (today known as Bioko).

Fernando Po is the largest of the so-called Guinea islands, but unlike its neighbors São Tomé and Príncipe, it was never actually settled by its Portuguese claimants due in part to the potential difficulty of subduing its thriving local population and in part to the hazardous approaches to the island that made it unsuitable as a trading colony. Still, the Portuguese exerted influence on the island: The language that developed there was a creole form of Portuguese, and Portugal administered Fernando Po as an extension of São Tomé until 1778, when they ceded the island to Spain.

Further reading: Tony Hodges and Malyn Newitt, *São Tomé and Príncipe: From Plantation Colony to Microstate* (Boulder, Colo.: Westview Press, 1988); Ibrahim K. Sundiata, *From Slavery to Neoslavery: The Bight of Biafra and Fernando Po in the Era of Abolition, 1827–1930* (Madison: University of Wisconsin Press, 1996).

— Marie Kelleher

feudalism

Feudalism is the term used by scholars to describe the political and economic ties among members of the warrior aristocracy in western Europe during the ninth through 13th centuries based on the exchange of military service for maintenance and protection.

The terms *feudalism* and *feudal* have been applied to a great number of phenomena of the medieval period, ranging from monarchical rights over noble tenants to noble rights over peasants. While historians continue to dispute the term, most now use it to refer only to the system of power relations among members of the warrior aristocracy, the main components of which were the personal tie of loyalty known as vassalage and the land grant, known as a fief, that the lord gave to his vassal in exchange for service.

The principal element of feudalism was the relationship between the lord and his vassals, who were free or noble followers bound to their lord by formal ties of loyalty. Vassals may also have promised service, usually military, in exchange for maintenance, often in the form of a grant of land. The tie between lord and vassal, sometimes referred to as homage, was typically both voluntary and reciprocal. Lords had obligations to protect and maintain their vassals in exchange for the vassals' loyalty and service and implied control over a deceased vassal's widow and minor children as well as over inheritance of any land the lord may have granted his vassal.

Feudal ties were solemnized by a ritual of formal commendation wherein the new vassal would kneel before his lord, who would clasp his hands around those of his vassal, symbolizing protection and dominance. The vassal would then verbally declare himself to be his lord's "man." This oath was often sealed with a kiss and followed by an oath of fealty, or loyalty. Fulbert of Chartres best summed up the implications of the oath of fealty. Writing in 1050 in response to a request from the duke of Aquitaine, Fulbert stated that a vassal's oath of fealty implied that he would neither injure his lord, nor betray his secrets or fortresses, nor impede the lord's justice, nor impugn his honor, nor cause him to lose his possessions. In addition, in order to be worthy of a benefice, or land grant, the vassal owed his lord aid and counsel, the former usually implying military service, the latter service in the lord's court.

The relationship between lord and vassal was personal, and even though there might be a hierarchy of feudal relationships stretching from the king through several layers of feudal bonds, the kings' position to their vassals' vassals (and so on) was that of nominal overlord, rather than sovereigns with universal power to command. In fact, the nature of the relationship between lord and vassal was such that a vassal would be expected unquestioningly to support his lord in battle against *his* lord, should the situation arise. As one medieval lord commented, "The man of my man is not my man." The relationship was also dyadic, although there was an implied bond of solidarity among vassals of the same lord. Finally, the relationship between lord and vassal was affective, superseding (in theory, at least) the relationship between husband and wife. It is important to bear in mind that the relationship between the two parties, whatever else it was, was at its core a contract, and the relationship could be broken only if one of the parties involved failed in obligations to the other.

The other phenomenon important to historians of feudalism is the fief, or the parcel of land that the lord granted as a benefice to his vassal. The lord's obligation to maintain his vassal had not always been exclusively in the form of a fief. Lords might offer their vassals employment or find some other way of maintaining them. By the 12th century the option of granting a fief had come to dominate this area of the feudal relation. Fiefs were units of property, normally landed, that vassals held and from which they reaped the profits. The ownership of these lands rested with the lords who granted them, even though they may have been in the possession of someone else. This split between landowner and landholder meant that the lords who granted the fiefs had the power to decide who would get the land upon the current beneficiary's death. Usually, this would be a son (or more infrequently, a daughter) of the former vassal, who would in turn become a vassal him- or herself. The heritability of tenure quickly became a matter of course, especially with the post-Carolingian decentralization of authority.

While the system outlined above seems relatively straightforward, the apparent simplicity of the picture is deceptive. There are a number of important factors to consider before applying any notion of "feudalism" to early and high medieval western Europe. The single problem that underlies all concerns about feudalism is that both the term and the concept were essentially inventions of 17th- and 18th-century jurists and historians who were struggling to find a pattern for the political systems they were attempting to contrast with their own. This desire for uniformity led to a wide variety of political relationships and landholding arrangements being forced into a model for a political system that, as such, never existed earlier. Type of terrain, degree of warfare, style of agricultural exploitation, level of commercial activity, and lay versus ecclesiastical lordship resulted in widely differing political and landholding relationships. Our "classic" picture of feudalism assumes that the rise of feudal relations was the function of a weak central government that was unable to prevent power from devolving to the local level. Although this picture fits well with much of post-Carolingian France, it can hardly be applied to England and Germany, both of which had strong central government and royal institutions during parts of the period of "classic" feudalism. In the end, "feudalism" may roughly describe the political and economic ties among the medieval nobility, but it is a term that should be used with an awareness of the differences it masks.

Further reading: D. Barthélemy, "Debate: The 'Feudal Revolution' I," *Past and Present* 152 (1996): 196–205; Marc Bloch, *Feudal Society,* trans. L. A. Manyon (Chicago: University of Chicago Press, 1964); Elizabeth A. R. Brown, "The Tyranny of a Construct: Feudalism and Historians of Medieval Europe," *American Historical Review* 79:4 (1974): 1063–1088; François Ganshof, *Feudalism,* 3rd English ed., trans. Philip Grierson (New York: Harper, 1961); Susan Reynolds, *Fiefs and Vassals* (Oxford, U.K.: Oxford University Press, 1994).

— Marie A. Kelleher

Florida

The Spanish province of La Florida included all of present-day Florida and portions of Alabama, Georgia, and South Carolina, and before the implementation of the Spanish mission system it contained approximately 500,000 indigenous inhabitants organized into chiefdoms spread throughout the province.

Before the arrival of Europeans, native groups throughout most of the La Florida participated in the MISSISSIPPIAN mound building culture that represented the apex of indigenous development in the eastern portion of North America. Primarily, the Mississippian presence extended throughout southeastern North America into peninsular northern Florida, but not to southern Florida. Except in southern Florida, native populations lived in sedentary villages and practiced intensive horticulture of a variety of crops with a primary reliance on CORN. They supplemented their diet by hunting and gathering wild plants and various aquatic resources. Most villages were palisaded and centered on a grouping of temple and funeral mounds built around a ceremonial square. The people in southern Florida lived in similarly organized towns. They did not practice horticulture on any significant scale, and they depended more upon the gathering of wild plants and aquatic resources. The indigenous groups that eventually had extensive and constant relationships with the Spanish were the Yamasee, Cusabo, Guale, Apalachee, and TIMUCUA in coastal South Carolina, southern Georgia and Alabama, and northern Florida, and the Ai, Calusa, Tekesta, and Key in southern Florida.

The Spanish first learned of Florida's existence in the early 1500s, and JUAN PONCE DE LEÓN named the region La Florida during his expedition there in 1513. The Spanish used this term to describe all the land they claimed in southeastern North America, from current-day North Carolina to Mississippi, but despite the extent of their alleged claims, they never moved far beyond settling the Atlantic coast of South Carolina, Georgia, and Florida, the interior of north Florida, and the Gulf coast of Florida and Alabama.

At first the Spanish could not exercise any real control over their claims in La Florida. The expeditions of Ponce de León in 1521, Lucas de Ayllón in 1526, PÁNFILO DE NARVÁEZ in 1528, HERNANDO DE SOTO in 1539, Lois Cancer de Barbastro in 1549, Juan Pardo in 1566, and Tristán de Luna in 1559 all failed to establish a permanent Spanish presence in La Florida. After French HUGUENOTS founded FORT CAROLINE near modern-day Jacksonville as a base to raid Spanish shipping, the Spanish launched a campaign with enough resources not only to annihilate the French presence but also begin the systematic development of missions and presidios (Spanish fortifications) up the Atlantic coast and across Florida to the Gulf coast. Pedro Menéndez de Avilés led this successful attempt in 1565 to create a permanent Spanish presence in La Florida. In the process he established the city of Saint Augustine, which remained the anchor of the Spanish presence in southeastern North America until 1763. La Florida, and specifically Saint Augustine, acted as a base to protect the shipping lanes off the east coast of the Florida peninsula for the Spanish GOLD fleet that annually left the Americas for Spain. It also was used as a base to maintain Spanish claims in eastern North America. Yet despite their efforts, Spanish influence deteriorated when native groups, the English, and the French challenged their control in the region.

The Spanish successfully incorporated the Apalachee, Timucua, Guale, Cusabo, and some Yamasee into their mission system before 1600, but they were never able to bring the indigenous groups of southern Florida into their fold. The JESUITS first attempted to christianize the Guale, Cusabo, and Yamasee along the Atlantic coast as well as the tribes of southern Florida, but after the indigenous uprisings among the Guale and Cusabo on the Atlantic coast in the late 16th century, the FRANCISCANS replaced the Jesuits throughout La Florida. After the initial establishment of missions and presidios in the region, the Spanish gradually began to lose their foothold on La Florida until they abandoned all the missions and presidios except those in the vicinity of Saint Augustine and Pensacola. During the period of Spanish occupation in Florida, indigenous populations decreased primarily through the introduction of new DISEASES from the Old World but also from famine, war, slave raiding (see SLAVE TRADE) by English-allied natives during the late 17th century, and the burden of supplying the Spanish presence with food and other vital supplies.

Further reading: Michael V. Gannon, *The Cross in the Sand: The Early Catholic Church in Florida, 1530–1870* (Gainesville: University Press of Florida, 1965); ———, *Florida: A Short History* (Gainesville: University Press of Florida, 1993); John H. Hann, *Apalachee: The Land Between the Rivers* (Gainesville: University Press of Florida, 1988); Eugene Lyon, *The Enterprise of Florida: Pedro Menendez de Aviles and the Spanish Conquest of 1565–1568* (Gainesville: University Press of Florida, 1976); Jerald T. Milanich, *Florida Indians and the Invasion from Europe* (University Press of Florida, 1995); ———, *Florida's Indians from Ancient Times to the Present* (Gainesville: University Press of Florida, 1998); ———, *Laboring in the Fields of the Lord: Spanish Missions and Southeastern Indians* (Washington, D.C.: Smithsonian Institution Press, 1999).

— Dixie Ray Haggard

flowery wars

The flowery wars (Nahuatl = *Xochiyaotl*) were semiritual battles that the Aztecs and their neighbors waged for the specific purpose of gaining captives for sacrifice.

In 1454–55, in response to four years of famine, either the Aztec great speaker Moctezuma I or his *cihuacoatl*, TLACACLA, established the flowery wars. Believing that regular and abundant human sacrifice was needed to propitiate the gods, the speaker and his *cihuacoatl* initiated a perpetual war with the other peoples of the Puebla-Tlaxcala valley in order that all might secure a source of sacrificial offerings. These battles were distinct from the concurrent wars of conquest: In this case, conquest would be self-defeating because it would leave no more enemy warriors to capture.

Combatants seem to have gone willingly in response both to the warrior ethos and the belief that only those who died in battle would attain a comfortable afterlife (see AZTECS). Participation also assured a comfortable existence on the earthly plane, given that Moctezuma I and Tlacacla had also established a system of privilege based on battlefield success allowing for exaltation of valiant commoners and debasement of less bellicose nobles.

There is some evidence that Moctezuma's idea was no innovation, but rather an adaptation of a practice long used by various peoples of ancient MEXICO. Nonetheless, it was a significant development, marking the beginning of more than half a century of continuous hostilities between the Aztecs and their neighbors, especially TLAXCALA, resulting not only in a climate of animosity toward the Aztecs but also a tendency toward monumental sacrifices and thus the need for increased warfare, flowery and otherwise. In the long run, the institution of the flowery wars left several independent states within the Aztec Empire that were both able and willing to aid the Spaniards when they arrived in 1519.

Further reading: Geoffrey W. Conrad and Arthur A. Demarest, *Religion and Empire: The Dynamics of Aztec and Inca Expansionism* (Cambridge, U.K.: Cambridge University Press, 1984); Nigel Davies, *Aztecs: A History* (Norman: University of Oklahoma Press, 1980); Kay Almere Read, *Time and Sacrifice in the Aztec Cosmos* (Bloomington: Indiana University Press, 1998).

— Marie A. Kelleher

Fon

Also known as the Agadja, the Fon are an ethnic group whose ancestors built the early kingdom of DAHOMEY in the southern part of modern-day BENIN.

The Fon were originally part of the Adja kingdom in Tado (present-day Togo). They separated from that kingdom early in the 17th century after an unsuccessful attempt to take control of the Adja throne. Legend states that Agasu, the son of an Adja princess and a leopard, attempted to usurp the throne. He and his Fon followers were forced to leave Adja when the coup failed. They fled to Allada, establishing their own kingdom, but succession struggles plagued the new Fon kingdom. Agasu's son Dogbari migrated to Abomey around 1620, establishing the kingdom of Dahomey. Dahomey's highly centralized monarchy and large army, made up in part by female warriors (known as Amazons), gave the Fon kingdom a powerful advantage over neighboring kingdoms. As part of their conquests, the Fon often took slaves from the conquered peoples for labor and sacrificial purposes as well as for use in the SLAVE TRADE.

Further reading: Elizabeth Heath, "Fon," in *Africana: The Encyclopedia of the African and African American Experience,* eds. Kwame Anthony Appiah and Henry Louis Gates, Jr. (New York: Basic *Civitas* Books, 1999), 760; ———, "The Peoples," in Roland Oliver and Michael Crowder, eds., *Cambridge Encyclopedia of Africa* (Cambridge, U.K.: Cambridge University Press, 1981), 57–86.

— Lisa M. Brady

Foxe's *Book of Martyrs*

John Foxe's popular *Actes and Monuments,* more commonly called *The Book of Martyrs,* helped convince English Protestants of their importance in the struggle between Protestantism and Catholicism.

The Book of Martyrs, although focusing on English Protestant martyrs during the reign of Mary Tudor, sought to show a connection between the simplicity of the early church and the reformed practices of 16th-century Protestants. According to Foxe, the Church of Rome had fallen to the Antichrist, but God had also raised up reformers to fight against the corruption of the church.

The Book of Martyrs was among the most important English Reformation works. In its effect on the religious ideas of English Protestants, it ranks behind only the English Bible and the *Book of Common Prayer.* It went through nine editions between 1563 and 1684, with later editions generally becoming longer and more complete. Foxe emphasized the role of the English church in the "Latter and Perilous Days" in which he believed he was living, but he also recognized the contributions of European reformers to the purifying of the church.

Foxe's work is the best-known of the books of martyrs, but it was part of a larger tradition. Both Protestant and Catholic authors wrote and compiled histories of their martyrs. These works, written in vernacular languages, emphasized the evil done by members of opposing churches and helped shape popular conceptions of religion.

Further reading: Patrick Collinson, "Foxe, John" in *The Oxford Encyclopedia of the Reformation,* vol. 2, ed. Hans J. Hillerbrand (New York: Oxford University Press, 1996), 122–123; Jean-François Gilmont, "Books of Martyrs" in *The Oxford Encyclopedia of the Reformation,* vol. 1, ed. Hans J. Hillerbrand (New York: Oxford University Press, 1996), 195–200; D. M. Loades, *The Oxford Martyrs* (London: B. T. Batsford, 1970); V. Norskov Olsen, *John Foxe and the Elizabethan Church* (Berkeley: University of California Press, 1973); Helen C. White, *Tudor Books of Saints and Martyrs* (Madison: University of Wisconsin Press, 1963).

— Martha K. Robinson

Franciscans

The largest order of friars in early modern Europe, the Franciscans were active in missionary work but in the Americas were torn by internal divisions.

The Franciscan order was founded in the early 13th century by Francis of Assisi. By the 16th century the Franciscans, like other religious orders, were being criticized for not living up to their vows of poverty, chastity, and obedience but instead living in luxury. These criticisms came both from within and without the order. From outside some secular leaders, most notably FERDINAND AND ISABELLA of Spain, tried to reform the order. More important reform impulses within the order led to its division. By the 14th century some Franciscans had come to believe that the order needed to adhere more closely to the vision of St. Francis, especially in the matter of poverty. These reformers came to be known as Observants. By 1517 the division between the Observants and the Conventuals had become so acrimonious that Pope LEO X issued a bull, *Ite et vos,* that separated them into distinct branches within the Franciscan order. This division left the Observants with about 30,000 members and the Conventuals with about 25,000. The same impulse to recover the purity of the original order would result in more divisions in the 16th century, leading to the creation of four new offshoots, the Discalced, Recollect, Reformed, and Capuchin Franciscans. Among the female orders of Franciscans, reform usually meant a greater emphasis on the strict cloistered life.

Roman Catholic friars, generally Franciscans, accompanied initial Spanish explorations of the New World. Franciscan missionaries landed with HERNÁN CORTÉS in 1525 in what is now La Paz, Mexico, ostensibly to introduce Christianity to Native American groups. The Franciscans abandoned this missionary effort due to difficult agricultural conditions. Beginning in 1540, Franciscan friars accompanied the expedition of FRANCISCO CORONADO, only to be murdered by Native Americans they attempted to convert. The Franciscans made another effort to establish missions among Native Americans in 1596, when five friars accompanied Spaniard Sebastián Vizcaíno. Ill-supplied and unsuccessful in recruiting neophytes, these missionaries again abandoned missionary efforts in Baja California. In general, the Franciscan friars were less willing than the JESUITS to think that converts could retain their cultural heritage while becoming Christian and were more likely to expect cultural as well as religious conversion.

Further reading: Jean Delumeau, *Catholicism between Luther and Voltaire: A New View of the Counter-Reformation* (London, Burns and Oates, 1977); John Patrick Donnelly, S. J., "Religious Orders" in *The Oxford Encyclopedia of the Reformation,* vol. 3, ed. Hans J. Hillerbrand (New York: Oxford University Press, 1996), 413–416; C. J. Lynch, "Franciscans" in the *New Catholic Encyclopedia,* vol. 4, ed. William J. McDonald, et al. (New York: McGraw-Hill, 1967), 38–46; Lyle N. McAlister, *Spain and Portugal in the New World, 1492–1700* (Minneapolis: University of Minnesota Press, 1984); John Moorman, *A History of the Franciscan Order: From Its Origins to the Year 1517* (Oxford, U.K.: Clarendon Press, 1968).

— Martha K. Robinson
— James Jenks

Frobisher, Martin (1539–1594)

An English explorer, knighted admiral, and occasional pirate, Martin Frobisher led three unsuccessful voyages to Greenland and Canada in the 1570s in hope of discovering GOLD and a NORTHWEST PASSAGE through North America to China.

An accomplished mariner who undertook two trading expeditions to West Africa before his 20th birthday, Frobisher earned favor with Queen ELIZABETH I for his naval skills and his role as a privateer, or licensed pirate, for the English government. Raised in an aristocratic Yorkshire family who told tales of the riches of the Orient, Frobisher offered to find a northwest passage to China for 15 years before gaining the support of the Muscovy Company and its director, Michael Lok. In June 1576 Frobisher and his crew of 35 men sailed two large ships, the *Gabriell* and the *Michaell,* and an additional small ship past a waving Queen Elizabeth on their way west across the Atlantic. A storm near GREENLAND claimed the smaller ship, and the *Michaell,* now separated from Frobisher and the *Gabriell,* returned to England. Frobisher continued westward around Greenland and discovered what became known as Frobisher's Strait, the bay at Canada's Baffin Island that he believed was the passage to Asia. After both peaceful and hostile encounters with the island's native Inuit population, Frobisher returned to England with a small amount of black ore and an Inuit prisoner.

Although the captive soon died and the efforts to refine the ore proved inconclusive, English interest in both led to a second voyage sponsored by the Cathay Company, Frobisher and Lok's newest venture, in May 1577. Frobisher added a third ship, the *Ayde,* and set off with 120

Sir Martin Frobisher, detail of an oil painting by Cornelius Ketel (1548–1616), dated 1577 *(The Granger Collection)*

men and orders to return with large amounts of ore. The crew of the *Ayde* brought back 200 tons of ore while Frobisher, unable to locate the members of his earlier crew missing on Baffin Island, captured three Inuits—a man, a woman, and a child—and returned to Europe.

Before refiners in England declared the ore from the second voyage to be of poor quality, Frobisher launched a third and final voyage around Greenland in May 1578 with the goal of obtaining 2,000 tons of ore and creating a mining colony on Baffin Island. This ambitious effort involved 15 vessels and an unprecedented crew of almost 400 men. While Frobisher took possession of Greenland in the name of Queen Elizabeth, naming it West England, he abandoned the plan to create a settlement after storms and ice sank one ship and convinced another to return to England. Before leaving Frobisher ordered the crew to build two homes, one of stone and one of wood, to determine the effects of arctic winters. The group also buried supplies and planted a few crops with the expectation of a return voyage in 1579. Frobisher continued to believe his discovery held the shortcut to Asia, but after years of failed attempts in England to refine the mysterious black ore into gold, enthusiasm and investors dissipated and the Cathay Company faced bankruptcy. Not until the early 1600s did George Waymouth and Henry Hudson prove that Frobisher's Strait led to Canada's Hudson Bay rather than Asia.

Frobisher's three voyages marked the first encounter between Europeans and North American Arctic peoples such as the Inuit. Explorers' accounts and Inuit folklore describe minimal trade of items such as food and furs during the first voyage. After five members of Frobisher's initial crew were lost and feared captured, the English and the natives limited later encounters to brief skirmishes and attempts to obtain or recover hostages. While none of the Inuits Frobisher took back to England survived more than a short time, the ethnographic accounts about their culture revealed, to the surprise of Europeans, a complex Arctic society with iron weapons and tools.

Despite his failures in the North Atlantic, Frobisher's reputation remained intact as he continued his naval duties with numerous campaigns against Ireland and Spain, including a lucrative privateering expedition in the West Indies with SIR FRANCIS DRAKE. In 1588 Queen Elizabeth knighted Frobisher, then an admiral of the seas, for his efforts in defending England from the SPANISH ARMADA. Six years later Frobisher died of a gunshot wound suffered while fighting the Spanish in the Battle of Brest. Although Frobisher died without discovering the pathway to the Orient or its elusive riches, his three failed voyages were important in encouraging Europeans, especially the British, to turn south for exploration and settlement rather than risk the dangers and costs of Arctic expeditions.

Further reading: John L. Allen, ed., *North American Exploration: A New World Disclosed,* vol. 1 (Lincoln: University of Nebraska Press, 1997); William W. Fitzhugh and Jacqueline S. Olin, eds., *Archeology of the Frobisher Voyages* (Washington, D.C.: Smithsonian Institution Press, 1993); James McDermot, *Martin Frobisher, Elizabethan Privateer*

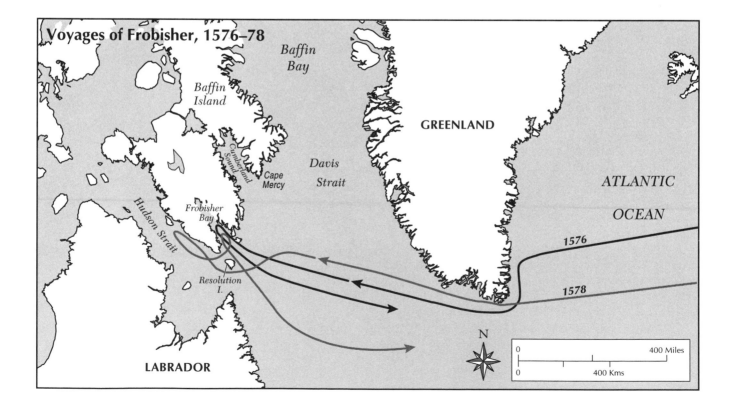

Voyages of Frobisher, 1576–78

(New Haven, Conn.: Yale University Press, 2001); William McFee, *Sir Martin Frobisher* (London: J. Lane, Bodley Head, 1928).

— Richard Hughes

Fulani (Peul, Fula, Fulbe)

Believed to have origins in the grasslands around the Senegal River, the Fulani are a largely pastoral ethnic group widely dispersed through West Africa, including present-day Senegal, Guinea, MALI, Niger, Nigeria, and CAMEROON.

Until the fall of the kingdom of GHANA in the 11th century, the Fulani were nomadic pastoralists composed of several autonomous bands each led by its own headman. They traced their descent patrilineally and maintained an animistic spiritual belief system. They lived on the western edge of Ghana and remained relatively independent until the Tarkur established a new Islamic (see ISLAM) state in Ghana. Under the new kingdom some Fulani abandoned their traditional pastoral lifestyles and became sedentary. This branch of the Fulani merged with the already settled population to form the Tukolor, a Fulfulde-speaking subgroup.

By the 14th century the Fulani began migrating eastward, away from their traditional homeland. They reached the Futa Djallon region of present-day Guinea and Mali by the 15th century, and by the 16th century they had arrived in Hausaland and Bornu in modern-day Nigeria. Previously a somewhat homogenous ethnic group in West Africa, migration brought cultural differentiation to the Fulani based on lifestyle choices. The *fulani bororo*, or cattle Fulani, retained their pastoral traditions. The *fulani gida*, or town Fulani, settled in towns along the route of migration through Mali, SONGHAI, and HAUSA.

During the 16th century many Fulani converted to radical forms of ISLAM influenced by SUFISM. These sects, including the *qadiriya* and *tijaniya* orders that were brought across the SAHARA by the TUAREG, upheld the right of the faithful to establish a society based on Islamic principles through rebellion against unjust rulers. Through *jihad,* or holy war, the Fulani replaced rulers they felt were corrupt with devout Muslim theocracies.

Further reading: Yaa Pokua Afriiyie Oppong, "Fulani," in *Africana: The Encyclopedia of the African and African American Experience*, eds. Kwame Anthony Appiah and Henry Louis Gates, Jr. (New York: Basic *Civitas* Books, 1999), 794; "Peul," in *Historical Dictionary of Mali*, 2nd ed., ed. Pasca James Imperato (Metuchen, N.J.: Scarecrow Press, 1986), 209–210.

— Lisa M. Brady

G

Gama, Vasco da (1469–1524)

The navigator Vasco da Gama succeeded in discovering a passage to India in 1498, an achievement that made possible the Portuguese monopoly over the spice trade with the Orient.

The likelihood of a passage to India had been paved by BARTHOLOMEU DIAS's rounding of the Cape of Good Hope in 1488. Then, in March 1496, as CHRISTOPHER COLUMBUS struggled to obtain approval for his third expedition to the NEW WORLD, Portugal made plans for an expedition to India under Vasco da Gama's leadership. The Spanish Crown's willingness to grant financing to Columbus stemmed in large part from the competition between Spain and Portugal and the knowledge of da Gama's planned journey.

Historians know very little about Vasco da Gama's life before his voyage to India. Born in Sines, Portugal, in 1469, da Gama grew up the son of the governor of the Order of St. James. Da Gama served in the royal court of King João II and later became a naval officer. Before his voyage to India, da Gama led the defense of Portuguese overseas possessions in Guinea.

Da Gama and his fleet of four ships departed LISBON harbor in July 1497, and in May 1498 the crew sighted the Malabar Coast of India. Along the way da Gama and his crew encountered conflict when they reached Muslim (see ISLAM) trading centers along the coast of Africa. Despite tensions between the Portuguese and Muslim traders, da Gama reached Calicut, India, on May 20, 1498.

Following an initial welcome from the indigenous Hindu ruler and his people, da Gama and his crew soon found themselves excluded from the Indian and Hindu trade networks. The indigenous people considered Portuguese goods to be of little or no value. As a result, in August 1498 da Gama began the difficult journey back to Lisbon having very little to show for his journey beyond recognition as the first European to reach India.

In a 1502 return trip to India da Gama equipped himself with better preparations and a much larger crew. During this expedition da Gama successfully pursued his goal of establishing a trade network between the Portuguese and East Indies through brutal and deadly force.

Vasco da Gama's discovery of a passage to India enabled the Portuguese to expand their commercial empire and establish dominion over the booming spice trade. Portugal owed much to da Gama, including important bases secured in Ceylon, Malacca, the SPICE ISLANDS of the Indonesian archipelago, and the colony of Macao on the Chinese mainland. Following da Gama's death in 1524 during his final journey to India, the Portuguese continued their extensive exploration of the NEW WORLD.

Further reading: Francis A. Dutra, "A New Look at the Life and Career of Vasco da Gama," *Portuguese Studies Review* 6:2 (1997–1998): 23–28; Sanay Subrahmanyam, *The Career and Legend of Vasco da Gama* (Cambridge, U.K.: Cambridge University Press, 1997); Edwin Williamson, *The Penguin History of Latin America* (New York and London: Penguin Press, 1992).

— Kimberly Sambol-Tosco

Gao

A city on the upper bend of the NIGER RIVER, Gao served as an important trading center for the MALI and SONGHAI Empires.

Gao likely arose as a city in the eighth century as a terminus for the trans-Saharan trade routes carrying GOLD, salt, slaves (see SLAVE TRADE), and other goods between North and East Africa and West Africa, with trade partners as distant as Algeria and Egypt. Gao probably began as a seasonal camp for the Sorko, a fishing people who grew crops on the banks of the Niger while in residence there. What the Sorko could not grow or harvest from the river, they traded for with the nomadic peoples living on the fringes of the SAHARA. Early connections between Gao's inhabitants and North African traders facilitated the spread

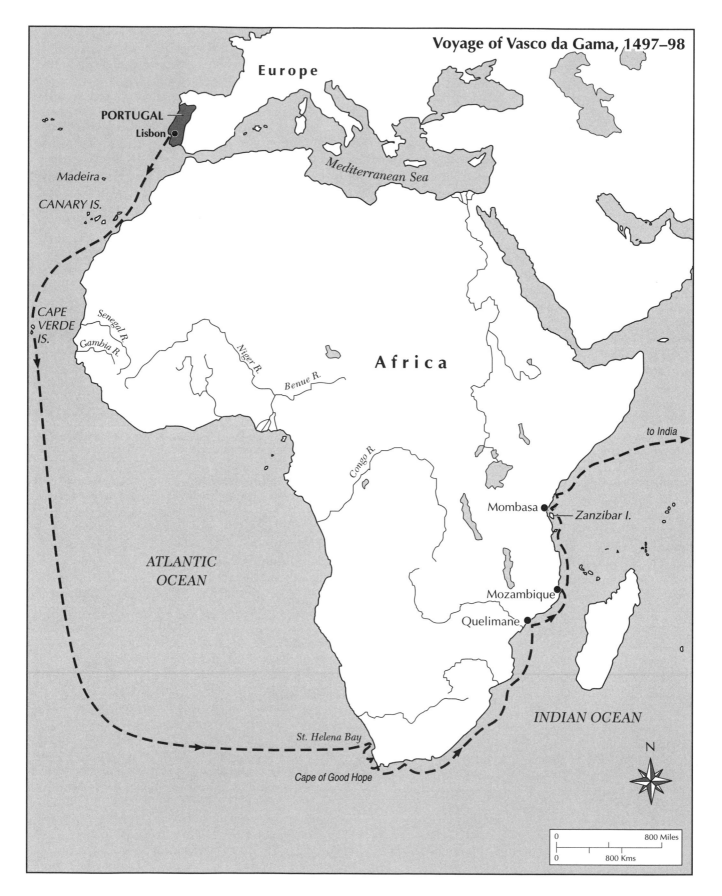

Voyage of Vasco da Gama, 1497–98

Europe

PORTUGAL
Lisbon

Madeira

CANARY IS.

Mediterranean Sea

CAPE
VERDE
IS.

Senegal R.

Gambia R.

Niger R.

Benue R.

A f r i c a

Congo R.

to India

Mombasa

Zanzibar I.

ATLANTIC
OCEAN

Mozambique

Quelimane

St. Helena Bay

INDIAN OCEAN

N

Cape of Good Hope

| 0 | | 800 Miles |
| 0 | | 800 Kms |

of ISLAM to the area, especially through the conversion of the royal rulers of the city. By the 13th century Islam was the dominant religion there.

The growth of the ancient kingdom of GHANA in the ninth century provided the necessary impetus for the fishing camp to become an influential trading center. By the 12th century Gao elicited intense competition among eastern traders, who wanted to control the growing gold trade, and western merchants, who wished to retain their monopoly of that lucrative commerce. By the 13th century Gao's importance to the trans-Saharan trade attracted the attention of powerful kingdoms, including Mali, which incorporated the city into its empire by the middle of that century.

Under the rule of MANSA MUSA I in the 14th century, Gao designated the eastern edge of the great Mali Empire. The Songhai, a tributary state to Mali, had its base in Gao and used the city's strategic location to aid them in their overthrow of the Mali kingdom in the 15th century. Under the Askia dynasty (see ASKIA MUHAMMAD I), Gao replaced Kikuya, the ancient royal capital of the Songhai, as the capital of the new empire. The famous chronicler LEO AFRICANUS visited Gao during the reign of Muhammad I and described the city as a large town whose king had numerous wives and concubines housed in a large, separate palace heavily guarded by slaves and eunuchs.

Eventually, the Songhai kingdom ended where it started, sealing the fate of Gao. Moroccan invaders under the leader Mansur defeated the Songhai Empire near its home city in 1589, expelling the Songhai from Gao in 1591. The Moroccans had a military advantage in the form of firearms, easily defeating the Songhai, armed only with hand weapons. With the invasion of the Moroccans and the expulsion of the Songhai, Gao declined rapidly in importance to the trans-Saharan trade.

Further reading: J. F. Ade Ajayi and Michael Crowder, *History of West Africa*, vol. 1, 3rd ed. (London: Longman, 1985); Basil Davidson, "Songhay Achievement" and "Kanem-Bornu and the Hausa States," in *West Africa before the Colonial Era: A History to 1800,* (London: Longman, 1998), 47–90; Elizabeth Heath, "Mali," in *Africana: The Encyclopedia of the African and African American Experience*, eds. Kwame Anthony Appiah and Henry Louis Gates, Jr. (New York: Basic *Civitas* Books, 1999), 1236–1241.

— Lisa M. Brady

Gedi

A coastal town in modern-day Kenya, Gedi's history from the 13th to the 17th century is one of periodic abandonment and reoccupation.

Located 10 miles south of present-day Malindi, Gedi has a mysterious past. Its outer wall, nearly nine feet tall, surrounded 45 acres, which were separated from the town proper by an inner wall. The city had a large mosque, a palace, three pillar tombs, several small mosques, and many private houses. Influenced by the Swahili culture of southeastern Africa, Gedi was not integrated into the Swahili coastal trading system. It lay four miles from the coast of the Indian Ocean and two miles from a navigable creek. This inland location may be explained by the tendency of water courses to shift their banks, but some have argued that it is because its focus was not on the sea but instead on the land that surrounded it. Because no written records from the city exist, not even from the period of Portuguese settlement (1512–1593) of nearby Malindi, its history remains ambiguous.

Archaeological evidence provides some insight into the physical structure of the city and thus into its society. Gedi's architecture ensured the comfort of its inhabitants. Long shadows created by sunken courts kept the palace cool, as did the thick walls and stamped red earth roofs of other buildings. Like the palace, all private residences had separate lavatories and strong rooms for storing valuables. Sumps throughout the town held surface water, ensuring the integrity of the structures' walls and protecting them from damaging runoff. The great mosque, built of stone and coral tiles in the mid-15th century and located near the palace, incorporated traditional Swahili symbols of kingship. Carved in the entry was a broad-bladed spear. The arched *quibla*—showing the direction of MECCA (see ISLAM)—was in the north wall of the mosque.

Archaeological evidence suggests Gedi was the site of a highly developed, complex, and wealthy society. Probably founded in the 13th century, it suffered from decline until it was rebuilt sometime in the 15th century, when it reached the height of its prosperity. The inhabitants of the city abandoned Gedi in the 16th century, reoccupied it briefly, but abandoned it permanently by the early 17th century. No clues exist as to why Gedi was abandoned; Portuguese or Galla attack, a decrease in the water tables, and epidemic disease represent only some of the tentative explanations.

Further reading: James de Vere Allen, *Swahili Origins: Swahili Culture and the Shungwaya Phenomenon* (London: James Curry, 1993); Robert Fay, "Gedi," in *Africana: The Encyclopedia of the African and African American Experience*, eds. Kwame Anthony Appiah and Henry Louis Gates, Jr. (New York: Basic *Civitas* Books, 1999), 823; Michael N. Pearson, *Port Cities and Intruders: The Swahili Coast, India, and Portugal in the Early Modern Era* (Baltimore: Johns Hopkins University Press, 1998).

— Lisa M. Brady

Gesner, Conrad von (1516–1565)

Swiss physician and naturalist whose five-volume *Historia Animalium* (1551–58 and 1587) attempted to systematically describe all known animals, providing science with a foundation for modern zoology.

Impressed by his son's prodigious intellectual abilities, Gesner's father, a poor furrier, sent young Conrad to live with an uncle who derived supplemental income by collecting medicinal herbs. The young Gesner thus grew up in an environment that fostered his interest in medicine and natural history. Gesner's intellectual aptitude so impressed his teachers that one acted as a foster father after Gesner's biological father died fighting for the Protestant cause in 1531. In 1533 Gesner won a traveling scholarship and spent two years of self-directed study in Bourges and Paris. A man of many languages, Gesner spoke Dutch, French, German, Greek, Hebrew, Italian, Latin, probably some English, and maintained a reading knowledge of Arabic. Such talents landed the 21-year-old Gesner an appointment as professor of Greek at the Lausanne Academy. After three years of teaching, Gesner left to study medicine and finish his doctoral degree in Basel; in his spare time he completed a Greek–Latin dictionary published in 1537. Gesner spent his professional career practicing medicine in Zurich, where, among many other activities, he served as lecturer in Aristotelian physics at the Collegium Carolinum and after 1554 as city physician.

Gesner's career as an author was astonishing. He wrote or edited at least 70 books during his lifetime, several of which were among the first contributions to their various disciplines. In an early work describing the virtues of milk, Gesner included a letter to a friend that lauded mountains as among the finest wonders of nature. This letter, along with a 1555 account of his summit climb of Mt. Pilatus, constitute some of the first literature on mountain climbing. In 1545 Gesner published his remarkable and justly famous *Bibliotheca universalis*, a reference work listing more than 1,800 authors and their works, widely regarded as the world's first modern bibliography. Ten years later he published *Mithridates: De differentis linguis*, an account of the approximately 130 languages then known.

Gesner's most lasting contributions related to his attempts to categorize human knowledge of nature. His *Historiae animalium* sought to compile all recorded knowledge of animal life, distinguishing between known facts and popular myths. Gesner's work revived the classical school of zoological description that culminated with the work of Carolus Linnaeus. Gesner's penchant for systematic thought infused his 1565 volume on minerals, *De omni rerum fossilium*, the first illustrated book on minerals. Although uncompleted, Gesner's comprehensive compendium of plant life that included his voluminous notes and more than 1,500 engravings informed scholarly work for more than two centuries after his death. Gesner's accuracy and systematic thinking were important contributions to early Enlightenment science. He died of PLAGUE on December 13, 1565.

Further reading: Willey Ley, *Dawn of Zoology* (Englewood Cliffs, N.J.: Prentice Hall, 1968).

— Kevin C. Armitage

Ghana

The ancient kingdom of Ghana, not to be confused with the modern-day nation-state, ruled over the area located in present-day western MALI and southeastern Mauritania during the ninth through 13th centuries.

Oral tradition describes the rise and fall of an ancient kingdom in the Sahel (see SAHARA) known as Wagadu. Founded by the Soninke, the most northern of the Mande peoples, Wagadu's rulers, the Magha, lived in the capital city of Kumbi. The basis of Wagadu's wealth was GOLD, replenished each year by the kingdom's guardian. This guardian, a powerful snake, demanded the annual sacrifice of a virgin to ensure the continued success of the kingdom. Catastrophe came to the kingdom when the lover of one virgin destined for sacrifice killed the snake, which cursed the kingdom with desiccation of its lands and cessation of the flow of gold. Unable to survive in the desert, the people of Wagadu dispersed to new lands.

Contemporary historical evidence and modern archaeological findings show that the legends of Wagadu closely correlate to the history of the ancient kingdom of Ghana. Although the snake does not play into the historical and archaeological records on Ghana, the role of gold in the formation and success of the kingdom and the location and name of the capital provide evidence that Wagadu and Ghana were the same.

Late eighth-century Arab historical sources show that Ghana, which was the name of both the kingdom and the rulers, emerged out of the growth of the trans-Saharan trade routes that transported slaves (see SLAVE TRADE), ivory, cloth, food products such as salt, and, most important, gold across the Sahara among North, West and East Africa. Ghana's merchants served as middlemen between the Berber and Arab traders of Northern Africa and the producers of gold and ivory in the south. Taking advantage of this central position, the kings of Ghana attained control over the highly lucrative gold trade by the end of the eighth century, inspiring the Baghdad (Iraq) chronicler Al-Farazi to describe the kingdom as the "land of gold." By the 11th century the tales of the riches of Ghana had reached Spain, where the Muslim historian al-Bakri, who never visited Ghana, took his information from traders and explorers who described the kingdom as one in which dogs wore collars of gold and the kings were called "lords of the gold." In fact, Ghana's kings served two functions and held the title of both "lord of the gold" *(kaya maghan)* as well as war chief *(ghana).*

Al-Bakri's descriptions of Ghana remain the best sources of information on the kingdom. In his histories he described Ghana's royal court, its army, and its economic and trading systems. Al-Bakri also described the royal city, built of stone, and its twin commercial city located approximately six miles distant, both named Koumbi-Saleh. In one of these cities lived the traditional kings of the empire, who adhered to their traditional pagan religion. The other city housed a wealthy merchant trader class, which was predominantly Muslim. These traders, buoyed by their success as middlemen in the trans-Saharan trade, imported luxury goods from Spain and Morocco. Koumbi Saleh was a type of "port city" (if the Sahara is taken as a "sea" of sand, the Sahel, in which the city was located, as its shore, and the camel its ships) and as such stimulated high levels of political organization and state formation.

At its height the kingdom of Ghana reached the Senegal River in the west, and its southern border was the confluence of the Senegal and Faleme Rivers. It controlled the rich Bambuk gold fields as well as the gold deposits at Wangara, between the upper NIGER RIVER and the Senegal River. By its apex in the ninth century, Ghana began trading slaves for salt from Teghaza in the Sahara and cloth from North Africa, further expanding its trading and political influence, but decline set in when the empire had to defend its control of the gold trade from competitors. By 1076 Ghana had weakened, leaving it open to attack from the north. In that year the Muslim Almoravids of the Maghreb attacked and destroyed the capital. The Almoravids, led by Abu Bakr, waged a *jihad* (Islamic holy war) against the pagan Ghana kingdom, converting many to ISLAM. After a short occupation by the Almoravids, Ghana recovered, but in 1203 Sumanguru, a leader of the Takrur people to the west, defeated Ghana again. His reign, known as the Sosso kingdom, was also short-lived because the Mande people of Mali under the leadership of SUNDI-ATA KEITA defeated him in a mythical battle. By the end of the 13th century, Ghana was subsumed into the more powerful Mali Empire.

Further reading: Basil Davidson, "Pioneers in Ancient Ghana," in *West Africa before the Colonial Era: A History to 1800* (London: Longman, 1998), 23–34; Nehemia Levtzion, "The Early States of the Western Sudan to 1500," in *History of West Africa,* vol. 1, 3rd ed., ed. J. F. Ade Ajiya and Michael Crowder (London: Longman, 1985), 129–166; Mark O'Malley, "Ghana," and Elizabeth Heath, "Ghana, Early Kingdom of," in *Africana: The Encyclopedia of the African and African American Experience,* eds. Kwame

Anthony Appiah and Henry Louis Gates, Jr. (New York: Basic *Civitas* Books, 1999), 828–835; Thurstan Shaw, "The Prehistory of West Africa," in *History of West Africa,* vol. 1, 3rd ed., eds. J. F. Ade Ajiya and Michael Crowder (London: Longman, 1985), 48–86.

— Lisa M. Brady

Gilbert, Sir Humphrey (1539?–1583)

Among the most influential promoters of the English colonization of North America, Sir Humphrey Gilbert was among the elite whom Queen ELIZABETH I sent to Ireland to secure her rule there, an assignment that Gilbert carried out with as much zeal as his long-term efforts to find the NORTHWEST PASSAGE.

Born near the end of the 1530s, Gilbert would have been in his 20s when he joined the mission of Sir Henry Sidney to Ireland in June 1566. That mission was part of a larger military campaign known to scholars as the Elizabethan conquest of Ireland, a campaign characterized by the bloody tactics English officers devised in an attempt to get native Catholic Irish men and women to accept the rule of the Protestant queen. Thomas Churchyard, an observer of English actions (and an Englishman himself), described the ways Gilbert hoped to subdue the Irish. According to Churchyard, Gilbert ordered "that the heddes of all those (of what sort soever thei were) which were killed in the daie, should be cutte of from their bodies and brought to the place where he incamped at night, and should there bee landed on the ground by eche side of the waie ledying into his own tense so that none could come into his tense for any cause but commonly he muste pass through a lane of heddes which he used *ad terrorem,* the dedde feelyng nothyng the more paines thereby: and yet did it bring grease terrour to the people when thei sawe the heddes of their dedde fathers, brothers, children, kinsfolke and freinds, lye on the grounde before their faces, as thei came to speak with the said collonell." After the campaign Gilbert returned to Ireland in 1570, and two years later he once again served with the queen's military forces when he led 1,100 men against Spanish troops in several inconsequential skirmishes.

Gilbert's service in Ireland and the Netherlands pleased the queen, who granted him a patent enabling him to control much of northeastern North America if he could establish settlements there. Because he was a half brother of SIR WALTER RALEGH, Gilbert seemed ideally situated for the task. By the time he set out on his first venture to the Western Hemisphere in 1578, he had already written *A Discourse of a Discoverie for a New Passage to Cataia,* published in London in 1576, which examined evidence for the existence of a water route to East Asia. With knowledge that he gathered from RICHARD HAKLUYT THE

ELDER and others about the bountiful fisheries off New-foundland, Gilbert hoped to create a colony between 40 and 42 degrees north latitude. Although his first effort failed in 1579, Gilbert arranged for a more substantial effort upon his return in 1583. Among his associates was the young Hungarian poet-adventurer, STEPHEN PARMENIUS, a close friend of RICHARD HAKLUYT THE YOUNGER. Once in Newfoundland, Parmenius and many of Gilbert's men realized that the territory was less pleasing and promising than they had been led to believe by their leader. With discontent on the rise and supplies running short, Gilbert decided that the time had come to return to England, but Gilbert's small squadron of ships ran into foul weather in September 1583. Parmenius went down on the *Delight,* and Gilbert himself died when a smaller ship, the *Squirrel,* sank.

Gilbert made extensive plans about how he would run his colony. Like other Elizabethans, he was convinced that settlements in North America would become profitable. He believed that many English people would choose to migrate there and those who did so would enjoy a better life than they had left behind in Europe. In the end, of course, his dreams died with him, but not before he had laid out his plans to his associates and in various reports. Little could he have known that the territory he desperately wanted to bring into the English realm would eventually become part of New France.

Further reading: Nicholas P. Canny, "The Ideology of English Colonization: From Ireland to America," *William and Mary Quarterly,* 3rd ser., 30 (1973), 575–598; David B. Quinn and Neil M. Cheshire, *The New Found Land of Stephen Parmenius: The life and writings of a Hungarian poet, drowned on a voyage from Newfoundland, 1583* (Toronto: University of Toronto Press, 1972); David Beers Quinn, ed., *The Voyages and Colonising Enterprises of Sir Humphrey Gilbert,* 2 vols., Works Issued by the Hakuyt Society, 2nd Ser., LXXXIII–LXXXIV (London, 1940).

gold

The precious commodity that drove rulers of kingdoms to sponsor colonizing expeditions so they could enrich themselves by gaining what was arguably the most universally recognized symbol of wealth in the early modern world.

Gold, found on every continent in the world, has had a timeless appeal to human beings. Whether used to make coins, jewelry, or paint for statues or mosaics, early modern peoples all appreciated and wanted gold. They recognized that gold was rare and that it was durable. As one modern commentator has observed, "almost all the gold ever mined is still around, much of it now in museums bedecking statues of the ancient gods and their furniture or in numismatic displays, some on the pages of illuminated manuscripts, some in gleaming bars buried in the dark cellars of central banks, a lot of it on fingers, ears, and teeth." If the entire known quantity of gold could be combined into one mass, it would weigh about 125,000 tons and fit on a single oil tanker.

The search for gold played an enormous role in the history of the world from the mid-15th century to the 17th century. Gold had, of course, a much longer pedigree, even in Europe: In 1257 the English king Henry III authorized the first use of gold in coins in his realm, and subsequent monarchs followed suit. (There were, in all, 14 different kinds of coin made from gold in England from 1257 to 1717.) The finest artisans on the continent used gold leaf to adorn priceless manuscripts and to make mosaics in churches shine, as they still do in glorious monumental displays in the Basilica of San Marco in VENICE.

Although Europeans knew about gold, they had less access to it than other peoples, especially Africans. Gold had benefited empire-builders in GHANA and MALI, among others, as well as traders in TIMBUKTU, Ualata, Tarudant, Sijilmesa, and Mesa. By the early 14th century Portuguese explorers began to find supplies of gold in North Africa; by mid-century, when some Portuguese had traveled to Senegal, Guinea, and Gambia, traders working through Morocco had begun to acquire gold along with slaves (see SLAVERY), indigo, and SUGAR. In 1471 Fernão Gomes began to acquire so much gold from Sierra Leone that the coat of arms he later received depicted three Africans wearing golden pendants. Soon the Portuguese built fortresses along the west African GOLD COAST to protect their investments, including an outpost at São Jorge da Mina that grew into a city.

Once Europeans set their sites on the Western Hemisphere, they hoped to find gold there also. CHRISTOPHER COLUMBUS was only the first of many Spanish CONQUISTADORES who hoped to find gold in the Americas. Fortunately for Columbus and those who supported his ventures, the Spanish did find gold in the West Indies. They began to process it in HISPANIOLA as early as 1494. Between 1503 and 1510, according to records in the CASA DE CONTRATACIÓN in SEVILLE, the Spanish imported almost 5,000 kilograms of gold. From 1511 to 1520 the amount increased to more than 9,000 kilograms, although during the 1520s the total hauled into Spain dropped to slightly less than 5,000 kilograms, but the decline was temporary. By the mid-1530s the Spanish had found other supplies of gold, and their imports in the 1550s totalled 42,500 kilograms. Much of this gold, of course, came not from mines but from the AZTECS and other indigenous peoples whom the Spanish plundered. Conquistadores were after gold above all else, observers recognized, and

Native Americans melting gold to pour into doll-shaped molds, engraved by Theodor de Bry, 1599   *(Hulton/Archive)*

they felt little apparent unease when they melted down religious icons that had had enormous meaning before 1492. Outright theft of gold made sense to conquistadores such as FRANCISCO PIZARRO who, after all, had killed the INCA king ATAHUALPA despite the fact that he received an enormous ransom of gold and SILVER.

Over time silver became a more important commodity for Europeans in the Americas, although the lure of gold persisted well beyond the colonial period. Perhaps the European desire for gold was most evident in the constant search for EL DORADO, a place that was, according to legend, made of gold and jewels. The dream of finding that city had enthralled many conquistadores, including FRANCISCO CORONADO, whose men searched for a golden civilization on the plains of the modern-day United States. They never found El Dorado, of course, but their quest signified the long-standing desire to find the most precious metal in the world.

Further reading: Peter Bernstein, *The Power of Gold: The History of an Obsession* (New York: Wiley, 2000); Roy W. Jastram, *The Golden Constant: The English and American Experience, 1560–1976* (New York: Wiley, 1977); Pierre Vilar, *A History of Gold and Money, 1450–1920* (London: NLB, 1976).

Gold Coast

The region in western Africa stretching along the coast between the Ivory Coast and Nigeria (modern-day Ghana) where Portuguese explorers and merchants first acquired gold for the European market in the 15th century and that remained, for generations, a crucial center for the export of precious commodities.

During the mid-14th century enterprising Portuguese explorers seeking to enrich themselves and their empire began to establish regular trade with African merchants. The

Europeans were especially interested in getting access to gold, and so they established themselves at crucial points on the west coast of Africa. At São Jorge da Mina (see Documents), Redes, and Axim they established forts that they used as bases for their gold-seeking operations. The Portuguese learned that the gold they wanted had to be brought to the coast (it was found farther inland) and so they purchased African slaves (see SLAVERY and SLAVE TRADE) in BENIN and brought them to the Gold Coast settlements, where they relied on their labor to haul gold, although they often then sold the slaves there, too. Much of the gold sold to Europeans along the Gold Coast had come from across the SAHARA, suggesting that the Arab merchants who organized the commerce recognized its great value. Although no one could have known how extensive trade in the region would become, the cloth that Europeans brought to the Gold Coast to trade might have clothed perhaps 1.5 million Africans by the mid-17th century. Surviving documents demonstrate that purchasers of cloth, which had originated in Asia as well as in Europe, wanted a wide variety of choices. Such evidence suggests the complexity of commerce in the early modern world and the fact that consumers of goods— the Europeans who wanted gold as well as the Africans who wanted cloth—often found ways to get what they wanted, usually in places like the Gold Coast, where merchants found ways to bring commodities to markets.

Further reading: Peter L. Bernstein, *The Power of Gold: The History of an Obsession* (New York: Wiley, 2000); John Thornton, *Africa and Africans in the Making of the Atlantic World, 1400–1800,* 2nd ed. (Cambridge: U.K.: Cambridge University Press, 1998); Pierre Vilar, *A History of Gold and Money, 1450–1920* (London: NLB, 1976).

Gomes, Diogo (ca. 1440–ca. 1482)

A Portuguese ship captain sent by Prince HENRY THE NAVIGATOR to explore commercial possibilities along the west coast of Africa.

In 1458 Prince Henry commissioned Gomes to follow the earlier route of the Venetian Alvise Ca'da Mosto, who had sailed from Portugal down the African coast as far as Senegal. Gomes went 900 miles farther: His expedition, consisting of three CARAVELS, rounded the Horn of Africa and got as far as Cape Palmas along the coast of Guinea. He returned to Portugal the next year with a cargo of slaves (see SLAVE TRADE) and GOLD, thus proving to the dying Henry that his commercial inclinations were on target. Although Henry had ordered Gomes not to kidnap anyone but, instead, to treat with local officials and set up trade with them, he admitted to capturing some Africans while they slept, herding them "as if they had been cattle towards the boats." That day he claimed he captured 650 Africans

to take them back "to Portugal, to Lagos in the Algarve, where the Prince was, and he rejoiced with us." In the years after the monarch's death, Gomes established commercial connections that sustained ties between LISBON, the Cape Verde Islands, and the coast of Guinea.

Further reading: Angus Konstam, *Historical Atlas of Exploration, 1492–1600* (New York: Facts On File, 2000); Hugh Thomas, *The Slave Trade: The History of the Atlantic Slave Trade, 1440–1870* (New York: Simon & Schuster, 1997).

Gonja

An ethnic group of diverse origins in modern-day northwestern Ghana and northeastern Côte d'Ivoire, the Gonja established a powerful trading kingdom in the 17th century but were conquered by the ASANTE in the 18th century.

Founded in the mid-16th century by a cavalry force of the declining but expansionistic MALI Empire, the Gonja's origins were based on conquest. Gonja's first ruler, Nabaga ("the one who arrived"), established the new kingdom's capital at Yagbum. The descendants of the Malian cavalrymen, called Ngbanya, formed a chiefly class overseeing the diverse territories the Gonja kingdom encompassed. The indigenous peoples of the region became a commoner class, the *nyamasi,* but retained ritual control over their lands through their land priests. As in the neighboring MOSSI kingdom, the indigenous traditions survived the period of conquest, but unlike the Mossi, the Gonja began as an Islamic state.

Located in the geographical interstice between the growing Mossi and AKAN kingdoms, the Gonja continued their expansionist tradition throughout the 16th and 17th centuries. These so called Gonja wars increased the Gonja territory to the Oti River (in the far eastern part of present-day Ghana and part of the Volta River basin), effectively isolating the Akan peoples who founded the powerful Asante kingdom from the Mossi kingdoms until the middle of the 18th century. Dynastic struggles in the late 17th century left the Gonja weakened and susceptible to invasion by the Asante in the mid-18th century.

Further reading: "Gonja," in *Africana: The Encyclopedia of the African and African American Experience* eds., Kwame Anthony Appiah and Henry Louis Gates, Jr. (New York: Basic *Civitas* Books, 1999), 845; "The Peoples," in *Cambridge Encyclopedia of Africa,* eds. Roland Oliver and Michael Crowder (Cambridge, U.K.: Cambridge University Press, 1981), 57–86; Ivor Wilks, "The Mossi and the Akan States, 1400–1800," in F. J. Ade Ajiya and Michael Crowder, eds., *History of West Africa,* vol. 1, 3rd ed. (London: Longman, 1985), 465–502.

— Lisa M. Brady

Gorée Island

An island off the coast of west Africa, first colonized by the Portuguese but later sold to the Dutch, who built two forts there and used it to supply their slave trading expeditions, Gorée Island eventually attracted the attention of various European states interested in maintaining trade with African states.

Further reading: Hugh Thomas, *The Slave Trade: The History of the Atlantic Slave Trade, 1440–1870* (New York: Simon & Schuster, 1997).

Greenland

The North Atlantic island of Greenland, settled first by Inuit and later by NORSE explorers, tested the durability of Norse culture and the adaptability of European peoples to new environments.

Two-thirds of Greenland, the world's largest island, rests within the Arctic Circle, and the island's northern extremity extends to 500 miles from the North Pole. Paleo-Eskimo people exploring from Canada first settled Greenland at least 3,000 years ago.

Around 1,000 a second wave of immigration came from two separate directions. A new wave of Eskimos reached Greenland across the frozen archipelago north of Canada, while in 982 Norwegian navigator Erik the Red, who had been banished from ICELAND for manslaughter, landed in southwest Greenland. He explored the southwest coast for three winters before returning to Iceland for more colonists. In an attempt to make the island attractive to European settlement, Erik the Red dubbed the island Greenland. Christianity arrived in the 11th century through Erik the Red's son, Leif Eriksson. By the 13th century the small Norse colonies grew to relatively prosperous communities of more than 2,000 people. Norse Greenland remained a republic until 1261, when the colonists swore allegiance to the king of Norway.

Little is known about the interaction between Norse and indigenous Greenlanders. The southwest coast of Greenland was apparently unoccupied when the Norse arrived, but contact between the two cultures increased as each explored new hunting grounds. The Inuit hunters acquired materials such as woolen cloth and bits of chain-metal armor from the Norse, but the curiosity toward new goods apparently was not reciprocated. The Norse did not adopt Inuit technology, including such potentially useful items as fur clothing, harpoons, and seal-hunting methods. The inability or refusal to adopt new bodies of knowledge may have precipitated Norse decline.

Despite the initial success of the Norse colonies, they deteriorated in the 14th century. The Little Ice Age (ca. 1250–1860) hurt farming, and malnutrition mounted as trade declined. According to one 14th-century court case, desperate Norse Greenlanders forced weather-stranded sailors to buy their trade goods. After 1410, when the last vessel sailed from Norway to Greenland, most communication with Europe ceased. As a result, little is known about Greenland until European explorers returned to its shores in the 16th century.

Seeking the NORTHWEST PASSAGE, the English navigator Sir MARTIN FROBISHER landed on the southwest coast in 1578. Another English explorer, John Davis, mapped much of the eastern coast during his voyages in 1585 and 1587 and described Greenland as "the Land of Desolation." Perhaps due to reports like Davis's, little exploration of the forbidding land took place for the next two centuries.

Further reading: Alfred Crosby, *Ecological Imperialism: The Biological Expansion of Europe, 900–1900* (Cambridge, U.K.: Cambridge University Press, 1986); Fin Gad, *The History of Greenland,* trans. Ernst Dupont (London. C. Hurst, 1970); Kirsten A. Seaver, *The Frozen Echo: Greenland and the Exploration of North America, ca. 1000–1500* (Stanford, Calif.: Stanford University Press, 1996).

— Kevin C. Armitage

Grijalva, Juan de (fl. 1517–1527)

The leader of an early expedition to the mainland of MEXICO that paved the way for HERNAN CORTÉS's campaign in 1519.

In 1517 the survivors of FRANCISCO HERNÁNDEZ DE CÓRDOBA's disastrous expedition arrived back in CUBA with tales of wealthy MAYA cities on the YUCATÁN PENINSULA. Many hoped to replenish their supplies and strike out again, but the powerful governor of Cuba, DIEGO DE VELÁZQUEZ, hoped to claim the lands for himself and thus organized and outfitted an expedition of his own to conquer the region in 1518. He provided four ships, wine, and arms for the campaign and hand-selected Grijalva (his nephew) to lead it. The foot soldier BERNAL DÍAZ DEL CASTILLO accompanied the party and wrote extensively about its progress.

Like Hernández de Córdoba before him, Grijalva made his first landfall along the Yucatán coast, but unlike Hernández de Córdoba, he was more concerned about reconnaissance than conquest. The natives chose not to attack the Spaniards directly, correctly assuming that this group was better armed than previous ones. Instead, they simply retreated into the wilderness, taking food, water, and anything of value with them. It proved difficult for Grijalva to restrain many of his men from attacking the Maya, for many of them wanted to punish the Maya for their attacks on previous expeditions. Finally, Grijalva arrived in TABASCO, where he met with local CACIQUEs and attempted to convey his peaceful intentions. Reluctantly, the local Maya agreed to trade supplies for Spanish trinkets. While the Spaniards smugly assumed the Maya were acquiescing because they recognized the Europeans' alleged superiority, it seems clear that the Maya were in fact following a long-established tradition of gracefully submitting to reasonable demands in order get the Spaniards to move on.

From Tabasco, Grijalva sailed up the coast of VERA-CRUZ to Pánuco, where he heard the first reports of the powerful AZTECS in central Mexico. The few battles the expedition fought were not brilliant successes, and the soldiers began to chafe under Grijalva's apparent inability to win decisive battles. Satisfied that he had fulfilled Velázquez's instructions, Grijalva returned to Cuba. By the time he arrived in Santiago de Cuba, Governor Velázquez had already organized a new expedition to explore the coast under Cortés. Hopeful that Cortés's campaign would be more profitable for them, many of Grijalva's men abandoned their captain and enlisted with Cortés.

Lacking the brilliance, daring, and success of his contemporaries, Grijalva quickly faded from the scene after 1518. He was incidentally involved in a political squabble with Cortés in 1521–22 regarding rights to explore and administer a region north of Pánuco, Veracruz. He later joined forces with Pedrarias Dávila in PANAMA, where he died after being ambushed by natives in 1527.

Further reading: Inga Clendinnen, *Ambivalent Conquests: Maya and Spaniard in Yucatan, 1517–1570* (Cambridge, U.K.: Cambridge University Press, 1987); Hernán Cortés, *Letters from Mexico* (New Haven, Conn.: Yale University Press, 1986); Bernal Díaz del Castillo, *The Discovery and Conquest of Mexico* (New York: Da Capo Press, 1996).
— Scott Chamberlain

Guerrero, Gonzalo (fl. 1511–1534?)

One of the more intriguing figures of the conquest era, Guerrero was a shipwrecked sailor who, after living among the MAYA for several years, became a leader in their struggle against the Spaniards.

Very little is known of Guerrero's early life or the events that brought him to the Western Hemisphere. Traditionally, scholars have believed that he was a sailor of humble origin. In 1511 a ship containing several hundred Spaniards sailing north from PANAMA foundered off the northern coast of the YUCATÁN PENINSULA. Most of the Spaniards made it to shore, where the local Maya captured and later sacrificed them. The local CACIQUE spared only a handful to remain as slaves (see SLAVERY), but hunger and DISEASE took the lives of all but two men: Guerrero and GERÓNIMO DE AGUILAR. While Aguilar remained rigidly loyal to his king and religion, Guerrero had a profound change of heart. He married a local Maya woman and offered his services as a warrior and tactician to the local cacique. In short order he

relocated with his family to Chetumal farther south and began preparing the Maya for what he saw as an inevitable war with the Spaniards. He began training warriors in how to fight his former countrymen, urging them to use the rugged landscape to their advantage. He traveled extensively across the Yucatán, building alliances and preparing for the oncoming invasion. At his instigation the Maya repeatedly attacked the expedition of FRANCISCO HERNÁN-DEZ DE CÓRDOBA when it arrived in 1517. When Cortés arrived in the Yucatán in 1519, Guerrero refused to be "rescued" along with Aguilar and stepped up his preparations. He continued to resist the Spaniards for the next 15 years.

Guerrero's defection caused enormous distress among the Spaniards. Convinced of their cultural superiority and the righteousness of the conquest, many saw his actions as the darkest of all betrayals. Over the course of his conquests in the Yucatán, Francisco de Montejo implored Guerrero to recall himself and his faith, but Guerrero rebuffed him. In time the Spaniards' fear prompted them to blame Guerrero for every reversal, every defeat, and every problem in Central America or the Yucatán. After a pitched battle in Honduras in either 1534 or 1535, the Spaniards discovered the body of a white man tattooed in the manner of the Yucatec Maya. Only with the discovery of his body did they believe that Guerrero's diabolical threat had ended.

Further reading: Inga Clendinnen, *Ambivalent Conquests: Maya and Spaniard in Yucatan, 1517–1570* (Cambridge, U.K.: Cambridge University Press, 1987); Friar Diego de Landa, *Yucatan Before and After the Conquest* (New York: Dover Publications, 1978).
— Scott Chamberlain

Guiana See Ralegh, Sir Walter

Guinea-Bissau

Located on the west coast of Africa just south of Senegal, Guinea-Bissau covers approximately 36,125 kilometers.

The history of Guinea-Bissau is closely linked to the Cape Verde Islands and Portuguese exploration. There are two possible origins for the name *Guinea*. It may stem from the Berber word "Aguinaou," which is a reference to "Land of the Blacks." The second possibility has its roots in European exploration. The Portuguese used *Guinea* to refer to the entire region from Senegal to Angola. The term may stem from a corruption of *Ghana*, the African empire known for its GOLD production that sparked Portuguese interest in the region.

According to the archeological record people settled the Guinea-Bissau area around 11,000 years ago, living in small communities subsisting on hunting and fishing. Over time events farther inland influenced the development of this coastal region. The rise of the medieval empires of GHANA and MALI had particular influence on the coastal region's politics, economy, and social order. The trans-Saharan trade that provided the basis of wealth for Ghana and Mali also brought new food products that could be grown in the west African tropics. Additionally, the expansion of trade brought ISLAM, which played a significant role in all parts of west Africa. Most influential was the development of Mali tributary states, such as the kingdom of Kaabu, which exacted slaves (see SLAVERY), gold, and other resources leading to the displacement of the people living in the Guinea-Bissau area.

In the 15th century Portuguese sailors began their steady move southward around the coast of Africa. By 1460 Antonio de Noli and Kiogo Gomes officially claimed the Cape Verde Islands for King Afonso V of Portugal. The Portuguese quickly established the islands as a major stronghold but were unable to develop a strong presence on the coast with the exception of a few fortified enclaves. Portuguese explorers immediately began trading for slaves (see SLAVE TRADE). Before the establishment of colonial outposts on the Cape Verde Islands only a few hundred Africans were enslaved each year and exported to Europe or the CANARY ISLANDS, but the numbers steadily grew when the Cape Verde settlements developed into slave trading stations.

Further reading: G. E. Brooks, Jr., *Kola Trade and State Building: Upper Guinea Coast and Senegambia, 15th–17th Centuries* (Brookline, Mass., 1980); Richard A. Lobban and Peter Karibe Mendy. *Historical Dictionary of the Republic of Guinea-Bissau* (Lanham, Md.: Scarecrow Press, 1997); Richard Olaniyan, *Guinea-Bissau in Anglo-Portuguese Relations, 1860–1870: A Study in the Diplomacy of Colonial Acquisition* (Ile-Ife, Nigeria: University of Ife Press, 1980).
— Tom Niermann

Gutenberg, Johannes Gensfleisch zum
(ca. 1397–1468)
A German metalsmith who discovered how to make moveable type, an invention that led to the proliferation of the PRINTING PRESS, a technological device that changed the world.

Johannes Gensfleisch zum Gutenberg was born in Mainz, Germany, around 1397. Despite his fame and significance, there is little surviving information about Gutenberg himself. He was a member of an elite family, Friele zum Gensfleisch, who remained in his birthplace until 1428. That year he moved to Strasbourg, and extant records reveal that he worked with a goldsmith there from 1434 to 1444. He apparently began to work on moveable type sometime in the mid-1430s and had perhaps begun to make letters out of lead by 1438.

By the late 1440s he had returned to Mainz, yet despite what seem (to modern audiences) the obvious benefits of the nascent printing technology, Gutenberg had financial problems that forced him to borrow money to continue his ventures. His debts accumulated, and by the mid-1450s he no longer had the assets to cover them. By that time he had produced his greatest achievement. a version of the Bible printed forty-two lines to the page. Gutenberg Bibles today are among the rarest of incunabula (the term used for books printed before 1500).

At the time of his death in 1468, Gutenberg had developed a working relationship with Adolf of Nassau, archbishop of Mainz. A Latin dictionary originally written in the 13th century and printed in Mainz in 1460 was quite possibly the work of Gutenberg, although no definite proof of his work on the volume survives. After his death the archbishop gave a local lawyer named Conrad Humery the printing press that was Gutenberg's, perhaps a final sign that the inventor of moveable type never escaped financial woes. The people of Mainz, for their part, eventually celebrated Gutenberg's achievements. On the 400th anniversary of the invention of the printing press, the city put on a three-day festival that included the appearance of a new statue, boat races, an artillery salute, and even processions lit by torchlight.

Further reading: Warren Chappell, *A Short History of the Printed Word* (New York: Knopf, 1970); Adrian Johns, *The Nature of the Book: Print and Knowledge in the Making* (Chicago: University of Chicago Press, 1998).

H

habitants

The *habitants* of New France (Canada) occupied the lowest rung of the social ladder in the colony and worked the land as peasants in a semifeudal fashion.

The officials of New France populated their colony primarily with a peasant class referred to as *habitants.* In general, *habitants* practiced limited husbandry and agriculture on land technically owned by others *(seigneurs).* They worked the land in family units and were for the most part self-sufficient. *Habitants* made their own decisions concerning how they used their assigned land, but a portion of what they produced, or rent, was owed to the *seigneurs,* or owners. Although *habitants* were more independent than peasants in France, *seigneurs* still exploited them. Some *habitants* participated as part-time *voyageurs* (licensed by the government) and *couriers de bois* (illegal operators) in the fur trade with New France's native allies, and others supplemented their income as merchants and craftsmen. Although *habitants* often feared falling into debt or being attacked by the IRO-QUOIS, they still became the backbone of the colony. Much of the limited early success of New France can be attributed to *habitant* hardiness.

Further reading: William J. Eccles, *Canadian Society During the French Regime* (Montreal: Harvest House, 1968); ———, *France in North America* (East Lansing: Michigan State University Press, 1990); Allan Greer, *Peasant, Lord, and Merchant: Rural Society in Three Quebec Parishes 1740–1840* (Toronto: University of Toronto Press, 1985); André Vachon, Victorin Chabot, and Andre Desrosiers, *Dreams of Empire: Canada before 1700* (Ottawa: Canadian Government Publishing Centre, Minister of Supply and Services Canada, 1982).

— Dixie Ray Haggard

hacienda

One of the hallmarks of Spain's empire in the Americas, the hacienda was a large rural estate that combined the medieval concept of the seigneurial manor with feudal and capitalistic practices. Haciendas became the dominant social and in some areas political organizing units in Spanish America.

Most of the large haciendas found in Spanish America originated in the 20 or 30 years after a specific territory or region came under the control of the Spanish. Many of the CONQUISTADORES and early settlers from Spain received land grants from the Crown. Others seized land from its indigenous inhabitants and eventually legalized their claims through payments to the Crown. These early grants and seizures laid the foundations for most of the haciendas that developed throughout Latin America. Most added to their holdings through various legal and illegal acquisitions through the centuries.

In Latin America a hacienda referred to large rural property or estate. These entities dominated the political and economic scene during the entire colonial period. Generally, those haciendas located in desolate, less fertile regions became quite large, and at the same time those situated in healthy agricultural areas tended to be smaller because of competition for the best land. Most sent what they produced to specific markets, and in some cases haciendas laid the foundations for significant wealth for individual families. This eventually translated into political clout and prestige. Over time haciendas came to represent the highest status in a community, and many who achieved wealth through other enterprises invested in haciendas to improve their standing in local communities.

Haciendas needed a dependable labor force, and these workers came from several different sources. Owners of haciendas that grew labor intensive crops such as SUGAR cane usually invested in large numbers of African slaves (see SLAVERY). Some of these plantations became quite large and operated as small towns. On other haciendas natives worked as part of an ENCOMIENDA or REPARTIMIENTO requirement, or Spaniards, creoles, mestizos, and mulattoes labored as wage earners.

Three types of haciendas existed: the staple crop farm, the mixed crop farm, and the livestock ranch. The staple crop farm usually produced one type of agricultural product for market. These products included sugarcane, rice, CACAO, and wheat. Most of these crops required some form of processing before they could be sent to the market. These haciendas thus needed some type of mill, animal- or water-powered, on the estate. This type of hacienda needed significant outlays of capital before it could become fully operational. For this reason most staple crop haciendas evolved from the mixed crop farm or the livestock ranch or developed from the exploitation of an *encomienda* or *repartimiento* indigenous labor requirement.

Owners of mixed crop haciendas grew several varieties of food plants for market, and in the early years they depended upon crops that did not need a significant amount of processing. This type of hacienda required some initial investment of capital but not as much as the staple crop farm.

The livestock hacienda required the smallest investment and fewest workers to begin operations. Furthermore, transportation costs were minimal because cattle could be driven to market. In the 16th century this type of farm needed only a few units of titled land on which the owner built a house, a shed, and corrals. The cattle grazed on the public domain and were only periodically kept in the corrals. As a result, livestock haciendas during the 16th century remained relatively small in size, although over time the Crown began to sell public pasture lands to raise money for the government.

Further reading: Robert G. Keith, *Conquest and Agrarian Change: The Emergence of the Hacienda System on the Peruvian Coast* (Cambridge, Mass.: Harvard University Press, 1976); Robert G. Keith, ed., *Haciendas and Plantations in Latin American History* (New York: Holmes & Meier, 1977); James M. Lockhart, "Encomienda and Hacienda: The Evolution of the Great Estate in the Spanish Indies," *Hispanic American Historical Review* 49(1969): 411–429; Eric R. Wolf and Sidney W. Mintz, "Haciendas and Plantations in Middle America and the Antilles," *Social and Economic Studies* 6 (1957): 380–412.

— Dixie Ray Haggard

Haida

The Haida, living on the Queen Charlotte Islands of British Columbia, were one of many northwestern peoples who developed sophisticated hierarchical cultures in the centuries before contact with Europeans.

It is not known how long the Haida lived in the northwest, although archaeologists have found traces of human settlement in the area dating back 12,000 years. The Haida language is unrelated to any other, but the Haida shared many cultural traits with their neighbors, including the Tlingit and Coast Tsimshian peoples.

Northwestern peoples, including the Haida and Tlingit, had a complex ceremonial life. Their society was divided into two moieties, Eagle and Raven, each of which included several lineages. There were three basic classes within Haida society: nobles, commoners, and slaves. Although some tasks, like canoe-making, were more prestigious than others, people from each of the classes performed many of the same tasks, and the Haida valued hard work. Men fished, hunted, and built houses and canoes. They also produced works of art, including totem poles. Women gathered foods, prepared food and skins, and made baskets and clothing.

The Haida produced impressive wooden items, including well-built canoes and large houses, some of which had a deep-set central fire pit surrounded by tiers of platforms. They were well known for their artwork, which included stylized depictions of animals, often painted red, black, and blue-green. They also decorated many objects in daily use, including canoes, houses, dishes, tools, boxes, and masks. The first recorded contact between Haida and Europeans took place in 1774, when the Spanish explorer Juan Pérez visited the Queen Charlotte Islands.

Further reading: Margaret B. Blackman, "Haida: Traditional Culture" in *Handbook of North American Indians*, William C. Sturtevant, gen. ed., vol. 7, *Northwest Coast*, ed. Wayne Suttles (Washington, D.C.: Smithsonian Institution, 1990), 240–260; Robin Fisher, "The Northwest from the Beginning of Trade with Europeans to the 1880s," in *The Cambridge History of the Native Peoples of the Americas*, vol. 1, part 2, eds. Bruce G. Trigger and Wilcomb E. Washburn (Cambridge, U.K.: Cambridge University Press, 1996), 117–182; Alvin M. Josephy, Jr., ed., *America in 1492: The World of the Indian Peoples Before the Arrival of Columbus* (New York: Knopf, 1992); Alice B. Kehoe, *North American Indians: A Comprehensive Account*, 2nd ed. Englewood Cliffs, N.J.: Prentice Hall, 1992).

— Martha K. Robinson

Hakluyt, Richard, the Elder (?–1591)

A lawyer, geographer, and economic essayist, Richard Hakluyt the Elder helped to lay the ideological groundwork for the English colonization of North America in the age of Queen ELIZABETH I.

Richard Hakluyt the Elder, working with his cousin known as RICHARD HAKLUYT THE YOUNGER, became a staunch advocate of the English colonization of North America during the late 16th century. Inhabiting a world that stretched from BRISTOL to Paris and centered on Oxford and London, the Hakluyts were members of an elite community of explorers and authors who constructed the Elizabethan policy of overseas expansion. Before the Hakluyts appeared on the scene, English efforts to understand North America were limited and disorganized, and English foreign policy paid little attention to America. As a result of the Hakluyts' efforts and the actions of their associates, the English came to embrace colonization.

The elder Hakluyt was in the 1560s a member of the Middle Temple, one of the Inns of Court in London where lawyers practiced their craft. The Middle Temple at that time had begun to be associated with overseas journeys, and it counted as members some of the most prominent explorers of the Elizabethan age, including SIR FRANCIS DRAKE, SIR WALTER RALEGH, MARTIN FROBISHER, and SIR JOHN HAWKINS. Perhaps Hakluyt gained the knowledge he needed at the Middle Temple, which stood hard by the Thames River in London.

Hakluyt's most important contribution to the English colonization of North America was an argument that he made around 1585 stressing the benefits that overseas settlements would have for the realm. In this document, known as "Inducements to the Liking of the Voyage Intended towards Virginia in 40. and 42. Degrees," Hakluyt provided a list of justifications for colonization and an itemization of the goods to be obtained or cultivated in North America. Hakluyt stressed, as did many other promoters, the religious value of colonization. In his enumeration of the benefits of colonization, he wrote that the first gain would be the "glory of God by planting religion among those infidels," a reference to the non-Christian indigenous population of the Americas. He added that colonization would "increase the force of the Christians," presumably through the conversion of Indians to Protestantism. Colonization, he argued, had other salutary benefits as well, including bringing glory to the queen, finding new markets for English manufactured goods, the possibility of discovering the fabled NORTHWEST PASSAGE, and providing jobs for unemployed and underemployed youth—"our people void of sufficient trades" as he put it—who might otherwise cause trouble at home. As he summarized his argument: "The ends of this voyage are these: 1. To plant Christian religion. 2. To trafficke. 3. To conquer. Or, to do all three." In order to make his plan seem plausible, he even provided his readers with a list of the skilled workers that a new colony would need and an enumeration of the agricultural goods they could hope to find in North America.

In the long run, Hakluyt's contributions faded in comparison to his younger cousin's. Even the *Dictionary of National Biography,* which aimed to list every significant English man or woman who ever lived, ignored the older Hakluyt entirely. By the time of his death in 1591, his cousin had already emerged as the leading proponent of the English colonization of the Americas, despite the fact that it was the older cousin who had set the younger on his life's mission.

Further reading: Lynden L. Macassey, *The Middle Temple's Contribution to the National Life* (London: Solicitors' Law Stationery Society, 1930); Peter C. Mancall, ed., *Envisioning America: English Plans for the Colonization of North America, 1580–1640* (Boston and New York: Bedford Books of St. Martin's Press, 1995); David Beers Quinn, ed., *The Hakluyt Handbook,* 2 vols., Works Issued by the Hakluyt Society, 2nd Ser., 144–145 (London, Hakluyt Society, 1974); E. G. R. Taylor, ed., *The Original Writings and Correspondence of the Two Richard Hakluyts,* 2 vols., Works Issued by the Hakluyt Society, 2nd Ser., 76–77 (London, Hakluyt Society, 1935).

Hakluyt, Richard, the Younger (1552?–1616)

Editor, translator, and minister, the younger Richard Hakluyt was arguably the most important promoter of the English colonization of the Western Hemisphere during the reign of Queen ELIZABETH I.

In the century following the voyages of CHRISTOPHER COLUMBUS, the English devoted little effort to establish colonies in North America. While JOHN CABOT and SEBASTIAN CABOT had traveled across the Atlantic in the years after Columbus's historic journeys, few if any English followed, although it is likely that English fishermen based in BRISTOL had made contact with the ALGONQUIAN peoples who inhabited the northeast coast of North America. Consumed by domestic affairs, such as the spread of the REFORMATION to Britain and hampered in their attempts to colonize Ireland, the English demonstrated a remarkable lack of interest in the Western Hemisphere. That lack of interest faded when Hakluyt the younger began his efforts to encourage the English to establish settlements across the Atlantic.

Raised in London, Hakluyt was a queen's scholar at Westminster School during his youth. At some point he paid a visit to his cousin, a lawyer of the Middle Temple (one of the Inns of Court in the city) known as RICHARD HAKLUYT THE ELDER. The Middle Temple was, during that time, one of the focal points for overseas navigation; among its members were SIR FRANCIS DRAKE, SIR WALTER RALEGH, MARTIN FROBISHER, and SIR JOHN HAWKINS. Years later the younger Hakluyt realized that this visit set the course for his entire life. When he arrived, he wrote that later, he noticed "certeine bookes of Cosmographie, with an univesall Mappe" lying on a table. Noticing his younger cousin's interest, the elder Hakluyt began to instruct him in geography, the discipline that became the passion of the younger Hakluyt for the rest of his days.

In 1570 Hakluyt was elected to attend Christ Church, at Oxford. While at Christ Church Hakluyt had the support of the Skinners' Company, one of England's merchant guilds that provided financial assistance to a select group of young men in the hope that their scholarship would someday provide material benefits to the nation. Hakluyt studied natural science, mathematics, and philosophy at Oxford and received his bachelor's degree in 1574. He stayed on to receive his master's degree in 1577, which he was able to do through support he had received from the Clothworkers' Company.

Hakluyt remained at Christ Church until 1582, gathering various documents relating to English knowledge of the Western Hemisphere. His first collection, entitled *Divers Voyages Touching the Discovery of America,* published in London in 1582, included copies of King HENRY VII's instructions to the Cabots to travel to the Western Hemisphere to discover new lands and claim them for the English, as well as accounts of various travelers who had returned to tell the tales of what they had seen.

Among the readers of *Divers Voyages* was SIR FRANCIS WALSINGHAM, Queen Elizabeth's principal secretary, who already had an interest in overseas affairs. Walsingham arranged for Hakluyt to become attached to the English diplomatic mission in Paris, where he studied available documents relating to long-distance navigation and settlement. In 1584 Hakluyt wrote a long manuscript entitled "A particuler discourse concerninge the greate necessitie and manifolde comodyties that are like to growe to this Realme of Englande by the Westerne discoveries lately attempted." The book, which remained unpublished until the 19th century, was the most thorough 16th-century argument for the English colonization of North America. Known as the "Discourse Concerning Western Planting," the book propelled Hakluyt to the forefront of English efforts to create colonies in North America. It circulated among the highest government circles at the same time the English were attempting to settle ROANOKE, an island off the shore of modern-day North Carolina. While that venture eventually failed, Hakluyt's star continued to rise.

By the late 1580s Hakluyt had become the greatest authority on overseas explorations in England. He had at some point acquired the third volume of GIOVANNI BATTISTA RAMUSIO's *Delle Navigationi e Viaggi Nel Quale Si Contegno Le Nauigationi al Mondo Nuouo,* first published in VENICE in 1556. Through this volume, which included travel accounts relating to the Western Hemisphere, Ramu-

sio provided Hakluyt with a model for understanding the world. In 1589, following Ramusio's lead, Hakluyt published a massive tract entitled *The Principall Navigations, Voyages, and Discoveries of the English Nation.* The texts provided ample justification for Hakluyt's belief that North America contained abundant natural resources and would be an ideal setting for English colonies. Hakluyt believed that the 15th-century royal patents to the Cabot family gave England the right to claim whatever explorers found, and many of the accounts testified to the ability of the English to reach North America and the success they would find there. English colonists would also be able, Hakluyt hoped, to convert America's indigenous peoples to Protestant Christianity, thus limiting the inroads of the Catholic Church across the ocean. His readers praised his efforts, including one who wrote that he believed "that there is no man living more eager in searching out the manner of voyages or who can say more about it." Hakluyt assisted in the publication of other travel accounts, including THOMAS HARRIOT's *A Briefe and True Report of the New Found Land of Virginia,* which was published in an illustrated edition in London in 1590 and became quite possibly the most significant short work describing any Native American population when it was simultaneously issued in English, French, German, and Latin so that it could reach a broad audience.

In 1590 Hakluyt became rector at Wetheringsett in Suffolk, although he never lost his interest in promoting colonization. Sometime between 1587 and 1594 he married Douglas Cavendish, who in 1595 gave birth to the couple's only child, a son named Edmund. By then Hakluyt was also presumably running affairs at his manor called Bridge Place, located between Ipswich and Wetheringsett. Whatever comfort he enjoyed was short-lived, because Douglas died in 1597, and Hakluyt remained a widower until 1604.

From 1598 to 1600 Hakluyt published a revised and expanded version of his work, now entitled *The Principal Navigations, Voyages, Traffiques and Discoveries of the English Nation.* This work, consisting of three enormous volumes, contained more travel accounts than any other individual had ever gathered together in a single place. His materials on the Western Hemisphere, which filled the third volume, included almost 200 documents, an enormous increase from the 77 texts that he had published in 1589. Although much of his effort went toward locating and preparing new texts for inclusion, he also removed the writings of two authors, SIR JOHN MANDEVILLE and DAVID INGRAM, whose work Hakluyt now apparently believed to be fraudulent.

During the final years of his life, Hakluyt continued to promote the efforts of the English nation. He became a member of the Virginia Company, the enterprise that organized the English settlement at Jamestown in 1607. In addition, he provided prefaces and supported the publication of accounts of travels abroad, translated part of Grotius's *Mare Liberum,* and even became interested in English-language translation of the language of the native peoples of Madagascar. In 1601 he served as a consultant to the EAST INDIA COMPANY and offered his views on such matters as the locations where rhubarb, pepper, and "the roote of China"—which he called the "most sovereigne remedie against the French poxe"—could be found. Eventually, his unpublished manuscripts fell into the hands of SAMUEL PURCHAS, who became the next generation's primary publisher of travel accounts and an avid promoter of colonization schemes.

Hakluyt died in 1616 and was interred in Westminster Abbey in London. His body, allegedly laid to rest in Poet's Corner, cannot be found.

Further reading: Tom Girton, "Mr. Hakluyt, Scholar at Oxford," *Geographical Journal* CXIX (1953); Peter C. Mancall, ed., *Envisioning America: English Plans for the Colonization of North America, 1580–1640* (Boston and New York: Bedford Books of St. Martin's Press, 1995); George B. Parks, *Richard Hakluyt and the English Voyages* (New York: American Geographical Society, 1961); David Beers Quinn, ed., *The Hakluyt Handbook,* 2 vols., Works Issued by the Hakluyt Society, 2nd Ser., 144–145 (London: Hakluyt Society, 1974); G. D. Ramsay, "Clothworkers, Merchants Adventurers and Richard Hakluyt," *English Historical Review* XCII (1977), 504–521; E. G. R. Taylor, ed., *The Original Writings and Correspondence of the Two Richard Hakluyts,* 2 vols., Works Issued by the Hakluyt Society, 2nd Ser., 76–77 (London: Hakluyt Society, 1935).

Hanno the elephant (1510?–1516)

A gift to Pope LEO X by King Manuel I of Portugal, the elephant named Hanno became a favorite of the pope himself and thousands of Romans who enjoyed watching his antics in the bestiary in Vatican City.

In the early 16th century rulers of nations across Europe vied with one another to present the reigning pope with extravagant gifts in order to show their devotion to the Church (known after the Protestant REFORMATION as the Catholic Church). Among those seeking the pleasure of the pope was the Portuguese King Manuel I. Because the Portuguese at that time were among the leading Europeans in the realm of long-distance exploration and trade, one of the benefits of Prince HENRY THE NAVIGATOR's earlier sponsorship of expeditions, Manuel knew that the shipment of an Indian elephant to Rome would dazzle anyone. He entrusted the job of overseeing the elephant's migration to Tristão da Cunha, a commander of the entire Portuguese fleet.

Hanno was not the first elephant to set foot in Europe, an honor that had taken place centuries earlier before the fall of the Roman Empire, but elephants (and other pachyderms) had almost mythic status to 16th-century Europeans, few of whom had ever seen a live specimen. With little practical experience with such animals, the Portuguese had much difficulty transporting the elephant to Rome. Even though they hired two men to guide the great beast, including a Moor who purportedly could be understood by the elephant, the actual shipment took enormous energy. At one point the elephant refused to set foot on the boat that was to take him to Europe, apparently (so the Portuguese believed at the time) because his trainer had told him about the unpleasantness that awaited him at the other end of the trip. When the Moor was threatened with death if the elephant would not board the ship, he somehow managed to convince the elephant to go along for the journey.

After an arduous sailing and then extensive overland travel across parts of Italy, the elephant finally reached Rome. By the time he got there, he had become a celebrity. Because the elephant walked slowly, crowds of people had advance word of his approach, and they lined the roads to catch a glimpse of him. According to contemporary sources, thousands of spectators managed to see him before his triumphant march into Vatican City. He arrived in front of the pope at Castel San Angelo on March 12, 1514, a bright Sunday afternoon. His trainer had the elephant stop in front of the pope, and the elephant proceeded to bark three times and then fill his trunk with water and spray it on the pontiff, who laughed in delight. Known for his love of excess, Leo X was the ideal recipient of such a gift. He soon did all he could to make the elephant, whom the Romans had named Hanno, comfortable in the Vatican's bestiary. He appointed one of his officials to take care of the elephant, an odd assignment indeed for a cleric in the pope's inner circle. The elephant seems to have recognized the pope, too: According to available evidence, he genuflected whenever he saw the pontiff. The people of Rome also became enamored with the beast and named inns after him. When the pope allowed Hanno outside of his enclosure to be paraded in the city, the locals cheered with delight. Poets, some in the employ of the pope, wrote verses to honor Hanno, and artists painted and sculpted his likeness.

Despite the attentions he received, Hanno fell ill and died in June 1516. The pope grieved for the loss of his favorite animal, an expression of sentiment that struck critics of the church, including MARTIN LUTHER, who mentioned the pope's elephant in one of his critiques of the papacy. Another critic, presumably Mario de Peruschi, who was then a financial adviser to the consistory of cardinals, wrote a long satiric last will and testament for Hanno in which he attacked various prominent political and clerical figures. Such attacks, while vicious, represented a minority view, at least of Hanno, whose brief sojourn in Rome endeared him to virtually everyone who saw him.

Further reading: Silvio A. Bedeni, *The Pope's Elephant: An Elephant's Journey from Deep in India to the Heart of Rome* (New York: Penguin, 2000); Donald F. Lach, "Asian Elephants in Renaissance Europe," *Journal of Asian History* I (1967): 133–176.

Harriot, Thomas (1560–1621)

English mathematician and ethnographer whose account of the Native Americans in modern-day coastal North Carolina provided Europeans with the most detailed sketch of any single Indian population during the 16th century.

Born in Oxford in 1560, Thomas Harriot entered St. Mary's Hall of the University of Oxford in 1577. After his graduation he was hired by SIR WALTER RALEGH to be a tutor in mathematics, a subject that then encompassed the disciplines of navigation and astronomy. In the early 1580s he offered guidance to English mariners traveling to North America. When they returned and brought back with them MANTEO and WANCHESE, two Indians, Harriot quite possibly tried to learn ALGONQUIAN from these captives. To breach the language barrier, Harriot created a phonetic alphabet of standardized English phonemes from Algonquian words that could be reproduced accurately. Harriot's goal was to find a way to preserve pre-contact Native languages for future study in the hope of finding the underlying features of what Renaissance linguists assumed was the primary language that existed before the Tower of Babel. Harriot's phonetic system lapsed into obscurity, but his manuscripts were probably used in the 1630s by English grammarians, such as Edward Howes, but, like much of Harriot's writing, they have since disappeared.

In 1585 Harriot went to ROANOKE, along with John Smith, and returned to England in 1586. Upon his return he wrote a detailed account of his travels, which was published in London in 1588. Two years later the book, entitled *A Briefe and True Report of the New Found Land of Virginia*, accompanied by illustrations based on White's watercolor paintings rendered by the Flemish engraver THEODOR DE BRY, became an instant sensation. Published with the assistance of RICHARD HAKLUYT THE YOUNGER, the 1590 edition of Harriot's book appeared in English, German, French, and Latin.

The *Report* described in detail the flora and fauna of the region around Roanoke, on the coast of modern-day North Carolina. It included the most detailed European map rendered of that region during the 16th century, its accuracy no doubt aided by Harriot's mathematical skills and knowledge of astronomy as well as input from White. Unlike many of the travelers' accounts published by Hakluyt, Harriot's descriptions contain much more precision, reflecting both his eye for detail and the fact that he,

Title page of Thomas Harriot's *A Briefe and True Report of the New Found Land of Virginia* (Dover)

unlike Hakluyt, was actually on the ground in the Western Hemisphere and did not have to rely on others' reports.

Harriot's *A Briefe and True Report* is a highly accurate and sympathetic ethnographic account of coastal Algonquians that gave England its first in-depth view of Native American life. The 1590 edition of Harriot's *Report* consists of four related parts. Part one describes the natural resources around Roanoke that could be shipped to Europe profitably. These goods included such commodities as silkworms, flax, pitch, turpentine, cedar, furs from various animals, iron, and copper. In the second part Harriot described the crops that Europeans could produce in the region. In his mind the region was ideal for maize (see CORN), pumpkins, peas, various herbs, an abundance of roots, nuts, fruits, animals with tasty flesh, fowl, and fish. Harriot based this part of the report on his understanding of the local environment and from observing the Carolina Algonquian who lived there and enjoyed these diverse goods. Harriot used the third part of his report to describe how potential colonists could take advantage of the area's resources for their own good. He was especially impressed by local trees, including oak (which he called "as good timber as any can be"), walnut, maple, beech, elm, cedar, willow, and sassafras, among others. The third part of the report also includes Harriot's description of the Indians he encountered, an account that touched on the nature of their towns and houses, how and when they conducted wars, their religious practices, and their views of the English men and women who had arrived unannounced on their shores. The 1590 edition also included a fourth part, arguably most famous of all, with de Bry's engravings of the local Indians. These illustrations depicted individual Indians; the ways that the Native peoples fished, cooked, ate, and prayed; the layout of two of the most important towns, the palisaded village of Pomeiooc and the unfenced town of Secota; the way the Algonquian tended their dead; and the various tattoos that individuals wore. At the end of these pictures Harriot added another section, again with de Bry's engravings. These illustrations portrayed the PICTS, the legendary ancient inhabitants of Britain. Why did he include these illustrations in a book about North America? Because, as Harriot put it, he was trying to show that "the Inhabitants of the great Bretannie have bin in times past as savage as those of Virginia." In other words, the pictures provided an anthropological lesson: Europeans always argued that American Indians lacked "civilization"; here were pictures that proved that earlier Europeans were equally "savage." If the Picts could become the British over time, Harriot argued, then the same sort of cultural evolution could take place in North America.

When Harriot and White returned to England in 1586, they hoped to gain more supplies for the 110 colonists they left behind in Roanoke, but the threat of war with Spain loomed so great that not even Ralegh, who had a claim to ownership of the region that he had inherited from his half brother, SIR HUMPHREY GILBERT (who had perished at sea on his return from Newfoundland in 1583) was willing to attempt a transatlantic journey. After the British defeated the SPANISH ARMADA in 1588 the way was finally clear for a return trip to Roanoke. However, by the time the English got back the settlers had vanished. Harriot's *Report* thus became a strange epitaph for the so-called lost colonists.

Little is known of Harriot in the last years of his life. At around the same time the illustrated edition of the *Report* was circulating in England, Ralegh introduced Harriot to Henry, ninth earl of Northumberland, who became Harriot's patron and provided him with financial support for the rest of his life. When Henry was imprisoned in the Tower of London in 1606, he allowed Harriot to move into Syon House, in Isleworth, where Harriot continued his study of mathematics. He became a correspondent of Johannes Kepler, the famous German astronomer whose work on planetary motion formed part of the basis for modern understanding of the evening skies.

Despite his world-class mind, Harriot's mathematical innovations remained little known in his own age. He died of cancer of the nose in 1621. Ten years later his most important treatise, after the *Report,* was published under the title *Artis Analyticae Praxis ad Aequationes Algebraicas Resolvendas.* The work helped provide the foundations for the modern study of algebra.

Further reading: Paul Hulton, "Introduction" to Thomas Harriot, *A Briefe and True Report of the New Found Land of Virginia* (New York: Dover, 1972); Peter C. Mancall, ed., *Envisioning America: English Plans for the Colonization of North America, 1580–1640* (Boston and New York: Bedford Books of St. Martin's Press, 1995); M. Rukeyser, *Traces of Thomas Harriot* (New York: Random House, 1970).

Hausa

An ethnic group now numbering around 22 million people who live primarily in northern Nigeria and southern Niger, the Hausa began to form distinct states during the medieval period.

The first Hausa states formed around 1,200 years ago. The first towns grew around traditional shrines that attracted pilgrims and developed into economic centers. Trans-Saharan trade expanded Hausa markets to include slaves (see SLAVERY), GOLD, and kola nuts. The wealth generated by the thriving markets allowed town leaders to create states. Seven states—Biram, Daura, Gobir, Kano, Katsina, Rano, and Zazzau—emerged from this period, creating the core of Hausaland. Hausa raiders acquired slaves from the south, providing the Hausa states with a valuable source of labor. By the 15th century Kano boasted a population of nearly 50,000 people and was one of the major trade centers in Africa.

ISLAM arrived in Hausaland near the end of the 11th century. Contact with MALI, SONGHAI, and Kanem-Bornu served to reinforce Muslim traditions. Most Hausa people had adopted Islam by the 19th century, although the Maguzawa, a rural Hausa subgroup, retained traditional African religious beliefs and remain non-Muslim today.

Around the middle of the 17th century, the independent Hausa states reached the peak of their power. The territory they controlled stretched from the borders of Bornu in the east to the Niger River, and from the Jos Plateau in the south to the edge of the Sahara desert. Hausa traders traveled far beyond the political boundaries of Hausaland, even taking part in the Atlantic SLAVE TRADE. As a result of the widespread Hausa trade network, Hausa enclaves still exist in present-day Ghana and Chad.

Further reading: R. A. Adeley, "Hausaland and Borno, 1600–1800," in *The History of West Africa,* 3rd ed., eds. J. F. Ade Ajayi and Michael Crowder (London: Longman, 1985); John O. Hunwick, "Songhay, Borno, and the Hausa States, 1450–1600" in *The History of West Africa,* 3rd ed., eds. J. F. Ade Ajayi and Michael Crowder (London: Longman, 1985); Murray Last, *The Sokoto Caliphate* (New York: Humanities Press, 1967); Yusufu B. Susman, *The Transformation of Katsina, 1400–1883: The Emergence and Overthrow of the Sarauta System and the Establishment of the Emirate* (Zaria, Nigeria: Ahmodu Bello University Press, 1981).

— Tom Niermann

Havasupai

The Havasupai, whose name means "People of the Blue-Green Water," lived at the bottom of a side branch of the Grand Canyon.

In summer the Havasupai irrigated the canyon floor to raise crops; in winter they hunted and gathered in the plateau region. In precontact times the Havasupai raised CORN, beans, and squash in their fields. They gathered wild foodstuffs to supplement their farming, and they dried their foods so they would last all winter. In the fall the Havasupai returned to semipermanent camps on the plateau. They spent the winter hunting animals and gathering wild plants on the plateau. After the arrival of the Spanish, they incorporated new foods, including peaches and apricots, into their diets.

Until the 19th and 20th centuries the Havasupai had no central government. The most important social unit was the nuclear family, and the Havasupai lived in bands of a few families. They had no clans, and kinship reckoning beyond the patrilocal extended family was limited. Religious beliefs seem to have occupied only a minor place in the lives of the Havasupai, who performed few rituals or rites of passage. Sixteenth-century Spanish observers noted Indian people in the region, but the first reference to the Havasupai by name was in 1665.

Further reading: Bertha P. Dutton, *American Indians of the Southwest* (Albuquerque: University of New Mexico Press, 1983); Douglas W. Schwartz, "Havasupai," in *Handbook of North American Indians,* William C. Sturtevant, general ed., vol. 10, *Southwest,* vol. ed. Alfonso Ortiz (Washington, D.C.: Smithsonian Institution, 1983), 13–24.

— Martha Robinson

Hawkins, Sir John (1532–1595)

An English merchant adventurer, John Hawkins participated in and promoted the growing 16th-century SLAVE TRADE between the coasts of West Africa and the West Indies.

Born to William Hawkins, Plymouth's leading merchant during the first half of the 16th century, John was raised amid the backdrop of trade and its connection to the Atlantic Ocean. At an early age he made "divers voyages to the isles of the Canaries," learning "that negroes were very good merchandise in Hispaniola, and that they might easily be had upon the coast of Guiana." Sometime in or around 1559, he married Katherine, the daughter of William Gonson, treasurer of the navy. With the backing of his father-in-law and other influential investors, Hawkins assembled three ships, sailing from England in October 1562 on the first of his slaving voyages. Although Spanish officials confiscated two of his three ships upon a return stop at SEVILLE, Hawkins profited handsomely from the venture.

A second successful slaving voyage, undertaken in 1564–65, earned Hawkins further riches as praise poured in from influential quarters. With little hesitation, investors commissioned Hawkins for a third voyage. Queen ELIZABETH I became personally involved, lending Hawkins the use of the ship the *Jesus.* Accompanied by kinsman SIR FRANCIS DRAKE, who commanded the *Judith,* Hawkins's fleet sailed out of Plymouth on October 2, 1567. After taking part in the native wars at Sierra Leone, the English crew captured more than 500 slaves and departed for Dominica. An initial round of successful trading in the early summer of 1568 was followed by the hurricane season. Already reeling from the elements, Hawkins's crew received a further setback at San Juan de Ulúa when the Spanish further battered their ships. Only two vessels escaped, making their way to the North American mainland where Hawkins and Drake allowed their crew a choice: Those who desired could try their fortunes on a return voyage to England; others could test their luck on the land.

DAVID INGRAM was among the 105 men who decided to stay as Hawkins and Drake led the rest of the crew back to England. By 1569 Ingram arrived back in England, offering a tall tale of his adventures. RICHARD HAKLUYT THE YOUNGER published his account in the 1589 edition of *Principal Navigation.* Perhaps questioning the authenticity of the story, he dropped it from the edition he later published in three volumes (London, 1598–1600). Hawkins's arrival back in England also met with mixed fortunes. His defeat at the hands of the Spaniards led some, including Lord Cecil, to question both his dealings in the slave trade and his semipiratical activities.

In 1572 Hawkins entered politics as a member of PARLIAMENT representing Plymouth. Shortly after, he was appointed to the office of treasurer of the navy, a post previously held by his father-in-law. The duties of comptroller of the navy were soon added to his responsibilities. Making use of his seafaring knowledge, Hawkins directed many improvements within the ships of the English navy, many of which saw service against the SPANISH ARMADA, a campaign in which Hawkins served as both a ship captain and as a member of the queen's council of war. Scholars have credited Hawkins, along with Drake, with instigating the fund known as the Chest of Chatham, a charity relief for disabled sailors. It was perhaps fitting that the two aged mariners both perished on an ill-fated venture that left Plymouth in the late summer of 1595 to capture and conquer PANAMA.

Further reading: J. W. Blake, *European Beginnings in West Africa 1454–1578* (London: Longmans, Green, 1937); Rayner Unwin, *The Defeat of John Hawkins: A Biography of His Third Slaving Voyage* (New York Macmillan, 1960); James A. Williamson, *Hawkins of Plymouth* (London: Black, 1969); ———, *Sir John Hawkins: The Time and the Man* (Oxford: Clarendon Press, 1927).

— Matthew Lindaman

headright

The headright system, which granted land in English colonial America to anyone funding a settler's voyage, was crucial for the success of Virginia and Maryland during the early 17th century.

The greatest problem the English faced in the early colonial period related to their need for workers to produce TOBACCO. Since local DISEASE often devastated settlers, many of whom were indentured servants, those who wanted to export tobacco required labor for their fields. In order to encourage migration, the English devised the headright system, which gave 50 acres of land to anyone who paid his or her own way across the Atlantic and an additional 50 acres to someone who paid for the journey of another. By arranging for the shipment of servants, some of the early colonists were able to gain large tracts of land, thereby helping to establish themselves in the nascent outposts.

Further reading: Alison Games, *Migration and the Origins of the English Atlantic World* (Cambridge, Mass.: Harvard University Press, 1999); Allan Kulikoff, *From British Peasants to Colonial American Farmers* (Chapel Hill: University of North Carolina Press, 2000); John J. McCusker and Russell R. Menard, *The Economy of British America, 1607–1789* (Chapel Hill: University of North Carolina Press, 1985).

— David P. Dewar

Henry the Navigator, prince of Portugal (Infante Henrique) (1394–1460)

A younger son in the royal family of early 15th-century Portugal, Henry gained fame for his interest in and sponsorship of numerous voyages of exploration southward along the west coast of Africa.

Prince Henry was the third son of the Portuguese king John (or João) I. The prince was born in Oporto in 1394 and soon developed an interest in exploration and expansion, becoming commander of the Order of Christ, a military order dedicated to fighting enemies of the Catholic faith. However, expansion was more than just a military and religious matter to Henry, who was also interested in developing and profiting from trade. He was in part stymied in his expansionist ambitions by older brothers who opposed further conquest, probably on the grounds that the Portuguese Crown could not bear the expense of defending its most recent acquisitions, let alone new ones. In 1437 he succeeded in persuading one of his younger brothers, Fernando, to help him undertake a campaign against the Muslim city of Tanger. King John approved the plan and even petitioned the pope to issue a crusading indulgence, granting remission of sins to all those involved in the campaign, but the venture failed. Fernando died in a Muslim (see ISLAM) prison, while Henry retired from court life.

After the disaster at Tanger, Henry retired to a residence near Segres, where he established an observatory. From this point on it becomes difficult to separate history from legend in the story of Henry's life. Legend depicts the navigator-prince as studious and intellectually vora-

Henry the Navigator, detail from painting by Nuno Goncalves *(Hulton/Archives)*

cious, a man who gathered around himself like-minded men to draw up new maps and charts and to develop advances in ship-building and navigational technology, all toward the end of finding a passage around Africa to Asia. Henry's contemporary Eanes de Zuara confirmed at least part of this story. According to his biography of his prince, Henry was interested in exploration for at least three reasons: simple curiosity, strategic interest in the extent of Muslim domains in Africa, and the desire to seek out any undiscovered Christian kingdoms to the south that might be enlisted as allies against the Muslims. This last hope reflected the power of a prevailing myth of a Christian kingdom located somewhere in either Africa or Asia, a belief common among medieval explorers and evident in their preoccupation with the figure of PRESTER JOHN. Despite such contemporary observations as Zuara's, it seems likely that the achievement for which Henry is best known—the establishment of a school for navigators—was an invention of a later era. There is no evidence dating from the period of Henry's life to substantiate the existence of such a school. In fact, the first mention of Henry's purported school for navigators dates from the 17th century.

Even if Henry did not establish such a school, there can be no doubt that he took more of an interest in voyages of exploration than did any of his Portuguese contemporaries. Fully one-third of the known Portuguese voyages between 1415 and 1460 were at Henry's initiative, and these voyages helped to advance an already solid foundation of Portuguese skill in navigation, cartography, and ship-building technology. He arranged for the establishment of trading posts along the west African coast, trading European grain, cloth, and HORSEs for GOLD, slaves, silk, and cotton from African trade routes. His ambitions to get to the gold trade of MALI at its source, bypassing often hostile Muslim middlemen, was consistent with the mercantilist economic thinking of the time. Adherents of such a belief thought that control of the African trade in precious metals could be translated into not only profit, but power.

Further reading: James M. Anderson, *The History of Portugal* (Westport, Conn: Greenwood Press, 2000); David Birmingham, *A Concise History of Portugal* (Cambridge, U.K.: Cambridge University Press, 1993); Eugene F. Rice, Jr., and Anthony Grafton, *The Foundations of Early Modern Europe, 1460–1559*, 2nd ed. (New York and London: Norton, 1994).

— Marie A. Kelleher

Henry IV, king of France (Henry of Navarre)
(r. 1589–1610)

A member of the Spanish house of Bourbon, the Protestant Henry, prince of Navarre, became Henry IV of France after his marriage into the Catholic house of Valois and rapidly became a focal point of religious tension within that country.

Henry of Navarre married into the French royal family as a part of the intricate matrimonial politics of Catherine de' Medici. Catherine, widow of the French King Henry II and mother of his sons and successors Charles IX and Henry III, married her daughter Marguerite to the Protestant prince of Navarre in 1572 in an attempt to end the civil wars between the houses of Valois and Bourbon. The interconfessional union, although undertaken in a climate of limited and uneasy tolerance of Protestantism, was governed by the shifting currents of religious tolerance and violence from its very beginning. Taking advantage of the fact that thousands of members of the Huguenot nobility had gathered in Paris for the wedding, French Catholics rose up in what was possibly the greatest single act of religious violence of the era, the St. Bartholomew's Day Massacre.

When the childless King Henry III's last surviving brother, the duke of Alençon, died, Henry of Navarre became heir presumptive to the French throne. The prospect of a Protestant king on the French throne threatened the balance of power in Europe between the Protestant ELIZABETH I of England and the Catholic PHILIP II of Spain. It also heightened religious tension within France itself. A power struggle known as the War of the Three Henries ensued, pitting Henry of Navarre, Henry of Guise (who claimed descent from Charlemagne), and the reigning Henry III against one another in a struggle for the Crown. The civil war eventually forced King Henry III into an alliance with Henry of Navarre, whom he recognized as his successor shortly before his own death in 1589.

Henry of Navarre, now Henry IV of France, remained a Protestant at the time of his accession, prompting worries at the court of Philip II that a Protestant king in France would tip the balance of power against Catholic Spain. Of more pressing concern, however, were the domestic consequences of Henry's accession. Catholics and HUGUENOTS fought one another over the religion of Henry IV not just because of religious differences, but because they were both convinced that the salvation of France depended on the outcome. There were even divisions among French Catholics, some of whom were primarily concerned that their king be a Catholic, while others were more concerned with an orderly succession.

Conversion of the monarch seemed France's only way out of domestic and foreign difficulties, but Henry moved slowly, determined not to alienate his Huguenot supporters. While Henry temporized on the conversion issue, he issued a declaration that he would maintain the Catholic Church in France, thus offering hope to his moderate Catholic supporters. However, such assurances did little to satisfy the members of the more extreme Catholic League, who believed that the restoration of civil order and moral harmony required the king's conversion to Catholicism. Henry eventually bowed to personal and national necessity, and at Saint-Denis on July 25, 1593, he abjured the Protestant faith.

Although Catholic preachers inveighed against what they felt was an opportunistic conversion, the populace lent them little credence, since Henry's conversion, sincere or not, seemed to be the only way to secure an end to decades of religious violence. Leaguers eventually accepted Henry's conversion, hoping that the presence of a Catholic king would banish heresy from the kingdom, much as it had been banished from the person of the king. Huguenots, for their part, were secure only after the king signed the Edict of Nantes in 1598, declaring "union, concord and tranquility" for all his subjects, both Catholic and Protestant. In final analysis, Henry IV's conversion may have been opportunistic, but it also provided long-sought domestic peace after years of civil war and restored confidence in the Crown as the guardian of order.

Further reading: David Buisseret, *Henry IV: King of France* (London and New York: Routledge, 1992); Keith Cameron, *From Valois to Bourbon: Dynasty, State and Society in Early Modern France* (Exeter, U.K.: University of Exeter, 1989); J. H. Elliott, *Europe Divided, 1559–1598* (London: Collins, 1968); Michael Wolfe, *The Conversion of Henri IV: Politics, Power and Religious Belief in Early Modern France* (Cambridge, Mass.: Harvard University Press, 1993).

— Marie A. Kelleher

Henry VII, king of England (1457–1509)

A descendant of one of the warring factions in the English Wars of the Roses, Henry VII founded the Tudor dynasty of England, put an end to civil war in his realms, temporarily freed the Crown from dependence on PARLIAMENT, and laid the foundations for England's political, economic, and cultural renaissance during the 16th century.

The future King Henry VII came to power at the end of the Wars of the Roses, a power struggle between contending factions of English nobles. The houses of Lancaster and York were both descended from King Edward III, and both were struggling to gain control of both Crown and countryside. Henry had inherited a tenuous claim to the throne through his mother, but his success at seizing the throne from the Yorkist Richard III and placing the house of Tudor on the English throne was due less to the legitimacy of Henry's claims than to the unpopularity of Richard himself. At the Battle of Bosworth Field in 1485, Henry defeated his rival, who died in battle, and became king

himself, inaugurating a new dynasty to replace both the Lancastrian and Yorkist parties.

Henry did more than found a new dynasty that was to include such potent historical players as HENRY VIII, MARY I, and ELIZABETH I. He also put an end to civil war in his realms. Descended from Lancastrians, the new king negotiated a marriage with Elizabeth, eldest daughter of the Yorkist Edward IV, and left many Yorkists in high office in his administration. Despite these overtures, Henry had to contend with numerous Yorkist plots to retake the throne. In the end he managed to legitimize his dynasty, not just by delicately balancing the interests of domestic factions with those of the Crown, but also by conducting shrewd matrimonial negotiations with established foreign dynasties: He married his daughter Margaret to King James IV of Scotland and secured a match between his eldest son, Arthur, and Catherine of Aragón, daughter of FERDINAND AND ISABELLA. When Arthur died only months after the wedding, Henry salvaged the alliance with the Catholic monarchs by managing to get a papal dispensation to have Arthur's widow married to Henry's younger son, the future Henry VIII.

Despite Yorkist resistance to his reign, Henry managed some domestic victories. He reasserted royal control over the king's advisory council, and by increasing Crown revenues he released himself and the Crown from financial dependence on Parliament. Freed from these two burdens, Henry established a position that allowed the king the initiative in policy making. Henry had seized control of a Crown in chaos, and he had not completely restored order by his death in 1509. Nevertheless, he was able to pass on to his son Henry a prosperous, well-governed, and generally stable realm.

Further reading: Stanley Bertram Chrimes, *Henry VII* (Berkeley: University of California Press, 1972); G. R. Elton, *England Under the Tudors,* 3rd ed. (New York: Routledge, 1991); Roger Lockyer, *Henry VII,* 3rd ed. (New York: Longman, 1997).

— Marie A. Kelleher

Henry VIII, king of England (1491–1547)

Second king in the English Tudor dynasty, Henry VIII is famous for his many marriages and divorces, the first of which prompted his break from the Catholic Church, and his establishment of the CHURCH OF ENGLAND.

As the younger son of HENRY VII, Henry VIII would normally not have succeeded to the throne, but when his older brother Arthur died in 1502 only months after his marriage to Catherine of Aragón, daughter of FERDINAND AND ISABELLA of Spain, Henry stepped into his late brother's role, both as husband to the Aragonese princess and his father's successor to the throne in 1509.

Henry VIII, portrait by Hans Holbein the Younger
(1497–1543)   *(The Granger Collection)*

The young Henry preferred amusing himself and others to governing and left most of the administrative work of the kingdom to Cardinal Thomas Wolsey. Henry also symbolically broke from his father's policies by executing two of the latter's chief tax collectors—a popular move, but one that, combined with Henry's lavish spending habits, began the slow process of eroding the secure fiscal base his father had worked to establish. Henry also differed from his father in his eager involvement in foreign war. In 1511, at age 19, Henry joined the efforts of the HOLY LEAGUE, an alliance with the pope, Spain, VENICE, and the Swiss, to drive France from northern Italy. He also captured two towns in France during this campaign, reviving England's continental pretensions. However, both lack of money and difficulties within the alliance eventually forced him to make peace with France in 1514.

Henry remains best known for his many marriages and divorces, the first of which caused a break with the Catholic Church and the beginning of a long rivalry between Tudor England and Habsburg Spain. Henry's efforts to divorce his first wife, Catherine of Aragón, were provoked by dynastic concerns. Catherine's only living child was a daughter, MARY, who, because of her sex, was excluded from the succession. Around 1525, plagued with worries about the future of his

dynasty as well as concerns that his marriage to his brother's widow was in violation of church law, Henry turned his attentions to Anne Boleyn, the daughter of one of his ministers. He began the process of seeking an end to his marriage to Catherine in 1527, but when the pope refused to grant an annulment for a marriage that had required a papal dispensation to go forward in the first place, Henry broke with the church. In a series of parliaments convened between 1529 and 1536, Henry won gradual independence from Rome and was eventually recognized by Parliament as "protector and only supreme head of the English Church." Henry's break with the church was in vain, at least as far as the succession was concerned. Anne's only child turned out to be a daughter as well—the future ELIZABETH I—and Anne herself soon faced the executioner.

Henry VIII's break with the Roman Catholic Church had far-reaching consequences. His move brought England into the contest between Protestantism and Catholicism that was being waged throughout Europe at the time. Henry's children and successors, the Catholic Mary and the Protestant Elizabeth and Edward (son of Henry's third wife, Jane Seymour), spent much of their reigns dealing with their father's ambiguous religious legacy, striving to solidify a religious identity for their realm. The religious crisis also had political ramifications. At home Henry's need for the cooperation of Parliament meant that the latter could establish itself as integral to the workings of the kingdom, putting an end to the absolutist course embarked upon during the reign of Henry VII. Abroad England was forced to forge new alliances as it shifted sides in the international conflict between Catholic and Protestant nations.

Further reading: G. R. Elton, *England Under the Tudors*, 3rd ed. (New York: Routledge, 1991); D. G. Newcombe, *Henry VIII and the English Reformation* (New York: Routledge, 1995); M. D. Palmer, *Henry VIII*, 2nd ed. (New York: Longman, 1983).

— Marie A. Kelleher

Hiawatha

The League of the IROQUOIS, which united the SENECA, CAYUGA, ONEIDA, ONONDAGA, and MOHAWK, originated when Hiawatha brought the Five Nations together in peace.

According to Iroquois histories, there was a time when the Five Nations were at war with one another and with outsiders. Because of the constant warfare, no one could feel safe. One man, Hiawatha, lost his reason when all three of his daughters died. Grief stricken, he left the people and went into the forest, where he lived as a cannibal. In the forest he met a man or supernatural being named

Deganawida, the "Peacemaker," who had been born of a virgin. The Peacemaker cleared Hiawatha's mind and restored him to sanity. He told Hiawatha of his plan to bring peace to the Iroquois nations by creating an alliance among them. Because the Peacemaker suffered from a speech impediment, Hiawatha spoke for him. Together they traveled through Iroquoia, speaking to the people. They convinced the nations to replace blood feuding and constant warfare with condolence rituals that relieved sorrow and restored grieving and angry people to reason. Hiawatha's greatest opponent was the fearsome Onondaga leader Thadodaho (or Atotarho), a sorcerer whose hair was made up of writhing snakes. Hiawatha overcame Thadodaho, combed the snakes out of his hair, and restored his reason. The resulting League of the Iroquois was probably founded in the 15th century.

Further reading: Matthew Dennis, *Cultivating a Landscape of Peace: Iroquois–European Encounters in Seventeenth-Century America* (Ithaca, N. Y.: Cornell University Press, 1993); Alice Beck Kehoe, *North American Indians: A Comprehensive Account* (Englewood Cliffs, N.J.: Prentice Hall, 1992); Daniel K. Richter, *The Ordeal of the Longhouse: The Peoples of the Iroquois League in the Era of European Colonization* (Chapel Hill: University of North Carolina Press, 1992); Anthony F. C. Wallace, *The Death and Rebirth of the Seneca* (New York: Knopf, 1973).

— Martha Robinson

Hidatsa

A sedentary and horticultural people, the Hidatsa lived along the Missouri and Knife Rivers in what is now North Dakota.

About 900 years ago people began to grow crops and build rectangular, earth-covered log houses on the bluffs over the Missouri River. These settlements were small, averaging 20 to 30 houses. The people who lived there grew CORN, beans, and squash, caught fish, hunted buffalo, and made pottery. They probably placed their dead on scaffolds. Over time some cultural traits changed: Around 1450 the inhabitants began to build round houses and to erect defensive fortifications around their villages.

At the time when Europeans first reached the Americas, there were three separate peoples who would later join to become the Hidatsa. These groups were the Hidatsa, the Awatixa, and the Awaxawi. Each of these peoples had a different origin story and spoke different, though related, Siouan languages. The Hidatsa believed they had come out of the earth near Devils Lake in North Dakota and then wandered for years before settling along the Missouri River. The Awaxawi told a similar story, but the Awatixa believed that they had always lived along the Missouri

River, ever since a sacred being, Charred Body, brought 13 couples from the sky to make their first village.

The Hidatsa shared many cultural traits with their near neighbors, the Mandan. Both hunted and farmed in similar ways, and their villages were popular trading sites. The Hidatsa were also closely related to the Crow, who may have split from the Hidatsa as late as A.D. 1700. Crow and Hidatsa families and bands often visited and traded with one another; the Crow brought HORSES to trade for agricultural products.

The first European to describe the Hidatsa and Mandan was the French-Canadian trader Pierre Gaultier de Varennes, who visited the Mandan in 1738. In 1797 the Canadian geographer David Thompson estimated the Hidatsa population at 1,330 and the Mandan population at 1,520.

Further reading: Peter Iverson, "Taking Care of the Earth and Sky," in *America in 1492. The World of the Indian Peoples Before the Arrival of Columbus*, ed. Alvin M. Josephy, Jr. (New York: Knopf, 1992), 85–117; Alice B. Kehoe, *North American Indians: A Comprehensive Account*, 2nd ed. Englewood Cliffs, N.J.: Prentice Hall, 1992); Mary Jane Schneider, *The Hidatsa* (New York: Chelsea House Publishers, 1989).

— Martha K. Robinson

Hispaniola

Originally the home of 1 million TAINO, Hispaniola became the base for Spanish conquest in the Americas during the first decades after contact in 1492.

The Taino originally inhabited the island of Hispaniola. Before the arrival of Europeans, they developed a complex society built on manioc horticulture and supported by trade on the island itself and with other islands in the vicinity. In a very unique environment and in isolation, the Taino established a hierarchical system of chiefdom leadership similar to those found in some mainland areas of the Americas. After contact with Europeans in 1492, Taino society collapsed in the face of the Spanish colonization effort.

CHRISTOPHER COLUMBUS landed at Hispaniola on his first voyage to the Western Hemisphere and established a garrison there called Navidad. He returned in late 1493 to find the town destroyed and the inhabitants dead. In January 1494 he founded the town of Isabella, which never developed into a significant settlement. After the Spanish established Santo Domingo in 1496, Hispaniola developed into the primary staging area for Spanish expansion into the Caribbean. From 1492 to 1530, the Spanish on Hispaniola developed the processes and methods by which they would successfully build and maintain their American empire.

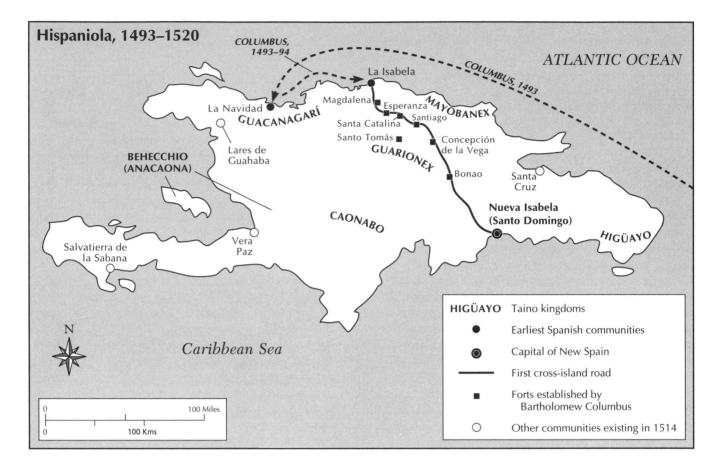

Santo Domingo served as the Spanish base of operations for 20 years as the Spanish conquered the nearby islands of CUBA and Puerto Rico and moved to the mainland territories of MEXICO, PANAMA, and PERU.

From the beginning the Spanish took advantage of the Taino inhabitants of the island by forcing them to work as slave labor (see SLAVERY) in GOLD mines on the island as well as on the plantations, or ENCOMIENDAs, of Hispaniola. For a period of time in the late 1490s, the Taino rebelled against Spanish control and ruthlessness, but ultimately their horticultural society disintegrated when they could no longer support both themselves and the voracious Spaniards. As a result of Spanish abuse and the introduction of epidemic DISEASEs from Europe, the Taino population in the first 20 years of Spanish occupation dropped from a precontact high of 1 million people to only a few hundred. Eventually, they became extinct. Later, the French established a colony on the western side of the island as the Spanish began to focus on their more productive holdings in the West Indies and on the mainland. The French side of the island eventually became the nation of Haiti, and the Spanish side became the nation of Santo Domingo (Dominican Republic).

Further reading: Sherburne F. Cook and Woodrow Borah, "The Aboriginal Population of Hispaniola," in *Essays in Population History,* vol. 1, eds. Sherburne F. Cook and Woodrow Borah (Berkeley: University of California, 1971), 376–410; Robert D. Heinl and Nancy G. Heinl, *Written in Blood: The Story of the Haitian People, 1492–1971;* revised and expanded by Michael Heinl (Boston: University Press of America, 1996); David Henige, "On the Contact Population of Hispaniola: History as Higher Mathematics," *Hispanic American Historical Review* 58 (1978): 217–237; Samuel M. Wilson, *Hispaniola: Caribbean Chiefdoms in the Age of Columbus* (Tuscaloosa: University of Alabama Press, 1990); Carl O. Sauer, *The Early Spanish Main, 2nd ed.* (Lanham, Md.: University Press of America, 1992); Irving Rouse, *The Tainos: Rise and Decline of the People Who Greeted Columbus* (New Haven, Conn.: Yale University Press, 1992).

— Dixie Ray Haggard

Hochelaga

The residents of Hochelaga, a fortified Indian settlement on the site of present-day Montreal, welcomed the French explorer JACQUES CARTIER in October 1535.

Cartier visited Hochelaga when he journeyed upstream on the St. Lawrence River. He had little understanding of the interior geography of the continent and hoped that the St. Lawrence would lead either to the NORTHWEST PASSAGE through the continent or at least lead to one of the fabled lands of riches that Europeans still hoped to find in the North American interior.

When Cartier arrived at Montreal Island, the Saint Lawrence Iroquoian who lived at Hochelaga welcomed him and his men and led them into their village. Cartier described Hochelaga as a fortified town of about 50 longhouses, each some 50 paces long and about 12 to 15 paces wide. The village was surrounded by a defensive palisade, with a single gate that could be barred against attack. When necessary, defenders could shut the gate and rain stones and other projectiles down on invaders. Hochelaga was surrounded by fields of CORN and other crops. A village of this size might have had a population of about 1,500.

Although the Hochelagans welcomed Cartier warmly, he did not stay long. To survey the surrounding country, he climbed Mount Royal. From its peak he could see that the Lachine Rapids would block any attempt to travel farther inland by water. After making this disappointing discovery he left almost immediately. Cartier gave the Hochelagans hatchets, beads, and knives but refused to stay for a feast they had prepared for him and his men. As the anthropologist Bruce Trigger has noted, this refusal to eat with his hosts probably struck the Hochelagans as "inexplicable and discourteous."

After Cartier's departure no European is known to have visited Hochelaga until Samuel de Champlain arrived in 1603. Champlain found no trace of the Hochelagans or the Stadaconans, another Iroquoian nation visited by Cartier. The disappearance of the Saint Lawrence Iroquoian remains a mystery. Various scholars have suggested that the Hochelagans and Stadaconans were destroyed in the 16th century by the HURON, ALGONQUIAN, or (most likely) the IROQUOIS.

Further reading: James Axtell, *The Invasion Within: The Contest of Cultures in Colonial North America* (Oxford, U.K.: Oxford University Press, 1985); W. J. Eccles, *France in America* (East Lansing: Michigan State University Press, 1990); James F. Pendergast and Bruce G. Trigger, *Cartier's Hochelaga and the Dawson Site* (Montreal: McGill-Queen's University Press, 1972); Carl Ortwin Sauer, *Sixteenth Century North America: The Land and the People as Seen by the Europeans* (Berkeley: University of California Press, 1971); Bruce G. Trigger, *The Children of Aataentsic: A History of the Huron People to 1660*, vol. 1 (Montreal: McGill-Queen's University Press, 1976).

— Martha K. Robinson

Hohokam

The Hohokam, a Native American people, practiced irrigation-based farming in the deserts of Arizona for centuries before disappearing in the first half of the 15th century.

The Hohokam were already gone when Spanish CONQUISTADORES entered the region in the 16th century, and neighboring peoples do not agree on who they were or what happened to them. As a result, many aspects of Hohokam history are controversial, and scholars have developed a variety of theories to explain their origin, describe their culture, and account for their disappearance.

The Hohokam adapted to an arid climate. The hot, dry deserts of southern Arizona usually receive less than 10 inches of rainfall per year, making farming difficult. As a result, the Hohokam tended to settle near rivers, which could provide the most reliable source of water for crops. Hohokam settlements existed along the Salt, Gila, Verde, Santa Cruz, and Agua Fria Rivers. The Hohokam are most famous for their elaborate canal systems, some of which were enormous. In the valley of the Salt River, which runs through modern-day Phoenix, the Hohokam built up to 350 miles of main canals, with perhaps 1,000 miles of smaller canals. Despite their successful canal systems, the Hohokam did not rely solely on farming. They also gathered wild plants and hunted game to supplement their diet.

The origin of the Hohokam is unknown. The earliest traces of the Hohokam date to about 500 B.C. Archaeologists disagree about whether the ancestors of the Hohokam migrated north from Mesoamerica or whether the Hohokam, although affected by Mesoamerican developments, were indigenous to the area. In either case, the Hohokam probably first acquired various crops, including CORN, beans, and squash, from Mesoamerica. Hohokam sites also include ceramic figurines, ornamental earspools, copper bells, platform mounds, and ball courts, all of which could also be found in Mesoamerica. Whatever the origins of the Hohokam, the similarities between their culture and Mesoamerican societies have led scholars to the consensus that the Hohokam can be described as "a northern frontier Mesoamerican society."

Hohokam culture changed over time. The archaeologist Emil Haury suggested four main stages of Hohokam development: the Pioneer (300 B.C. to A.D. 550), Colonial (550 to 900), Sedentary (900 to 1100), and Classic (1100 to 1450). During the Pioneer period the Hohokam lived in large square or rectangular houses. Even in this early period, the Hohokam grew corn, beans, and cotton in irrigated fields. They produced pottery, ceramic figurines, and shell ornaments. They also cremated their dead. In the Colonial period, the Hohokam expanded into new territories. Hohokam settlements appeared farther north, near modern-day Flagstaff and Prescott, and also farther east and west. In this period the Hohokam first constructed ball courts and platform mounds, which probably had religious or ceremonial significance. Hohokam arts and crafts also suggested Mesoamerican influence. The Hohokam of the Colonial period also produced highly decorated objects of stone and shell as well as mosaic plaques. During the Sedentary period, few major changes took place. The boundaries of Hohokam territory remained more or less stable, and artwork became less flamboyant and original. During this epoch they constructed additional platform mounds. The Classic period was a time of great change. Many Hohokam settlements outside the core area of the Salt and Gila River basins were abandoned. The Hohokam began to build houses with solid clay walls and later built large multistory buildings resembling pueblo architecture. The purpose of these "Great Houses" is unknown. Some of these changes may have resulted from contact with a people known as the Salado, but archaeologists disagree about whether the Salado invaded Hohokam territory, moved into it peacefully, or simply influenced their neighbors.

Much about the Hohokam remains unknown. Population estimates, for example, vary widely. Some archaeologists have suggested that only 12,000 people lived in the Salt River valley, the center of Hohokam culture, while others argue that at least 50,000 people lived there. The total population of the Hohokam territory is unknown. Nothing is known about Hohokam government or political authority. Some scholars have suggested that only a powerful central authority could have provided the labor necessary to build and maintain such large canal systems, but other scholars disagree.

What accounts for the disappearance of the Hohokam? Scholars have proposed a variety of theories, including earthquakes, internal dissent, a failure of leadership, and invasion by outsiders. More widely accepted theories focus on environmental issues. The Hohokam may have been affected by a series of droughts that made farming more difficult. Irrigation without adequate drainage might have led to a build-up of salts and minerals in the land, making it unusable. Floods could have overwhelmed their canal system, making it unworkable. Although the disappearance of the Hohokam remains a mystery, scholars have suggested that their descendants might be either the Akimel O'odham (Pima) or the Tohono O'odham (Papago) peoples of southern Arizona.

Further reading: Paul R. Fish, "The Hohokam: 1,000 Years of Prehistory in the Sonoran Desert," in *Dynamics of Southwest Prehistory,* ed. Linda S. Cordell and George J. Gumerman (Washington, D.C.: Smithsonian Institution Press, 1989); George J. Gumerman and Emil W. Haury, "Prehistory: Hohokam" in *Handbook of North American Indians,* William C. Sturtevant, gen. ed., vol. 9, *Southwest,* vol. ed. Alfonso Ortiz (Washington, D.C.: Smithsonian Institution, 1983), 75–90; Randall H. McGuire and Michael B. Schiffer, eds., *Hohokam and Patayan: Prehistory of Southwestern Arizona* (New York: Academic Press, 1982); J. Jefferson Reid and David E. Doyel, eds. *Emil W. Haury's Prehistory of the American Southwest* (Tucson: University of Arizona Press, 1992).

— Martha K. Robinson

Holy League

The Holy League was a short-lived alliance of several of Europe's Catholic nations formed to fight Muslim incursions into Christian lands.

The Holy League was in many ways the creation of Pope Pius V (1566–72), who envisioned a new crusade against ISLAM led by a coalition of Catholic nations: Spain, France, VENICE, and the Italian states. Pius attempted to put his plan into action at the beginning of his pontificate but met with little immediate success because Spain was attempting to quash religious and political dissent in the Netherlands (see PHILIP II), and Venetians were unwilling to risk their lucrative trade with the Levant by disturbing the delicate peace they had established with the Ottoman Turks.

The catalyst for Spain's final entry may have been the 1568 revolt of the Moriscos, Spain's indigenous Muslim population. Although Spain's Moriscos and their revolt were unconnected with the Ottoman Turks, contemporaries were likely to have viewed the events in the context of a larger struggle between Christian Spain and Islam (see RECONQUISTA). At the same time, Venice's relations with the Muslim East, long dependent on the good relations between its ally France and the Ottoman Turks, became precarious when French civil wars (see HUGUENOTS) forced that country to shift its priorities away from the East, leaving Venice vulnerable. Pius V seized the opportunity to send a papal nuncio to Philip in 1570 promoting his idea of the Holy League. Philip, encouraged by successes in the Netherlands and embarrassed by failures at repelling attacks by Muslim corsairs, quickly agreed.

The Venetian–Spanish armada set sail with papal blessing in September of the following year. At the Battle of Lepanto they captured the Turkish flagship and more than one-third of the fleet and killed perhaps 30,000 Turkish soldiers. The Christian forces suffered casualties as well—15 or 20 ships sunk, 8,000 men killed, another 15,000 wounded. The success at Lepanto, subsequently captured by Renaissance artists consumed by the battle's drama, seems to have been an important psychological victory for the beleaguered Catholic nations of Europe, although, as one contemporary observer noted, the battle gained no land whatsoever for Christendom.

The Holy League did not disband after Lepanto, but its aims became less focused. Philip wanted the league's future campaigns to focus on North Africa, where they would be of immediate benefit to CASTILE. Pius's successor, Pope Gregory XIII, wanted to maintain the league as a more general crusading force. However, Venice's trade-based economy had only suffered in the wake of Lepanto, and in 1573 the republic's rulers signed a peace treaty with the Ottoman Turks, effectively putting an end to the league.

Further reading: J. H. Elliott, *Europe Divided, 1559–1598* (London: Collins, 1968).

— Marie A. Kelleher

Holy Roman Empire

Although it was the largest political unit in western Europe, the Holy Roman Empire was for most of its history a loose confederation of from 30 to 300 independent principalities nominally ruled by an elected Emperor who struggled with both nobles and the papacy to assert his authority in his own territories.

The Holy Roman Empire was a political entity born in the wake of the fragmentation of the Carolingian Empire in ninth-century Europe. In exchange for aid against a northern Italian Germanic tribe that had been menacing the papal territories, Pope Leo III crowned Charlemagne "Emperor of the Romans" on Christmas Day of the year 800. During Charlemagne's reign the empire consisted of most of modern-day France, Germany, and the Low Countries as well as portions of northern Italy and eastern Europe. This empire did not long outlive Charlemagne himself; after his death his grandchildren divided the empire: the western portion became France, and the eastern evolved into the entity that would become known as the Holy Roman Empire.

While the western Frankish kingdom deteriorated into about 30 independent territories, the eastern Frankish kingdom, now the empire, remained relatively unified, evolving into four duchies—Bavaria, Franconia, Saxony-Thuringia, and Swabia—whose leaders traced their bloodlines back to Carolingian nobility. During the ninth century the dukes who ruled these territories were technically subject to the will of the Carolingian king in the west, but the 10th-century decline of the Carolingian kings combined with their inability to assist their eastern neighbors against the invading Magyars resulted in the German dukes mak-

ing a definitive break from Frankish authority. In 911 the dukes elected Conrad I as their king, establishing the elective nature of the imperial monarchy as well as the contentious politics that governed the choice of the four (eventually seven) imperial electors.

Much of the history of the high medieval empire is dominated by the Investiture Controversy, a struggle between the Holy Roman emperors and the popes over who would have the power to appoint bishops to vacant dioceses within the empire. By the late 10th century the royal power of investiture had become an essential pillar of support against the dukes and other nobles, most of whom preferred to keep power in their own hands, keeping the emperor as their lord in name only. During the 11th century Pope Gregory VII challenged the right of the new emperor, Henry IV (r. 1056–1106), to make episcopal appointments. Henry eventually deposed Gregory, but the conflict over investiture of bishops continued throughout the 11th and 12th centuries and was eventually resolved by a compromise at the Concordat of Worms in 1122.

By the late medieval period centuries of struggle among emperor, papacy, and German princes had weakened imperial government to such a degree that royal officers withdrew from most principalities within the empire. The political entities both large and small that made up the Holy Roman Empire were able to operate more or less independently, to the point that many territorial lords coined their own currency and administered justice within their own territories, independent of any overarching imperial jurisdictional claims. Local autonomy during this period culminated with the "Golden Bull" of 1356, which emphasized the territorial sovereignty of the great magnates, granting seven major territorial lords the right to elect the emperor as well as complete immunity from imperial jurisdiction. By 1500 the Holy Roman emperor was a junior partner in the ruling of the empire, which at that time consisted of more than 300 political entities. Supreme among them were the electoral principalities, followed by half a dozen more major principalities such as Bavaria and Saxony, then the territories of about a hundred counts, 70 bishops and abbots, and 66 free and imperial cities. Simply put, at a time when monarchs such as the king of France were beginning to consolidate territory under royal authority, the Holy Roman Empire was a decentralized mass of particularist interests that the emperor ruled in little more than name.

During the first half of the 16th century, the Holy Roman Empire was ruled by CHARLES V, a Spanish Habsburg whose domains encompassed much of western Europe and extensive territories in the NEW WORLD as well, yet within the empire Charles was merely the nominal overlord of hundreds of cities and principalities of varying sizes and degrees of independence, many of which possessed territorial princes who worked to solidify the sovereign authority that they had wrested from the imperial power. To accomplish this task, the German princes embraced techniques that rulers of more established European monarchies had long used to consolidate and extend their own power: the adoption of PRIMOGENITURE to maintain territorial integrity, the use of strategic marriages to forge alliances and expand territorially, and the development of administrative institutions. Lack of resources slowed the pace of the princes' centralization program, but by the 18th century they had created "national" government and institutions comparable to many more established European monarchies.

Further reading: Uta-Renate Blumenthal, *The Investiture Controversy: Church and Monarchy from the Ninth to the Twelfth Century* (Philadelphia: University of Pennsylvania Press, 1988); Horst Fuhrmann, *Germany in the High Middle Ages,* trans. Timothy Reuter (Cambridge, U.K.: Cambridge University Press, 1986); Eugene F. Rice, Jr., and Anthony Grafton, *The Foundations of Early Modern Europe, 1460–1559,* 2nd ed. (New York and London: Norton, 1994).

— Marie A. Kelleher

Hopewell culture

Before the ascendance of the MISSISSIPPIAN peoples, the Hopewell peoples created a complex civilization in the region now encompassed by the states of Ohio and Illinois.

The Hopewell cultural pattern originated about 100 B.C. and was flourishing by A.D. 1. Its rise may have been related to a shift in the climate that made the region warmer. In a warmer climate maize (see CORN) could be more reliably grown. With more food available the population grew. Even after maize cultivation increased, Hopewellians never relied entirely on it for their diet. They also hunted animals and ate a wide variety of plant foods, including sunflowers, squash, nuts, and berries. Hopewell communities were often built on river terraces near flood plains where women could gather wild plants to supplement the food supply.

Hopewell culture was hierarchical. Elites could draw on the labor of ordinary people to construct large earthworks, including conical burial mounds and geometric embankments. High-ranking people were buried, sometimes in mounds, with valuable and exotic trade goods, including sheet mica, SILVER, TOBACCO pipes, ornaments, beads, and weapons. The tombs of some elite men suggest that their wives, servants, or retainers were sacrificed to accompany the dead, and Hopewell religion may have included a cult of the dead. The trading network that allowed for the accumulation of such objects was extensive.

Hopewellians acquired copper from Lake Superior; mica, quartz, and other minerals from the Appalachians; and shells, shark teeth, and turtle shells from Florida. Hopewell art included stone pipes carved in the shapes of humans, animals, birds, and fish. Archaeologists have also found clay figurines, embossed copper sheets, and engraved bones.

Hopewell culture was in decline by A.D. 500. The reasons for its decline are obscure but may be linked to a cooler phase in the climate, which made growing maize more difficult. Anthropologists speculate that as resources dwindled Hopewell groups fought one another over resources and territories. The trade routes that had linked Hopewell sites collapsed, and autonomous, more egalitarian villages replaced the network of Hopewell groups. Aspects of the Hopewell cultural pattern survived among southern peoples, who would have been less affected by a shift in climate.

Further reading: David S. Brose and N'omi Greber, eds. *Hopewell Archaeology: The Chillicothe Conference* (Kent, Ohio: Kent State University Press, 1979); Patricia Galloway, *Choctaw Genesis 1500–1700* (Lincoln: University of Nebraska Press, 1995); John A. Walthall, *Prehistoric Indians of the Southeast: Archaeology of Alabama and the Middle South* (University, Ala.: University of Alabama Press, 1980); Biloine Whiting Young and Melvin L. Fowler, *Cahokia: The Great Native American Metropolis* (Urbana: University of Illinois Press, 2000).

— Martha K. Robinson

Hopi

Located in the northeastern portion of modern-day Arizona, the Hopi homeland has been inhabited for at least 10,000 years by a people who mastered a complex and difficult environment and survived periodic incursions from European colonizers.

There is little archaeological evidence for any Hopi communities before the year A.D. 1, but there are remains that suggest that the Hopis inhabited small communities, or even individual farms, for the period up to 1300. At that point Hopi population grew, and some areas became much more populous, although Hopi abandoned some sites, in all likelihood because drought made some regions uninhabitable. Hopi also had conflicts with other indigenous nations, notably the Navajo, Apache, and Ute. Still, despite hardships, the Hopi homeland emerged as one of the three principal Pueblo centers from approximately 1300 to 1600.

Long before Spanish CONQUISTADORES arrived, the Hopi had become master farmers. Like other peoples in the region, they learned how to extract great yields from CORN, which became the staple of their diet, along with beans. To battle the ferocious winds of the area, the Hopi built windbreaks from stones and plants, many of which survived hundreds of years. Hopi farmers also found ways to cope with the region's limited rainfall. They planted on floodplains of local streams, and, perhaps more significant, they practiced irrigation. Hopi success went beyond agriculture. In the centuries before Europeans arrived, Hopi became perhaps the only indigenous people in the region to use coal for cooking and heating and to use coal fires to heat their painted pottery, which became among the most celebrated in the world.

The Spanish arrived in 1540 searching, as they so often were, for the great riches they believed existed in the region. Spanish explorers sent out by FRANCISCO CORONADO first arrived under the direction of Pedro de Tovar in the Hopi town of Awatovi. Coronado sent Tovar there from his base at ZUNI because the Zuni had told him that there was a place lying to the west similar to theirs. Coronado hoped that they meant that the fabled city of Cíbola could be found there, but he also recognized that an exploratory venture to the west might achieve one of his other goals: to discover a water route to the Pacific Ocean. Tovar reported back that his men, who included a Franciscan named Juan de Padilla (probably the first emissary of the Catholic Church to visit the region) had heard about a major river farther west. Coronado then sent another mission, under the direction of García López de Cárdenas, with the hope of finding a passage to the sea. Although they were perhaps the first Europeans to see the Grand Canyon, they could not figure out how to descend to the Colorado and so had to abandon the search.

The Spanish returned in 1583 led by Antonio de Espejo, who followed clues left by Tovar. Espejo encountered Hopi at Awatovi and, in classic Conquistador fashion, claimed the region for the king of Spain (presumably after reading the REQUERIMIENTO to the Hopi, who probably had no clue about its meaning). For the next generation the Spanish paid only occasional attention to the emerging colony of NEW MEXICO, although FRANCISCANS believed the region ripe for their spiritual attentions. In 1629 30 Franciscans took up residence in the area and found converts among the Acoma, Zuni, and Hopi. One of the missionaries, Francisco Porras, who had arrived at Awatovi in August 1629, allegedly performed a miracle by restoring sight to a blind boy by placing a cross on his eyes. That act apparently helped the Franciscans to establish themselves in the region and perhaps explains why they had more followers in Awatovi than in other parts of the Hopi homeland as late as 1700.

Despite the miracle, the Franciscans never had a large following among the Hopi, but the importance of New Mexico to the Spanish could not be measured in converted souls alone. Like other peoples in the southwest, the Hopi world changed as a result of long-term contact with Europeans, who brought new goods and foods into the region at the same time that their DISEASEs, part of the COLUMBIAN EXCHANGE, often devastated indigenous communities. Perhaps it was lingering tensions about the changes in their world that fueled the hostilities known as the Pueblo Revolt of 1680, a resistance movement that swept across the Hopi homeland and elsewhere and became the greatest indigenous resistance movement of the 17th century and a signal that European colonization would not always be tolerated by the peoples Europeans hoped to Christianize and control. The survival of Hopi ceremonies and religious beliefs, which demand that humans pay proper attention and respect to divine forces, suggests that the Franciscans had little chance to eradicate religious beliefs that stretched back hundreds of years to a time when the world was in order.

Further reading: J. O. Brew, "Hopi Prehistory and History to 1850," in *Handbook of North American Indians*, William C. Sturtevant, gen. ed. vol. 9, *Southwest*, ed. Alfonso Ortiz (Washington, D.C.: Smithsonian Institution Press, 1979), 514–523; Arlette Frigout, "Hopi Ceremonial Organization," in Ortiz, ed., *Southwest*, 564–576; Louis A. Hieb, "Hopi World View," in Ortiz, ed., *Southwest*, 577–580.

horse

The history of the horse reveals many major technological, social, and ecological consequences for the various interactions between peoples in Europe, the Americas, and Africa.

Ancestors of the modern horse, *Equus*, actually originated in North America, and from approximately 1 million to 9,000 B.C. migrated over the various continental land bridges into Asia, South America, Europe, and Africa. Approximately 1,000 years after the disappearance of the Bering Strait land bridge in 9000 B.C., these early ancestors of the horse—along with the sloths and mastodons—became extinct throughout the Americas for reasons that remain unclear. Not until 1519, when HERNÁN CORTÉS arrived in MEXICO with 16 horses (11 stallions and five mares), would modern *Equus* return to its ancestors' continent. As early as CHRISTOPHER COLUMBUS's first expedition in 1492, however, when he left 30 horses on the island of HISPANIOLA, Europeans had begun introducing horses to the islands of the West Indies.

Since 1519 the horse population in the Americas has grown to be the largest in the world; within 400 years it reached its peak, more than 25 million. Even during the early colonial period, this growth rate was significant. For example, 50 years after Pedro de Mendoza brought 100 horses to Río de la Plata, Argentina, the total herd size there reached an estimated 20,000. A similar exponential growth also occurred in PERU. By 1579 wild horse herds roamed as far north as northern central Mexico, and by 1582 many American Indians were mounting horses and introducing them into the southern Great Plains of the present-day United States.

The horses that Cortés introduced into the Americas in 1519 came from Spain (Iberia). Throughout Europe the Spanish were known for their horsemanship, especially their military and fighting skills. The horsemanship skills of the early modern period drew heavily on the medieval tradition of the "armed knight," a knight riding on horse-back using bits and spurs. By far the most common use of the horse in Europe was as beasts of burden in both agricultural and commercial economies. In the Americas Europeans used horses as a source of both food and labor in their explorations.

In Africa horses were apparently introduced from Asia over an almost 2,000-year period ending around A.D. 1000. In West Africa horses played important roles in ongoing traditions of military and economic expansion, especially in the mounted cavalries of various dynasties. Horses did not arrive in central Africa until the coming of the Portuguese in the late 15th century. Further information on

Spanish conquistadores on horseback depicted in this watercolor found in the Lienzo de Tlaxcala   *(Hulton/Archive)*

the spread of the horse through Africa is rather sparse until the 19th century, but it seems likely that the gradual spread of the horse throughout the entire continent took place either through military invasions or trade routes. Interestingly, the native stock of African horses, including those that interbred with the Portuguese animals during the 16th century, were able to survive DISEASEs that decimated later livestock that Europeans imported, thus holding off most of the colonization of Africa until the 1850s.

Altogether, in the processes of colonization and cultural interaction among Europe, the New World, and Africa, the most significant consequences of the horse were technological, social, and ecological in nature. For example, the technological advantage of the horse significantly changed the lifestyles and social systems of many American Indian groups as well as their interactions with one another. The introduction of the horse, for example, allowed many tribes (such as the Lakota, Dakota, Santee, and Navajo) to pursue new resources in new ecosystems, such as hunting buffalo in the Great Plains, or to carry out new strategies for raiding or intertribal warfare. Others have suggested that these technological changes in economic and subsistence activities eventually also changed the social and gender structures of these groups, with the increased emphasis on the traditionally male activities of hunting and warfare often resulting in a loss of status for American Indian women.

For many years historians also thought that the primary advantage that the horse gave to the European colonization of the Americas was military; even Columbus claimed that in warfare his horses "terrified" the natives he encountered, thus aiding his conquest. But the European transport of the horse to the Western Hemisphere was only one of the most visible symbols of the ecological changes that allowed the immigrants to gain a foothold in the Americas. With their grazing and foraging habits, horses and other Old World domestic animals (including sheep, cattle, goats, and pigs) forever changed the ecosystems of the Americas, the forests, savannas, and steppes. Horses not only competed with local species for resources, they also brought disease-bearing microorganisms in their food, feces, and fluids. The combination of hooves and overgrazing also destroyed native ground covers, allowing Eurasian and North African grasses and weeds to take their place. Without the help of the horse and other biota, it is possible that the European invasion of the New World would have failed.

Further reading: Alfred W. Crosby, *Germs, Seeds, & Animals: Studies in Ecological History* (London: M. E. Sharpe, 1994); Elwyn Hartley Edwards, *The Encyclopedia of the Horse* (London: Dorling Kindersley, 1994); Robin Law, *The Horse in West African History* (Oxford, U.K.: Oxford University Press, 1980); Eliot West, *The Way West: Essays on the Central Plains* (Albuquerque: University of New Mexico Press, 1995).

— Maril Hazlett

Huguenots

The Huguenots, or French Protestants (see REFORMATION), survived persecution and war to achieve the right to practice their religion.

In the first half of the 16th century, French reformers drew inspiration from MARTIN LUTHER and biblical humanism, but from midcentury the Protestant churches in France drew their most important theological ideas from JOHN CALVIN and modeled their church organization after the Genevan model. Calvinist literature, aided by the PRINTING PRESS, also spread rapidly.

Protestants never became a majority in France, but their churches grew rapidly. By the middle of the 16th century, modern scholars suggest that between one-tenth and one-fourth of the population had become Protestant. These converts included members of every social class, but artisans, members of the professions, and the nobility predominated. Relatively few peasants became Protestants, possibly because low literacy rates slowed the rate at which Protestant ideas could spread.

By 1562 about one-third of the nobility had either converted to Protestantism or supported the Huguenot cause. Religious differences accented previously existing rivalries among noble families, which helped lead to the French Wars of Religion. At the same time that Protestant churches were growing, the French Crown was distracted with problems of its own. King Henry II died in 1559, leaving his widow, Catherine de' Medici, and four young sons. Catherine de' Medici put an end to persecution of Protestants, issuing the Edict of Saint-Germain-des-Près in 1562. By the terms of this edict, Huguenots were permitted limited rights of worship and assembly.

The Catholic nobles were incensed at this declaration of toleration. In 1562 Francis of Guise, a member of a leading Catholic noble family, led an attack on a congregation of Protestants worshiping in the town of Vassy, and 74 Protestants died. This incident touched off the Wars of Religion, which continued intermittently until 1598. In addition to the declared wars, every province in France also suffered from massacres and riots. The most infamous episode of the Wars of Religion was the St. Bartholomew's Day Massacre in 1572. On August 23 and 24, many of the leading Huguenots in Paris were murdered, and the violence spread to other cities. The number of dead is unknown, but may have reached 30,000.

This blow changed the shape of French Protestantism. Within the Protestant community a division had existed between those who favored the oligarchic, authoritarian model of Genevan Calvinism and those who supported a more congregationalist church structure. Many of the leaders of the congregationalist party died in the massacres, thus strengthening the Genevans. In addition, the massacres led to new developments in Huguenot political thought. Huguenot thinkers, including Théodore de Bèze, began to articulate theories that justified resistance to tyrannical leaders.

In 1598 King HENRY IV (Henry of Navarre) issued the Edict of Nantes. This edict established limited toleration for French Protestants. It recognized freedom of conscience, allowed Protestants to form their own churches (although not within Paris), and stated that education and high government offices were open to Protestants. The Edict of Nantes ended the Wars of Religion, but French Protestantism never fully recovered. In the next century the percentage of Protestants in the French population dropped from one-tenth to one-sixteenth.

Further reading: Euan Cameron, *The European Reformation* (Oxford, U.K.: Clarendon Press, 1991); Natalie Zemon Davis, *Society and Culture in Early Modern France* (Stanford, Calif.: Stanford University Press, 1975); Barbara B. Diefendorf, *Beneath the Cross: Catholics and Huguenots in Sixteenth-Century Paris* (New York: Oxford University Press, 1991); Hans J. Hillerbrand, ed. *The Oxford Encyclopedia of the Reformation* (New York: Oxford University Press, 1996), Lewis W. Spitz, *The Protestant Reformation, 1517–1559* (New York: Harper & Row, 1985).

— Martha K. Robinson

Huitzilopochtli (Huichilobas)

Huitzilopochtli was the god of war in the central Mexican pantheon, especially revered by the AZTECS as their patron god.

Huitzilopochtli, whose name literally means "southern hummingbird" or "hummingbird on the left," was the supreme god of the Aztecs, associated with sun, fire, and ruling lineage. According to the mythology of the central Mexican valley, Huitzilopochtli's mother, Coatlicue, was miraculously impregnated by a ball of down that she tucked into her shirt while cleaning. Her children, furious with her perceived dishonor, proceeded to murder her, but at the moment of her death she gave birth to the fully armed Huitzilopochtli, who avenged his mother's death by killing his 400 siblings.

According to Aztec myth, Huitzilopochtli led his people on the journey from AZTLÁN to TENOCHTITLÁN. Modern historians speculate that the special Aztec cult of Huitzilopochtli may have originated with a living ruler bearing this name who was deified by his followers.

Huitzilopochtli's main shrine at the time of the Spanish arrival had one of the most prominent locations in Tenochtitlán, the so-called great pyramid that dominated the temple precinct of the Aztec capital, surmounted by twin temples, one to Huitzilopochtli, the other to TLÁLOC. This temple was the site of an annual festival commemorating Huitzilopochtli's (re)birth as a god, apparently including large numbers of ritual sacrifices. Native chronicles report that some 80,000 captives were sacrificed at the dedication ceremonies for this structure. Even if these figures were exaggerated, they give an idea of the impressive scale of Mesoamerican sacrificial rites. Aztecs believed that their patron was nourished by blood sacrifice, both from self-mutilation and from the many captives obtained for sacrifice in the so-called FLOWERY WARS. The cult of Huitzilopochtli was thus one major reason behind the Aztecs' territorial expansion, allowing them to obtain the victims required to satisfy their patron deity. This expansion caused the Aztecs to be both feared and hated by their neighbors, a situation that must have facilitated the Spanish conquest in the early 16th century because it provided the latter with ample allies against the dominant political power in MEXICO at the time of their arrival.

Further reading: Geoffrey W. Conrad and Arthur A. Demarest, *Religion and Empire: The Dynamics of Aztec and Inca Expansionism* (Cambridge, U.K.: Cambridge University Press, 1984); Nigel Davies, *The Aztec Empire: The Toltec Resurgence* (Norman: University of Oklahoma Press, 1987); Mary Miller and Karl Taube, *The Gods and Symbols of Ancient Mexico and the Maya* (London: Thames & Hudson, 1993).

— Marie A. Kelleher

Huron

The Huron, who called themselves the Wendat, created a powerful confederacy in the area between Lake Huron and Lake Ontario.

The Huron Confederacy was made up of four nations: the Attignawantan, Attigneenongnahac, Arendaronon, and Tahontaenrat. In the 16th century, before European contact, their population probably numbered between 18,000 and 22,000. They lived in villages of varying size, most of which seem to have had a population of 800 or less.

A Huron village consisted of several longhouses clustered closely together. The longhouses were made by setting up a framework of poles and covering the poles with bark sheets. The average longhouse was about 100 feet long and 25 feet wide, with doors and storage space at each end. Within the longhouse long sleeping platforms ran the length of the building, with more storage space below the platforms. Each longhouse also had several fire pits along the central axis. In the summer people slept on the platforms; in the winter they slept on the floor in order to be closer to the fire. The size of longhouses varied, but, on average, most probably held about six families. The Huron sought to build their villages, some of them palisaded, in areas with ready access to water, wood, and arable land.

The Huron believed that all things, both living and inanimate, had a spirit. Powerful spirits were known as *oki*. The most powerful *oki* was the sky, but unusual human beings, such as noted warriors, shamans, and the insane, were also called *oki*. Next in importance were AATAENTSIC, who was believed to be the creator of human beings, and her son or grandson, Iouskeha. The Huron also believed in magic and witchcraft (see WITCHES). A witch was a person, either male or female, who sought to injure an individual or the tribe through magical means. If caught, a witch could expect to be killed without mercy, for such crimes against the community placed one outside the bounds of protection, even by family.

The Huron participated in a variety of feasts, dances, and rituals. Dreams played an important role in Huron life, as the Hurons believed that they reflected personal desires that must be gratified. The most important Huron ritual was the Feast of the Dead. At death a Huron was either buried in the ground or placed in a bark coffin on a scaffold. Every eight to 12 years, apparently when the village was going to move, the Huron held a ceremony in honor of the dead. The bodies of those who had died were disinterred and reburied in a common grave. This ritual both honored the dead and symbolized the unity of the living.

Each Huron belonged to one of eight clans: Bear, Beaver, Deer, Hawk, Porcupine, Snake Turtle, or Wolf. A child was born into the clan of his or her mother, and Huron were expected to marry someone from another clan. When a child was born, his or her ears were pierced and he or she was given a name. As a child grew, he or she was encouraged to begin to perform the tasks he or she would perform as an adult. Since the Huron had clearly defined sex roles, these tasks were different for boys and girls.

Among the Huron women were largely responsible for agriculture, food preparation, and child care. Women raised CORN, beans, squash, pumpkins, and sunflowers. Farmland belonged to particular individuals or families for as long as they used it. Unused land could be taken and cultivated by any member of the community. Men cleared new fields using slash and burn techniques, which had the benefit of enriching the land with ash. Stumps that were left after burning remained until they rotted and could be easily removed. To plant corn, women made holes in the ground with a digging stick. In each hole they placed up to 10 grains of corn. As the corn grew, the women hoed up the earth around the stalks to form hills and then planted beans in the hills. When a village's fields were exhausted or when

supplies of firewood became distant, the Huron migrated to a new site. Such moves apparently took place every eight to 12 years. Women also gathered wild plants, especially berries, but these were not a large part of the Huron diet. In addition, women made many household items, including pottery, baskets, and mats. These items might be decorated with paint or colored porcupine quills.

As a general rule, men performed tasks requiring greater strength or ones that took them far from home. Men cleared the fields and constructed palisades and houses. They made fish nets, tools, weapons, and wooden armor. They also hunted and fished. Fish was an important element in the Huron diet, meat less so. According to archaeologists and anthropologists, corn made up about 65 percent of the Huron diet, and other crops, such as beans, squash, and pumpkins, made up 15 percent. Fish made up another 10 or 15 percent, and meat about 5 percent. Nonetheless, hunting was a prestigious activity, and men were honored for providing meat.

Men had primary responsibility for martial activities. The Huron had a number of enemies, the most important of whom were the IROQUOIS. Warfare seems to have been endemic. Among both the Huron and neighboring tribes, men fought to gain prestige, avenge the deaths of other members of their communities, and gain captives to adopt. Usually, war parties attacked in the summer or fall, when leaves were still on the trees and could help a war party to hide. Ordinarily, warriors tried to capture or kill individuals or isolated groups of people fishing or working in the fields. For this reason the Huron tried to provide male protection for women working in the fields. Warriors might also creep into an enemy village at night to try to kill enemies. To prove their bravery, they sought to return with enemy captives or the heads or scalps of enemies. Because the death of an individual at the hands of an enemy called for revenge, and because young men sought to gain prestige as warriors, the cycle of killing continued. Prisoners might be killed on the spot, brought back to the Huron's village to be tortured and killed, or formally adopted into Huron families to replace dead members. A victim condemned to die was often first adopted into a Huron family, in which members would then address the condemned as "brother" or "nephew." The torture might last one or several days, during which the prisoner tried to demonstrate his bravery by singing songs and taunting his captors.

Men also ran Huron government. A typical village had families belonging to several clans. The part of any clan in a given village was known as a "clan segment." Each clan segment within a village had both a civil chief and a war chief. Both of these positions were filled largely on the basis of merit, although candidates had to be chosen from the proper clan and some lineages within the clan appear to have been more prestigious than others. The Huron valued wisdom, generosity, and skill in oratory in their leaders. Both civil and war chiefs lacked coercive power and gained followers only as long as they retained support. Decisions made by civil or war councils were not binding on individuals because the Huron valued individual freedom.

Confederacy councils met at least once a year. Each village sent its clan segment chiefs to this council. Action could not be taken without consensus, which often meant that the assembled reached no decisions. Although this governing structure provided room for opposition and relied on a willingness to reach consensus, it was not well suited to make binding decisions that could compel the nations or the confederacy as a whole to act. This loose structure, lacking coercive power, became a problem in the 17th century, when the Huron proved unable to respond effectively to the threat posed by the Iroquois.

The first contact between Europeans and the Huron took place in 1609, when a group of Huron warriors met with the French explorer Samuel de Champlain along the St. Lawrence River.

Further reading: Nancy Bonvillain, *The Huron* (New York: Chelsea House Publishers, 1989); Conrad E. Heidenreich, "Huron," in *Handbook of North American Indians,* William C. Sturtevant, gen. ed., vol. 15, *Northeast,* ed. Bruce G. Trigger (Washington, D.C.: Smithsonian Institution, 1978), 368–393; Elisabeth Tooker, *An Ethnography of the Huron Indians, 1615–1649* (Syracuse: Syracuse University Press, 1991); Bruce G. Trigger, *The Children of Aataentsic: A History of the Huron People to 1660* (Montreal: McGill-Queen's University Press, 1976); ———, *The Huron: Farmers of the North* (New York: Holt, Rinehart & Winston, 1969).

— Martha K. Robinson

I

Ibn Battuta (1304–1369)

Born in Tangier in 1304, Sheikh Abu Abdallah Muhammad ibn Abdallah ibn Muhammad ibn Ibrahim al-Lawati, otherwise known as Ibn Battuta, became the most famous African traveler of the medieval period.

Ibn Battuta began his travels in 1325, when he set out on a pilgrimage to MECCA. According to his memoirs, Ibn Battuta received a vision while on his pilgrimage that foretold his future travels. After completing the necessary rites pilgrims were required to perform, Ibn Battuta left Mecca to visit every country in the Islamic world (see ISLAM). He traveled through the Middle East recording events along the way. He returned to Mecca on a second pilgrimage and remained there for two years engaged in academic study. While in Mecca, tales of India intrigued the young scholar, so he set out to see India for himself. Preferring to travel by land instead of sea, he journeyed to India across Anatolia and the steppes of central Asia. He arrived in India and remained for seven years, even becoming a judge in Delhi. Although he became destitute, the Indian sultan Muhammad ibn Tughluq appointed Ibn Battuta India's ambassador to China. Although Ibn Battuta described his China adventures in his memoirs, most scholars believe he never actually visited the country.

He returned to Morocco in 1349, having traveled through North Africa, the east African coast, the Middle East, and central Asia. He decided to embark on two more trips, one to Muslim Spain and the other to the SUDAN. Ibn Battuta easily completed his trip to Spain the following year, then set out from Sijilmasa across the SAHARA to MALI. Upon arrival in Mali, Ibn Battuta won an audience with the ruler Mansa Sulayman, the grandson of MANSA MUSA I, whose wealth and generosity achieved legendary status after his famed pilgrimage to Mecca in 1324. Ibn Battuta found Mansa Sulayman much less impressive than his grandfather, but Ibn Battuta's observations of Mali culture and society provide historians with one of the most valuable resources on medieval West African history. Ibn Battuta wrote with admiration when he described the high standards of justice and security in the Mali Empire. Crime appeared almost nonexistent, while citizens valued scholarship and learning. In a more judgmental tone, he recounted the roles of men and women, noting that people traced their ancestry matrilineally. He also noted that the citizens of Mali observed the practices and rituals of Islam faithfully but wondered at their custom of allowing both men and women to enjoy "companions" outside the bonds of marriage and the total lack of jealousy directed toward these partners.

In 1353 Ibn Battuta returned home for the last time. At the command of his sultan, Ibn Battuta dictated his travel memoirs. Upon completion he became a judge near Fez and died in 1369 at the age of 64. If all of Ibn Battuta's travels are to be taken as the truth, he traveled approximately 75,000 miles through 44 different modern-day countries.

Further reading: Basil Davidson, *The Lost Cities of Africa* (Boston: Little, Brown, 1959); Ross E. Dunn, *The Adventures of Ibn Battuta: A Muslim Traveler of the 14th Century* (London: Croom Helm, 1986).

— Tom Niermann

Ibn Khaldûn, 'Abd-ar-Rahmân Abû Zayd ibn Muhammad ibn Muhammad (1332–1406)

A historian and statesman whose history of the world represented one of the most important works of scholarship of its age and was among the first "scientific" historical works ever written.

Born to an aristocratic Moorish family in Tunis on May 27, 1332, Ibn Khaldûn had a traditional education. Like other members of elite scholarly Muslim (see ISLAM) families, he learned the Koran, Arabic poetry, and the law. He entered government service in 1352, but by the time he was 22 he had decided to move to other pursuits. Thus, in

1354 he left Tunis for Fez, where he began to work for the Merinid Sultan Abû ʿInân. He continued his education there and made contacts with a wide range of scholars. Three years into his work at Fez his employer had him jailed for disloyalty, and he remained in prison until Abû ʿInân died in late 1358. Once he gained his freedom, he then sought new opportunities, and he decided to leave Africa. He arrived in Granada in late 1362, where he soon entered the service of Ibn al-Ahmar, Muhammad V, who in 1364 sent him as an emissary to the king of CASTILE, Pedro the Cruel, with the goal of establishing peace between the Arabs of Granada and Castile. He did not remain long in Castile and soon after his departure he returned to northwest Africa, where, among other things, he helped to organize a military force from Arabs in the desert to serve the sultan of Tlemcen. Frustrated by the demands and risks of public life, he retreated into a monastery at Tlemcen, although he was there but a short time before he was again pressed into service, this time by ʿAbd-ad-ʿAzîz, who ruled Fez. After ʿAbd-al-ʿAzîz died, Ibn Khaldûn remained in Fez until he had an opportunity to return to Spain in 1374.

Ibn Khaldûn spent the mid-1370s at Qalʾat Ibn Salâmah in Oran. There he wrote the long introduction (known as the *Muqaddimah*) to his history of the world. This section of his longer *History* (the *Kitâb al-ʿIbar*) "can be regarded," one modern commentator has noted, "as the earliest attempt made by any historian to discover a pattern in the changes that occur in man's political and social organization." Before Ibn Khaldûn, those who wrote about the past either did so by trying to describe the relation between divine forces and worldly events (evident, for example, in the description of the ancient Israelites' flight from Egypt in the Book of Exodus), or they were content to provide a listing of events, in chronicles and annals, that told when things had happened but offered no explanation of why they had occurred. Ibn Khaldûn, by contrast, tried to explain why things changed in the ways that they did. He offered his readers abundant details about the world that he knew, including explanations for why some people were different from others based on the climate of the region they inhabited. He spoke about the rise of cities and civilizations and about the relationship between nature and culture.

"History is a discipline widely cultivated among nations and races," he wrote in the beginning of the *Muqaddimah*. "It is eagerly sought after. The men in the street, the ordinary people, aspire to know it. Kings and leaders vie for it." Although there had been scholars who had offered information about past dynasties, some of whom had provided material to entertain those who would pay attention, they eschewed explanations. Ibn Khaldûn, by contrast, wanted to explain the "inner meaning of history," a task that, he explained, "involves speculation and an attempt to get at the truth, subtle explanation of the causes and origins of existing things, and deep knowledge of the how and why of events." He recognized that there had been important Muslim historians who wrote earlier, but too many of them had become bound by tradition and, worse still, had allowed their histories to become polluted by myth. The time had come to lay out a new way to look at the past. He thus tried to write "an exhaustive history of the world" that would force "stubborn stray wisdom to return to the fold."

Successful as he was, Ibn Khaldûn realized his own limitations. "A person who creates a new discipline does not have the task of enumerating all the problems connected with it," he wrote near the end of the *Muqaddimah*. "His task is to specify the subject of the discipline and its various branches and the discussions connected with it." He left it to those who followed him to add yet other problems that needed to be solved.

In the years following the completion of the *Muqaddimah* Ibn Khaldûn continued to work as a scholar. In 1384 he moved to Cairo, where he became professor of Mâlikite Jurisprudence in the Qamhîyah College and Grand Cadi of the Mâlikite Rite. At the end of that year his family drowned when their ship from Tunis sank. Three years later he made his pilgrimage to MECCA, and in 1400, after holding yet other official posts, he traveled to Jerusalem, Hebron, and Bethlehem. He finally settled in Cairo in 1401, where he remained until his death on March 17, 1406, his remains destined for the local Sufi cemetery.

Further reading: Ibn Khaldûn, *The Muqaddimah: An Introduction to History*, trans. Franz Rosenthal, ed. N. J. Dawood (Princeton, N.J.: Bollingen Series, Princeton University Press, 1967).

Iceland

The remote North Atlantic island of Iceland, settled by NORSE explorers, tested the durability of European political systems and the adaptability of European peoples to new environments.

The first known human inhabitants of Iceland, situated between Norway and GREENLAND, were Irish hermits, but some scholars speculate that travelers from the classical Mediterranean world knew about the island. All historians agree that immigrants from Norway established Iceland's first permanent settlement. Early Icelandic sources credit Ingólfur Arnarson and his wife with homesteading on the site of present-day Reykjavik in 874. Early Icelandic settlers were mostly Norse immigrants. Many fled Norway to Iceland during the attempt by King Harold the Fairheaded to consolidate separate chieftainships into a unified Norwegian kingdom.

The Norse chieftains who made Iceland their home were determined to use negotiation to prevent such abuse of power. In 930 they created an assembly called Althing that met for two weeks every summer to promulgate laws and settle differences. The greatest threat to chieftain power came from a rapidly spreading Christianity. In 1000 the chieftains agreed to build Christian churches, which resulted in an independent church that played a prominent role in spreading literacy to wealthy Icelandic families.

Norway attempted to rule the island from the 10th century onward, gaining control in 1262 following the Icelandic civil war. The 1380 union of Denmark and Norway transferred governance of Iceland to Denmark, yet Iceland remained relatively independent until the middle of the 17th century, when the Danish Crown asserted stricter control over its island possession.

Environmental factors, including DISEASE, played a pivotal role in Icelandic history. The distance of Iceland from continental Europe ensured that when diseases reached Icelandic shores they spread with the ferocity of so-called virgin soil epidemics. The Black Death (see PLAGUE) arrived in Iceland in 1402. SMALLPOX repeatedly swept the island, most disastrously in a 1707 epidemic that killed 18,000 people, one-third of the population. Overgrazing by imported cattle and sheep also triggered soil erosion that transformed once-fertile land into barren rocky outcrops.

Further reading: Kirsten Hastrup, *Nature and Policy in Iceland, 1400–1800* (Oxford, U.K.: Clarendon Press, Oxford University Press, 1990); Sigurdur A. Magnússon, *Northern Sphinx: Iceland and Icelanders from the Settlement to the Present* (Montreal: McGill-Queen's University Press, 1977).

— Kevin C. Armitage

Igbo (Ibo)

Also know as the Ibo, the Igbo are a major ethnic group in present-day Nigeria who have lived in their traditional homeland, known as Igboland, along the banks of the lower NIGER RIVER for thousands of years.

Archaeological evidence shows that the traditional metalwork, weaving, and woodcarving that the Igbo are known for today have been an integral part of their culture for more than 10 centuries, with sophisticated bronze and textile artifacts dating from the ninth century. The traditional Igbo religion included ideas about the afterlife and reincarnation, incorporated sacrificial elements, and maintained a system of spirit and ancestor worship. Elaborate ceremonies accompanied funerals and other rites of passage for the Igbo. In contrast to other peoples in the region, the Igbo did not develop a centralized monarchy, but instead relied on fairly autonomous, democratic villages for their governance, regulated by complex kinship structures, secret societies, oracles, and religious leaders. This decentralized political system prevented any single person from gaining too much power and maintained the basic democratic principles of the Igbo.

Beginning in the 15th century the Igbo homeland became a major center for the SLAVE TRADE. Coastal Igbo became slave traders, often capturing neighboring ethnic groups and even other inland Igbo for sale on the slave market. Igboland remained an important source for the transatlantic trade in slaves throughout the 17th and 18th centuries.

Further reading: E. J. Alagoa, "The Niger River Delta States and Their Neighbors to c. 1800," in *History of West Africa,* vol. 1, 3rd ed., eds. J. F. Ade Ajiya and Michael Crowder (London: Longman, 1985), 372–411; David P. Johnson, Jr., "Igbo," in *Africana: The Encyclopedia of the African and African American Experience* eds. Kwame Anthony Appiah and Henry Louis Gates, Jr. (New York: Basic *Civitas* Books, 1999), 988; Ade Obayemi, "The Yoruba and Edo-speaking Peoples and Their Neighbors before 1600," in *History of West Africa,* eds. Ajiya and Crowder, 255–322; "The Peoples," in *Cambridge Encyclopedia of Africa,* eds. Roland Oliver and Michael Crowder (Cambridge, U.K.: Cambridge University Press, 1981), 57–86.

— Lisa M. Brady

Inca

From approximately 1200 to 1532 the Inca conquered and controlled an Andean empire in South America that covered portions of modern-day Argentina, Bolivia, Chile, Ecuador, and PERU only to see it collapse in the face of the twin disasters of a pandemic introduced by the arrival of Europeans in South America and a Spanish invasion in 1532.

According to Inca legend, their people emerged from three caves near the town of Pacaritambo near CUZCO. Following their first emperor, Manco Capac, the Inca moved into the valley containing Cuzco, and from there over the next several centuries they spread out and conquered much of the territory in the ANDES MOUNTAINS. Until the time of the ninth emperor, Pachacuti Inca, the Inca empire did not extend beyond the Cuzco valley. After defeating the Chanca, who threatened to overrun the Inca, Pachacuti Inca reorganized the empire and rebuilt Cuzco into a suitable capital for the empire. He also built several new cities and palaces throughout the empire, including MACHU PICCHU. Pachacuti Inca promoted advances in architecture and built the royal highway system, which improved transportation and communication. This made it possible for the

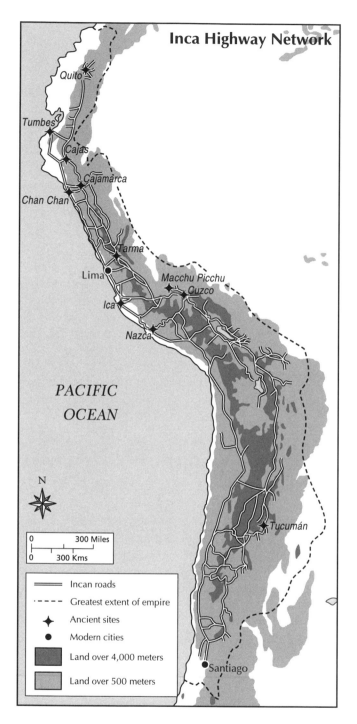

Inca Highway Network

Quito

Tumbes

Cajas

Cajamarca

Chan Chan

Tarma

Lima

Macchu Picchu
Cuzco

Ica

Nazca

PACIFIC

OCEAN

N

Tucumán

| 0 | 300 Miles |
| 0 | 300 Kms |

Santiago

Incan roads

Greatest extent of empire

Ancient sites

Modern cities

Land over 4,000 meters

Land over 500 meters

out the empire be held by only those of pure Inca blood. Inca adopted from allies in the Cuzco valley filled other valued positions in the hierarchy. Below this rank the Inca incorporated localized nobility of conquered people into their system. At this level families that functioned as economic units within the Inca system were systematically grouped into units of 10, 50, 100, 500, 1,000, 5,000, and 10,000 and controlled from the top down. These various levels of organization provided specific services and tribute to the Inca state based on their location and resources. The Inca government in turn provided protection from invasion and relief during emergencies from surpluses set aside for these types of crises.

The wide range of environments found within the Inca Empire influenced its economic system and dictated the type of resources collected. The tribute collected by the empire included chiles, coca, cotton, maize, TOBACCO, and yucca from the valleys and grains, wool, and tubers from the highlands. Coastal areas provided a wide variety of aquatic resources, and mining districts provided GOLD, SILVER, and other metals used by the empire. CORN (maize) and different types of potatoes provided the bulk of the Inca diet. These potatoes could be grown throughout an extended range of altitude, thus ensuring that in any given year, regardless of weather conditions, at least a portion of the potato crop would be harvested.

The Inca kept track of this expansive economic system by using a mnemonic device known as a *quipu*. *Quipus* consisted of main cords with smaller strings of varying colors attached. Each string contained a collection of knots at differing intervals. The different lengths, spacing of the knots, and colors indicated specific numbers. With these devices the Inca kept track of the resources of the empire and made sure that resources were dispersed whenever they were needed. *Quipus* could also be used to aid in the recitation of narratives and important oral traditions associated with religious practices. Unfortunately, only those who knew what the specific *quipu* recorded could use them, but the system was nonetheless sufficient to aid in keeping the empire running smoothly.

The Inca religion centered on worship of a sun god and an earth-mother goddess within an ever increasing pantheon of other gods and goddesses. They also revered special spirits that inhabited the mummies of their ancestors, mountains, stone idols, and a wide range of other aspects of the natural world. In general, their religion was highly ritualized, their annual calendar filled with ceremonies and festivals associated with it. When they conquered a new people, they usually incorporated the religion of the new group into their pantheon and thus partially guaranteed the loyalty of their new subjects rather than further antagonizing them. They also allowed local leaders to retain some

Inca to rule such a far-flung empire. Those emperors who followed Pachacuti expanded upon the boundaries of the empire and continued refining the infrastructure of state until its defeat at the hands of the Spanish.

The Inca emperors rigidly controlled their society by requiring that all important government positions through-power, a strategy that proved to be a source of strength and stability for the empire.

The beginning of the end for the empire started with the arrival of a Spanish *entrada* under the command of FRANCISCO PIZARRO in 1532. As it happened, Pizarro arrived just as a civil war was being waged between two brothers, Huascar and ATAHUALPA, for the imperial throne. The premature death of the emperor, their father, and his heir, their older brother, from the pandemic introduced to South America by the arrival of Europeans precipitated this civil war. In the wake of the devastation created by the pandemic and the civil war, Pizarro, with 168 men, arrived in the region and took advantage of the situation. Having won the civil war, the emperor Atahualpa met Pizarro at the city of Cajamarca. After Atahualpa rejected the *REQUERIMIENTO*, the Spanish attacked the Incan entourage and took the ruler captive. Bargaining for his freedom, Atahualpa promised Pizarro a room filled with gold and silver. It took several months to meet this goal. In 1533, after the Inca delivered the ransom, Pizarro reneged on the deal and had Atahualpa executed. He then marched on the Inca capital of Cuzco and took it, although Inca resistance continued for more than a century. In 1535 the most successful rebellion was led by Manco Inca, a brother of Atahualpa who had been used by the Spanish as a puppet ruler of the Inca Empire. Manco Inca laid siege to Cuzco and Lima and almost took both cities. The Spanish finally quelled this stage of the rebellion in 1537, and Manco Inca fled to eastern Peru and formed the rump state of Vilcabamba. This particular insurgence ended after the Spanish captured and executed Manco Inca. In the end the Spanish were never able to conquer the entire domain of the Inca Empire, but they successfully ended Inca control of the region.

Further reading: Juan de Betanzos, *Narrative of the Incas,* trans. and eds. Roland Hamilton and Dana Buchanan (Austin: University of Texas Press, 1996); Brian S. Bauer, *The Development of the Inca State* (Austin: University of Texas Press, 1992); Bernabe Cobo, *History of the Inca Empire: An Account of the Indians' Customs and their Origin Together with a Treatise on Inca Legends, History, and Social Institutions,* trans. and ed. Roland Hamilton (Austin: University of Texas Press, 1979); John Hemming, *The Conquest of the Incas* (New York: Harcourt Brace Jovanovich, 1970); Gary Urton, *The History of a Myth: Pacariqtambo and the Origin of the Incas* (Austin: University of Texas Press, 1990).

— Dixie Ray Haggard

Ingram, David (fl. 1568–1582)

A sailor on an English mission to North America in the late 1560s, David Ingram wrote an account of his escapades during which he claimed he walked approximately 2,000 miles from the Gulf of Mexico to Cape Breton, a story that received wide notice when RICHARD HAKLUYT THE YOUNGER printed it in 1589.

According to his account, Ingram, from Barking in Essex, was perhaps 50 years old when he joined the English expedition led by SIR FRANCIS DRAKE and SIR JOHN HAWKINS in the late 1560s. The ships under Drake and Hawkins fared poorly in a naval encounter with Spanish ships off the coast of Florida, a territory that then encompassed not only the modern-day state but also much of the northern rim of the Gulf of Mexico. After they reached the North American mainland, Drake and Hawkins gave their men a choice: Those who wished could try their luck in a return voyage to England in a small and battered fleet, and the others could fend for themselves on land. Although the return expedition did manage to reach Cornwall, most of those aboard had perished from famine or disease.

Ingram was one of 105 men who decided to stay. Those who remained found survival difficult. Ingram wrote about near-starvation conditions during which the men ate parrots, monkeys, cats, mice, rats, and dogs. For unknown reasons, the men on land broke into small groups, and Ingram left the others in the company of Richard Browne and Richard Twide. Starting their journey at what Ingram called the Rio de Minas, the men walked northward, "by land two thousand miles" in Ingram's accounting. Along the way they traveled through a number of Indian villages, none of them well described in the surviving account. Ingram provided his readers with descriptions of the flora and fauna of the mainland, as well as tales about the Indians' religious beliefs and their social mores, noting that some were polygamous but had strict rules against adultery. At one point he and his companions even came face-to-face with the Indians' devil, a creature he called "Colluchio." This beast, which appeared in the shape of a black calf or a black dog, terrified Ingram and his companions, but when they blessed themselves in "the name of the Father, and of the Sonne, and of the holy Ghost," it "shrancke away in a stealing maner" and never bothered them again.

Historians have long suspected that Ingram made up his account, but Hakluyt, an expert on travel accounts, nonetheless included it in the 1589 edition of his *Principall Navigations, Voiages, and Discoveries of the English Nation.* However, when Hakluyt revised this work and published a far larger volume on American travels in 1600, he no longer included Ingram's account. Although Hakluyt never stated why he dropped Ingram's tale, his successor, SAMUEL PURCHAS, suggested that he believed that Ingram had, in fact, created the improbable story.

David Ingram, along with Browne and Twide, traveled back to England, apparently on a ship commanded by a French captain, who picked the trio up somewhere near modern-day Halifax, Nova Scotia. Upon their return the three visited Hawkins to tell him of their journey. By the time Hakluyt published Ingram's tale in 1589, Ingram was the only one of the three still alive. Although Ingram did publish his own version of his travels in a book entitled *A true discourse of the adventures & travaile,* no copy of the work has survived.

Further reading: "Examination of David Ingram," in David Beers Quinn, ed., *The Voyages and Colonising Enterprises of Sir Humphrey Gilbert,* 2 vols., Works Issued by the Hakluyt Society, 2nd Ser., LXXXIII-LXXXIV (London: Hakluyt Society, 1940), II: 281–283; "The Relation of David Ingram of Barking, in the County of Essex," in Richard Hakluyt, *The Principall Navigations, Voiages, and Discoveries of the English Nation* (London: Hakluyt Society, Extra Series XXXI) II: 557–561; Samuel Purchas, *Purchas His Pilgrimage, Or Relations of the World and the Religions Observed in All Ages and Places Discovered, from the Creation unto this Present,* 2nd ed. (London: W. Stansby, 1613).

inquisition

Beginning as a legal procedure for prosecution of "hidden crimes" such as heresy and clerical sexuality, inquisition in early modern Europe became associated with national and religious identities and became a tool for eliminating enemies of the state or of the Catholic faith.

Inquisition began not as a national institution for the prosecution of religious dissenters but rather as a legal procedure for civil trials. The procedure, which had begun in antiquity, was relatively uncommon during the first few centuries following the fall of the Roman Empire but was revived during the rebirth of Roman law and legal thought in western Europe during the late 11th and early 12th century. In the prosecution of certain crimes, such as clerical sexuality or heresy, where "full proofs" such as those offered by eyewitnesses were absent, a "partial proof," such as hearsay or general reputation, could be considered justification for seeking a confession, thus bringing the inquisitorial procedure into play. Inquisition differed from other legal proceedings of the time in four major ways. First, the identity of witnesses was kept secret. Second, counsel for the defense was restricted or nonexistent. Third, the goal of the proceedings was penitential rather than punitive. Fourth, inquisitors and their agents were allowed to resort to torture to extract a confession but would only do so when there was enough partial proof to indicate that a confession would likely be forthcoming.

The inquisitions from the 13th through the 15th centuries operated differently throughout Europe, giving lie to the myth of a monolithic medieval inquisition. Not until the late 15th century was there a move toward institutionalization of inquisition. Around this time the pursuit of heterodoxy became more closely identified with national interests.

Probably the best known of these "national" inquisitions was the inquisition in Spain, which arose out of a tradition of Castilian identity, Christian military nobility, and Christian superiority over Muslims (see ISLAM) and JEWS, all of which had roots in the RECONQUISTA. The Spanish Inquisition began as a national venture in 1478 and condemned more than 3,000 people to death by its end in 1800. The original targets of this particular inquisition were *conversos*—Spanish Jews and Muslims who had converted to Christianity—who had apostatized, reverting to the practices of their former faiths. The office of the Inquisition in Spain soon cast its net more broadly, seeking to root out any possible enemies of the Catholic Church. Once Protestant revolts broke out throughout Europe, inquisitors used their methods to keep unorthodox beliefs out of Spain and the Spanish Empire. Even Catholics were not above suspicion: Ignatius of Loyola was called before the Inquisition twice. Those accused of heterodoxy were subject to secret trial, often including torture, and if found guilty, they were sentenced to public execution in an AUTO-DA-FÉ, or "act of faith." Reactions to the Inquisition within Spain included the flight of between 600 and 3,000 *conversos* and occasional violent resistance, as in the case of the murder of inquisitor Pedro de Arbués in the cathedral of Zaragoza.

Any analysis of the Spanish Inquisition must take into account the religiously plural composition of that empire. Spain had been home to members of three religious traditions—Jewish, Christian, and Muslim—throughout most of the medieval period, and the REFORMATION added Protestants into the equation in various portions of the Spanish empire under CHARLES V and PHILIP II. In this context the Spanish Inquisition might be interpreted as a means to unification of a religiously plural empire, a reflection of a belief that maintaining the empire's religious unity was the only way to maintain its political unity.

Further reading: Henry Kamen, *The Spanish Inquisition: A Historical Revision* (New Haven, Conn.: Yale University Press, 1997); Edward Peters, *Inquisition* (New York: Free Press, 1988).

— Marie A. Kelleher

invention and technology

Advances in certain kinds of invention and technology, particularly relating to the flow of information, shipping, weaponry, and urban architecture and planning, enabled

"The way they built their boats in Virginia," wrote Thomas Harriot in his report of the new land, "is very wonderful." Without metal tools, the Indians of Virginia used fire and clam shells to make canoes. A fire was kindled at the roots of a tall tree and carefully tendered until the tree fell. Then the leaves and branches were burned off. Small fires were carefully lit along the length of the trunk to hollow it out. Finally, the charred wood was cleared away with sharpened shells. Engraving by Theodore DeBry, from a watercolor by John White   *(Library of Congress)*

early modern Europeans to develop specific advantages over other peoples in the Atlantic basin and provided crucial assistance for exploratory and colonizing efforts.

One of the reasons that Europe came to dominate the Atlantic world in this period was its ability to take inventions from various peoples and turn them into pragmatic technologies. Perhaps one of the best examples of this was the PRINTING PRESS. Although it was the Chinese, by historical consensus, who can lay claim to the invention of printing, it remained largely unused owing to the complex nature of Chinese ideograms. Those European alphabets based on Roman letters had less than thirty simple characters. JOHANNES GENSFLEISCH ZUM GUTENBERG transformed the baked clay of Chinese printing blocks into movable steel blocks in his printing press. In a period when European guns and sailing ships were to play a significant role in conquering Atlantic cultures, it is easy to overlook the power of

the printed word, yet without the ability to mass produce cheap, short pamphlets, the teachings of MARTIN LUTHER would not have spread as quickly, and it may have proved easier for a pope such as LEO X to contain his influence. When CHRISTOPHER COLUMBUS and others reached the Western Hemisphere, their reports spread across Europe far quicker than had they been reproduced by hand. When English promoters of colonization such as RICHARD HAKLUYT THE YOUNGER and THOMAS HARRIOT began to encourage English settlements in the Americas, the availability of printing gave them a wider audience.

Technological advances in shipping also proved vital for early modern Europeans. Improvements in such vessels as BRIGANTINES and CARAVELS, as well as better navigational techniques and added knowledge about wind patterns, facilitated long-distance voyages. Such developments proved particularly significant for the Portuguese, whose seaborne empire stretched from the Iberian Peninsula around Africa to the SPICE ISLANDS off southeast Asia and BRAZIL, as well as for the Dutch. With its limited land area, the Dutch were compelled to seek foodstuffs from other sources. This need pushed them to develop shipping technology, and their full-rigged *flute* ships were the result. These ships enabled the Dutch to transport desperately needed grain from the Baltic states. As the Dutch maritime reach lengthened, they found themselves shut out of more lucrative routes by the British and Spanish fleets. Relegated to carrying bulk goods such as lumber, the Dutch developed designs for simple ships that could be constructed far quicker than those of their competitors and positioned them for their 17th-century efforts.

The absence of raw materials, of course, played a decisive role in technological change. Most of the states of West Africa had developed the ability to make iron products long before Europeans arrived to offer them as trade items, but, by an environmental quirk, very few of these states found both iron mines and timber in close enough proximity to produce tools and weapons, thus encouraging them to trade with Europeans for these goods. In the absence of gunpowder and large quantities of iron weapons, the African states developed large oar-powered vessels for use in coastal trade. When confronted with the superior weaponry of the European ships, African rulers dispatched several of these vessels armed with up to 100 archers per ship, using their technology to overcome the technology of the Europeans.

In some cases it was not necessary to use the full extent of one's technology. This was the case of the Spanish conquest of the American empires. Although much of the Spanish triumph can be attributed to the spread of infectious DISEASEs, technology undoubtedly played a part. However, it was not their gunpowder that proved decisive. Rather, it was their possession of steel thrusting weapons—swords, pikes, and sabres—that enabled the Spanish to defeat indigenous peoples who possessed superb technological knowledge (evident, for example, in much Mesoamerican architecture). A crucial problem for the AZTECS and others was the absence of natural resources that would have allowed them to develop weapons equal to those of the Spanish.

Invention could also take the form of discovering something of the way nature worked. For decades European sailors had practiced a technique called *volta do mar,* by which they would sail west into the Atlantic in order to pick up a westerly wind to bring them home. In 1487 BARTHOLOMEU DIAS, trapped near the western coast of southern Africa, sailed west and south into the Atlantic until he picked up a westerly wind that enabled him to lay claim as the first European to sail to the Indian Ocean. Ten years later VASCO DA GAMA put his knowledge of the winds

to work and sailed southwest into the Atlantic from the Cape Verde Islands until he picked up the winds that brought him around the southern coast of Africa en route to Asia. Da Gama's inventive route remained the standard for as long as sailing ships traveled from Europe to Asia.

Why was it that Europeans seemed to develop some of these skills quicker than other Atlantic cultures? There are multiple possible answers. Europeans, long fragmented into dozens of kingdoms, principalities, and city-states, lived in a state of on-going warfare for centuries. When they sought better weapons to attack their foes, they were able to apply some the lessons to other fields. Thus, steel produced for swords could also be used in agricultural implements to increase productivity. Further, some Europeans (unlike Native Americans and Africans) believed that because they owned land (and not only what the land produced), they needed ways to protect their holdings, and this need served as a further goad to military inventions. Geography also played a vital role. Those nations with access to the ocean, especially the English, Portuguese, Dutch, and Spanish, developed maritime technologies to assist their military and commercial ventures. Such technologies, necessary for maintaining transoceanic trade, had little obvious appeal to states or communities whose political and economic horizons remained fixed to their homelands and adjacent territories. The concentrations of Europeans into large cities also facilitated technological advances, especially in architecture, although Europeans had no monopoly on urban design. The great city of TENOCHTITLÁN, for example, possessed buildings that could rival any in the world at the time, and other Aztec and MAYA settlements had pyramids that towered as impressively as the spires of St. Paul's Cathedral in LONDON.

Finally, for better or for worse, European financial and economic systems propelled technology faster there than elsewhere. In the early 15th century Chinese technology appears to have been far ahead of European, but the Chinese rulers decided to prohibit certain technologies, which dampened further innovation. In the Islamic states (see ISLAM) of the Middle East, a commitment to invention was often held back by an arbitrary approach to taxation, which could see the fruits of labor forfeited. While both government prohibitions and arbitrary seizure occurred in Europe, the political fragmentation meant that they were not practiced in all of Europe at the same time. Thus, if one city-state banned an innovative technique, its practitioners could move somewhere else. The proliferation of printing presses across the continent also facilitated the spread of information about new inventions.

Further reading: Alfred W. Crosby, *Ecological Imperialism: The Biological Expansion of Europe, 900–1900* (Cambridge, U.K.: Cambridge University Press, 1986); Jared Diamond, *Guns, Germs and Steel: The Fate of Human Societies* (New York: Norton, 1999); David Landes, *The Wealth and Poverty of Nations: Why Some Are So Rich and Some So Poor* (New York: Norton, 1998); John Thornton, *Africa and Africans in the Making of the Atlantic World, 1400–1800*, 2nd ed. (Cambridge, U.K.: Cambridge University Press, 1998).

— John Grigg

Iroquois

Although Iroquoian cultural patterns and linguistic commonalities extended to a myriad of Native American groups in what is now the United States and Canada, the tribal designation *Iroquois* specifically refers to the peoples of the Five Nations (MOHAWK, ONEIDA, ONONDAGA, CAYUGA, and SENECA), whose principal settlements in the area of modern-day New York State enjoyed considerable social, economic, and political linkage. (They later became the Six Nations in the early 1720s, when the Tuscarora came north and joined the Iroquois Confederacy.)

The word *Iroquois* derives from the ALGONQUIAN Irinakhoiw (translated as "real adders," although other terms from this language family simply referred to the fact that the Iroquois spoke a foreign tongue), which French voyageurs and missionaries changed to the more familiar spelling. The Iroquois called themselves by other names, the best-known being the Seneca Haudenosaunee, or "people of the longhouse," referring to the communal living structures that were the centerpiece of village life.

By the time Europeans first encountered them, during the first half of the 16th century, the Iroquois had already established themselves in villages clustered near Lake Erie and Lake Ontario. Over time they grew into a political and military force to be reckoned with in the region. Although contact with the newcomers often exacted a heavy price, they drew on cultural strengths and patterns of response familiar to them in their dealings with other native groups to meet the challenges of European encroachment. Politically savvy and strategically well located, they retained a degree of hegemony and autonomy few of their neighbors knew.

Early Iroquois

Long before 1492 the Iroquois developed the complex cultural traditions that helped to sustain them. The archaeological record suggests that the Five Nations Iroquois (or their progenitors) resided in the eastern Great Lakes region for centuries before whites arrived, coalescing into their respective tribal entities by the year 1200 at the latest. As a result, what Europeans witnessed in their sojourns among and relationships with the Iroquois reflected a series of settlement patterns, community structures, and group interactions that had evolved much earlier.

Iroquois subsistence patterns, relying on a mixture of horticulture, especially CORN (but also beans and squash and later sunflowers and TOBACCO), and fishing and hunting, were firmly in place by 1000 C.E. (and perhaps much earlier). Within this gendered economy women tended crops, and men had responsibility for procuring game. Early artifacts, including ceramic bowls and pipes adorned with human faces and animal forms, suggest not only utilitarian function but also the rise of craftsmanship and ties to ritual purposes, including tobacco use and the Harvest or Green Corn festivals celebrating the bounty of women's work. After the introduction of copper and brass implements from Europe, pottery figured less prominently among the Iroquois, yet such changes did not signify abandonment of traditional beliefs in exchange for technological advances; metal tools helped add elaborate detail to the wooden masks worn by the Society of Faces (or False Faces, often previously depicted in the clay objects) during cleansing and healing ceremonies, an indication that the Iroquois, like other Native American groups, adapted innovations according to their own social needs and beliefs.

The rise of fortified villages, including prototypical forms of the longhouse structure, predated the introduction of agriculture, suggesting that the ancestors of the Iroquois had taken steps to limit internecine warfare. Over time village and longhouse size increased (the latter sometimes growing to several hundred feet), with the palisaded towns affording protection against outside invasion and serving as trading centers. Although pre-Columbian trade was not as extensive among the Iroquois as it was with their HURON neighbors, archaeological evidence of imported luxury items such as marine shells and native copper suggests the Iroquois were not economically isolated, either. By the early contact period village life was vibrant, with the dozen or so major Iroquois towns home to 50 to 1,000 people inhabiting 30 to 150 multifamily longhouses.

The Iroquois traced descent matrilineally, and their communal living arrangements expressed matrilocal residence. Each extended longhouse family had at its core a group of women (mothers, sisters, and daughters), with men moving into the homes of their wives upon marriage. Women retained ownership of these structures, and inheritance and succession to political offices moved along the maternal line. The eldest female in the group acted as the matriarch, directing the work and daily activities of the home. Down the central aisle of the longhouse ran a series of hearths, each marking the existence of semi-private cubicles occupied by the nuclear family units who made up the basic components of the whole.

Each longhouse family further identified with a clan structure based on an animal crest or spirit, so that members of the group became fictive siblings with other maternal families from separate villages. Clan members had an obligation to welcome and provide for outsiders who shared their affiliation and became blood relatives in a legal sense. (Marriage among those of the same clan was taboo.) The nine clans of the Iroquois were the Turtle, Bear, Wolf, Hawk, Heron, Beaver, Deer, Snipe, and Eel. Two or more clans composed a moiety, or what the Iroquois today call "the sides," which added greater cohesion to the entire community by connecting these larger groupings as siblings. Those joined by the moieties performed ceremonial functions such as preparing and burying each other's dead, hosting games and feasts, and conducting other rituals meant to underscore and solidify their relationship.

The Iroquois Confederacy

The internal links unifying the Iroquois socially had their political counterpart in the overarching alliance fusing the Five Nations together. Although certainly in existence before the arrival of Europeans, the League of the Iroquois did not reach full florescence until after contact, by about the late 16th century. The story of its origins survives in the lengthy oral tradition known as the "Great Law of Peace," which recounts the vision of the prophet Deganawida, or the Peacemaker, who sought an end to the bloodshed, divisiveness, and warfare that threatened the social order of the region in precontact times. Joined in his crusade by the exiled Onondaga chief HIAWATHA, the two carried a plan to the people for political organization and the end of intertribal violence.

Their proposals initially met opposition in the person of Tadodaho, an Onondaga war chief, who mounted a campaign against Hiawatha, killing his daughters. Returning to exile, Hiawatha devised an alternative to revenge for the loss of loved ones. In his new scheme members of the appropriate moiety would console and care for the family who lost a member, a strategy aimed to replace traditional blood feuds. If these condolence rituals did not satisfy the afflicted, an outsider could come to serve in the place of the deceased. This gave rise to the so-called mourning wars, raids specifically geared toward the seizure of captives from other tribes who might either be killed or adopted by the stricken relatives. After his own period of mourning, Hiawatha returned undaunted with Deganawida, and they at last succeeded in persuading Tadodaho to accept the path of diplomacy by offering him a leadership role in their Great League.

Foremost in this arrangement was the establishment of a grand council composed of 50 sachems, or chiefs—eight Seneca, nine each from the Mohawk and Oneida nations, 10 Cayuga, and 14 Onondaga—who, acting together, sought diplomatic solutions to the blood feuds and enmity plaguing the region. The linkage of the nations found its symbol in the wampum belt, or string of shells held together by a common strand; this "chain" featured the Onondaga at the center surrounded by the remaining four tribes, and it was at Onondaga, under the Great Tree of Peace, that the grand council would meet. In addition, the confederacy represented the longhouse writ large, with the metaphorical structure of roof (sky) and floor (earth) safely containing the fires of the Five Nations. Furthermore, the league observed the familiar clan divisions, and clan mothers selected the men who would represent these interests in the council. This arrangement underscored the primacy of matrilineage and kinship in Iroquois culture.

At the village level a headman and council of elders made decisions about local matters, yet it was the clan chiefs who acted as tribal leaders and spoke for their people in the grand council. In keeping with the delineation of the moieties, the league representatives occupied different chambers, or houses, within the confederacy's political configuration. These "brotherhoods" dictated that the Mohawk and Seneca (elder brothers) sit on one side and the Cayuga and Oneida (younger brothers) on the other, much like the bicameral systems of parliamentary bodies. The former group first conferred on issues brought to the council before sending them to the latter for consideration. In the case of disagreement, the Onondaga, or "Firekeepers," had the final vote. Invested with the power to strike agreements or alliances with foreigners and keep peace within the Five Nations, the grand council expressed a complex political order that unified the Iroquois and helped them face the challenges wrought by contact with Europeans.

The Iroquois in a Changing World

The French were the first Europeans whom the Iroquois encountered, but JACQUES CARTIER's initial meetings with Iroquoian peoples near Quebec in the summer of 1534 did not translate into sustained contact with the Five Nations until significantly later, with the intensification of the fur trade. Heavy demand for the *castor gras*, or coat beaver, and the popularity of beaver hats in Europe by the 1580s increasingly drew the southern Iroquois into the French sphere of influence. As trade relations developed around the port of Tadoussac, the Mohawks penetrated northward, effectively driving out the St. Lawrence Iroquois by 1603, but failed to settle in the area, probably due to the strength of the Huron, Algonquian, and other French trading partners. Instead, they staged raids to obtain the knives, mirrors, and metal goods exchanged for pelts at trading centers. Whether they sought the role of middlemen occupied by these northern tribes is not clear, but warfare was their method of entry into the region. The French, for their part, instead allied with groups they knew better, supplying them with weapons (but not yet firearms) to repel the Iroquois attacks.

During the first years of the 17th century, the Montagnais allied with the Algonquian and Huron to protect the trade and rout the Mohawk, and conflicts between indigenous nations increased. Others from the Five Nations likely began to join the Mohawk in these forays as the clamor for goods won through raiding helped to solidify the strength of the league. This economically motivated war soon brought the Iroquois into more continuous contact with Europeans. Samuel de Champlain received orders in 1608 to build a fort at Quebec and the next year joined France's Indian allies in pursuing the Iroquois. Soon, the French–Huron alliance held the Iroquois at bay in the western trade.

At nearly the same time the Iroquois found access to another source of goods among the Dutch, who came to control the wampum trade around Long Island. To secure this exchange, the Iroquois mounted a protracted campaign against eastern tribes living in the vicinity of Fort Orange. Emerging victorious, they were now intermediaries to all trade with the Dutch, a coup that secured their strength but quashed the hopes of the Dutch to expand their own influence into French trading territory. This turn of events shored up the power of both the Five Nations and the French, and the Dutch fell victim to growing competition with English traders who supplied the Iroquois with guns and began to establish inroads among them.

While the Iroquois increased their use of European trade goods, they maintained the integrity of traditional social structures and beliefs. Village life continued to be a source of vibrancy and renewal, military and economic power was in ascendance, and warfare had actually invigorated the league. However, over the course of the 17th century, so-called virgin soil epidemics, particularly SMALLPOX, began to take a heavy toll, reducing the pre-contact population of the Five Nations by as much as half (to about 10,000) by the end of the 17th century and claiming specialists and elders whose arts and wisdom could not be easily replaced. Nevertheless, they escaped the social and political fragmentation of the Huron confederacy that resulted from that tribe's alliance with the French. They likewise kept their homeland essentially intact. In fact, for the remainder of the colonial period they successfully exploited the animosities that existed between England and France, holding onto a delicate "middle ground" between the two empires, and managed to preserve relative autonomy until after the American Revolution. Even today, the social and political cultures of the Five Nations Iroquois still thrive, an indication of their power to adapt to difficult circumstances and maintain strength in the face of adversity.

Further reading: José António Brandão, *"Your Fire Shall Burn No More": Iroquois Policy Toward New France and Its Native Allies to 1701* (Lincoln: University of Nebraska Press, 1997); Daniel Richter, *The Ordeal of the Longhouse: The Peoples of the Iroquois League in the Era of European Colonization* (Chapel Hill: University of North Carolina Press, 1992); Elisabeth Tooker, ed., *An Iroquois Source Book*, 3 vols., (New York: Garland, 1985); Elisabeth Tooker, "The League of the Iroquois: Its History, Politics, and Ritual," in William C. Sturtevant, gen. ed., *Handbook of North American Indians*, vol. 15, *Northeast*, ed. Bruce G. Trigger (Washington, D.C.: Smithsonian Institution Press, 1978), 418–441; Anthony F. C. Wallace, "Origins of the Longhouse Religion," in *Northeast*, ed. Trigger, 442–448.

— Eric P. Anderson

Isabella See Ferdinand and Isabella

Islam

A monotheistic religion based on the revelations of Muhammad as written in the Qur'an (Koran), Islam arose in the seventh century C.E. in the city of MECCA, spread quickly through southwest Asia, northern Africa, and the SUDAN in the seventh through 11th centuries, and was well established as a world religion by the 16th century, with adherents as distant as Europe, Asia, and the Americas.

Origins

Muhammad, considered by Muslims (followers of Islam) to be the final prophet in the line of Abraham and whose divine revelations between the years 610 and 632 form the text of the Qur'an, was born in Mecca in or around the year 571. He was a member of the Quraysh tribe, who controlled the *haram*, or sacred area, around the local shrine. The Ka'ba, reputedly built by Abraham and his son Ishmael, was the site of a long-standing tradition of pilgrimage by followers of various local and regional faiths. In 623, after Muhammad had returned victorious from his forced exile in Medina (his flight from Mecca in 622 is known as the *Hijrah* and marks the beginning of the Muslim calendar), he purged the Ka'ba of all its idols and claimed it solely for the worship of Allah (Arabic for God). The Ka'ba became the primary destination for Muslims making the *hajj*, or pilgrimage, one of the five pillars of Islam.

Islam is based on the Qur'an, the written version of Allah's revelations through the angel Gabriel to Muhammad. The Qur'an is organized into 114 chapters, or *surahs*, and 6,236 verses. It is the source of Islamic law and establishes rules for daily living. The Qur'an served to unify Muslims the world over, regardless of their local customs and cultural differences. This unity is based in part on the practice of the five acts of worship, or pillars, of Islam: first, the open profession of faith through the statement "There is no god but Allah, and Muhammad is the Prophet of Allah"; second, prayer—usually five times per day, always in the direction of Mecca; third, almsgiving; fourth, fasting during the month of Ramadan (the ninth lunar month); and fifth, making the *hajj* to the sacred sites of Mecca and Medina during Dhu al-Hijjah (the twelfth lunar month). The *hajj* is only required once during an individual's lifetime and only of those who are physically and financially able to perform this important act of worship. For some Muslims *jihad*—holy war or striving for faith—became a pillar as well.

In addition to the Qur'an, Muhammad established many traditions (*hadith*) that form the basis of Islamic custom (*sunnah*) pertaining to law, religion, education, worship, and devotion. Al-Sha'fi (d. 820), a Muslim lawyer in Cairo, wrote the *Risalah* to record the *sunnah*, bringing unity to a diverse religious following that placed community at the center of tradition. The *Risalah* in essence created a living tradition that spanned the cultural and geographic separation of the broader Muslim community. However, whereas the Qur'an is the word of Allah and therefore law, the *hadith* are associated with the actions and words of Muhammad and are less strictly and more selectively applied by various Muslim communities. The flexibility of the *hadith* and their application allowed for regional diversity within Islam and accommodated local traditions, thus making conversion to Islam easier and more appealing to a variety of peoples.

Differences between Muslim communities based on the *hadith* are only one source of diversity in the broader Muslim world. More significant is the split between the Sunni, who follow the tradition of electing the caliph (the spiritual and temporal leader of the Muslim community) from Muhammad's companions, and the Shi'i, who believe that the caliphate belonged to the descendants of Muhammad through his cousin and son-in-law 'Ali, husband of Muhammad's only surviving child, Fatima. 'Ali was the fourth elected caliph but was assassinated in 651, giving rise to the succession issue. The Sunni–Shi'i split formed the basis of many of the power struggles by various of the competing Islamic dynasties well into the 16th century.

Islam in the Sixteenth Century

By the 16th century Islam dominated southwest Asia, North and West Africa, and parts of Europe. Its spread outside the Hijaz (see Mecca) can be attributed to several factors, including trade, migration—both permanent and temporary—political conquest, and cultural assimilation. Of these factors, trade had perhaps the farthest reaching and longest-lasting effects. Some of the earliest converts to Islam were Arab traders who followed trade routes between the Arabian Peninsula and the African continent through cities such as Cairo, Egypt, and Zeila on the Horn of Africa (see DJIBOUTI) and along the Mediterranean Ocean into southern Europe. With the introduction of the camel, Muslim traders began to cross the SAHARA to the Sudan, encouraging the spread of Islam to areas previously isolated from the Islamized north African and east African peoples. Goods traded on these routes included GOLD, ivory, kola nuts, and slaves from Africa for salt, HORSES, cloth, copper, metal weapons, and beads from the Middle East, Europe, and Asia. Even Mecca, a city virtually closed to all non-Muslims, became a principal market for slaves from Africa by the 16th century. Accompanying these nomadic traders were teachers and holy men who traveled to cities like Djenne and TIMBUKTU and established mosques, converting and educating the local populations in the principles of Islam.

Although the spread of Islam often followed the path of trade routes, its adoption in various regions took different forms. In North Africa, the nomadic Berbers converted to Islam in the 11th century, establishing the Almoravid Dynasty in the Maghreb. From their base in what is today Morocco, the Almoravids (derived from the Arabic *al-murabit* referring to their association with the border fortresses, or *ribat*) were instrumental in the spread of Islam to Spain under the leadership of Yusuf ibn Tashfin and to the Sudan under Abu Bakr. The Almohads replaced the Almoravids in the 12th century and encouraged the growth of Sufi brotherhoods in the region. They fell from power in the late 13th century. SUFISM became popularized in the 13th century in the Maghreb, especially through the actions of the MARABOUT, who grew in importance in the region into the 16th century. After the RECONQUISTA in Spain and the expulsion of Muslims from Granada in 1492, Muslims in North Africa became increasingly militarized, fighting the Christian Europeans who began infiltrating the region. Maghrebi Muslims began looking to the south as well, to the empires of the Sudan such as the SONGHAI, for the purposes of controlling the lucrative trades in gold and salt and eager to supply the Egyptian and North African SLAVE TRADE with men and women from West and central Africa.

Islam in the Sudan (West Africa) took on more of an elite cast. In many of the Sudanic empires, including GHANA, MALI, and Songhai, only the kings and their courtiers converted to Islam, and even then it was often nominal in character. By the time of MANSA MUSA I of Mali, who made a famous pilgrimage to Mecca in 1324, Islam began to gain more popular acceptance, but according to the chronicler IBN BATTUTA, traditional forms of religion persisted and were even integrated with the laws and customs of Islam. By the 16th century and the apex of the Songhai Empire, Islam was firmly ingrained in Sudanic society.

Conversion to Islam in European cultures was less prevalent than in African and frequently was achieved only through *jihad.* Muslim forces arrived on the Iberian Peninsula in 710 from Morocco and retained control over parts of the region until they were ousted from Granada in 1492. Ottoman Turks attacked eastern Europe beginning in the 11th century and nearly captured Vienna under the leadership of SULEIMAN I in 1529. Islam posed a threat to Christian Europe for nearly 1,000 years (both physically and ideologically), but in the 16th century the tide turned. The rise of European commercial powers shifted the balance of power against the Islamic states. European cities such as VENICE, entrenched in trade with the Levant, often showed only minor toleration for Muslim merchants. Despite this seeming disdain, the Islamic Mamluks of Egypt had diplomatic relations with Venice beginning in 1506, and by the end of the 16th century envoys between Venice and Istanbul (the capital of the Ottoman Empire, which defeated the Mamluks in 1517) were a regular occurrence.

As in Europe and Africa, the major means of Islam's spread to the Americas was trade. However, in this instance Muslims were the traded, not just the traders. The majority of slaves taken to the Americas came from west and central African kingdoms, including CAYOR, SENEGAMBIA, and CAMEROON, many of them held at the port of CALABAR to be shipped across the Atlantic. These regions had long histories of Muslim influence, and it is probable that a significant number of the humans forced into bondage and taken across the ocean on the MIDDLE PASSAGE were practicing Muslims. Although many of them were forced to give up their names and their cultural and social practices, the influence of Islam remains evident in some African American traditions that can be traced back to the 16th century.

Further reading: Peter B. Clarke, *West Africa and Islam: A Study of Religious Development from the 8th to the 20th Century* (London: Edward Arnold, 1982); L. P. Harvey, *Islamic Spain, 1250–1500* (Chicago: University of Chicago Press, 1990); Mervyn Hiskett, *The Development of Islam in West Africa* (London: Longman, 1984); Albert Hourani, *A History of the Arab Peoples* (Cambridge, Mass.: Belknap Press of Harvard University Press, 1991); Bernard Lewis, *Islam and the West* (Oxford, U.K.: Oxford University Press, 1993); ———, *The Muslim Discovery of Europe* (New York: Norton, 1982); I. M. Lewis, *Islam in Tropical Africa,* 2nd ed. (Bloomington, Ind.: International African Institute in association with Indiana University Press, 1964); Nabil Matar, *Islam in Britain, 1558–1685* (Cambridge, U.K.: Cambridge University Press, 1998); Maxime Rodinson, *Muhammad,* 2nd ed., trans. Anne Carter (London: Penguin Books, 1996); J. Spencer Trimingham, *The Influence of Islam upon Africa,* 2nd ed. (London: Longman, 1980).

— Lisa M. Brady

Itzcóatl (1381–1440)

Itzcóatl was fourth great speaker of the AZTECS, whose military leadership led to the overthrow of their Tepaneca overlords, the establishment of the Aztecs as an independent nation, and the beginnings of the expansion that would leave them the dominant power in central MEXICO.

Itzcóatl ascended to the throne as an experienced military leader, having held the office of *tlacochcalcatl,* or supreme commander of the army, for more than 20 years. He was proclaimed lord of the Aztecs (Mexica) on April 3, 1427, but Maxtla, lord of the Tepanecs (of whom the Mexica were tributaries at the time) refused to recognize his authority, prompting Itzcóatl to forge an alliance with Nezahualcóyotl, lord of neighboring Texcoco. The two leaders conquered the Tepaneca capital of Azcapotzalco in 1428, killing Maxtla and sacking and burning the city. This event marked the beginnings of the Mexica as a sovereign people, with a capital established at TENOCHTITLÁN.

Itzcóatl governed from 1427 to 1440, going on to conquer, according to the Codex Mendoza, 24 neighboring cities in the valley of Mexico and beyond. Although many of these conquests did not bring the conquered lands directly under Aztec control, they did provide levies and dependencies within easy range of Tenochtitlán that gave the Aztecs a springboard for farther ranging campaigns. In 1431 Itzcóatl formed a more permanent alliance, both defensive and offensive in character, with the lords of Texcoco and TACUBA. The military leadership of this "triple alliance" was reserved to the Aztec great speaker.

Together with his adviser TLACACLA Itzcóatl introduced a series of reforms based on an extensive rewriting of his people's history to reflect a mystic-visionary view that placed them as the true heirs to the TOLTECS and ordained lords of the region, whose responsibility it was to keep the sun moving across the sky by means of captive sacrifices gained in many wars of conquest.

Itzcóatl also worked to improve the quality of life in his capital, ordering the construction of temples to Cihuacóatl and HUITZILOPOCHTLI as well as construction of the causeway linking the island-city to the lake's northern shore. To reinforce the idea that his reign began a new era, he ordered the destruction of all existing records containing any reference to his people's existence as a tributary state.

Further reading: Michael Coe, *Mexico: From the Olmecs to the Aztecs,* 4th ed. (London: Thames & Hudson, 1994); Nigel Davies, *The Aztec Empire: The Toltec Resurgence* (Norman: University of Oklahoma Press, 1987); Susan D. Gillespie, *The Aztec Kings: The Construction of Rulership in Mexica History* (Tucson: University of Arizona Press, 1989).

— Marie A. Kelleher

J

Jamaica

One of the islands of the Greater Antilles located on the northern edge of the Caribbean Sea just to the south of Cuba, Jamaica became one of the most profitable SUGAR islands in the English realm by the end of the 17th century.

Jamaica has a land mass of 4,471 square miles and a predominantly mountainous terrain, with a peak height of 7,400 feet. The TAINO first inhabited the island, but scholars know little of their history on the island. Archaeologists have garnered most of this knowledge by study of kitchen middens, burial caves, and other artifacts.

CHRISTOPHER COLUMBUS arrived in Jamaica on his second transatlantic trip. He landed at Discovery Bay on May 5, 1494. Upon his arrival he found the natives on the western side of the island more hospitable than those on the eastern side. The defensiveness of the eastern end islanders was based on the fact that attacks from island CARIB usually came from the east. The indigenous inhabitants of Jamaica suffered the same fate as their other relatives in the Greater Antilles: enslavement by the Spanish and the introduction of epidemic DISEASEs that wiped out a majority of their population within the first three decades of contact with Europeans.

The Spanish used Jamaica primarily as a supply base because they did not find any substantial mineral wealth on the island. The first Spanish settlement on the island, Sevilla la Nueva, proved unsuccessful, but eventually they established a foothold on the island and created their largest settlement at St. Jago de la Vega. The Spanish introduced the cultivation of bananas and citrus fruits to the island as well as traditional Spanish agricultural crops. The Spanish forced the Taino to work their fields, but under Spanish control Jamaica never amounted to more than an insignificant farming community on the periphery of their colonial world. As a result, Jamaica became the first Spanish Caribbean possession taken by another European power when the English seized the island in the mid-17th century.

Further reading: Clinton V. Black, *The Story of Jamaica from Prehistory to the Present* (London: Collins, 1965); Carl O. Sauer, *The Early Spanish Main* (Berkeley: University of California, 1966); Allan S. R. Sumnall, "Jamaica," in *Encyclopedia of Latin American History and Culture*, vol. 2, ed. Barbara A. Tenenbaum (New York: Scribner's, 1996), 310–311; Peter Bakewell, *A History of Latin America: Empires and Sequels, 1450–1930* (Malden, Mass.: Blackwell, 1997), 73, 213.

— Dixie Ray Haggard

James I, king of England (1566–1625)

James I ascended to the English throne upon the death of ELIZABETH I, inheriting a feckless Parliament, difficult fiscal circumstances, and a church still unsure of its identity.

James came to the English throne after a protracted royal dispute. James's father, Henry Stuart, Lord Darnley, was murdered for his boorish and murderous behavior within the Scottish court, perhaps with the complicity of his wife, Mary, Queen of Scots, who was Elizabeth's first cousin. After Darnley's death Mary married one of Darnley's alleged assassins. The Scottish nobility was outraged and demanded her abdication. At 13 months old, James came to the Scottish throne. Mary fled to England, where she became entangled in a plot to assassinate Elizabeth. She was imprisoned and, 19 years later, executed by Elizabeth in 1587. In 1603 Elizabeth died, and her oldest male blood relative was the 37-year-old Scottish monarch. He never knew his mother or his mother's cousin, but he arrived in LONDON with long experience of being a ruler.

James received an excellent education as a child in Scotland from tutors who substituted for his parents. One of them was a strict Calvinist named George Buchanan, who inspired the intellect of the young king. James spoke Greek, Latin, French, and English as well as his native Scottish tongue. He was an accomplished rhetorician and writer. Through his intellectual capabilities James gained a reputation as a learned and capable orator and legislator. He also adhered to a personal style of rule—informal and unpolished—that would make him confusing and confounding to his new subjects in England.

James was a man and a king full of inconsistencies and paradoxes. Despite his history of capable rule, he was continually concerned that he could not generate affection either in those closest to him or his subjects. A tireless hunter, James exhibited courage bordering on recklessness as a horseman but harbored an irrational fear of knives and other drawn weapons. Other than the Gunpowder Plot of 1605, there were no legitimate threats to his life, but he wore inordinately heavy clothing to protect himself against knife attacks. He fathered children with his wife, Anne of Denmark, including two sons who both, in turn, became Prince of Wales, yet he was an unabashed homosexual. His sexual orientation brought anxiety to court, as his favorites often gained title and power at court based solely on James's affections. The most obvious recipient of such largesse was George Villiers, who became Duke of Buckingham, Lord High Admiral, and a primary royal diplomat abroad.

Controversy marked James's relationship with the English church, as well. Having been raised a Calvinist within the Church of Scotland, he accepted the doctrine of double predestination. As a result, the CHURCH OF ENGLAND, with its traditional rituals and liturgy, posed a theological problem for the intertwined relationship of church and king as James came to the throne, yet he turned out to be quite tolerant. Theology was something of a hobby for the new king, and he wrote on the subject often. By applying his political skills to his theological encounters, James was able to balance traditional factions within the church against the reformers who wanted to make the Anglican Church more recognizably Protestant. He worked to strike this balance early in his reign by calling both factions together at the Hampton Court Conference in 1604. Here James disappointed the reformers by asserting the importance of the Anglican episcopacy, but he also worked behind the scenes to make bishops understand the reformers' ideas. Further, he was able to treat nonconformist—that is, Catholic—practitioners with a tolerance unimaginable during Elizabeth's reign. Indeed, James suggested that persistent Catholicism was more a political decision among nonconformists than a religious one.

James I was an enigmatic ruler who was remarkably successful given his penchants for excess in his personal life and the financial life of England. Nevertheless, he was not responsible for the problems within the Church of England that would escalate into civil war and the execution of his son and successor.

Further reading: Christopher Durston, *James I* (London: Routledge, 1993); Lori Anne Ferrell, *Government by Polemic: James I, the King's Preachers, and the Rhetorics of Conformity, 1603–1625* (Stanford, Calif.: Stanford University Press, 1998); S. J. Houston, *James I* (London: Longman, 1995).

— David P. Dewar

Jenne-Jeno   See Djenne-Djeno

Jesuits

The Society of Jesus, a Roman Catholic religious order founded by IGNATIUS LOYOLA, played an important role in the 16th-century drive to counter Protestantism and to promote reform within the Catholic Church.

The history of the Jesuit order began in Paris, where, between 1528 and 1535, Ignatius Loyola gathered a group of six fellow students, all of whom took vows of poverty and chastity. These companions planned to travel to Jerusalem to convert the Muslims. War prevented this mission, but Ignatius and nine followers were ordained priests and resolved to offer their services to the pope. Ignatius admired the 13th-century saints Francis of Assisi and Dominic (see FRANCISCANS and DOMINICANS), both of whom had inaugurated new religious orders and sought to rejuvenate the church.

The Jesuits initially saw themselves as itinerant preachers and focused their energies on preaching, hearing confessions, and teaching. A distinctive element in Jesuit practice was Ignatius's *Spiritual Exercises,* a kind of religious guidebook. The *Exercises* laid out a plan for a 30-day program of meditation and self-analysis. All Jesuits had to work through the *Spiritual Exercises* at least once, and they encouraged other Catholics to complete the *Exercises* as well.

The *Spiritual Exercises* encouraged Jesuits to cultivate an indifferent or detached attitude toward the world. This detachment was not meant to encourage monastic withdrawal from the world. Rather, by ridding the Jesuit of fear and anxiety about his future, the *Exercises* promoted an active life in the world. Ignatius, in contrast to other Catholic thinkers of the 16th century, did not approve of excessive penances, fasts, or vigils. Such practices, he thought, weakened the body and thus could render a Jesuit incapable of serving others. As the historian A. Lynn Martin has observed, Ignatius "would rather a Jesuit seek God in visiting the sick than in passing a sleepless night of prayer and mortification."

Pope Paul III confirmed the existence of the Jesuit order in September 1540. The original petition, written by Ignatius, pledged each Jesuit "to abandon his own will, to consider ourselves bound by special vow to the present pope and his successors to go, without complaint, to any country whither they may send us, whether to the Turk or other infidels, in India or elsewhere, to any heretics or schismatics, as well as to the faithful, being subject only to the will of the pope and the general of the order." The original members of the order chose Ignatius as their general, a post he held until his death in 1556.

The order grew rapidly. By 1556 it numbered about 1,000, and by 1615 had some 13,000 members. By the middle of the 16th century, the order was divided into 12 provinces: nine in Europe and one each in BRAZIL, India, and ETHIOPIA. The largest number of Jesuits resided in Spain, Portugal, and Italy, but the Jesuits soon turned to missionary work. During the 16th century they sent missionaries to Africa, India, China, Japan, the Philippines, Brazil, PERU, and MEXICO. In their missionary work they were often flexible about cultural differences. In China, for example, the Jesuit MATTEO RICCI wore mandarin clothing, permitted ceremonies that honored Confucius and the dead, and adapted the observance of Sundays and fasts to make them more acceptable to Chinese customs. Such adaptations earned the Jesuits the ire of more traditional orders, including the Dominicans and Franciscans, who feared that cultural adaptation would destroy Christian missions by allowing potential converts to conflate Christian and non-Christian practices.

Within Europe the Jesuits' primary interest was education. They opened their first school in Messina, Sicily, in 1548 and by 1560 regarded education as their primary ministry. By 1615 the Jesuit order operated about 370 schools. This early commitment to education had two major effects: It made the order more sedentary, because schoolteachers could not move around as much as itinerant priests, and it made the Jesuits more learned. As the scholar John W. O'Malley observed, this 16th-century turn to education "largely explains why and how the society began to earn its reputation for learning. Other orders had teachers and erudite members, but in the Jesuits learning became systemic in ways and to a degree different from the others."

In the REFORMATION debate over whether grace perfects human nature or overcomes it, the Jesuits tended to side with the Scholastic theologian Thomas Aquinas against the more negative views of St. Augustine. While many of the Protestant reformers, including MARTIN LUTHER, argued that human nature was so corrupted by sin that human good works had no value, the Jesuits generally held that God's grace perfected a human nature that was already created in the image of God.

The Reformation was not initially of great concern to the Jesuits. Most lived and worked either in areas of Europe that were largely Catholic or in overseas missions where the population belonged to no Christian church, but by the 1550s the Jesuits turned more of their attention to the Catholic battle against Protestantism. In the German territories they founded schools and sought the support of rulers, including Emperor Ferdinand I. The order also sent missionaries to Protestant areas, including England, Scandinavia, and Holland, both to instruct and encourage Catholics in those territories and in the hopes of reclaiming the countries for the Catholic Church. Jesuit theologians, including Peter Canisius, Alfonso Salmerón, and Diego Laínez, reemphasized Catholic teaching on such matters as the authority of the pope and the presence of Christ in the Eucharist against Protestant challenges. Jesuits also participated at the COUNCIL OF TRENT.

Despite its commitment to battling Protestantism, the order faced opposition from within the Catholic Church. Its rapid growth and rejection of traditional monastic practices made members of other orders suspicious, as did the Jesuits' special vow of obedience to the pope (rather than to local Catholic authorities). Dominicans and members of other orders attacked the Jesuits' theological grounds. The Faculty of Theology of Paris condemned the order in 1554 as "a disturber of the peace of the church."

Controversy over the Jesuits increased in the 17th and 18th centuries as the order grew in size and influence. Pope Clement XIV suppressed the order in 1773, although the order was able to start again in 1814.

Further reading: J. F. Broderick, "Jesuits," in the *New Catholic Encyclopedia*, vol 7, ed. William J. McDonald et al. (New York: McGraw-Hill, 1967), 898–909; Jean Delumeau, *Catholicism between Luther and Voltaire: A New View of the Counter-Reformation* (London, Burns and Oates, 1977); Hans J. Hillerbrand, ed., *The Oxford Encyclopedia of the Reformation* (New York: Oxford University Press, 1996); John C. Olin, *Catholic Reform: From Cardinal Ximenes to the Council of Trent, 1495–1563* (New York: Fordham University Press, 1990); John W. O'Malley, *The First Jesuits* (Cambridge, Mass.: Harvard University Press, 1993); A. Lynn Martin, *The Jesuit Mind: The Mentality of an Elite in Early Modern France* (Ithaca: Cornell University Press, 1988); Steven Ozment, *The Age of Reform, 1250–1550* (New Haven, Conn.: Yale University Press, 1980).

— Martha K. Robinson

Jews (Judaism)

The history of Jews in the 16th century begins with their expulsion from Spain in 1492 and the victories of the Ottoman Empire in the Mediterranean world and ends after the publication of one of the great works of Jewish law: the *Shulhan Arukh* (1571).

Most of the world's Jews still lived in the Middle East in the 16th century, where the Muslim Turks allowed them to maintain communities in relative safety and freedom. In

Christian countries the medieval Crusades, a series of blood libels over several centuries, pogroms, and increasing ecclesiastical and secular legal restrictions contributed to the deteriorating social and economic status of the Jews. Throughout Europe Jewish numbers decreased, and intellectual life declined. The famous scholarly disputations among Christian and Jewish leaders of the 13th and 14th centuries no longer occurred; many Christian theologians and high-ranking clerics became convinced that Jews, like heretics and other infidels, were better restricted and controlled than engaged in argument. The INQUISITION, the holy office endowed with the power to search out and prosecute unbelievers, was an international police force at the disposal of any princeling who wished to harass Jews in his territory. Although the popes in Rome repeatedly issued decrees banning Christians' unproven accusations against their Jewish neighbors (e.g., Martin V in 1418), local kings and lords did not always follow the letter of the Christian law. The constitution of the German empire granted electors (princes and bishops) the ability to maintain and tax Jewish communities in their lands in a decree called the "Golden Bull" (1356). Jews had been gradually limited to few professions in Christendom, primarily in finance and rag-collecting. Rulers in Germany and elsewhere protected their Jewish citizens when it suited them but constantly remitted the debts of Christian businessmen and businesswomen to Jewish lenders and even occasionally encouraged mob attacks on Jewish communities in order to discharge their own debts or to pacify political factions threatening their rule. Extraordinary events, such as plagues, famines, wars, or the Jubilee declared by the pope in 1450 aggravated the already tense coexistence of groups of Jews within larger Christian towns. In addition, the recent gathering of Christian leaders at the Council of Basel (1421–43) had repeated anti-Jewish measures of previous church councils and had ordered further restrictions, such as that Jews be kept out of universities and that baptized Jews be prevented from marrying among themselves to prevent "apostasy" to Judaism.

The Iberian Peninsula had long provided a haven for Sephardic Jews. But as the RECONQUISTA of territory from the Muslims (see ISLAM) by the Christian kings of such kingdoms as Aragón and CASTILE advanced during the 15th century, the great flourishing of Jewish theology, literature, politics, and fortunes waned. As elsewhere, some Jews in Spanish kingdoms submitted to Christian proselytizing and became what Christians called *maranos.* Although new Christians intermarried with old Christian families and integrated more fully into the civic life of the Spanish towns of Barcelona, Toledo, SEVILLE, and Cordoya, political strife often implicated *maranos,* rightly or wrongly. In Castile, when townsfolk refused to pay taxes to supply a defending army in the 1440s, churchmen summoned a mob by ringing bells; the mob burned down *marano* houses. Jews in Segovia died at the stake or on the gallows after a blood libel in 1471. Legal decrees followed this kind of occurrence in many cities of the Iberian Peninsula, forbidding *marano* participation in city or ecclesiastical government, partially in order to prevent further reactive violence. Other laws forbade Christian and Jewish marriage or prevented Jews from having Christian servants. By the time Queen Isabella took the throne of Castile (1474) and her husband, Ferdinand, became king of Aragón (1479), uniting the kingdoms of Spain, both rulers were ready to deal decisively with Jews and former Jews. The Dominican monk Torquemada, Isabella's confessor, headed the Inquisition for the queen in 1481 (he was inquisitor general in Spain from 1485) and held his first AUTO DA FÉ in the following year. By November 1481, 300 *maranos* had died at the stake for returning to Judaism while almost 100 more languished in prison for life. Although many Christians, especially those married into *marano* families, sympathized with Jews, the Inquisition urged all Christians to watch for the signs of Judaizers: those new Christians, or *conversos,* who used clean linens on Friday nights for the Sabbath, refused to light fires on Saturday, or bought all their food from Jews. Finally, in 1492 Ferdinand and Isabella decreed that all Jews (including *maranos* suspected of Judaism) were to leave their kingdoms at penalty of baptism or death. Families that had lived in Spain for centuries were to pack their belongings—except all their money—and leave. "In the same month in which their Majesties issued the edict that all Jews should be driven out of the kingdom and its territories, in the same month they gave me the order to undertake with sufficient men my expedition of discovery to the Indies," wrote CHRISTOPHER COLUMBUS.

Although Jewish money helped finance the explorer's expedition and some Spaniards of Jewish descent went with him to the NEW WORLD, most Jews left Spain and Portugal (1496) for other parts of Europe, especially Navarre, the Lowlands, and Italy. They were followed by a migration of *maranos* in the 1550s and 1560s. Although Jews landing in Genoa were required to convert to Christianity and expulsions of Jewish communities occurred sporadically throughout the early 16th century, some Italian cities accepted immigrants more or less willingly. In Italy, birthplace of the Renaissance, Hebrew learning still flourished, and even Christian scholars had begun to study the language and its literature. The first printed Hebrew appeared in VENICE before 1500, although the first gated Jewish ghetto was also introduced there in 1516. (The word *ghetto* probably comes from the Venetian *getàr,* "to smelt," because the 700 or so Jews of Venice lived where iron foundries had once stood.) Soon presses existed in Reggio di Calabria, Naples, Mantua, Ferrara, Bologna, Rome, and wherever else humanism flowered. Jews and Christians could buy copies of the Torah, midrash, Mishnah, and parts of the Talmud as well as prayer books, dictionaries, and philosophy. The first complete edition of both Babylonian and Palestinian Talmud appeared in Venice, printed by Daniel Bomber, known as Aldo Manuzio (1449–1515), the first Italian printer. Together with interested Christians such as Pico della Mirandola, Jews of the Italian Renaissance pursued the study of kabbalah. Although the discrimination of the later 16th century brought Venetians to burn the Talmud in 1553, and Hebrew works were banned for 13 years, Jewish publishing revived in Venice and continued until the 1800s.

Jewish communities throughout Italy gained immigrants from persecuted communities in Germanic territories and Iberia who contributed to both the religious and economic life of their new homes. Doña Gracia Nasi, for instance, born a new Christian in Portugal had been born Beatriz de Luna in 1510; after marrying a wealthy man from the Benveniste family in 1528 and becoming a widow in 1536, Gracia left Portugal with her daughter and her fortune for Antwerp and then the cities of Italy. She supported scholars and rabbis in Italy, paid for the publication of Jewish books, helped other Jews and *conversos* escape Iberia, and planned a Jewish resettlement in Israel. She ended her days a rich woman in Constantinople. Doña Gracia was both typical of Jewish women in the age of *maranos* and the Inquisition and extraordinary for her wealth, mobility, political contacts, and support of scholarship. At a time when the open practice of Judaism gained the attention of the Inquisition, especially for "crypto-Jews" who rejected recent baptism for their original faith, maintenance of Judaism at home was crucial for embattled communities. Without rabbis, schools, and texts, women's rituals at home, especially the keeping of Sabbath and dietary laws, the lifeline through which Judaism passed from one generation to the next in Spain, Portugal, and the Iberian colonies of MEXICO and South America. When these women escaped to new lives, as did Gracia Nasi, they carried Judaism with them.

The relatively peaceful interlude of Italian Jews came to end in the mid-16th century, when the Inquisition gained power in Italy. Whereas previous popes had stood fairly firm against the determination of political leaders who wished to expel Jews, Paul IV (1555–59) enacted restrictions on Jews in the papal states and supported Christian rulers elsewhere who wished the Jews harm. Jews could not own land, take up professions, leave the ghettos at night, or go into public without yellow hats or veils. They were taxed, forcibly converted, and forced to watch the Talmud burn. Rome, which had the most ancient Jewish community in Europe, escaped the most severe persecutions only because of the economic interests of the papacy there.

Two developments turned Christian mentalities toward anti-Judaism and antisemitism in the 16th century: the advance of the Turks and the success of the Protestant REFORMATION. Only the pressing requests of the Ottoman sultan, Suleiman II, brought about the release of the *maranos* of Ancona in 1558, when papal officials took them prisoner. Beginning in 1453, when they took Constantinople, and continuing with the triumphs of SULEIMAN I, "the Magnificent" (1520–66), the sultans of the empire invaded northern Africa, Greece, Venice's islands, and the Balkans. They threatened the very heart of the Habsburg Empire and controlled the Mediterranean. Only after their defeat by combined European forces in the Battle of Lepanto (1571) did they relinquish their gains and withdraw from Europe. However, during the Turkish threat Jewish refugees constantly found their way to Turkish territory, making the Jewish community in Constantinople the largest in Europe, at about 30,000 by 1500; the synagogue there still carries the name of Gracia Nasi. Jews continued to move back and forth between the Ottoman state and the kingdoms of Europe. As a result, Christians in Venice and elsewhere blamed the Jews as agents of the Turks.

It was in Turkey that Joseph Karo spent his childhood after the expulsion from Spain, where his family had once lived. From 1422 to 1542 Karo worked to collect and annotate every legal statement in Talmud. He researched and interpreted the opinions of all the earlier experts, from the rabbis of ancient Palestine to Rashi and beyond. He spent more years revising his work until in 1567 he published the great "Prepared Table" or *Shulhan Arukh.* Even today this work remains the basis of legal training for orthodox rabbis. The code appealed to both Sephardic and Ashkenazic Jews at a time when their differences in custom and belief were becoming ever more pronounced, primarily because Karo's work was annotated and expanded by an Ashkenaz named Rabbi Moses Isserles of Poland (the *Rama.*) The *Shulkhan Arukh* contains four volumes, divided as follows: *Orakh Hayyim,* dealing with prayer and holidays; *Yoreh Deah,* laws concerning charity (*tzedaka*), the study of Torah, dietary, and other laws; *Even ha-Ezer* regarding marriage and divorce; and *Khoshen Mishpat,* civil law. The great code immediately went through many editions and, thanks to the effects of printing, spread throughout the Jewish communities of the world.

Although the dispute among Christians that came to be known as the Reformation brought tolerance for the Jews in some Protestant states, such as the Netherlands and England, elsewhere it brought reinvigorated persecutions. By the early 17th century the English reopened their island to Jews as companion devotees of the (Old Testament) Bible, while the Dutch Calvinists became the most hospitable of Christian nations, allowing Jews almost total integration into Dutch society. There in the 17th century, Sephardic Jews built beautiful synagogues in the spare Dutch style, Uriel da Costa and Baruch Spinoza theorized, and Rembrandt painted members of the Jewish community. But in Catholic and Lutheran states the era of MARTIN LUTHER brought more trouble for the well-established communities of Jews and their new Iberian immigrants. Luther, who began by embracing Jews as people of the Old Book, began to revile them in the 1540s, when he realized that Jews were not susceptible to his revisions of Christianity and were not likely to convert en masse. "What shall we Christians do with this rejected and condemned people, the Jews?" Luther demanded in print. "Since they live among us, we dare not tolerate their conduct, now that we are aware of their lying and reviling and blaspheming." His solutions were multiple: "First to set fire to their synagogues or schools and to bury and cover with dirt whatever will not burn. . . . Second, I advise that their houses also be razed and destroyed. . . . Third, I advise that all their prayer books and Talmudic writings, in which such idolatry, lies, cursing and blasphemy are taught, be taken from them. . . . Fourth, I advise that their rabbis be forbidden to teach henceforth on pain of loss of life and limb. . . . Fifth, I advise that safe-conduct on the highways be abolished completely for the Jews. For they have no business in the countryside, since they are not lords, officials, tradesmen. . . . Sixth, I advise that usury be prohibited to them, and that all cash and treasure of silver and gold be taken from them. . . . Seventh, I commend putting a flail, an ax, a hoe, a spade, a distaff, or a spindle into the hands of young, strong Jews and Jewesses and letting them earn their bread in the sweat of their brow."

Luther provided material for later antisemites, but communities of German Jews survived his accusations and recommendations. At the end of the 16th century, after the religious wars that tore apart the Christian states of the Habsburg Empire, France, and England, Jews were on the move again to the frontiers of eastern Germany, Poland, and Russia. At the beginning of the 16th century 50,000 Jews had lived in Poland and Lithuania; by 1660 the number was 500,000. Jews found that they could engage with freedom in professions denied them in western Europe, once again protected by the local lords of dukedoms and principalities, as in the Middle Ages. Kings and gentry once again competed to borrow from or exploit the Jews at will. Rabbinic Judaism, regulated by Karo's *Shulhan Arukh,* flourished in the towns of Lublin, Krakow, Vilna, and in many smaller villages of the region. Synagogues and yeshivas appeared across the towns east of the Danube, and Jewish learning began yet another great revival that would produce scholars such as Solomon Luria and Moses Isserles. With printing and relative freedom, even women had access to books, if not much

Hebrew literacy, and could offer up their own Yiddish prayers *(tkhines)* and exchange them in printed pamphlets: "Send an angel to guard the baking," prayed one central European woman, "as you blessed the dough of Sarah and Rebecca our mothers."

Jews in the following decades would also move westward across the Atlantic, following in the wake of Columbus, and settling with other Europeans in *marano* and Jewish communities in BRAZIL, Suriname, and throughout the far side of the Atlantic world where they found both new freedoms and old prejudices.

Further reading: Judith R. Baskin, *Jewish Women in Historical Perspective* (Detroit: Wayne State University Press, 1991); Nicholas De Lange, ed., *The Illustrated History of the Jewish People* (New York: Harcourt Brace, 1997); Benjamin R. Gampel, ed., *Crisis and Creativity in the Sephardic World, 1391–1648* (New York: Columbia University Press, 1997); Max Margolis and Alexander Marx, *A History of the Jewish People* (New York: Atheneum, 1969); Paul R. Mendes-Flohr and Jehuda Reinharz, eds., *The Jew in the Modern World: A Documentary History* (New York: Oxford University Press, 1980); Cecil Roth, *A History of the Jews in England,* 3rd ed. (Oxford, U.K.: Clarendon Press of Oxford University Press, 1964); ———, *The Jews in the Renaissance* (New York: Harper & Row, 1965).

— Lisa M. Bitel

John III, king of Portugal (João) (1502–1557)

John III was king of Portugal during neighboring Spain's "Golden Age," a period in which his own country was pushing the frontiers of exploration abroad but was foundering at home in a sea of debt.

Born in 1502, son of King Manuel of Portugal and his Spanish queen Maria, John III ascended to the throne in 1521. King Manuel had worked to expand Portugal's empire, including incursions into Morocco and the construction of forts in East Africa. John opposed many of his father's expansionist policies, and their relationship must have worsened even further when King Manuel, upon the death of his second wife, married the Spanish princess Leonor, daughter of CHARLES V, even though Leonor had originally been promised to John. John was eventually married to Leonor's sister Catarina in 1526, but the negotiation of a second Spanish match came at great expense to the Portuguese.

One of John III's most important contributions to the history of the Atlantic world was the initiation of large-scale colonization in BRAZIL. Brazil was important not only as a military base to protect trade between Portugal and Asia but also as a source of trade goods. The profitability of trade in goods like brazilwood, which was used in cloth dyeing, aroused the interest of rival countries like France, who tried to institute their own trade with Brazil. The Portuguese attempted to mount a coast guard, but the crenellated topography of Brazil's coastline made this unworkable.

Faced with the possible loss of a profitable trade monopoly, John III made the decision to promote colonization, sending Martím Afonso De Sousa and a large group of colonists to establish a settlement at São Vicente and a second settlement at São Paulo in 1532. To secure the new colonies, John divided Brazil into 15 captaincies, each about 150 miles wide and extending all the way to the line demarcated by the TREATY OF TORDESILLAS. The captaincy system was similar to the classic model of FEUDALISM: Captaincies were distributed as grants of land that could not be sold or given to anyone except an oldest son. The owners could impose taxes, dispense justice, and distribute land within their territories. In exchange they were expected to render military service, holding and defending their territories in the name of the monarch. Unfortunately, although some captaincies were run efficiently and profitably, most became mired in warfare and corruption. Mindful of this situation, John eliminated all but the best-run of the captaincies and instituted a system of governors general and viceroys that would allow more centralized control of the colonies.

Historians have generally regarded John as an incompetent ruler. His nobles were able to wrest power from him, and he spent much of the Crown's commercial income on luxuries rather than investing in some of the commercial activities that were enriching so many other countries at the time. He adopted a nonconfrontational foreign policy, attempting to buy his way out of problems. One example of the spectacular failure of this policy was his attempt to pay off the organizers of French pirates, who happily took John's payments while continuing to plunder his shipping interests. Existing Portuguese colonies were the only matter in which he attempted to act more assertively, authorizing Jesuit missions to Portuguese colonies and employing VASCO DA GAMA as viceroy in India in an attempt to reassert royal control.

John's private affairs were nearly as troubled as his public life: Of his nine children, only one, sickly Prince John, survived long enough to marry at age 15. The prince lived only two more years, but his widow was pregnant at the time of his death and gave birth to a son named Sebastião who was slated to continue the dynasty. King John died a few years later in 1557, leaving his three-year-old grandson as heir and his widow Catarina as regent.

Further reading: James M. Anderson, *The History of Portugal* (Westport, Conn.: Greenwood Press, 2000); David Birmingham, *A Concise History of Portugal* (Cambridge, U.K.: Cambridge University Press, 1993); E. Bradford Burns, *A History of Brazil*, 3rd ed. (New York: Columbia University Press, 1993).

— Marie A. Kelleher

Kaabu, kingdom of

The Kaabu kingdom, from its capital Kansala, controlled what is today northeastern Guinea-Bissau and southern Senegal for more than six centuries.

Founded in 1250 by Tiramakhan Traore, a Mandinke general from the kingdom of MALI, Kaabu dominated small chiefdoms and enslaved the indigenous peoples of the region. Kaabu was a socially stratified kingdom that determined its royal succession through matrilineal descent. It expanded its power and territory slowly, unable to shed its initial dependency on the Mali Empire. The Kaabu kingdom remained an important source of salt, GOLD, and slaves for the larger state until the SONGHAI kingdom conquered Mali in the mid-15th century. Kaabu asserted its independence, gaining much of its power through waging war against its neighbors in efforts to supply the increasing European demand for the transatlantic SLAVE TRADE. Kaabu ruled over 44 provinces at its peak but deteriorated rapidly when the slave trade declined in the late 18th century. By the mid-19th century the Kaabu kingdom was subject to internal and external pressures, including holy wars, or *jihads* (see ISLAM), waged by the FULANI, an Islamic people of the area. In 1867 the Fulani, with an army of 12,000 soldiers, forced the surrender of the last Kaabu king from his throne in Kansala.

Further reading: Jean Boutlegue and Suret-Canale, "The Western African Coast," in *History of West Africa,* 3rd ed., eds. J. F. Ade Ajayi and Michael Crowder (London: Longman, 1985), 1: 503–530; Eric Young, "Kaabu, Early Kingdom of," in *Africana: The Encyclopedia of the African and African American Experience,* eds. Kwame Anthony Appiah and Henry Louis Gates, Jr. (New York: Basic *Civitas* eds. Books, 1999), 1073.

— Lisa M. Brady

Kayor See Cayor

Kongo

The Kongo, an ethnic group located in what is today Angola, the Democratic Republic of Congo, the Republic of Congo, and Zaire, founded a highly centralized kingdom in the 14th century that declined in the 18th century due to Portuguese slave raiding.

The ancestors of the Kongo most likely migrated north to the Congo plateau before the 12th century, settling in organized farming communities. By the 14th century these villages formed a semicohesive federation that was the basis for their kingdom. The kingdom's founder, Ntine ("King") Wene, married into the local clan that held spiritual rights over the land, uniting his people with the area's indigenous people. He used conquest and intimidation to expand his stronghold in the region, which extended at its peak south from the Congo River to the Kwanza River and east from the Atlantic Ocean to the Kwango River. The Kongo kingdom established its capital at the successful farming village of Mbanza Kongo, near the mouth of the Congo River. The kings organized the area into political districts, created a monetary system based on shells, or *nzimbu,* harvested on the island of Luanda, and exacted taxes and tributes from the subjects. In return the kings protected the kingdom and its people and performed religious rituals. Long a tradition with the Kongo people, iron work became a prerogative of the royal family. The iron industry formed an important part of the Kongo economy, but the kingdom's environment provided the mainstay for its source of wealth. In the western part of the kingdom, salt lagoons and shell fisheries abounded, and in the east millet farming predominated. The forests of the Kongo kingdom supplied the raffia for the region's textile industry. Woven raffia squares became a major commodity in the region, providing a source of political and economic influence for the Kongo kingdom.

The Kongo's first documented contact with Europeans was in 1483, when the Portuguese explorer Diogo Cão arrived. When Cão returned to Portugal, he took with him

Kongo emissaries, who returned to their kingdom in 1491 with priests, soldiers, and European trade goods. The priests baptized the Kongo king, Nzinga a Nkuwu, and his son, Nzinga Mbembe. Although Nzinga a Nkuwu later abandoned Christianity, Nzinga Mbembe adopted the name Afonso (or Alfonso) and made Catholicism the state religion of the Kongo kingdom. Afonso maintained strong ties with the Portuguese, trading slaves and ivory for European goods and guns. He also invited missionaries to his kingdom and renamed the capital São Salvador. When JESUITS arrived in Kongo territory in 1548 (after Afonso's death), they opened schools and converted many Kongolese to Catholicism.

Afonso's grandson, Diogo I (r. 1545–61), tried to limit Portuguese influence in the Kongo economy but encouraged religious and political ties with the European power. Diogo attempted to assert Kongo control over Portuguese settlers in the region and to reassert the kingdom's dominance over inland trade. In 1555 he banned all but a few Portuguese traders from his kingdom in an attempt to reassert his economic control, but the Portuguese on the nearby island of São Tome continued to engage in trade, undermining Diogo's success. In another bid for control, Diogo expelled the Jesuits in 1558.

The SLAVE TRADE ultimately undermined the Kongo kingdom when the neighboring peoples who were the targets of Kongo slave raiders retaliated. The resulting instability weakened the Kongo, forcing the kingdom into dependence upon the Portuguese. By the mid-17th century the Kongo kingdom had lost much of its power in the region, although it remained intact and influential through the 19th century.

Further reading: "Diogo I," "Kongo, Kings of" and "Wene," in *Dictionary of African Historical Biography,* 2nd ed., eds. Mark R. Lipschutz and R. Kent Rasmussen (Berkeley: University of California Press, 1986), 58, 113, 247; Elizabeth Heath, "Kongo," in *Africana: The Encyclopedia of the African and African American Experience,* eds. Kwame Anthony Appiah and Henry Louis Gates, Jr. (New York: Basic *Civitas* Books, 1999), 503–511 and 1104–1105; Joseph C. Miller, "The Paradoxes of Impoverishment in the Atlantic Zone," in David Birmingham and Phyllis M. Martin, eds., *History of Central Africa,* vol. 1 (London: Longman, 1983), 118–159; "The Peoples," in *Cambridge Encyclopedia of Africa,* eds. Roland Oliver and Michael Crowder (Cambridge, U.K.: Cambridge University Press, 1981), 57–86.

— Lisa M. Brady

Kotoko

The Kotoko, an ethnic group in present-day CAMEROON, Chad, and Nigeria, ruled a kingdom in West Africa that controlled large areas of northern Cameroon and northeastern Nigeria until the 15th century, when they were conquered by the Kanuri of the Bornu kingdom.

Made up of several smaller kingdoms, including the Makari, Mara, Kousseri, and Logone-Birni, the Kotoko kingdom was organized into a large state ruled by a single king. The kingdom included a northern and southern division, making it easier for the kingdom's policies to be administered. Before its defeat and incorporation into the Bornu kingdom, the Kotoko peoples converted to ISLAM, introduced into the region by Muslim missionaries.

Further reading: "Kotoko," in *Africana: The Encyclopedia of the African and African American Experience,* eds. Kwame Anthony Appiah and Henry Louis Gates, Jr. (New York: Basic *Civitas* Books, 1999), 1106; "Kotoko," in *Historical Dictionary of the Republic of Cameroon,* 2nd ed., eds. Mark W. DeLancey and H. Mbella Mokeba (London: Scarecrow Press, 1990), 118.

— Lisa M. Brady

L

Lane, Ralph (?–1603)

Known more as military commander than a maritime adventurer, Lane served as the first governor of Virginia in 1585–86.

Little is known of Lane's early life. After serving Queen ELIZABETH I in a number of capacities in the realm of public security from 1570 to 1585, he sailed for North America under the command of Sir Richard Grenville. Holding a royal patent to the Virginia area of mainland North America, the expedition was initiated and funded by SIR WALTER RALEGH. After a harried voyage that stopped at HISPANIOLA, the expedition passed up the coast of FLORIDA, arriving in June at Wokokan, one of the many islands off the coast of North Carolina, or "Virginia," as the English then termed the region. Here the party established a colony with Lane as governor. Grenville departed two months later, but not before the two brash personalities clashed in a bitter dispute.

Following Grenville's departure, the colony was moved to ROANOKE, and Lane's party of 107 men quickly faced a number of urgent problems. The fact that no women and children were among the colonizers coupled with little evidence of Lane's party cultivating the land displayed how far the English were from the concept of planting a self-sustaining society at this time. As provisions withered, frustrations mounted. Many of the men under the employ of Ralegh arrived hoping to find riches in precious metals. Lane was also gravely disappointed that the area yielded neither the immediate prospect of riches nor an inland water route to CATHAY. Further difficulties arose when the relations between the settlers and the native population became strained as Wingino, chief of the neighboring Secota Indians, grew increasingly frustrated with the English colonizers.

In 1586, following a difficult winter, Lane led a search expedition north to the Chesapeake Bay area hoping to find a narrow land mass leading to the Pacific, much like the Isthmus of PANAMA. In addition, he had heard an alluring tale about a tribe in the north that possessed copper in abundance and lived near a great sea. Lane's hopes were quickly dashed on both fronts, and the expedition party returned to Roanoke. Weeks later, SIR FRANCIS DRAKE, fresh off a triumph in the Caribbean, arrived off the coast of Roanoke to check on Ralegh's colony. Frustrated, Lane convinced Drake to return all the colonists home to Portsmouth. Although there is no direct evidence, it is possible that Lane and his fellow colonizers first brought TOBACCO and potatoes to England at this time.

Upon his arrival home, Lane prepared to defend his motives for the decision to abandon Virginia, citing the area's harsh conditions. Two of Lane's party left a more memorable impression: chroniclers THOMAS HARRIOT and JOHN WHITE, whose maps of the landscape and sketches and depictions of the Native Americans were quickly circulated in the promotional literature of RICHARD HAKLUYT THE YOUNGER. Following stints in which he served under expeditions of both Drake and SIR JOHN HAWKINS, Lane was appointed to the office of muster-master in Dublin, a post occupied until his death in 1603.

Further reading: Stephen Coote, *A Play of Passion: The Life of Sir Walter Raleigh* (London: Macmillan, 1993); Robert Lacey, *Sir Walter Ralegh* (London: Weidenfeld & Nicholson, 1973); Peter C. Mancall, ed. *Envisioning America: English Plans for the Colonization of North America, 1580–1640* (Boston: Bedford, 1995); David Beers Quinn, ed., *The Roanoke Voyages, 1584–90* (New York: Dover, 1991).

— Matt Lindaman

Las Casas, Bartolomé de (1474?–1566)

A former *encomendero* (holder of an ENCOMIENDA) who, after experiencing the plight of the native peoples under Spanish rule in the early 16th century, took the vows of a

Dominican friar and became an energetic champion of native rights on both sides of the Atlantic.

Las Casas remains one of the most controversial figures in Latin American history. His attempts to convert and protect the indigenous peoples of the Americas earned him the adulation of missionaries and several key figures in the Catholic Church. Religious and secular leaders in England, France, and the Netherlands argued that he was a courageous figure for standing up to the corrupt, destructive actions of his countrymen, and his works were widely read in these countries. In Spain he faced a more mixed reaction. Many Spaniards felt that he was unpatriotic, soiling the reputation of national heroes. His later writings seemed to undermine the legitimacy of the conquest, causing Las Casas to lose favor with the royal government. Many of the CONQUISTADORES and their families felt personally attacked by his writings and moved to have them denounced at court. One 16th-century polemic against Las Casas bore a revealing title: *Against the Premature, Scandalous, and Heretical Assertions which Fray Bartolomé de Las Casas Has Made in His Book About the Conquest of the Indies, Which He Has Had Printed Without the Permission of the Authorities.* The controversy over his life and writings has continued through the 20th century, in which he has been called "mentally ill" (1927), "a pigheaded anarchist" (1930), a "leveler possessed by the Devil" (1946), and "a pathological liar" (1963). Those who doubt the veracity of his works have argued that he created a BLACK LEGEND about Spain's actions in the NEW WORLD, while his supporters claim that he is perhaps the only reliable figure of the conquest era.

Early Life and Conversion

Las Casas was born in SEVILLE, Spain, in either 1474 or 1484. His mother's family was considered to be "old Christian," meaning that they had no trace of Jewish or Moorish blood in their background. His father, however, was from a family of *conversos,* or JEWS who had converted to Christianity during the RECONQUISTA. His family was sufficiently wealthy to provide a Latin education at the cathedral academy. Las Casas's father, Pedro, accompanied CHRISTOPHER COLUMBUS on his second voyage and received a native slave as a reward for his efforts. Apparently, Pedro gave his son custody of this slave, because the younger Las Casas freed him and had him sent back to the Indies. In 1502 Las Casas journeyed to the Caribbean for the first time as a *doctrinero* (teacher of Christian doctrine), although he returned to Europe shortly thereafter. He arrived back in the Caribbean in 1512, settling on the island of HISPANIOLA, where he became the first priest ordained in the New World. The following year he took part in the conquest of CUBA, serving as the expedition's chaplain. During these early years he mingled freely with several conquistadores, including HERNÁN CORTÉS and PEDRO DE ALVARADO.

Significantly, as part of his reward for the successful campaign in Cuba, Las Casas received an *encomienda,* which gave him the use of native labor. At first he felt this was a just, honorable grant. Over time, his firsthand observations about *encomiendas* and *encomenderos* began to change his mind. He personally witnessed several *encomenderos* brutally overworking their natives and became concerned that many Spaniards were not converting the natives at all. Gradually, he became convinced that the *encomienda* system was exploitative and would never truly bring the indigenous people to Christianity. According to his writings, he read a passage from Ecclesiasticus 34 that turned him against the *encomienda* forever: "Tainted the gifts who offers in sacrifice ill-gotten goods."

In 1514 Las Casas began a new life dedicated to protecting the natives of the New World. He began by dissolving his own *encomienda.* On Pentecost Sunday he preached a fiery sermon against the *encomienda* and demanded that fellow *encomenderos* abandon theirs, too, lest they face the wrath of God. He approached the colonial authorities demanding that they hold the *encomenderos* responsible for their abusive actions and take more rigorous steps to protect the natives. Initially, his actions were treated with shock, then polite dismissal. The *encomienda* was too entrenched to be dislodged, the officials responded, and besides, the natives were simple-minded heathens who needed discipline. Las Casas was not discouraged but realized that it was not enough to pressure single *encomenderos:* he had to end the *encomienda* system altogether. To this end, he traveled back to Spain, where he enlisted the support of two powerful figures at court, the co-regents Francisco Jiménez de Cisneros and Adrian of Utrecht. With their backing Las Casas became the official protector of the Indians in 1516. He began proposing several alternatives to the *encomienda* system, including the development of African SLAVERY—a decision he later regretted.

Las Casas the Colonizer

In 1520 Las Casas entered a more active phase of his career. He had become a well-known figure in the intellectual circles of Spain, and his writings came to the attention of the king, CHARLES V. With the support of a number of missionaries from the New World, Las Casas presented his ideas before the king in 1520. He argued that the time for conquest by "fire and sword" had passed. Instead, he argued, the Crown should focus on peaceful conversion of the natives, who would make loyal subjects and Christians if given the chance. Las Casas pointed out that putting them to work for individual *encomenderos* did not contribute to the public good or even the development of the colony. Moreover, *encomenderos* who had unlimited power over the natives abused them, leading to the depopulation of the colony. Las Casas argued that the natives should be put under the protection of missionaries, who would convert them to Spanish culture as they Christianized them. Under this system the colonies would continue to be productive. Although there were many voices of dissent, Charles decided to give Las Casas a chance to put his ideas into practice, assigning the cleric to colonize the newly discovered territories of Venezuela.

Despite his high hopes, the new Venezuelan colony was a disaster. Las Casas's goals were simple: to convert the natives and create a self-sustaining agricultural colony. However, congregating the natives actually helped spread European DISEASES because they had no immunity to scourges such as SMALLPOX, measles, and mumps. Also, colonial officials in the area were hostile to Las Casas's ideas, arguing that the natives were heathens who did not deserve royal protection. They attempted to stifle Las Casas's project through bureaucratic means, denying or delaying requests or claiming they were waiting for official instructions. Spanish conquistadores were even less subtle and began raiding the colony for captives. The natives began to feel that they had been corralled so that the Spaniards could capture them more efficiently, and they began to revolt. The uprising brought on the full wrath of the conquistadores, who argued that because the natives had rebelled against their Spanish king, they were justified in enslaving them. By 1522 the colony had collapsed, and conquistadores had dragged away most of the natives to serve in Caribbean *encomiendas*. Dismayed, Las Casas temporarily abandoned his project, taking vows as a Dominican monk and removing himself from politics as a penance.

In time Las Casas turned again to the problem of colonization and made an effort to develop his utopian plans more fully. First and foremost, he created a clear agenda and methodology for building a new colony and articulated these ideas in his work *The Only Method of Attracting Everyone to the True Religion (Del único modo de atraer a todos los pueblos a la verdadera religión)*. In this book Las Casas argued that the Spaniards would never be able to convince the natives of God's love while the natives viewed all Europeans with fear and hatred. He demanded an end to violence, even when Spaniards themselves were threatened. He also forbade the Spaniards to confiscate land from native communities and, in fact, advocated returning land already confiscated by Europeans. Ultimately, Las Casas realized that his proposed colony would have to be well removed from the conquistadores; the colony had to be either in an area where colonists could not go or that they considered so worthless that they would leave it alone. He selected for his next project a dangerous area in the Guatemalan highlands called Tuzultán, meaning "land of war."

This new experiment was far more successful than the Venezuelan venture. Las Casas was able to secure an agreement that no secular Spaniard would enter the region for five years and that no *encomiendas* would be created from the territory. Because no Spaniard entered the unstable region willingly, the royal officials did not object. In 1537 Las Casas and a handful of DOMINICANS arrived, having composed a series of educational hymns regarding the creation, the fall of man, and the life of Jesus in the natives' own language. They taught these hymns to several local traders and convinced them to travel throughout the region teaching others in turn. After repeated concerts the local leaders were sufficiently impressed to invite the Dominicans in themselves. Over time Las Casas was able to convince the local population of the Spaniards' honesty and sincerity. The native leaders were particularly impressed to discover that Las Casas had stopped the Spanish raids in the region. The local CACIQUE, or native chieftain, converted, ordering an end to animal sacrifice and the worship of stone idols. The Spaniards were shocked that Las Casas and his fellows had not been killed, and eventually PEDRO DE ALVARADO wrote to the king commending his actions. By royal decree the "Land of War" was renamed Verapaz ("True Peace"), a name it has retained to the present time.

The Decline of the Encomienda

Buoyed by the success of his Guatemalan colony, Las Casas redoubled his efforts to end the *encomienda* system once and for all. He developed a two-pronged assault: first to turn public opinion in Spain against the institution, and second to petition the king to end it directly. For both these ends, he wrote and later published his most famous work, *The Very Brief Account of the Destruction of the Indies (Brevísima relación de la destrucción de las Indias)*. Las Casas was fairly successful in both his goals. His short book created a sensation, particularly when he read sections of it to the royal court. His writing style was firm and direct, using numerous examples to show how the Spaniards' actions were annihilating the native populations of the New World. He named names, places, and events with horrifying accuracy. The king and his advisers were not only appalled, but convinced by his rhetoric. In response the king promulgated the New Laws of 1542, which forbade the enslavement of the natives and greatly curtailed the *encomienda* system. Moreover, it forbade *encomenderos* from bequeathing their *encomiendas* to their heirs, effectively ending all *encomiendas* after a generation.

Although this was a victory for Las Casas, the war over the *encomienda* was far from over. Spanish colonists reacted with outrage over the New Laws. *Encomenderos* felt that the *encomiendas* were justifiable rewards for their actions of conquering territories for the Spanish Crown. Additionally, they had begun to see them as personal property. Even those colonists without *encomiendas* were angered, for many hoped to earn an *encomienda* of their own. Across Spanish America the colonists rose up in violent protest against the New Laws. With royal backing Las Casas returned to the New World as the bishop of Chiapas. He provoked further hostility by threatening any Spaniard who maintained an *encomienda* with excommunication. The *encomenderos* responded by threatening Las Casas's life. Those members of the church with ties to *encomenderos* refused to support him. Again, Las Casas pushed the envelope by publishing a confessional that instructed priests to withhold absolution from *encomenderos*, while declaring that all wealth derived from *encomiendas* was tainted by sin. Because much of Spain's wealth in the New World derived from *encomiendas*, many saw this as a direct assault on the entire Spanish colonial system. Opposition grew to the point that in 1545 Charles was forced to modify the New Laws, allowing some inheritance rights. In the face of violent hostility, Las Casas resigned from his post in 1550.

This same year Las Casas took part in a famous debate over the future of the natives. Back in Spain, Las Casas's ideas came under fire from the influential JUAN GINÉS DE SEPÚLVEDA. Sepúlveda was an ardent scholar who was well versed in the works of Aristotle. Using Aristotle's classification of humans, Sepúlveda argued that the indigenous peoples of the Americas were inherently inferior to Europeans and as such could be subjected to slavery. His ideas circulated widely in Spain and ultimately came to the attention of the king. In an attempt to decide how best to proceed in the New World, Charles invited both Las Casas and Sepúlveda to present their cases before the royal court in the city of Valladolid. Some modern observers believe that during this unprecedented spectacle the two great figures argued their cases together, using withering cross-examination, heated objections, and rhetorical attacks against their opponent. In reality, both men spoke separately and did not address each other's points directly. Sepúlveda spoke first, arguing for three hours that the natives were barbarians who would only turn away from their savagery if forced to do so at sword point. Las Casas responded over the course of five days by reading aloud from his writings. His use of specific examples and eyewitness testimony on the realities of the colonial system made much more of an impact on the court than did Sepúlveda's abstract reasoning. Although there was no official winner of the debate, the Crown sided with Las Casas, and many of his proposals were later codified in the Ordinances of Discovery and Settlement of 1573, which prohibited conquest by "fire and sword."

After the great debate, Las Casas began to retreat from public life. He continued to be an advocate for native rights, but his ceaseless travels (including 14 transatlantic voyages) began taking their toll. Most of his efforts went into completing and publishing his various writings, again hoping to win public approval for his ideas. In the late 1550s a group of Peruvian conquistadores offered the new King PHILIP II a substantial sum of SILVER to eliminate all restrictions on inheriting *encomiendas*. Las Casas used his influence to delay a final decision on the matter. In the meantime he organized a collection among native nobles that produced an even larger amount of silver, which he successfully used to bribe Philip into maintaining the restrictions. Still, his constant denunciations eroded his popularity at court, as did the constant efforts against him by *encomenderos*. He died in 1566, expressing dismay that he did not do more on the natives' behalf.

Las Casas's Legacy

Perhaps the most enduring legacy Las Casas left behind was his voluminous collection of writings. His most famous work was the *Destruction of the Indies*, which was translated into every major European language by 1560. Spain's enemies pounced on the book as proof that the Spaniards were depraved, cruel, and undeserving of a colonial empire, which has hurt his stature in Spain ever since. More valuable to modern scholars were his writings on the events of the conquest. His *History of the Indies (Historia de las Indias)* still provides a great deal of information on the important events of the conquest. Because Las Casas either witnessed these events directly or spoke to the principal actors, this book has been invaluable in reconstructing the past. The book also continues to provide a sustained criticism of the actions of Spain, questioning the morality of violent conquest, slavery, and the obligations of secular governments toward their people. From an anthropological perspective, the most valuable of Las Casas's writings is the *Apologetica Historia*, which documents how a number of native cultures lived around the time of the conquest. While not nearly as comprehensive as such works as the Florentine Codex, the *Apologetica* did provide information on groups across Latin America who were vanishing even as Las Casas wrote. Amazingly, many of Las Casas's works were not published until 1990, and several have yet to be translated from the original Spanish.

Las Casas has also been instrumental in uncovering what exactly happened to native cultures after the arrival of the Europeans. He wrote that tens of thousands had died in the Caribbean area alone and that within 50 years of the conquest the region's indigenous peoples disappeared. For centuries scholars scoffed at these accusations, relying on other Spanish accounts to suggest Las Casas was mistaken or possibly delusional. Modern work has confirmed that the native populations were every bit as extensive as Las Casas claimed and that the native population *did* decline by as much as 90% between 1500 and 1600. Disease seems to have been the greatest single factor in this demographic collapse, but in substantiating Las Casas's claims scholars have begun to place more weight on the rest of his observations. Because most of the accounts of the conquest and early colonial period were written by the conquistadores or their supporters and naturally tended to glorify the Spaniards' actions, Las Casas's writings provide a critical second opinion about the conquest. As a direct or near-direct witness, Las Casas often gave a more complete and unvarnished description of Spain's actions in the Americas.

Las Casas was one of the most remarkable figures of the 16th century. He was a prolific writer, gifted public speaker, and one of the earliest human rights activists. Alternately praised and damned throughout history, he provides crucial insights into the process of Spain's conquest and colonization of the New World.

Further reading: Lewis Hanke, *The Spanish Search for Justice in the Conquest of America* (Philadelphia: University of Pennsylvania Press, 1949); ———, *All Mankind Is One: A Study of the Disputation Between Bartolomé De Las Casas and Juan Ginés De Sepúlveda in 1550 on the Intellectual and Religious Capacity of the American Indians* (DeKalb: Northern Illinois University Press, 1974); Benjamin Keen, *The Aztec Image in Western Thought* (New Brunswick, N.J.: Rutgers University Press, 1971); Bartolomé de Las Casas, *The Devastation of the Indies: A Brief Account* (Baltimore: Johns Hopkins University Press, 1992); ———, *History of the Indies* (New York: Harper & Row, 1971).

— Scott Chamberlain

Laudonnière, René de (1562–1582)

René de Laudonnière served as the initial leader of the ill-fated French Huguenot colony of FORT CAROLINE established near the mouth of the St. Johns River in present-day FLORIDA in 1564.

René de Laudonnière was born into a prominent family in the French city of Dieppe in 1529. Before his involvement in French colonization efforts in the Western Hemisphere, Laudonnière served in the French navy. During the 16th century religious civil wars divided France between French Protestants (HUGUENOTS) and Roman Catholics. Laudonnière was a Huguenot and a protégé of Admiral Gaspard de Coligny. Coligny, also a Huguenot, hoped to use colonization to strengthen France's position in Europe and create a haven for persecuted Huguenots. In 1555 the French attempted to establish a colony on the northeast coast of South America, but it failed miserably.

In 1562 Laudonnière sailed as the second in command of an expedition headed by Jean Ribault to Florida to find an appropriate site for a colony. First, they explored the area around the St. Johns River and made friends with the local TIMUCUA Indians. Eventually, they moved up the coast and left a garrison on modern-day Parris Island, South Carolina, before returning to France. The men left behind mutinied and killed their commander, built a makeshift boat, and attempted to sail back to France. After being lost at sea and having to resort to CANNIBALISM, an English ship rescued them and took them back to Europe.

Because Ribault was imprisoned in England in 1564, Coligny placed Laudonnière in command of the expedition to create a permanent colony on the St. John's River in Florida. That year he sailed for America on three ships— the *Falcon, the Petit Briton*, and the *Isabel of Honfleur*— with 300 settlers, including four women and the artist JACQUES LE MOYNE. Upon arrival the French constructed Fort Caroline, fortified it with seven pieces of artillery, and proceeded to make an alliance with the local Timucua, led by their *mico*, or chief, Saturiba. Because the colony had not been funded properly, it quickly began to run low on supplies. Fortunately, Jean Ribaut (having been released from jail in England) arrived in August 1565 with supplies and new colonists. Unfortunately, the Spanish had already learned of the little French colony's existence and had sent out an expedition under Pedro Menendez de Aviles to eradicate the colony.

Menendez landed in Florida on the same day that Ribaut arrived at Fort Caroline. Menendez threw up entrenchments around an abandoned Timucua hut to create a base of operations. This post eventually became the city of SAINT AUGUSTINE. He then sailed north and engaged the French in a naval battle that ended in a stalemate. Menendez then returned to his base at Saint Augustine and marched overland to Fort Caroline. At the same time, Ribaut, against Laudonnière's advice, took the French ships south to attack Saint Augustine, only to lose the fleet in a hurricane. When Menendez reached the French garrison, he easily took the post and proceeded to execute all the male captives. Along with other survivors, Laudonnière escaped into the woods and made his way to a French ship in the river. Two months later the ship sailed into Swansea Bay, Wales. Because of the failure of the colony and his Huguenot faith, Laudonnière fell out of favor with the French Crown and was never to receive prestigious appointments again. In an effort to justify his actions, and fortunately for historians, he recorded his experiences in *L'Histoire notable de la Floride*. Because of this book and Le Moyne's illustrations, historians know specific details surrounding the establishment and demise of Fort Caroline and important ethnohistoric information about the Timucua.

Further reading: Charles E. Bennett, *Laudonnière and Fort Caroline: History and Documents* (Gainesville: University of Florida Press, 1964); René de Laudonnière, *A Foothold on Florida: The Eye Witness Account of Four Voyages Made by the French to That Region and Their Attempt at Colonisation, 1562–1568*, trans. Sarah Lawson with annotations and appendices by W. John Faupel (East Grinstead, U.K.: Castle Cary Press for Antique Atlas Publications, 1992).

— Dixie Ray Haggard

Le Moyne, Jacques (c. 1533–1588)
An artist who participated in the ill-fated French attempt to establish a colony in FLORIDA, Jacques Le Moyne made maps of the region and drew illustrations of TIMUCUA Indian culture that continue to have significant ethnohistoric value.

In 1565 Jacques Le Moyne journeyed to Florida as part of the RENÉ DE LAUDONNIÈRE's expedition to create a base to raid Spanish treasure fleets and as a haven for French HUGUENOTS. Upon arriving at the mouth of the St. Johns River, the French built a small fortification called FORT CAROLINE. In 1565 the Spanish ordered Pedro Menendez de Aviles to destroy Fort Caroline. Le Moyne escaped and took refuge with the local Timucua. He lived with them until he was rescued by a French expedition headed by Dominique de Gourges in 1567. Gourges, allied with the Timucua, destroyed the Spanish presidio established at the former site of Fort Caroline and then moved north to attack Spanish installations located on the coast of modern-day Georgia and South Carolina to gain revenge for the murder of the French colonists at Fort Caroline two years earlier.

Le Moyne's illustrations of Timucua life remain valuable evidence of a culture and a people that have long since vanished. Further, the Appalachian Mountains received

Using watercolors, Le Moyne depicted Native American life, as shown in this engraving (after one of his paintings) of Timucua Indians planting their fields *(Hulton/Archive)*

their name from an error made by Le Moyne on his maps of the region. Based on information provided by the Timucua, he mistakenly thought that the mountain range to the northwest of Florida ended in the territory of the Apalache, the enemies of the Timucua located near modern-day Tallahassee, Florida. Therefore, he labeled the mountains the "Apalatci Mountains."

Further reading: Charles E. Bennett, *Laudonnière and Fort Caroline: History and Documents* (Gainesville: University of Florida Press, 1964); Paul Hulton, *The World of Jacques Le Moyne de Marjues: A Hujucanat Artist: France, Florida and England,* 2 vols. (London: British Museum Publications, 1977). René de Laudonnière, *A Foothold on Florida: The Eye Witness Account of Four Voyages Made by the French to That Region and Their Attempt at Colonisation, 1562–1568,* translated by Sarah Lawson with annotations and appendices by W. John Faupel (East Grinstead, U.K.: Castle Cary Press for Antique Atlas Publications, 1992).

— Dixie Ray Haggard

Leo X, Pope (Giovanni de' Medici) (1475–1521)

The second son of Lorenzo ("the Magnificent") de' Medici of Florence, Giovanni de' Medici became Pope Leo X in 1513, and his reign became revered by many for his patronage of the arts and of scholars.

From his childhood the man who became Pope Leo X was groomed for a life in the hierarchy of the Catholic Church. He became an archbishop when he was seven years old and was created a cardinal in 1488, when he was only 13. Other than his time as a captive during the Battle of Ravenna in 1512, he spent much of his life in the higher circles of the Italian church. As a cardinal he traveled to the Low Countries, France, and Germany before returning to Italy and the Vatican in 1500. A favorite of Pope Julius II, Leo became pope when he was 37 years old. Rome celebrated his accession with a triumphal procession of musicians, standard bearers, and 200 mounted lancers.

During his eight-year pontificate Pope Leo helped the Vatican to become what one historian termed "a treasure house of talent" filled with artists, poets, and scholars. Among those he supported was LEO AFRICANUS. A scholar himself (his portrait by Raphael d'Urbino from ca. 1514, now on display at the Uffizi Gallery in Florence, depicts him reading an illuminated manuscript with a magnifying glass in his right hand) he cultivated Latin scholars and musicians and provided increased support for the faculty at the University of Rome. Leo X also played a crucial role in foreign affairs, first helping to force the French from Italy and then suffering defeat at the hands of King Francis I when the French returned in 1515. European monarchs were desperate for his favor. Among those who strove to please him was the Portuguese King Manuel, who wanted to make sure that Leo X would support the actions of Pope ALEXANDER VI, whose TREATY OF TORDESILLAS of 1494 demarcated much of the world between Spain and Portugal. Knowing that Leo appreciated the wonders of nature, King Manuel arranged for an elaborate gift: HANNO THE ELEPHANT, a pachyderm that Leo came to adore when the beast joined the Vatican menagerie in 1514.

Leo X worked tirelessly to prevent any break in the church during a period of strife. As a result he recognized the threat posed by the REFORMATION, and so in 1520 he excommunicated MARTIN LUTHER. The next year the Pope, still youthful, went on a hunting expedition at La Magliana, his villa in the Italian countryside in late November. He returned exhausted and died on December 1. All of Rome seemed to grieve for the youthful pontiff, and his own relatives (like the kin of earlier popes) soon arrived at the Vatican to ransack his dwelling. Although he could not be buried in St. Peter's Basilica, which was being renovated at the time, there is a magnificent memorial to Leo X in Santa Maria Sopra Minerva in Rome.

Further reading: Silvio A. Bedini, *The Pope's Elephant: An Elephant's Journey from Deep in India to the Heart of Rome* (New York: Penguin, 2000).

Leo Africanus (Giovanni Leoni; al-Hassan ibn Muhammad al-Wazzan al-Zayyati) (ca. 1493–ca.1552)

The most important chronicler of the western SUDAN and Mediterranean Africa since IBN BATTUTA's accounts of the area in the 14th century, Leo Africanus wrote *The History and Description of Africa and the Notable Things Therein Contained,* providing a detailed account of 16th-century African cultures and kingdoms, including the MALI, SONGHAI, and HAUSA Empires.

Born al-Hassan ibn Muhammad al-Wazzan al-Zayyati to a wealthy Muslim family in Granada (Spain), Leo Africanus and his family moved to Fez, Morocco, in the wake of the RECONQUISTA. There he gained an education and traveled throughout North Africa, working as a clerk and a notary. At age 17 (ca. 1513), Leo Africanus (still al-Hassan ibn Muhammad al-Wazzan al-Zayyati) traveled with his uncle to the Sudan as part of a diplomatic and commercial trip to the Songhai Empire. On these travels he visited TIMBUKTU, describing its geography, architecture, and social and political cultures. In 1518, returning from a journey to Egypt and a pilgrimage to MECCA (or *hajj,* see ISLAM), Leo Africanus was captured near Tunis by Christian corsairs and taken as a slave to Pope LEO X. Soon after Leo X freed him and baptized him as Johannis Leo de'Medici (also written as Giovanni Leoni), from which the moniker Leo Africanus comes. Seven years later, in 1526, Leo Africanus completed his book about his African travels, which was published in 1550 by GIOVANNI BATTISTA RAMUSIO in Italian, then translated into French and Latin six years later, and into English by 1600. Although some of Leo Africanus's descriptions of West Africa were adapted from extant accounts of the region and some of his information was incorrect (for example, he stated that the NIGER RIVER flowed east to west, a misconception prevalent in Europe until 1796, when the Dutch explorer Mungo Park corrected the error), his chronicle was the most important account of the region's political and cultural history since Ibn Battuta's history written two centuries earlier. Leo Africanus remained in Italy for some time, occasionally teaching the Arabic language at Bologna University. He eventually returned to Africa, most likely reverted to Islam, and died in Tunis sometime between 1552 and 1560.

Further reading: Elizabeth Heath, "Leo Africanus," in *Africana: The Encyclopedia of the African and African American Experience,* eds. Kwame Anthony Appiah and Henry Louis Gates, Jr. (New York: Basic *Civitas* Books, 1999), 1146–1147; John O. Hunwick, *Timbuktu and the Songhay Empire: Al-Sadis Tarikh al-Sudan down to 1613 and Other Contemporary Documents* (Boston: Brill, 1999); "Leo Africanus," in *Dictionary of African Historical Biography,* 2nd ed., eds. Mark R. Lipschutz and R. Kent Rasmussen (Berkeley: University of California Press, 1986), 120–121.

— Lisa M. Brady

Leonardo da Vinci (1452–1519)

An Italian artist, scientist, mathematician, and engineer, da Vinci established a reputation as the most versatile genius of the Renaissance.

Born on April 15, 1452, near the small Tuscan hill town of Vinci, Leonardo was the illegitimate son of the prominent Florentine notary Ser Piero da Vinci and a peasant woman known as Caterina. By 1469 his father sent Leonardo, who displayed a proclivity for the arts at an early age, to Florence, where he apprenticed at the workshop of Verrochio. Under Verrochio's mentorship da Vinci trained both in sculpture and painting, beginning what is known as his first Florentine period. By 1478 he established his own studio in Florence. Three years later the monks of San Donato a Scopeto commissioned Leonardo to create the altarpiece the *Adoration of the Magi*, but before completing the project he left for the court of Milan because the intellectual currents of Florence under Lorenzo the Magnificent focused on philosophical speculation, a spiritual

system at odds with Leonardo's interest in mathematics and the applied sciences.

Between 1482 and 1499 Leonardo served at the court of the duke of Milan, Lodovico Sforza. It was Leonardo who first initiated the contact, writing to the duke and advertising himself as a military and civil engineer. In what is known as his first Milanese period, he worked as an architect, directed court pageants, served as a building consultant, and accepted commissions for paintings. Among his first commissions in Milan was an altarpiece for the Confraternity of the Immaculate Conception, the *Virgin of the Rocks.* His stay at Milan also allowed him to complete the mural of the *Last Supper,* which he painted between 1495 and 1497.

In 1499 the French invaded Milan, interrupting Leonardo's stay. After brief stints in Mantua and VENICE, he returned to Florence in 1500. For a period of 10 months he entered the service of Cesare Borgia. During this time he traveled widely throughout central Italy, producing a series of maps that quickly added to the discipline of cartography. By 1503 he returned to Florence, where he was commissioned to design one of the large murals in the council hall of Palazzo della Signoria. Incidentally, MICHELANGELO competed with him on the opposite wall. For his subject Leonardo chose the *Battle of Anghiari.* Although vehemently opposed to warfare, he depicted the brute character associated with battle on more than one occasion. Finishing the *Battle of Anghiari* by 1506, Leonardo began exhibition of his work when King Louis XII of France called upon him to return to Milan.

Leonardo remained in Milan from 1506 to 1513, where he served as the artistic adviser to the French governor Charles d'Amboise. Da Vinci's connection to the French government at this time provided an important impetus for France's growth as a patron of the arts, a status the country would build upon in the coming centuries. It is of little surprise, therefore, that Leonardo's *Mona Lisa*—created during his second stay in Florence—eventually found a permanent home in the Louvre, France's world-famous museum. In 1517 King Francis I invited him to move to France. The French king proclaimed the venerable master royal painter, architect, and engineer. Although no longer active in these roles, Leonardo remained surrounded by a respectful and admiring court as he established residence at Cloux, near Amboise. Amid these surroundings he died on May 2, 1519. Within a few decades Giorgio Vasari honored his achievements in a glowing biography.

Although Leonardo is mostly remembered as a painter, sculptor, and architect, his genius did not stop in the realm of the arts. His intellectual curiosity in natural phenomena led him away from the practice of art during the latter decades of his life. While turning down numerous commissions for paintings and sculptures, Leonardo drifted toward mathematics and science, filling volumes of notebooks with his observations, many of which were ahead of his time. Unparalleled in his era, Leonardo's range of scientific studies encompassed geometry, optics, mechanics, physiology, anatomy, botany, zoology, paleontology, and geology. He anticipated many of the attitudes and intellectual discoveries of later epochs. Interested in the human body, he investigated and described the processes of breathing, digestion, blood flow, and reproduction. Although he failed to define many of the phenomena he observed, his mechanical and optical observations ranked him as a forerunner to the likes of Newton, Galileo, and Kepler. Perhaps most indicative of his prescient ability, Leonardo's notes toward a treatise on the flight of birds inspired him to investigate the possibilities of a flying machine for humans.

Further reading: Margeret Cooper, *Inventions of Leonardo da Vinci* (New York: Macmillan, 1965); Paolo Galluzzi, ed., *Leonardo da Vinci: Engineer and Architect* (Boston: Northeastern University Press, 1988); Bruno Santi, *Leonardo da Vinci* (New York: Riverside Book Company, 1990).

— Matthew Lindaman

Léry, Jean de (1534–1613)

Born in a France dominated by the Catholic Church, Jean de Léry traveled to BRAZIL in 1556 to help found the first Protestant colony in the Western Hemisphere, and upon his return to Europe he produced a narrative of his stay in South America that remains one of the most important 16th-century descriptions of what to Europeans was a NEW WORLD.

Jean de Léry was born in Burgundy in 1534, and at some point in his youth he left France for Switzerland, where he joined the church of JOHN CALVIN, who had during the early 16th century established himself as one of the leaders of the REFORMATION, the movement intended to transform the Catholic Church. Léry was among a group of young clerics who studied with Calvin in the belief that they would travel to France to spread the Reformation in that Catholic nation. But in 1516 Léry instead joined a Huguenot mission to Brazil intended to establish a Protestant colony among the TUPINAMBA, who inhabited that portion of South America.

From 1552 to 1558 Léry lived among the Tupinamba and paid close attention to their daily lives. Like THOMAS HARRIOT, who later in the century traveled to ROANOKE and left a vivid description of the Carolina ALGONQUIAN who lived there, Léry's published writings on the Tupinamba constitute one of the most in-depth ethno-

graphies that survive for any 16th-century population. Like many European observers of Native American Indians, Léry often found these indigenes barbaric. Because they had no knowledge of Christianity, they were by definition heathens whose religious beliefs needed to be eradicated and replaced by what Europeans believed was a proper theology that emphasized the tenets of monotheism. The Indians he observed also practiced CANNIBALISM, a practice that Europeans everywhere feared. However, unlike some visitors who believed that Indians ate human flesh for its nutritional value, Léry recognized that the act had specific social purposes: Carried out in prescribed ways, those who ate their victims did so because they believed such an act would "strike fear and terror into the hearts of the living." Although such an act terrified many observers, Léry interpreted it as a sign of a people living with an inferior culture. No matter how odd or culturally deficient the Indians seemed, he argued, their deficit was not intellectual. In his mind the Tupinamba were quite "teachable" and thus capable of learning "knowledge of God," which was the principal goal of all missionaries. When he wrote about them mourning lost kin, he conveyed not a static portrait of a primitive people but instead a complex portrait of humans quite capable of experiencing the same range of emotions and thoughts as Europeans.

When he returned to Europe, Léry stopped first in France and then made his way back to Geneva to continue his studies for the ministry and to begin his account of his expedition. But he returned at a difficult time, when Catholics and Protestants were often battling each other. Léry continued to move about serving the cause of the Reformation, working at Nevers in the mid-1560s and then at La Charité-sur-Loire in 1569, when he had to flee for his life after a group of Catholics attacked local HUGUENOTS, killing 22 of them. Léry eventually landed at Sancerre in 1573, a city under peril from royalist Catholic troops whose control of food supplies had led to a famine. Once he made his escape to safer territory, Léry traveled in both Switzerland and France, finally settling back in Burgundy, where he completed his book on Brazil, which was published in 1578 in Geneva with the title *Histoire d'un voyage faict en la terre du Bresil autrement dite Amerique*. The book quickly found an audience, and Léry lived long enough to oversee four more editions, all of them published in Geneva. Along with the royal cosmographer ANDRÉ THEVET, Léry helped to teach the French-reading public about the peoples and resources of the Americas.

Léry's account contained more than a report of the Tupinamba and their social practices. His book also included detailed information about the creatures that inhabited the Atlantic, the birds to be found at sea and on land, and the animals that roamed Brazil. These parts of his account make Léry's achievement all the more notable and presumably more useful to 16th-century Europeans, who could use it as a guidebook to know what they could expect to find on a transatlantic journey. His chapters on his return to Europe aboard a ship that got lost and ran out of supplies serve as a remarkable testimony to the hazards of long-distance travel, a testimony all the more poignant because of Léry's descriptions of the chaos that often enveloped those on board and the necessity of dumping corpses into the ocean.

Jean de Léry completed his life as he had intended: as a minister. Working in Switzerland in the Vaud region, he died of PLAGUE in 1613, yet another victim of the DISEASE that continued to haunt the Old World.

Further reading: Jean de Léry, *History of a Voyage to the Land of Brazil*, trans. and ed. Janet Whatley (Berkeley: University of California Press, 1990).

Levant Company

The company established during the reign of Queen ELIZABETH I to organize commerce between the Levant (modern-day Turkey) and England.

During the course of the 16th century, the English, like other western Europeans, wanted to acquire goods from the East. In earlier times Venetian merchants, sitting astride the critical meeting place of East and West (see VENICE), had controlled much of this commerce. However, by the late 16th century, when various commercial enterprises such as the DUTCH EAST INDIA COMPANY and the English EAST INDIA COMPANY began operations, the time was ripe for a venture to organize trade with the Levant. Thus, on September 11, 1581, Elizabeth granted to Sir Edward Osborne and Richard Staper a patent for the Turkey Company to organize trade with the Levant. The patent was to last seven years, although it could be extended if the trade became a success. By 1590, when the company reviewed its operations, it found that since the mid-1580s it had used 19 ships, which together had sailed back and forth 27 times; their efforts and those of the 787 men they employed had led to £11,359 added to the nation's customs houses, a testament to the potential of the business. A parallel venture, known as the Venice Company, aimed to organize trade between England and that Italian republic.

After a series of political disputes, members of the two companies joined their efforts and received a patent for the Levant Company on January 7, 1592. The company had the right to organize trade with Venice and the East, including the East Indies. Once again, success followed, especially when demand for currants boomed in the early 17th century.

Further reading: Mortimer Epstein, *The English Levant Company: Its Foundation and Its History to 1640* (New York: Burt Franklin, 1968); H. G. Rosedale, ed., *Queen Elizabeth and the Levant Company: A Diplomatic and Literary Episode of the Establishment of Our Trade with Turkey* (London: Henry Frowde, 1904).

Lima

Lima served as an important religious center for the INCA before the arrival of the Spanish, and it became capital of the Spanish Viceroyalty of PERU during the colonial era.

Before Spanish arrival in the region, the valley in which the city of Lima would be founded served as the location of the sanctuary dedicated to the Inca god responsible for earthquakes. In 1535 FRANCISCO PIZARRO established Lima as the capital of the Viceroyalty of Peru. At the time it was known as the Ciudad de los Reyes ("City of the Kings"). The city housed the residences of government officials, a major cathedral, and the important municipal buildings of the viceroyalty. Most of the architecture of the early city reflected Spanish rather than Inca styles because the city proper did not exist there before the establishment of the viceroyalty. By the beginning of the 17th century, Lima's native population consisted mostly of several thousand residents, most of them of indigenous heritage and more than a third of them migrants from other areas in the viceroyalty.

Further reading: Peter Bakewell, *A History of Latin America: Empires and Sequels, 1450–1930* (Malden, Mass.: Bakewell Publishers, 1997); Pedro de Cieza de León, *The Discovery and Conquest of Peru: Chronicles of the New World Encounter*, ed. and trans. Alexandra Parma Cook and Noble David Cook (Durham N.C.: Duke University Press, 1998); David Collier, *Squatters and Oligarchs: Authoritarian Rule and Policy Change in Peru* (Baltimore: Johns Hopkins University Press, 1976).

— Dixie Ray Haggard

Linschoten, Jan Huygen van (1563–1611)

Jan Huygen van Linschoten, a Dutch explorer and writer, went as far as Goa in Indonesia but never managed to find the NORTHEAST PASSAGE, which 16th-century Europeans had hoped would transport them through the frigid arctic waters north of Russia to the lucrative markets of east Asia.

Born in Haarlem in the province of Utrecht in Holland, Linschoten grew up among a Dutch community eager to break free of Spanish control. Despite a brief period from 1572 to 1573, when Haarlem achieved its independence from Spain, Linschoten spent his early years under Spanish rule. Only 16 years old, he left home in 1579 and headed for Spain to join two of his brothers who had become merchants there. After a stop in SEVILLE to learn Spanish, he went to LISBON, where he eventually became interested in a job in the fleet of ships that carried goods and news between Portugal and India. In 1583 he joined a Dutch mission headed for India and eventually found a position as an aid to Vincente de Fonseca, who had just received an appointment as the new archbishop of Goa. After his arrival in Goa, Linschoten became so happy there that he wanted to remain for the rest of his life. But after the archbishop died on a return voyage to Europe in 1588, Linschoten believed that the time had come for his own return. After a long and arduous journey, which included two years on the island of Tercera, Linschoten arrived in Lisbon in early January 1592. Soon after he booked passage back to Holland, where he arrived in early September.

Linschoten's significance lies less in his journey than in the fact that upon his return to Europe he wrote a detailed account of his travels. Entitled *Itinerario, Voyage ofte Schipvaert naer Oost ofte Portugaels Indien,* the book was published first in Dutch in 1596. It contains information on routes from Europe to India and the East, including details about the Malay Archipelago and the coast of China as well as routes to the Americas. He included as well a list of the Spanish king's overseas dominions, the territories that owed dues to the monarch. A final part includes accounts from other travelers, a strategy employed earlier by GIOVANNI BATTISTA RAMUSIO and RICHARD HAKLUYT THE YOUNGER, among others. Here Linschoten included writings about the Congo, BRAZIL (by JEAN DE LÉRY), and the Americas (by GONZALO FERNÁNDEZ DE OVIEDO Y VALDÉS). He also provided descriptions of the Atlantic and Indian Ocean coasts of Africa. Recognizing the potential utility of visual evidence, Linschoten included 36 illustrations in his work in addition to six large fold-out maps. The pictures depict the people of Goa, including the goods that they produced; city plans detail the places Linschoten traveled—Goa, Mozambique, St. Helena, Ascension, and Tercera. Also, the maps included a chart of the world, with a depiction of prominent northern and southern constellations. Like THEODOR DE BRY, Linschoten recognized the importance of including illustrations in his work. When his book appeared in an English edition published in LONDON in 1598 under the title *Iohn Huighen Van Linschoten his Discours of Voyages into ye Easte and West Indies,* the printer maintained the pictures without even changing the captions from their original Latin and Dutch. His illustrations of the Portuguese in the East suggest how Europeans adapted to regions well beyond their continent at the same time that other images depicted exotic fauna, indigenous peoples riding on elephants, and the kinds of icons to be found in Eastern temples.

The publication of his *Itinerary* brought Linschoten honor among the Dutch and constituted his major contribution to the expansion of knowledge in Europe in the late 16th century. Although he maintained his interest in finding the Northeast Passage, Linschoten spent time in the Netherlands engaged as a translator. Among his works was a Dutch edition of JOSÉ DE ACOSTA's history of the West Indies, which Linschoten translated and published under the title *Historia naturael ende morael van de Westersche Indien.* By 1610 Linschoten realized that his *Itinerary* had been a great boon to the Dutch, and so he approached the States-General for an annual pension to support him in recognition of the feat. They refused his request.

By the time of his death in February 1611, Linschoten's fame had spread widely throughout western Europe, due in large part to the translations of the *Itinerary* into other languages. As a result, Linschoten took on a place in history remarkably similar to that of the younger Hakluyt: an eager seeker of information about the world beyond Europe, a believer that long-distance trade would benefit Europeans, and a man who advanced the age of discovery not through his own actions but more directly through his words and their appearance in printed books.

Further reading: Arthur C. Burnell and P. A. Tiele, eds., *The Voyage of John Huygen van Lischoten to the East Indies,* 2 vols., Works Issued by the Hakluyt Society, 1st Ser., 70–71 (London, Hakluyt Society, 1885); *Iohn Huigen Van Linschoten his Discours of Voyages into ye Easte & West Indies* (London, 1598).

Lisbon

Capital of Portugal, Lisbon was one of that country's main commercial centers and a crucial center for Portuguese commercial successes during the empire's age of expansion.

The strategic importance of Lisbon was apparent from ancient times, when the Romans built a major road running between the settlement and the highlands. During the Middle Ages the city was occupied first by Muslims (see ISLAM), who enjoyed its hot public baths and its good sanitation, then by Christians, who continued to exploit the commercial potential of the area.

Over time Lisbon continued to grow in importance. By the late 16th century it was one of only a dozen or so European cities with more than 100,000 inhabitants. Although Portugal as a whole was not wealthy, especially in comparison with neighboring Spain, Lisbon was the spice capital of the Western world and the hub of a commercial empire that stretched from BRAZIL to the Indian Ocean. Commercial wealth from Africa passed through the seaports of Lisbon and Lagos on its way to the royal residences in the provinces, enriching the city's haute bourgeoisie, whose wealth financed countless commercial ventures. Lisbon's wealth and commercial position were probably the primary motivations behind the Spanish annexation of Portugal engineered by PHILIP II.

Further reading: David Birmingham, *A Concise History of Portugal* (Cambridge, U.K.: Cambridge University Press, 1993); J. H. Elliott, *Europe Divided, 1559–1598* (London: Collins, 1968).

— Marie A. Kelleher

London

London, founded by the Romans as Lundinium, became by the 16th century the economic, cultural, and political core of an English nation ready to expand its territory.

With its favored location on the River Thames, London was always a commercial hub. Even before Roman times, merchants living on the Thames engaged in trade with people of northern Europe. With its mouth emptying into the North Sea, the Thames provided excellent access to the European continent and the Low Countries. These connections dating from pre-Christian antiquity laid a firm foundation for flourishing trade by the Middle Ages.

By the time of the Norman Conquest of 1066, farmers had turned London into a market town. In the following centuries artisans and laborers also brought their wares to the city. Artisans in specific trades gravitated to particular areas where they worked. Thus, the corn market was on Cornhill, tailors clustered along Threadneedle Street, and Vintry Row was the place to find wine.

The construction of London Bridge in 1176 began London's rise to modern economic and cultural prominence in Europe. It was the height of architectural design and engineering technology, with 19 stone arches and myriad tall houses that sheltered people and shops. Once the bridge was built, ships began docking at the site because it provided the best means of transporting commercial goods north and south. The Romans had, as part of their imperial vision, built roads to and from the London Bridge area to transport soldiers and material necessary to rule. These roads, maintained and expanded, became crucial for the transportation of goods throughout England by the 16th century. Over time London became a magnet for men and women eager to establish professional and ethnic enclaves. JEWS came to London to set up financing houses despite the fact they found hostility, including expulsion in 1290.

During the 16th century enterprising citizens built the first Royal Exchange, and entire industries grew to meet the needs of merchants. Workers flooded into the city, many of them from foreign lands. Native Londoners' penchant for bigotry and persecution was rekindled when immigrants began inhabiting neighborhoods on the outskirts of the city's commercial center. Priests decried the invasion during Sunday services, and riots often ensued. HENRY VIII even had a few rioters hanged following one incident. The city's commercial success also attracted emigrants from around England, and a population explosion resulted. In 1500 London boasted 75,000 residents. By 1600 that figure grew to 220,000. In the mid-17th century nearly a half million people called London home.

The social consequences of such growth were immense. Aristocrats, uncomfortable living near the increasing number of laborers, began moving west, beyond the city limits. With the dissolution of the English monasteries during the REFORMATION, much land that was not used to house laborers became part of large estates. Pastureland, once abundant, became covered with housing, an early episode of urban sprawl that suggested that urbanization could pose substantial challenges across the Continent. Queen ELIZABETH I, according to the history recorded by WILLIAM CAMDEN, wanted to halt any further expansion of the city. Immigrants arrived despite the fact that by 1550 the city had to import most of its food and that urban growth had polluted available water supplies, although the invention of the pump and a 40-mile canal to import water from Hertfordshire helped to solve the problem.

Christianity, like commerce, throve in London. Church spires came to dominate the skyline. St. Paul's Cathedral, destroyed by fire time and again, rose each time upon the foundations of the earliest Roman basilica. In the 12th century St. Paul's was finally constructed of stone, all except its spire, and rose to mammoth proportions: The wooden spire reached to 450 feet, nearly 100 feet higher than did Christopher Wren's dome built after the fire of 1666. Mendicant friars who arrived in the 13th century became successful evangelists who also established hospitals and charitable societies. For these works London's elite contributed time and money, hoping to attain the salvation the friars promised.

By the end of the 16th century, London had become the center for the nation's economic and cultural life. Home to many PRINTING PRESSes as well as individuals such as RICHARD HAKLUYT THE YOUNGER and SAMUEL PURCHAS, London also became the place where the English most frequently discussed the benefits of colonization and dreamed about the wealth to be made from establishing colonies in the Americas.

Further reading: Robert Gray, *A History of London* (New York: Barnes & Noble Books, 1978); Roy Porter, *London: A Social History* (Cambridge, Mass.: Harvard University Press, 1995); Geoffrey Trease, *London: A Concise History* (London: Thames & Hudson, 1975); Ben

Weinreb and Christopher Hibbert, eds. *The London Ency-clopaedia* (London: Macmillan, 1983).

— David P. Dewar

Loyola, Ignatius (1491–1556)

The founder of the Jesuit order (see JESUITS), Ignatius Loyola sought to extend the reach of the Catholic Church into new lands and to promote deeper devotion within the church.

Ignatius, baptized Iñigo, was the youngest child in a family of 13. His family was noble, and as a young man he sought a career as a soldier and courtier. His military career was cut short when he was wounded in both legs at the siege of Pamplona during a war between Francis I of France and the Holy Roman Emperor CHARLES V. During a lengthy convalescence Ignatius read religious books, including a collection of saints' lives called *The Golden Legend* and Ludolphus of Saxony's *Life of Christ*. These books made a deep impression on the young soldier, and he resolved to imitate the example set by St. Francis and St. Dominic. After recovering from his wounds, Ignatius made a pilgrimage to the shrine of the Virgin Mary at Montserrat. There he dedicated himself to a life of religion. He spent 1522–23 in fasting, prayer, and contemplation near Barcelona. While there, he wrote down some of his thoughts on religion. These early writings formed the core of the *Spiritual Exercises,* a manual for individual religious devotion and development. He continued to develop and revise the *Exercises* throughout his life.

In 1523 Loyola made a pilgrimage to Jerusalem and then returned to Spain. As a young man he had not been well educated, and he resolved to remedy this deficit. He studied Latin in Barcelona and then attended school in Alcalá and Salamanca.From 1528 to 1535 he studied at the University of Paris, receiving a master's degree at the Collège de Montaigu in 1534. In Paris he gathered a group of six fellow students and guided them through the *Spiritual Exercises*. These men included the future Jesuits Francis Xavier, who would later serve as a missionary in India and Japan, and Diego Laínez and Alfonso Salmeron, both of whom would attend the COUNCIL OF TRENT. By 1534 the group took vows of poverty and chastity and determined to travel to Jerusalem, if the pope permitted, to convert the Muslims (see ISLAM). In 1537 Ignatius and most of his colleagues were ordained as priests in VENICE. War prevented them from traveling to the Holy Land, and so they offered their services to Pope Paul III.

In September 1540 Paul III approved the foundation of a new order, the Society of Jesus. In 1541 Ignatius became general of the society for life. The order resembled older monastic orders in some ways but introduced new ideas as well. It was highly centralized and placed great emphasis on obedience to the pope and the church. Jesuits were also more flexible than other orders: They did not wear a distinctive habit, recite the daily prayers of the office together, or encourage ascetic penances and fasts. From the early years of the order, the Jesuits emphasized missionary work and education. The order grew rapidly. From the original 10 members in 1540, the order had a thousand members by the time Ignatius died in 1556. Its motto was "ad majorem Dei gloriam," or "For the greater glory of God."

Although Jesuits became active in the COUNTER-REFORMATION, Ignatius's initial focus was not on combating Protestantism. More of a mystic than a theologian, he did not address the theological ideas of the REFORMATION, nor, for most of his career, did he pay great attention to Protestant religious developments in Germany. Near the end of his life he began to stress the importance of the struggle against Protestantism. Nonetheless, his focus was not on the fight against Protestantism. His two most important goals were the promotion of a more deeply felt and sincere Catholicism and the development of Jesuit missions around the world.

Ignatius of Loyola died in 1556 and was declared a saint of the Roman Catholic Church in 1622.

Further reading: Cándido de Dalmases, *Ignatius of Loyola, Founder of the Jesuits: His life and Work,* trans. Jerome Aixalá (St. Louis: The Institute of Jesuit Sources, 1985); John C. Olin, *Catholic Reform: From Cardinal Ximenes to the Council of Trent, 1495–1563* (New York: Fordham University Press, 1990); John W. O'Malley, *The First Jesuits* (Cambridge, Mass.: Harvard University Press, 1993); ———, "Ignatius Loyola" in *The Oxford Encyclopedia of the Reformation,* vol. 2, ed. Hans J. Hillerbrand (New York: Oxford University Press, 1996), 307–310; J. Ignacio Tellechea Idígoras, *Ignatius of Loyola: The Pilgrim Saint,* trans. Cornelius Michael Buckley, S.J. (Chicago: Loyola University Press, 1994).

— Martha K. Robinson

Luba

Founded by the powerful warrior Nkongolo (Kongolo), the Luba Empire spanned territory in what is today the Democratic Republic of the Congo and Zambia from the 14th century until the late 19th century.

The Luba peoples, one of the earliest iron-working peoples in central Africa from whom the later empire took its name, settled as farmers near the Lake Kisale region in the fourth century. During the 14th century small chiefdoms arose among the Luba peoples, but by 1400 they were subsumed under the larger entity of the Nkongolo dynasty, established when the warrior Nkongolo invaded the southern part of the modern-day Democratic Republic of the Congo. Soon thereafter, according to oral tradition, the huntsman Ilunga Kalala overthrew the Nkongolo dynasty and established the Luba Empire. Ilunga Kalala expanded the kingdom greatly, conquering important trade routes between eastern and central Africa and gaining control over copper mines and fishing and palm oil industries. The Luba kingdom also participated in the SLAVE TRADE in the region, increasing their wealth and power. By 1700 Luba spanned the Upemba Depression (in the southern parts of the modern-day Democratic Republic of the Congo) over the Congo River to Lake Tanganyika.

Further reading: Elizabeth Heath, "Luba," in *Africana: The Encyclopedia of the African and African American Experience,* eds. Kwame Anthony Appiah and Henry Louis Gates, Jr. (New York: Basic *Civitas* Books, 1999), 1206; "Luba," in *African States and Rulers: An Encyclopedia of Native, Colonial, and Independent States and Rulers, Past and Present,* John Stewart (London: McFarland & Co., 1989), 144–145.

— Lisa M. Brady

Luhya

A heterogeneous ethnic group in Kenya, the Luhya area related to the larger BANTU ethnic group and were an essential part of Bantuizing the region between the 16th and 18th centuries through assimilating and absorbing newcomers to the area, like the Kalenjin and the Maasai.

The Luhya's ancestors most likely migrated to their traditional lands near Mount Elgon and Lake Victoria around the end of the first century A.D. The Luhya traced their descent to Mugoma and Malabe, who, according to Luhya tradition, were created by the supreme being, Wele. They were an agricultural people who have historically organized their society into *oluhia,* or clans, that occupy a defined territory and take their identity and clan name from a single prominent ancestor.

The Luhya typically organized themselves into decentralized clan groups, not into kingdoms. The Tiriki clan founded the Wanga kingdom in the 17th century, ruling over two dozen other clans. The majority of the Luhya people remained outside the power of this unique kingdom, keeping to traditional forms of social and political organization.

Further reading: Robert Fay, "Luhya," in *Africana: The Encyclopedia of the African and African American Experience,* eds. Kwame Anthony Appiah and Henry Louis Gates, Jr. (New York: Basic *Civitas* Books, 1999), 1207–1208.

— Lisa M. Brady

Luther, Martin (1483–1546)

The first great Protestant reformer, the German monk and theologian Martin Luther triggered the REFORMATION with his protest against the sale of indulgences.

Luther was born November 10, 1483, in Eisleben and grew up in nearby Mansfeld. He received his bachelor's degree from the University of Erfurt in 1502 and his master's in 1505. His parents wanted him to study for a career in law, but although Luther originally agreed, their wishes came to nothing. Returning to Erfurt after visiting his parents in July 1505, Luther was caught in a violent thunderstorm. In great fear, he cried out "Help, St. Anne, I will become a monk!" When he arrived in Erfurt, Luther fulfilled this vow, entering the Augustinian monastery against the wishes of his father. In 1506 Luther took his monastic vows and the following year was ordained a priest. In 1510 he traveled to Rome, where he was shocked at the worldliness and corruption of the Roman clergy. After returning from Rome, he studied theology in Wittenberg, receiving his doctorate in 1512.

As a monk and a priest Luther suffered from feelings of guilt and inadequacy. He felt that his best efforts to live a pure life were insufficient and feared that God would reject him. Frequent confession did not resolve his fears, nor did obedience to the rules of his order. The expression "the righteousness of God" frightened him, for he thought of God as a judge whom he could not face. Probably between 1513 and 1515, Luther began to understand terms such as "righteousness" and "justification" in a new way. In *Christian Liberty* (or *The Freedom of a Christian*), a treatise published in 1520, Luther argued that all human beings are sinners and therefore cannot fulfill the laws that God gave them in scripture. Since, Luther argued, "it is equally impossible . . . to keep any one of [the commandments]," God did not give them to human beings with the expectation that they would live up to them. Instead, the commandments "are intended to teach man to know himself, that through them he may recognize his inability to do good and may despair of his own ability." The recognition that one cannot live without sin, according to Luther, should then lead the Christian to rely on the grace and mercy of God, rather than attempting to earn salvation through human works.

This belief that humans were justified through faith alone *(sola fide)* and the accompanying rejection of the value of human works led Luther to become involved in a dispute over indulgences. According to the medieval Catholic Church, Jesus, his mother Mary, and the saints had lived such holy lives that they had accumulated a spiritual "treasury of merit." The church claimed the authority to draw on this treasury through indulgences in order to help people avoid punishment in purgatory and thus gain salvation. By buying an indulgence, a sinner could escape the "temporal penalty" of purgatory for sins that had been forgiven through the sacrament of confession.

Technically, an indulgence did not forgive sins, nor was it intended to be a way to buy one's salvation. The theory behind indulgences, however, was complicated and widely misunderstood. Because people wanted to ensure their own salvation, and because the church found that it could raise a great deal of money by selling indulgences, the system became corrupt. Preachers sometimes suggested that buying an indulgence made contrition and confession unnecessary or sold indulgences that claimed to remit the penalty for sins not yet committed. The Dominican indulgence preacher Johann Tetzel, who sold indulgences near Wittenberg, asked his listeners "Do you not hear the voices of your dead parents and other people, screaming and saying: 'Have pity on me, have pity on me . . . for the hand of God hath touched me?' We are suffering severe punishments and pain, from which you could rescue us with a few alms, if only you would. Open your ears, because the father is calling to the son and the mother to the daughter."

On October 31, 1517, Luther presented a series of 95 "Theses on the Power of Indulgences" to Archbishop Albert of Mainz. The archbishop forwarded the theses to Rome, and in the summer of 1518 Luther was summoned to Rome to face allegations of heresy. Through the intervention of Luther's patron and protector, Elector Frederick III of Saxony (Frederick the Wise), Luther's examination took place in Augsburg rather than in Rome. In Augsburg Luther refused to retract his attacks on indulgences.

The controversy over Luther's ideas spread, and in 1520 Pope LEO X excommunicated him, denouncing his works as "heretical, offensive, and false." In 1521 Luther appeared at the Diet of Worms, where, before the Holy Roman Emperor CHARLES V, he refused to recant his views on indulgences and justification, saying "it is neither safe nor right to go against conscience." Luther left the Diet of Worms with a guarantee of his safety for three weeks, after which he would be subject to capital punishment as a heretic. After leaving the Diet of Worms, Luther went into hiding at Wartburg Castle under the protection of Frederick the Wise. There, he completed an influential translation of the New Testament into German and wrote a treatise against monastic life. As the historian Steven Ozment observed, Luther was fortunate that the "manifold distractions of imperial politics" kept the emperor too busy to carry out a campaign against him. While the emperor was occupied in fighting his European rivals and the Ottoman Turks, reformers' ideas spread widely, making Luther a famous man.

In at least one case, Luther's ideas spread farther than he would have wished. German peasants who heard Luther's defense of Christian freedom interpreted his message as one promising political freedom. The peasants' sit-

Martin Luther *(Hulton/Archive)*

uation in the early 16th century was poor: Harvests had failed in 1523 and 1524, land they had traditionally held in common was being expropriated by aristocrats, and they were subject to onerous taxes. In 1525 a group of Swabian peasants composed a list of grievances. Among other things, they demanded release from serfdom, new rent assessments, the return of expropriated lands, and free access to fish, game, and firewood. The peasants drew inspiration from Luther's message, and Luther's response to them was initially favorable, although mixed. He blamed the German princes for their oppression of the peasants but warned the peasants that they did not have the right to rebel against legitimate authority. Luther's moderation ended when the peasants rebelled. In April 1525, when the dissenters rose up, Luther wrote a treatise titled "Against the Murderous and Plundering Hordes of the Peasants." "Let everyone who can smite, slay, and stab [the peasants], secretly and openly, remembering that nothing can be more poisonous, hurtful, or devilish than a rebel," he declared. "It is just as when one must kill a mad dog; if you do not strike him, he will strike you, and a whole land with you." Although Luther's call to action was unnecessary because the German princes were not listening to his commands, the harshness of his appeal—which came in the wake of the deaths of between 70,000 and 100,000 peasants killed in the suppression of the uprising—forever damaged his reputation.

In 1530 the emperor summoned reform leaders to the Diet of Augsburg. Luther, still threatened with execution, was unable to attend. He sent instructions with Philipp Melanchthon, the leader of the reformers' delegation. Melanchthon presented a compromise document, the Confession of Augsburg, that was intended to appeal to a variety of reformers while simultaneously muting points of controversy with the Catholic Church. The Augsburg Confession, while important to the development of Protestant faiths, was not successful in convincing the emperor to tolerate Protestantism. Charles V ordered Protestant territories to return to the Catholic faith by April 1531, but by then the Reformation had become too well established to end abruptly. Religious controversy continued.

After the Diet of Augsburg, Luther reevaluated his position on resistance to secular authority. Previously he had advised his followers to suffer tyranny without resistance, but he now began to argue that Protestants must resist authority for the sake of their consciences. In 1531 Protestants organized a defensive alliance, the Schmalkaldic League. Fighting between Catholic and Protestant forces continued until the Peace of Augsburg in 1555 established the principle *cuius regio, eius religio*—"who reigns, his religion."

In his later years Luther grew more critical of the Catholic Church, which he came to believe was incapable of reform. In 1545, when Pope Paul III encouraged the emperor to wage war against the Protestants, Luther responded with a treatise entitled "Against the Papacy in Rome Founded by the Devil." He also grew increasingly anti-Semitic as he aged and in 1543, in a treatise titled "On the Jews and Their Lies," argued that Christians should burn Jewish homes, schools, and synagogues, adding that the JEWS should be banished from Christendom.

Luther's central and most influential theological argument was that of justification by faith. His treatises, sermons, and letters influenced the shape of the Reformation not only in Germany but across Europe. His most important works include *Christian Liberty* (1519), the *Address to the Christian Nobility of the German Nation* (1520), *On the Bondage of the Will* (1525), and the *Small Catechism* (1529). When Luther died in 1546 his friends, including Melanchthon, mourned the loss of the "charioteer of Israel."

Further reading: Hans J. Hillerbrand, ed. *The Oxford Encyclopedia of the Reformation* (New York: Oxford University Press, 1996); Martin Luther, *Christian Liberty* (Philadelphia: Fortress Press, 1957); Richard Marius, *Martin Luther: The Christian Between God and Death* (Cambridge, Mass.: Harvard University Press, 1999); Heiko A. Oberman, *Luther: Man Between God and the Devil* (New Haven, Conn.: Yale University Press, 1989); Steven Ozment, *The Age of Reform, 1250–1550* (New Haven: Yale University Press, 1980; W. D. J. Cargill Thompson, *The Political Thought of Martin Luther*, ed. Philip Broadhead (Totowa, N.J.: Barnes & Noble Books, 1984). For Luther's own writings see Jaroslav Pelikan and Helmut T. Lehmann, eds., *Luther's Works*, 55 vols. (Philadelphia: Fortress Press, 1955–1986).

— Martha K. Robinson

M

Mabila

A MISSISSIPPIAN town located in central present-day Alabama, Mabila served as the location in which the paramount chief Tascaluza ambushed HERNANDO DE SOTO's expedition in 1540.

During Soto's march through Alabama in 1540, he continually forced natives to serve as porters and slaves of his *entrada*. Additionally, his army devoured food reserves of the towns through which it passed, thus guaranteeing a time of starvation for those unfortunate enough to encounter this expedition. Responding to the high-handed manner in which Soto's army moved through the territory and after he had been taken hostage by Soto, the paramount chief Tascaluza laid plans to ambush the Spaniards at the town of Mabila.

On the secret orders of Tascaluza, the natives took time in the weeks before Soto's arrival at Mabila to strengthen the palisades that surrounded the town and to clear the area immediately surrounding the town of all underbrush. Warriors from surrounding towns and chiefdoms gathered and hid in the village awaiting the arrival of the Spanish. Being wary of his host and captive, Tascaluza, Soto had the town reconnoitered so he knew in advance about the ambush. After the army arrived at Mabila on the morning of October 18, 1540, the battle began when one of Soto's soldiers entered a building to capture Tascaluza and discovered it filled to the rafters with armed warriors. In the end the Mabilians and their allies could not resist the mounted soldiers on the open ground outside of town, and as a result they retreated to the safety of the walls of the town. Eventually the Spanish broke through the palisades and began to burn the town while they slaughtered the warriors. The Mabilians and their allies had the Spanish outnumbered by as many as 20 or 25 to one, but the cramped interior of the town and metal armor and weapons gave the Spanish the tactical advantage. The battle lasted nine hours. Soto's army suffered 22 killed and 148 wounded. The Mabilians and their allies suffered as many as 3,000 dead and perhaps as many as 1,000 wounded. The fight with the Mabilians was the worst confrontation encountered by the Soto *entrada* after their battles with the APALACHEE in FLORIDA a year earlier and before their future encounter with the Natchez. This battle severely hindered the expedition. From this point forward there would be a steady drain on its manpower. The natives of central present-day Alabama were devastated by this incident, and it was still evident to Tristan de Luna when his expedition moved into the region 20 years later.

Further reading: Lawrence A. Clayton, Vernon James Knight, Jr., and Edward C. Moore, eds., *The De Soto Chronicles: The Expedition of Hernando de Soto to North America in 1539–1543*, 2 vols. (Tuscaloosa: University of Alabama Press, 1993); Charles Hudson, "The Hernando de Soto Expedition, 1539–1543," in *The Forgotten Centuries: Indians and Europeans in the American South, 1521–1704*, eds. Charles Hudson and Carmen Chaves Tesser (Athens: University of Georgia Press, 1994), 74–103; Charles Hudson, *Knights of Spain, Warriors of the Sun: Hernando de Soto and the South's Ancient Chiefdoms* (Athens: University of Georgia Press, 1997).

— Dixie Ray Haggard

Machu Picchu

A beautiful and isolated Incan city located in the ANDES MOUNTAINS 9,000 feet above sea level, Machu Picchu served as an estate for the INCA emperor Pachacuti, and it was an important ceremonial site in the Inca religion.

Machu Picchu is one of the few Inca sites not discovered by the Spanish during their conquest of the Inca Empire or during the era of Spanish colonial control. It therefore is an example of pure Inca architecture and material culture not tampered with by the Spanish. Its location on a mountain ridge high in the Andes kept it hidden until the 20th century. The Inca emperor Pachacuti built it as a personal estate, and for a time it may have held an important place in the ceremonial life of the Inca. Today some scholars think that it may have been abandoned at the time of Spanish conquest, but others believe that the last of the Inca to resist the Spanish may have briefly occupied it.

Further reading: Hiram Bingham, *Machu Picchu: A Citadel of the Incas* (New Haven, Conn.: Yale University Press, 1930); ———, *Lost City of the Incas* (Lima, Peru: Librerias A. B. C., 1948); Paul Fejos, *Archaeological Explorations in the Cordillera Vilcabamba* (New York: Viking Fund Publications in Anthropology, 1944); John Hemming, *Machu Picchu* (New York: Newsweek, 1981); and Johan Reinhard, *Machu Picchu: The Sacred Center* (Lima, Peru: Nuevas Imágenes, 1991).

— Dixie Ray Haggard

Madeira

The name given to both a group of islands and the main island of the group lying in the Atlantic Ocean at 17° W 22°45′ N.

Madeira offers, perhaps, one of the clearest examples of how ecological factors contributed to the transformation of lands newly discovered by Europeans. Madeira was almost entirely covered by trees when the first Portuguese settlers arrived, and this timber proved to be a valuable export. However, despite potential profit, the newcomers decided to clear land by setting fire to the forests. More than one of these fires went out of control, and at least one group of settlers had to take refuge in the ocean for several days until a fire burnt itself out. Because Europeans brought pigs and cattle to the islands (see COLUMBIAN EXCHANGE), these ecological changes ensured that the region would never return to the state in which the Europeans found it.

On the smaller island of Porto Santo, the villains were rabbits. Released by Europeans in the very early days of colonization, the rabbits bred rapidly. Porto Santo lacked the natural DISEASES and predators the animals had known in Europe, and the rabbit population grew to such a degree that they actually forced the Portuguese off the island for a number of years. When they returned the original ecosystem of Porto Santo had ceased to exist, and the introduction of European weeds and organisms transformed it into an environmental clone of the Old World.

Politically, control of the Madeira group was divided into three captaincies—two on Madeira and one on Porto Santo. Madeira's route to becoming a prosperous colony owed everything to the introduction of SUGAR. Unlike the future plantations in places like BRAZIL, Europeans planted sugar in Madeira not on plains but on narrow hillside terraces. Planters also needed irrigation to bring sufficient water from the higher elevations to the cane fields. They thus constructed *levadas*, a handmade irrigation network that ran an estimated distance of 700 km on an island 60 km in length. By the early 1450s Madeira's planters were already exporting raw sugar to England and Flanders. By the end of the 15th century, the island was the world's largest sugar producer, and the price of sugar had fallen by more than 50 percent. Madeiran sugar dominated the market until the late 16th century when the numerous advantages of Brazilian sugar planters enabled them to undercut Madeiran prices. Although sugar would enjoy a brief resurgence in importance during the Dutch occupation of Pernambuco, by the end of the 17th century Madeira's main export was wine.

The Madeira planters' dedication to cash crops meant that they did not produce enough food to feed the human population of the island. Although some grew wheat in western parts of the island, the island was short of many food products. Its only reliable source of wheat, the most essential need, was the nearby island of Porto Santo. Too dry to grow sugar, the island was able to support livestock as well as produce surpluses of basic cereal crops. Although never able to supply even half the demands of its larger neighbor, a good harvest on Porto Santo always pushed wheat prices down on Madeira.

Like other sugar producing plantation owners, those on Madeira came to rely on slaves (see SLAVERY) to produce their exports. It is likely that in the early years of the 17th century, the majority of Madeira's slaves were not of African descent. Rather, their numbers possibly consisted of Berbers as well as JEWS and Muslims (see ISLAM) whose conversion to Christianity was deemed suspect by Portuguese authorities. A large number of Madeiran slaves appear to have been Guanches—the original inhabitants of the Canary Islands who were extinct by the end of the 16th century.

Madeira remained profitable during the following centuries, and planters there maintained an extensive trade that had among its clients the Virginia planter George Washington, the first president of the United States. Its decline began in the 19th century, when the vital American trade suffered at the hands of both American whiskey producers and the temperance movement. Several blights that all but destroyed the grapevines signaled the final end to the once-thriving island sugar economy.

Further reading: Alfred W. Crosby, *Ecological Imperialism: The Biological Expansion of Europe, 900–1900* (New York: Cambridge University Press, 1986); T. Bentley Duncan, *Atlantic Islands: Madeira, the Azores and the Cape Verde Islands in Seventeenth Century Commerce and Navigation* (Chicago: University of Chicago Press, 1972).

— John Grigg

Magellan, Ferdinand (1480?–1521)

Ferdinand Magellan (Fernão de Magalhães), a Portuguese explorer, commanded the first voyage to circumnavigate the globe.

Magellan was born in Portugal to a noble family. As a young man he was involved in Portuguese expeditions to the Far East, sailing to Malacca (modern Melaka) and the Moluccas, or SPICE ISLANDS. By 1510 he had become captain of a ship and sailed as far east as Ambon and Banda, two Indonesian islands. On his later westward voyage around the world, he passed beyond these islands before dying in the Philippines. Thus, although he did not live to complete the circumnavigation of the globe that his men accomplished from 1519 to 1522, he is credited with being the first person to circle the world.

When Magellan sailed, the Portuguese already knew of a sea route to the Spice Islands, but this route was difficult, involving a trip around the Cape of Good Hope. Magellan thought that it might be possible to reach the Moluccas more easily from the other direction, that is, by sailing westward from Europe. The king of Portugal, Manuel, refused to support such a venture. Not only did the Portuguese already have one route to the islands, but another Portuguese explorer, Gonçalo Coelho, had twice tried to find a westward route through or around America and failed.

Rejected by Portugal, Magellan turned to Spain. He arrived in SEVILLE in 1517 and offered his services to the Spanish king Charles I, who would later become the Holy Roman Emperor CHARLES V. While in Spain Magellan also married Beatriz Barbosa, a wealthy young woman. He showed the Spanish court a map, perhaps by MARTIN BEHAIM or the cartographer Johannes Schöner, that depicted the Pacific Ocean as relatively small, which made a westward voyage seem likely to succeed.

In 1518 Charles agreed to provide Magellan and a joint captain of the expedition, Rui Faleiro, with five ships. They would command about 250 sailors and receive one-fifth of the profits from the journey. Charles also promised to make them ADELANTADO of any new lands they discovered. The preparations for the voyage took longer than expected. Magellan had a difficult time assembling a crew for his five ships, the Trinidad, San Antonio, Concepción, Victoria, and Santiago.

Magellan's officers proved troublesome from the start. Juan de Cartagena, the son of a powerful bishop, became opposed to Magellan from the beginning of the voyage. This faction included Cartagena, who was the captain of the San Antonio, Gaspar de Quesada, captain of the Concepción, and Luis de Mendoza, captain of the Victoria. Three of Magellan's five ships, then, were commanded by men hostile to him and who were plotting against him even before they left Spain.

The fleet left Spain on September 20, 1519. Magellan set course for the CANARY ISLANDS, which they reached on September 26. While still in the Canaries, Magellan received a message that warned him that Cartagena, Quesada, and Mendoza were plotting to kill him. After leaving the Canaries, the fleet was becalmed in the doldrums, where Cartagena first challenged Magellan's authority. Magellan removed Cartagena from command of the Victoria, replacing him with Antonio de Coca.

The ships reached the coast of BRAZIL in December 1519. The crew stopped at Rio de Janeiro for two weeks, where they traded with the Indians. After leaving Rio de Janeiro Magellan followed the coast southward. He stayed close to the shore, exploring large inlets in an attempt to find a way through the continent. He sailed up the Rio de la Plata, hoping that it would reach the western ocean. After this excursion the ships continued down the coast, passing through difficult waters and enduring dangerous storms. They spent the winter at San Julián, Patagonia, where they met natives whom ANTONIO PIGAFETTA, who later wrote a chronicle of the journey, described as "giants." The sailors, who had endured weeks of navigating through hazardous waters, doubted that Magellan would ever find a passage through the continent and wanted to return to Spain. The captains of the San Antonio, Concepción, and Victoria, in concert with Juan de Cartagena, led a mutiny, which Magellan and men loyal to him suppressed. Magellan hanged Quesada and sentenced other conspirators, including Cartagena, to hard labor for the rest of the winter. When the ships left San Julián in September Magellan left Cartagena and another conspirator behind. Their fate is unknown.

After leaving San Julián the ships continued southward, spending two months at the Rio Santa Cruz. From there they traveled south again. The Santiago was wrecked in a storm, but soon after Magellan found the strait he had sought. Magellan faced a dilemma. Although he had found a way through the continent, he had provisions for only two more months. Although some of the sailors and pilots wanted to return to Spain, he chose to continue. During the course of sailing through the strait, the San Antonio vanished. Magellan searched but found no trace of the missing ship. The San Antonio was not lost; rather, a successful mutiny had deposed its captain, and it returned to Spain, arriving safely in March 1521.

After passing through the strait that would later bear his name, Magellan still faced the ocean between South America and the Spice Islands. Magellan named the ocean the Pacific ("peaceful"). Like other Europeans of the day, he believed the Pacific to be smaller than it is. Unfamiliar with the Pacific, he chose an unlucky course across it. As the historian Samuel Eliot Morison observed, "the fleet could not have sailed a more lonely course across the

Pacific if Magellan had been the captain of a modern solo, non-stop cruise looking for publicity and prizes." Magellan missed Tahiti, the Marshall islands, and other ports. Before he and his men found land again, they ran out of supplies, suffered from scurvy, and were reduced to eating leather from the ships' rigging. According to Pigafetta, 19 men died.

On March 6, 1521, the travelers sighted Guam and Rota, which Magellan named Las Islas de Velas Latinas, the "Islands of Lateen Sails." The Polynesian people who lived there, the Chamorro, visited the ship, where, according to the sailors, they stole everything they could reach. Magellan's men killed several with crossbows, and the Chamorro fled. Magellan then attacked their village, driving the people away, burning their homes, and taking their food stores. The *Trinidad, Concepción,* and *Victoria* next sailed toward the Philippines and areas that were already known to Europeans. Near one island Magellan's slave Enrique conversed with native people in Malay, and the sailors traded for goods of Chinese design.

Magellan met and traded with a Malay ruler, Rajah Colambu. The Europeans and the islanders exchanged gifts, and the islanders treated Magellan and his men to a feast. Magellan also met peacefully with a ruler whom the

Europeans called Sultan Humabon. Humabon agreed to be baptized with all his people. In April 1521 Magellan and Humabon sealed their alliance in a ceremony in which Humabon, Rajah Colambu, and other islanders agreed to be baptized.

At this time Magellan became embroiled in the islanders' politics and promised to attack Humabon's enemies. Humabon did not want to go to war, but Magellan apparently hoped to prove his good intentions by attacking his new allies' enemies. On April 27, 1521, Magellan led a force of 60 of his men in three longboats, combined with the islanders' forces, to Mactan Island. He sent a message to Lapu Lapu, the leader of Humabon's enemies, ordering him to recognize the king of Spain as his lord and pay tribute. When Lapu Lapu refused, Magellan and his men began to wade toward the shore. There, a much larger opposing force waited. In the ensuing battle Magellan and seven of his men died, as did four natives who fought with them and about 15 of their opponents.

Historians have harshly criticized Magellan's behavior in the Philippines. Having established good relations with Rajah Colambu and Sultan Humabon, he had no need to fight, and they had not asked him to go to war

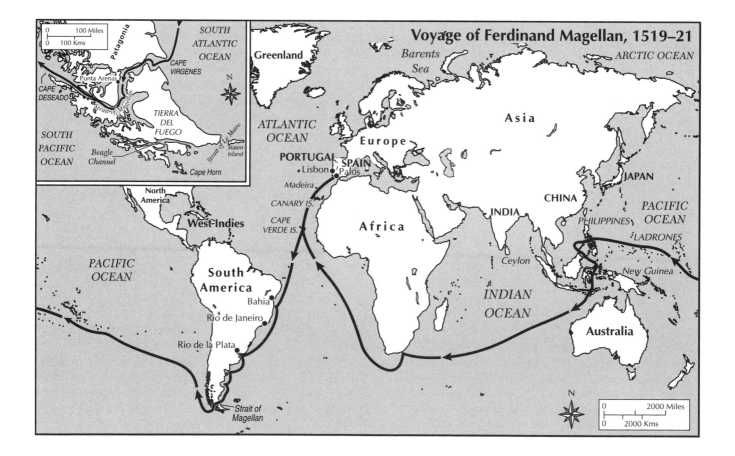

on their behalf. After Magellan's death relations with Humabon deteriorated, and some 25 Europeans were killed in fighting before the remains of Magellan's fleet left the Philippines.

The remnants of the fleet successfully reached the Spice Islands, crossed the Indian Ocean, traveled around the Cape of Good Hope, and returned to Spain. When they completed their circumnavigation of the globe in 1522, they had been traveling for three years. The losses of the journey were great. Of the original fleet of five ships, only one, the *Victoria*, survived the circumnavigation and returned to Spain. Crew members suffered and died from cold, sickness, and warfare. Of the 277 men who sailed with Magellan, only 19 survived. The voyage was a remarkable feat, but its results were meager. Although Magellan had discovered a new route to the islands of the East, the Strait of Magellan was so distant and dangerous and the Pacific so large that his route was longer and more difficult than the old one.

Further reading: Samuel Eliot Morison, *The Great Explorers: The European Discovery of America* (New York: Oxford University Press, 1978); Paula Spurlin Paige, trans. *The Voyage of Magellan: The Journal of Antonio Pigafetta* (Englewood Cliffs, N.J.: Prentice Hall, 1969); J. H. Parry, *The Discovery of South America* (London: Paul Elek, 1979); Donald Payne, *Magellan and the First Circumnavigation of the World* (London: Weidenfeld & Nicolson, 1974); Antonio Pigafetta, *The First Voyage Around the World: An Account of Magellan's Expedition,* ed. Theodore J. Cachey, Jr. (New York: Marsilio Publishers, 1995).

— Martha K. Robinson

Mahfuz, emir of Adal   See Ethiopia

maize   See corn

Mali

The early west African empire Mali controlled the trans-Saharan trade in GOLD, slaves (see SLAVERY), and other goods from the 13th century through the mid-15th century, reaching its zenith of power under the leadership of MANSA MUSA I in the early 14th century.

Mali emerged as an empire in the mid-1200s, after SUNDIATA KEITA defeated the Sosso, a minor successor to the first great Sudanic empire, GHANA. Established in about A.D. 600, the kingdom of Ghana reached its height of power in the mid- to late 10th century. In 1076 the Moroccan Almoravids overthrew the ancient kingdom, with

important consequences for the region. Although in power for less than two decades, the Islamic Almoravids were instrumental in converting the local people to ISLAM, which became a major force in the region's cultural and political development. Most of the succeeding Sudanic empires, including Mali, were based on Islamic principles, and many of the rulers were at least nominally Muslim.

The first Malian king to convert to Islam was Baramendana, in 1150. Only half a century later, Moussa, also known as Allakoi for his habitual exhortation that God causes all ("Alla koi"), reportedly made four pilgrimages to MECCA, one of Islam's holiest cities. Although doubtful in its accuracy, the account may have been an attempt to portray Mali as a Muslim dynasty of long standing. IBN KHALDÛN, the 14th-century Arab historian, described Mali's second imperial king, Mansa Uli Keita (ca. 1260–?, Sundiata Keita's son and successor), as a great leader and a devout Muslim, documenting his pilgrimage to Mecca. The most famous of Mali's Muslim rulers was Mansa Musa I, who made a legendary pilgrimage to the holy city in 1324–25.

Ranging at its peak from the Atlantic Ocean east to the city of GAO and spanning the SAHARA south to the forested regions along the Gulf of Guinea, Mali's territory incorporated some of the most important and lucrative trade routes in West Africa. Established in the region in the 11th and 12th centuries, these trade routes stimulated the growth of independent political kingdoms, of which Mali was only one. Although historical accounts of its early history are fragmented and unclear, Mali's rise to empire is much better documented. The Mandinka (Mande) people of the Kangaba kingdom were important middlemen in the gold trade late in ancient Ghana's history. They were dependent on Ghana for their livelihood and their safety on their trading journeys from the Wangara gold fields to the empire's trading centers. When Ghana fell, Kangaba established itself as an independent kingdom. Threatened by other kingdoms' bids for power in the region, Kangaba relied on the leadership of Sundiata Keita to maintain its independence. After defeating the rival king Sumanguru, Sundiata founded the Mali Empire around the year 1240, although he was not the first of Mali's kings because they traced their leadership through the Kangaba line to Baramendana.

Mali's success resulted from the strategic location of its capital on the Upper NIGER RIVER and its extensive use of rivers for communication, empire building, and trade. Gold was an especially important resource for the empire, and much of Mali's wealth came from control of the Boure gold fields located in the empire's heartland. The Niger River, with its major cities DJENNE-DJENO (Djenne), TIMBUKTU, and Gao, lay at the center of Mali's mercantile enterprise and provided the kingdom with the means for transporting trade goods such as gold, copper, salt, cola nuts, spices, and slaves. Mali's trading system brought the empire into contact with diverse peoples in the SUDAN and North Africa, including the AKAN, HAUSA, and SONGHAI, as well as with Moroccan and Arab merchants. Most of Mali's traders, called Dyula or Wangara after the major gold mining districts, were Muslim and provided an important link in the spread of Islam within Mali's as well as to other areas of Sudanic West Africa.

Although Islam eventually became the official and predominant religion in Mali, indigenous spiritual beliefs and practices remained intact and continued to influence the development of Malian society. IBN BATTUTA, the Moroccan traveler and chronicler, commented on the social freedoms Malian women enjoyed. Like men, women in Mali were free to choose "friends" or "companions" of the opposite sex outside their own families. Furthermore, succession and descent continued to be determined through matrilineal relations, not through the father's line, as was practiced in most other Islamic societies. Ibn Battuta described this practice of matrilineal succession and remarked on its singularity in the Muslim world.

An elaborate kinship system existed in Mali based on lineages and clans and organized territorially into villages and districts. Noble clans composed the top echelon of political power, ruling over other social groups such as freemen, serfs, slaves, and non-Mande peoples. Slavery was an essential dimension of ancient Mali's social and economic structures, as it had been and would be to other Sudanic societies. Slaves cultivated land to support local administrative functions, served in the army as bowmen, and often held important administrative posts, as their lack of family or clan ties lent them an aura of objectivity.

Mali eventually surpassed its predecessor, Ghana, in geography and in influence. By the reign of Mansa Musa I, Mali had ambassadors in Morocco, Egypt, and elsewhere, and its capital Niani (no longer in existence) was a prosperous, populous city with more than 6,000 families according to the chronicler LEO AFRICANUS. Mali developed a complex system of government headed by the king but administered by various departmental ministers. Top officials at Niani were typically noblemen who oversaw specific departments or activities within the larger governmental structure.

The larger Mali power structure consisted of a confederation of various kingdoms under the overall direction of one king, or mansa. The Mali confederation was a loose one, plagued by frequent challenges to the central power. One of the most persistent sources of discontent came from the Songhai peoples, who controlled transportation on the Niger River. The Songhai, based in Gao, enjoyed a long tradition of autonomy and were unhappy with Mali rule. By the early 15th century the Songhai separated from Mali, establishing themselves as an independent kingdom under the rulership of Sonni Ali Ber. By 1465 Sonni Ali Ber conquered much of Mali. Weakened by the Songhai invasion as well as by succession disputes and unrest in peripheral territories, the empire went into decline in the early 16th century. In 1589 the last vestiges of the Mali Empire fell to a Moroccan invasion.

Further reading: "Before Colonization," in *Cambridge Encyclopedia of Africa,* eds. Roland Oliver and Michael Crowder (Cambridge, U.K.: Cambridge University Press, 1981), 57–86; Basil Davidson, ed., "Mali," in *The Lost Cities of Africa,* (Boston: Little, Brown, 1987), 90–98; Nehemia Levtzion, "The Early States of the Western Sudan to 1500," in J. F. Ade Ajayi and Michael Crowder, eds., *History of West Africa,* 3rd ed. (London: Longman, 1985), Vol. 1, 129–166, esp. 138–143; "The Majesty of Mali," in *West Africa before the Colonial Era: A History to 1850,* ed. Basil Davidson (London: Longman, 1998), 35–45.

— Lisa M. Brady

Malinche (ca. 1500–?)

Malinche, later baptized as Doña Marina, was a young woman from the TABASCO region who, after having been given as a slave to HERNÁN CORTÉS, became his lover and soon learned enough of the Spanish language to become his interpreter as well as his adviser on internal affairs of the native peoples.

Malinche, or Malintzin, was descended from a royal family in the Tabasco region, but internal conflicts had left her reduced to near-slavery. She, along with 19 other young women, formed part of a gift from the Tabasco leaders to Cortés and proved her worth by becoming his interpreter and expert adviser on regional political affairs.

Her information was instrumental in the destruction of CHOLULA, instigated when an old woman informed her of a plot purportedly instigated by MOCTEZUMA II to surprise and kill the Spaniards. Acting on her information, Cortés ordered the execution of the native nobles and warriors present in the city.

Malinche also served as liaison between the Spaniards and the native peoples along the route from the coast to TENOCHTITLÁN, convincing them to deliver provisions when, left to themselves, they seemed to fear even approaching the newcomers. Most historians consider her aid to have been instrumental in the Spaniards' conquest of the AZTECS.

Further reading: Cordelia Candelaria, "La Malinche, Feminist Prototype," *Frontiers,* 5 (1980): 1–6; Joanne Danaher Chaison, "Mysterious Malinche: A Case of Mistaken Identity," *Americas* [Academy of American Franciscan History], 32 (1976): 514–523; Nigel Davies, *Aztecs: A History* (Norman: University of Oklahoma Press, 1980); Anna Lanyon, *Malinche's Conquest* (London: Allen & Unwin, 1999).

— Marie A. Kelleher

Maliseet

An ALGONQUIAN-speaking tribe that lived along the modern-day eastern border between Canada and the United States, the Maliseet established contact with the French before 1535 and maintained an alliance with them throughout the political existence of New France.

The Maliseet (also known as the Amalecite, Etchemin, Malecite, and Maleschite) inhabited Passamaquody Bay, the lower St. John River, and St. Croix River in what is today northeast Maine and western New Brunswick. They lived in oval-shaped wigwams made from sapling poles covered with birch bark and grass matting. In the winter bands broke up into small family units to hunt the solitary moose. In the summer families came together to form bands along the coast and rivers, where they fished and cultivated TOBACCO. During the warm months the Maliseet used canoes to move among bands to socialize, to perform religious ceremonies, and to arrange marriages.

Their first recorded contact with Europeans occurred in 1535, when they met JACQUES CARTIER at Passamaquoddy Bay and offered to trade furs with the French for various goods produced in Europe. More than likely, the Maliseet had already encountered French fishermen on the coast of New Brunswick and learned what these new people had to offer them. At the time that Samuel de Champlain formally made an alliance with the Maliseet in 1604, they seem to have been at war with the ABENAKI, but eventually they participated in an alliance system with the Abenaki, Micmac, PASSAMAQUODDY (which some consider to be a subgroup of the Maliseet), and Penobscot. The French used this confederacy during the colonial era to keep English expansion in New England in check. Eventually, the French built Fort La Tour on the St. John River. They used this post to keep the Maliseet supplied with guns and ammunition and to promote the fur trade with the nation. Descendants of the Maliseet still live in New Brunswick, Canada, and continue to perpetuate their rich cultural heritage.

Further reading: Charles George Hebermann, ed., *The Catholic Encyclopedia: An International Work of Reference on the Constitution, Doctrine, Discipline, and History of the Catholic Church,* vol. 9 (New York: Appleton, 1910); Michel R. P. Herisson, *An Evaluative Ethno-historical Bibliography of the Malecite Indians* (Ottawa: National Museums of Canada, 1974); Reuben Gold Thwaites, ed., *The*

Jesuit Relations and Allied Documents: Travels and Explorations of the Jesuit Missionaries in New France, 1610–1791, 3 vols. (Cleveland: Burrow Bros., 1896–1901); Carl Waldman, *Atlas of the North American Indian* (New York: Facts On File, 1985).

— Dixie Ray Haggard

Mandeville, Sir John (fl. 1322–1356?)

Long deceased by the time CHRISTOPHER COLUMBUS sailed across the Atlantic in 1492, the 14th-century writer Sir John Mandeville left an account of his alleged journeys beyond the boundaries of Europe that had a remarkable impact on those who hoped to expand the continent's intellectual and economic horizons.

Little is known of Mandeville other than the few personal clues he left behind in his account of his travels. He tells his readers that he was an English knight who journeyed from 1322 to 1356 and that during those decades he came to serve the sultan of Egypt and the "Great Chan," the purported leader of China. Many scholars believe that Mandeville never left England at all but was simply a master writer whose account fascinated everyone who saw it. In that age, before the advent of the PRINTING PRESS, it is difficult to know exactly how many people ever had any encounter with Mandeville's story. Because approximately 300 surviving manuscripts have existed since at least 1500, and because they exist in virtually every language spoken or read in Europe (including Irish, Czech, and Dutch), there is no doubt that the book had many readers. Given the difficulty of producing extensive texts in an age when each manuscript had to be copied by hand, often in a monastic scriptorium where copyists tended to focus on religious texts, the mere fact that so many manuscripts of Mandeville's travels survive suggests its extraordinary popularity.

Mandeville took it upon himself to describe what Europeans termed the East, the lands that stretched from Muslim-dominated North Africa through China and Japan. Mandeville's was not the only account circulating in the 14th century; during those same years manuscripts of the Venetian MARCO POLO's travels also spread across Europe. Although there were other sources of information, it would have been difficult for any writer to top the incredible phenomena that appeared in Mandeville's text, such as his memorable account of MONSTERS who ranged from midgets to giants, some of whom lacked heads, others of whom had only a small hole for a mouth and had to suck their nutrition through narrow reeds, and still others of whom had ears so long that they touched their knees or lips so large that they covered their faces while they slept. Yet even Mandeville admitted that he had not seen everything. "Of Paradise I cannot speak properly," he wrote at one point, "for I have not been there; and that I regret."

It would be easy to agree with scholars who have dismissed Mandeville and termed him a "travel liar" instead of a traveler. His claims are, after all, preposterous and impossible, but whatever judgment modern readers might claim, there is no doubt that Mandeville helped to shape Europeans' expectations of the world beyond their borders. LEONARDO DA VINCI, one of the great intellectuals of the age, possessed a copy of Mandeville's book, and it was the only travel book that he had in his library at the end of the 15th century. Columbus studied Mandeville so that he would have a better understanding of the peoples he was sure he would find at the end of his journey in 1492. Mandeville's popularity was so great in England that MARTIN FROBISHER took a copy with him on his journey to North America in 1576, and RICHARD HAKLUYT THE YOUNGER even included the text, in Latin, in the 1589 edition of his *Principal Voiages, Navigations, and Travels of the English Nation*. More than 600 years after the initial appearance of the manuscript, Mandeville's *Travels* remain in print, a testimony indeed to the staying power of some 14th-century tales.

Further reading: Malcolm Letts, *Mandeville's Travels: Texts and Translations,* Works Issued by the Hakluyt Society, 2nd Ser., CI–CII (London, Hokluyt Society, 1950); C. R. D. W. Mosley, trans. and ed., *The Travels of Sir John Mandeville* (Harmondsworth, England: Penguin Classics, 1983).

Mansa Musa I (Kankan Musa) (r. 1307–1337)

Emperor of MALI at the zenith of the kingdom's power and nephew to the empire's founder, SUNDIATA KEITA, Mansa (king or emperor) Kankan Musa I made legendary journeys to MECCA and Cairo and established Mali as a center for Islamic learning and culture.

A devout Muslim, Kankan Musa made a pilgrimage to Mecca in 1324–25. On this hajj (see ISLAM), he traveled across the SAHARA to Cairo, where he expended so much GOLD in gifts and purchases that the city's gold prices remained depressed for years. According to Arab historians, Mansa Musa's entourage included more than 60,000 servants and porters, 500 of them dressed in gold and carrying gold staffs. Kankan Musa's journey to Mecca, although primarily a religious pilgrimage, also served a political purpose by acquainting him with his growing empire. Under the leadership of Kankan Musa, the kingdom of Mali reached its geographic peak, stretching from the Atlantic Ocean to the middle bend of the NIGER RIVER and from the Sahara to the southern forests along the Gulf of Guinea. Kankan Musa's Mali was geographically diverse, rich in valuable resources such as gold, and incorporated important trade centers such as DJENNE-DJENO and TIMBUKTU. While the Mansa was on his pilgrimage, one of his generals conquered the SONGHAI city of GAO, an important trade center on the trans-Saharan route. Kankan Musa traveled to Gao to establish his power there, receiving the submission of the king, Za Yassibou. While there, Kankan Musa built a mosque designed by the Andalusian architect and poet Abou-Ishaq Ibrahim Es Saheli. Es Saheli, who also designed Kankan Musa's great Dyingerey Ber mosque in Timbuktu, was only one of the many Muslim artists and scholars Kankan Musa attracted to Mali during his reign. Kankan Musa's role in establishing Mali as a center of Islamic culture and religion was one of his most important accomplishments. His patronage of Islamic art, literature, and education laid the foundation for the African-Arabic literary tradition that came out of Timbuktu beginning in the 14th century. Kankan Musa died in 1337 and was succeeded by his son Magha I.

Further reading: "Musa," in *Africana: The Encyclopedia of the African and African American Experience,* eds. Kwame Anthony Appiah and Henry Louis Gates, Jr. (New York: Basic *Civitas* Books, 1999), 1360; "Mansa Musa," in *Encyclopedia of Islam* (Leiden, The Netherlands: E. J. Brill, 1988); Pascal James Imperato, *Historical Dictionary of Mali,* 2nd ed. (Metuchen, N.J.: Scarecrow Press, 1986).
— Lisa M. Brady

Manteo (fl. 1580s)

A member of an important Croatoan Indian family, Manteo traveled to England, helped the ROANOKE colonists survive, and provided ethnographic and environmental information to THOMAS HARRIOT.

Manteo and another man, WANCHESE, were brought to England, apparently willingly, by ARTHUR BARLOWE and Philip Amadas in 1584. While in England they learned English and taught some ALGONQUIAN to Harriot. Both Manteo and Wanchese returned to Roanoke with the 1585 colonizing expedition. There, Manteo seems to have tried to help the colonists and Indians understand each other, although he was unable to stop hostility from arising. His mother was apparently the leader of the Croatoan Indians, and the Croatoan may have been glad to have a representative within the English colony, one who could keep them informed about English actions and intentions. In 1587 Manteo was baptized at Roanoke and received the title "Lord of Roanoke and Dasemunkepeuc." By ordering this ceremony, SIR WALTER RALEGH apparently intended to establish Manteo as a lord over his people and so formalize his authority. Nothing is known of Manteo after the disappearance of the Roanoke colony.

Further reading: Karen Ordahl Kupperman, *Indians and English: Facing Off in Early America* (Ithaca, N.Y.: Cornell University Press, 2000); ———, *Roanoke: The Abandoned Colony* (Totowa, N.J.: Rowman & Allanheld, 1984); Michael Leroy Oberg, "Gods and Men: The Meeting of Indian and White Worlds on the Carolina Outer Banks, 1584–1596," *North Carolina Historical Review* 76 (October 1999): 367–390; David Beers Quinn, *Set Fair for Roanoke: Voyages and Colonies, 1584–1606* (Chapel Hill: University of North Carolina Press, 1985).

— Martha K. Robinson

Mantoac

The ALGONQUIAN of what is today North Carolina believed in the existence of spiritual forces known as Mantoac, Montóac, or Manitou.

When English colonists settled at ROANOKE, they met people who believed in a variety of spiritual powers. The term *Mantoac* has no precise translation in English, but European observers, most notably THOMAS HARRIOT, wrote that the Indians believed in both a single god who had always existed and in other gods and spirits. Similar beliefs seem to have been commonly held by Algonquian peoples along the Atlantic seaboard. In the 17th century Roger Williams reported that the Narragansett in Rhode Island called "Manittóoes, that is, Gods, Spirits, or Divine powers, . . . every thing which they cannot comprehend" and when seeing "any Excellency in Men, Women, Birds, Beasts, Fish, &c, they cry out *Manittóo* A God."

Indians who negotiated with the English sometimes took names that apparently indicated having Montoac or having a relation to Montoac. Thus, the name MANTEO appears to be related to Montoac, as did Pocahontas's name Amonute and one of her father's titles or names, Mamanotowick.

Further reading: Christian F. Feest, "North Carolina Algonquians" in *Handbook of North American Indians,* William C. Sturtevant, gen. ed., vol. 15, *Northeast,* vol. ed. Bruce G. Trigger (Washington, D.C.: Smithsonian Institution, 1978), 271–281; Thomas Harriot, *A Briefe and True Report of the New Found Land of Virginia* (New York: Dover Publications, 1972); Karen Ordahl Kupperman, *Indians and English: Facing Off in Early America* (Ithaca, N.Y.: Cornell University Press, 2000); ———, *Roanoke: The Abandoned Colony* (Totowa, N.J.: Rowman & Allanheld, 1984); David Beers Quinn, *Set Fair for Roanoke: Voyages and Colonies, 1584–1606* (Chapel Hill: University of North Carolina Press, 1985).

— Martha K. Robinson

mappae mundi

Mappae mundi, literally "cloths of the world," were medieval Europeans' depictions of the lands and peoples of the Earth.

The term *mappae mundi* can refer either to maps, such as medieval T-O MAPS, or to written works of geography. Medieval maps did not follow modern conventions of mapmaking. They seldom portrayed coastlines, rivers, or other geographical features accurately. *Mappae mundi* were primarily intended to depict religious and spiritual concepts, not to provide accurate charts for travelers. In general, *mappae mundi* included illustrations of distant regions of the globe and populated them with figures who were important to Christian history, especially people who might be expected to play a role in the coming of the end of the world. Thus, medieval mapmakers placed Gog and Magog, the 10 lost tribes of Israel, the Magi, and the legendary king PRESTER JOHN on their maps. The maps also depicted fabulous MONSTERS and strange races of human beings, such as the Sciapodes, who had only one foot, which they stretched over their heads to shade themselves from the sun, and headless people whose faces were in their chests. Such maps, scholars assert, helped medieval Christians appreciate the wondrous powers of their God.

Mappae mundi generally depicted a round world, with water surrounding the known continents of Africa, Asia, and Europe. Some map readers argued that with such a round world, there must be only a short stretch of ocean separating Europe from Asia. Such maps and arguments helped convince CHRISTOPHER COLUMBUS that he could reach Asia by sailing west from Europe.

Further reading: Evelyn Edson, *Mapping Time and Space: How Medieval Mapmakers Viewed Their World* (London: British Library, 1977); Valerie I. J. Flint, *The Imaginative Landscape of Christopher Columbus* (Princeton, N.J.: Princeton University Press, 1992); William D. Phillips, Jr., and Carla Rahn Phillips, *The Worlds of Christopher Columbus* (Cambridge, U.K.: Cambridge University Press, 1991); R. V. Tooley, *Maps and Map-Makers,* 7th ed. (London: B. T. Batsford, 1987).

— Martha K. Robinson

marabout

Taken from the Arabic word *murabit,* the term *marabout* describes a variety of Muslim spiritual and political leaders active in spreading ISLAM through North and West Africa beginning in the 12th century.

Murabit originally identified only residents of the *ribat,* Muslim monastic communities in North Africa that flourished in the 12th century. As Islam gained followers across the Maghreb (North Africa), the term *marabout*

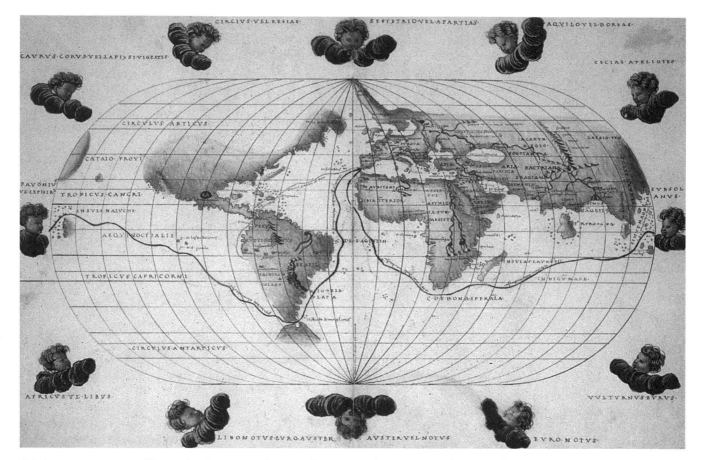

This large *mappae mundi* bears the date 1544, showing the tropics of Capricorn and Cancer, the Arctic and Antarctic Circles, and the nine winds   *(Hulton/Archive)*

expanded to include disciples of Islamic teachers, members of Sufi fraternities, and mystical spiritual teachers of Islam. By the 19th century *marabout* evolved to incorporate anyone associated with the orthodox Muslim faction in the religious wars in the SENEGAMBIA. Its development as a term illustrates the increasing and changing role of Islam in spiritual, cultural, and political life in North and West Africa.

The marabout, along with merchants and traders, played an essential role in the dispersion of Islam in the Maghreb. Seen as an alternative to the intellectual, elite Islam of urban Arab migrants, the marabout were known for their miracles and magic, gaining popularity especially among rural populations. Described as populist in their politics, the marabout became highly influential, gaining followers and integrating into regional political and social structures. Although they gained much popular support, some Islamic kingdoms, including the Almoravid dynasty in Morocco, persecuted them as heretics as early as the 12th century. Under the Almohad dynasty, successors to the Almoravids, the marabout gained power, increasing their

influence until the century, when they again faced persecution by Moroccan political and religious leaders.

While some marabout established themselves as resident teachers and spiritual leaders, becoming powerful leaders in Islamic dynasties, others remained wandering teachers, bringing Islam to rural areas. Part of their success came through their willingness and ability to incorporate pre-Islamic beliefs with the teachings of the Qur'an. This led to local variations among the marabout, following regional differences in indigenous spiritual practices. Despite these regional differences, the marabout remained priests and scholars of the Qur'an, making Islam the dominant political and spiritual force throughout North and West Africa by the end of the early modern period.

Further reading: Marían Aguían, "Marabout," in *Africana: The Encyclopedia of the African and African American Experience,* eds. Kwame Anthony Appiah and Henry Louis Gates, Jr. (New York: Basic *Civitas* Books, 1999), 1249–1250; Jean Boulegue and Jean Suret-Canale, "The Western Atlantic Coast," in *History of West Africa,* vol. 1, 3rd, eds. J. F. Ade Ajayi and Michael Crowder (London: Longman, 1985), 503–530; "Marabout," in *Dictionary of African Historical Biography,* 2nd ed., Mark R. Lipschutz and R. Kent Rasmussen (Berkeley: University of California Press, 1986), 136.

—Lisa M. Brady

Maravi

Called Malawi by the Portuguese who colonized their homeland, the Maravi controlled a powerful confederacy in the 15th and 16th centuries in what is today Malawi, Zambia, and Mozambique.

The Maravi, meaning "people of the fire flames," a heterogeneous group comprising several distinct ethnic groups such as the Chewa, Chipeta, and Nyanja, migrated to the area between the Shire and Zambezi Rivers from Katanga (now the Democratic Republic of the Congo) around the 13th century. By the 15th century they controlled a powerful alliance that dominated the ivory trade in the region. The Maravi Confederacy included connections with the Lundu peoples to the north and, after 1497 and the arrival of VASCO DA GAMA, the Portuguese. Ruled by hereditary kings from the Phiri clan, the Maravi Confederacy collected tribute in the form of grain, which was redistributed in times of famine. These kings also controlled the lucrative trade in ivory and iron, valuable goods demanded by Swahili traders engaged in markets along the eastern coast from Mogadishu to Mozambique. As the Portuguese made their way farther up the Zambezi River, they increased their trade with the Maravi peoples for guns, ammunition, cloth, and beads. Although this new avenue of trade brought the Maravi prosperity, it also brought conflict over who would control the trade in ivory and GOLD. The Maravi attempted to open new Trade routes to the Indian Ocean free from Portuguese interference by conquering Makua territory in Mozambique. Lundu opposition forced the Maravi Confederacy to ally with the Portuguese, resulting in a Lundu defeat and open access for the Maravi to the Indian Ocean. By the late 17th century the Maravi Confederacy was in decline and in the process of disintegrating into several smaller political entities.

Further reading: "Before European Colonization," in *Cambridge Encyclopedia of Africa,* eds. Roland Oliver and Michael Crowder (Cambridge, U.K.: Cambridge University Press, 1981), 77–155; "Malawi," in *Historical Dictionary of Malawi,* Cynthia A. Crosby (London: Scarecrow Press, 1993), 80–81; "Mozambique," in *Africana, The Encyclopedia of the African and African American Experience,* eds. Kwame Anthony Appiah and Henry Louis Gates, Jr. (New York: Basic *Civitas* Book, 1999), 1351–1356; Ari Nave, "Malawi," in, *Africana: The Encyclopedia of the African and African American Experience,* eds. Kwame Anthony Appiah

and Henry Louis Gates, Jr. (New York: Basic *Civitas* Books, 1999), 1229–1233; "The Peoples," in *Cambridge Encyclopedia of Africa,* eds. Oliver and Crowder, (Cambridge, U.K.: Cambridge University Press, 1981), 57–86.

— Lisa M. Brady

Martinique

One of the islands of the Lesser Antilles and originally inhabited by Island CARIB at the time of first contact with Europeans, Martinique eventually developed into one of France's most important SUGAR islands.

Island Carib disappeared from Martinique due to epidemics caused by the introduction of European DISEASES, for which the natives had no immunities, Spanish slave raiding (see SLAVE TRADE), and warfare with French colonists, who first settled Martinique in 1635. Because of active Island Carib resistance and little support from France, the colony grew slowly in its early years. Additionally, Dutch trading with the colonists limited French profits and hindered investments from France. Martinique's position was so precarious that in 1653 Carib almost drove the French from the island. Finally, from 1664 to 1674, the French government, under the guidance of the finance minister Jean-Baptiste Colbert, successfully initiated measures that promoted the production of sugar on the island, eliminated the Dutch trade with Martinique, and ended the Island Carib threat to the island. The importation of African slaves increased rapidly as Martinique's economy centralized on the production of sugar, and SLAVERY continued as the primary labor force until the institution was permanently abolished by French law in 1815.

Further reading: Nellis Maynard Crouse, *French Pioneers in the West Indies* (New York: Columbia University Press, 1940); William J. Eccles, *France in America,* rev. ed. (East Lansing: Michigan State University Press, 1990); Leo Elisabeth, "The French Antilles," in *Neither Slave Nor Free: The Freedman of African Descent in the Slave Societies of the New World,* eds. David W. Cohen and Jack P. Greene (Baltimore: Johns Hopkins University Press, 1972); Walter Adolphe Roberts, *The French in the West Indies* (New York: Bobbs Merrill, 1942).

— Dixie Ray Haggard

Mary I, queen of England (1496–1558)

First child of King HENRY VIII and later queen herself, Mary's attempts to bring England back to the Roman Catholic Church were to result in religious and political divisiveness in her kingdom.

Mary Tudor was born in 1496, the only of child of Henry VIII and his first wife, Catherine of Aragón, herself the daughter of the Spanish monarchs FERDINAND AND ISABELLA. Although she would eventually ascend the throne of England, her position was precarious throughout most of her life. She had lived in exile with her mother since childhood, a victim of her father's repudiation of her Catholic mother for the Protestant Anne Boleyn. Mary's lot was made even more difficult by the fact that she remained a fervent Catholic, even in the face of opposition by her father and his supporters and subsequently throughout the reign of her younger brother Edward and his ultra-Protestant guardians.

Edward died at a young age in 1553, leaving Mary next in line for the throne, according to her father's act of succession. However, the Protestant partisans who had enjoyed power throughout the reigns of both her brother and her father feared that the ascension of Catholic Mary would entail a loss of power for them and perhaps persecution for all Protestants in England. To forestall what they saw as impending disaster, the Protestant magnates, led by the earl of Northumberland, named Henry VIII's Protestant grandniece Jane Grey as queen. Mary resisted this usurpation, declaring herself queen and raising her supporters to take the throne. Support for the Protestant regime melted away at the news of Mary's sudden and immense following, and no battle for the throne ever took place. On July 19, less than two weeks after Edward's death, Mary was proclaimed queen.

Mary took the throne to widespread acclaim but proceeded to make blunders that alienated her subjects and prevented her from governing effectively. The first of her mistakes was to contract a marriage with PHILIP II of Spain. A Habsburg–Tudor match had been proposed when Mary was only six years old, to Philip's father, the young CHARLES V. The marriage was canceled when Henry set aside Mary's mother. On July 25, 1554, the alliance was renewed when Mary married Philip, a reluctant tool of his father's foreign policy, in which an alliance with the English was necessary for the defense of the Low Countries. Mary was looking for an ally in her plans to restore England to the Catholic Church as well as an heir who would continue her religious policy. The envisioned heir could also be counted on to protect the Low Countries from France, freeing up Don Carlos, Philip's son by a previous marriage, to concentrate on Spain and the Mediterranean. Unfortunately for the plans of both sides, Mary, 39 years old at the time of her marriage and rarely visited by her unenthusiastic spouse, never bore any children. In fact, far from solving England's deepening religious schism, the match only worsened it, making the Spaniards highly unpopular in England. English magnates had resisted the match, feeling that a foreign marriage—especially one to a power as strong as Spain—would reduce England to a subject position, much like Scotland's relationship to France. When the House of Commons petitioned against the match, Mary dissolved PARLIAMENT and went

through with the marriage on her own, alienating many supporters in the process. Resistance soon turned to open rebellion, resulting in the execution of 100 rebels as well as Jane Grey, whom Mary's supporters believed might become a flash point for future uprisings. Mary's supporters also urged her to execute her half sister Elizabeth on the same grounds, but although Mary imprisoned her in the Tower of London, she could never bring herself her to sign her execution warrant. In the end, Mary survived a major crisis early in her reign, but at the cost of identifying English Catholics with Spanish overlordship and Protestantism with anti-Spanish English patriotism.

Mary's other major mistake was to identify popular enthusiasm for her succession with support for the Catholic cause she championed. During the first year of her reign, she convinced Parliament to repeal most of the reforms from her brother Edward's reign, although with the stipulation that seized church properties be allowed to remain with their new owners. However, neither Parliament nor the people were ready to accept Catholicism as a state religion again. Protestantism continued to thrive underground, and Mary and her supporters responded by taking stronger action, eventually resulting in the public burnings of 286 Protestants, commemorated in FOXE'S BOOK OF MARTYRS. Mary's heavy-handed attempt to bring her subjects back to the Roman Church and the resultant publicity, far from achieving the desired effect, merely served to create sympathy for the Protestant cause and to deepen the religious divide between her subjects. This precarious religious situation was to be Mary's principal legacy to her half sister and successor, ELIZABETH I, when Mary died on November 17, 1558

Further reading: G. R. Elton, *England Under the Tudors,* 3rd ed. (New York: Routledge, 1991); David Loades, *Mary Tudor: A Life* (Oxford, U.K.: Oxford University Press, 1989); Robert Tittler, *The Reign of Mary I,* 2nd ed. (New York: Longman, 1991).

— Marie A. Kelleher

Massachusett

The Massachusett Indians, who probably had a precontact population of about 22,000, were among the first North American native peoples to have sustained contact with English settlers.

The Massachusett and their neighbors, including the Pequot, Mohegan, Wampanoag, Pokanoket, and Nipmuck, spoke related eastern ALGONQUIAN languages. Precontact boundaries between native peoples in the region are difficult to determine, but before contact the Massachusett apparently lived on the south side of Massachusetts Bay, between the Pawtucket to the north and the Pokanoket to the south.

Like other Indian groups in present-day southern New England, the Massachusett relied on a combination of farming, hunting, and gathering to obtain their food. Women planted and tended fields of CORN, beans, pumpkins, squash, TOBACCO, and sunflowers. They also gathered a wide variety of edible wild plants, including roots, strawberries, blackberries, grapes, walnuts, acorns, and chestnuts. Men used bows and arrows to hunt animals, particularly deer, but also bear, turkey, and other wildlife. Communities also relied on fish, shellfish, seals, and stranded whales.

The Massachusett moved seasonally within a restricted area in order to take advantage of resources available at different times of the year. In the spring they planted their fields, then moved to the banks of rivers or to the ocean to catch fish. They returned to harvest their fields in the autumn, and the harvest was followed by winter hunts. They did not move together as one large "tribe." Rather, groups of extended families moved together, coming together at some times of the year and splitting up at others.

The Massachusett lived in homes called wigwams. These were semicircular lodges formed by tying a circle of bent poles at the top and covering the resulting framework with woven mats or sheets of bark. The average wigwam was about 14 to 16 feet in diameter and could house two families. The Massachusett also sometimes built larger houses, which might be 100 feet long and 30 feet wide. These bark-covered longhouses could hold 40 to 50 people.

Political authority among the Massachusett was held by men (and sometimes women) known as sachems. A sachem was a village leader who held office through a combination of hereditary status and desirable personal qualities, including charisma, courage, and political skill. Sachems generally held office for life unless they lost the community's confidence. They led primarily through persuasion, and their coercive powers were limited. Although a few sachems were women, in general, Massachusett life was male-dominated. Men held greater authority both in politics and within the family, and residence patterns were commonly patrilocal.

Religious leaders, known as powwows, were important to the Massachusett. The Massachusett believed in two major deities, Kiehtan (or Chepian) and Hobbamock (or Abamacho), as well as other spiritual beings. Communities relied on powwows to interpret dreams, predict the future, and cure disease. They also believed that powwows could change their shape or take the form of an animal. The Massachusett respected the powwows for their ability to influence the spiritual world but also feared them, for the same power that allowed powwows to cure allowed them to cause DISEASE. A powwow who failed to protect the people from a disaster, such as an epidemic, might be accused of witchcraft.

The Massachusett probably first encountered Europeans in the early 16th century. European explorers who saw the Massachusett or nearby Indian groups include GIOVANN IDA VERRAZANO (1524), Bartholomew Gosnold (1602), Martin Pring (1603), and John Smith (1614). Between 1600 and 1620 the Massachusett and other New England Indian nations probably lost at least half their population to European disease, which made them less able to resist Puritan incursions into their lands.

Further reading: James Axtell, *The Invasion Within: The Contest of Cultures in Colonial North America* (New York: Oxford University Press, 1985); William Cronon, *Changes in the Land: Indians, Colonists, and the Ecology of New England* (New York: Hill & Wang, 1983); Karen Ordahl Kupperman, *Indians and English: Facing Off in Early America* (Ithaca, N.Y.: Cornell University Press, 2000); Howard S. Russell, *Indian New England Before the Mayflower* (Hanover, N.H.: University Press of New England, 1980); Bert Salwen, "Indians of Southern New England and Long Island: Early Period," in *Handbook of North American Indians*, William C. Sturtevant, gen. ed., vol. 15, *Northeast*, ed. Bruce G. Trigger (Washington, D.C.: Smithsonian Institution, 1978), 160–176.

— Martha K. Robinson

Maya

One of the most brilliant, sophisticated cultures of the ancient NEW WORLD, whose civilization encompassed the YUCATÁN PENINSULA, Guatemala, Belize, and Honduras.

The "discovery" of the Maya by modern scholars is an interesting story in and of itself. To most of the outside world, it was a "lost" civilization, despite the fact that almost 7 million Maya still live in their ancestral lands. Writer John L. Stephens visited many of the larger ruins in 1839, such as COPÁN, CHICHÉN ITZÁ, Uxmal, and PALENQUE. His travel writings became international best-sellers and led to scholarly interest in the Maya. Although the Maya ruins contained many carved hieroglyphs, archaeologists were unable to make sense of them. Sir Eric Thompson realized that many of the glyphs contained numbers and developed a hypothesis that the Maya were a peaceful people who were concerned only about the abstract movement of time, calenders, and mathematics. This vision of the Maya survived until the 1980s, when a new generation of scholars began investigating these people. In one of the 20th century's great scientific discoveries, scholars investigating the glyphs were able to crack the code, enabling them to translate Maya writing. These new advances, along with more sophisticated archaeological studies, have revolutionized our understanding of the Maya. Instead of being an ethereal, philosophical culture, it is clear that the Maya were a

Map legend:
- Ancient Mayan sites
- Modern cities
- BELIZE — Modern nations and borders
- Izapan culture

Maya Territory

Isla Cerritos
Dzibilchaltún
Mérida
Chichén Itzá
Coba
Uxmal
Kabah
Labna
Savil
Tulum
Isla Cozumel
Campeche
Edzna
Gulf of Mexico
NORTHERN LOWLANDS
Becan
Río Bec
MEXICO
Calakmul
Lamana
El Mirador
Nakbe
San José
Belize City
Palenque
Uaxacrun
Holmul
Piedras Negras
Tikal
Barton Ramie
BELIZE
SOUTHERN LOWLANDS
Taxchilan
Altar de Sacrificos
Bonampak
GUATEMALA
Naco
NORTHERN HIGHLANDS
HONDURAS
Izapa
Copán
Guatemala City
Kaminaljuyú
SOUTHERN HIGHLANDS
PACIFIC OCEAN
Monte Alto
EL SALVADOR

0 — 100 Miles
0 — 100 Kms

violent, complex people very much interested in the workings of the real world.

Brief Chronology

Archaeologists have divided the cultures of ancient MEXICO into three major periods: the preclassic (or formative), the classic, and the postclassic. The culture of the Maya spans all three of these periods, making it one of the longest-lasting in the region. The preclassic (roughly 1500 B.C. to A.D. 200) was an era of great experimentation that led to the development of many of the cultural traits that defined the later Maya culture. The Maya's slash-and-burn farming, in which community members cleared a field of trees and vegetation and then burned it to add a layer of nutrient-rich ash, provided sufficient food to support a growing popu-

lace. Maya leaders began to develop the symbols and rituals of kingship, borrowing heavily from their neighbors the OLMECS. These royal trappings remained remarkably stable over the centuries, with Maya kings using the same symbols of authority until the Spanish conquest. Maya religion also took shape during this time. The great Maya cities of the preclassic were Nak'be and El Mirador. The latter city was perhaps the largest Maya city ever built, containing enormous temples, raised platforms, and plazas. Its decline around A.D. 100 led to the development of new cities that flourished during the classic period.

Many developments that began in the preclassic reached their apogee in the classic era, which ran from A.D. 200 to 900. The population continued to grow, supported by intensive agricultural systems that converted many of the outlying regions into farmland. Moving away from simple slash-and-burn agriculture, the Maya constructed elaborate terracing systems, irrigation, and raised field networks to turn marginal areas into productive farmland. A number of Maya sites developed into densely populated cities, including Palenque, Dos Pilas, Kalakmul, Quiriguá, Copán, and TIKAL. The residents of these cities traded extensively among themselves and with many other regions of Mesoamerica. A clear example of this trend is that a number of Maya cities established contact with the great city of TEOTIHUACÁN in central Mexico, which led to cultural, religious, artistic, and military transformations across the region. The hallmark of this period was the development of writing. While it is clear that numerals, royal names, and city symbols had been developed many years before, it was in the classic period when true writing with syntax, complex signs, and grammar appeared. Through the decipherment of these texts, epigraphers have been able to chart the rise and fall of kings, the vicissitudes of war, and the religious beliefs of the Maya.

Around 900 the classic period came to an end. Written records abruptly cease, and over time the Maya abandoned their great cities in the lowlands. A great deal of scholarly attention has focused on the "collapse" of the classic Maya. Recent discoveries have shed light on this crucial era. It appears that as the population grew, competition between the cities also intensified. Warfare, which had been a highly ritualized affair, became more violent, destructive, and widespread. A number of cities engaged in what has been called "total war," which led to the wholesale destruction of sites. It seems that large-scale immigration away from the lowlands began at this time as residents fled from the demands of warmongering rulers and marauding armies.

The final era of the ancient Maya was the postclassic. While many archaeologists view this as a step backward in terms of culture, it is clear that many of the traditional elements of Maya society continued, although adapted to meet new circumstances. Most of the postclassic period was characterized by militarism. Postclassic Maya culture centered on two main areas: the Guatemalan highlands and the northern portion of the Yucatán Peninsula. In the highlands two powerful kingdoms emerged: the Quiché (K'iche') and the Kachiquels. Both were highly militaristic, containing heavily fortified cities and allowing a degree of upward social mobility for successful warriors. The kingdoms of the Yucatán were smaller but created a series of shifting military alliances to protect their interests. By the high standards of the classical era, art and architecture were of lesser quality. This period was also characterized by more extensive incursions by groups from central Mexico. Around 1000 the TOLTECS exerted considerable pressure on the northern Maya kingdoms, conquering Chichén Itzá and using it as a power base of their own. In the early 1500s the AZTECS began penetrating the Maya region. Evidence suggests that they captured the Putún Maya city of Xicallango in TABASCO as well as Xoconusco, a region of southern Guatemala, from which they put pressure on the Quiché. The postclassic ended with the Spanish conquest.

With the arrival of the Spaniards, the colonial era began. A popular misconception suggests that the Maya simply vanished after the Spaniards moved into the region, but the Spaniards had great difficulty in conquering and holding the Maya area. PEDRO DE ALVARADO succeeded in conquering the Quiché and Kachiquel kingdoms, but rebellions against Spanish rule in the Guatemalan highlands were so frequent that the area became known as the "Land of War." Francisco de Montejo had no better luck in the Yucatán. In both these areas the lack of precious metals and the tenacious resistance of the Maya forced the Spaniards to all but abandon the region. Essentially, the Maya continued to live on their ancestral lands following traditional customs with relatively little interference. The interior of the Maya area was not even tentatively conquered until quite late in the colonial period: The Itzá Maya kingdom of Tayasal (modern Flores, Guatemala) fell to the Spaniards in 1697, almost 200 years after the Spaniards first arrived.

Political Structure

The modern understanding of the Maya's political systems has changed rapidly in recent years. Earlier, scholars believed that the Maya kingdoms were small, peaceful entities ruled by a "philosopher king." Decipherment of the Maya's writing system has allowed for a fuller, more realistic assessment. Unlike the Aztecs and INCAS, the Maya did not have a single empire ruled over by a single ruler. Maya kingdoms were smaller, more along the lines of the city-states of Renaissance Italy. The kingdoms consisted of forests, farmland, and outlying villages that were all ruled from a larger capital city. The urban centers were densely populated, and residents used much of the surrounding land for intensive agricultural purposes. Most kingdoms were divided into provinces of some sort, with a noble of royal lineage set up as a local magistrate or governor. A small number of states became more powerful and absorbed a number of their neighbors to form larger "empires." The most powerful of these empires during the classic era were Tikal and its rival, Kalakmul. To achieve greater power and position, many Maya kingdoms formed alliances with distant kingdoms. This strategy secured borders or trade routes and provided a defense against a potentially hostile state. Tikal and Kalakmul both tried to use alliance networks to outflank each other, often urging their surrogates to fight wars on their behalf.

At the center of each kingdom was the holy king, called the *ahaw* (or *ahau*). Like the pharaohs of Egypt, these *ahaws* were sacred—the living embodiment of the gods. As

A monument to Mayan warriors, from Oaxaca in Mexico (Hulton/Archive)

such, they were able to communicate directly with the gods, petitioning for the gods' continuing benevolence. The sacred aspect of the *ahaw* ensured that bloodlines were strictly guarded. Both men and women inherited this divine blood, and marriages were arranged so that heirs would have as much of this sacred element as possible. The *ahaw* held absolute power within the kingdom. At times he would consult with counsels of elders (who were usually princes of the blood), but in his guise as divine representative his word was final. The *ahaw* was expected to be a competent general and bring military glory to his realm. Frequently, he celebrated his ascension to power by attacking a rival kingdom in order to capture victims for sacrifice. He was also expected to pray and offer sacrifices on behalf of his people. In ceremonies of national importance or in times of national emergencies, the *ahaw* would perform a series of blood-letting ceremonies. After days of fasting, he would pierce his tongue, ears, or penis with a knife or stingray spine and pass a rope of thorns through the wound. The object was to splatter the blood onto sacred strips of paper, which were then burned over ritual fires of incense. The Maya believed that visions of gods or ancestral spirits would appear in the smoke and communicate with the *ahaw*. These bloodletting rituals were the fundamental connection between the people, their ruler, and the gods.

Religion

One of the most pervasive elements of Maya religion was the idea that the cosmos was governed by cycles of time that were constantly in motion. Some of these cycles were very long, while others were brief. In practical terms this meant that nothing truly ended, and nothing truly began. The cosmos was created, later destroyed, only to be created anew. Agricultural gods died but through their death ensured rebirth of new crops. On the human level parents died, but children continued their legacy on earth. Death and destruction were never permanent, nor was life eternal. All people, gods, and events were bound on a great cosmic wheel that turned endlessly. The present creation, just one in an endless series, began August, 13, 3114 B.C. It is not clear why the Maya chose this particular date, as the first recognizable Maya villages did not appear for thousands of years afterward. Nevertheless, they considered this point the beginning of the present cycle of creation, which would end on December 23, 2012. The Maya felt that the end of the great cycle would not bring about an absolute Apocalypse, but the death of this era of creation would serve to give birth to a new one.

The importance of these cycles is evident in the *Popol Vuh,* a great compendium of Maya thought and belief written down shortly after the Spanish conquest. In this work humans were not simply created ex nihilo. First, the gods experimented by making people of mud. These specimens were imperfect and ultimately destroyed. Later, the gods fashioned new humans from wood. These, too, proved inadequate and, again, needed to be destroyed. Finally, the gods made people from their own flesh. They were the most successful, although the act of creation greatly weakened the gods themselves. Therefore, it became the duty of humans to make sacrifices to the gods, who continued to support the cosmos.

Unfortunately, the Maya gods themselves remain poorly understood. The main problem in understanding the roles and characteristics of the Maya gods has been that most of the information regarding them dates from the postconquest period and was often colored by the prejudices of the Spanish missionaries who recorded information from indigenous informants. There were as many as 166 named gods in the pantheon, although their duties and spheres of influence were seldom mentioned in the texts that have survived. Moreover, it is clear that there were vast religious differences between Maya regions. At the time of the conquest, Kukulcán, the Feathered Serpent, was an important royal god in the Yucatán, but it seems clear that he was a Maya version of the central Mexican god QUETZALCÓATL brought by Toltec invaders in the 10th century. Therefore, he was all but unknown in the Maya cities to the south during the classic era. Several of the Maya gods had some connection with food and fertility, which is not surprising in a culture that depended on intensive agriculture. One of the oldest, most important Maya gods was Chak, the rain god. It is possible that he was adopted from the Olmecs during the preclassic period. Whatever his origin, Chak the Thunderer was among the most venerated and most frequently depicted of Maya gods; his cult has survived to the present day.

One final aspect of Maya religion was its preoccupation with Xibalba, the underworld. For the Maya, Xibalba was a bleak, watery realm where most living things went after they died. Even the sun and the moon passed through this dismal land on their constant journeys through the skies. Caverns and pools of water were seen as gateways to this dark land and thus became both venerated and feared. Among the most frequently depicted gods in Maya art were the nightmarish Lords of Xibalba—nine lords of death, disease, and filth who were the constant scourge of humans. Many of these images survive in tombs, depicted in ceramics, paintings, and royal carvings, either alone or in conjunction with the Hero Twins, who defeated them in one of the most memorable sections of the *Popol Vuh*.

The Maya Writing System

The Maya writing system was the most fully developed in the Americas. Other cultures, such as the Zapotecs, Mixtecs, and Aztecs developed rudimentary writing, but the

Maya had an integrated system that used complex grammar. Much of the writing dealt with religion. The texts were in books made of long strips of beaten bark paper, folded accordion-style to make individual pages. For the most part these books were religious almanacs that listed the cycles of the sun, moon, and Venus, ascribing ritual significance to the days, and explaining which gods were associated with the various cycles. Only four books of this type have survived from the Maya area. Many decayed naturally in the hot, tropical climate of the Maya region, but most were destroyed by Spanish missionaries, who felt they were heretical and ordered them burned. Maya also used writing to commemorate completed cycles of time. Maya rulers set up stone monuments to mark important anniversaries of the Maya calendar. These monuments have helped clarify the reigns of Maya kings and have provided some of the most notable Maya sculpture in existence.

The majority of Maya texts, historical in nature, were carved on stone monuments, plaques, and tomb walls. These texts detail the great events of rulers' lives, list the *ahaws'* ancestors, and relate the great deeds of former rulers as well. This material has helped scholars to reconstruct Maya political history and to understand the relationships among Maya states. The texts also describe the great rituals of the Maya world, particularly those associated with coronation and warfare. These monuments at times create problems for scholars because they often discuss the reigns of certain rulers, leaving large gaps in the historical record. Additionally, these monuments list only the important moments of an *ahaw's* life. It would be much like trying to reconstruct the life of Abraham Lincoln based on the inscribed text of the Lincoln Memorial. Further, because the chroniclers tended to depict their rulers in a favorable light, much of the writing consists of propaganda. Readers who encounter descriptions of the length of an *ahaw's* reign, his conquests, and his lineages must cross-reference particular parts to ensure that the information is accurate.

All surviving evidence confirms that the Maya were a highly sophisticated people living in ancient Mesoamerica. They developed an advanced system of writing and calendrics, which has allowed modern scholars to unravel the mysteries of Maya history. Although their civilization had been in long decline by the time the Spaniards arrived, they were much more successful than most native groups in resisting the Spanish CONQUISTADORES and maintaining their culture under Spanish rule. They continue to survive today, with more than 7 million Maya living in Mexico and Central America.

Further reading: *General works:* Michael Coe, *The Maya,* 6th ed. (London: Thames & Hudson, 1999); Robert J. Sharer, *The Maya,* 5th ed. (Stanford, Calif.: Stanford University Press, 1994); Linda Schele and David Freidel, *A Forest of Kings: The Untold Story of the Maya* (New York: William Morrow, 1990); Gene S. Stuart and George E. Stuart, *Lost Kingdoms of the Maya* (Washington D.C.: National Geographic Society, 1993). *On Maya religion:* Linda Schele, David Freidel, and Joy Parker, *Maya Cosmos: Three Thousand Years on the Shaman's Path* (New York: William Morrow, 1993); Dennis Tedlock, ed. *Popol Vuh: The Maya Book of the Dawn of Life* (New York: Simon & Schuster, 1985). *On Maya art:* Linda Schele and Mary Ellen Miller, *The Blood of Kings: Dynasty and Ritual in Maya Art* (Fort Worth, Tex.: Kimbell Art Museum, 1983). *On Maya writing:* Michael Coe, *Breaking the Maya Code* (London: Thames & Hudson, 1992). *On the Maya after the conquest:* Nancy M. Farriss, *Maya Society Under Colonial Rule* (Princeton, N.J.: Princeton University Press, 1984).

— Scott Chamberlain

Mbundu

Despite heavy involvement in the SLAVE TRADE with the Portuguese, the Mbundu resisted Portuguese attempts at colonization of their territory throughout the 16th and 17th centuries.

Mbundu oral tradition describes how three separate Bantu-speaking ethnic groups migrated in the 15th century from central and east central Africa to the northern coast of present-day Angola and coalesced into a larger single ethnic group. The Mbundu ancestors brought with them sophisticated ironmaking techniques, an agricultural tradition, and a unifying belief in a divine kingship. *Ngola,* or lineage emblems passed down in matrilineal succession, formed the basis of the Mbundu political structure. By 1500 the Ndongo monarchy, largest of the Mbundu kingdoms, established its capital at Kabasa. The Ndongo had a three-part mixed economy based on agriculture, artisanry, and trade.

Proximity to the coast and control of major trade routes brought the Ndongo into contact with Portuguese traders early in the 16th century. In 1520 the Portuguese issued a royal decree requiring Mbundu conversion to Christianity. Catholic missionaries established a mission near present-day Luanda, but the Mbundu of Ndongo proved indifferent to the new religion, unlike their Kongo counterparts to the north. The Ndongo king was interested in trading with the Europeans, not in adopting their religion, and outlawed preaching of the gospel. Later Ndongo rulers, such as NZINGA, also resisted Portuguese colonization but desired to maintain trade relationships with the Europeans. The major source of trade between the Mbundu and the Portuguese was in humans bound for the transatlantic slave trade. Resistance to and participation in the slave trade destroyed many of the Mbundu kingdoms, including the Ndongo, whose capital fell to the Portuguese in 1669.

Further reading: Eric Young, "Mbundu," in *Africana: The Encyclopedia of the African and African American Experience,* eds. Kwame Anthony Appiah and Henry Louis Gates, Jr. (New York: Basic *Civitas* Books, 1999), 1280; "The Peoples," in *Cambridge Encyclopedia of Africa,* eds. Roland Oliver and Michael Crowder (Cambridge, U.K.: Cambridge University Press, 1981), 57–86.

— Lisa M. Brady

Mecca

The holiest of cities in the Islamic world, Mecca was the birthplace of Muhammad and served in the 16th century, as it does now, as the primary destination for Muslims making the hajj (pilgrimage) in accordance with the tenets of ISLAM.

Centuries before Islam's founding, Mecca was a trading town on the caravan routes through the part of the Arabian Peninsula known as the Hijaz. Arabic for "barrier," the Hijaz is part of a geologic fault between Africa and Asia. Its landscape, formed in part by volcanic activity, sustains little vegetation except in isolated areas. Although bounded by mountains on the east, and despite its forbidding climate and topography, the Hijaz was in a prime location to access various trade routes of the Red Sea, which formed its western edge. Mecca, most likely founded in the fifth century by one of Muhammad's ancestors, Qusayy ibn Kilab, became a trading center by the sixth century, but its importance stemmed less from its commercial activity than from its connection to the Ka'ba—a local shrine built near the famous well of Zamzam.

The Ka'ba, which means cube, is a small, houselike structure reputedly built by Abraham and his son Ishmael, but probably built by Arab pagans in the first or second century. It has as its cornerstone a small black stone of meteoric origins and was already a place of pilgrimage and worship for numerous local and regional religions, including Christianity, by the time of Mecca's founding. The shrine's draw as a pilgrimage site proved to be lucrative for the traders who controlled the *haram,* or the sacred area of the shrine. These traders were the Quraysh, Muhammad's ancestors. When Muhammad began preaching against the practice of any religion but Islam, which forbids the worship of any god but Allah (the Muslim word for God), he was forced out of Mecca because his teachings threatened the continuance of the lucrative pilgrimage. Muhammad went north to escape from his persecutors in 622 to the trading city of Yathrib, renamed Medinat an-Nabi, or Medina, "City of the Prophet." This flight to Medina, called the *hijrah,* marks the beginning of the Muslim

calendar and the beginning of Medina's rank as the second holy of Islam. Muhammad returned to Mecca at the head of an army, defeating the Meccan army at the battle of Badr in 623. He removed all idols from the Ka'ba, claiming it for the sole use of Muslims, and established it as the primary pilgrimage site for all who adhere to Islam.

Mecca's importance as a pilgrimage site increased as Islam spread to Africa, Asia, and Europe. From the 13th to the 16th century, Mecca was under the control of the Islamic Mamluk Empire of Egypt, whose links to Spain, North Africa, the SUDAN, India, and Malaysia encouraged greater pilgrimage numbers from those areas. Perhaps the most famous hajj was that of MANSA MUSA I of MALI in 1324, during which this African king distributed so much GOLD in Cairo on his way to Mecca that he depressed the gold market in the Egyptian city. By the end of the 15th century, 30,000 to 40,000 pilgrims gathered annually in Cairo to make the hajj, 20,000 to 30,000 in Damascus, and smaller numbers traveled via other cities linked to the Hijaz.

From early on Mecca was closed to all but the faithful. This situation became more important with the growing threat of *renegados* (adventurers) to the Hijaz after the opening of the sea route around the Cape of Good Hope by VASCO DA GAMA. One of these *renegados,* Ludovico di Varthema from Bologna, disguised himself as a Mamluk and traveled through the Muslim holy land in 1503. He visited the Prophet's tomb in Medina, made the hajj to Mecca, and left the first account of the cities written by a European, included in collections of travel accounts edited by RICHARD HAKLYUT THE YOUNGER. Di Varthema's tales were inaccurate on some counts (he described two "unicorns" kept in a pen near the Ka'ba) but were nonetheless important descriptions of the cities, the hajj, and the pilgrims themselves. In 1517 the Ottoman Empire took control of the Hijaz and the holy cities, which opened the region to greater European contact. The Ottomans, under SULEIMAN I conquered large areas of southern and eastern Europe, taking slaves from the region and converting them to Islam. Some of these European slaves were taken to the Muslim holy land either to sell or as part of the entourages of those making the pilgrimage to Mecca. Much of European understanding of the Hijaz during this period came from the accounts of these enslaved Europeans.

Further reading: Albert Hourani, *A History of the Arab Peoples* (Cambridge, Mass.: Belknap Press of Harvard University Press, 1991); F. E. Peters, *Mecca: A Literary History of the Muslim Holy Land* (Princeton: N.J. Princeton University Press, 1994); John Sabini, *Armies in the Sand: The Struggle for Mecca and Medina* (London: Thames & Hudson, 1981).

— Lisa M. Brady

Mendoza, Antonio de (1490–1552)

The first viceroy of NEW SPAIN, who was instrumental in establishing the colonial administration of the Spanish empire in the Western Hemisphere, Mendoza also set the standard to which all subsequent officials aspired.

Mendoza was born in Granada, Spain, in 1490, the son of a powerful aristocratic family. He began his career as a diplomat in the court of CHARLES V, serving as an administrator and royal ambassador in Flanders and Hungary. His actions suggest that he was intensely loyal to the king and frequently used his talents to strengthen royal authority wherever he worked. He was intelligent and a skilled politician, which allowed him to rise through the ranks of the bureaucracy without making powerful enemies. He had become a trusted adviser to the king, and his talents and political finesse made him a natural selection in 1535 to be the first viceroy of the newly conquered territories in MEXICO.

From the beginning Mendoza realized he had an extremely dangerous task. New Spain had only recently been conquered, and several native groups were all too willing to rebel against Spanish rule. Moreover, the CONQUISTADORES were ranging across the area, ransacking villages and setting themselves up as regional powers in their own right. HERNÁN CORTÉS was particularly dangerous; the Crown was deathly afraid that this charismatic leader was becoming too powerful and too independent. Thus, Mendoza had the difficult job of establishing royal authority, developing the colony, pacifying the natives, and slowly quieting the conquistadores.

In many regards Mendoza succeeded admirably. He promoted the creation of royal officials such as the CORREGIDOR, which would reign in the powers of the CABILDOS and monitor the ENCOMIENDAS of the region. Mendoza enhanced the power of the royal treasury by improving record keeping, creating a mint in Mexico City, and streamlining the collection of taxes and tribute. He also codified laws regarding the SILVER trade and built a foundry in the capital. Concerned with the plight of the natives, he curtailed the activities of the conquistadores, attempted to regulate native working conditions, constructed a school for sons of the indigenous nobility, and made it a point to hear their grievances regularly. He also sponsored further explorations of NEW MEXICO, Guatemala, and the YUCATÁN PENINSULA, in part to occupy the time of some of the more restless conquistadores. Finally, he commissioned native informants to produce a document that would inform Charles about his newly conquered subjects: the Codex Mendoza. Today, the Codex Mendoza is one of the most important sources of information regarding the culture and politics of the former Aztec Empire.

In order to maintain royal power, Mendoza at times had to go against the express wishes of the king. For example, Mendoza realized that Charles's elimination of the *encomiendas* in 1542 could lead to open rebellion in New Spain, as it had in PERU. Hoping to defuse the situation, he developed a political philosophy that is best expressed in his famous statement—"I obey but I will not comply." In other words, while maintaining his loyalty to the Crown, he would not implement any law that would seriously undermine royal authority. Instead, he would send royal orders back to Spain for "clarification" or bury them in bureaucratic paperwork. As time went on, he became more and more cautious of passing controversial laws and delayed action on issues he considered "reckless." While caution was not necessarily a bad thing, it did create a tradition whereby the government often avoided taking decisive action. At the end of his term in office, he proudly proclaimed a maxim that became a mantra for future viceroys: "I did little, and I did it slowly." The Crown assigned him to become the viceroy of Peru in 1551, but he died a year later.

Mendoza became the ideal royal bureaucrat. Subsequent viceroys followed his political philosophies and closely examined his legal briefs and opinions. In office Mendoza stabilized the government, helped develop the colony, and maintained good order. On the negative side, his actions produced substantial bureaucratic tangles that tended to limit the effectiveness of the government he helped create.

Further reading: Arthur S. Aiton, *Antonio de Mendoza, First Viceroy of New Spain* (Durham, N.C.: Duke University Press, 1927); Frances F. Berdan and Patricia Rieff Anawalt, *The Essential Codex Mendoza* (Berkeley: University of California Press, 1997); Michael C. Meyer and William L. Sherman, *The Course of Mexican History* (Oxford, U.K.: Oxford University Press, 1995).

— Scott Chamberlain

Mercator, Gerhardus (1512–1594)

A geographer, Mercator pioneered the 16th-century boom in mapmaking while also contributing to Europeans' better understanding of the earth's spherical nature.

A pair of 15th-century events led to the 16th-century evolution and growth of the mapmaking business. Leading the way was the rediscovery of Ptolemy's *Geography*, an event that advanced the profession of the mapmaker, making theirs a respectable trade. In addition, JOHANNES GENSFLEISCH ZUM GUTENBERG's Bible, printed with moveable type (see PRINTING PRESS), first rolled off the presses in 1454. Shortly thereafter, printers produced illustrative maps combined with texts, offering readers a rich combination of geographical images, illustrations, and printed material about sea voyages and exotic places in

Gerhardus Mercator   *(Hulton/Archive)*

convenient packages during the age of growing curiosity and discovery. Ptolemy's *Geography* led the way, possessing all the requirements of a beautiful book and a saleable product, all the while spreading knowledge about the planet. Printers turned out seven folio editions of the *Geography,* cementing its place in the geographical canon well into the 16th century.

Born in Flanders, Mercator studied philosophy and theology at the University of Louvain before turning to studies of mathematics and astronomy. Combined, the disciplines served him well as he added the skills of engraving, instrument making, and surveying to his résumé. In 1537, at the age of 25, he produced a small-scale map of Palestine. Over the next three years he worked on a map of Flanders. Emperor CHARLES V was so impressed with the end product that he commissioned Mercator to make a terrestrial globe.

Because of religious fanaticism, Mercator found Louvain of the 1540s a dangerous place. Ruled by the Catholic regent Mary, the queen dowager of Hungary, Flanders was a hotbed of persecution. In 1544 authorities caught Mercator and 42 others in a roundup of suspected Lutherans. Two of the accused were buried alive, two burned at the

stake, and one beheaded. Although all were supposed to be burned at the stake, the officials offered those willing to repent an escape from the torture. Instead, the men would be put to death by sword and the women buried alive. While imprisoned and awaiting his fate for months, Mercator was saved by the efforts of a parish priest who lobbied for and secured his release. Cognizant of the best route out of the area, Mercator left for safer territory.

In 1552 Mercator was invited to become professor of cosmography at a new university in the Prussian town of Duisburg on the Rhine. After the professorship failed to materialize, he assumed the duties of cosmographer to the duke of Cleves. He settled permanently in Duisburg, producing the first modern maps of Europe and Great Britain. In 1568 he published *Mercator's Chronology . . . from the beginning of the world up to 1568, done from eclipses and astronomical observations.* One year later he unveiled his highly influential first world map based on the projection he invented. Building from knowledge based on Ptolemy's grid of latitudes and longitudes, Mercator imagined the lines of longitude to be like cuts on an orange. This allowed him to peel the segments off the rind and lay them down next to one another on a table, thus allowing sailors to align their compass projections while gazing at a rectangular sheet of paper laid out on a table. Using this process, the shapes on the surface could keep their form, although their dimensions were slightly enlarged.

Along with his map of the world, Mercator established a new standard for map engraving and lettering. With the help of Abraham Ortelius, Aegidiuss Hooftman, and Chrisophe Plantin, Mercator and his friends helped bring forth the first modern, marketable atlas. An early version of the new medium rolled off Plantin's Antwerp presses in 1570. Theirs was a product with immediate commercial success. Appearing in more than 40 editions by 1612, the atlas was translated into Latin, German, Dutch, French, Spanish, English, and Italian. Combined, the early cartographers, map makers, and printers brought the discoveries of CHRISTOPHER COLUMBUS, FERDINAND MAGELLAN, AMERIGO VESPUCCI, VASCO NÚÑEZ DE BALBOA, and others to countless people once the atlas became portable, although early versions adorned with fancy binding became expensive showpieces on noble and royal bookshelves.

Mercator had planned a three-volume atlas, of which he published two parts before his death in 1594. Mercator's son Rumold completed the project under the title *Atlas, or cosmographical meditations upon the creation of the universe and the universe as created.*

Further reading: Leo Bagrow, *History of Cartography* (Chicago: Precedent, 1985); Lloyd A. Brown, *The Story of Maps* (Boston: Little, Brown, 1949); Robert W. Karrow, Jr., *Mapmakers of the Sixteenth Century and their maps:*

Biobibliography of the cartographers of Abraham Ortelius, 1570 (Chicago: Speculum Orbis Press, 1993); John N. Wilford, *The Mapmakers,* rev. ed. (New York: Knopf, 2000).

— Matt Lindamann

mestizaje

An initial shortage of Spanish women and families in 16th-century Latin America, combined with the increasing reliance on imported African slaves by Spanish settlers, contributed to the widespread practice of *mestizaje* (interracial sexual relations).

According to some estimates, the proportion of Spanish women to Spanish men never exceeded 10 per 100 in colonial Latin America. Most married Spanish men left their wives behind in Europe, and of the small number of Spanish women who journeyed to the NEW WORLD during the 16th century, many encountered great difficulty in adjusting to the high altitude (the Andean plains) or to the tropics. As a result, reproduction among the Spanish proved almost nonexistent during the early years of conquest and colonization. Largely because of the low numbers of available Spanish women adapted to the rigors of life in the Western Hemisphere, the first *criollo* (an individual of European parentage born in the Americas) birth in POTOSÍ did not occur until 53 years after the initial conquest. In the absence of Spanish women, beginning with the CONQUISTADORES, Spanish men engaged in sexual relations with and in some cases married native women.

The acceptance of the practice of concubinage (the cohabitation of persons not legally married) also contributed to the pervasiveness of *mestizaje*. While indigenous women were sometimes forced or coerced into sexual relations with Spanish men, Indians also offered female daughters and wives as gifts or tribute to the Spanish, usually with the intent of consolidating amiable relations with the conquistadores. In turn, particularly during the early years of conquest and settlement, Spanish men took Indian women of good lineage as their wives. Although the Spanish benefited from such relationships, through their associations with the Spanish, Native women enjoyed certain advantages as well, particularly when the Spanish men legitimized their MESTIZO children by embracing them in their homes and wills. More frequently, however, interracial relationships were more casual in nature, including, but not limited to, concubinage. For example, records indicate that Spanish men in 16th-century Paraguay kept up to 20 to 30 Indian women as concubines.

The complex, confusing terminology developed and used by Spanish settlers to describe the various racial amalgamations hints at the pervasiveness of *mestizaje* in the Western Hemisphere. Although perhaps the most prevalent type, interracial sexual relationships between Indians

and Spaniards were not the only type of *mestizaje* in early Latin America. The Spanish began to import Africans as a primary labor source in the colonies more extensively and at a much earlier date than did their English counterparts. Moreover, because the number of available Spanish women remained low, Spanish-African *mestizaje* grew to be a very common practice. With the introduction of Africans to various parts of Latin America, the term ZAMBO came to refer to the Indian-African mixture. Still, the most widespread racial mixture during the 16th century, mestizo, referred to persons of Indian-white parentage. The second generation born following the arrival of the Spanish included *castizos,* individuals of mestizo-white mixture.

At times during the 16th century, the Spanish Crown, although ideally in favor of marriage between Spanish men and Spanish women, promoted intermarriage. Under penalty of losing their ENCOMIENDAs, the Crown instructed married men to send for their wives still living in Spain and for unmarried settlers to marry within three years of their arrival in the Americas. On occasion such a policy led to formalization of unions between Indian women and Spanish men. In contrast, the Crown strongly opposed intermarriage of persons of African descent with either Spanish or Indian persons. Royal authority, the church, and local ordinances worked to prohibit the most prevalent type of *mestizaje* involving blacks, that between Spanish men and African-descended black female slaves, although such relations persisted throughout the colonial years, especially when the Spanish imported more African slaves as a source of sustainable labor.

Further reading: Claudio Esteva-Fabregat, *Mestizaje in Ibero-America,* trans. John Wheat (Tucson: University of Arizona Press, 1995); Magnus Mörner, *Race Mixture in the History of Latin America* (Boston: Little, Brown, 1967); Gary B. Nash, "The Hidden History of Mestizo America," *Journal of American History* 82:3 (December 1995): 941–964.

— Kimberly Sambol-Tosco

mestizo

The initial shortage of Spanish women and families in 16th-century Latin America contributed to frequent occurrences of MESTIZAJE (interracial sexual relations), and as a result, many mestizos (mixed-race persons of Indian and Spanish parentage).

Interracial sexual relations, far more prevalent in colonial Latin America than in British North America, produced a large, racially diverse stratum in the area under Spanish influence. The Spanish devised nomenclature to distinguish among the various amalgamations resulting from sexual relationships among persons of European, African, and Native

American descent. Terms used to denote racial differences included, among others: mestizo, or Indian-white mixture; *castizo,* mestizo-white mixture; and ZAMBO, Indian-African mixture. Although seemingly firm categories, the Spanish applied such labels in a casual and unpredictable way, basing most assumptions on skin color. In addition, settlers in different regions of Latin America used different terms for similar hybrids. For example, settlers used the term *zambo* in MEXICO but used *chino* in BRAZIL to refer to individuals of Indian-African heritage.

The majority of mestizo individuals were the products of unions between Spanish men and Indian women, and a large percentage of the mestizo population resulted from casual sexual encounters and concubinage. Nevertheless, some Spanish males married Indian women. In such cases the Spaniards benefited through the acquisition of land rights or other tribute from the woman's family. In a number of cases Spanish men acknowledged their mestizo children by providing an inheritance and/or rearing them in the white community, but as a general rule, particularly during the late colonial period, most fathers did not welcome their mixed-race children. As a result, many mestizos made lives for themselves as part of the Indian community of their mothers. Others traveled to Europe, where they sought low-level positions on the outskirts of the Spanish economy as part of the church or state bureaucracy.

As a whole, mestizo men and women fared better in colonial society than did their Indian counterparts. They tended to occupy more skilled positions and roles, such as that of a master artisan, in which they supervised or delegated tasks to others. Such fluidity existed to a larger extent during the early years of conquest and colonization, when Spanish men more regularly acknowledged their mestizo children and thus gave them many of the privileges enjoyed by whites. Nevertheless, as the mixed-race population grew over the course of the 16th and 17th centuries, the social status of mestizos declined.

In the racial hierarchy devised by the Spanish, the mestizo population ranked above Indians and African-descended individuals but below the Spanish. During the mid-16th century the Spanish Crown issued various orders that linked mestizos with unemployment, poor instruction, adultery, and other crimes. During the later years of the century, the Crown continued to characterize mestizo individuals as a "vicious and lost people" whose very existence jeopardized the colonial social order.

During the 17th century free mixed-race individuals represented a growing presence in rural areas and the largest group in most mining districts and urban centers. As early as 1650, due primarily to the relatively small number of Spaniards who immigrated to the Americas, mestizos outnumbered Spaniards in NEW SPAIN.

Further reading: Mark A. Burkholder and Lyman L. Johnson, *Colonial Latin America,* 3rd ed. (New York: Oxford University Press, 1998); Claudio Esteva-Fabregat, *Mestizaje in Ibero-America,* trans. John Wheat (Tuscon: University of Arizona Press, 1995); Magnus Mörner, *Race Mixture in the History of Latin America* (Boston: Little, Brown, 1967); Gary B. Nash, "The Hidden History of Mestizo America," *Journal of American History* 82:3 (December 1995): 941–964.

— Kimberly Sambol-Tosco

Mexico

Mexico is the modern term for a country that at one time was the site of several ancient empires, as well as the core of the Spanish Empire in North America.

The name *Mexico* is derived from the AZTECS' name for themselves (the *Mexica*) and was a shortened reference to their capital city of TENOCHTITLÁN. After the conquest HERNÁN CORTÉS rebuilt the city, retaining this nickname as its official name. The Spanish called the colony as a whole NEW SPAIN. *Mexico* was not used to denote the country until after it gained independence from Spain in 1821. In recent years there has been a new use for the term. Modern archaeologists frequently use the term *Mexican* to refer to the non-MAYA peoples of northern Mesoamerica, such as the Aztecs, TOLTECS, and TARASCAN.

Mexico is a large, geographically diverse area. The main geographical feature of the country is the Mexican Plateau, also known as the central highlands. Throughout history this area has had the greatest concentration of human settlements. The highlands are shaped like a large "V," with the tip some miles to the south of Mexico City and the arms continuing northward to the border with the modern-day United States. Except at its outer edges, the area is mostly level. Elevations are highest in the southern part of this zone (8,000 feet) and lowest at the U.S. border (4,000 feet). While the southern part of this zone (around Mexico City) receives adequate rainfall, the north is considerably drier and characterized by extensive deserts. The Southern Highlands begin at the Pacific Ocean and run north, including the modern-day Mexican states of Oaxaca and Guerrero. Mountain peaks in this region are at about 8,000 feet. Since most of the region is mountainous, humans have tended to congregate in small valleys that lie around 3,000 feet. The Gulf Coastal Plain is another major geographic zone, running from the Rio Grande in the north to the YUCATÁN PENINSULA. It is a low-lying region that is wet and swampy in the south, becoming drier in the north. VERACRUZ and TABASCO are two of the most important subregions in this large area. The final major area of Mexico is the Yucatán Peninsula, consisting of the modern-day Mexican states of Campeche, Yucatán, and Quintana Roo. This is a large, flat table of limestone that is dry in the north and wetter in the south.

This range of geographical zones has given rise to a number of distinct cultures. Mexico is part of a large cultural area called Mesoamerica by modern anthropologists. This region covers most of modern-day Mexico along with Guatemala and parts of El Salvador, Honduras, Nicaragua, and Costa Rica. The arid borderlands in the north before 1492 were mostly peopled by nomadic hunters and gatherers. The center of the country, dominated by the Mexican Plateau, saw the rise of complex agricultural societies and eventually large empires such as the Aztecs. In the south broken topography and scattered valleys led to the development of small city-states focused mostly on the fertile valley floors. Both the low-lying Tabasco and Yucatán regions were home to the Maya people.

Mexico was the most important region within New Spain, containing most of the educational, health, and economic infrastructure. Arts such as music, metalworking, painting, and architecture thrived and were the equal of those in Europe. Mexico City itself remained one of the largest cities in Spanish America throughout the colonial period. The SILVER mines in ZACATECAS were crucial to the colonial economy of New Spain and the Spanish Empire as a whole. Throughout the colonial period Mexico was one of the most developed, most densely populated regions of the New World.

Further reading: Peter Gerhard, *A Guide to the Historical Geography of New Spain* (Norman: University of Oklahoma Press, 1993); Michael C. Meyer and William L. Sherman, *The Course of Mexican History* (Oxford, U.K.: Oxford University Press, 1995).

— Scott Chamberlain

Michelangelo (1475–1564)

An Italian sculptor, painter, architect, engineer, and poet who personified the highest ideals of the Renaissance.

Michelangelo di Buonarroti Simoni was born on March 6, 1475, in the Tuscan village of Caprese. Because of his mother's frail health, he was raised in the family of a stonemason at the village of Settigano. Following his mother's death and the remarriage of his father in 1485, Michelangelo rejoined his family in Florence and began school. At the time the Florence he experienced was rich and powerful. It was also a patron and symbol of the arts, a home to numerous cathedrals, churches, and palaces adorned with sculptures by Donatello, Verrochio, and Granacci and with paintings by Giotto, Fra Angelico, Botticelli, and Masaccio. Amid the rich artistic atmosphere Michelangelo fraternized with art students, practicing art by copying smuggled drawings of the masters' works.

Clinging to an impoverished noble title, his father, Lodovici, was aghast that his son desired to learn a trade. Nevertheless, he reluctantly apprenticed his son to Ghirlandaio in 1488.

Between 1489 and 1492 Michelangelo learned the rudiments of sculpture, apprenticing in the Medici gardens patronized by Florence's unofficial ruler, Lorenzo the Magnificent. During this time he produced his first two sculptures, reliefs of the Christian *Madonna of the Stairs* and the classical *Battle of the Centaurs.* Following Lorenzo's death in 1492, the political and religious climate of Florence changed and so did Michelangelo's work. Reflecting the growing European demand for moral reform, the citizenry of Florence expelled the Medici family and looted their palace. Bereft of the art community's most important patrons, many artists fled the city. Michelangelo drifted from VENICE to Bologna and Rome, taking on commissions for sculptures. With his reputation solidified as an artist, he returned to Florence in 1501 at the request of the city. Wishing to regain prestige as a center for the arts, the city commissioned Michelangelo to turn a four-meter block of marble into a sculpture that was to adorn the outside of a cathedral. Following three years of work, much of it in the secrecy of a locked shed, Michelangelo unveiled *David,* a sculpture of the biblical figure portrayed as an ideally formed classical hero. During his stay in Florence from 1501 to 1506, he also completed reliefs of the *Pitti Madonna* and the *Taddei Madonna,* produced the marble *Madonna of the Burghes,* and painted *Doni Madonna.* Moreover, he painted his cartoon for the *Battle of Cascina* (1504–05) to adorn the Palazzo Vecchio as a fresco opposite LEONARDO DA VINCI's *Battle of Anghiari.*

In 1505 Pope Julius II invited Michelangelo to Rome, commissioning him to design his burial tomb. The project dragged on for more than 40 years. Equally frustrating for Michelangelo was Julius's demand to fresco the ceiling of the Sistine Chapel. "Foul I fare and painting is my shame," stated the artist as he began the project, but the result was an elaborate composition composed of 343 colossal figures from the Bible and classical times, proving Michelangelo's brilliance in the medium of painting. Influenced by Neoplatonism, the muscular figures on the ceiling of the Sistine Chapel revealed an ideal type of human being whose beauty reflected their divine stature.

Between 1513 and 1534 Michelangelo served the Medici popes, Lorenzo the Magnificent's son Giovanni (LEO X) and the bastard nephew Giulio (Clement VII). As in his relationship with Julius II, Michelangelo found little in common with the Medici popes. Following Clement VII's death in 1534, Michelangelo moved permanently to Rome, where he lived in a comfortable house provided by the heirs of Julius. He continued to serve the Vatican during the reigns of Popes Paul III and Julius III. The former, who waited impatiently for more than 30 years for the services of the master artist, commissioned Michelangelo to paint *The Last Judgement* over the altar wall of the Sistine Chapel and the *Conversion of Saul and the Crucifixion of St. Peter* in the Vatican's Pauline Chapel. Combined, the work on these frescoes lasted from 1535 to 1550. In 1547 Paul named Michelangelo the architect in chief of the new, partially completed St. Peter's Basilica, often referred to as the greatest single project of the Renaissance. Completed after the artist's death, St. Peter's was constructed close to Michelangelo's original plans.

Eccentric and finally independent, Michelangelo died in Rome on February 18, 1564, shortly before his 89th birthday. Supported by four popes and numerous other important patrons of art, his rise from artisan to artistic genius helped elevate the status of artists during the High Renaissance.

Further reading: Charles De Tolnay, *Michelangelo*, 6 vols. (Princeton, N.J.: Princeton University Press, 1969–1975); Frederick Hartt, *The Sistine Chapel* (New York: Knopf, 1991); R. M. Letts, *The Cambridge Introduction to the History of Art: The Renaissance* (Cambridge, U.K.: Cambridge University Press, 1981); David Summers, *Michelangelo and the Language of Art* (Princeton, N.J.: Princeton University Press, 1981).

— Matthew Lindaman

middle passage

The term *middle passage* referred to the forced relocation of an African man, woman, or child from his or her native community to SLAVERY in the Western Hemisphere.

The middle passage began when an individual was captured and sold as part of the SLAVE TRADE. Although slavery had long existed in Africa (and in other parts of the world), before the mid-15th century an individual captured and sold into slavery normally traveled a limited distance; the farthest journeys, in all likelihood, took a slave from sub-Saharan Africa across the SAHARA. However, the growth of the slave trade after the mid-15th century, first promoted by Portuguese slavers, extended the distance that a captive traveled. As a result, the passage from freedom to slavery in the Americas, which invariably involved a weeks-long journey in miserable conditions onboard ships crossing the Atlantic, took on a meaning unto itself. Conditions on the slaving vessels were notorious. Recent historical scholarship has revealed that perhaps 10 percent of the enslaved men and women rose up in protest despite the fact that the cost of such protests was often death.

Well after 1607, when some Europeans began to organize protests against the slave trade, stories were told of the deprivations caused by the middle passage in an attempt to awaken humanitarian sympathies in the great mass of Europeans who had long accepted the enslavement of Africans. Graphic illustrations of conditions on slave ships circulated in the United States well into the 19th century, an enduring legacy of the horrors of the middle passage.

Further reading: "New Perspectives on the Transatlantic Slave Trade," special issue of *William and Mary Quarterly*, 3rd ser., LVIII (2001): 3–251; Hugh Thomas, *The Slave Trade: The History of the Atlantic Slave Trade, 1440–1870* (New York: Simon & Schuster, 1997).

Mississippian

Mississippian culture represents the apex of indigenous culture in the lower Midwest and Southeast of what is today the United States from 900 to 1600, and after flourishing for approximately 700 years, it finally collapsed in the face of contact with Europeans and the epidemic DISEASES they introduced.

The Mississippian era lasted from A.D. 900 to 1600. Characteristics of this cultural period include the expanded use of platform mounds, population nucleation, the development of chiefdoms, the increased importance of maize (see CORN) horticulture in subsistence systems, an extensive trade in prestige goods, and a ceremonial complex with a shared iconography.

From 900 to 1200 Mississippian culture spread throughout the lower Midwest and Southeast of what is now the United States. During this early Mississippian period native societies began to reorganize from an egalitarian society to a ranked society known as a chiefdom, with residents gathering in palisaded towns. Several types of chiefdoms existed: simple, complex, and paramount. A simple chiefdom developed when an elite group exercised influence over several villages from a ceremonial center implementing a single decision-making level. A complex chiefdom had two decision-making levels in which one chiefdom controlled two or more simple chiefdoms. A paramount chiefdom maintained influence over several complex chiefdoms indirectly and several simple chiefdoms directly. However, chiefdom levels were inherently unstable, and the constant rise and fall of chiefdoms over a given area created long-term political instability. For most of the early Mississippian era, chiefdoms rarely moved to the complex level.

Throughout this era dependence on maize horticulture spread, and two basic types of subsistence systems developed, riverine and coastal. Those Mississippians living in river valleys depended upon beans, gourds, maize, marsh elder, squash, sunflower, and TOBACCO, with maize being the most important crop. They supplemented their horticultural production by gathering local wild plants, collecting aquatic resources, and organizing hunting parties to pursue game, primarily deer, in the late fall and winter. These societies tended to be sedentary. Mississippians who participated in the coastal subsistence systems tended to depend less on growing crops and more on gathering wild plants, aquatic resources, and hunting. As a result, for part of the year these peoples had to be more mobile than sedentary.

The middle Mississippian period, from 1200 to 1400, saw the development of more complex and paramount chiefdoms and the spread of an iconograph-laden religious complex know as the Southeastern Ceremonial Complex. This led to an increase in population nucleation, the size of ceremonial centers, and the number of platform mounds built within these towns. Platform mounds demonstrated and reinforced the position of chiefly elites as the leaders of their communities and religious ceremonies. In general, control of the trade in religious and prestige items expanded and perpetuated the authority of these chiefly/priestly elites. Toward the end of this era, leadership in warfare started to replace control of religious life as a means to legitimize political authority.

Localized population dislocation and warfare marked the late Mississippian period, from 1400 to 1600. Chiefdoms continually rose and fell whenever war disrupted the ability of chiefly elites to provide protection for their people and challenged elites' claims to ceremonial legitimacy. During this period of turmoil, Europeans first appeared in the Southeast and added to native problems. In some areas Europeans threw off the balance of power through slave raiding (see SLAVERY) and warfare. They also introduced epidemic diseases that caused demographic collapse in some areas, which led to political reorganization by the survivors. Thus, the arrival of Europeans ultimately caused or hastened the end of the Mississippian era.

Further reading: J. Daniel Rogers and Bruce D. Smith, *Mississippian Communities and Households* (Tuscaloosa: University of Alabama Press, 1995); John F. Scarry, ed., *Political Structure and Change in the Prehistoric Southeastern United States* (Gainesville: University Press of Florida, 1996); Bruce D. Smith, *Mississippian Settlement Patterns* (New York: Academic Press, 1978); Bruce Smith, ed., *Mississippian Emergence* (Washington, D.C.: Smithsonian Institution Press, 1990).

— Dixie Ray Haggard

Moctezuma II Xocoyotzin (Montezuma)
(r. 1502–1520)

Moctezuma II was *huei tlatoani* (great speaker) of the AZTECS when HERNÁN CORTÉS arrived and died in 1520 during the Spanish occupation of the Aztec capital, TENOCHTITLÁN.

Son of Axayácatl (r. 1468–81) and nephew of the previous speaker Ahuitzotl, Moctezuma ascended to the rulership of the Aztec Empire at age 34. His main function, like that of other great speakers, was dealing with external relations of Aztec politics, including relations with tributaries and enemies. He governed his realm with the assistance of the *cihuacoatl* ("woman snake," although the officeholder was always male), who dealt with internal affairs of the Aztec state. Like his predecessors, he was elected from the royal lineage by a council of nobles, priests, and top military officers of Tenochtitlán as well as rulers of neighboring cities.

Spanish chroniclers noted that the Aztecs treated Moctezuma as divine rather than human. The fact that Moctezuma carried this aspect of the Aztec ideology of kingship further than had any of his predecessors stands in sharp contrast to his reaction to the arrival of Cortés and his troops. Moctezuma sent humbly attired representatives to present the newcomers with fine gifts, causing some historians to speculate that this semidivine ruler capitulated to the invaders sight unseen. However, his response may also be interpreted not as an act of submission but rather as a gesture fitting the Aztecs' belief in their own supremacy over all other peoples, of the great speaker over his people, and of this speaker in particular, who developed the ideology of divine rulership to a degree not seen under other rulers. The sumptuousness of the gifts may have been meant as a display of disposable wealth as well as the power needed to acquire that wealth, the humble state of the presenters merely a gesture to emphasize what a trifling impact such a gift had on the overall wealth and power of the giver.

Spaniards may have missed the point of the lavish gift giving, but they could not help but be impressed by Moctezuma's lifestyle. Chroniclers noted the scope of his palace, garden, zoo, and aviary as well as the number of people supported at the palace. Moctezuma's power over his subjects was also a source of awe: Cortés asserted in his letters to the emperor CHARLES V that the Aztecs both revered and feared their leader to a degree that might make him the envy of any European monarch.

Moctezuma's opulence was not the only thing that set him apart from his predecessors. Although Spanish chronicles emphasized the bellicose character of Aztec society, Moctezuma was actually much less preoccupied with warfare than were his predecessors. Instead, he devoted himself more to the religious aspects of leadership and was especially consumed by the study of the old Toltec religious philosophy. Later sources assert that he believed that Cortés, or perhaps one of his lieutenants, was the reincarnation of QUETZALCOATL, returned to destroy the Mexican peoples if they did not somehow appease him, and that this idea proved instrumental in the intruders' conquest of Tenochtitlán.

Many accounts portray Moctezuma as an ineffective leader who presided over the downfall of his people. Such a judgment does not fit the available evidence. At the time of his ascension to the throne, the Aztec Empire had in many ways reached the limits of its outward expansion. Previous administrations had already extended the Aztec domains south to the Pacific and east to the defensible Isthmus of Tehuantepec. In addition, Aztecs were hemmed in on the west by both mountainous terrain and the armies of the TARASCAN, and in the north the empire already bordered on desert, the conquest of which would have brought very little profit at huge expense. Moctezuma thus turned to the internal consolidation of his empire, focusing his efforts on subduing long-standing pockets of resistance and rebellion within his own borders. External expansion had long been the engine of the Aztec Empire's prosperity and the foundation upon which earlier generations had built the social, economic, and political structures of their state. Moctezuma thus faced the unenviable task of creating a stable monarchy out of a society based on physical expansion and a warrior ethos. His reforms included a general purge of the plebeians whom his predecessor had raised to high office, reinforcing the notion of the great speaker as the representative of or substitute for the gods and forcefully reasserting the privilege of the hereditary nobility. (This latter effort might have contributed to his downfall; according to some chronicles, Moctezuma chose his bodyguard more on the basis of impeccable breeding than on military valor, and was thus ill protected when captured by Cortés.) The resulting economic and social dislocations contributed to the new ruler's unpopularity with both subjects and neighbors. Regardless of Moctezuma's intentions, the internal tensions that his policies created or exacerbated weakened his empire at a time when it would be most in need of strength and stability. In light of these facts, it is not surprising that Moctezuma probably died of wounds inflicted by his own subjects during a riot that was as much a rebellion to overthrow their own leader as it was a revolt against the occupying Spanish forces.

Further reading: Francis J. Brooks, "Motecuzoma Xocoyotl, Hernán Cortés, and Bernal Díaz del Castillo: The Construction of an Arrest," *Hispanic American Historical Review* 75 (1995): 149–183; Geoffrey W. Conrad and Arthur A. Demarest, *Religion and Empire: The Dynamics of Aztec and Inca Expansionism* (Cambridge, U.K.: Cambridge University Press, 1984); Nigel Davies, *The Aztec Empire: The Toltec Resurgence* (Norman: University of Oklahoma Press, 1987); Susan D. Gillespie, *The Aztec Kings: The Construction of Rulership in Mexican History* (Tucson: University of Arizona Press, 1989).

— Marie A. Kelleher

Mohawk

The easternmost tribe of the IROQUOIS Confederacy, the Mohawk originally lived in the middle Mohawk Valley of present-day New York State.

Probably the second-largest of the Five Nations (numbering perhaps 8,000) at the time of contact with whites, the Mohawk maintained three principal villages and several smaller satellite towns. As "keepers of the eastern door" of the metaphorical Five Nations longhouse, the tribe was closest in proximity to Albany and therefore the Dutch and English traders who sought their wares in the fur trade. This circumstance afforded them wealth and influence disproportionate to the other members of the Iroquois League.

Within the grand council, or governing political body, of the Five Nations, the Mohawk held nine seats, or chieftainships, three each for their three clan structures: Turtle, Wolf, and Bear. According to Mohawk oral tradition, it was their chief Deganawida who first proposed the Iroquois alliance and brought the governing laws to the people, while other tribal histories claim this figure as their own. Nevertheless, the fact that the Mohawk were the first of the Iroquois to engage in trade relations with Europeans does lend credence to the theory that they probably played an integral role in developing and strengthening the league during the early historic period. Seeking the iron weapons and metal tools brought by the newcomers, the Mohawk spearheaded early campaigns to relieve indigenous rivals of these goods. After French–Indian alliances in the early 17th century made Mohawk raiding parties to the west too costly and dangerous, the Mohawk established ties with the merchants who followed in the wake of Henry Hudson's 1609 expedition and helped secure Iroquois ascendancy in the eastern trade. Afterward, they maintained economic connections to the English, who came to supplant the Dutch.

Further reading: Nancy Bonvillain, *The Mohawk* (New York: Chelsea House, 1992); William N. Fenton and Elisabeth Tooker, "Mohawk," in William Sturtevant, ed., *Handbook of North American Indians,* vol. 15, *Northeast,* ed. Bruce G. Trigger (Washington, D.C.: Smithsonian Institution Press, 1978), 466–480; Dean R. Snow, T. Gehring, and Willam A. Starna, eds., *In Mohawk Country: Early Narratives about a Native People* (Syracuse, N.Y.: Syracuse University Press, 1996); Elizabeth Tooker, ed., *An Iroquois Source Book,* 3 vols. (New York: Garland, 1985).

— Eric P. Anderson

Monardes, Nicholas (1493–1588)

A physician from SEVILLE, Nicholas Monardes wrote an influential tract extolling the natural wonders to be found in the Western Hemisphere.

Born in Seville in 1493, only a year after the historic passage of CHRISTOPHER COLUMBUS, Nicholas Monardes learned medicine in an age when there were few medical schools. He studied at Alcalá de Henares, a famous Spanish center for medical science at the time, and soon after receiving his degree in April 1533, he returned to Seville. He published his first medical tract, *De secanda vena in pleuritide,* in Seville in 1539. After marrying in 1540, he and his wife had seven children, including one son who emigrated to PERU and another son and one daughter who vowed their lives to the church. Monardes became one of the leading physicians in the city, and his clients included the archbishop as well as other members of the Seville elite.

Monardes's chief achievement was the publication of a book that described the benefits to be had from harvesting American crops for medicinal uses. Published originally in Seville in 1574, the book appeared in LONDON in 1577 under the title *Joyfull Newes out of the Newe Founde Worlde.* Here Monardes told his readers about such medical marvels as a root found in FLORIDA called the beads of Saint Elen that helped alleviate stomach and urinary problems as well as eased the pain of kidney stones, and the cures to be wrought from medicines made from sassafras, also found in Florida. He was most enthusiastic in his endorsement of TOBACCO, which he believed could help to cure virtually any affliction. Consuming tobacco would heal infected breasts and stomach pains, reduce pain associated with kidney stones, eradicate troublesome gas, expel worms, take the pain away from toothaches, lessen any pain in joints, and cure all manner of wounds, including bites from venomous beasts. However, he did more than enumerate tobacco's benefits: He also instructed his readers how to use these botanical products, thereby providing crucial information for Europeans who witnessed the growth of the tobacco trade during their lifetimes.

Nicholas Monardes died in Seville on October 12, 1588. With his earthly remains buried at the monastery in San Leandro, his legacy lived because of his efforts to encourage Europeans to use the plants of the Western Hemisphere to improve their lives.

Further reading: Nicholas Monardes, *Joyfull Newes out of the Newe Founde Worlde,* trans. John Frampton, 2 vols., ed. Stephen Gaselee (New York: Arno Press, 1977).

monsters

Sixteenth-century Europeans, living in an age when their intellectual horizons seemingly expanded by the day, believed that monsters inhabited their world and posed dangers to anyone who crossed their paths.

The belief in monsters was not new in the early modern period. Europeans had long known about monsters from such classical authorities as Solinus and Pliny the Elder, who described monsters for their audiences in antiquity. By the time CHRISTOPHER COLUMBUS sailed across the Atlantic, most Europeans would have had some sense of what monsters looked like because visual depictions of various monstrous beasts could be found in the carvings of churches and along the edges of *MAPPAE MUNDI.* The monsters included cyclopes, which had only one eye positioned in the middle of their forehead; hermaphrodites, who were half male and half female; Sciopodes, who possessed only one leg with a massive foot at the end of it that they would use to shade themselves from the sun; and cynocephali, a creature with the body of a man and the head of a dog. Gerald of Wales's late 12th-century description of Ireland included his observations on monsters, such as a woman with a beard and mane and a creature who was half ox and half man, who roamed the island and haunted the minds of his local informants.

The master of medieval monster tales was SIR JOHN MANDEVILLE. His 14th-century ethnographic fable, which circulated widely in Europe, warned his readers about the range of monsters who inhabited the East. He told them about cyclopes and cannibals, "ugly folk without heads, who have eyes in each shoulder" with round mouths, "like a horseshoe, in the middle of their chest." "And there are in another place folk with flat faces," he wrote, "without noses or eyes; but they have two small holes instead of eyes, and a flat lipless mouth. In another isle there are ugly fellows whose upper lip is so big that when they sleep in the sun they cover all their faces with it." He claimed he had evi-

Sebastian Muenster's depiction in *Kosmographic Universalis* of what people in far-off places were assumed to look like *(Hulton/Archive)*

dence of a place where dwarfish people lacked mouths and had to inhale their nutrition through reeds. In isolated parts of the East a traveler might find humans with ears so long that they reached their knees, or men and women with feet like horses that enabled them to catch animals for their meals, or hermaphrodites who could either impregnate females or give birth depending on which sex organs they decided to use at a given moment.

The invention of the PRINTING PRESS and the increase in the number of books spreading across the continent expanded knowledge about monsters, many of whom took on new lives in the pages of books. The publication in Latin and German in 1493 of Hartmann Schedel's *Liber chronicarum,* known as the *Nurenberg Chronicle,* spread information about monsters to a sizable audience. The volume contained illustrations along the left margin of one map that showed readers the monsters of the world, including a woman covered in fur, a centaur, a hermaphrodite, a man with the head of a crane, a man with three arms, another with six fingers on each hand, and another with four eyes.

Over the course of the 16th century, literature about monsters proliferated on the Continent. Perhaps the most notable of these works was Ambroise Paré's *Des Monstres et prodiges,* first published in Paris in 1573 (see Documents). Paré's freaks were of a new sort in that he focused not on the exotic East but, instead, on the monsters who could have lived next door to his readers. As a master barber–surgeon and an anatomist, Paré's career spanned most of the century, during which he cared for the wounded and the ill on the battlefield and in Parisian hospitals. He saw, it could be argued, the full range of the human species, and he took notes. His observations on European monsters became the most well known of his works, and for good reason: The book, with its vivid depictions of freaks, was riveting. He wrote about conjoined twins and hermaphrodites, including a pair of conjoined hermaphroditic twins. He described what happens when a man had insufficient "seed" to produce an entire child: The resulting offspring lacked limbs. In one notorious case, a female "monster" born in 1562 in Ville-France-de-Beyran in Gascony even lacked a head. He wrote as well about "sodomists and atheists who 'join together' and break out of their bounds—unnaturally—with animals," whose lust produced creatures that were half human and half animal. He told about a creature, half pig and half man, born to a sow owned by Joest Dickpert on Warmoesbroeck Street in Brussels in 1564, and of a being that came from the woman living at the sculptor Jean Mollin's house on Camerstrate in Antwerp in 1571 that had the body of a dog and the head of a bird. Although much of the book contained information that could be found in more traditional bestiaries, such as descriptions of flying fish, ostriches, and whales, the sense of wonder never faded from the pages.

Like other 16th-century authors and chroniclers, Paré borrowed freely from antiquity and more recent works, often telling his readers when he derived his views from St. Augustine or Pliny, among the ancients, or JEAN DE LÉRY or ANDRÉ THEVET among the moderns.

In a world so crowded with monsters and books, Paré argued that there were multiple causes for the oddities he described. "There are several things that cause monsters," he informed his readers. "The first is the glory of God. The second, his wrath." But divine origins accounted for only some of the beasts that lurked in his pages. Paré also believed that monsters could be caused by "too great a quantity of seed" and "too little a quantity." They could be caused by "the imagination," by "the narrowness or smallness of the womb," and by "the indecent posture of the mother, as when, being pregnant, she has sat too long with her legs crossed, or pressed against her womb." Injury during pregnancy could create monsters if a pregnant woman fell down or had "blows struck against the womb." Yet monsters could also spring from "hereditary or accidental illnesses," or "rotten or corrupt seed," or "through mixture or mingling of seed." Finally, monsters could be caused by "the artifice of spital beggars" (a reference to those who begged in public locations or went door-to-door seeking donations) or, predictably, "through Demons and Devils." Yet at the end of this list, Paré added a cautionary note to his readers. "There are other causes that I leave aside for the present," he warned, "because among all human reasons, one cannot give any that are sufficient or probable, such as why persons are made with only one eye in the middle of the forehead or the navel, or a horn on the head, or the liver upside down. Others are born having griffin's feet, like birds, and certain monsters which are engendered in the sea; in short, countless others which it would take too long to describe." The details in the text, based on the case studies that Paré claimed to have seen firsthand or that he had heard about from reliable sources, typically provided explanations that fell into one of these 13 categories. Monsters, a reader would realize, could occur anywhere, not just remotely, although they were especially likely in places where humans lacked a firm understanding of the Bible. Those who did not know God's prohibition on intercourse during menstruation, as explained by Moses in Leviticus (chapter 16) and by the prophet Esdras, were thus likely to produce monsters since they copulated "like brutish beasts, in which their appetite guides them, without respecting the time, or other laws ordained by God and Nature."

Paré's readers might have been entranced by his descriptions and perhaps alarmed at the multitude of monsters prowling the world, but they would not have been shocked. By the 16th century knowledge about monsters was so widespread that some observers no longer felt it necessary to make any comment on their existence. Sebastian Brant, the author of two late 15th-century broadsides (one in Latin, the other in German) that dealt with monsters, refused to write about a child born with two heads, informing his correspondent that he saw no reason to issue such a report since "monsters have become so frequent. Rather than a wonder, they appear to me to represent the common course of nature in our time." The publication during the 16th century of text after text describing monsters proved that Brant understood all too well that the freakish had become commonplace in both folklore and the printed books that together created the common language of western Europeans.

In this world where monsters were common, it is worthy of note that travelers to the Western Hemisphere did not encounter any member of any of the monstrous races that classical writers had told them about or that physicians such as Paré warned existed everywhere. The native peoples of the Americas might have seemed like "savages" or cannibals to Europeans, but those were cultural defects that could be overcome and not a sign that Indians were monsters.

Further reading: Lorraine Daston and Katherine Park, *Wonders and the Order of Nature, 1150–1750* (New York: Zone Books, 1998), esp. 173–214; John B. Friedman, *The Monstrous Races in Medieval Art and Thought* (Cambridge, Mass: Harvard University Press, 1981); *Ambroise Paré on Monsters and Marvels,* trans. Janis L. Pallister (Chicago: University of Chicago Press, 1982); C. W. R. D. Moseley, trans. and ed., *The Travels of Sir John Mandeville* (Harmondsworth: Penguin Classics, 1983); Katherine Park and Lorraine Daston, "Unnatural Conceptions: The Study of Monsters in Sixteenth- and Seventeenth-Century France and England," *Past and Present* 92 (1981): 20–54; Rudolf Wittkower, "Marvels of the East: A Study in the History of Monsters," *Journal of the Warburg and Courtauld Institutes* 5 (1942): 159–197.

Montagnais-Naskapi (Innu)

The people whom the French called Montagnais and Naskapi, and who called themselves Innu, lived in the Quebec–Labrador peninsula of Canada.

Before European contact probably at least 4,000 Innu lived in river valleys and around lakes in Canada. When the Innu first encountered Europeans, they lived in a number of bands of varying sizes that moved with the seasons. The French called the bands they knew best the "Montagnais," or "mountaineers," and by the mid-17th century referred to more northerly Innu bands as Naskapi. Both the Montagnais and the Naskapi spoke Innu-aimun, a dialect of the ALGONQUIAN language family, and thought of themselves as one people.

Culturally, the Innu people had much in common with other northern Algonquian peoples. They lived in conical tents covered with birch bark or caribou hide. Bands traveled throughout the year, moving when food became short. Band composition was not permanent. During the winter groups of a few families traveled to hunt, reuniting with other Innus in the summer. During following winters, families might join other bands.

Sex role distinctions were not rigid among the Innus, but men generally hunted large game animals, especially caribou, and made canoes, toboggans, and other wooden items. Women might set snares to trap smaller animals. They also made clothing and gathered wild foods. The Innus also fished and hunted seals, and some traded with the HURON for CORN and TOBACCO. Early French observers were surprised by the relatively egalitarian relationships between Innu men and women and by the absence of any central authority with the power to command individuals.

The Innu people may have had contact with Viking explorers some 500 years before Columbus. The Viking settlement was short-lived, but the Innu met Europeans again in the 1500s. In 1534 they encountered JACQUES CARTIER, and throughout the middle of the 16th century traded with Basque fishermen, who offered metal goods for furs. The Innu were on good terms with the Basque traders and sometimes warned them of planned Inuit attacks. Innu success in the fur trade led to increased tensions with the IROQUOIS because both the Innu and the Iroquois sought to position themselves as middlemen in the lucrative fur trade. Trade with Europeans was so frequent that the Innu came increasingly to depend on trade goods. By 1623 they no longer made their own baskets or adzes and often preferred French clothing to their own leather garments. In the 17th century French Jesuit and Recollét priests (see JESUITS) established missions among the Innu, although without great success.

Further reading: Peter Armitage, *The Innu (The Montagnais-Naskapi)* (New York: Chelsea House, 1991); Eleanor Leacock, "The Montagnais-Naskapi of the Labrador Peninsula" in *Native Peoples: The Canadian Experience,* ed. R. Bruce Morrison and C. Roderick Wilson (Toronto: McClelland & Stewart, 1986), 140–171; Alan D. McMillan, *Native Peoples and Cultures of Canada: An Anthropological Overview* (Vancouver: Douglas & McIntyre, 1988); Bruce G. Trigger, *Natives and Newcomers: Canada's "Heroic Age" Reconsidered* (Kingston, Ontario: McGill-Queen's University Press, 1985).

— Martha K. Robinson

Monte Albán

One of the most remarkable pre-Columbian centers in southern MEXICO, whose ceremonial importance was so great that it was used as a royal burial site long after the city itself had been abandoned.

Monte Albán was located in the Valley of Oaxaca, where the three great branches of the valley converge. Zapotec Indians from the valley selected the site because of its strategic and ceremonial importance, not because the site was particularly practical. It was perched on an artificially flattened mountaintop 1,300 feet above the valley floor, which would have made it extremely difficult for its inhabitants to secure adequate supplies of food, water, and fuel.

The city rose to prominence in the preclassic era and shows strong Olmec influences. Some of the earliest written texts from Mesoamerica are located at Monte Albán, showing calendrical information as well as actual history. The importance of astronomy and calendrics is evident from the precise location and orientation of several buildings in Monte Albán's main plaza, and it is clear that at least one building served as an astronomical observatory. Monte Albán's greatest period was during the classic period (beginning around A.D. 200), along with TEOTIHUACÁN, CHOLULA, and the MAYA. During this time the city reached a population of 15,000 to 20,000. The Zapotec developed a unique art style that was highly valued in Mesoamerica, and it is clear that there were trade links between Monte Albán and the other great cities. For example, Zapotec appear to have established an ethnic enclave in the mighty city of Teotihuacán. Monte Albán also established its own sphere of influence, but it is not clear how tightly the surrounding regions were controlled. The city had great ceremonial importance, and several gods are depicted at the site. Prominent among these are the rain god Cociyo, the Bat God, the Corn God, and a local variant of the Feathered Serpent (see QUETZALCOATL). More than 170 royal tombs were located at Monte Albán, giving it great importance as a royal necropolis.

After 600 the city began a long, mysterious decline. The city's dramatic site probably worked to its disadvantage—in times of economic recession or drought, it would have been difficult to keep the city adequately supplied. Some time around 700, Monte Albán was all but abandoned. It remained a holy site for centuries thereafter. By 1350 Mixtec Indians from western Oaxaca had taken control of the rich Valley of Oaxaca through a system of conquest and royal marriage. The Mixtecs maintained Monte Albán as a sacred center and buried their own kings in the old Zapotec tombs. Several of these tombs, undisturbed since antiquity, were rediscovered in the mid-20th century. The large assortment of Mixtec goldwork from Monte Albán is the only testimony we have of the ancient Mexican's skills at metallurgy. After the conquest, the Spaniards built the city of Oaxaca at the foot of Monte Albán's mountain.

Further reading: Michael D. Coe, *Mexico: From the Olmecs to the Aztecs*, 4th ed. (London: Thames & Hudson, 1994); Joyce Marcus and Kent V. Flannery, *Zapotec Civilization: How Urban Society Evolved in Mexico's Oaxaca Valley* (London: Thames & Hudson, 1996).

— Scott Chamberlain

Monte Verde

The discovery of Monte Verde, a prehistoric settlement site in Chile, has led some archaeologists to suggest that humans may have lived in South America more than 33,000 years ago.

Archaeologists have found a number of sites of human occupation in North and South America that date to approximately 11,200 years ago. The North American, or Clovis, sites show that people in widely separated settlements made virtually identical tools. These similarities have led some archaeologists to theorize that Clovis people were migratory hunters who entered the Americas relatively recently and spread across North America very rapidly. Other scholars have suggested that such rapid population movement in an unfamiliar continent would have been impossible. They suggest that dental, linguistic, and genetic diversity within modern Indian populations suggest that humans must have been present long before Clovis. The similarity of technology at Clovis sites, in this view, may represent the development of new toolmaking methods, not population movements.

Many candidates have been suggested as pre-Clovis sites, but most have been discredited. The most likely pre-Clovis site is Monte Verde, Chile. At Monte Verde, discovered in the 1970s, archaeologists found two sites that indicated early human occupation. One dated to about 12,500 years ago, more than a thousand years before Clovis. This site contained evidence of a group of about 20 to 30 people who hunted mastodons, made tools, gathered medicinal plants, and lived in a long structure made of animal hides and wood. If the dating of this site is correct, it would suggest that humans may have crossed into the Americas from Asia more than 20,000 years ago. Their second discovery was even more controversial. In another area of the same site, they found charcoal from burned clay. Subjected to radiocarbon dating, the charcoal suggested that humans may have occupied the site 33,000 years ago. The Monte Verde findings remain highly controversial, but if authenticated will require archaeologists to rethink their theories on the migration of early peoples to the Americas.

Further reading: Thomas D. Dillehay, *Monte Verde: A Late Pleistocene Settlement in Chile*, 2 vols. (Washington, D.C.: Smithsonian Institution Press, 1989); ———, *The*

Settlement of the Americas: A New Prehistory (New York: Basic Books, 2000); Ruth Gruhn and Christy G. Turner II, "On the Settlement of the Americas: South American Evidence for an Expanded Time Frame," and "Reply," *Current Anthropology* 28 (1987): 363–365; David J. Meltzer, "Clocking the First Americans," *Annual Review of Anthropology* 24 (1995): 21–45.

— Martha K. Robinson

Montserrat

A small island located to the southwest of Antigua in the Lesser Antilles of the West Indies, Montserrat experienced a colonial era of conflict between, first, the Island CARIB and its initial Irish colonists and, later, the French and the British.

Originally inhabited by Island Carib, CHRISTOPHER COLUMBUS first explored Montserrat in 1493, but Europeans ignored the island until the English claimed it in 1625. The Irish colonized the island in 1643 in the name of the English and suffered constant raids by Island Carib. Over time Montserrat became a valuable SUGAR-producing island dependent upon the institution of African SLAVERY. By the end of the 16th century the Island Carib threat ceased, but Montserrat became a pawn in the colonial wars for empire fought between the French and English.

When hostilities broke out between the French and English in 1666, the taking of Montserrat became one of the focal points of French strategy in the Lesser Antilles. The French captured Montserrat in 1667, and the Irish colonists immediately swore oaths of allegiance to the French Crown. The French controlled the island for over a century until they relinquished control under the terms of the Treaty of Versailles in 1783.

Further reading: Alan Burns, *History of the British West Indies* (London: Allen & Unwin, 1954); Jean-Baptiste Labat, *The Memoirs of Père Labat*, trans. John Eaden (London: F. Cass, 1970); Howard A. Fergus, *History of Alliouagana: A Short History of Montserrat* (Plymouth, Montserrat: University Centre, 1975).

— Dixie Ray Haggard

Mossi

The Mossi people, an ethnic group in modern-day Burkina Faso, Cote d'Ivoire, GHANA, Togo, and BENIN, founded a powerful kingdom in 1495 at the city of Ouagadougou, Burkina Faso, that remained powerful throughout the 16th century and into the 19th century.

The origins of the Mossi are the subject of some debate. According to one oral tradition, the Mossi descended from a single ancestor, Na Gbewa, who established himself in the early 15th century as political leader in Pusiga, an urban center in the extreme northeast of present-day Ghana. This tradition holds that Na Gbewa's four offspring—sons Tusugu, Sitobu, and Nmantambu and daughter, Yanenga—are the apical ancestors of the major Mossi kingdoms, whose political relations mirror the family positions of their founders. The Mamprussi, founded by Tusugu, the eldest, is the "senior brother" kingdom in the Mossi family. The DAGOMBA and the Nanumba, founded by Sitobu and Nmantambu, respectively, are "junior brothers." Na Gbewa's daughter, Yanenga, married the hunter Riale and bore Wedraogo (Ouedraogo), who founded the "grandchildren" kingdoms of Wegadugu (Ouagadougou) and Yatenga. In this account, the founding dates of the five kingdoms center on the mid-15th and early 16th century.

According to another oral tradition, Wedraogo is the apical ancestor of the entire Mossi Empire. He and his Dagomba followers migrated north from their homeland and established the village of Tenkodogo as the first capital of the Mossi kingdom. Three of Wedraogo's sons captured additional territory in the Volta River basin, beginning a long tradition of Mossi cavalry-led conquest. By the 15th century Wedraogo's descendants comprised more than 20 kingdoms with diverse ethnic populations. In 1495 Wegraogo's grandson Oubry founded the most important Mossi kingdom at Ouagadougou, establishing himself as *mogho naaba,* or "king of the world." (The *mogho naaba* is still a respected leader in Ouagadougou today.)

Regardless of which tradition is accepted, both demonstrate that the Mossi were expansionistic, at their peak extending their political and economic influence into the Sahel, the borderland region south of the SAHARA. Before the Mossi conquest, the indigenous peoples of the region were organized around "land priests," called after Mossi conquest *tengasoba* in the north and *tengdana* in the south, who had custody of the earth shrines. According to the first oral tradition discussed above, the Dagomba killed these priests, but other Mossi kingdoms integrated them into the new political structures. The rest of the indigenous population assimilated into Mossi society as commoners, or *tengdamba* (*tengbisi* in the south). In Dagomba those indigenous peoples who did not flee became incorporated into the new state, some as bowmen in the army.

Mossi power depended on the HORSE and an excellent command of cavalry warfare techniques. The Mossi successfully increased their territory, but not without resistance. The SONGHAI Empire, centered at GAO on the NIGER RIVER, challenged Mossi dominance of the western SUDAN first under Sunni Ali Ber and later under ASKIA

MUHAMMAD I. Mossi struggles with the Songhai over domination of the Niger Bend are documented in two important histories of the region, the *Ta'rikh al-Sudan* and the *Ta'rikh al-fattash*. Beginning in the 1430s with Mossi incursions into Songhai territory, conflict between the two kingdoms lasted more than a century. The 1490s represented a second period in the contest over the Niger, during which Askia Muhammad led a jihad (see ISLAM) against the Mossi. He failed in this attempt to convert the Mossi from their form of ancestor worship to the Muslim religion. The third period of conflict between the Mossi and the Songhai occurred during the reign of Askia Dawud of Songhai. He waged three wars against the Mossi, first in 1549, then in 1561–62, but it was not until 1574, the final war, that Askia Dawud effectively eliminated the Mossi threat to the Songhai Empire.

As the two oral traditions also show, Mossi society, like its political structure, was hierarchical. In the case of the Ouagadougou, Wedraogo's direct descendants, the *nakombse*, were at the top of the social structure as nobles. Under the nobles were the commoners, or *talse*, and at bottom, the *yemse*, or slaves. Those who claimed descent from the original Dagomba settlers had privileged status as *tengabiise*—"children of the earth"—which entitled them to land and made them responsible for harvest rites.

Mossi agricultural production consisted predominantly of yams, cereals, and legumes and was the basis of its economy until the 18th century, when its isolation from major trading centers ended. The *yarse*, assimilated Mande Muslims, traded GOLD, kola nuts, salt, and livestock with the Mossi. They paid tribute to the various kingdoms for safe passage through their territories and for space to sell their goods in local markets. Trade with Muslim societies became the most common factor in Mossi conversion. Adoption of the Muslim faith led to significant social changes in the Mossi kingdoms, including increased social class divisions. Commoners in Mossi society typically retained their traditional beliefs, while those of the noble class converted to Islam. The most prevalent form of Islam in the Mossi kingdoms was the "Suwarian" tradition, which rejected jihad as a method of conversion, minimized the role of proselytizing, and did not limit political involvement as long as the Muslim community was not compromised by such action. In these ways Mossi conversion to Islam opened channels of communication, both diplomatic and commercial, with other kingdoms, effectively ending Mossi isolation from the major centers of trade in the western Sudan.

Further reading: Elizabeth Heath, "Mossi," in *Africana: The Encyclopedia of the African and African American Experience,* eds. Kwame Anthony Appiah and Henry Louis Gates, Jr. (New York: Basic *Civitas* Books, 1999), 1346; "Mossi" and "Mossi Kingdoms," in *Historical Dictionary of Burkina Faso,* 2nd ed., eds. Daniel Miles McFarland and Lawrence A. Rupley (London: Scarecrow Press, 1998), 86–87; "The Peoples," in *Cambridge Encyclopedia of Africa* eds. Roland Oliver and Michael Crowder (Cambridge, U.K.: Cambridge University Press, 1981), 57–86; Ivor Wilks, "The Mossi and the Akan States, 1400–1800," in *History of West Africa*, vol. 1, 3rd ed., eds. J. F. Ade Ajiya and Michael Crowder (London: Longman, 1985), 465–502.

— Lisa M. Brady

mound builders

Mound building cultures developed in the Southeast and the lower Midwest of what is today the United States from 2200 B.C. to A.D. 1600, and they represent the most sophisticated indigenous cultural development east of the Great Plains.

Poverty Point, the first mound building culture, developed in the lower Mississippi Valley and part of the coast of the Gulf of Mexico. Residents there participated in an extensive trade network, developed pottery, and cultivated gourds. The Poverty Point culture is most famous for one set of mounds built at Macon Ridge in present-day Louisiana, also known as Poverty Point. This site consists of six midden ridges that formed six semicircles and two large mounds. The mounds seem to have had some ceremonial significance, and the society apparently developed into an early form of a chiefdom. The Poverty Point culture lasted from 2200 to 1000 B.C.

The Adena were the next mound building people to arise. Their culture developed in the central Ohio River Valley around 500 B.C., where these people created a ceremonial system that centered on a burial complex. At first, the mortuary systems consisted of simple mounds built over grave pits. By 200 B.C. they began to place the dead in charnel houses until the house filled. Then the charnel housed were burned and mounds were built over them. Finally, another charnel house was constructed on top of the mound, and the process began again. The Adena also built effigy mounds that related to the ceremonial complex. They practiced a hunting and gathering subsistence, but they were primarily sedentary. The Adena ceremonial complex lasted until approximately A.D. 1, when it was absorbed by the HOPEWELL CULTURE.

The Hopewell ceremonial complex originated in two locations, south-central Illinois and central Indiana and Ohio. Eventually these two cultural groups merged with the Adena complex to form the Hopewell ceremonial complex. The Hopewell people used conical platform mounds as staging areas for religious ceremonies. Burials began to contain a wide range of artifacts. The more important individuals had the largest and most elaborate burials with the most grave goods. The Hopewell used charnel houses like the Adena but on a larger scale, and their funeral mounds were also bigger. Many of the ceremonial items used in burials came from raw materials acquired in an extensive trade system that contained materials gathered from the Rocky Mountains, the Great Lakes, and the Gulf and Atlantic coasts. They also developed a limited form of horticulture but were not completely dependent upon it. The Hopewell complex faded between A.D. 700 and 900 primarily because its trade network collapsed and possibly because warfare in the Midwest increased due to the introduction of the bow and arrow to the region. Mound build-

ing continued in the Mississippi Valley and along the Gulf Coast, and this led to the development of the MISSISSIPPIAN culture.

Further reading: Judith A. Bense, *Archaeology of the Southeastern United States: Paleoindian to World War I* (New York: Academic Press, 1994); Jon L. Gibson, "Poverty Point: The First American Chiefdom," *Archaeology* 27 (1974): 95–105; R. Barry Lewis and Charles Stout, eds., *Mississippian Towns and Sacred Spaces: Searching for an Architectural Grammar* (Tuscaloosa: University of Alabama Press, 1998); Bruce Smith, ed., *Mississippian Emergence* (Washington, D.C.: Smithsonian Institution Press, 1990).

— Dixie Ray Haggard

Aerial view of the Great Serpent Mound in Adams County, Georgia

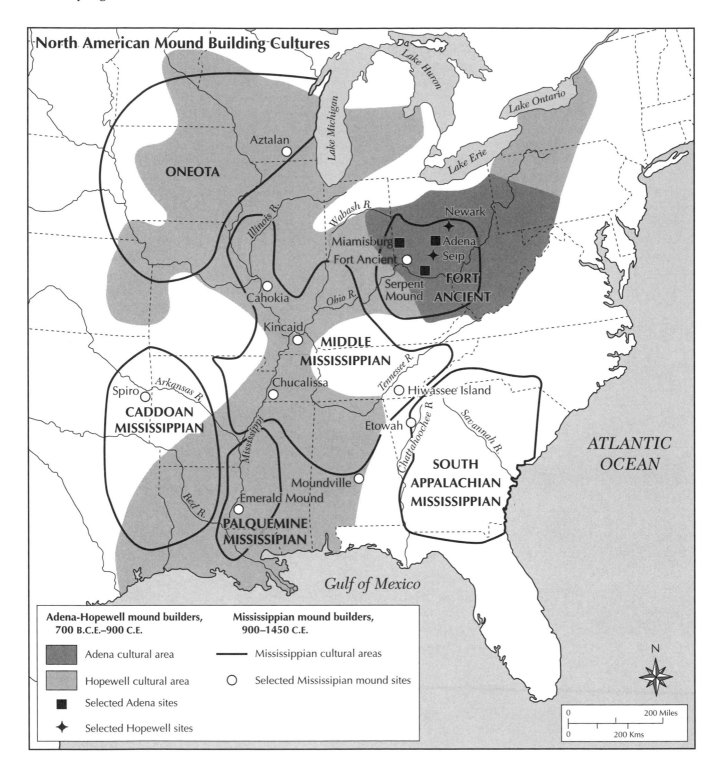

North American Mound Building Cultures

Adena-Hopewell mound builders,
700 B.C.E.–900 C.E.

- Adena cultural area
- Hopewell cultural area
- Selected Adena sites
- Selected Hopewell sites

Mississippian mound builders,
900–1450 C.E.

- Mississippian cultural areas
- Selected Mississipian mound sites

Mpongwe

The Mpongwe, an ethnic group in northwestern modern-day Gabon, served as middlemen in the SLAVE TRADE in the 16th century.

The earliest inhabitants of what is known as the Estuary, the mouth of the Ogooue River, the Mpongwe established clans in the area beginning in the 16th century. Organized into numerous clans led by *ogas*, or chiefs, the

Mpongwe hunted, fished, and grew crops such as yams. They were also craftspeople, ironworkers, and boat builders. A largely coastal people and accomplished sailors, the Mpongwe navigated their dugout canoes along the Atlantic coast from their homes on the Ogooue River delta to as far north as CAMEROON. Early trading with the Bakele and FANG for ivory and later trading for copper, dyewood, and ivory with the Loango kingdom to the south provided the Mpongwe with essential connections for their later roles as middlemen in the transatlantic slave trade. Slave-holders themselves, the Mpongwe became slave brokers in the slave trade with European merchants, who established themselves in the region beginning in the 15th cen-tury. By the 16th century the Mpongwe were deeply involved in the trade as middlemen but were pushed by the neighboring Orungu peoples out of the region to the Gabon estuary in the north.

Further reading: "Mpongwe," in *Historical Dictionary of Gabon,* David E. Gardinier (London: Scarecrow Press, 1994), 233–325; Eric Young, "Mpongwe," in *Africana: The Encyclopedia of the African and African American Experience,* eds. Kwame Anthony Appiah and Henry Louis Gates, Jr. (New York: Basic *Civitas* Books, 1999), 1356.

— Lisa M. Brady

N

Nahua

The general name scholars have given to those indigenous people of central MEXICO who spoke NAHUATL as their primary language, including such specific groups as the TOLTECS, Tlaxcalan, and AZTECS.

Nahua had lived in central Mexico at least since the end of the classic period, roughly A.D. 600 to 800. They formed one of the largest ethnic groups in Mesoamerica, with several million members. The Nahua retained a strong ethnic identity, regarding themselves as the most "civilized" people of Mexico. The first group of Nahua who rose to political prominence was the Toltecs. Under the Toltecs Nahuatl became the lingua franca of Mesoamerica, with soldiers, politicians, and merchants using it from the American Southwest to Guatemala. After the Toltec kingdom disintegrated after 1150, little political unity existed among the Nahua. Over the next 200 years several Nahua kingdoms emerged and faded. Although they were not politically unified, these petty states did maintain a basic cultural uniformity that survived the political upheavals of the time. By 1450 two large Nahua states arose to dominate Mexico again—the Aztecs and the Tlaxcalan. Although culturally similar, these two states were bitter political rivals.

The basic political organization of the Nahua was the *altepetl,* which usually centered in a large town and its hinterland. For organizational purposes, the *altepetl* usually had four, eight, or 16 components (called *calpulli*). Instead of direct, universal taxation, one *calpulli* supported the administrative and religious costs of the *altepetl* as a whole for one year, before another *calpulli* took its turn. Scholars refer to this as a form of rotating, cellular organization that was particular to the Nahua. The *altepetl* was the basis for everything in Nahua society. Each *altepetl* had its own patron god, organized its own armies, and administered justice through its own courts. If through conquest, marriage, or some other mechanism a series of *altepetls* merged, they would often keep their judicial, administrative, and religious apparatus distinct. Thus the Aztec "Empire" was not a unified state like the Roman Empire, but instead a series of Nahua *altepetls* that all paid tribute to the city of TENOCHTITLÁN. This loose confederate system ultimately doomed the Aztecs, who had no real control over their territories and no efficient way to marshal their territories' resources. Once the Spaniards arrived, many of the *altepetls* were only too happy to break with the Aztecs and throw their support behind the invaders.

The Nahua are one of the best understood cultures of the NEW WORLD. Because they were the dominant culture at the time of the Spaniards' arrival, most of the early descriptions of native culture focus on the Nahua. Further, the Spaniards concentrated their settlements in Nahua areas, and the newcomers came into closer contact with them than with any other ethnic group in Mexico. Missionaries, historians, and early natural scientists used Nahua informants for their works, preserving many aspects of Nahua culture, politics, and religion in works such as the Florentine Codex. No other group in ancient Mesoamerica is so well documented. Additionally, many Nahua communities kept copious records in both Spanish and Nahuatl. These have proven to be a gold mine for colonial historians, who have been able to use the wills, court cases, and memoranda to reconstruct Nahua life under Spanish rule. It is clear from these records that the Nahua sense of ethnic identity survived well into the colonial period. Contrary to popular opinion, the Nahua did not abandon their culture while embracing the Spaniards', but continued to follow their own traditions. Notably, the *altepetl* system survived as the way to pay taxes, support religious ceremonies, and divide administrative costs.

Although various Nahua political states rose, fell, and fought among themselves, there always remained a clear Nahua identity that served to unify them. This Nahua identity survived the Spanish conquest and slowly adapted to the new regime. Today there are between 1 and 2 million Nahua living in Mexico who continue to speak Nahuatl and maintain their ethnic identity.

Further reading: Michael Coe, *Mexico: From the Olmecs to the Aztecs,* 4th ed. (London: Thames & Hudson, 1994); Charles Gibson, *The Aztecs under Spanish Rule* (Stanford:, Calif.: Stanford University Press, 1964); James Lockhart, *The Nahuas after the Conquest* (Stanford, Calif.: Stanford University Press, 1992).

— Scott Chamberlain

Nahuatl

The language spoken by the AZTECS, which served as a lingua franca in MEXICO both before and after the Spanish conquest in 1521.

Nahuatl is part of the Uto-Aztecan language group, a broad family of languages spoken by people from the northwestern United States to PANAMA. Linguists believe that the heartland of this language family was in northwestern Mexico. The most important language group within the Uto-Aztecan family was Nahua, with Nahuatl being the most widespread language within this group. Nahuatl primarily differs from other languages in the family by its use of the *tl* sound. Most of the inhabitants of Mexico's central valley spoke an early form of Nahuatl and referred to all those who spoke the language as NAHUA, an ethnic designation that persists to this day. The first Nahual-speaking group that rose to prominence was the TOLTECS. As the Toltecs conquered or colonized substantial portions of Mexico, Nahuatl spread throughout the region, becoming the language of international diplomacy. For example, ancient manuscripts from the Mixtec Indians of southern Mexico differentiated Nahuatl speakers from local Mixtecs, and frequently depicted the Nahua as diplomats or ambassadors. The Aztecs also spoke Nahuatl, and once they seized control over much of Mexico, Nahuatl clinched its position as the dominant language of Mesoamerica.

Nahuatl is a lyrical, highly expressive language that often relies on metaphors to convey ideas. This gives it a poetic feel that sets it apart from most European languages. Nahuatl's development reached its apogee between 1400 and 1500, which scholars refer to as its classical age. Aztec boys learned Nahuatl rhetoric as part of their basic education, and a remarkable series of gifted poets made use of its expressive qualities. Perhaps the most famous poet was Nezahuacóyotl, the king of Texcoco (1402–72). Acknowledged as the greatest proponent of the classical style, Nezahuacóyotl wrote about the transience of existence and the fragile beauty of nature. Besides using it for poetry, Aztec scholars used the language to record history in the form of elaborate oral songs that were similar in style and content to the *Iliad.*

Contrary to popular belief, Nahuatl did not die out in the wake of the Spanish conquest. In fact, the conquest actually promoted the use of Nahuatl. Because most natives already used it as a second language, the Spaniards encouraged the use of Nahuatl as a convenient, standard language for all legal transactions involving non-Spanish speakers. In this way Spanish officials and translators would have to work with only one universal language, rather than almost 100 smaller ones. Additionally, when the Spaniards began exploring and mapping Mexico, they relied almost exclusively on Nahuatl-speaking guides and informants. Therefore, royal officials gave Nahuatl names to hills, rivers, and cities throughout the colony of NEW SPAIN. These Nahuatl names persist in Mexico and Guatemala today, although many of the communities never actually spoke Nahuatl. Also, a number of Spanish scholars such as BERNARDINO DE SAHAGÚN interviewed Nahuatl speakers and used these interviews to construct their histories of ancient Mexico. Many of the most important works on Aztec culture, such as the Florentine Codex and the Codex Mendoza, were originally written in Nahuatl, and many colonial writers, musicians, and poets used Nahuatl in their works. A number of Nahuatl songs, theater pieces, and sonnets survive from colonial Mexico.

Nahuatl studies continue to be important today. Many of the documents of colonial Mexico, including histories, wills, court transcripts, and dramas, were not written in Spanish, but Nahuatl. Historians who concentrate on Spanish sources often end up with a distorted view of postconquest Mexico. Nearly 1.5 million people speak Nahuatl today, making it among the most widely spoken indigenous languages in the Americas. English words that derive from Nahuatl include *tomato (tomatl), coyote (coyotl),* and *chocolate (xocolatl).*

Further reading: J. Richard Andrews, *Introduction to Classical Nahuatl* (Austin: University of Texas Press, 1975); Miguel León-Portilla, *Fifteen Poets of the Aztec World* (Norman: University of Oklahoma Press, 1992); James Lockhart, *The Nahuas after the Conquest* (Stanford, Calif.: Stanford University Press, 1992).

— Scott Chamberlain

Narváez, Pánfilo de (ca. 1478–1528)

A Spanish explorer and CONQUISTADOR, Pánfilo de Narváez helped conquer CUBA and later led a disastrous expedition into FLORIDA.

Narváez first came to the Americas as a young man, probably around 1498. He fought in JAMAICA and helped lead the Spanish soldiers who conquered Cuba in a war that lasted from 1510 to 1514. The governor of Cuba, DIEGO DE VALÁZQUEZ, feared that HERNÁN CORTÉS, the conqueror of the AZTECS, was growing insubordinate. In 1520 Velázquez sent Narváez to Mexico at the head of almost a thousand soldiers with instructions to arrest Cortés. Cortés, in a surprise attack, defeated Narváez and recruited many of his soldiers into his own army. He then imprisoned Narváez for more than two years. Once freed, Narváez returned to Spain.

In 1526 Narváez received a commission to conquer the Gulf coast of Florida. As a reward for leading this expedition, he was named both ADELANTADO and governor for life of Florida. His party landed near Tampa Bay on April 14, 1528.

The expedition faced severe problems from the beginning, which were probably exacerbated by conflicts between Narváez and his second-in-command, ÁLVAR NÚÑEZ CABEZA DE VACA. Narváez did not bring enough food and supplies for the expedition, and the men suffered from hunger and thirst. As they headed north they fought with Indians they encountered. The Spanish survivors eventually reached the chiefdom of APALACHEE, in northern Florida. Ill and exhausted, they decided to build boats and return to Mexico. They launched five boats, but their attempt to return to Mexico failed. Some boats were washed out to sea, while others washed ashore. Only four men, including Cabeza de Vaca, survived to return to New Spain eight years later.

Cabeza de Vaca, in his account of the expedition, wrote that Narváez was among those lost at sea. He heard from another Spanish survivor of the expedition that one night "the governor stayed in his boat and refused to go ashore . . . and a mate and a page, who was ill, stayed with him; and they had no water in the boat or anything to eat, and in the middle of the night the north wind began to blow so fiercely that it took the boat out to sea without anyone seeing it go, for they had no anchor but a stone."

Further reading: Rolena Adorno and Patrick Charles Pautz, *Álvar Núñez Cabeza de Vaca: His Account, His Life, and the Expedition of Pánfilo de Narváez,* vol. 3 (Lincoln: University of Nebraska Press, 1999); Jerald T. Milanich, "Narváez, Pánfilo de" in *Encyclopedia of Latin American History and Culture,* vol. 4, ed. Barbara A. Tenenbaum (New York: Scribner's, 1996); Enrique Pupo-Walker, ed., *Castaways: The Narrative of Alvar Núñez Cabeza de Vaca,* trans. Frances M. López-Morillas (Berkeley: University of California Press, 1993); Stuart B. Schwartz, ed. *Victors and Vanquished: Spanish and Nahua Views of the Conquest of Mexico* (Boston: Bedford/St. Martin's, 2000).

— Martha K. Robinson

Natchez

An extinct indigenous nation whose members inhabited territory near modern-day Natchez, Mississippi, the Natchez Indians had enormous power in the Mississippi Valley when they first encountered Europeans in the mid-16th century.

The Natchez, like other indigenous nations in the southeast of the modern-day United States, had strong cultural links to the MISSISSIPPIAN peoples. They inhabited a theocracy in which the head chief, known as the great sun, had the responsibility for the rising of the sun each day. Because the Natchez believed that the sun itself was the supreme deity, the link between its daily movements and the human who headed the nation made obvious sense. The Natchez also believed in other minor deities, and they constructed houses to honor the sun and the great sun. On certain occasions, such as the death of the great sun, the Natchez sacrificed humans to propitiate the divine forces that governed their world. In one of the temples the Natchez kept a fire always burning.

In many respects Natchez communities resembled nearby indigenous groups. CORN agriculture, supplemented by beans, pumpkins, peaches, and melons, was the basis of their diet. The Natchez also grew TOBACCO and gathered locally available plants, including wild rice and grapes. Women tended the crops while men had responsibility for hunting deer, buffalo, and other game. They traveled through the region in canoes, some of them up to 40 feet long, and engaged in trade with other native peoples.

The Natchez first met Europeans when HERNANDO DE SOTO traveled through the region in 1542. The natives and newcomers did not get along, although there is little evidence of any overt hostility. Nonetheless, contact with Europeans and with Old World DISEASEs that had come to the Western Hemisphere as part of the COLUMBIAN EXCHANGE, devastated the nation. From a population of perhaps 4,500 in 1650, the Natchez declined to only 300 in 1731. Eighteenth-century conflicts with French colonists proved disastrous, especially when the Europeans defeated the Natchez in battle in 1731 and sold the survivors, including their last leader, into SLAVERY. Some Natchez survived the French assault and migrated to nearby indigenous communities of Chickasaw, Cherokee, and Creek.

Perhaps the best written source of evidence for the Natchez is the account written by the French colonist Antoine Simon le Page du Pratz, who documented elements of Natchez culture and society during the early 18th century. His account, entitled *Histoire de la Louisiane,* was published in Paris in 1758, although it contains information du Pratz gathered in the early 1730s. Like other European observers, du Pratz made drawings of some of the things he saw, including the main temple and the house of the great sun.

Over time the surviving Natchez married members of other native nations. The last speaker of the Natchez language died in 1965, and the last Natchez ceremony took place in 1976, although a group of several hundred claiming some Natchez ancestry maintained a ceremonial site in eastern Oklahoma into the 1980s.

Further reading: Patricia Galloway, *Choctaw Genesis, 1500–1700* (Lincoln: University of Nebraska Press, 1995); Barry M. Pritzker, *A Native American Encyclopedia* (New York: Oxford University Press, 2000); Charles D. Van Tuyl, *The Natchez: Annotated Translations from Antoine Simon le Page du Pratz's* Histoire de la Louisiane *and A Short English–Natchez Dictionary,* Oklahoma Historical Society Series in Anthropology no. 4 (Oklahoma City: Oklahoma Historical Society, 1980).

Native American religion

Long before Europeans and Africans arrived in the Western Hemisphere, indigenous peoples of the Americas possessed rich religious traditions, many of them tied to specific homelands.

Like other peoples across the globe, every native group in the Americas created, developed, and maintained a set of religious ideas. These sets of ideas varied from place to place, although in most instances religious traditions included stories of the origins of human beings and guidelines for propitiating the divine forces that often exert control over life on earth, including the actions of humans and animals. Like the peoples of Europe who built places of worship to honor the Judeo-Christian God, indigenous peoples across the Americas constructed temples to honor their deities. Unlike Europeans, Native American peoples tended to believe in more than a single divine force in the universe.

Given the diversity of lifestyles and histories across the Western Hemisphere, there is no simple way to describe Native American religious practice. In the Southwest of the modern-day United States, for example, some HOPI have long believed that there was (and is) a spiritual dimension to the planting and tending of CORN, and their tradition tells of a link between the planting of blue corn and the origins of the Hopi themselves. The Anishinaabe of modern-day northern Minnesota celebrated the central role that wild rice played in their economy. The IROQUOIS in the northeast, like the Hopi, celebrated the planting of corn, and long before Europeans arrived they had created sacred ceremonies in which they would ritually smoke TOBACCO or consume unripe (or green) corn to please the deities responsible for the annual corn crop. Farther north, where agriculture played a less crucial role in native people's lives because the growing season was too short and unpredictable, indigenous traditions spoke about the power that certain animal spirits possessed. Thus, some sub-Arctic peoples like the Micmac and Cree believed that there were great "bosses" or "keepers" of bears and beavers, enormous spirits that kept watch over their counterparts on earth. In order to have a successful hunt, those who wanted to kill large game needed to engage in certain behaviors to please the animal bosses. They would not let their dogs chew on the bones of an animal killed in the hunt, for example, or allow menstruating women to share in the first feast that they made after a hunt. By obeying such rules these native peoples maintained peaceful relations with the bosses who, in return, would often instruct real-world animals where they should go so they could be captured and killed by humans. Maintaining harmony with these spirits also prevented sickness because the animal bosses tended to control the spread of infectious diseases. In central Alaska the Koyukon people, who rely on hunting for their livelihoods, also believe in animal forces, including the power of Raven to shape the flow of the rivers in their homeland.

Across the Americas indigenous peoples reshaped their landscape to reflect their religious beliefs. The MISSISSIPPIAN peoples, for example, built enormous mounds (such as those at CAHOKIA) that had multiple religious purposes; such structures, constructed of tons of earth, could be used for ceremonies and for the interment of the remains of community members. Natives of the HOPEWELL tradition constructed a massive mound at Fairgrounds Circle near modern-day Newark, Ohio. They built this mound, which they used for cremation of human remains, around A.D. 300, long before Europeans ever had the idea of building a substantial cathedral. Another vast mound located near Monroe, Louisiana, dates from approximately 3000 B.C.

If North American mounds can still impress visitors, imagine what it must have been like for Spaniards who arrived in Mexico and found themselves staring upward at great Mayan temples such as the so-called Temple 5C-49 and Temple IV at TIKAL, the Temple of the Sun at PALENQUE, or the Temple of the Warriors at CHICHÉN ITZÁ. These enormous stone buildings tower over the surrounding fields and jungle; each is the product of hundreds of thousands of hours of labor and architectural genius. Carvings within sacred buildings reveal the religious practices of inhabitants. At the Aztec site at Yaxchilan in Chiapas, for example, one carving shows a bloodletting ritual in which the queen, Lady Xoc, pulled a rope through her tongue. Because the rope was lined with thorns, it drew copious amounts of blood, a vital part of the ritual. Women alone did not suffer in religious ceremonies. A sculpture at another Aztec site depicts a high-status man making ritual incisions into his penis to draw blood for a ritual.

There is no obvious link between each of these forms of religious expression other than the fact that all indigenous communities participated in rituals in order to preserve their existence. Many of these rituals reflected ties to local environments, such as rites associated with agriculture or hunting. Many ceremonies also symbolized the intimate connections that logically existed between indigenous peoples and the land they inhabited. For many peoples the landscape itself was a sacred text that could be read by those who knew the traditions. Thus, in the northwest of the modern-day United States, ancient oral histories tell how the great coyote spirit created the Columbia River and then changed its course. The Spokane Indians told a story about a sleeping monster assaulted by members of the community; when the monster awoke and fled, he carved a deep path to Lake Coeur d'Alene that became the Spokane River. White Mountain Apaches told stories about particular parts of their homeland, stories so specific that mention of a place evoked not only what it might look like but also a lesson that that place offered to those who knew how to pay attention. Across the eastern woodlands indigenous peoples believed in spirits they called MANTOAC, Montóac, or Manitou.

Virtually every European who arrived in the Americas was convinced that the religious practices of indigenous peoples reflected the natives' ignorance. "Some religion they have alreadie," the English ethnographer THOMAS HARRIOT wrote about the Carolina ALGONQUIAN he met at ROANOKE in his *Briefe and True Report of the Newfound Land of Virginia,* published first in LONDON in 1588, "which although it be farre from the truth, yet being as it is, there is hope it may bee the easier and sooner reformed." Recognizing that native religious beliefs would be of enormous interest to his European audience, Harriot enumerated some of the defining features of the Carolina Algonquian's beliefs. "They beleeve that there are many Gods which they call *Mantóac,* but of different sortes and degrees," he wrote, "one onely chiefe and great God, which hath bene from all eternitie," as well as lesser deities. "For mankind they say a woman was made first, which by the woorking of one of the goddes, conceived and brought foorth children: And in such sort they say they had their beginning." These peoples believed in the immortality of the soul and that gods had human form and "therefore they represent them by images in the formes of men, which they call *Kewasowok* one alone is called *Kewás*[.] Them they place in houses appropriate or temples which they call *Mathicáomuck*[,] where they woorship, praie, sing, and make manie times offerings unto them." When JOHN WHITE painted his memorable watercolors of the Carolina Algonquian, he was careful to document the ways that these Native people prayed and danced using rattles and provided a careful rendering of an idol in human form that presided over the bodies of deceased leaders. When THEODOR DE BRY engraved these paintings for the 1590

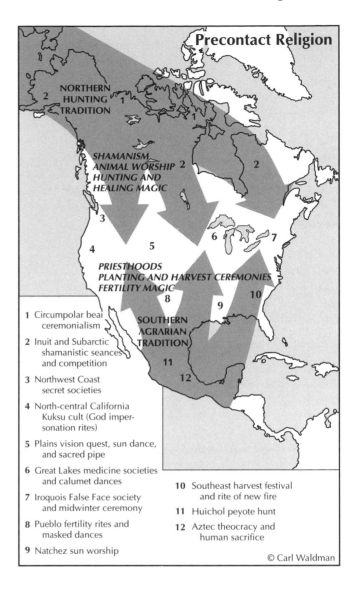

Precontact Religion

NORTHERN HUNTING TRADITION

SHAMANISM ANIMAL WORSHIP HUNTING AND HEALING MAGIC

PRIESTHOODS PLANTING AND HARVEST CEREMONIES FERTILITY MAGIC

SOUTHERN AGRARIAN TRADITION

1 Circumpolar bear ceremonialism
2 Inuit and Subarctic shamanistic seances and competition
3 Northwest Coast secret societies
4 North-central California Kuksu cult (God impersonation rites)
5 Plains vision quest, sun dance, and sacred pipe
6 Great Lakes medicine societies and calumet dances
7 Iroquois False Face society and midwinter ceremony
8 Pueblo fertility rites and masked dances
9 Natchez sun worship
10 Southeast harvest festival and rite of new fire
11 Huichol peyote hunt
12 Aztec theocracy and human sacrifice

© Carl Waldman

edition of Harriot's book, these images of Native American religion spread across Europe.

The existence of indigenous religious practices presented a challenge to Europeans, who wanted to bring Christianity to the Western Hemisphere. JESUITS, FRANCISCANS, DOMINICANS, and missionaries from every other religious group all had to devise strategies whereby indigenous peoples would abandon their ancestral practices and adopt the rituals and beliefs of the newcomers. At times their methods worked, and some native peoples converted. More often, at least during the period before 1607, native peoples did not embrace the spiritual offerings of the "black robes" or others promising everlasting redemption in exchange for abandonment of indigenous ways, although some native peoples did adopt elements of the missionaries' programs. European missionaries often bemoaned the syncretic practices that emerged when religious traditions from the Old World arrived in the Americas, but such adaptations only reflected indigenous peoples' longstanding respect for the spiritual forces that guided their world and their ability to adapt to changing circumstances.

Further reading: James Axtell, *The Invasion Within: The Contest of Cultures in Colonial North America* (New York: Oxford University Press, 1985); Sam D. Gill, "Religious Forms and Themes," in Alvin M. Josephy, Jr., ed., *America in 1492: The World of the Indian Peoples Before the Arrival of Columbus* (New York: Knopf, 1992), 277–303; John S. Henderson, *The World of the Ancient Maya,* 2nd ed. (Ithaca, N.Y.: Cornell University Press, 1997); Calvin Martin, *Keepers of the Game: Indians, Animals, and the Fur Trade* (Berkeley: University of California Press, 1978); Joel W. Martin, *The Land Looks After Us: A History of Native American Religion* (New York: Oxford University Press, 2001); Linda Schele and Mary Ellen Miller, *The Blood of Kings: Dynasty and Ritual in Maya Art* (New York: George Braziller with the Kimbell Art Museum, 1986).

Nevis

One of the Leeward Islands among the Lesser Antilles in the Caribbean Sea, Nevis contained an indigenous population for several centuries until they abandoned the island just before English colonization in 1628.

An oval volcanic island located at the northwest end of the Lesser Antilles near St. Kitts, Nevis was originally covered with forests, and it contains three volcanic cones, with the tallest, Nevis Peak, rising to a height of 985 meters. Indigenous people first populated the island around approximately 1000 B.C. This first group did not practice horticulture and depended upon hunting and gathering terrestrial and aquatic resources. Finally, around 200 B.C., a sedentary horticultural people moved to the island. These people eventually developed into the Eastern TAINO, who occupied the island at the time of contact with Europeans. From this point until just before English colonization, these Taino suffered slave raids by Europeans to the north and west in the Greater Antilles and Island CARIB to the south in the Leeward Islands of the Lesser Antilles. For unknown reasons the island was uninhabited by the time the English initiated colonization in the Leeward Islands in 1624.

In 1628 the English founded a colony on Nevis. The English became attracted to colonial development in the region due to the success of the Spanish and Dutch in the Caribbean. At first the English did not develop Nevis as a plantation colony, but they finally adopted a SUGAR planta-

tion economy after Portuguese JEWS introduced sugar cultivation to the Windward Islands between 1640 and 1650. Because of the limited acreage of flat land, these plantations tended to remain small, family-run enterprises.

Further reading: Helmut Blume, *The Caribbean Islands,* trans. Johannes Maczewski and Ann Norton (London: Longman, 1974); Irving Rouse, "The Tainos," in *Migrations in Prehistory: Inferring Population Movement from Cultural Remains* (New Haven, Conn.: Yale University Press, 1986), 105–156; ———, *The Tainos: Rise and Decline of the People Who Greeted Columbus* (New Haven, Conn.: Yale University Press, 1992); Samuel M. Wilson, "The Prehistoric Settlement Pattern of Nevis, West Indies," *Journal of Field Archaeology* 16 (1989): 427–450.

— Dixie Ray Haggard

New Mexico

A large area in what is today the southwest United States that saw the rise of a variety of native groups and served as the northern frontier of the Spanish colony of NEW SPAIN.

The name "New Mexico" was given to the area around 1580 by Spanish explorers who thought that the PUEBLOs, or apartmentlike residential complexes, of the local natives were reminiscent of the great Aztec cities such as TENOCHTITLÁN, TACUBA, and Texcoco in the central valley of MEXICO. With few natural boundaries, New Mexico was a poorly defined province. Many Spaniards used the term to refer to the entire northern zone of New Spain, although in late colonial times the separate territories of CALIFORNIA and Texas were removed from its jurisdiction. In reality, the province of New Mexico was centered on the Rio Grande, starting at El Paso and running north into Colorado. Most European settlements, like the native communities before them, were within a short distance of this river or its tributaries, leaving the other areas to nomadic groups such as the Apache and Navajo. Along with Spanish FLORIDA, New Mexico was one of the earliest areas in what is now the United States to have been settled by Europeans, and its capital of SANTA FE is the second-oldest European city in the modern-day United States.

Ancient New Mexico

New Mexico boasts some of the oldest human remains in North America. According to the geological and archaeological record, New Mexico was considerably wetter in ancient times than it is now. The area was covered with grasslands and forests that supported a variety of animals. Early humans were nomadic hunters following the trail of big game that inhabited the region. Two important groups of hunters were named for the sites in New Mexico where their remains were first found: Clovis Man and Folsom

Man. Archaeologists have dated these groups to around 9200 B.C. During this time they hunted large animals such as bison, which provided both meat and material for clothing. As the Ice Age ended, the climate became drier and hotter, forcing the people of New Mexico to adapt to new conditions. This developing "desert culture" gravitated toward the rivers of the region and turned slowly to agriculture as they supplemented their diet with smaller game such as deer, antelope, and fish. In time these settlements developed into sophisticated societies.

One of the first great cultures to develop in the region was the Mogollon Culture centered in the southwestern portion of New Mexico. Through ancient links to Mexico, Mogollon farmers learned to grow CORN between 3000 and 750 B.C., adding squash and red kidney beans to their diet by 400 B.C. Around 300 B.C. they began constructing pithouses, which were large oval or round pits overlaid with timber and earth roofs. Residents dug smaller pits within the houses for storing food, pottery, and votive offerings. A subgroup of the Mogollon culture created spectacular ceramic pots with distinctive geometrical and natural designs called Mimbres ware, which remains some of the Southwest's most sophisticated pottery. These pots were often included in household offerings interred with deceased members of a community but were systematically broken, suggesting that the beautiful, finely crafted ceramics were ritually "killed" before being buried, perhaps to release the pot's spirit. The Mogollon culture, protected by numerous mountain ranges, reached its apogee around A.D. 500. It had a great influence on the area around it, evident especially in the appearance of pit houses as ceremonial areas among later cultures.

The other great culture that developed in the region was the Anasazi, whose name means both "Ancient Ones" or "Ancestral Enemies" in the Navajo language. This culture developed more slowly than did the Mogollon but ultimately spread to an area covering modern-day New Mexico, Arizona, Colorado, and Utah. Over time the culture changed greatly. From around A.D. 1 to 500 the Navajo were primarily a basket-making people who did not use ceramics. They used their sophisticated baskets for everything—storage, cooking food, and carrying water. Between 500 and 700 the Anasazi built larger settlements and developed agriculture as well. After 700 they began dwelling in pueblos, which were villages consisting of residential apartment complexes and ceremonial pit houses called kivas. Traditionally the houses and above-ground spaces were associated with women, but the underground kivas were strictly used by men. Scholars have been able to trace the development of Anasazi sites by examining the well-preserved timber used to construct the pueblos. By examining the patterns of tree ring growth, archaeologists have been able to establish a basic chronology for the Anasazi area.

The Anasazi pueblos reached their peak after 1050. The greatest of Anasazi sites was Chaco Canyon, located in northwestern New Mexico, begun around 850 and completed by 1130. It consisted of a series of well-built pueblos linked with roads. Recent investigators have concluded that the roads were not just used to facilitate travel and communication, but also had ritual and cultural significance. The Anasazi built large-scale agricultural projects, including dams and irrigation ditches, which enabled them to increase food production. The largest pueblo at Chaco Canyon was Pueblo Bonito, which housed 1,200 people in a four-story, D-shaped complex. It was the largest apartment complex in the United States until the late 19th century. The Anasazi had numerous links with neighboring cultures in the Southwest, and there is evidence to suggest that this area of New Mexico had close trading contacts with central Mexico (particularly with the Toltec culture), along the so-called Turquoise Road.

Despite their success, by 1200 the Anasazi had started their long decline. Scholars have suggested that a series of droughts caused widespread famine. Other settlements, such as Mesa Verde in Colorado, reveal that the Anasazi were abandoning their great open pueblos and creating more defensible ones under cliffs, suggesting that Anasazi towns were under attack. Slowly the great pueblos were abandoned, and refugees began gravitating toward more fertile areas. Further droughts in 1450 sparked off another wave of migrations, with most of the remaining population clustering around the Rio Grande and its tributaries. By 1500 the Anasazi culture had disintegrated, leaving a legacy of puebloan culture focused on the ZUNI-Acoma area of New Mexico, the central Rio Grande valley, and scattered settlements in Arizona. These cultures, ancestors to today's HOPI and Zuni people, continued to live in adobe apartments and build underground kivas for ceremonies. Like others in the region, they were skilled at ceramics and basketweaving. Likewise, they practiced agriculture, but on a smaller scale than their ancestors.

The last main group of people located in ancient New Mexico were the nomadic hunters and raiders. There were two cultures in this category, the Apache and the Navajo. With linguistic roots in Canada, these two groups migrated into the region around 1200, leading some to speculate that their raids helped bring down the great Anasazi centers (which would account for the Navajo term). Both groups relied heavily on hunting, although over time the Navajo became more sedentary, developing agriculture as well. Both groups were nomadic, creating small temporary communities. Both groups apparently traded animal hides and dried meat with the puebloans, gaining cotton, corn, and utensils in return. Along with these more peaceful contacts, violence often flared between the puebloans and the nomads, and these internecine tensions intensified when Europeans began moving into the area.

Early Exploration

A few years after HERNÁN CORTÉS conquered the AZTECS, expeditions began leaving central Mexico to explore the continent. However, paradoxically, the first European explorers to enter New Mexico did not do so from the south, but rather from the east. ÁLVAR NÚÑEZ CABEZA DE VACA was part of an ill-fated expedition that became stranded in the Tampa Bay area of FLORIDA in 1528. The 300 survivors attempted to make their way west through country never before explored by Europeans in an attempt to reach Mexico. After several disasters and a period of enslavement, Cabeza de Vaca gained fame as a mystic healer whose Catholic prayers cured the sick. With four survivors, Cabeza de Vaca continued his westward search for the Spanish settlements in Mexico, reaching present-day New Mexico in 1534. Crossing over from what is now west Texas, the party briefly followed the Pecos River northward, although once they felt they were moving too far in that direction, they struck out west. They reached the Rio Grande and followed it south, passing near the site of modern-day El Paso and continuing south and west toward Mexico City. While Cabeza de Vaca's main concern was survival, he did take notes on the surrounding area, proclaiming that the people were skilled artisans with productive agricultural lands and in so doing providing an invaluable account of New Mexico on the eve of the Spanish conquest. He also reported that they had supplies of precious metals, which sparked more determined efforts to explore the land.

After the 1530s New Mexico became associated with a series of legends that lured Spaniards to explore the region. Enthusiasts suggested that various refugees fleeing from Europe and the Middle East (including Christians, survivors of Atlantis, and the Lost Tribes of Israel) had crossed the Atlantic and set up kingdoms in exile in the NEW WORLD. Cabeza de Vaca's suggestion that there were sophisticated societies to the north caused great interest among royal officials. Particularly seductive were the stories about the Seven Cities of Cíbola. In 1539 the viceroy of NEW SPAIN, ANTONIO DE MENDOZA, organized an expedition to explore the territories to the north. He selected Friar Marcos de Niza, a Franciscan priest who had accompanied FRANCISCO PIZARRO on his conquest of PERU, to lead the party. Esteban the Moor (Estevanico), who was one of the survivors who accompanied Cabeza de Vaca, served as the expedition's guide, partially retracing his steps into New Mexico. Friar Marcos's explorations were largely failures, and the natives who were friendly to Cabeza de Vaca killed Esteban in southern New Mexico. Still, Friar Marcos called it an unqualified success, claiming to have seen cities of gold in the distance. He urged others to follow, and the viceroy accordingly drew up new plans.

The leader of the next expedition was FRANCISCO CORONADO, who paid for most of its expenses himself. Coronado organized a huge enterprise that consisted of 336 men, 559 HORSES, and at least 100 native porters. Additionally, he provided for naval support from the Gulf of California. Several clergymen volunteered to ensure the peaceful conversion of the indigenous people. Friar Marcos, who had provided such glorious accounts of the area, served as the guide. Traveling northward through what is today Arizona, Coronado cut eastward and arrived in the Zuni area, where Friar Marcos claimed Cíbola lay. Instead of golden cities and hordes of precious stones, the CONQUISTADORES found adobe pueblos. Coronado pushed forward and, hearing good reports of the fertility of the Rio Grande valley, moved to set up a base camp there for the winter of 1540–41. Friar Marcos sensed the bitter disappointment of the campaign and chose to return to Mexico. Eventually, Coronado pushed east toward a legendary land called Quivira. After traveling to central Kansas in search of this equally mythical realm, Coronado returned to his base in New Mexico. Injured before he could mount any further expeditions in the area, he had no choice but to return home. The lack of any wealthy kingdoms to the north led the Spaniards to all but abandon New Mexico for the next 40 years.

Colonization

In the 1580s many Spaniards showed new interest in exploring New Mexico, with the particular intent to establish a permanent presence in the region. A native rebellion called the Mixton War convinced many that New Spain's frontier needed to be secure, and the new mining operations around ZACATECAS remained vulnerable to raids. With Coronado's campaign a distant memory, a new group of Spaniards entered the region. In 1580 the Franciscan lay brother Agustín Rodríguez proposed a new venture that would set up a line of fortified missions in New Mexico designed simultaneously to protect the frontier and convert the local population. In 1581 three FRANCISCANS accompanied by 19 soldiers under the command of Francisco Chamuscado moved into New Mexico, following the Rio Grande as far as modern-day Taos. They explored the Rio Grande Valley intensively, also scouting the Pecos River. Again, the expedition was far from successful, with one Franciscan and several soldiers dying before they abandoned the region in 1582. The two other friars remained in New Mexico, although they quickly met martyrs' deaths. Still, the careful records and surveys of the local populations they left behind were instrumental for future colonization efforts.

News of the voyages of SIR FRANCIS DRAKE led the Spanish to renew their interest in New Mexico. Geographers assumed that the area lay close to the sea and was thus vulnerable to attack. If Spain's enemies gained a foothold on the northern frontier of New Spain, they might be able to attack the colony as a whole. Thus, the royal government directed JUAN DE OÑATE in 1597 to subdue and colonize New Mexico. Like Coronado, Oñate financed much of the expedition himself. In addition to establishing a military presence in the area, the Crown directed Oñate to set up missions to Christianize the locals, who would serve as a buffer against external assault. In 1598 the expedition moved forward, containing 400 men (130 of whom had wives and children), 7,000 head of cattle, and 10 Franciscans. Oñate set up a base camp at the site of the Ohke pueblo, which he renamed San Juan de los Caballeros. Space was limited at the site, and many Spaniards felt ill at ease near the natives. Oñate established other settlements nearby, including San Gabriel. Population pressure remained a problem, and in 1609–10 the Spaniards built up the new city of Santa Fe as their permanent capital.

Power within the colony was divided between civil and ecclesiastical authorities. The nominal head of the secular government was a governor appointed by either the king or the viceroy in Mexico City. The remote location made it possible for ambitious governors to become enormously powerful. He ruled with the support of the *CABILDO*, or town council, located in Santa Fe, as well as a small number of judges who traveled through the colony. The royal governor also oversaw local governors who administered pueblos under Spanish jurisdiction. Besides this secular government, there was a parallel religious government based in Santa Fe as well. This role was taken up by the Franciscans, who continued to be the dominant religious order in New Mexico. They organized missions based in or near the pueblos and instructed the natives in Christian doctrine. The clerics also attempted to reshape indigenous communities. They imposed a strict schedule on the natives designed to create a European work ethic and demanded that local indigenous people perform a number of duties for the benefit of the colony, such as tending herds, growing food, and building churches. Missionaries also attempted to suppress local traditions and impose European morality, particularly in areas of marriage and sexuality. If the natives failed to comply with the Franciscans' demands, they received heavy punishment. Although the two main branches of government were closely interrelated, ecclesiastical and civic figures often fought over who held the ultimate power in the colony, and both claimed the authority to organize, administer, and punish the local natives.

Life in the early colonial days was difficult for the Spanish. Because New Mexico was, in the opinion of imperial bureaucrats, to be a military stronghold, most of the settlements and missions had a distinct military character. Still believing the region had rich metal deposits, many of the colonists spent an inordinate amount of time scouring the hills and mountains for GOLD. Agriculture was more successful than prospecting, but most of the Spaniards were unwilling to till the soil themselves. They conscripted local natives to work the land for them, but this did not endear the Spaniards to the indigenous people. Several villages, including Acoma, resisted Spanish law and raided the Spanish settlements. Because Oñate could not afford to appear weak, he sent an army that attacked and destroyed Acoma, killing 800 natives in the process. Franciscan friars did establish a successful network of missions among the puebloan people, but resentment against the cultural intrusion simmered for more than a century. Further, Apache and Navajo raiders periodically attacked both the pueblos and the Spanish settlements. The distance between the colony and the seat of the royal government in Mexico meant that the Spaniards in New Mexico were isolated both militarily and culturally, leading to the development of a siege mentality. Tensions between Spaniards and natives smoldered for most of the 1600s, finally erupting during the Pueblo Revolt of 1680, in which native rebels drove the Spaniards from New Mexico, holding the territory for 13 years before the Spaniards returned in force.

While often inhospitable, New Mexico became a home for various native peoples as well as Spanish colonists. As a strategic stronghold guarding the frontier of New Spain, the colony served an important military role. As a frontier province away from the centers of Spanish culture, New Mexico was a place where native and European elements mingled. The Spaniards tried to convert the indigenous peoples to European ways, but in the process the newcomers also adopted native architecture, building materials, and art forms. Even today, the area maintains important elements from native and European cultures. This mingling of cultures has provided New Mexico with a unique, rich heritage.

Further reading: *General works:* Calvin A. Roberts and Susan A. Roberts, *New Mexico* (Albuquerque: University of New Mexico Press, 1988); David J. Weber, *The Spanish Frontier in North America* (New Haven, Conn.: Yale University Press, 1992). *On the native past:* Kendrick Frazier, *People of Chaco: A Canyon and Its Culture* (New York: Norton, 1999); Joe S. Sando, *Pueblo Nations: Eight Centuries of Pueblo Indian History* (Santa Fe: Clear Light Publishers, 1991). *On society and the church:* Ramón Gutiérrez, *When Jesus Came, the Corn Mothers Went Away: Marriage, Sexuality, and Power in New Mexico, 1500–1846* (Stanford, Calif.: Stanford University Press, 1991).

— Scott Chamberlain

New Spain

New Spain was one of the great territorial divisions of the Spanish Empire in the NEW WORLD, based in MEXICO and encompassing most of the Spanish territories north of PANAMA, including the Caribbean islands and the Philippines.

The first Spanish claim on the American mainland occurred when HERNAN CORTÉS landed at VERACRUZ in 1519. He established a settlement (more accurately, a base camp) and claimed the area for Spain. The following year the Spaniards adopted the term *New Spain* to refer to central Mexico. As the conquest progressed, the territory's boundaries expanded. By 1524 the Spanish had pushed to Honduras in the south and Colima in the north. A number of these areas became autonomous provinces, including Honduras in 1526, Guatemala in 1530, and the northern district of New Galicia in 1531. Soon the Spaniards recognized the need for greater integration of their new territories. In 1535 the entire area was formally transformed into a viceroyalty called New Spain, which was governed by a viceroy from Mexico City (the AZTECS' former capital of TENOCHTITLÁN). Local governments in the provinces were given varying degrees of autonomy, but all remained loyal to the viceroy in Mexico City. Almost immediately, the Spanish placed the Caribbean under the administration of New Spain, and by the 1560s FLORIDA, NEW MEXICO, and the Philippines were added as well.

Spanish Conquest and Settlement

The core of New Spain was the old Aztec Empire, which fell to Cortés in 1521. With the conquest of this powerful state, most of the surrounding areas fell as well. The TARASCAN were quickly absorbed within a year. PEDRO DE ALVARADO led troops into the Guatemalan highlands, where he subdued the Quiché MAYA kingdom in 1523. Only the Maya kingdoms in the YUCATÁN PENINSULA offered sustained resistance, although by 1537 the CONQUISTADORES had established tentative control over the area.

The administrators of New Spain naturally favored the rapid construction of cities. For one, many of the native groups were urban themselves, and the first great Spanish cities were built on or around large indigenous communities. Mexico City, for example, was constructed on the ruins of Tenochtitlán. Additionally, Cortés was an active promoter of colonization and greatly encouraged construction of cities, which would serve as military strong points in a hostile land. By 1531 there were 15 official Spanish cities in central Mexico alone. From the central highlands several waves of city building spread across the region. One line led south and west, following the conquests of Pedro de Alvarado. By 1535 an additional 15 cities had been founded in Guatemala, in the heart of Maya territory. The difficult conquest of the Yucatán reduced the number of Spanish towns in the region, and it was only after 1570 that the Spanish established four communities there. Cities sprang up in the north as well, particularly after the Spanish crushed a rebellion by the Mixton Indians. Guadalajara was built in 1531 and ZACATECAS founded in 1546. By 1600 the most important cities in New Spain were Mexico City (the capital), Puebla, Guadalajara, Zacatecas, Antequera (Oaxaca), and Guatemala City.

From the beginning the Crown was concerned about how best to bring the natives into the Spanish fold. Conquest was not enough; imperial promoters wanted to acculturate the natives as well. One of the first attempts to do so was with the ENCOMIENDA. Under this system Spanish settlers had limited jurisdiction over a number of native communities. The *encomendero* was to convert, protect, and educate the natives, and in return he was allowed to make use of their labor. While the natives were not formally enslaved, they were coerced into working for the benefit of the *encomendero*. This system failed miserably. Most *encomenderos* usually made no attempt to fulfill their duties, and their excessive demands led to the deaths of thousands of overworked natives. Another attempt by the Crown to acculturate the natives was to force them into Spanish-style cities (see REDUCCIONES). Those who conceived the scheme believed that if natives were surrounded by Spanish culture and forced to interact in a Spanish-style environment, they would become more Spanish themselves. To put this plan into action, the Spanish uprooted many natives and forced them into new cities, a process that accelerated after the 1540s when great PLAGUES devastated the native population.

The Administrative System

From the beginning the Spanish Crown knew it would face enormous difficulties in establishing and maintaining its control over New Spain. One of the most significant hurdles was the distance between Spain and its new colony; it took months for messages to reach their destinations on the other side of the ocean, if they arrived at all. Moreover, the area had been recently conquered, and there was the lingering possibility of native revolts. Further, the Crown feared that the conquistadores, the most active Spaniards in the region, might decide to set up kingdoms of their own. Rewarding these men for their efforts was also fraught with peril. During Spain's war against the Moors (called the RECONQUISTA), conquering heroes were sometimes given lands and titles (see ADELANTADO). The Crown feared that if it followed this model in the New World, it would be creating a new landed aristocracy that could block its interests.

Faced with these potential problems, the Spanish Crown developed an unusual political system based on overlapping authority that contained considerable checks and balances. Imperial bureaucrats' overarching concern was to build a political system that could adequately meet the needs of the colony but that would not create institutions or politicians that could ever effectively challenge the king. The first step in this process was to slowly, graciously remove the conquistadores from power and replace them with bland bureaucrats. The most important of these royal officials was the viceroy. In principle, he was the king's representative in New Spain, speaking for the king, administering the king' justice, and executing the king's commands. Because this position was so strong, the king was cautious about whom he selected for it. The holder was always a person from Spain itself (never from a local family) who was forbidden from acquiring property or engaging in economic activities. He was even discouraged from becoming too friendly with the local population lest he become overly involved in local affairs. In 1535 ANTONIO DE MENDOZA became the first viceroy of New Spain, and his successful tenure became a model for all those that followed him.

The Crown remained concerned that despite its precautions, the viceroy might still become too powerful. To avoid this potential crisis, the Spanish established other institutions to counterbalance the viceroy. The most important of these was the AUDIENCIA, a council that primarily functioned as a court of appeals, although it took on other responsibilities as time went on. A limited *audiencia* was established in Mexico City in 1528, but the system was substantially altered after the arrival of the viceroy. It became an official advisory council to the viceroy and had the power to enact laws. The *audiencia* in Mexico City remained the ultimate judicial and legislative council for New Spain, but subordinate *audiencias* were established in most of the large cities, where they functioned as first courts of appeal. The Crown deliberately blurred the spheres of influence of the viceroy and the *audiencia.* The question of who had the ultimate authority to decide an issue, promulgate laws, collect taxes, and so forth became divided between the groups. This division led to fierce political in-fighting, which frequently paralyzed the colonial government. The only way to resolve an issue was to appeal to the COUNCIL OF THE INDIES (a royal advisory board in Spain) or the king himself. This overlapping authority kept any groups from becoming too powerful and subtly reinforced the power of the king because he remained the final arbiter of disputes.

Local government in New Spain consisted of two branches, which also served as checks on the viceroys and *audiencias.* First, there was the CORREGIDOR. He was a district administrator who presided over a subdivision of an *audiencia.* There were two types: the municipal *corregidor,* who was assigned to Spanish towns, and the *corregidor de indios,* who was associated with native towns. In both cases their functions were essentially the same. They were supe-

rior judges, head of the municipal councils, and had a fair degree of latitude in enforcing laws. Skilled *corregidores* often played off both the viceroys and *audiencias,* offering to support one against the other or blocking enforcement of laws championed by either side. Below the *corregidores* were the CABILDOs, or town councils. These councils, located in every official city, had local authority to maintain defense, collect local taxes and tariffs, and to enact municipal codes. *Cabildos* frequently challenged the authority of the other administrators, refusing to enforce laws that they felt infringed upon their lives. In addition, Spanish bureaucrats devised two other regulatory mechanisms: the *visita,* which consisted of a surprise inspection by a neutral crown official, and the *residencia,* a requirement that anyone who served in office had to remain in place for six months after the duration of their term so that anyone with a complaint could come forward. While such actions were well intended, they did not prevent corruption and did little to improve the government of New Spain.

Ethnicity and Social Status

There were several ethnic groups present in New Spain. The Spaniards, conquerors of the region, had the highest social status of all the ethnic groups, but even within the category of *Spaniard* were two groups of very unequal status. The highest group was the *peninsulares,* or Spaniards who came directly from Spain. The Europeans felt that America was a land of laziness, sloth, and "bad air." Therefore, people born in the New World would absorb these negative traits, making them inferior to people born in Europe. The *peninsulares* were considered more loyal to the Crown, more intelligent, and more sophisticated. Trusting their loyalty, the Crown decreed that only *peninsulares* could hold key positions in the government. Additionally, they were given preferential treatment in applying for trading licences. Much of the transatlantic trade remained firmly in the hands of the *peninsulares.* Although they never accounted for more than 1 percent of the population of New Spain, they held a monopoly of political, economic, and social power within the colony.

Directly below the *peninsulares* in status were the *criollos.* These people were of pure Spanish descent but were born in the New World. Generally, they were indistinguishable from the *peninsulares* in terms of dress, physical appearance, and customs, but the simple fact that they were born in America reduced their status within the colony. Despite their secondary rank, life for the *criollos* was relatively good. Although blocked from most of the overseas trade with Spain, they were frequently able to take part in the local economy, and many became wealthy. Some were able to acquire large tracts of land, establishing HACIENDAs. While they were forbidden from serving in the large, important government offices, they were able to obtain lucrative minor positions within the royal bureau-cracy and were allowed to hold office in the *cabildo*. While not able to take part at the highest levels of New Spain's economy, politics, or society, their fair skin and Spanish background gave them a privileged position within the colonial system.

Natives constituted the largest ethnic group in New Spain. In recent years there has been a large debate over the size of the native population. Many scholars have con-cluded that in 1519 there were approximately 25 million natives in central Mexico and several million more in the Maya areas to the south. Within a few years of the con-quest, the native population all but collapsed, a result of the violence of the conquest itself—tens of thousands died in the siege of Tenochtitlán alone—and the spread of Euro-pean DISEASES. The Europeans brought several diseases from the Old World for which the people of the New World had no natural immunity (see COLUMBIAN EXCHANGE). SMALLPOX, measles, mumps, bubonic plague, and typhus devastated the region, with particularly virulent plagues occurring in 1520, 1529, 1545, and 1576. By 1600 the native population had fallen to only 1 million people, a decline of more than 90 percent. Natives occupied a rela-tively low position in the colonial hierarchy. Although they were nominally protected by the Crown, they were fre-quently exploited and forced into coercive labor systems such as the REPARTIMIENTO.

Africans formed another important ethnic group in New Spain. A handful of Africans accompanied Cortés and the first few expeditions across Mexico. Small num-bers of Africans came to New Spain as indentured ser-vants as well, but they remained a tiny minority for the first few years of the colony's existence. However, as the native population declined the Spaniards began to look

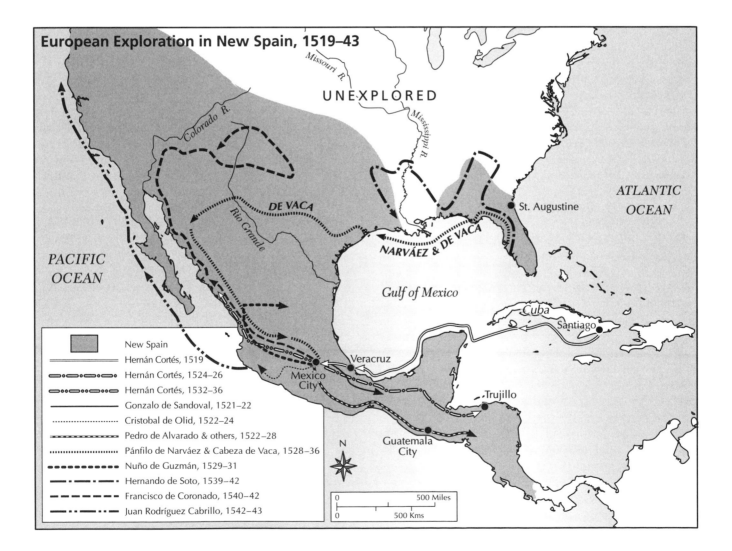

European Exploration in New Spain, 1519–43

for other sources of cheap labor. Between 1521 and 1650 120,000 Africans entered New Spain, and by 1560 Africans outnumbered Spaniards in Mexico. African labor was much more important in the Caribbean, and after the 1650s they became the backbone of the SUGAR industry there. Fear of slave revolts caused the government to pass several restrictive laws against the Africans in the 1540s. They were forbidden to carry arms, subjected to early curfews, and not allowed to gather in groups of three or more. Despite these precautions, slave revolts occurred between 1560 and 1570, particularly in the northern mining and agricultural zones. Several reports state that rather than submit to Spanish control, some slaves fled into the northern deserts to set up free communities, a process known as maroonage.

After years of intermarriage (the process of MESTI-ZAJE), other ethnic groups emerged in New Spain: the CAS-TAS, or mixed races. The various combinations of European, native, and African led to three major mixed groups—MESTIZOS, formed from the union of Spaniards and natives; mulattoes, the offspring of Spaniards and Africans; and ZAMBOS, the children of native and African parents.

The Colonial Economy

Mercantilism—the idea that colonies exist to serve the mother country and to provide it with precious goods—dominated the economy of New Spain. Essentially, the only economic activities that imperial bureaucrats encouraged in New Spain were those that did not interfere with the activities of Spain itself. They thus opposed the creation of industries such as textile factories but supported extractive efforts aimed at producing raw materials for export to Spain, where they could be sold or processed. To ensure the colony did not compete with Spain, the Crown maintained strict control over the economy. It did so primarily through Crown monopolies, whereby certain individuals were given the exclusive right to trade in specific commodities. The most famous monopoly was the *asiento*, or privilege of selling slaves, a lucrative trade granted to the highest bidder. The Crown also established geographic monopolies for international trade. In New Spain Mexico City became the official entrepôt for the colony, while Acapulco was designated the official Pacific port to receive goods from the Philippines, and Veracruz was the Atlantic port for the European trade.

The primary focus of New Spain's economy was mining. By Spanish law the sovereign was legally entitled to one-fifth of the precious metals discovered in the Indies (the *quinto*), so the kings actively promoted the search for GOLD and SILVER in New Spain. Colonists also recognized that finding precious metals was the most effective way of earning a fortune and were every bit as diligent in searching for metals as the Crown. Despite the dreams of finding cities of gold (typified in the search for the mythical city EL DORADO), it was silver that ultimately formed the basis of mining in New Spain. Within 50 years of the conquest, major silver strikes were found in Zacatecas, San Luis Potosí, and Guanajuato. These centers were quite removed from the major population centers of New Spain, making it difficult to find enough workers to keep the mines fully operational. The crown attempted to force the natives to work in the mines through labor systems such as the *repartimiento,* but they were only marginally effective. Ultimately, imperial officials came to rely on wage labor, a stark contrast to the mines of PERU.

The other major economic activity of New Spain was agriculture. Residents of New Spain produced two of the most valuable dyes in the world: cochineal and indigo. Cochineal was derived from a tiny insect that lived on the prickly pear cactus; when crushed, its body released a vivid, colorfast red dye. Indigo was a dark blue vegetable dye that was highly prized for maintaining its rich color. Vanilla and CACAO (from which chocolate was made) also were lucrative exports that were unique to New Spain. Sugar was the final important cash crop. Sugar production was never particularly important on the mainland, but it remained one of the Caribbean's major exports throughout the colonial period. In addition to these exports, CORN continued to be the staple crop, and natives typically grew it on small plots of land. The Spaniards also introduced a number of new domestic animals, and animal husbandry became an important way of life. Most small farmers supplemented corn production with poultry. In the north large ranches developed to raise cattle and sheep. Most of the meat went to the mining towns. As the native population declined, land formerly used by indigenous communities was bought by wealthy stockmen, who turned much of central Mexico into grazing land, although their actions had devastating consequences for the land when farmers paid insufficient attention to their herds and their livestock overgrazed some regions. Erosion became an ecological problem, especially in the drier expanses of northern New Spain.

The Church of New Spain

A final important element of the colonial system in New Spain was the Catholic Church. The importance of the church permeated everything but was particularly influential in the conquest of the natives. In 1492 Spain had finished the Reconquista, reclaiming Spanish territory from the Islamic Moors (see ISLAM), who had held it for almost 700 years. This crusading mentality, in the opinion of imperial policy makers, could work in the Western Hemisphere as well. As a result, those who sought to conquer the Americas often employed religious arguments to justify their efforts to subdue the hemisphere. This is evident in the REQUERIMIENTO, a document that was officially read before any military campaign. It demanded that in the name of God natives should put aside their idolatry, embrace Christianity, and accept the dominion of the church, God's instrument on earth. It also required fealty to God's secular leader, the king of Spain. Once they conquered the natives, the Spaniards felt that it was their divine duty to convert them to Christianity. Clerics and their allies built a vast number of missions, and missionaries performed mass baptisms to bring natives into the fold. At times those promulgating this religious campaign had unlikely assistance. In 1531 the Virgin of Guadalupe appeared to a native boy named Juan Diego on a hill sacred to the Aztec earth mother goddess. She told him in NAHUATL that she had come for him and all the people of the New World, not just the Spaniards. This miraculous sighting convinced many natives to accept Christianity.

The church was involved in the lives of the Spaniards as well, its position strengthened by its participation in local and imperial politics. One manifestation of clerics' interest in politics was evident in the *patronato real,* an agreement between the Crown and the pope whereby the Spanish king could appoint church positions in the New World. This doctrine meant that most church officials were loyal to the king rather than to the pope, and the church became essentially another branch of the Spanish government. Clerics also wielded considerable power as the ultimate arbiter of morality and social conduct in New Spain. Priests worked to control drunkenness, lewd behavior, gambling, and violence, threatening to withhold the sacraments to those who acted against church teachings. Moreover, the Church used its close connection with the royal government to turn proscribed sins into illegal activities. Church law and secular law became indistinguishable.

In the end church and state often were inextricable in New Spain. The alliance between these two institutions helped New Spain become Spain's first great viceroyalty, providing the model for government elsewhere in the New World. Its economy was relatively strong, based on a number of export crops. New Spain remained one of the most stable, wealthy, and well-developed regions in the New World.

Further reading: General works: Michael C. Meyer and William L. Sherman, *The Course of Mexican History* (Oxford, U.K.: Oxford University Press, 1995); David J. Weber, *The Spanish Frontier in North America* (New Haven, Conn.: Yale University Press, 1992). *On the conquest period:* Patricia de Fuentes, *The Conquistadors: First Person Accounts of the Conquest of Mexico* (Norman: University of Oklahoma Press, 1993); Miguel León-Portilla, *The Broken Spears: The Aztec Account of the Conquest of Mexico* (Boston: Beacon Press, 1992). *On native life after the conquest:* James Lockhart, *The Nahuas After the Conquest* (Stanford, Calif.: Stanford University Press, 1992). *On the economy:* Ross Hassing, *Trade, Tribute, and Transportation: The Sixteenth-Century Political Economy of the Valley of Mexico* (Norman: University of Oklahoma Press, 1985). *On the environment:* Elinor Melville, *A Plague of Sheep: Environmental Consequences of the Conquest of Mexico* (Cambridge, U.K.: Cambridge University Press, 1994).

— Scott Chamberlain

New World

The term used by Europeans to refer to the Western Hemisphere.

When CHRISTOPHER COLUMBUS arrived in the Caribbean in October 1492, he recognized that he had not, in fact, made it to East Asia. As a result, he determined that he had found territory Europeans had never known about earlier. He thus did what Europeans always liked to do in such circumstances: He decided to give new names to the places he found. That act of renaming made sense to Columbus and other Europeans because he had, in their minds, discovered new territory. AMERIGO VESPUCCI used the term for the title of his 1505 report about his ventures: *Novo mondo retrovato*—"New world found." RICHARD HAKLUYT THE YOUNGER had a clear understanding of the term. In the preface to his collection of travel accounts relating to America published in London in 1600, Hakluyt wrote that the reports that followed dealt with "The New World. New, in regard to the new and late discovery thereof made by Christopher Colon, alias Columbus, a Genoese by nation, in the year of grace 1492. And world, in respect of the huge extension thereof, which to this day is not thoroughly discovered." From the perspective of the indigenous peoples of the Western Hemisphere, by contrast, the renaming was only the first in what became a series of acts of appropriation of territory that did not, to them, need to be discovered because they already knew of its existence.

It is impossible to overestimate the significance of the Western Hemisphere—this new world—to Europeans. Because ancient authorities did not know of its existence, Columbus's reports and those that followed necessitated a reconceptualization of the earth's geography, a task that proved difficult to people who did not easily abandon an intellectual construction of the world that placed Jerusalem at its center and rested on the belief that there had to be a balance of territory to the east and west (see T-O MAPS). Every exploratory venture to the Western Hemisphere brought back news about the wonders to be found there. Such reports were often inaccurate, but even exaggerated accounts of the enormous natural bounties enticed further exploratory ventures. Because the peoples of the Western Hemisphere lacked Christianity, Europeans eager to profit from the material resources of the Americas also justified their expeditions on religious grounds: They would be, in their own way, a new generation of evangels bringing the word of their God to a people who, so Europeans repeatedly claimed, needed to be enlightened. Although Europeans routinely failed in their efforts to get the indigenous peoples of the Western Hemisphere to accept their religion and culture in the precise ways the newcomers intended, there is no question that the ships carrying various commodities from the Americas enriched Europeans. By the end of the 16th century, promoters of colonization could argue that Europeans should establish settlements in the Americas because this territory had become, to them, a grand shopping emporium where whatever Europeans wanted could be found. Reports of travelers printed across the continent (see PRINTING PRESS) made knowledge about American resources common and encouraged further colonizing ventures.

In recent years the term *New World* has become problematic, and many scholars prefer not to use it. To this new generation of observers, many of them made more sensitive to the arrogance of the term as a result of the enormous discussion of the age of discovery that took place in the 1990s as a result of the quincentennial of the Columbus voyages, the old terminology is an unacceptable relic from the colonial era.

Further reading: J. H. Eliot, *The Old World and the New, 1492–1650* (Cambridge, U.K.: Cambridge University Press, 1970); Anthony Grafton, *New Worlds, Ancient Texts: The Power of Tradition and the Shock of Discovery* (Cambridge, Mass.: Harvard University Press, 1992); Stephen Greenblatt, *Marvelous Possessions: The Wonder of the New World* (Chicago: University of Chicago Press, 1991); Peter C. Mancall, "The Age of Discovery," in Louis P. Masur, ed., *The Challenge of American History* (Baltimore: Johns Hopkins University Press, 1999), 26–53.

Niger River

Located in western Africa, the Niger River is the third largest river on the continent, flowing eastward approximately 2,600 miles (4,180 km) from the Futa Djalon Mountains through present-day MALI, Niger, and Nigeria to the Gulf of Guinea in the Atlantic Ocean.

In Yoruba cosmology, the Niger River is the domain of the goddess Oya, and the river itself is called Odo Oya, or "container of Oya." Oya was the favorite wife of Chango (or Shango), the god of fire, thunder, and lightning. In addition to its spiritual and cultural meanings to the peoples who lived near it, the Niger River was an important link between these peoples and the rest of the Atlantic world. The Niger was a major means of travel and transportation on the southern leg of the trans-Saharan trade routes. It carried GOLD, spices, cotton, ivory, salt, and slaves between important regional market centers such as TIMBUKTU and Djenne (see DJENNE-DJENO) and the Atlantic Ocean. Control of the Niger River was disputed several times during the early modern period, resulting in a succession of several empires, including GHANA, Mali, and SONGHAI. The gold mined in Bure, at the headwaters of the Niger, stimulated the rise of the Mali Empire in the 13th century; over the next two centuries the Mali Empire gained power and wealth from control of both trade on the river and the resources found near it. The Niger was also a means of spreading cultural and religious traditions. Trade and political disruption along the river contributed to the spread of ISLAM in the region and to the establishment of Islamic centers in the cities along its course.

Further reading: Robert Fay, "Niger River," in *Africana: The Encyclopedia of the African and African American Experience,* eds. Kwame Anthony Appiah and Henry Louis Gates, Jr. (New York: Basic *Civitas* Books, 1999), 1438; Jacob U. Gordon, "Yoruba Cosmology and Culture in Brazil: A Study of African Survivals in the New World," *Journal of Black Studies* 10 (1979): 231–244.

— Lisa M. Brady

Norse

Scandinavian peoples who exerted a powerful influence on early modern history by settling North Atlantic islands and briefly appearing in North America.

By the late eighth century Scandinavian craftsmen had perfected the design of Viking seafaring ships. At once light and strong, Viking ships could land on almost any beach and navigate many rivers as well as survive brutal ocean storms. Vikings put these ships to use exploring and settling the North Atlantic. According to tradition Norse peoples settled the Shetland and Orkney Islands around the year 800. In 874 the Norse explorer Ingólfur Arnarson established a Norse outpost on ICELAND at the present-day site of the capital city of Reykjavik. GREENLAND received its first Norse settlers when Erik the Red, banished from Iceland for manslaughter, explored its southwest coast in 892; he returned with colonists in 895. Leif Eriksson, Eric's son, explored North America from Greenland around the year 1000, landing at a spot the Norse termed VINLAND.

Much of the Norse success in the North Atlantic came from their catch of COD, the fish that provided the settlers with the nutrition they needed to survive in the inhos-

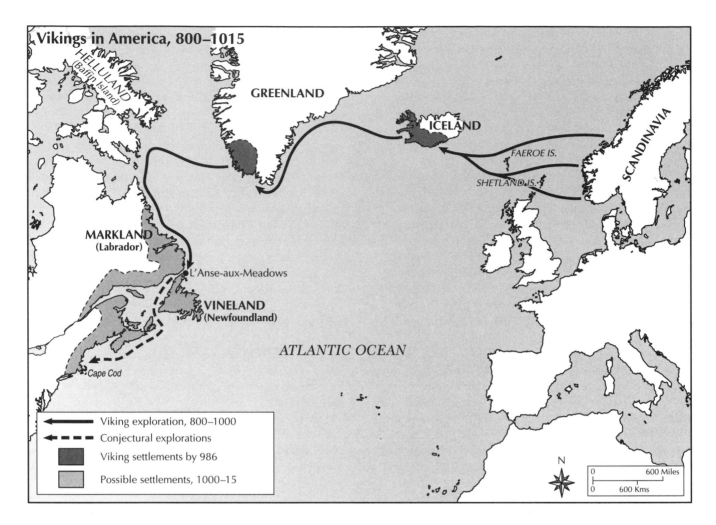

Vikings in America, 800–1015

HELLULAND (Baffin Island)

GREENLAND

ICELAND

FAEROE IS.

SCANDINAVIA

SHETLAND IS.

MARKLAND (Labrador)

L'Anse-aux-Meadows

VINELAND (Newfoundland)

ATLANTIC OCEAN

Cape Cod

→ Viking exploration, 800–1000
--→ Conjectural explorations
■ Viking settlements by 986
■ Possible settlements, 1000–15

N

0　　　　600 Miles
0　　　　600 Kms

pitable climates of Greenland and Iceland. The Norse learned to preserve cod by hanging the fish in the cold, dry winter air. After the cod had lost most of its weight, settlers could break off pieces of the flesh to eat. Soon the Norse began to ship dried cod to Europe.

Norse settlers initially enjoyed modest success on Iceland and Greenland. By the 12th century Iceland's population was between 30,000 and 60,000 people. The population of Greenland reached 6,000 in the 12th century, and it never grew again. Despite their small numbers, Norse Greenlanders traveled hundreds of miles north to hunt walrus herds. Walrus hide and ivory became Greenland's primary exports. Christianity reached both islands around 1000, and by 1100 most Norse were at least nominally Christian. Sagas and family histories were composed in Iceland and Greenland, and continental courts embraced Norse storytellers and poets.

Despite these successes, the settlers experienced difficult times. In 1264 Iceland and Greenland became part of the Norwegian kingdom just as Norway entered a long period of decline. Exchange between the North Atlantic Norse settlements and the European continent dwindled, at least in part from the success of cod fishermen leaving from ports such as BRISTOL, who began to supply the continental market. Further, a cooling shift in climate sometime after the mid-13th century made conditions in the North Atlantic more difficult. Winters became longer and ice floes impeded ship lanes, making the settlements even more precarious. Because Norse settlers tended to allow their livestock to graze freely, the settlers also began to have to cope with erosion of soil caused by overgrazing. Although the Norse might have fared better in Vinland, in all likelihood modern-day Newfoundland, they never had the resources to establish long-lasting settlements there. By the time CHRISTOPHER COLUMBUS sailed across the Atlantic, the Norse had abandoned any real efforts to set up colonies in North America.

Further reading: Alfred Crosby, *Ecological Imperialism: The Biological Expansion of* Europe, 900–1900 (Cambridge, U.K.: Cambridge University Press, 1986); Gwyn Jones, *The Norse Atlantic Saga* (New York: Oxford University Press, 1986); Thomas McGovern, "Norse Settlements," in *Encyclopedia of the North American Colonies*, 3 vols., ed. Jacob E. Cooke, (New York: Scribner's, 1993).

— Kevin C. Armitage

Northeast Passage

During the 16th century the Dutch and English explored a proposed northern sea route through the Arctic Ocean and along the northern coast of Russia known as the Northeast Passage.

Europeans had long had a fascination and attraction toward the Far East. Throughout the Middle Ages myths and legends of Far East riches and magic circulated throughout the European continent. By the end of the 15th century, European states achieved a level of technology and wealth that allowed them to explore the world beyond the European coasts. Numerous expeditions set out with the goal of discovering an accessible route to the Far East, with Portugal and Spain setting the early pace. As the 16th century progressed, the English, Dutch, and French began to resent the Spanish–Portuguese overseas monopoly. With the Southwest Passage in firm control of Iberian hands, these countries explored the possibilities of a NORTHWEST PASSAGE over—and preferably through—the North American continent and a Northeast Passage over the top of Europe and Asia.

Ironically, it was the Portuguese who first explored the possibility of a northeast route in 1484. The voyage reached Nova Zembla but did not draw many imitators for more than half a century. Beginning in the middle of the 16th century, English merchants began exploring the possibility of expanding their commercial opportunities. Goaded by promoters of long-distance trade, merchants paid close attention to any venture that promised rapid movement along (or through) the northern edge of Europe and Asia. In 1553 the Merchant Adventurers commissioned SEBASTIAN CABOT to organize an enterprise bound for Malay via the Arctic Ocean. Although he did not take part in the voyage due to his old age, Cabot set forth the general instructions for the expedition. Weeks into the voyage the ships directed by Sir Hugh Willoughby and Richard Chancellor separated off the Norway coast, never to meet again. Willoughby and his crew froze to death near Kola in Lapland, while Chancellor rounded the North Cape and undertook a daring trip through the White Sea before moving downriver from Dwina to Moscow. There, he met with Ivan the Terrible, and although Cabot's planned expedition did not reach CATHAY, Chancellor opened up communication and trade with Russia, as evidenced by the formation of England's Muscovy Company.

English advances in Arctic waters soon found imitation from their Dutch neighbors. The Dutch explorer Willem Barents's voyages in the 1590s convinced contemporaries that China could be reached by sailing north of Nova Zembla. Privy to Barents's geographical notebooks, Henry Hudson's second major voyage, sponsored by the Muscovy Company, explored the possibilities of the Northeast Passage. Leaving England in 1608, his advance knowledge of the Scandinavian coastline was readily apparent, but he had little accurate information about Nova Zembla and the Siberian coast on the Kara Sea, nor any warnings about a series of foreboding promontories jutting into icy waters. As a result, Hudson had to return to England, where interest in a Northeast Passage faded, although attempts to discover a Northwest Passage continued over the next few centuries.

Further reading: Benson Bobrick, *East of the Sun: The Epic Conquest and Tragic History of Siberia* (New York, Poseidon Press, 1992); Richard Bohlander, ed. *World Explorers and Discoverers* (New York: Da Capo Press, 1998); J. Gamel, *England and Russia*, trans. John Studdy Leigh (New York: Da Capo Press, 1968); Donald S. Jackson, *Charting the Sea of Darkness: The Four Voyages of Henry Hudson* (New York: Kodansha, 1995); Henry C. Murphy, *Henry Hudson in Holland* (New York: B. Franklin, 1972).

— Matthew Lindaman

Northwest Passage

A mythical water route through northern North America, the Northwest Passage became the object of repeated exploratory ventures during the 16th century.

Contrary to modern legend, Europeans even before the 1492 voyage of CHRISTOPHER COLUMBUS knew that the world was round. They also knew that the markets of East Asia contained abundant valuable resources and that transporting them overland across Asia, through the Middle East, and into Europe, normally via VENICE, was expensive and problematic. Although Portuguese and Dutch sailors who ventured to the SPICE ISLANDS had found an oceanic route to the Far East, such journeys were also long and often dangerous. Many who ventured on such expeditions never returned.

Although Europeans had a somewhat clear sense of the geography of the Old World, they had much less precise knowledge of what lay to the west. Once reports of Columbus began to circulate in 16th-century Europe, followed by accounts of Spanish CONQUISTADORES, Europeans began to speculate about a possible water route through North America that would take sailors directly to Asia. This idea had particular appeal for northern Europeans—the Dutch, French, and English—who had been left out of the TREATY OF TORDESILLAS and thus lacked any papally sanctioned claim to territory in the Western Hemisphere, yet the notion hinged on the belief that the world was smaller than it turned out to be. However wrong Europeans might have been about the size of the earth, and thus in error about the length of any possible expeditions, the basic lure remained: Because it was cheaper and quicker to travel by sea than overland, any route through North America would be worth finding.

Try as they might, Europeans never found the Northwest Passage. Of course, some did think they had found it. Whenever sailors ventured far up rivers, deep into modern-day Canada, they believed they might have found the route. Mysterious lands and communities found along such journey, such as NORUMBEGA and HOCHELAGA, seemed possible resting stations for any adventure to Asia. SEBASTIAN CABOT was desperate to find the Northwest Passage, and on a voyage that ended back in BRISTOL in 1509 he thought he had found it, although later investigations proved that he had sailed perhaps as far as modern-day Hudson Bay, an enormous body of water that he reasonably believed might be an ocean. JACQUES CARTIER and MARTIN FROBISHER each believed they had found the Northwest Passage, although they had in fact made substantial additions to European knowledge of the modern-day Maritime Provinces and subarctic waterways that lay west of GREENLAND. The English sailor John Davis (ca. 1550–1605) also hoped to find the passage by sailing along the western coast of Greenland deep into Baffin Bay in the mid-1580s, although he, too, failed.

Despite repeated failures to find the way through, the goal remained. As RICHARD HAKLUYT THE ELDER, a lawyer with an avid interest in geography, recognized the situation in 1585, the English should send settlers to North America because there was a "great possibilitie of further discoveries of other regions from the North part of the same land by sea, and of unspeakable honor and benefit that may rise upon the same, by the trades to ensue in Japan, China, and Cathay, &c." With such heady promise, it is little wonder that Europeans continued to look for the Northwest Passage well beyond 1607.

Renewed interest in a passage emerged in the 18th century. Impelled by the efforts of exploration promoter Arthur Dobbs, British expeditions under Christopher Middleton in 1742 and William Moor in 1747 combed the western shores of Hudson Bay for the entrance of a passage to the Pacific. Between 1774 and 1779, Spanish concern about Russian encroachments on the North Pacific and about possible British discovery of a Northwest Passage led to another series of Spanish expeditions along the Pacific coast. Led by figures such as Juan Pérez and Ignacio de Arteaga, Spanish ships sailed as far north as Alaska's Hinch-

inbrook Island. British expeditions, motivated by both scientific curiosity and by interest in the strategic and commercial value of a Northwest Passage, also appeared in the waters of the North Pacific in the final decades of the 18th century. Captain James Cook, in 1778, and George Vancouver, from 1792 to 1794, surveyed the Pacific coast for the western entrance of a Northwest Passage. Cook carried his exploration through the Bering Strait to the Arctic Ocean, where he encountered the northern ice that made a journey along the top of the continent from the Pacific to the Atlantic impractical for early modern ships. These explorations made it clear that no Pacific entrance to a Northwest Passage existed.

Further reading: Angus Konstam, *Historical Atlas of Exploration, 1492–1600* (New York: Facts On File, 2000).

— Paul Mapp

Norumbega

The name used by various Europeans during the 16th century usually to refer to territory in the northeastern portion of the North American mainland.

The first person to use the term *Norumbega* (or one of its variants) was probably GIOVANNI DA VERRAZANO after his exploratory voyage of 1524 along the eastern coast of North America. The term, in the form *Oranbega*, first appeared in print on a map created by the explorer's brother, Girolamo da Verrazano in 1529. Later cartographers altered the spelling, rendering it as *Anorombega* and *Anorobegua*, often located near what might be modern-day Penobscot Bay in Maine. Because 16th-century maps were created from information gleaned from travelers who often spent little time in the territory they described, it is not surprising that Norumbega often shifted place from map to map. Various Europeans speculated that Norumbega was the bountiful land described by Verrazano. Giacomo Gastaldi's map labeled "Tierra Nueva," which appeared in a 1548 edition of Ptolemy's *Geografia*, demarcated Nurumbega as a land well north of FLORIDA but south of Labrador. Michael Lok's map of the North Atlantic that appeared in RICHARD HAKLUYT THE YOUNGER's *Divers Voyages Touching on America,* published in LONDON in 1582, had Norumbega as a large island just east of the coast of North America. To promoters such as Hakluyt, the existence of this Norumbega helped to prove the validity of Verrazano's claims, including his belief in the existence of the NORTHWEST PASSAGE. By the time Cornelius Wytfliet had created his map entitled "Norumbega et Virginia, 1597," Norumbega had become an extensive part of a well-watered North American coastline as well as a city sitting across the largest river to flow into the Atlantic from the interior.

Unable to find a location that matched Verrazano's description, Europeans during the 17th century became skeptical about the existence of Norumbega. When Samuel de Champlain explored the region in the early 17th century, he believed that the settlement was a fiction, although, of course, it is possible that he landed in some place other than that seen by Verrazano earlier.

Further reading: Emerson W. Baker, et al., eds., *American Beginnings: Exploration, Culture, and Cartography in the Land of Norumbega* (Lincoln: University of Nebraska Press, 1994).

Nzinga, queen of Angola (Nzinga Mbande, or Ana de Sousa, or Dona Anna de Sousa) (ca. 1581–1663)

Ruler of the Ndongo (1624–26) and the Matamba (ca. 1630–63) kingdoms in what is today northwestern Angola, Nzinga Mbande led armies against the region's Portuguese colonizers in a struggle to maintain her people's independence.

By the early 17th century the Mbundu-speaking Ndongo kingdom dominated northwestern present-day Angola, deriving its power from the lucrative SLAVE TRADE with the Portuguese. Although trade with the Portuguese was the basis for much of the kingdom's wealth, it was also the source of its problems when the Europeans attempted to establish a permanent presence in the area. Born during a war between her father, King Kiluangi, and the Portuguese, Queen Nzinga spent much of her life struggling against European colonizing efforts.

Popular with her people and recognized early on as a powerful leader, Nzinga's brother, who had become king after their father died, exiled her and assassinated her son in an effort to stem any opposition to his rule. Faced with another Portuguese invasion, Nzinga's brother recalled her from exile in 1622 and sent her as emissary to the Portuguese governor in Luanda. She negotiated in the interest of her brother, exacting several concessions from the Portuguese. In exchange for Portuguese recognition of Ndongo independence, Nzinga promised the return of Portuguese prisoners and Ndongo assistance in the slave trade. To solidify the agreement, Nzinga agreed to a Christian baptism by JESUITS and took the name Dona Ana de Sousa (or Dona Anna de Sousa).

The alliance with the Portuguese was short-lived because the Europeans reneged on their part of the agreement. Nzinga's brother attempted to rectify the situation on his own but failed. Nzinga rallied her own supporters, renounced the Christian faith, allied with the reputedly cannibalistic Jaga people in the north, killed her brother, whom she saw as a traitor, and became queen of the Ndongo kingdom in 1624. Nzinga is frequently called the Cannibal Queen because of her connection to the Jaga, but any practice of CANNIBALISM by her or by the Jaga cannot be substantiated. Continued conflict with the Portuguese over trade forced Nzinga to flee eastward in 1629. She conquered the Matamba kingdom (a non-Mbundu kingdom) and established herself as queen. Nzinga's success as ruler was based on her military savvy as well as on her political élan. Nzinga created her own army of Jaga slaves, to whom she promised freedom after their service. According to one Dutch source, Nzinga dressed in men's clothing and kept a harem of male "wives." She led her own troops, made up partially by women warriors, and was the primary military strategist for her army. Through her alliances with the Dutch in Luanda and with the KONGO kingdom and by maintaining almost absolute control over the region's interior slave trade, Nzinga forced the Portuguese to negotiate with her. In 1656 Nzinga and the Portuguese created a fairly stable treaty, facilitating trade relations between them and allying them against other African states. Before she died in 1663, Queen Nzinga again embraced the Christian faith. Her sister, Dona Barbara, succeeded her to the throne.

Further reading: Eric Young, "Nzinga," in *Africana: The Encyclopedia of the African and African American Experience,* eds. Kwame Anthony Appiah and Henry Louis Gates, Jr. (New York: Basic *Civitas* Books, 1999), 1452; "Nzinga Mbande," in *Dictionary of African Historical Biography,* 2nd ed., eds., Mark R. Lipschutz and R. Kent Rasmussen, (Berkeley: University of California Press, 1986), 181–182.

— Lisa M. Brady

O

Olmecs

One of the first great cultures of Mesoamerica, whose art, religion, and iconography remained influential until the Spanish conquest.

The term *Olmec* has been a controversial one in Mesoamerican archaeology. In the AZTECS's language of NAHUATL, it simply means "People of the Land of Rubber," referring to the coastal areas of VERACRUZ and TABASCO. It apparently had no specific cultural connotation during Aztec times. The term itself was first used by archaeologist George Vaillant to describe local cultures along the Gulf Coast. Recent ethnohistorical investigations have suggested that the Aztecs did maintain a dim memory of this ancient culture, describing a coastal land called Tamoanchan, where good government began. Recently, linguists have argued that the language spoken by the Olmecs was a prototype of the modern Mixe and Zoquean languages. Thus, some scholars have considered abandoning the term *Olmec* for *Mixe-Zoquean,* although the original term remains in common use.

Whatever they are called, the Olmecs were the first great culture in ancient MEXICO. While it is clear that there were small, isolated cultures that predated the Olmecs in Mesoamerica, the Olmecs were the largest, most fully developed of these early societies. The Olmecs first emerged in the early preclassic period, around 1700 B.C. The most important site during this time was San Lorenzo, located along the flatlands of the Coatzacoalcos River. The settlement was relatively small, containing only 1,000 people at its height. It seems clear that the site offered many advantages to the early settlers. For one, the abundance of water and alluvial soils from the river would have greatly facilitated agriculture. Other cultures based in the more arid highlands required extensive irrigation systems whose construction and maintenance served as a steady drain on labor. Also, the area formed a natural trading corridor for cultures in the Mexican highlands with those in the YUCATÁN PENINSULA and Central America. By 1400 B.C.

San Lorenzo had a reasonably well-developed system of housing platforms and public architecture. The site was built over a large, artificially constructed platform about six feet high, a feat requiring extensive labor to construct. Around 1200 B.C. the city was at its height, and most of the visible architecture of San Lorenzo dates from this period. The most widely recognized feature of the site was its series of Olmec heads. These massive heads were carved from single boulders of basalt, were nine feet tall, and weighed many tons apiece. Analysis of the rock reveals that it came from the Tuxtla Mountains, more than 50 miles away. The simple effort of moving them to San Lorenzo required considerably more effort than the actual carving of the stones' features. These heads are all unique and presumably represent actual, historical rulers. Artists also depicted royal figures in a series of carved stone altars, often holding lines of bound captives.

Around 1100 B.C. San Lorenzo was destroyed by human hands. Some have speculated that there was a revolt from below, while others believe the city was sacked by one of its rivals. The monumental artwork was systematically defaced, then buried in long trenches. Another Olmec site, La Venta, arose to fill the political vacuum. This city was larger than San Lorenzo, and its architecture is considerably more impressive. The dominant feature of the site was a cone-shaped pyramid built of clay rising 110 feet above the jungle floor. It appears to be a sort of votive volcano, a scaled-down version of one of the volcanoes of the Tuxtla Mountains, which supplied the basalt for Olmec buildings. The city and its hinterlands supported 15,000 to 18,000 people, most of whom were involved in agriculture. Architectural features of La Venta are considerably more sophisticated than those of San Lorenzo, with elaborate stone carvings, mosaic floors, and elaborate tombs. At several points in La Venta, the Olmecs dug deep pits, laid in elaborate figurines, filled in the soil, and constructed elaborate mosaics over the spots, which became focal points for sacred rituals.

Colossal Olmec head   *(The Granger Collection)*

As was the case in San Lorenzo, La Venta was sacked and destroyed in roughly 400–300 B.C. Several other Olmec sites survived, most notably Tres Zapotes, 100 miles to the northwest of La Venta. This site contains some of the earliest dated monuments of the NEW WORLD. Stela C had an elaborate date that used the same calendrical system as the classic MAYA, reading September 3, 32 B.C. Another monument still bears the date March 14, A.D. 162. These monuments, using a "Maya" system hundreds of years before the Maya, suggest that it was the Olmecs who developed the calendrical and astronomical systems usually credited to the Maya. Despite these survivals, Olmec culture was waning by A.D. 200, and the region they controlled came under the influence of other groups, including the Maya.

The defining feature of the Olmec culture was its distinctive artwork. A recurring theme of Olmec art was the close connection between humans and nature. Time and again, carvings depict human or humanlike figures with animalistic features. Some have suggested that these sculptures depict Olmec shamans in the process of transform-

ing into their spirit guides. The most common combination was between humans and jaguars, leading to the term *were-jaguar* to describe the scenes. The humans have animal snouts and long, snarling features with curved fangs. Many pieces of Olmec art depict animals in reverential fashion. These animals tend to be the largest, most impressive predators known: the harpy eagle, the jaguar, the crocodile, and the shark. In Olmec culture both gods and men used elements from these animals as symbols of their power. Normal humans depicted in stone usually had unusual features—often puffy and resembling snarling, toothless babies. Heads were often cleft at the top. The Olmec heads themselves have large lips, causing some to speculate that they depict ancient African mariners, although there is no evidence to support the theory that Africans journeyed to Latin America in ancient times. Despite these unusual characteristics, Olmec art remains much more natural than much of the later art of Mesoamerica, which relied on harsh lines and baroque ornamentation.

By the beginning of the classic era (around A.D. 200), the Olmecs had faded as a distinct culture, but they left an enormous legacy. The Maya, who began to develop while the Olmec were at their height, borrowed many elements of Olmec culture. They were particularly taken with the Olmecs' symbols of status and royalty. The Maya adopted Olmec-style regal headbands, staffs of authority, and jewelry, and these symbols remained potent in Maya culture until the Spanish conquest. The sacred animals continued to be royal symbols throughout Mesoamerica, and the physical remains of the Olmecs also continued to have importance. In many early Maya sites, rulers reshaped Olmec carvings, frequently drilling holes into them so that they could be worn as pendants or pectorals. Excavations of the Great Temple of the Aztecs in TENOCHTITLÁN show that the Aztecs were great collectors of Olmec artifacts and buried these treasures in sacred caches throughout the complex. Even La Venta itself remained a pilgrimage site well into the colonial era. Such finds suggest that the Olmecs were one of the originators of Mesoamerican culture and that their influence lasted for centuries after their decline.

Further reading: Ignacio Bernal, *The Olmec World* (Berkeley: University of California Press, 1969); Michael Coe, *Mexico: From the Olmecs to the Aztecs*, 4th ed. (London: Thames & Hudson, 1994); Michael Coe and Richard Diehl, *In the Land of the Olmec* (Austin: University of Texas Press, 1980); Jacques Soustelle, *The Olmecs: The Oldest Civilization in Mexico*, trans. Helen R. Lane (Garden City, N.Y.: Doubleday, 1984).

— Scott Chamberlain

Oñate, Juan de (ca. 1551–1626)

Four centuries ago, in 1598, Juan de Oñate led a group of settlers out of modern-day Chihuahua, MEXICO, to colonize NEW MEXICO. Previous white explorers had visited New Mexico before Oñate, most notably FRANCISCO CORONADO in 1540, but none of these earlier expeditions led to successful long-term European settlement. Although he is largely forgotten today, Oñate settled the first colony in New Mexico, at San Juan de los Caballeros, nearly a decade before the English founded their first permanent settlement at Jamestown, Virginia, in 1607.

Oñate, the heir to a mining fortune, arrived in New Mexico in 1598 at the head of an expedition consisting of several hundred settlers, soldiers, servants, and missionaries. His instructions were to found towns and pacify the Indians in order to facilitate their conversion to Catholicism. He also received permission to profit from whatever trade or mining he could develop in New Mexico.

Oñate's initial encounters with the Indians were peaceful. As he traveled through the pueblos along the Rio Grande, he enacted dramas intended to illustrate to the Indians their subjection to the king of Spain. He reported that at Santo Domingo pueblo in July 1598 the leaders of 31 pueblos swore obedience to the king of Spain and also promised to obey Oñate and the Franciscan priest Fray Alonso Martínez. It is impossible to know how the Indians interpreted this ceremony, but Oñate's relations with most of the pueblos were peaceful, despite Spanish abuses. Oñate then moved on to San Juan, where he settled. From there he sent expeditions that unsuccessfully sought to find GOLD and other precious metals.

The colony, like others in the Americas, was not self-sufficient. The colonists complained that the climate was harsh, that no precious metals were to be found in the region, and that Oñate was a harsh commander. The Spanish demanded food, clothing, and other goods from the Indians, who did not have the resources to support several hundred extra people. In December 1598 the colony's demands for food and its arrogance toward the Indians provoked a rebellion at Acoma pueblo, where the Indians killed Captain Don Juan de Zaldívar and 12 of his men.

Oñate, reasoning that any rebellion must be punished immediately before the spirit of resistance spread, dispatched a force of 70 soldiers to attack the pueblo. Eight hundred Indians died in the resulting battle, and 500, including men, women, and children, were taken prisoner. The captives were convicted on charges of murder and of failing to give the Spanish the supplies they demanded. All prisoners over the age of 12 were sentenced to 20 years of slavery, and all men over the age of 25 had one foot cut off. The children were given as servants to Spanish settlers and monasteries.

By 1600, less than two years after its founding, the colony faced serious problems: Morale was low, the climate remained harsh, and initial hopes of finding wealth had foundered. Nonetheless, when 73 men arrived as reinforcements in December 1600, Oñate left the colony in hopes of finding the fabled land of Quivira. He reached the Great Plains, traveling as far east as Kansas, but found nothing. When he returned to New Mexico, he found the colony nearly deserted. Many of the colonists had returned to NEW SPAIN, where they complained to the viceroy that Oñate was a harsh and power-hungry commander. The Franciscan missionaries supported the colonists' claims and added that Oñate had abused the Indians and allowed his soldiers to do the same. In 1607 the viceroy ordered Oñate to resign his position. Oñate left New Mexico in 1609. He eventually returned to Spain, where he died in 1626.

Further reading: Elizabeth A. H. John, *Storms Brewed in Other Men's Worlds: The Confrontation of Indians, Spanish, and French in the Southwest, 1540–1795* (College Station: Texas A&M University Press, 1975); John L. Kessell, "Oñate, Juan de" in *Encyclopedia of Latin American History and Culture*, vol. 4, ed. Barbara A. Tenenbaum (New York: Scribner's, 1996), 228; Marc Simmons, "History of Pueblo–Spanish Relations to 1821," in *Handbook of North American Indians*, William C. Sturtevant, gen. ed., vol. 9, *Southwest*, vol. ed. Alfonso Ortiz (Washington, D.C.: Smithsonian Institution, 1979), 178–193; Edward H. Spicer, *Cycles of Conquest: The Impact of Spain, Mexico, and the United States on the Indians of the Southwest, 1533–1960* (Tucson: University of Arizona Press, 1962).

— Martha K. Robinson
—Donald Duhadanay

Oneida

A member tribe of the Five Nations IROQUOIS, the Oneida (or On'yote,' "People of the Standing Stone") lived to the west of their MOHAWK neighbors in the upper Mohawk Valley of modern-day New York near the lake that today bears their name.

Occupying one central village, the Oneida were the least populous group within the Iroquois Confederacy when Europeans arrived and shared the status of "younger brother" with the CAYUGA in the grand council uniting the five tribes. Nonetheless, the Oneida shared equal representation with the significantly larger Mohawk, each having nine sachems, or chiefs, in the governing body. In addition, their small numbers belied their prowess on the warpath. As a 17th century Jesuit priest observed, it was "a marvel that so few people work such havoc and render themselves so redoubtable to so great a number of tribes who, on all sides, bow before this conqueror." They particularly earned this reputation due to continual practice of the mourning war ritual to replenish war casualties they could ill afford to lose.

As did the other Iroquois nations, the Oneida became intensely involved in the fur trade early in the 17th century and prospered after securing intermediary status in the trade routes that linked key western tribes and the Dutch and English. They likewise became increasingly reliant on the new European goods won in exchange while maintaining the bulk of their traditional beliefs and customs. Nevertheless, while they adopted foreign clothing, tools, and weapons, the Oneida continued to funnel their use toward established standards of adornment, artistic and religious expressions, and hunting and warfare techniques. Such innovation and adaptation has been a hallmark of Iroquois culture, and the Oneida offer no exception.

Further reading: Jack Campisi,"Oneida," in William Sturtevant, ed., *Handbook of North American Indians*, vol. 15, *Northeast*, ed. Bruce G. Trigger (Washington, D.C.: Smithsonian Institution Press, 1978), 481–490; Jack Campisi and Laurence Hauptman, eds., *The Oneida Experience: Two Perspectives* (Syracuse, N.Y.: Syracuse University Press, 1988); Cara E. Richards, *The Oneida People* (Phoenix, Ariz.: Indian Tribal Series, 1974); Elizabeth Tooker, ed., *An Iroquois Source Book*, 3 vols. (New York: Garland, 1985).

— Eric P. Anderson

Onondaga

Geographically located at the center of the region occupied by the Five Nations IROQUOIS, the Onondaga ("People of the Hills") were one of the smaller of these tribes at the time of contact by Europeans but played a critical role in the formation and maintenance of the Iroquois Confederacy.

Situated in what is now central New York State near Onondaga Lake, the group's two main villages were well protected on the eastern and western flanks by their allies but remained vulnerable to attack by the French–HURON alliance in the north and other indigenous enemies from the south. It was the Onondaga chief HIAWATHA who helped found the Iroquois League and overcame the resistance of a rival leader in establishing this political structure.

Within the league's grand council, or governing body, the Onondaga were represented by the largest number of chiefs (14), who acted as the "Firekeepers" of the Five Nations and had veto power over the two "houses" of this political system in cases of disagreement. Furthermore, due to its central location, the grand council convened its meetings in Onondaga country. This key role in the confederacy gave the Onondaga a prestige in Iroquoia that extended far beyond their small numbers.

Like the other Five Nations, the Onondaga became heavily involved in the fur trade with competing European powers by the early 17th century. This commerce increased the tribe's wealth and power but in time brought with it disruptions and calamities in the form of growing reliance on new goods, repeated exposure to Old World DISEASES (such as SMALLPOX), and eventual displacement.

Further reading: Harold Blau, Jack Campisi, and Elisabeth Tooker, "Onondaga," in William Sturtevant, ed., *Handbook of North American Indians*, vol. 15, *Northeast*, vol. ed. Bruce G. Trigger (Washington, D.C.: Smithsonian Institution Press, 1978), 591–599; Daniel K. Richter and James H. Merrell, eds., *Beyond the Covenant Chain: The Iroquois and Their Neighbors in Indian North America, 1600–1800* (Syracuse, N.Y.: Syracuse University Press, 1987); Daniel K. Richter, *The Ordeal of the Longhouse: The Peoples of the Iroquois League in the Era of European Colonization* (Chapel Hill: University of North Carolina Press, 1992).

— Eric P. Anderson

Oviedo y Valdés, Gonzalo Fernández de (1478–1557)

A chronicler of the Spanish colonization of the Western Hemisphere, Gonzalo Fernández de Oviedo y Valdéz wrote a monumental history entitled *Historia General y Natural de las Indias Occidentales* that provided Europeans with crucial information about the Americas during the first half of the 16th century.

A child of an Asturian family, Oviedo met CHRISTOPHER COLUMBUS at the royal court in Madrid when he was 14 years old, and he met him again later at Granada. He was present in Barcelona when Columbus brought back captured natives from the Western Hemisphere, and then he spent time with Columbus's sons when they, like him, became pages to Infante Don Juan, heir to the Spanish Crown. After Don Juan's death in October 1497, Oviedo traveled to Italy, where he remained from 1499 to 1502, traveling and working in Genoa, Milan, and Rome before traveling back to Spain. In 1514 he made his first trip to the Western Hemisphere as inspector of the GOLD mines of the mainland in the service of Pedrarias Dávila, and the Americas became, from that moment onward, the central focus of his scholarship and life. Oviedo held various posts in the Spanish imperial bureaucracy, including inspector general of trade and governor of Cartagena (appointed in 1526). Oviedo's scholarship so pleased King CHARLES V that he became chronicler of the Indies in 1532, a title befitting his expertise in the complex history of Spain's overseas ventures. In 1535 he became governor of Santo Domingo, a post he held until 1545.

Oviedo's *Historia General y Natural de las Indias* included details on myriad aspects of the lives of the indigenous peoples of the Americas and their natural world. He provided the prices of goods and services, noting at one point that a prostitute cost eight to 10 CACAO beans (used for money), and he told in great detail about the abundant resources to be found in the West Indies. Convinced that this natural wealth could be transformed into great profits, in the late 1530s he became partners with GIOVANNI BATTISTA RAMUSIO, secretary of the Council of Ten (one of the ruling bodies of VENICE) and Antonio Priuli, procurator of the Basilica of San Marco in Venice, to establish a company that would transport goods, via Messina and Cádiz, from HISPANIOLA to Venice. No evidence survives about the successes or failures of the venture.

Twice widowed, Oviedo spent his last years working on his scholarship, although his great *Historia* remained mostly unpublished at the time of his death on June 26, 1557. Scholars disagree on where he died, with some claiming he breathed his last in Valladolid and others asserting that he passed away in Santo Domingo. Wherever he perished, his work survived, both in Spain and elsewhere, forming a major part of Ramusio's *Navigationi E Viaggi,* published in Venice in the 1550s, a work that had an enormous influence on the English promoter of colonization RICHARD HAKLUYT THE YOUNGER. Such chains of information, made possible by the spread of the PRINTING PRESS and the subsequent dissemination of books across Europe, assured Oviedo's prominence among the 16th-century chroniclers of the Western Hemisphere's peoples, resources, and history.

Further reading: Antonello Gerbi, *Nature In The New World: From Christopher Columbus to Gonzalo Fernández de Oviedo,* trans. Jeremy Moyle (Pittsburgh: University of Pittsburgh Press, 1985).

Oyo

The most powerful kingdom of YORUBA peoples by the 17th century, the Oyo dominated the area of West Africa now known as Nigeria.

According to Yoruba tradition, the Oyo became a distinct people in the 13th century, when Oranyan, an Ife prince from the Yoruba homeland, left the city to found his own kingdom. Oranyan was the son of Oduduwa, the ruler of the city of Ile Ife, or Ife, and the common ancestor of the principal Yoruba kingdoms. Oral and written sources disagree about the origins of the kingdom, claiming direct dynastic links to Oduduwa and Oranyan. Shango, Oranyan's son and the god of thunder, was crucial to the establishment of a legitimate power structure for the fledgling Oyo kingdom's rulers, or *alafins.* The Oyo estab-

lished their capital in the northeastern part of their kingdom, at the city of Oyo Ile (now known as Old Oyo).

Before the 16th century the Oyo were in frequent conflict with neighboring kingdoms such as the Owu and Nupe, attempting to establish their dominance in the region. Around 1550 the Nupe sacked the Oyo capital, forcing the Oyo *alafin* Onigbogi to flee to the Borgu kingdom to the north. This invasion of the Oyo kingdom effectively, but temporarily, caused the downfall of Oyo dominance in the area, but the Oyo regained power around 1600 under *alafin* Orompoto, who created a cavalry and a standing trained army. The maintenance of a cavalry was extremely difficult in the Oyo territory because two types of tse-tse fly made HORSE breeding impossible. The Oyo developed a strong trade in horses with their neighbors north of the NIGER RIVER and through their cavalry became the dominant power in Yorubaland. The Oyo established their capital at Igbohu but were again forced out by invading forces. They returned to the capital in the 17th century and became the most powerful state in the region, dominating all but BENIN.

The Oyo kingdom's location made it particularly well suited for controlling various types of trade. Oyo trade extended from the HAUSA kingdom to the cities of GAO, TIMBUKTU, and Djenne (see DJENNE-DJENO). The Oyo were skilled artisans as well, with sophisticated forms of spinning, dyeing, and weaving cloth, smelting and working of iron, and creating bowls and jugs from calabash gourds, yet the Oyo power base, like that of other contemporary African kingdoms such as DAHOMEY and ASANTE, rested on another sort of trade. The Oyo participated extensively in the transatlantic SLAVE TRADE, and its period of ascendancy can be dated accordingly, from the beginning of the 17th century until its disintegration in the 1830s.

Further reading: Basil Davidson, *West Africa before the Colonial Era: A History to 1850* (London: Longman, 1998), 113–117; Robin Law, *The Oyo Empire c.1600–c.1836: A West African Imperialism in the Era of the Atlantic Slave Trade* (Oxford, U.K.: Clarendon Press, 1977); "Oyo, Early Kingdom of," in *Africana: The Encyclopedia of the African and African American Experience,* eds. Kwame Anthony Appiah and Henry Louis Gates, Jr. (New York: Basic *Civitas* Books, 1999), 1474; "Oyo, rulers of," in *Dictionary of African Historical Biography,* 2nd ed., eds. Mark R. Lipschutz and R. Kent Rasmussen (Berkeley: University of California Press, 1986), 188.

— Lisa M. Brady

P

Palenque

A municipality in the northern part of present-day Chiapas, MEXICO, the city-state of Palenque flourished in the seventh and eighth centuries, becoming one of the great centers of classical MAYA civilization.

Palenque, a Hispanic name meaning "fortified place" (the Maya called Palenque B'aakal, or "Bone"), lies among thick tropical rain forest at the junction of a chain of low hills and the green floodplain of the Usumacinta River. The Palenque kingdom maintained cordial relations with other great classic kingdoms such as TIKAL but antagonistic ones with Calakmul, Tonina, and Piedras Negras. Palenque prospered during the second half of the classic period of Maya civilization (ca. A.D. 514–784). During this time denizens of Palenque led the Maya world in artistic and architectural accomplishment, particularly stucco work, and possessed a great deal of celestial knowledge as well.

The growth and arrangement of Palenque could only occur after its residents figured out how to solve pressing problems. Palenque Mayans overcame the difficult terrain by constructing an elaborate series of terraces designed to provide buildings with level platforms. They also modified the terrain by diverting a small river that coursed through the site underground through a vault-roofed aqueduct. One notable terrace housed three related temple pyramids that archaeologists have named the Temples of the Sun, Cross, and Foliated Cross, collectively known as the Group of the Cross. These structures served various ideological purposes. Recently, scholars have surmised that the three buildings symbolize the Maya creation myth.

The architectural and political achievements of the Palenque Maya did not insulate them from the dramatic decline in Maya civilization that scholars designate the Great Collapse. Despite the difficulty of reconstructing the complex events that precipitated the decline, scholars agree that by the end of the eighth century the population of the Maya had exceeded the carrying capacity of the land. Over-hunting and deforestation likely contributed to endemic internecine warfare; the final devastating blow may have resulted from a drought that began around 800 and did not end until 1050.

The collapse was remarkably fast. At Palenque the final words written into the classical Maya historical record occur on a small vase found in an ordinary residential apartment, rather than as an inscription on a towering pyramid that the recording of historical memory once required. The vase inscription boasts of a great and powerful king, but scholars have discovered that the vase was made in a town north of Palenque, hardly the sign of a thriving empire. Palenque was entirely abandoned during the early 900s and reoccupied only by wandering tribesmen who lived atop the disintegrating buildings. The ruins at Palenque served as shelter for itinerant travelers for the next millennium.

Further reading: Michael D. Coe *The Maya*, 6th ed. (New York: Thames & Hudson, 1999); Simon Martin and Nikolai Grube, *Chronicle of the Maya Kings and Queens: Deciphering the Dynasties of the Ancient Maya* (London: Thames & Hudson, 2000); Linda Schele and David Freidel, *A Forest of Kings: The Untold Story of the Ancient Maya* (New York: William Morrow, 1990).

— Kevin C. Armitage

Panama

Once resting between two great Indian civilizations, what today is Panama was first settled by Europeans in 1508 and crossed by VASCO NÚÑEZ DE BALBOA in 1513.

Geographically situated between present-day Colombia to the south and Costa Rica, Honduras, and MEXICO to the north, the Isthmus of Panama stood between the great INCA and MAYA civilizations. In the more immediate vicinity, the Chibchas lived in the mountainous Colombian region. Already established in the West Indies, the Spanish planters of HISPANIOLA looked longingly at the mainland for riches and more important, manpower, because the enslaved natives under their control were perishing in great numbers. Accordingly, the Spanish sent a number of exploratory expeditions to the mainland whose end goals included colonization and subjugation of the native population. The "discovery" of the Isthmus of Panama played an important role in Spanish expansion because the establishment of a permanent settlement on Tierre Firme, the northern coast of South America, allowed Spain's empire to spread to the Pacific and into South America.

Yet, however promising, Panama was not an easy place for the Spanish to succeed. In 1508 Alonso de Ojeda and Diego de Nicuesa obtained permission to organize and lead a large expedition to explore and settle the coast. Splitting up to cover more territory, Ojeda began his settlement after landing at the Gulf of Urabá, where present-day Colombia and Panama come together, referring to his settlement as Darién. Nicuesa sailed farther to the north, landing at Panama, where he enthusiastically, not to mention hopefully, dubbed his settlement Golden Castile. The horrors met by both parties soon became legendary throughout the Indies and even back in Spain. In addition to uncooperative natives, land crabs, flies, jungle cats, crocodiles, mosquitoes, and DISEASE combined to make life uncomfortable and often deadly. Within a year the combined number of nearly 1,000 settlers within the two camps was reduced to a few dozen ill-tempered Spaniards within each settlement. After he was wounded, Ojeda returned to Hispaniola, becoming a monk. His spirit broken, he soon died.

A small party ventured out of Darién in search of Nicuesa. Finding him in near-skeletal form, they helped revive him. Possibly insane from his experiences, Nicuesa demanded that he should take over Darién and the GOLD and pearls that the CONQUISTADORES had managed to gather. Indignant at the request, the remaining settlers of Darién chased Nicuesa away, putting him out to sea, where he disappeared from the annals of history. The remaining men quickly organized a city, electing the ablest amongst them ADELANTADO. In the process they allowed an official who was legally in charge to sail away. Returning to Spain, he informed the Crown of the rebellious and defiant attitude of Darién.

Eventually, Vasco Núñez de Balboa, who had originally joined the expedition as a stowaway after fleeing his creditors in Santo Domingo, became its improbable leader. Balboa, who possessed rare leadership qualities, soon rallied the unruly colonists and gained the friendship of the native population. With the colony in order, he set about investigating reports of a great sea to the west. In September 1513 he left with nearly 200 Spaniards and 1,000 native guides and porters. Slogging their way through swamps and jungles, the expedition soon reached the mountainous ridge separating the two great oceans. Approaching the crest of

the ridge, Balboa reportedly preceded the rest of the party, becoming the first European to "discover" the "South Sea," later known as the Pacific Ocean. With pomp and circumstance, the Spaniards took possession of the Pacific for Spain, erecting a cross and signing an affidavit that the discovery occurred on September 25, 1513. Before returning to Darién, Balboa received a gift of pearls and gold from the natives on Panama's western coast.

In Spain news of Nicuesa and Ojeda's colonization debacle was well circulated, leading the Crown to believe that a firm hand was needed to control the area. Accordingly, the Crown commissioned a large expedition of 19 ships and more than 2,000 men to set sail in April 1514. The elderly yet strong-willed Pedro Arias de Ávila, otherwise known as Pedrarias Dávila, commanded the expedition. Accompanying Pedrarias was a long list of famous conquistadores of later years including HERNANDO DE SOTO, Diego de Almagro, Hernado de Luque, and FRANCISCO CORONADO.

The expedition's arrival began a bitter conflict of interest between Balboa and Pedrarias, one in which the latter possessed, by decree of the Crown, the upper hand. Although he was appointed *adelantado* of the South Sea and ruler of Panama, Balboa's power was ultimately subsumed under that of Pedrarias's, resulting in an acrimonious feud resembling a modern-day soap opera. Among other bizarre events, Pedrarias captured the popular Balboa and brought him to his house, where he had him caged for a time. The two came to a truce after Balboa agreed to marry, by proxy, Pedrarias's oldest daughter in Spain and remove himself from Darién. Released from Pedrarias's possession, Balboa moved to the north, where he spent three peaceful years constructing ships while he learned of great civilizations to the south. Ever jealous of Balboa's increasing popularity, his father-in-law called him for a meeting at the town of Alca. Upon his arrival, Pedrarias ordered Balboa seized and charged with treason. His captors soon beheaded him.

Pedrarias continued to control the area until his death in 1531, much to the indignity of the area's natives. During his tenure as governor of Panama, he oversaw the establishment of the first bishopric on the American mainland at Darien in 1513, yet his rule was anything but benevolent for the native population. In Panama the Spaniards followed their conquest with the establishment of their form of agriculture and the enslavement of captives. This process devastated the native population. Leaving behind a systematic description of Panama before and after conquest, the early 16th-century chronicler Cieza de León wrote in harsh terms of the destruction of the Indians. At the same time he noted the growth of farms and ranches with herds of cattle and groves of oranges, citrons, and figs, all imported from Spain.

As the native population died out or migrated, the Spanish imported African slaves (see SLAVERY and SLAVE TRADE) to Panama. Accepted not only as an economic necessity in Spanish America, slavery was also defended by the church as being compatible with Christian ethics. In 1531 the Spanish suppressed a general slave uprising in Panama only with great difficulty, creating insecurity in the isthmus throughout the colonial period. Because of the inaccessible hills and forests of the interior, the isthmus also became an inviting haven for escaped African slaves. Known as *cimarrones,* they formed independent communities within Panama's interior, thereby contributing to Panama's present-day ethnic heritage.

Beyond expanded production, Panama served as a center for Spanish trade. By the middle of the 16th century, Panama's Nombre de Dios ranked as one of Spain's three principal ports for the reception of merchandise in America (the others were VERACRUZ and Cartagena). Merchants at the port received goods that they then sent across the isthmus to Panama City and transshipped to Callao and other ports in Ecuador, Chile, and PERU. The conquest of these South America regions came shortly after the conquest of Panama. Between 1509 and 1554 the Spanish brought Venezuela, Colombia, Ecuador, Peru, Bolivia, and Chile under their control. Many conquering missions used Panama as a geographical springboard for these conquests. Such was the case in 1531, when a pair of illiterate explorers, FRANCISCO PIZARRO and Diego de Almagro, left Panama en route to Peru. Theirs was an expedition that signaled not only the demise of the Inca civilization but also the Spanish exploitation of the Peruvian SILVER mines.

The Spanish conquistadores used Panama as a weigh station in the trade of Peruvian silver en route to Spain, thus providing an inviting target for piracy. Perhaps the most intriguing raid on Panama's silver warehouses occurred in 1572–73, when England's SIR FRANCIS DRAKE, known to the Spanish as *El Draque,* landed and captured a large store of riches, leading to a hero's welcome back home. Not all the English pirates were as successful as Drake. Attempting a similar raid, John Oxenham was captured by the Spanish and executed by the INQUISITION in LIMA as a heretic. Drake himself met defeat and death in 1595 while leading 2,500 men on an attempted conquest of Panama. Despite its jungles, mountains, and swamps, which combined to make transportation difficult, control over Panama gave the Spanish remarkable power in the Western Hemisphere.

Further reading: L. G. Anderson, *Life and Letters of Vasco Núñez de Balboa* (New York: Fleming H. Revell, 1941); Bailey W. Diffie, *Latin-American Civilization: Colonial Period* (New York: Octagon Books, 1967); John Edwin Fagg, *Latin America: A General History* (New York: Macmillan, 1969); Kathleen Romoli, *Balboa of Darien* (Garden City, N.Y.: Doubleday, 1953); Dominic Salandra, "Pedrarias Davila and the Spanish Beginnings on the Isthmus," Ph.D. diss. (University of California at Berkeley, 1933).

— Matthew Lindaman

Parliament

The English legislative body known as Parliament evolved from Saxon traditions that required a king to rule with the advice of his nobility, the great men of the realm.

The body that sat in Westminster during the reigns of the HENRY VIII and ELIZABETH I traced its lineage to the system of FEUDALISM as it developed in England. Lords granted freedmen land in trade for service. Lords, in turn, were responsible to tenants. Feudalism created a social system of fealty to regional monarchs and their courts that was supported by the advice tenants could provide about local political and social conditions.

Gatherings of tenants occurred on a semiregular basis and became assemblies in which all members of society were, in theory, represented. Such gatherings offered the opportunity to advise the monarch. From that body a few special advisers became members of the monarch's council, emerging as the PRIVY COUNCIL by the time of the Tudors. These men did the day-to-day work of the government, along with the monarch, and became part of the executive operations of government. Parliament remained responsible for legislation.

As early as 1242, clerics, earls, and barons who were called to a *parliamentum* advised the king. By 1258 Parliament was to meet three times a year. Knights of the shires were desirable allies for clerics, earls, and barons by 1264, and they came to be called the House of Commons. By the early 16th century towns as well as shires were demanding representation. In 1530, 236 representatives in commons represented 117 English boroughs. The figure nearly doubled during the reign of Elizabeth I. By the turn of the 17th century Parliament had two distinct houses within its legislative body, one closely associated with subjects and one closely associated with the king.

Further reading: Christopher Hollis, *Parliament and Its Sovereignty* (London: Hollis & Carter, 1973); Kenneth Mackenzie, *The English Parliament* (Baltimore: Penguin Books, 1959); Edward Miller, *The Origins of Parliament,* General Series Number 44 (London: Historical Association of London, 1960); J. G. A. Pocock, *The Ancient Constitution and the Feudal Law* (Cambridge, U.K.: Cambridge University Press, 1957).

— David P. Dewar

Parmenius, Stephen (1555?–1583)

The first Hungarian to see the Western Hemisphere, Stephen Parmenius was an intimate of various Elizabethan explorers and promoters of colonization who intended to write a great epic about the European exploration of North America but managed to leave behind only two poems and a short prose piece before his death at sea leaving Canadian waters in 1583.

Born in Buda when that Hungarian city was under the control of the Turks, Parmenius was an intelligent young man who left his homeland in 1589 to travel to western Europe, where he quickly came into contact with a number of men who had an interest in overseas exploration. Raised in a Calvinist family, Parmenius presumably intended to return to Hungary once he had completed his tour of various Protestant churches in Germany and perhaps beyond. He studied at Heidelberg and then quite possibly traveled to other well-known destinations for young men seeking a broad humanist education. If so, he would have traveled to Rome, Florence, VENICE, and the Netherlands. Whether he made this predictable trip is unknown, but Parmenius did arrive in Oxford in 1581, one of the centers of learning in the Western world and a city renowned for its concentration of individuals with an interest in matters of state policy in Elizabethan England.

Soon after his arrival in Oxford, Parmenius met RICHARD HAKLUYT THE YOUNGER, the avid promoter of the English colonization of the Americas, and eventually he came to the attention of SIR HUMPHREY GILBERT, who in the early 1580s was busy preparing for a venture to establish a colony in North America in modern-day Newfoundland. The two men shared common interests, especially their fascination with America. Parmenius subsequently spent his time writing a poem celebrating the exploration of North America. Eventually, Gilbert offered Parmenius a chance to live out his life's dream: He enticed him to join the English mission to Newfoundland in 1583, an invitation the young Hungarian did not refuse. After a successful crossing the *Delight,* the ship Parmenius sailed on, ran aground in August of that year, and he was lost at sea along with most of those onboard. Soon after Gilbert himself perished when his small vessel, the *Squirrel,* also sank on his return to England.

Parmenius's loss mattered deeply to Elizabethans who cared about the potential colonization of the Americas, especially to Hakluyt. Parmenius's written pieces survive as testament both to his interest in Atlantic exploration and to the literary abilities of a young man whose death was one of many when Europeans sailed in unfamiliar—and thus to them dangerous—American seaways.

Further reading: David B. Quinn and Neil M. Cheshire, eds., *The New Found Land of Stephen Parmenius: The life and writings of a Hungarian Poet, drowned on a voyage from Newfoundland, 1583* (Toronto: University of Toronto Press, 1972); David B. Quinn, "Stephen Parmenius Budaeus: A Hungarian Pioneer in North America," in Quinn, ed., *Explorers and Colonies: America, 1500–1625* (London: Hambledon Press, 1990), 225–238.

Passamaquoddy

An ALGONQUIAN-speaking people, the Passamaquoddy Indians lived in modern-day Maine and New Brunswick.

The Passamaquoddy Indians shared close contact and many cultural similarities with their neighbors, especially the ABENAKI and the MALISEET peoples. The early history of these "Dawnland Peoples" who lived along the eastern coast of North America is often obscure, for early European accounts are sparse and contradictory, and many Passamaquoddy sites have been lost to rising sea levels. Later tribal divisions are not always appropriate for the early years of contact, and the Maliseet and Passamaquoddy, if not the same peoples, were very closely related.

It is possible that the Passamaquoddy first met Europeans in the early 16th century, when European fishermen sought to trade metal goods for furs. In 1603 Samuel de Champlain met Passamaquoddy warriors at Tadoussac, an important trading site. The question of early contact between Europeans and the Passamaquoddy remains complicated because early French writers often referred to a group of people called the Etchemins, who have been variously identified as the Passamaquoddy, Maliseet, and eastern Abenaki peoples.

The Passamaquoddy lived along the coast of current-day Maine and New Brunswick, where they relied on fishing and hunting. Like other Indian peoples of the region, they moved seasonally, living in hunting camps during the winter and larger communities in the summer. In the 17th century they used both conical wigwams and larger rectangular lodges, each of which might house several families.

Further reading: Colin G. Calloway, *Dawnland Encounters: Indians and Europeans in Northern New England* (Hanover, N.H.: University Press of New England, 1991); Vincent O. Erickson, "Maliseet-Passamaquoddy," in *Handbook of North American Indians,* William C. Sturtevant, gen. ed., vol. 15, *Northeast,* ed. Bruce G. Trigger (Washington, D.C.: Smithsonian Institution, 1978), 123–136; Dean R. Snow, "Late Prehistory of the East Coast," in *Northeast,* ed. Bruce G. Trigger (Washington, D.C.: Smithsonian Institution, 1978), 58–69.

— Martha K. Robinson

Peckham, Sir George (?–1608)

Sir George Peckham, a close associate of SIR HUMPHREY GILBERT, promoted the English colonization of North America and hoped to profit from the establishment of trading posts in current-day Newfoundland as well as from his lands at Narragansett Bay.

Little is known of the early life of Sir George Peckham. By the late 1570s he had become a familiar of Gilbert, but unlike his friend Peckham did not engage in any serious military engagements either in Ireland or on the Continent. Unlike most of the English who dreamed of colonizing North America, Peckham was a Catholic who had hoped to establish a refuge in the Western Hemisphere for his coreligionists in England, who were suffering persecution as a result of the Protestant REFORMATION and its spread to Britain. That plan eventually failed, but Peckham continued to try to promote colonization, especially after Gilbert had given him an extensive tract of land along Narragansett Bay, an area that would later become crucial for the English fur trade with the indigenous peoples of coastal New England.

Despite the presumed demise of Gilbert in 1583, Peckham wrote a book about his patron's efforts to create a colony in Newfoundland. Entitled *A True Reporte of the Late Discoveries and Possession, Taken in the Right of the Crown of Englande, of the Newfound Landes: by that Valliant and Worthye Gentleman, Sir Humphrey Gilbert*, the book was published in LONDON in 1583. Peckham hoped that his book would inspire English settlement in the Western Hemisphere. With that goal in mind, he decided that the way to convince his fellow English to join the cause would be to demonstrate the obvious benefits of colonization. He thus likened the pursuit to the struggles of biblical times and drew on the Book of Joshua and other bits of Scripture to provide an ideological argument supporting the venture. He rhetorically dismissed the claims of the Spanish, believing, as other English promoters did, that the queen's subjects had the right to lay claim to much of North America. He also noted that commerce with Native Americans would be crucial and profitable. He emphasized that such trade would be to the Indians' benefit as well, in large part because the presence of Protestants in the area would mean that Indians could, as he put it, "be brought from falsehood to truth, from darknes to lyght, from the hieway of death, to the path of life, from superstitious idolatry, to sincere Christianity, from the devill to Christ, from hell to Heaven." To make sure that others would accept the challenge, he told his readers about the commodities to be found in North America and assured them that the passage to the northeast would be safe since the ships would not have to cross "the burnt line, whereby commonly both beverage and victuall are corrupted and mens health very much impaired, nor doo we passe the frozen Seas, which

yeelde sundrey extreme daungers." Confident that his enticements would work, Peckham went on to lay out a feudal (see FEUDALISM) type of society in which those who invested in the establishment of the colony would have legal as well as economic authority over others who arrived later. Although such legal arrangements had already become archaic in England, Peckham believed such a system would be an ideal way to administer the new settlements. Peckham lived long enough to hear about the origins of Jamestown in 1607, but not long enough to know that the plans of Europeans often meant little on the ground in North America.

Further reading: Peter C. Mancall, ed., *Envisioning America: English Plans for the Colonization of North America, 1580–1640* (New York: Bedford Books of St. Martin's Press, 1995); Sir George Peckham, *A True Reporte of the Late Discoveries and Possession, Taken in the Right of the Crown of Englande, of the Newfound Landes: by That Valiant and Worthye Gentleman, Sir Humphrey Gilbert*, in *New American World*, 5 vols., ed. David Beers Quinn and Alison O. Quinn, (London: Macmillan, 1979). 3:34–60.

Peru

One of the great territorial divisions of colonial Latin America, Peru formed a distinct geographical and cultural zone that became the core of several native kingdoms as well as of the Spanish Empire in South America.

The most important geographical feature of Peru is the ANDES MOUNTAINS. As the second-highest range of mountains in the world, the Andes formed an effective barrier between climate zones and human cultures. In particular, they block the wet, humid air of the AMAZON RIVER region from reaching western Peru, leaving the Pacific coastal areas arid while the eastern slopes are covered with rain forests. Another important factor in shaping Peru's climate is the Humboldt Current, a cold water current that flows north along the coast. The Humboldt Current makes the sea much colder than the land, which forces the rain to fall at sea and keeps the coastal zone a desert. In certain areas moisture from the upper slopes of the Andes runs down toward the Pacific in a series of small rivers, such as the Ica and Nazca. These river valleys are fertile agricultural zones that have always attracted human settlers. Most human settlements, however, congregated in the mountain valleys of the Andes themselves. In general, these valleys were flat enough to facilitate agriculture and frequently received adequate water from mountain streams or cloud vapor. Although a series of valleys could be only a few miles apart, the differences in elevation between them could radically change the types of plants and animals that could flourish there. This has given rise to the term "vertical ecology" to describe the Andes, a place where altitude, not latitude, is the primary factor in determining the local climate.

In this unusual world of stark contrasts, several native cultures flourished. Two main cultural areas emerged over time: the highlands and the coastal zone. The people of the coast generally relied on fishing and growing beans, squash, and CORN in the river valleys. In the highlands, natives grew CACAO, potatoes, and quinoa while raising llamas for wool and meat. Each zone produced powerful kingdoms, and the balance of power shifted from the highlands to the lowlands many times until the INCA united the region under their control after the 1430s. Andean societies never developed true systems of trade to move goods from one zone to another. Instead of bartering for the goods of other regions, individual clans, called *ayllus*, would send colonists to spend one-year shifts living in another region, producing a particular good that the *ayllu* desired. A coastal *ayllu*, for example, would send colonists into the mountains to grow potatoes and cacao. These colonists would return at year's end with their goods, and a new group of colonists would take their place. This notion of *ayllu* continued under Inca rule.

With FRANCISCO PIZARRO's conquest of the region from 1531 to 1533, Peru became the core of the Spanish empire in South America. Pizarro established the city of LIMA on the Pacific coast to be the colony's capital, fearing the Incas' former capital of CUZCO was too remote and vulnerable to possible native rebellions. For the next half century many Spanish CONQUISTADORES went out from Lima in search of other kingdoms of GOLD (see EL DORADO). In terms of political administration, colonial Peru closely followed the model of NEW SPAIN. In fact, the first viceroy the Crown appointed to Peru was none other than ANTONIO DE MENDOZA, the first viceroy of New Spain, who had just completed his term of office in Mexico City. Within a short time the Crown also established AUDIENCIAS, CORREGIDORES, and CABILDOs throughout the colony to maintain order. Peru's colonial economy depended on the export of SILVER. Explorers discovered massive silver veins at POTOSÍ in 1545, which quickly became the most important mining zone in the Western Hemisphere.

Considered to be Spain's most valuable possession in the NEW WORLD because of its size and great mineral wealth, Peru was also one of the most difficult to govern. Population centers were isolated, and the Andes hindered effective communication. There was also no easy way to trade directly with Spain; merchants had to unload their goods at PANAMA and haul them overland to ships waiting on the other side. Moreover, the great wealth generated by the mines inspired greed, smuggling, and, at times, open rebellion among the colonists. The situation of the native peoples was particularly grim. Both the Crown and the colonists wanted to use them as a cheap labor force to work in the mines. Ultimately, to satisfy the mines' needs, the Crown developed a coerced labor system called the REPARTIMIENTO, which was essentially a labor draft that forced young males to work at the mines for one year. Working conditions at Potosí and other mines were so unsafe that few survived their year-long shift. Infuriated at this exploitation, many natives rose up in rebellion or retreated ever farther into unsettled areas. Despite these problems, Peru flourished throughout the colonial period, producing not only great wealth, but gifted scholars, notable architecture, and accomplished works of art.

Further reading: Adrian von Hagen and Craig Morris, *The Cities of the Ancient Andes* (London: Thames & Hudson, 1998); James Lockhart, *Spanish Peru 1532–1560: A Colonial Society* (Madison: University of Wisconsin Press, 1968); Sabine MacCormack, *Religion in the Andes: Vision and Imagination in Early Colonial Peru* (Princeton, N.J.: Princeton University Press, 1991); Lyle N. McAlister, *Spain and Portugal in the New World, 1495–1700* (Minneapolis: University of Minnesota Press, 1984); Karen Spalding, *Huarochirí: An Andean Society under Inca and Spanish Rule* (Stanford, Calif.: Stanford University Press, 1984).

— Scott Chamberlain

Peter Martyr (Pietro Martire d'Anghiera) (1457–1526)

An early chronicler of the voyages of CHRISTOPHER COLUMBUS, whose writings on European travelers in the Western Hemisphere circulated widely across Europe during the 16th century.

Born in Italy, Peter Martyr became attached to the court of FERDINAND AND ISABELLA in 1487, a position that enabled him to interview Columbus and other Spaniards returning from the Americas. Although he later became dean of the cathedral of Granada, his most significant work was the publication in 1516 of *De Rebus Oceanicis et Nove Orbe decades tres*. This work contained the most extensive descriptions of the Americas then available in Europe, much of it intended for religious officials including, not surprisingly, Pope LEO X. Across the continent, astute editors and translators recognized the potential significance of the work. Among those who published translations were the Venetian civil servant GIOVANNI BATTISTA RAMUSIO, who included an Italian translation in the third volume of his *Navigationi E Viaggi* (published in VENICE in 1559) and Richard Eden, who in 1555 published in LONDON an English translation with the title *The Decades of the newe worlde or west India;* Eden also translated other, related works written by, among others, AMERIGO VESPUCCI,

ANTONIO PIGAFETTA, GONZALO FERNÁNDEZ DE OVIEDO Y VALDÉS, and SEBASTIAN CABOT.

Further reading: Edward Arber, ed., *The First Three English Books on America* (Birmingham, 1885); Ernesto Lunardi, Elisa Magioncalda, and Rosanna Mazzacane, eds., *The Discovery of the New World in the Writings of Peter Martyr of Anghiera,* trans. Felix Azzola (Rome: Instituto Poligrafico e Zecca della Stato/Libreria dello Stato, 1992); Pietro Martire d'Anghiera, *The Decades of the Newe Worlde or West India,* trans. Richard Eden (Ann Arbor, Mich.: University Microfilms, 1966).

Philip II, king of Spain (1527–1598)

King of Spain and ruler of numerous other European lands, Philip II was a skillful administrator who played a key role in most of the important political events of his age, including European political conflicts, colonization and exploitation of the wealth of the Americas, and the European Wars of Religion.

Born May 21, 1527, son of CHARLES V, Holy Roman Emperor and king of Spain, and Isabella, sister to the king of Portugal. While Charles ceded his Habsburg domains to his brother Ferdinand, his son Philip was undisputed heir to his western European and overseas possessions. In October 1555 Charles gave Philip control of the Low Countries, followed three months later by all Spanish possessions on both sides of the Atlantic, relinquishing control of Franche-Comté to Philip the following year. Charles's abdication managed to forestall the political chaos that an improvised succession after his death might have brought but did little to remedy Spain's economic problems, leaving Philip 20 million ducats of debt at a time when the Crown's ordinary revenue was only 2 million ducats a year.

Philip's inherited domains were smaller than his father's, but he may have been fortunate to inherit a more manageable empire. Although Philip's empire was far from unified, it was distinctly Spanish, centered in Madrid, almost completely Catholic, and had a constant infusion of wealth from the Americas. Like his father, Philip ruled a composite monarchy, even in the Iberian peninsula, where he ruled the Spanish kingdoms of CASTILE, Aragón, and Navarre as separate kingdoms, rather than a unified whole. Philip ruled his more distant territories by means of appointed viceroys, usually drawn from the great families of the Castilian nobility, each of whom reported to a supervisory council in Madrid. Philip did not normally attend these council sessions himself but did review their decisions, all of which were subject to royal approval.

Philip continued many of his father's policies, with mixed results. Like his father, he won great military victories for Spain, but with limited long-term results. In general, Philip was a reserved intellectual much more interested in the administrative duties of kingship than in the warrior ideal so common to the Spanish nobility. He never personally led his troops in battle, a fact that caused some to comment that he "tried to govern the world from a chair." Even his marriages—all four of them—reflected his gift for political strategy, yet none of these unions turned out to be the dynastic master stroke that he had planned. Philip outlived all four of his wives as well as six of his nine children. His first son, Don Carlos, was both physically deformed and mentally unbalanced and resented his father deeply enough to run off and join the Dutch revolt against Philip. Philip's subsequent arrest of his own son, who died in exile, resulted in open criticism and not-so-thinly-veiled accusations from other European courts.

In the Americas Philip strove more or less successfully to prevent colonists from achieving political independence from Castile and its king. He accomplished his goals in part by encouraging the AUDIENCIAS, or royal courts, to challenge the authority of the viceroys. The COUNCIL OF THE INDIES in Madrid operated as a further check on colonial autonomy, monitoring both the viceroys and the *audiencias* and reporting ultimately to Philip.

Still, colonists and traders in the Indies and the Americas benefited from the strong royal presence. During Philip's reign the Spanish navy was the strongest in Europe and was able to prevent Dutch, English, and French pirates from disrupting shipping and harassing colonies. Philip's formidable navy also enforced his exclusionary policies, effectively preventing Spain's Atlantic rivals from establishing colonies in the Indies until after 1600.

Despite its prosperity from the Indies trade, there were economic weaknesses built into Philip's empire. The Castilian ethic of Christian military expansionism, based on the centuries-long RECONQUISTA, meant that Castilians generally valued military activity over mercantile ventures. As a result commercial enterprises never became highly developed among Castilians. Not even the Castilian-monopolized Indies trade was truly Spanish; its European exports generally originated outside Castile, rendering Castilian merchants little more than well-positioned middlemen. The inherent economic deficiencies of the Castilian economy meant that very little of the GOLD and SILVER that arrived from the Americas actually stayed in Castile and instead went to importing manufactured goods that the Castilians were forced to buy from other countries.

Spaniards generally remember Philip as their "Prudent King," but some of his policies were more daring. The most successful of these was his Mediterranean campaign against the Muslims (see ISLAM). Philip authorized a series of battles against the Ottoman-backed Barbary pirates that failed to stop the raids but did manage to provide greater protection for Spanish shipping in the eastern Mediterranean. Spain, along with VENICE and the papacy, formed the HOLY LEAGUE, an international alliance dedicated to fighting the Turks. The combined Catholic forces won a decisive victory at the Battle of Lepanto in October of 1571, effectively halting Turkish expansion into the Mediterranean. Finally, and closer to home, Philip managed to crush an uprising of the Muslim community in Granada.

Another daring move was Philip's annexation of Portugal and its empire in 1580. Philip's mother had been sister to the king of Portugal, and when the latter died with no direct heir, Philip's claim to the throne was as good as that of many other contenders. His agents overcame the Portuguese nobility's traditional hatred of Castile with a combination of donations of silver and promises of future rewards. Philip dispatched Spanish troops to quell any violent resistance to his candidacy and soon secured the throne for himself. Although the absorption of the Portuguese empire augmented Spain's Iberian and American holdings and added profits from the Portuguese spice trade to Spain's coffers, Portugal remained politically and economically autonomous. In the final analysis, its acquisition may have been much less profitable than it seemed.

The annexation of Portugal and the near-elimination of the Turkish threat combined with the sudden doubling of silver revenues had the secondary effect of giving Philip the confidence to pursue his Protestant adversaries in northern Europe. This planned venture had three complementary goals: the suppression of Calvinism in the Spanish Netherlands, the resolution of the French Wars of Religion in favor of the Catholic Church, and the conquest of England, whose privateers had been raiding the Spanish Indies and whose queen, ELIZABETH I, followed her father, HENRY VIII's, policy of declaring herself head of the English church, thereby flouting papal authority. However, despite favorable circumstances, Philip failed in all three of these ventures. In 1593 Henry of Navarre converted to Catholicism as a part of the agreement by which he was crowned HENRY IV of France. This move both frustrated Philip's plans to place a Spanish princess on the throne and constituted a further roadblock to his vision of a unified Catholic Europe when Henry promised toleration of French HUGUENOTS. In the Netherlands Dutch Protestants rebelled, fled, or resisted but refused to be unified under a Spanish king and, more important, a Roman church. Most disastrous of all, Philip's invasion of England—finally provoked by Elizabethan assistance to the Dutch rebels—ended in utter failure in 1588 when the SPANISH ARMADA met defeat as a result of a combination of the skill of the English navy, the inexperienced leadership of the Spanish forces, and a chance storm that scattered the remnants of the Spanish fleet into the North Sea. The loss of the armada marked the end of Spain's dominance of Europe. Philip's multiple defeats during the last 10 years of his reign also signaled the end of Catholic hopes of eradicating Protestantism in Europe.

Further reading: John Elliott, *Imperial Spain, 1469–1716* (New York: St. Martin's Press, 1977); Henry Kamen, *Philip II of Spain* (New Haven, Conn.: Yale University Press, 1997); John Lynch, *Spain 1516–1598: From Nation State to World Empire* (Oxford: Blackwell, 1992); Eugene F. Rice, Jr. and Anthony Grafton, *The Foundations of Early Modern Europe, 1460–1559,* 2nd ed. (New York: Norton, 1994).

— Marie A. Kelleher

Picts

Legendary inhabitants of Britain, the Picts dyed themselves blue in an effort to scare off enemies, a strategy that solidified their place in myth.

The origins of the Picts remain unknown. They appeared in history as one of the neolithic peoples who inhabited northern Britain and modern-day Scotland in the centuries before the Romans arrived at the end of the first century A.D. When the Romans under Hadrian conquered much of Britain from 78 to 142, they eventually built an enormous structure known as Hadrian's Wall to separate the Romanized, and thus civilized, parts of the island from those the Romans deemed barbaric, such as the Picts.

The Picts eventually faded into obscurity as a people, but they remained in British history. When THOMAS HARRIOT published the illustrated edition of his *Briefe and True Report of the Newe Found Land of Virginia* in LONDON in 1590, he included a series of pictures by the Flemish engraver THEODOR DE BRY of the Picts. In the de Bry engravings the Picts appeared bellicose and savage; men and women alike were naked, heavily tattooed, and holding weapons, and one man was shown holding the head of an enemy still dripping blood while another head lay at his feet. Harriot added these renderings of a bloodthirsty people at the end of the illustrations of Carolina ALGONQUIANS, who seemed peaceful by comparison. He did so to demonstrate to his audience that the native peoples of North America might seem unlikely converts to European "civilization," but in fact they were no more "savage" than the Picts had been. The lesson? If the Picts could become modern-day Britons, then Indians could also be converted to English ways.

Further reading: Thomas Harriot, *A Briefe and True Report of the Newe Found Land of Virginia* (New York: Dover, 1972).

Pigafetta, Antonio (fl. 1480s?–1532?)

Antonio Pigafetta's account of FERDINAND MAGELLAN's circumnavigation of the globe is the most important contemporary account of the voyage.

Little is known about Pigafetta's life. His birth is placed variously in the 1480s and 1490s, and the date of his death is unknown, although most scholars believe he died young, perhaps by 1532. An Italian, Pigafetta apparently joined Magellan's expedition in search of adventure. During the voyage Pigafetta was loyal to Magellan, eulogizing him after his death as "our mirror, our light, our comfort, and our true guide."

Pigafetta's account of the peoples he encountered provided vivid, sometimes accurate, geographic and ethnographic information. He described the TUPINAMBÁ Indians of Brazil, claimed to have seen giants in Patagonia, and provided a detailed account of the peoples of the Philippines.

Pigafetta's account of the journey was first published in French in 1525. It was translated into Italian in 1536 and into English in 1555. Because Magellan's papers, letters, charts, and logs were lost or destroyed, Pigafetta's work is of immense value as the most valuable of the few surviving sources on the voyage.

Further reading: Samuel Eliot Morison, *The Great Explorers: The European Discovery of America* (New York: Oxford University Press, 1978); J. H. Parry, *The Discovery of South America* (London: Paul Elek, 1979); Donald Payne, *Magellan and the First Circumnavigation of the World* (London: Weidenfeld & Nicolson, 1974); Antonio Pigafetta, *The First Voyage Around the World: An Account of Magellan's Expedition,* ed. Theodore J. Cachey, Jr. (New York: Marsilio Publishers, 1995)

— Martha K. Robinson

Pizarro, Francisco (ca. 1478–1541)

The CONQUISTADOR who led the Spanish conquest of the INCA Empire in the 1530s.

Born in the town of Trujillo of Extremadura, Spain, around 1478, Francisco Pizarro was the illegitimate son of Gonzalo Pizarro, who had several illegitimate sons with different women. Because of his illegitimacy, Pizarro never received an education and eventually sought his destiny in military affairs. While still young he probably served with Spanish forces in Italy in the late 15th century. Eventually, Pizarro made his way to HISPANIOLA in 1502.

Pizarro garnered considerable experience in the Caribbean as a conquistador. He participated in the Spanish exploration of the Gulf of Uraba in 1509 and 1510 and went with VASCO NÚÑEZ DE BALBOA across PANAMA to the Pacific Ocean in 1513. Pizarro helped found Panama in 1519 and was eventually rewarded with an ENCOMIENDA.

He also acted as an administrator at various levels for the city of Panama.

Finally, with Diego de Almagro and Hernando de Luque, Pizarro began to make preparations for the expedition that would make him famous, the conquest of PERU. Not really knowing what lay below Panama, he moved into South America for the first time in 1524. He did not find much during this first foray, but in his second effort in 1526–27, Pizarro survived a mutiny on the Isla del Gallo and made contact with the northern border of the Inca Empire. Realizing what potentially lay before him, he returned to Spain to get financial support for his *entrada* into the Inca Empire, acquire additional soldiers he could depend upon, and clear his title to the territory he would conquer. By doing so, Pizarro effectively cut his erstwhile partners out of the spoils he planned to garner.

In 1530 Pizarro's expedition set off for Peru. In 1532 Pizarro encountered the Inca emperor, ATAHUALPA, at the city of Cajamarca. After Atahualpa rejected the REQUERIMIENTO, the Spanish attacked the Incan entourage and took the ruler captive. To ransom his freedom, Atahualpa promised Pizarro to fill a room with GOLD and SILVER. It took several months to meet this goal. In 1532, after the Inca delivered the ransom, Pizarro decided Atahualpa no longer served a purpose and had him executed. Pizarro then marched on the Inca capital of CUZCO and seized it.

The Spanish were able conquer the Inca Empire, numbering approximately 14 million subjects, because they appeared on the scene immediately after the empire had suffered a major SMALLPOX epidemic that killed tens of thousands, including Atahualpa's father and his older brother, the heir to the throne. As a result of this situation, Atahualpa and his brother, Huascar, fought a civil war over their claims to the throne. Additionally, many of the people whom the Inca had conquered were willing to side with the Spanish to rid themselves of Incan rule. All of these elements came together to help the Spanish gain the upper hand.

After seizing control of a majority of the empire, Pizarro decided to move the administrative center from Cuzco to the newly created Spanish city of LIMA, which was closer to the coast and easier for the Spanish to control. He also began granting *encomiendas* to his supporters and brought in missionaries to convert the Spanish Empire's newest subjects. Pizarro's former partner, Almagro, eventually reached the Andes as the governor of New Toledo, which was located to the south of Pizarro's territory. Conflict continued between Almagro's faction and Pizarro's faction until Pizarro defeated Almagro at Salinas in 1538 and had him executed. In 1541 followers of Diego de Almagro the Younger broke into Francisco Pizarro's home in Lima and assassinated him.

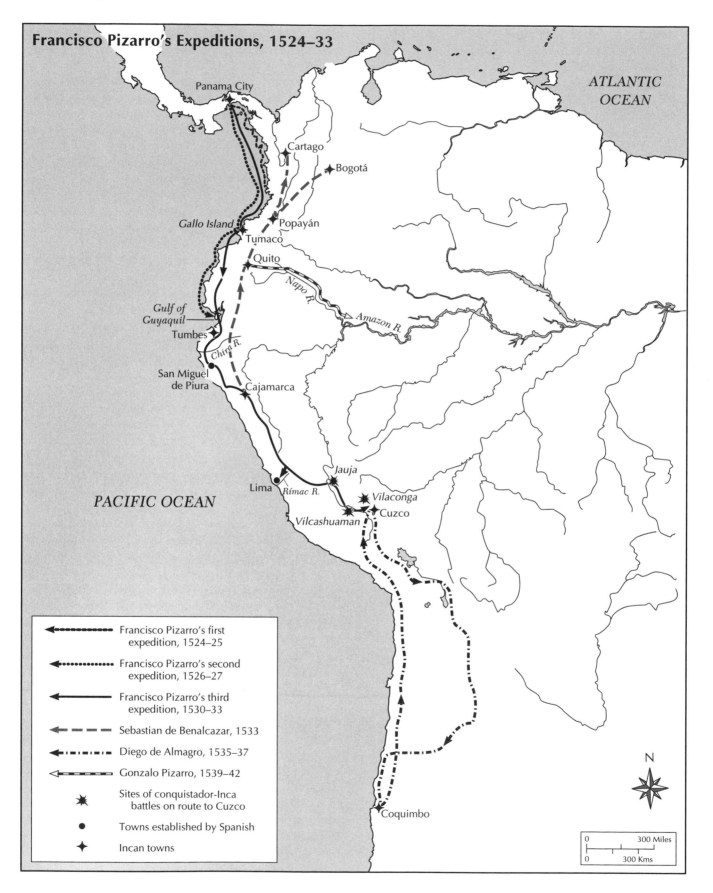

Francisco Pizarro's Expeditions, 1524–33

ATLANTIC OCEAN

Panama City

Cartago

Bogotá

Gallo Island

Popayán

Tumaco

Quito

Napo R.

Gulf of Guyaquil

Amazon R.

Tumbes

Chira R.

San Miguel de Piura

Cajamarca

PACIFIC OCEAN

Jauja

Lima

Rímac R.

Vilaconga

Cuzco

Vilcashuaman

Coquimbo

Francisco Pizarro's first expedition, 1524–25

Francisco Pizarro's second expedition, 1526–27

Francisco Pizarro's third expedition, 1530–33

Sebastian de Benalcazar, 1533

Diego de Almagro, 1535–37

Gonzalo Pizarro, 1539–42

Sites of conquistador-Inca battles on route to Cuzco

Towns established by Spanish

Incan towns

N

Francisco Pizarro   (Hulton/Archive)

Further reading: Pedro de Cieza de Leon, *The Discovery and Conquest of Peru: Chronicles of the New World Encoutner,* eds. and trans. Alexandra Parma Cook and Noble David Cook (Durham, N.C.: Duke University Press, 1998); John Hemming, *The Conquest of the Incas* (New York: Harcourt, Brace Jovanovich, 1973); James Lockhart, *Spanish Peru, 1532–1560: A Colonial Society* (Madison: University of Wisconsin Press, 1968); ———, *The Men of Cajamarca: A Social and Biographical Study of the First Conquerors of Peru* (Austin: Institute of Latin American Studies, University of Texas, 1972).

— Dixie Ray Haggard

plague (bubonic)

From the 14th to the 17th centuries, the bubonic plague repeatedly swept through Europe and North Africa, reaching up to 50 percent mortality in some regions and throwing Europeans' social, political, and economic structures into disarray (see DISEASE).

The bubonic plague is caused by the bacillus *Yersina pestis,* which lives in the bloodstream of fleas that feed on black rats, pests that were commonly found on the ships and in the cities of Europe. Once the flea contracts the bacillus, it can no longer digest the blood of the rat, and so, voraciously hungry, it goes in search of a new host, such as a human body. Humans cannot transfer bubonic plague among themselves; it takes the flea to infect human hosts and transfer the bacillus. These fleas can survive up to 50 days by hiding in grain or cloth, which were both major trade items in medieval Europe and probably major causes of the transmission of the plague. In humans the plague manifests as the swellings of the lymph nodes. In many victims of the plague in medieval Europe, these swellings, particularly in the throat and groin areas, reportedly reached the size of grapefruits.

The bubonic plague first migrated from Asia to Europe and northern Africa in the 14th century. During the winter of 1347–48, rats and fleas bearing the bubonic plague stowed away onboard European merchant ships docked along the coast of Asia. Within months, a new disease—a pestilence—had entered the ports of Europe. The Black Death, as it came to be called, spread quickly among a population whose defenses had already been lowered by poor nutrition and a harsh winter. The Black Death was actually a combination of bubonic plague (carried by rats and their fleas) and pneumonic plague (a respiratory version spread by humans). From 1348–49 the Black Death spread throughout Europe and North Africa, killing approximately one-third of the total population, with mortality rising to more than 50 percent in many crowded, unsanitary urban areas. The highest mortality rates from the plague occurred in the summer months, when the fleas bred in especially high numbers. Through the 16th and 17th centuries this devastating disease repeatedly revisited Europe.

The ravages of the bubonic plague had many different social, religious, and economic effects. Above all, the high mortality rate stunned the population and sent many communities into disarray, looking for both an explanation and an escape from this pestilence. Doctors could not explain the plague or cure it. Many people fled the disease, abandoning their homes and even shunning members of their own families. As entire artisan and commercial communities were wiped out, Europe's economy changed as well. In Italy and Spain religious explanations for the plague were especially prevalent. Clerical and secular officials often claimed JEWS caused epidemics. During the 14th century such accusations led Christians to burn many Jews alive. Because of the disease's many recurrences, Europe's population only began to rise again near the end of the 15th and beginning of the 16th century, despite waves of the plague and other epidemic diseases (see SMALLPOX) still attacking at times. To this day, no one is quite sure why the bubonic plague lost its potency, except to speculate that it might have finally evolved into a less virulent strain.

The bubonic plague affected Europe's colonization efforts during the 16th century as well. The loss in Europe's population translated to severe lack of labor for reaping the resources of the NEW WORLD. The need for labor at home led to the Spaniards' efforts to enslave the indigenous peoples as well as to the European colonizers' eventual decision to enslave Africans (see SLAVERY).

The bubonic plague was also one of the diseases that entered the Western Hemisphere as a result of the COLUMBIAN EXCHANGE. The first potential sighting of the plague in the Americas came in the late 1610s, when French sailors shipwrecked in Massachusetts Bay released the disease. However, given the ambiguity of the historical sources, this disease may have been smallpox. The bubonic plague is also suspected to be the disease that later killed Squanto, the Pawtuxet Indian who helped the Pilgrims when they landed in New England.

Further reading: Kenneth F. Kiple and Stephen V. Beck, eds., *Biological Consequences of the European Expansion, 1450–1800, an Expanding World,* vol. 6 (Aldershot, U.K.: Ashgate Publishing, 1997); Sheldon Watts, *Epidemics and History: Disease, Power, and Imperialism* (New Haven, Conn.: Yale University Press, 1997).

— Maril Hazlett

Polo, Marco (1254–1324)

The son of Nicolo Polo of VENICE, Marco Polo at the age of 17 accompanied his father on a trip overland through Asia to present letters of Pope Gregory X to Khubilai, the Great Khan of the Mongols in Northern China; his account of what he saw in the East shaped Europeans' understandings of Asia for generations.

Despite Marco Polo's widespread fame, little is known about him, his actual activities in China, or the circumstances surrounding the writing of his book. Information on Marco is so scarce, in fact, that reputable scholars continue to argue that Marco never traveled to China at all. Virtually the only information about his famous trip comes from the book itself. (No Chinese documents have ever been found that mention him.) Scholars believe that Marco's father and uncle, Nicolo and Maffeo, left a Venetian trading post on the Black Sea around 1260 to trade in jewels with the Mongol Khanate of the Golden Horde. Starting about 1209 the Mongols under Temüchin, or Genghis Khan, began expanding from their base in the plains of Central Asia, and in time he and his successors conquered territories ranging from the plains of Hungary in Europe to central and southern China. The Golden Horde was one of four khanates into which the vast Mongol conquests had been divided. Supreme among all the khans at this time was Khubilai, who reigned from 1260 to 1294.

Wars and other disturbances prevented Nicolo and Maffeo from returning the way they had come, so they accompanied an embassy traveling farther east to meet Khubiali at his palace in Beijing (Khanbalikh in Mongolian). They were then commissioned by the khan to carry messages to the pope in Rome and return with his reply, 100 Christian missionaries, and other items. They returned to Venice sometime around 1269, but the reigning pope had died, and it was not until 1271 that Gregory X became pontiff. The Polo brothers took papal messages and young Marco but no missionaries with them back to Beijing. They arrived around 1275, two years after Khubilai had completed his conquest of southern China. During the 17 years Marco remained in China he seems to have been used in various administrative duties. This is not so unusual as it sounds because the Mongols used foreign administrators over the conquered Chinese territories as a way to break the power of the local gentry.

The Polos supposedly returned to Europe by sea around Southeast Asia and through the Indian Ocean, escorting a Mongol princess who was to be married to a lesser khan in Persia (modern-day Iran). From there the Polos were able to make their way to Venice around 1295. Marco was then 42 years old. Sometime around 1297 Marco, in command of a ship, was captured on the high seas and imprisoned for a time in Genoa. There he met a fellow prisoner, Rustichello of Pisa, who had already gained a fair reputation as a writer. The two collaborated on a book based on Marco's experiences. Marco was released from prison in 1299, lived quietly but comfortably as a modest trader and moneylender, and died, aged 69, on January 8, 1324.

As much uncertainty as there is about Marco Polo's life and travels, there is even more uncertainty about his book, to the extent that scholars have difficulty even agreeing on what its title should be. No original manuscript exists, and the existing copies and later printings have important differences, omissions, and additions. Quite a bit of controversy exists over the role Rustichello played in compiling the book. Did he simply write as Marco dictated? Did he rewrite a manuscript previously written by Marco? Or did he do both? Did he also make use of documents Marco had brought back with him from China? Perhaps the best way to describe the book is as a difficult collaboration between a writer of highly stylized romantic poetry and fiction (Rustichello) and a through, impersonal, and somewhat detached Mongolian civil servant (Marco). In the end the book does not belong to any existing Western writing tradition, but it does have many things in common with official Chinese gazetteers. Marco, who spent almost all his adult life in Asia prior to writing his book, doubtless absorbed considerable Asian cultural influences.

The exact impact of the book on the science of geography and exploration in the West remains a matter of debate. A number of European traders and missionaries made journeys similar to Marco's afterward, but with the conversion of the khans of central Asia to ISLAM and the coming of the Black Death (see PLAGUE), it became virtually impossible to recreate Marco's journey after the 14th century. Interest in the book was spurred by the humanist movement, during which European scholars studied, translated, and distributed many previously unknown or forgotten ancient texts. Among these were works of geography against which Marco's story could be compared. Marco's story and others influenced a number of 15th-century mapmakers, among them Paolo dal Pozzo Toscanelli, who united Marco's description of Japan with his own ideas on mapmaking. Toscanelli was among the first to advocate that voyages from Europe to Asia could be made by sailing due west, across the Atlantic. These ideas possibly inspired Columbus's plans for his voyages of exploration.

During the 16th and 17th centuries European exploration of East and Southeast Asia served both to confirm much of what Marco's book said as well as to engender doubts. Since the 17th century scholars—basing their arguments on items in the text that were wrong or misleading and other items that are not in the text but which, they feel, should have been—have continued to charge that Marco never actually traveled to China. In this view, his book was an elaborate hoax. Some scholars continue to level such charges today. For instance, doubters ask, why doesn't the book contain any mention of the Great Wall of China or the practice of binding young women's feet or almost anything about Chinese culture? Supporters of Marco's journey note that these omissions can be accounted for by the fact that the Great Wall, in its present form, was not built until 200 years later and that the practice of foot binding did not become general among women until about 100 years later. Marco's inability to speak or read Chinese, a matter on which virtually all scholars agree, also explains his general lack of knowledge of Chinese culture. His position as a functionary of the Mongol overlords helps explain his lack of interest. The exaggerations in published versions of the account could also have come from Rustichello, who might have felt compelled to add adventure and chivalrous deeds to what is otherwise a dull accounting of Marco's alleged journey.

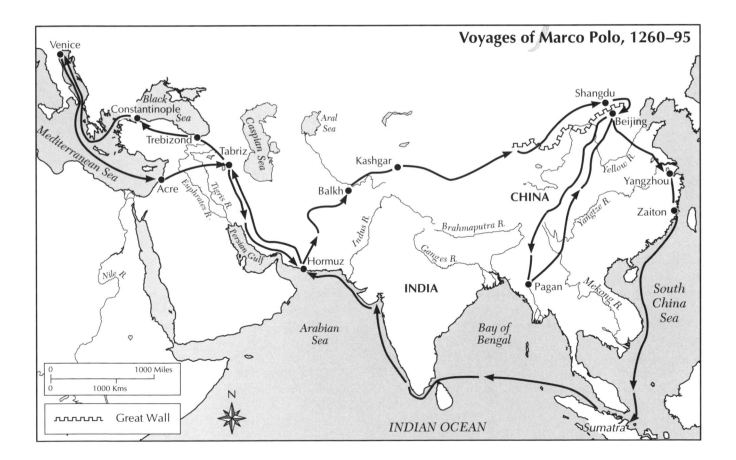

During the 19th century, when European, particularly British and Russian, imperialists began to open up and colonize the areas of Central, South, and East Asia that Marco described, interest in the book once again peaked. This was partly because Marco's account remained virtually the only one generally known in the West. Today, by contrast, Marco's book is something that far more people are likely to know about than ever to have actually read, although the book will continue to hold an honored place as an original work of geography and a remarkable, if sometimes annoyingly laconic, epic traveler's tale.

Further reading: John Critchley, *Marco Polo's Book* (Aldershot, U.K.: Variorum, 1992); John Larner, *Marco Polo and the Discovery of the World* (New Haven, Conn.: Yale University Press, 1999); Frances Wood, *Did Marco Polo Go to China?* (London: Secker & Warburg, 1995); Henry Yule, ed., *The Book of Ser Marco Polo the Venetian*, 3rd ed., edition, rev. by Henri Cordier (London: J. Murray, 1929).

— Paul Dunscomb

Ponce de León, Juan (ca. 1460–1521)

A Spaniard who accompanied CHRISTOPHER COLUMBUS on the expedition of 1493 and who remained in the Western Hemisphere as a Spanish official, Juan Ponce de León is best known for his search for the fountain of youth in FLORIDA.

Born in Spain around 1460, Ponce de León had become known in CASTILE before Columbus made his first voyage to the west. He joined the 1493 journey, and in 1502 he enrolled on a mission led by Nicolás Ovando to HISPANIOLA. Ponce de León soon became governor of the western portion of the island. Enthralled by the kinds of tales of riches and fame that frequently enticed CONQUISTADORES, Ponce de León sailed to PUERTO RICO in 1508; three years later he became governor of the island. While in Puerto Rico, Ponce de León enriched himself by drawing profits from GOLD mining carried out by the indigenous residents of the island.

But success did not satisfy his desire for gain. In 1511 he sought permission to establish a settlement in the BAHAMAS, where he hoped to find more gold and use Indian slaves (see SLAVERY) to mine it. In 1513 he led an expedition of three ships to, as he asked King Ferdinand (see FERDINAND AND ISABELLA), "discover and settle" this new territory. But he continued beyond the northwest tip of the Bahamas, apparently to find another island that local natives in the islands had told him had a magical spring where those who drank the water would remain forever young; there was also gold rumored to be in the region. Ponce de León's search for that fountain of youth and other riches took him to the North American mainland, where he arrived, possibly near modern-day Daytona Beach, on April 2, 1513, and claimed this previously uncharted land for the Spanish monarchy. Later the Spanish would build SAINT AUGUSTINE nearby. Ponce de León named this land "Tierra La Florida" after *Pascua Florida,* the Spanish name for Easter Sunday. Although JOHN CABOT and SEBASTIAN CABOT, as well as an unknown number of NORSE sailors had earlier reached North America, Ponce de León was the first from his country to land along the east coast of the continent.

While in Florida, Ponce de León and his companions sailed along the coast, a journey that eventually took them through the Florida Keys (which he called Los Martyres) and into the Gulf of Mexico. No one now can determine the northernmost point he reached, though it seems likely that the expedition went as far as Pensacola Bay or Charlotte Harbor before turning back and sailing toward CUBA before their return to Puerto Rico, which they reached about six months after their initial departure. He returned to Spain in 1514, concerned in part with the fate of his daughters because his wife had died.

Ponce de León never found the fountain of youth, but his exploits nonetheless earned him a knighthood in Spain and the opportunity to return to the Western Hemisphere with the right to colonize Florida and Bimini. He left Spain again in 1521, and after a stop in Puerto Rico he returned to Florida and attempted to settle an area near modern-day Sanibel Island. Injured in a battle with local CALUSA Indians, he sailed back to Havana, where he died of his wounds in July, 1521.

Ponce de León's failed quest was not an unusual occurrence in the 16th century. Other Spanish conquistadores, notably FRANCISCO DE CORONADO and HERNANDO DE SOTO, had also been inspired by rumors of the fabulous treasures to be found in North America. There were, of course, riches to be found in the Americas, as the Spanish conquerors of the AZTECS and INCA discovered. But no fountain of youth could ever be found, despite Ponce de León's obsessive search for it. Still, as the first Spaniard to wield power as *ADELANTADO*, he had an enduring legacy in the Caribbean basin. He died without learning that the island of Florida he had found was actually a peninsula attached to the modern-day United States.

Further reading: Angus Konstam, *Historical Atlas of Exploration, 1492–1600* (New York: Facts On File, 2000); David Weber, *The Spanish Frontier in North America* (New Haven, Conn.: Yale University Press, 1992).

population trends

During the long 15th century, from approximately 1492 to 1607, population shifts in the Atlantic basin reshaped societies in the Old World and in the Western Hemisphere.

It is impossible to put precise figures on the number of people who inhabited the Atlantic basin at the time of CHRISTOPHER COLUMBUS's initial crossing of the ocean. No society possessed the kinds of sophisticated tools necessary to make accurate estimates of the size of the local population, and many peoples kept no real count of the number of men, women, and children residing in particular communities. As a result, scholars have had to devise methods to estimate how many people lived in a given locale at a certain time and then use those figures to measure the rate of population growth or decline over time. To estimate the number of individuals in a Native American community, for example, demographers and anthropologists have used the number of people, usually men in arms, identified in early European travel accounts. They then take that number and multiply it by some figure to deduce an estimate of the total population. Because the populations of many indigenous groups shifted before anyone actually saw a European, scholars also make inferences about population size based on groups' economies: Communities that practiced agriculture tended to be larger than those that relied on hunting, and people who inhabited fertile river valleys often had more substantial populations than did groups who inhabited more arid regions. Historical demographers have used any kinds of records they can find to estimate populations in the Old World. They thus turn to tax lists and the records of baptisms and burials and to the number of slaves imprisoned on ships heading from Africa to the Western Hemisphere. From myriad pieces of information, scholars have assembled rough estimates of population trends. None of their figures are as precise as those to be found in a modern-day census, but the numbers at least provide a starting point for understanding the ebb and flow of populations in particular places.

Putting aside the detailed estimates for specific communities or nations, scholars have identified two fundamental trends for the 16th century. First, the population of the Western Hemisphere declined as a result of the spread of infectious DISEASES that arrived as a result of the COLUMBIAN EXCHANGE. Second, no population was particularly stable. Contrary to an age-old notion that peoples in Europe and Africa inhabited traditional communities where individuals tended to spend their entire lives, newer research reveals enormous domestic population movements. As the historian Bernard Bailyn has suggested for Europe for the period after 1607, the "peopling of British North America was an extension outward and an expansion in scale of domestic mobility in the lands of the immigrants' origins, and the transatlantic flow must be understood within the context of these *domestic* mobility patterns." The same notion applies to the earlier period as well and to places beyond the boundaries of Europe.

The decline in numbers of indigenous peoples in the Americas is perhaps the most frightening and dramatic demographic trend for the 16th century. Before 1492 the peoples of the Western Hemisphere tended to be healthy. To be sure, some diseases, including some caused by nutritional deficiencies, afflicted native peoples. Hence, while CORN agriculture provided abundant food, overreliance on maize could lead to diseases (such as pellagra) with debilitating health consequences. Nevertheless, infectious diseases tended to be rare. The lack of contagions can be explained in various ways. First, the original peopling of the Americas took place between 40,000 and 10,000 years ago, when the Bering Strait was frozen and groups of people from East Asia walked from modern-day Russia into Alaska and then dispersed from there. As these peoples moved inland, those who traveled to the south found conditions ideal for agriculture, and the initial abundance of food allowed populations to grow. However, just as important was the fact that these original migrants tended to be healthy, because only able-bodied people could have made the trek across the land bridge. Further, although some Native American peoples developed cities, especially in MEXICO, the majority tended to live in dispersed communities. As epidemiologists have explained, smaller communities tend to be poor breeding places for the pathogens that cause infectious diseases because the human populations in them are not large enough to sustain the diseases over time. From a demographic perspective this residential strategy contributed to the increase of populations by reducing the threats that these people might otherwise have encountered. Finally, most Native American peoples kept no domesticated livestock, another protection against diseases often associated with close human-to-animal contact.

But the phenomena that helped with the initial increase in population for indigenous peoples in the Americas also provided the ideal conditions for any imported diseases to wreak havoc. Thus, while scholars continue to disagree about the population of the Western Hemisphere before 1492, there is no doubt that the number of native peoples shrank when Europeans inadvertently introduced diseases to peoples who had had no opportunity to develop immunities to ward off their dangers.

Ever since the first systematic estimates for the Western Hemisphere began to appear in 1924, scholars have argued that the population of this part of the globe before Europeans arrived ranged between a low of 8.4 million and a high of 75 million. Whatever the exact numbers, all agree on the trend: The arrival of infectious diseases led to a decrease in population by perhaps as much as 90 percent from 1492 to 1800, with much of the decline taking place before 1700. The catastrophe struck different peoples at different times. Some indigenous populations, including many of the native peoples in the Caribbean whom Columbus encountered, disappeared, as did some groups on the mainland, including the Carolina ALGONQUIAN at ROANOKE described by THOMAS HARRIOT and JOHN WHITE. The disappearance of an entire group did not necessarily mean that every individual died. Rather, as historians now believe, demographic catastrophe led to the weakening of particular communities, and those who believed they could no longer maintain their settlements migrated outward, usually to other like-minded indigenous peoples. Thus, the NATCHEZ, who at one point were among the most dominant groups in the lower Mississippi Valley, disappeared as a distinct entity, a fate sealed by a military defeat at the hands of the French in 1731 but invariably begun with the spread of infectious diseases such as SMALLPOX. However, individuals who were Natchez did not all perish at once. Instead, they joined other indigenous communities, part of a trend that continued well beyond 1607.

Unlike the Americas, the continents of Europe and Africa did not suffer from the same kind of population loss because individuals had already built up resistance to some potentially lethal diseases. Of course, the SLAVE TRADE robbed Africa of hundreds of thousands of men, women, and children during the 16th century. According to one estimate, British and Portuguese slave traders hauled approximately 266,000 individuals across the Atlantic Ocean during the 16th century. That trade followed an earlier commerce that took Africans to the East in what the historian Ronald Segal has termed "the other black diaspora." From the mid-seventh century until the end of the 16th century, perhaps 4.82 million Africans traveled across the SAHARA bound for destinations outside the continent, many of them sold during the peak period of this commerce in the 10th and 11th centuries. During the 16th century this eastern slave trade led to the forced relocation of approximately 5,500 individuals each year, a total of more than 500,000 people for the century. Still, despite the horrendous demographic consequences of this vile trade in human beings, the introduction of new food crops into Africa from the Americas, notably manioc and maize, quite possibly increased the population, thereby making the demographic consequences of the slave trade less obvious. Thus, the population of Africa, which was perhaps 85 million in 1500, possibly reached 90 million a century later, although the lack of precise data makes such an estimate especially imprecise. According to one scholar, the population of sub-Saharan Africa grew from 79 million in 1500 to 95 million in 1750, in addition to another 5 million in northern Africa by the mid-18th century.

In Europe, by contrast, populations across the continent grew, often at a fevered pace, during the 16th century. In part, this demographic increase constituted a final stage in the long-term recovery from the notorious pandemic of PLAGUE known as the Black Death that killed at least one-third of all Europeans during the mid-14th century (and killed even more people farther north, where famine often followed in the wake of pestilence). Population increase could also be attributed to increased cultivation of available land and an improvement in diet, especially with the arrival of American foodstuffs.

In the age of Columbus, the population of Europe stood at approximately 60 to 70 million. By applying modern-day geographical boundaries, it is possible to measure the rough distribution of this population. There were approximately 15 million people in France, 10 million in Italy, 5 million in the British Isles, between 6.5 million and 10 million in Spain, and lesser numbers in other nations. By the end of the century, Europe's population stood at perhaps 90 million, demonstrating far more rapid demographic growth than was experienced elsewhere in the Atlantic basin during this time.

Continental estimates, however useful, tend to mask local variations, as is evident in the estimates of population for England, arguably the most thoroughly studied place in the world during the early modern period. The population of England increased from approximately 2,774,000 individuals in 1541 to 3,271,000 in 1571 and to 4,110,000 in 1601. According to the most detailed estimate, the population of England in 1606—the year before the founding of Jamestown—stood at 4,253,325, but while the overall trend was positive (in a demographic sense), fluctuations nonetheless occurred. Disease still hit periodically, of course, and years of inadequate rainfall or some other natural calamity could produce an agricultural disaster that diminished the rate of population increase. Even during England's rapid demographic increase, the population of the country declined by almost 175,000 from 1551 to 1556, although it immediately recovered, and the nation experienced no further serious declines until the years of plague and fire in the 1660s.

From a demographic perspective Europeans fared best in the Atlantic world during the century following 1492. That result is not surprising given the fact that the Columbian Exchange brought the greatest benefits to Europeans. Africans, although they did not apparently suffer from the same kinds of disease-related mortality as Native Americans, also fared well during the 16th century, at least in the sense that the population of the continent grew. However, here again the overall positive trend masks the horrors of the slave trade. Without that noxious commerce, Africa's population would have been even greater, although problems of overpopulation in the modern world suggest that growth is not always positive. Without doubt, those who fared the worst in the shifting demography of the Atlantic basin were the indigenous peoples of the Americas, who succumbed in large numbers to imported diseases. Native American populations reached their nadir in 1800 or so, and since then have climbed steadily back toward the precontact numbers. That fact demonstrates the importance of assessing population trends from the long term.

Further reading: Nicholas Canny, ed., *Europeans on the Move: Studies on European Migration, 1500–1800* (Oxford, U.K.: Oxford University Press, 1994); Philip D. Curtin, *The Atlantic Slave Trade: A Census* (Madison: University of Wisconsin Press, 1969); John D. Durand, "Historical Estimates of World Population: An Evaluation," *Population and Development Review* 3 (1977): 253–296; David Eltis, "Volume and Structure of the Transatlantic Slave Trade: A Reassessment," *William and Mary Quarterly,* 3rd ser., LVIII (2001): 17–46; Colin McEvedy and Richard Jones, *Atlas of World Population History* (New York: Facts On File, 1978); Ronald Segal, *Islam's Black Slaves: The Other Black Diaspora* (New York: Farrar, Straus & Giroux, 2001); John W. Verano and Douglas H. Ubelaker, eds., *Disease and Demography in the Americas* (Washington, D. C.: Smithsonian Institution Press, 1992); E. A. Wrigley and R. S. Schofield, *The Population History of England 1541–1871: A Reconstruction* (Cambridge, Mass.: Harvard University Press, 1981).

Porres, St. Martín de (1575–1639)

St. Martín de Porres, the son of an African woman and a Spanish man, was the first person of mixed African and European heritage to be recognized as a saint by the Catholic Church.

Born in LIMA, PERU, Martín began life at a disadvantage. As a child of mixed race in the hierarchical society of Latin America, his opportunities were limited, especially because his father, Don Juan de Porres, neither married his mother, Ana Velázquez, nor formally recognized his two children by her. Because membership in the DOMINICANS was forbidden to blacks, Indians, and their descendants, Martín was unable to join the order as a friar but was accepted as a *donado,* or servant. Martín served in this capacity for nine years. He showed such piety, dedication, and devotion to the poor that the order made an exception and admitted him as a lay brother in 1603.

As a friar Martín was known for his ability to heal and care for the sick and the suffering. He helped establish an orphanage and hospital and was responsible for distributing food to the poor. He also worked among African slaves in Peru.

St. Martín died in 1639 at the age of 60. Although he lived in a hierarchical society divided by color, he worked among the poor and suffering of all races. Because of this aspect of his work, the Catholic Church recognizes him as the patron saint of social justice and race relations.

Further reading: "Porres, Martin de," in *Dictionary of the Saints,* John J. Delaney (Garden City, N.Y.: Doubleday, 1980), 477; Carlos Parra, "Porres, San Martín de," in *Africana: The Encyclopedia of the African and African American Experience,* eds. Kwame Anthony Appiah and Henry Louis Gates, Jr. (New York: Basic *Civitas* Books, 1999), 1540–1541; "St. Martin de Porres," in *Butler's Lives of the Saints,* vol. 11, November, new full edition, rev. by Sarah Fawcett Thomas (Collegeville, Minn.: Liturgical Press, 1995), 11–20.

— Martha K. Robinson

Potosí

A city and region located in the eastern range of the ANDES MOUNTAINS in southern Bolivia, the name Potosí became synonymous with the production of SILVER for the Spanish Empire during the colonial era.

One of the most famous silver mining centers of the Spanish Empire, the Villa Imperial of Potosí developed around one of the richest silver deposits in the Andes Mountains. In 1545 the Spanish discovered rich silver ore deposits in Cerro Rico, and the town of Potosí quickly grew on the northern slope as a support center for the mining operations. Most of its inhabitants engaged in activities to support the production of silver, such as mining and refining the raw mineral into ingots and bars. The workers for these activities came from indigenous draft labor called the *REPARTIMIENTO,* a system developed from the Incan *mitia,* which assigned laborers on a temporary basis to perform community service.

The ore obtained from Cerro Rico supplied more than 50 percent of Spain's American silver production before 1650. Its most productive decade occurred from 1575 to 1585. The Spanish refined most of the ore mined from Cerro Rico in 80 mills located in the vicinity. By 1600 most of the easily reached ore had been mined, but the Spanish found veins in the surrounding area and continued to exploit the lower grade ore left in Cerro Rico. The remaining silver proved more expensive to acquire and refine, but the process continued to be profitable. The silver acquired from Potosí helped to make Spain a world power in the 16th and 17th centuries, and the wealth it helped to create for Spain enticed other European powers into colonizing the Americas.

Further reading: Peter Bakewell, *Miners of the Red Mountains: Indian Labor in Potosí, 1545–1650* (Albuquerque: University of New Mexico Press, 1984); ———, "Mining in Colonial Spanish America," in *Cambridge History of Latin America,* vol. 2 (Cambridge U.K.: Cambridge University Press, 1984), 110–151; Jeffery A. Cole, *The Potosí Mita, 1573–1700* (Stanford, Calif.: Stanford University Press, 1985); Enrique Tandeter, *Coercion and Market: Silver Mining in Colonial Potosí, 1662–1826* (Albuquerque: University of New Mexico Press, 1993).

— Dixie Ray Haggard

Powhatan

An ALGONQUIAN-speaking chiefdom located in the present-day Chesapeake Bay area, the Powhatan had built an empire that controlled the region before the arrival of the English in 1607 at Jamestown, and through their interactions with the English, they became a cornerstone of the folklore and popular history surrounding the English colonies in North America.

At the time of contact with Europeans, the Powhatan occupied the fertile coastal plain to the west of what is today Chesapeake Bay. The forests of the region provided abundant game, which they hunted primarily in the late fall and winter and food plants such as nuts, berries, and roots. The bay also provided a rich supply of aquatic resources. The Powhatan practiced intensive maize, beans, squash, and TOBACCO horticulture using the slash-and-burn technique to clear land. They lived in semisedentary villages with significant populations located near rivers and streams. Powhatan homes were multiple family lodges built of bark or reeds and rectangular in shape, with curved roofs.

In the era before the arrival of the English in the region, Wahunsonacock, called Powhatan by the English, had conquered a succession of 30 ethnically and culturally related local chiefdoms and forged a paramount chiefdom on the western shore of the Chesapeake Bay, with a total population of approximately 15,000 people living in 200 towns. Wahunsonacock received tribute from subject towns in the form of shell beads, deerskins, and food. Local groups conquered by Wahunsonacock kept their tribal names, but the chiefdom as a whole was referred to as Tsenacomocco. The English began the practice of calling the people and their leader by the name of Powhatan. The chiefdom had a polytheistic religious structure whose complexity reflected the amalgamation of different identities within the paramount chiefdom. At the time of contact, Wahunsonacock's empire faced a constant challenge from hostile, ethnically different groups west of the fall line in Virginia; other Algonquian chiefdoms such as the Piscataway and the Roanoac contested its position of prestige in the tidewater region. Although these native groups posed a serious threat to the Powhatan, the arrival of the English ultimately caused the final collapse of this chiefdom by the mid-17th century. Despite the conflicts, some of this group's descendants still live in the area of the Chesapeake Bay and retain their identity and some aspects of the aboriginal culture.

Further reading: J. Frederick Fauz, "Pattern of Anglo-Indian Aggression and Accommodation along the Mid-Atlantic Coast, 1584–1634," in *Cultures in Contact: The Impact of European Contacts on Native American Cultural Institutions, A.D. 100–1800* (Washington, D.C.: Smithsonian Institution Press, 1985), 225–270; Helen C. Rountree, ed., *Powhatan Foreign Relations, 1500–1722* (Charlottesville: University Press of Virginia, 1993); Frederic W. Gleach, *Powhatan's World and Colonial Virginia: A Conflict of Cultures* (Lincoln: University of Nebraska Press, 1997).

— Dixie Ray Haggard

Prester John

Beginning in the 12th century, European travel writers assured their readers that Prester John, the mythical ruler of a distant country, was the most powerful and wealthiest Christian king on earth.

The first report of Prester (or Presbyter) John reached Europe in 1145. A bishop returning to Europe from the Middle East told the pope of Prester John, whom he identified as the king of India and a descendant of the Magi. The bishop reported that Prester John was fighting his way toward Jerusalem. According to the story, he had already defeated the Medes and the Persians and might be able to join the Crusaders and help them defeat the Muslims. Because medieval Christians believed that the Apostle Thomas had preached in India and won many converts, they found it easy to believe that a Christian king ruled in distant and little-known India. The idea that a mighty Christian king from the East was willing to help Europeans conquer Jerusalem soon gained popularity and helped motivate Europeans to explore Asia.

Rumors and stories about Prester John spread for centuries. In the 1160s a letter purportedly from Prester John himself circulated in Europe, reaching both the Byzantine emperor and the pope. The pope, Alexander III, even sent an envoy to meet Prester John. This unsuccessful mission was only one of many attempts to find the mythical king. As rumors and stories spread, Europeans heard fantastic tales of the king. According to the 14th-century writings of SIR JOHN MANDEVILLE, Prester John's land was so far away that the inhabitants "have day when we have night, and night when we have day." India, in this version, consisted of many islands, and Prester John was emperor over 72 men who were themselves the kings of various peoples. The people of Prester John's kingdom were Christians and more honest than Europeans. His land was also full of marvels, including a sea of sand that behaved like water but that no boat could sail on. This sea, although it had no water, was somehow full of fish. Prester John's land also held a river of precious stones, and trees that grew, reached maturity, and returned back into the earth in a single day. His army was so large that he had 110,000 men whose sole duty was to guard his standard—three jewel-encrusted crosses of gold—when he went into battle.

The myth of Prester John proved durable. In the 15th century an expedition sent by King João II of Portugal sought Prester John in the Middle East but failed to find him. As explorers failed to find Prester John in Asia and the Middle East, they began to look elsewhere. By the early 14th century one treatise claimed that Prester John's kingdom was in ETHIOPIA, which cartographers sometimes placed in Asia, and Portuguese explorers in Africa searched for him. Portuguese emissaries to Ethiopia in 1520 met a wealthy Christian king, LEBNA DENGEL, and claimed that they had finally found the legendary Prester John.

Further reading: Francisco Alvares, *The Prester John of the Indies: A True Relation of the Lands of the Prester John,* ed. C. F. Beckingham and G. W. B. Huntingford (Cambridge, U.K.. Hakluyt Society, 1961); C. F. Beckingham, "The Quest for Prester John," in *The European Opportunity,* ed. Felipe Fernández-Armesto (Aldershot, U.K.: Variorum, 1995); William D. Phillips, Jr., and Carla Rahn Phillips, *The Worlds of Christopher Columbus* (Cambridge, U.K.: Cambridge University Press, 1991); Vsevolod Slessarev, *Prester John: The Letter and the Legend* (Minneapolis: University of Minnesota Press, 1959).

— Martha K. Robinson

Príncipe

Located 160 miles off the western coast of Africa, Príncipe was claimed by Portuguese explorers in the late 15th century, who enjoyed a brief period of prosperity because of its participation in the trade in SUGAR and West African slaves and created plantations similar to those later to appear in the NEW WORLD.

Like its neighbor SÃO TOMÉ, Príncipe was blessed by a climate that allowed for year-round sugar cultivation and a location that put it in a prime position to capitalize on the transatlantic SLAVE TRADE. The Portuguese Crown granted the administration of the island to the Carniero family in 1500 but reserved taxes on sugar production for itself, thus making Príncipe a source of profit for colonists and Crown alike.

Príncipe never realized the same profits from the sugar trade as did São Tomé, but it was equal to its neighbor in the slave trade. Príncipe's profits from the slave trade in the 17th and 18th centuries were great enough to attract interest from foreign powers, especially France, which raided the island in 1706 and occupied it until 1753. Even in the 19th century, when many countries were banning importation of new slaves, the trade remained profitable for

Príncipe and São Tomé: Between 1809 and 1815 alone the two islands exported more than 33,000 West Africans to the Americas.

Further reading: Tony Hodges and Malyn Newitt, *São Tomé and Príncipe: From Plantation Colony to Microstate* (Boulder, Colo.: Westview Press, 1988).

— Marie A. Kelleher

printing press

The printing press, one of the greatest technological advances of the early modern age, changed the world in such far-reaching ways that it is impossible to understand the meeting of Europe, Africa, and the Americas without some consideration of a device that first came into its own in the 1440s.

Before the year 1400 various peoples had devised ways to circulate information. During antiquity trained scribes had preserved vital texts, such as the epic poems of Homer and the Bible, and they did so with great labor. In that world there were no printing presses, and paper had not yet become common, at least not in the West. The greatest advances in the production of paper occurred in China, thousands of miles from Europe, when, during the second century A.D. Ts'ai Lun figured out how to make a pulp from various plants (such as bamboo and mulberry) and then spread it flat so that it became, with the help of threads to hold it together, paper. Over time knowledge about how to make paper spread to the West, reaching Samarkand in the eighth century and, sometime in the late 11th century, Europe. By the end of the 13th century, paper mills had started to appear in Italy, and as a result Europeans had greater access to paper, although it remained relatively rare. Scribes on the Continent tended to use parchment (typically the skin of a sheep) or vellum (the skin of a calf) for the words they chose to commit to writing.

In the early 15th century a German metalsmith named JOHANNES GUTENBERG began to craft individual letters out of lead and discovered these letters could be used to print. Although Gutenberg had various personal financial problems, his invention of moveable type signaled the dawning of a new age. Before Gutenberg printers could publish items, such as playing cards or broadsheets, only by making a block, normally out of wood, for each page. That process was time consuming and, as a result, expensive. By contrast, moveable type allowed a printer to purchase a set of metal letters and then simply reset them whenever he or she wanted to print a new page. As the historian of print Warren Chappell has pointed out, before moveable type it could take an army of 55 writers to produce 200 books in two years; with moveable type one printer could run off 24,000 copies of a text in a matter of months. Although scribes continued to craft books page by page by hand for centuries, normally in monastic scriptoria affiliated with the Catholic Church, moveable type transformed the flow of information in Europe. From its origins in Gutenberg's shop in Mainz, Germany, in the middle of the 15th century, printing spread rapidly across the Continent: by 1470 printers had set up presses in Strasbourg, Bamberg, Cologne, Rome, Augsburg, Paris, and VENICE, which over time became arguably the most important center for publishing in Europe. The earliest printed books, those published before the year 1500, are now known as incunabula, and they originated in the almost 150 towns and cities that had presses by the end of the century. By 1500 such major European centers as LONDON, LISBON, Munich, Stockholm, and Copenhagen had printers, as did many smaller communities. Although printers still used woodblocks to print illustrations, including magnificent images by such luminaries as ALBRECHT DÜRER, moveable type became

Illustration of a printer's press, dated 1528   *(Hulton/Archive)*

the defining achievement of the first half century of the printing press.

Over the course of the 16th century, printing presses spread even farther across Europe and well beyond. The first press in Turkey set up shop in 1503, five years before a printing establishment appeared in Romania. Greece got its first printing press in 1515, but it was a generation later when Ireland (1550) and Russia (1553) had their own. By that time a printing press had been operating in MEXICO (part of NEW SPAIN) for almost 20 years, and the Spanish established another in PERU in 1584. Presses appeared in India in 1556, in Palestine in 1563, and in Japan in 1590. From the countless presses across Europe, the major Protestant theologians of the age, such as MARTIN LUTHER and JOHN CALVIN, launched their assaults against the Catholic Church. Presses also became crucial for spreading news about the NEW WORLD. News of the discoveries of CHRISTOPHER COLUMBUS spread through the publication of the so-called Barcelona Letter of 1493, which reached audiences across the continent by the end of the 15th century, as did the report by BARTOLOMÉ DE LAS CASAS that helped to spawn the BLACK LEGEND of the Spanish conquest. Europeans' interest in things American remained intense, and publishers sought to satisfy readers' demands. In 1601 73 Europeans wrote tracts about the Americas and published them. A quarter century later 179 authors published works that dealt, at least in part, with the Western Hemisphere. These books, now crucial for understanding the encounter between America and Europe, were published in European cultural capitals such as Barcelona, Rome, and Amsterdam, but they also came from presses located in Naples, Oxford, Lisbon, Frankfurt, Madrid, Toulouse, Edinburgh, Cádiz, Cologne, Utrecht, Padua, Milan, Stockholm, Halle, Ulm, Ingolstadt, Pisa, The Hague, Rostock, Basel, Leiden, and Valladolid. It was the existence of the printing presses that accounted for the publishing successes of editors and authors such as the Venetian civil servant GIOVANNI BATTISTA RAMUSIO, the French royal cosmographer ANDRÉ THEVET, and the English geographer RICHARD HAKLUYT THE YOUNGER.

The existence of the printing press did more than make texts available. By reducing the costs of disseminating information across Europe and, eventually, across the entire world, the printing press created a revolution in the ways that individuals understood the world around them. Information once confined to universities and monastic communities became, through printed books, available to hundreds of thousands of people. Images of the world beyond Europe, which in the Middle Ages had been confined to those elite members of society who could see the paintings and drawings brought back by explorers, became part of the common visual language of Europeans when the

Flemish engraver THEODOR DE BRY and others made it possible for pictures to appear in books. Although the politics of patronage often played an enormous role in what got printed in certain places, and although 16th-century Europeans and their colonists across the globe lacked the kind of routine access to books that became available to ever-wider numbers of people by the 19th century, such limitations were less important than the fact that the printing press ushered in a revolution in the printed word and in the ways that humans communicated with one another. The "Gutenberg Galaxy," to use a term from the communications theorist Marshall McLuhan, spread across the world and transformed every society it touched.

Further reading: Warren Chappell, *A Short History of the Printed Word* (New York: Knopf, 1970); Elizabeth L. Eisenstein, *The Printing Press as an Agent of Change*, 2 vols. (Cambridge, U.K.: Cambridge University Press, 1979); ———, *The Printing Revolution in Early Modern Europe* (condensed version of *The Printing Press as an Agent of Change*) (Cambridge, U.K.: Cambridge University Press, 1983); Adrian Johns, *The Nature of the Book: Print and Knowledge in the Making* (Chicago: University of Chicago Press, 1998).

Privy Council

The Privy Council of England became, by the reign of ELIZABETH I, the most powerful force in English politics, dictating policy in both government and English society.

The rise of the Privy Council to great power in the 16th century could not have been anticipated earlier. Although a private council was a feature of English government as far back as the reign of William I, whose *curia regis* was the conqueror's private set of councillors, the curia had little actual authority other than the management of certain kinds of legislation. However, by the late Middle Ages PARLIAMENT had emerged, and the council settled into the work of administering a government that was in the process of becoming larger and more complex. By the time of HENRY VIII, the council had established offices, accumulated records, and become a significant bureaucracy within Westminster Palace. Councillors' importance waxed during the short reign of Edward VI, partly due to the king's youth, but Elizabeth relied on their advice during the important years when the English secured secular rule, achieved a religious settlement in a post-REFORMATION world, and started the colonization of the Western Hemisphere.

In Elizabeth's time the council was often labeled "the government." The council had vast powers: It appointed men to government offices and had the power to expel them, it oversaw the military affairs of England, it regulated domestic and international trade, it negotiated with foreign nations, and it possessed judicial authority. At Elizabeth's death the Privy Council even smoothed the transition of power from one dynastic family to another.

Further reading: G. R. Elton, *England Under the Tudors*, 3rd ed. (London: Routledge, 1991); D. E. Hoak, *The King's Council in the Reign of Edward VI* (Cambridge, U.K.: Cambridge University Press, 1976); Michael B. Pulman, *The Elizabethan Privy Council in the Fifteen-Seventies* (Berkeley: University of California Press, 1971); Alan G. R. Smith, *The Government of Elizabethan England* (New York: Norton, 1967).

— David P. Dewar

Pueblo

The term referring to the indigenous peoples of what is now the American Southwest and the distinctive architecture of their houses and communities.

The term *pueblo* derives from the Spanish word for village. The Native Americans in the region now located in NEW MEXICO and northern Arizona along the Colorado Plateau shared certain characteristics that made them seem, to the Spaniards who first encountered them in the mid-16th century, similar to each other. The tendency to submerge the distinctive identities of indigenous communities into an undifferentiated mass was common in the 16th century and after, but in historic terms these peoples who shared aspects of their cultures also possessed specific cultural traditions. HOPI and ZUNI were among the Pueblo peoples whom Spaniards encountered, as were the residents of Acoma Pueblo and Tewa Pueblo.

The Pueblo peoples shared certain economic practices. All had long practiced agriculture by the time Europeans arrived, and like native peoples in much of the Americas they relied on CORN (maize), beans, and squash (the "three sisters" to the IROQUOIS). They all produced their own distinctive kinds of pottery, and to the present day the styles of design on pots differ from one pueblo to another. They used irrigation to provide sufficient water for their crops, and they engaged in trade to obtain goods that could not be found locally. The Pueblo peoples also produced such fine cotton that native peoples across the Southwest knew of it before Europeans arrived.

The first knowledge that any Europeans received about the Pueblo came in 1528, when the shipwreck victim ÁLVAR NÚÑUZ CABEZA DE VACA and his companions heard about—but never saw—Indians who lived to the west, along the upper reaches of the Rio Grande, who were expert blanket makers. When Fray Marcos de Niza and an African named Esteban (who had traveled with Cabeza da Vaca) traveled into Zuni territory in 1539, he thought he had found the Seven Cities of Cíbola, but when Esteban was killed in Hawikuh Pueblo, Marcos fled back into safer, already colonized parts of NEW SPAIN. FRANCISCO CORONADO and those who traveled with him became the first Europeans to spend any significant time among Pueblo peoples when they traveled through the Southwest from 1540 to 1542. Colonists arrived during the administration of JUAN DE OÑATE, who came to New Mexico in 1598. The Spanish brought missionaries with them to teach the Pueblo peoples the benefits of Christianity and European ways. Try as they might, neither the missionaries nor the colonists could make the indigenous peoples abandon their ancestral beliefs and practices. Although some communities adopted at least some elements of Christianity (and continue to observe some elements today, as is evident in the survival of the large church atop the mesa at Acoma Pueblo), the native peoples of the region rose up against the intruders in 1680. That event, now known as the Pueblo Revolt, was the most successful indigenous rebellion against any European colonizing power in North America. Joined together under the leadership of Popé, from Tewa Pueblo, the natives destroyed colonial settlements, murdered missionaries, and desecrated churches. Their actions drove the Spanish from New Mexico, at least for a time, although the colonizers returned and managed to suppress any further insurrections. By the end of the colonial period, many Pueblos that existed when the Spanish first arrived had ceased to exist, yet another sign of the costs of colonization for the native peoples of the Western Hemisphere.

Further reading: Fred Eggan, "Pueblos: Introduction," in William C. Sturtevant, gen. ed., *Handbook of North American Indians*, vol. 9, *Southwest,* ed. Alfonso Ortiz (Washington, D.C.: Smithsonian Institution Press, 1979), 206–223; Barry M. Pritzker, *A Native American Encyclopedia: History, Culture, and Peoples* (New York: Oxford University Press, 2000); Marc Simmons, "History of Pueblo–Spanish Relations to 1821," in *Southwest,* ed., Ortiz, 178–193; Albert H. Schroeder, "Pueblos Abandoned in Historic Times," in *Southwest,* ed., Ortiz, 236–254.

Puerto Rico

During the 15th and 16th centuries Puerto Rico remained a second-rate colony as the Spanish focused their attention on their more lucrative holdings in the viceroyalties of MEXICO and PERU.

Before contact with Europeans, at least thirty thousand TAINO inhabited Puerto Rico. The island seems to have been the cultural hearth for the eastern Taino. The ancestors of the Taino first reached the island around 200 B.C. The ceremonial ballgame played by the Taino seems to have begun on Puerto Rico. They also built substantial dance courts and ceremonial temples. Petroglyphs often adorned large stones that lined the dance and ball courts, and in some cases they carved effigies of their gods on these stones. The Taino also built roadways as their population expanded into the interior to make transportation and communication easier.

Taos Pueblo in New Mexico   *(Hulton/Archive)*

CHRISTOPHER COLUMBUS first landed on the smallest member of the Greater Antilles in November 1493. The first colonization of the island began in 1508, when JUAN PONCE DE LEÓN brought 42 colonists to the island and founded the village of Caparra. Immediately there was a dispute over who controlled Puerto Rico. In 1511 the highest Spanish court, the Consejo de Castilla, gave administration of the colony to Diego Columbus. He sold his interest in the colony to the Crown in 1536, and over time native labor assignments, DISEASE, and abortive rebellions significantly reduced the Taino population on the island. The Crown used civilian authorities to administer to the colony from 1545 to 1564, and in 1564 a captain-general was put in command of Puerto Rico. San Juan, the capital of the colony, experienced constant raids and threats from Dutch, English, and French privateers, with the worst attacks coming in 1595 and 1598 by the English and in 1625 by the Dutch.

The colony's economy depended upon the mining of placer GOLD until the 1530s, when the gold ran out, and then the island shifted to a subsistence mode. In 1512 the Spanish introduced SUGAR cultivation, but the colony did not have the resources to support its growth as an economic base. As a result, the colonists shifted to growing ginger in the early years and TOBACCO and CACAO by the 1600s. It was not until the 18th century that Puerto Rico became a major sugar producer and an important cog in the Spanish colonial system.

Further reading: Helmut Blume, *The Caribbean Islands,* trans., Johannes Maczewski and Ann Norton (London: Longman, 1974); Arturo Morales Carrion, ed. *Puerto Rico: A Political and Cultural History* (New York: Norton, 1983); Peter Hulme, *Colonial Encounters: Europe and the Native Caribbean, 1492–1797* (New York: Methuen, 1986); Irving Rouse, *The Tainos: Rise and Fall of the People Who Greeted Columbus* (New Haven, Conn.: Yale University Press, 1992).

— Dixie Ray Haggard

Purchas, Samuel (1577–1626)

A LONDON-based minister who edited and published travel accounts in order to encourage the English colonization of North America.

Born in Thaxted, Essex, Purchas attended St. John's College, Cambridge, receiving his B.A. in 1597 and his M.A. in 1600. Although he held various ministerial positions, Purchas spent much of his time and energy gathering travel accounts. In 1613 he published *Purchas his Pilgrimage* in London, an account based on his reading of perhaps 700 distinct accounts. In his note to the reader at the front of the book, he made his intentions clear: "I here bring Religion from Paradise to the Arke," he wrote, "and thence follow her round about the World, and (for her sake) observe the World it selfe, with the severall Countries and peoples therein; the Cheife Empires and States; their private and publique Customes; their manifold chances and changes; also the wonderfull and most remarkable effects of Nature; Events of Divine and Humane Providence, Rarities of Art; and whatsoever I find by relations of Historians, as I passe, most worthie the writing. Religion is my more proper aime, and therefore I insist longer on the description of whatsoever I finde belonging thereto[.]" He then proceeded to lay out the contents of his massive book in four parts. The first part dealt with the "Relations and Theologicall discoveries of Asia, Africa, and America." The second section included texts relating to Europe. He filled the third and fourth parts with what he called a "Christian and Ecclesiasticall Historie" from antiquity to the present. Purchas relied on 700 different sources for this book, but the text reflects his rewriting and use of these accounts. In that sense it was a dramatic departure from the strategy used earlier by the Venetian compiler GLOVANNI BATTISTA RAMUSIO or Purchas's English predecessor, RICHARD HAKLUYT THE YOUNGER.

Sometime after he completed the work for his book, Purchas met Hakluyt, who offered Purchas the use of books and manuscripts that Purchas used for a second edition of his *Pilgrimage,* published in London in 1614. Those loans, in addition to other materials Purchas had gathered, allowed him to draw on approximately 1,000 authorities for the second edition. He spent the mid-1610s acquiring more works, quite possibly from Hakluyt, who died on November 23, 1616. In 1617 he published the third edition of his *Pilgrimage.* This volume included yet more new accounts, including accounts of events during the early 1610s. His versions of travel accounts, like those that had appeared in Hakluyt's work, shaped other commentators' understanding of the earth. Thus, when Peter Heylyn published his *Microcosmus, or a little description of the great world* in Oxford in 1621, he drew much of his material from Purchas's work.

In January 1625 the London printer Henry Fetherstone printed Purchas's greatest effort, a work now entitled *Hakluytus Posthumus or Purchas his Pilgrimes.* Published in four volumes, this book represented two kinds of shifts for Purchas. First, he had access to a far greater number of travel accounts than he had earlier. Second, he followed Hakluyt's strategy of publishing versions of travelers' accounts in their own words. When Purchas gave a copy of his work to King JAMES I, the king asked him the difference between the new work and the old (which, he mentioned, he had read seven times). Though the books were similar in many ways, they "differ in the object and subject," Purchas responded, the 1625

Pilgrimage "being mine own in matter (though borrowed) and in forme of words and method: Whereas my *Pilgrims* are the Authors themselves, acting their owne parts in their own words, onely furnished by me with such necessaries as that stage further required, and ordered according to my rules; here is a *Pilgrimage* to the Temples of the Worlds Citie, religionis ergo, with obvious and occasionall view of other things; there is a full Voyage, and in a method of Voyages, the whole Citie of the World, propounded together with the Temples; here the soule and some accessories, there the body and soule of the remoter World[.]" Or, as one scholar later noted, the first book was a work of religious geography, the second a collection of materials to be used to compile a history.

Purchas never gained the reputation that Hakluyt achieved, but whatever the relative merits of their work, one fact is clear: An audience existed to purchase these enormous collections of travel accounts. Purchas, like Hakluyt, brought to the attention of readers the exploits of travelers such as the Englishman ANDREW BATTEL, who went to Africa, cast doubt on the report of DAVID INGRAM's alleged journey from FLORIDA to Canada, and provided, in a remarkable part of his 1625 work, an entire history of MEXICO told through a series of pictures. By the time he died the English settlements at Virginia had become more stable after their precarious start, and a group of English PURITANS, known as Pilgrims, had begun their colonization of New England. Purchas died in September 1626 and was buried at St. Martin's Church in Ludgate.

Further reading: Loren E. Pennington, ed., *The Purchas Handbook: Studies in the Life, Times, and Writings of Samuel Purchas, 1577–1626*, Works Issued by the Hakluyt Society, 2nd Ser., 185–186 (London, Hakluyt Society, 1997).

Puritans

English Protestants who believed that the REFORMATION had not sufficiently rid the church of Catholic influences were called first by their enemies and later by themselves Puritans.

The Reformation in England began in the reign of HENRY VIII (1509–47) and continued in the short reign of his son, Edward VI (1547–53). MARY I (1553–58), a Catholic, attempted to re-establish Catholicism, an effort that led some religious dissenters to flee England for the Continent, where they gained greater knowledge about Reformation ideas from JOHN CALVIN, Huldrych Zwingli, and Martin Bucer. After Mary's death ELIZABETH I (1558–1603) promoted Protestantism and aimed to settle religious disputes by establishing a theologically Protestant church that retained some liturgical elements of Catholicism.

From the beginning of the English Reformation, there were those who argued that the English church must be further purified. These Puritans, as they were later called, objected to certain holdovers from Catholic practice such as the use of the sign of the cross in baptism, the wearing of priestly vestments during the liturgy, and the retention of the office of bishops. Further, these religious dissenters disagreed with the open membership policies of the CHURCH OF ENGLAND. By law, each person born in England was a member of the national church (unless he or she adhered to a non-Christian faith), and every person was thus obligated to support the church through taxation. Dissenters disagreed with this aspect of Anglican theology. Following the logic put forth by St. Augustine, they believed that there were two churches. One church included everyone God had designated for salvation (the "invisible" church); the other included all individuals who adhered to the tenets of Christianity but who might or might not be destined for salvation (the "visible" church). As a result, reformers who objected to certain features of the Anglican church had to decide whether the Church of England, despite its flaws, was a "true" church, or whether its failings obligated believers to leave it and congregate with other true Christians (those destined for salvation). Puritans answered the question both ways: many stayed within the established church, although they might also meet with other like-minded worshipers for private prayer and study. Others, known as Separatists, rejected the Anglican Church and formed their own churches, which were generally small and prone to further division. All Puritans thought of themselves as a holy community of "elect" Christians who sought to live in holy brotherhood. Their theology was noteworthy for its commitment to the doctrine of predestination, the idea that God had, from the beginning of time, chosen some human beings to be saved and others to be damned.

Elizabeth I, hoping to end religious contention during her reign, persecuted both Catholics and Puritans to ensure the survival of her religious settlement. Archbishop John Whitgift, with Elizabeth's support, required ministers to swear to their support of the Anglican Church, including the monarch's status as "Supreme Governor" of the church and the use of the *Book of Common Prayer*. Many Puritans objected to the *Book of Common Prayer*, and their refusal to subscribe to this text led to the suspension of hundreds of Protestant ministers.

At the end of the 16th century, dissenters continued to find defects in the Church of England and its clergy. In 1600 the Puritan theologian Francis Johnson enumerated 91 erroneous elements of Anglican practice. Among the dissenters' objections was the fact that many individuals who became priests lacked the necessary training for their posts. Some who held office were, according to Puritan protests, "Dumme Doggs, Unskilful sacrificing priestes, Destroyeing Drones, or rather Caterpillars of the Word"— features that would not have been surprising among a people whom one Puritan writer identified as being artisans (such as tailors and shoemakers) or uneducated workers before receiving their appointments. In one of their characteristically caustic volumes, a Puritan writer catalogued the sins committed by clerics in one county in 1586. One was "a notorious swearer, a dicer, a carder, a hawker and hunter, a verie careless person" who had had "a childe by a maid since he was instituted and inducted," while another "kept a whore long time in his house" and was "unable to preach," while yet another was "thrice presented for a drunkard." "With such men for ministers," the historian Edmund Morgan concluded, "the Puritans foresaw that the membership of the Church of England could never be anything but ignorant, degraded, and corrupt."

Puritans made repeated protests about the systemic flaws in the Church of England. They argued that local churches needed the authority to punish an individual who had committed a sin, but that power lay vested in the higher officials of the clerical establishment. Unable to purge themselves of individuals whose presence in church would have been, they argued, an insult to God, the dissenters claimed that the Church of England could never be improved, let alone purified. Such beliefs led Puritans to embrace the concept of congregationalism, in which each church would choose its own officers and keep its members in line. Such an organization would also allow the Puritans to do what they wanted most of all: to exclude individuals they deemed unworthy.

Given their criticism against clerical authorities in England, the Puritans often found themselves persecuted. In response, some chose to leave England for the Continent, where they settled among like-minded Protestants. Others chose to stay in England, where they often suffered for their views until after the English civil war of the 1640s. Yet others, arguably the most famous, decided to take their chances in the new English colonies on the eastern shores of North America. Puritans thus came to dominate the so-

A Puritan Family: woodcut, 1563, from *The Whole Psalms in Four Parts* *(The Granger Collection)*

called Great Migration to New England, which began with the founding of Plymouth in 1620 and extended to 1642. It was thus in New England that Puritans had the opportunity to create churches along the lines they had envisioned, to fulfill their spiritual goals. Over time they would discover how difficult it could be to gather the members of the invisible church together and to maintain godly communities.

Further reading: Patrick Collinson, "Puritans," in *The Oxford Encyclopedia of the Reformation,* vol. 3, ed. Hans J. Hillerbrand (New York: Oxford University Press, 1996), 364–370; A. G. Dickens, "The Early Expansion of Protestantism in England, 1520–1558" in *The Impact of the English Reformation, 1500–1640,* ed. Peter Marshall (London: Arnold, 1997), 85–116; Christopher Durston and Jacqueline Eales, ed., *The Culture of English Puritanism, 1560–1700* (New York: St. Martin's Press, 1996); Edmund S. Morgan, *Visible Saints: The History of a Puritan Idea* (Ithaca, N.Y.: Cornell University Press, 1965).

— Martha K. Robinson

Q

Quetzalcoatl

Literally "Plumed" or "Feathered Serpent," the patron god of the city of CHOLULA and one of the major gods in several Mesoamerican pantheons.

Most often portrayed as a mixture of serpent and bird, Quetzalcoatl was prominent in Mesoamerican pantheons as far back as the OLMECS, and a temple dedicated to this god at TEOTIHUACÁN suggests that his cult in the central Mexican region dates back to at least the third century A.D. In his aspect as wind, he is referred to as Ehécatl. According to many Mesoamerican creation accounts, it was he, along with TEZCATLIPOCA, who rescued the bones of the people from the underworld after the previous extinction of all life on earth, thereby creating the present race of humanity. Other accounts portray these two gods as adversaries. Quetzalcoatl was patron of rulers, priests, and merchants, inventor of agriculture and writing, as well as patron of the city of Cholula, which was to become the main pilgrimage center for devotees of this god during the late postclassical period.

Sixteenth-century European documents tend to conflate the god Quetzalcoatl with the historical Ce Acatl Topiltzin Quetzalcoatl, a notably pacifist king of the TOLTECS. It is possibly because of this conflation that Spanish accounts of Aztec religion tend to portray the god Quetzalcoatl as averse to bloodshed. This does not, in fact, seem to have been the case, because his priests participated in the sacrificial rites of most festivals in TENOCHTITLÁN, including the bloody days-long dedication of the great temple to HUITZILOPOCHTLI and TLÁLOC during the reign of Ahuítzotl. Earlier generations of historians repeated the tale told in Spanish chronicles that the AZTECS, or at least MOCTEZUMA II, believed that HERNÁN CORTÉS or one of his men was Quetzalcoatl incarnate and that this was one of the reasons for the invaders' easy entry into Tenochtitlán and subsequent imprisonment of its great speaker. However, historians tend to put this theory far down the list of possible explanations for the Aztecs' defeat. If nothing else, any belief that Cortés was indeed that (or any other) god would have been called into question by the time the Spaniards reached Tenochtitlán, having slaughtered many of the inhabitants of Quetzalcoatl's sacred city of Cholula along the march from the coast.

Further reading: Alfredo López Austin, et al., "The Temple of Quetzalcoatl at Teotihuacán," *Ancient Mesoamerica* 2 (1991): 93–105; Nigel Davies, *The Aztec Empire: The Toltec Resurgence* (Norman: University of Oklahoma Press, 1987); Mary Miller and Karl Taube, *The Gods and Symbols of Ancient Mexico and the Maya: An Illustrated Dictionary of Mesoamerican Religion* (London: Thames & Hudson, 1993); William M. Ringle, et al., "The Return of Quetzalcoatl: Evidence for the Spread of a World Religion during the Epiclassic Period," *Ancient Mesoamerica* 9 (1998): 183–232.

— Marie A. Kelleher

R

Ralegh, Sir Walter (Raleigh) (1552?–1618)

The adventurer, poet, and close associate of Queen ELIZA-BETH I whose efforts to establish English settlements along the Atlantic coasts of North and South America failed and led to his execution.

Early in his life, perhaps when he was as young as 15, Ralegh joined a group of English soldiers who took it upon themselves to fight in France to help persecuted HUGUENOTS there. After his return he enrolled at Oriel College, Oxford, but took no degree and three years later was studying law at the Middle Temple, one of the Inns of Court in LONDON (and a place inhabited by, among others, RICHARD HAKLUYT THE ELDER). He later rose to prominence from his actions during the Elizabethan conquest of Ireland when he, along with his half brother, SIR HUMPHREY GILBERT, led devastating raids against Irish Catholics. When he returned to England, Queen Elizabeth became interested in him and in the early 1580s gave him a patent for territory along the east coast of North America. In 1584 Ralegh led an expedition across the Atlantic and sailed along the coast from present-day FLORIDA to the Carolinas. In honor of his patroness, he named the territory Virginia. In 1585 he led another expedition and left a party of English colonists at ROANOKE, although the colony failed and the colonists could not be found when the English came to look for them in 1588, after the defeat of the SPANISH ARMADA made transatlantic voyages safer. In addition to his disappointment in America, Ralegh also fell out of favor with the queen when he fell in love with Elizabeth (Bess) Throckmorton, daughter of Elizabeth's late ambassador to Paris and herself an attendant of the queen. She was possibly pregnant when they married in secret, and the queen was so furious when she found out about their relationship that Ralegh lost his standing in court.

Despite these shortcomings, he had the support of Elizabeth for a venture to Guiana, along the northern coast of South America, in 1595. He led an expedition up the Orinoco River and returned to England with high hopes for a more sustained expedition. Like other promoters of colonization, he claimed religious motives first. In a pamphlet he apparently wrote, known as "Of the Voyage for Guiana" and probably written in 1596, Ralegh noted that it was an "honorable" venture because English success in Guiana would mean that "infinite numbers of souls may be brought from their idolatry, bloody sacrifices, ignorance, and incivility to the worshiping of the true God[.]" Victory for England also would mean victory for the Protestant cause, a campaign dear to the heart of the queen. As Ralegh put it, conversion to Protestant religion would free Indians "from the intolerable tyranny of the Spaniards whereunto they are already or likely in short space to be subjected, unless her Majesty or some other christian prince do speedily assist and protect them." Such a development would stop the Spanish from boasting "of their great adventures for the propagation of the gospel" and thus add to the reputation of Elizabeth herself "upon the earth to all posterity[.]" Ralegh also added that establishing a colony in Guiana would enable the English to gain access to GOLD, SILVER, pearls, and precious stones. Through Guiana they might also reach PERU and other territory then under Spanish control. Finally, an English presence in Guiana would thwart any further Spanish designs on England because it would force the enemy to maintain a military presence there and thus lessen their force elsewhere.

However, Guiana became a disaster for Ralegh. The publication of his book entitled *The Discoverie of the Large, Rich, and Beautiful Empire of Guiana* in 1596 allowed Ralegh to become the acknowledged leader of an adventure crucial to the English state, yet enthusiasm did not translate into success. Although he had proven himself a superb military commander during English attacks on Cádiz in 1596 and in the AZORES in 1597, support for his Guiana venture faded when Elizabeth died in 1603. Upon her death he lost his property and, accused of a plot to murder King JAMES I, was jailed in the Tower

Sir Walter Ralegh   *(Library of Congress)*

of London along with his family. He remained there for 13 years. During that time he wrote his massive *History of the World.*

When he got out of the Tower in 1616 he once again led a mission to Guiana, but this mission proved more disastrous than any other in his life. James, unlike England, had no desire to annoy the Spanish, and so he ordered Ralegh not to trespass on Spanish territory but, instead, to explore areas (such as the Orinoco) where the Spanish had not yet established colonial settlements. On the voyage across the Atlantic, storms weakened and delayed his fleet, and a fever raced among the men, killing many, including Ralegh's son. The expedition was also a financial disaster. A mine Ralegh had believed would be a source of great stores of gold could not be worked because the route to the mine was almost impassable and he could not get the local Indians to work for him. When Ralegh returned to England in 1618, he arrived in disgrace. Worse still, the Spanish had interpreted his actions as a threat to their American property. When the ambassador to England complained that Ralegh and his forces were responsible for destroying a Spanish post at San Tomás, Ralegh was again committed to the Tower of London. Tried on various charges, including an accusation that he tried to bring

England and Spain into war against each other, that he had deceived others about the potential of the mine, and that he had been "unfaithful" to the king, James ordered his execution.

On October 29, 1618, the day after he received his final sentence, Ralegh was beheaded in front of a large crowd. After showing his head to the crowd, the executioners presented it to Bess, who allegedly put it in a red leather bag. She had the head embalmed and later displayed it to visitors.

Further reading: Stephen Coote, *A Play of Passion: The Life of Sir Walter Ralegh* (London: Macmillan, 1993); Agnes Latham and Joyce Youings, eds., *The Letters of Sir Walter Ralegh* (Exeter, U.K.: University of Exeter Press, 1999); Charles Nicholl, *The Creature in the Map: A Journey to El Dorado* (New York: William Morrow, 1995); Robert H. Schomburgh, ed., *The Discovery of the Large, Rich, and Beautiful Empire of Guiana . . . by Sir W. Ralegh,* Hakluyt Society, 1st Ser., no. 3 (London, Hakluyt Society, 1849).

Ramusio, Giovanni Battista (Giambattista)
(1485–1557)

A Venetian civil servant whose massive collection of travel accounts, published in VENICE in the 1550s, became a vital source of knowledge about the world beyond Europe's borders for readers across the Continent.

Born in Treviso in July 1485, Giovanni was the son of Paolo Ramusio, who was trained in the law but worked as a translator, publishing Valturio's *Precepta Militaria* in Verona in 1483. Paolo died in 1506. By that time his son, who had gone to Padua for study, was well on his way to a career in the Venetian civil service. In 1505 he began work as a chancellery clerk, traveling with Alvise Mocenigo, the Venetian envoy to France. During the trip he went to Blois, Tours, and probably Paris. By the time of his return in May 1507, he was such an expert in French that his linguistic skills became renowned in the republic. His knowledge put him into contact with the highest echelons of the Venetian state because the doge himself called upon the young Ramusio to serve as a translator for him. In 1515 he became a secretary to the senate, where he remained for 18 years. In 1533 he took a position as secretary to the Council of Ten, one of the ruling bodies of the Venetian republic that worked from the ducal palace. He kept that position for the rest of his working life. During his time in Venice he became close to a number of leading scholars of his day, including Girolamo Frascatoro (1483–1553), Andrea Navagero (1483–1529), and Pietro Bembo (1470–1547). When Navagero and Bembo, each of whom served time as the curator of the Biblioteca Marciana, traveled, Ramusio substituted in running Venice's marvelous library, work that often entailed finding material for the absent curators.

There are few extant details about Ramusio's life, but there is no doubt about his greatest achievement: the publication of an enormous three-volume set of travel accounts published under the title *Navigationi e Viaggi.* The books included the reports of travelers across the world. Ramusio at one point recorded why he decided the project was so important. "Seeing and considering that the maps of Ptolemy's *Geographia* describing Africa and India were very imperfect in respect of the great knowledge that we have of those regions," he wrote in the first volume of the *Navigationi,* published in 1550, "I thought it proper and perhaps not a little useful to bring together the narrations of writers of our day who have been in the aforesaid parts of the world and spoken of them in detail, so that, supplementing them from the description in the Portuguese nautical charts, other maps could be made to give the greatest satisfaction to those who take pleasure in such knowledge."

Ramusio apparently had little initial interest in publishing the results of his scholarly research. During his age many scholars were content to circulate their manuscripts to small groups of like-minded individuals. But by the late 1540s he had decided that publication made sense. Because Venice was one of the publishing centers of Europe (see PRINTING PRESS), and because its merchants were the crucial intermediaries between East and West, he could not have been in a better place. Because he knew Greek, Latin, Hebrew, Spanish, French, and Portuguese, he was able to translate a wide variety of texts into Italian. The decision to publish in Italian instead of Latin meant that his texts would have readers who were not scholars. Perhaps as a result of Ramusio's decision, other sets of travel accounts published in the 16th century also appeared in vernacular instead of classical languages.

Ramusio's books gave to European readers information that none had ever seen before. In the first volume of the *Navigationi,* published in 1550, Ramusio included LEO AFRICANUS's masterful and detailed description of Africa, as well as other writings such as the Venetian Alvise Ca'da Mosto's account of his trip to Africa, PEDRO ÁLVARES CABRAL's report of his journey to India, the report of VASCO DA GAMA, and AMERIGO VESPUCCI's so-called Soderini letter describing South America. The second volume, published in 1559 (after the publication of the third volume), included the account of MARCO POLO and various accounts of travelers across Europe. The third volume, published in 1556, included accounts of the Western Hemisphere. Ramusio included a summary of PETER MARTYR's *Decades of the New World,* accounts relating to the expeditions of FRANCISCO CORONADO in search of the Seven Cities of Cíbola, reports on HERNÁN CORTES's conquest of MEXICO, and a report by one of FRANCISCO PIZARRO's men of the Spanish conquest of PERU. This volume also included the first publication of some of the reports of JACQUES CARTIER's expeditions to Canada, which Ramusio translated from French into Italian before the accounts were published in France, and also the "Natural and General History of the West Indies" by his associate GONZALO FERNÁNDEZ DE OVIEDO Y VALDÉS, a work that included a depiction of CORN (maize) that became the standard view of the plant in early modern Europe.

Ramusio's collection had an enormous influence on others who decided to publish travel accounts, such as RICHARD HAKLUYT THE YOUNGER and SAMUEL PURCHAS. Unlike those later English editors, however, Ramusio did not link the translation and publication of reports to any obvious political agenda. Instead, he seemed interested primarily in promoting the better understanding of geography and recognized the invaluable contributions that firsthand accounts made in expanding knowledge about the nations and resources of the earth. He wanted his texts to commemorate, as he put it, "the greatest and most marvellous things which our age has seen"—things about the "many and varied countries of this globe never known to the ancients." Still, although he made no obvious link between his translations and any desire to reignite imperial ambitions in Venice, Ramusio did hope to profit from a venture he set up with Oviedo. According to the scheme, Oviedo would arrange for the shipment of goods from HISPANIOLA to Venice, where Ramusio and others would sell them. There is little evidence that this commerce had much success.

Ramusio died in July 1557 and was buried in the Chiesa della Madonna dell' Orto. Although his grave can no longer be identified, the church sits on a quiet edge of Venice, its bell tower looking out over the Adriatic Sea. The great Renaissance painter Jacobo Tintoretto (1518–94) is buried there, also, and his paintings alone, including his series of the "Last Judgment," make a pilgrimage to the church well worth the effort.

Further reading: Antonello Gerbi, *Nature in the New World: From Christopher Columbus to Gonzalo Fernández de Oviedo,* trans. Jeremy Moyle (Pittsburgh: University of Pittsburgh Press, 1985); George B. Parks, "Ramusio's Literary History," *Studies in Philology* 45 (1955): 127–148; ———, "Contents and Sources of Ramusio's Navigationi," *Bulletin of the New York Public Library* 59 (1955): 279–313; Gian Battista Ramusio, *Navigationi et Viaggi* (Amsterdam: Theatrum Orbis Terrarum, 1970); ———, *Navigationi E Viaggi,* ed. Marica Milanesi, 6 vols. (Rome: Giulio Einaudi, 1986).

Reconquista

Beginning in the late eighth century and ending in 1492, the Reconquista, or reconquest, was a campaign aimed at reclaiming the Iberian Peninsula from Muslims, who had invaded in 711.

The Reconquista began almost immediately after the Muslims had solidified their hold on the Iberian Peninsula, or modern-day Spain and Portugal. Muslim forces had crossed into Spain from present-day Morocco in 711 as a part of the dramatic expansion of ISLAM during the first 100 years after the prophet Muhammad's death in 632. Under the command of the general al-Tariq (after whom the Strait of Gibraltar would later be named in honor of his crossing) and his successors, a combined Arab-Berber army pressed northward, to be stopped only between Tours and Poitiers in 732 in a confrontation with Frankish forces under the command of Charles Martel.

The first phase of the Reconquista took place under the leadership of the grandson of Charles Martel. Charlemagne, or Charles I, dispatched a force southward from France across the Pyrenees to create a "Spanish march," or frontier in northeastern Spain. The progress of the Reconquista for the next several centuries was slow. The turning point came between 1010 and 1031, beginning with the Christian victory over and sack of the Muslim capital of Cordoba and ending with the collapse of the entire caliphate into fragmented *taifa* kingdoms. Many of these entities became tributary states to the Christian kingdoms, making regular payments, known as *parias,* in exchange for protection from both Christian and Muslim foes.

The relationship between Christian and Muslim states in the Iberian Peninsula during the 10th through the 15th century defies simple characterization. Despite gradual Christian advances and occasional important victories, an eventual Christian victory was never assured. Christian advances were often the impetus for Muslim religious and political revivals that shifted the balance of power for a time. On the other hand, relations were never exclusively inimical; both Christian and Muslim states were home to members of the other religion, as well as large Jewish communities. Both Muslim and Christian governments tried to limit interaction between the religious factions, but with little success. Normal political activity was also part of the relations between the two sides in the Reconquista. For example, there were Catalan ambassadors at the court of the caliph of Cordoba as early as the mid-10th century.

The Reconquista stalled temporarily during the political troubles endemic to the Christian kingdoms during the first half of the 15th century but received a boost when the fall of Constantinople to the Ottoman Turks in 1453 revived the moribund crusading ideal—the idea of papally sanctioned holy war against enemies of the faith. The marriage of FERDINAND AND ISABELLA in 1479 helped to cre-ate the political stability necessary for a successful Christian effort, and the combined kingdoms of Aragón and CASTILE were now able to lay aside their centuries'-old differences and unite their armies in the common cause of conquering the kingdom of Granada, the last Muslim-ruled political entity in the peninsula.

The final phase of the Reconquista began with the Christian conquest of Alhama in 1482 and continued over the next 10 years, detaching one region after another from the kingdom of Granada until only the capital city remained. The success of the Christian advance was in part due to the internal political struggles of the Muslim kingdom, dissension that the Catholic monarchs skillfully manipulated to their advantage.

The capture of the city of Granada in January of 1492 ended the reconquest on Spanish soil, but it gave birth to a new phase of fighting to vanquish or convert enemies of the faith beyond the water's edge. Spanish forces attempted—and largely failed—to establish a Christian foothold across the Strait of Gibraltar. Although these efforts were largely unsuccessful, it is worth noting that it was only three months after the Christian entry into Granada and only six miles away, in the town of Santa Fe, that an agreement was reached on the terms for the voyage of the Genoese sailor CHRISTOPHER COLUMBUS. The establishment of NEW SPAIN and the activities of both CONQUISTADORES and Christian missionaries would carry the ideal of the Reconquista into the early modern period.

Further reading: L. P. Harvey, *Islamic Spain, 1250–1500* (Chicago: University of Chicago Press, 1990); Derek W. Lomax, *The Reconquest of Spain* (London: Longman, 1978); Joseph F. O'Callaghan, *A History of Medieval Spain* (Ithaca, N.Y.: Cornell University Press, 1975); Bernard Reilly, *The Contest of Christian and Muslim Spain: 1031–1157* (Oxford, U.K.: Blackwell, 1992).

— Marie A. Kelleher

reducción

A Spanish policy demanding that Native Americans live apart from colonial society so that missionaries could convert indigenous peoples to Christianity and Spanish culture.

In northern Argentina and Paraguay FRANCISCANS first began the process of *reducción,* or reduction, of Native Americans. This process involved isolating native communities from outside influences other than missionaries. Although the Franciscans started the process, JESUITS perfected the method. With the *reducciones* Jesuits hoped to eliminate negative influences by Spanish colonists upon the native population. In this way they hoped to use intensive indoctrination to convert natives to Christianity and Spanish culture. Not only did the isolation promote the conversion process, it also protected indigenous peoples from slave raiders. However, by congregating Native Americans onto reserves, the missionaries increased their exposure to European DISEASES and inadvertently promoted the spread of epidemics.

Although *reducción* was the official Jesuit mission policy and became common in South America, many aspects of *reducciones* were used throughout Spanish America during the colonial era. Most of the *reducciones* were self-sufficient from cultivating European and American crops, raising cattle, HORSES, sheep, and various other items, and what they could not produce for themselves they bought with the surplus that they created.

Further reading: Philip Caraman, *The Lost Paradise: The Jesuit Republic in South America* (New York: Seabury Press, 1976); Magnus Mörner, *The Political and Economic Activities of the Jesuits in the La Plata Region: The Hapsburg Era* (Stockholm: Victor Petterson, 1953).

— Dixie Ray Haggard

Reformation

In the 16th century a series of reforms, attempted reforms, and religious crises led to a permanent split in the historic unity of western European Christianity, creating a permanent split between Catholic and Protestant churches.

The Reformation, scholars note, began in 1517, when the German monk MARTIN LUTHER protested against the sale of indulgences, but the roots of the Reformation extend further back. Many observers have noted that the thought of the 14th-century English reformer John Wycliffe, the 15th-century Bohemian reformer Jan Hus, and the lay religious movement known as the Modern Devotion all contributed to its origins. Such reformers sought a simpler, more egalitarian faith and complained of corruption within the church. Reaction to these movements was varied: While the Modern Devotion faced relatively little opposition, Wycliffe was convicted of heresy, and Hus was burned at the stake.

On the eve of the Reformation, critics and reformers complained about the wealth and corruption of Rome, about the sale of indulgences and church offices, and about absentee priests who lived off money collected in their parishes but did no pastoral service there. They also objected to a system of fees and tithes that redistributed money into the church's coffers, and some complained about the dry formalism of scholastic theology. These calls did not lead inevitably to the Reformation; many critics stayed within the church and sought internal reforms (see COUNTERREFORMATION). Nor was the church universally reviled. One historian has suggested that critiques of the church coexisted with "extravagant lay devotion to a con-

ventional, ritualized, often materialistic piety." Another has even argued that the term *Reformation* be used with care, in part because the term itself implies that the Reformation replaced "a bad form of Christianity [with] a good one."

Important reformers included Luther, JOHN CALVIN, Huldrych Zwingli, HENRY VIII, and John Knox. The early reformers initially sought to rescue a church that they believed had strayed, not to cause a schism in Christianity. But the church did not accept the reformers' theological ideas or implement their proposed reforms, and as religious wars spread across much of Europe the reformers tended to grow more convinced that the Catholic Church could not be rehabilitated.

The Reformation itself was characterized by great diversity of opinion, but most Reformation thinkers and movements can be placed into one of four groups: Lutherans, Reformed, Anglicans (see CHURCH OF ENGLAND), and radicals.

Lutherans

Luther was the first great theologian of Protestantism. He introduced two crucial theological ideas that most reformers came to defend: the belief in justification by faith alone *(sola fide)* and the conviction that the church should base itself on scripture alone *(sola scriptura)*. He also rejected papal claims to authority, proclaimed the centrality of the Bible (and translated the New Testament into German), redefined the significance of the Eucharist, and rejected the cult of the saints and the veneration of relics. His ideas roused great controversy, and Pope LEO X excommunicated him in 1520. The following year, upon his refusal to recant his beliefs, he was condemned as a heretic and declared an outlaw by Holy Roman Emperor CHARLES V at the Diet of Worms.

Luther's ideas spread rapidly, aided by popular sermons, religious plays, and the publication of pamphlets via the new technology of the PRINTING PRESS. Luther's ideas of Christian liberty helped spark a devastating Peasants' Rebellion in 1525, although Luther himself condemned the revolt. Intermittent religious wars continued in the Holy Roman Empire until 1555, when the Peace of Augsburg decreed that a region would be Catholic or Lutheran depending on the personal religious affiliation of its prince. By 1560 Lutheranism had become the dominant religion in Scandinavia and much of Germany, especially in urban areas.

Reformed Churches

Theologically, the Reformed churches had much in common with Lutheranism. Like Luther, they accepted justification through faith and the authority of scripture. Likewise, they placed great emphasis on Christianity as a

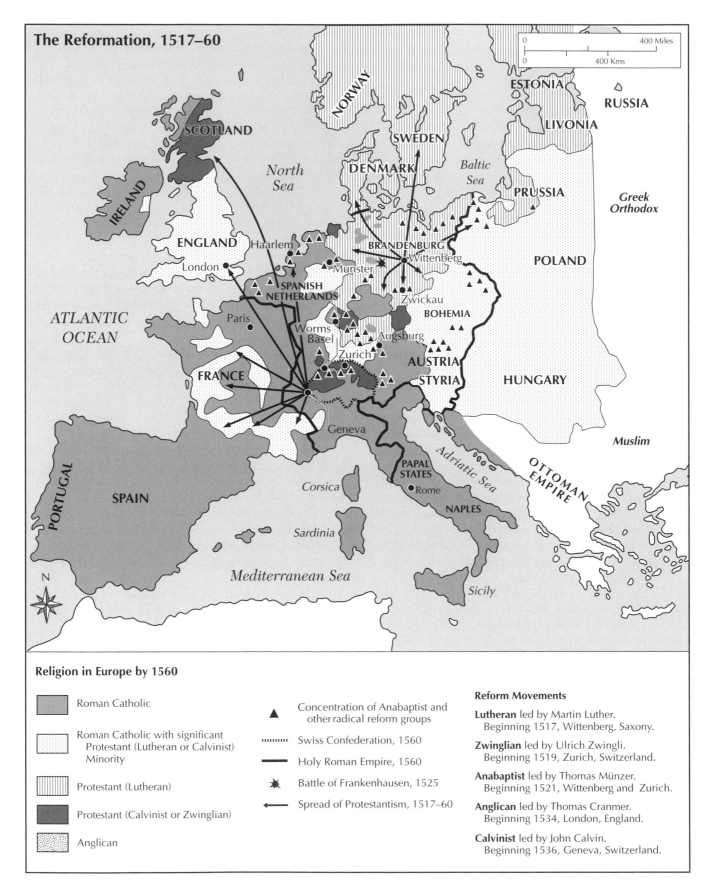

The Reformation, 1517–60

| 0 | 400 Miles |
| 0 | 400 Kms |

NORWAY
SWEDEN
DENMARK
ESTONIA
RUSSIA
LIVONIA
Baltic Sea
PRUSSIA
Greek Orthodox
North Sea
SCOTLAND
IRELAND
ENGLAND
Haarlem
London
SPANISH NETHERLANDS
Munster
BRANDENBURG
Wittenberg
Zwickau
POLAND
BOHEMIA
ATLANTIC OCEAN
Paris
Worms
Basel
Augsburg
Zurich
AUSTRIA
STYRIA
HUNGARY
FRANCE
Geneva
Muslim
OTTOMAN EMPIRE
PAPAL STATES
Rome
Adriatic Sea
PORTUGAL
SPAIN
Corsica
NAPLES
Sardinia
Sicily
Mediterranean Sea

Religion in Europe by 1560

- Roman Catholic
- Roman Catholic with significant Protestant (Lutheran or Calvinist) Minority
- Protestant (Lutheran)
- Protestant (Calvinist or Zwinglian)
- Anglican

▲ Concentration of Anabaptist and other radical reform groups

.... Swiss Confederation, 1560

—— Holy Roman Empire, 1560

✸ Battle of Frankenhausen, 1525

← Spread of Protestantism, 1517–60

Reform Movements

Lutheran led by Martin Luther.
Beginning 1517, Wittenberg, Saxony.

Zwinglian led by Ulrich Zwingli.
Beginning 1519, Zurich, Switzerland.

Anabaptist led by Thomas Münzer.
Beginning 1521, Wittenberg and Zurich.

Anglican led by Thomas Cranmer.
Beginning 1534, London, England.

Calvinist led by John Calvin.
Beginning 1536, Geneva, Switzerland.

religion of the word, and so emphasized literacy, preaching, and teaching over ritual. Congregants in the Reformed churches generally felt that Luther had been too willing to compromise with Catholic custom in such matters as the retention of images in churches. They were perhaps most notable for their emphasis on religion as a community matter.

The city of Geneva, where John Calvin's ideas had transformed the church and the community, was particularly important in Reformed religion. It served as a home for refugees and a training ground for ministers. These missionaries then founded congregations in France and elsewhere, spreading Reformed patterns of religion. The Genevan pattern of close cooperation between civil and church authorities influenced Reformed churches in other cities, as did its fourfold division of church offices into pastors, teachers, elders, and the consistory. Reformed churches emphasized duty and the need to live an orderly life, one of obedience, modesty, temperance, and diligence. This religious pattern had particular relevance for urban artisans, lawyers, and tradesmen, and scholars have observed that the devotion to secular duty and hard work promoted by Reformed churches proved to fit well in a capitalist economy. Reformed churches, like Lutheran ones, thrived in urban environments. Reformed cities included Basel, Bern, Constance, Geneva, and Zurich. Although the Reformed movement was strongest in western Germany, Holland, and Switzerland, it also reached Scotland and parts of France and England.

Anglicans

Lutheran ideas reached England by the 1520s, but clerical authorities initially suppressed them. By the late 1520s King HENRY VIII was enmeshed in matrimonial difficulties. His wife, Catherine of Aragón, had borne several children, but only one, a daughter, had survived. Henry hoped for a son and petitioned the pope to annul his marriage, freeing him to marry his mistress, Anne Boleyn. The pope, under pressure from Holy Roman Emperor Charles V, refused. This problem, combined with political rivalries between England and other states and the king's irritation at the English clergy, convinced Henry that he should assert his dominance over the church in England. In 1534 PARLIAMENT passed the Act of Supremacy, declaring the king to be "the supreme head of the Church of England."

The Reformation took greater shape during the reign of Henry VIII's daughter, Queen ELIZABETH I. Religious controversies had worsened during the reigns of Edward VI and MARY I, and Elizabeth sought to end religious disputes in England. Her Act of Supremacy of 1559 established her status as "Supreme Governor" of the church and mandated the use of the *Book of Common Prayer.* Nonetheless, the Anglican church also retained some Catholic elements, such as a governing structure of bishops and a greater use of ritual than was common in Lutheran or Reformed churches. Elizabeth was not a religious zealot, but she wanted stability and expected English subjects to adhere, at least nominally, to the Church of England. Those who publicly refused, whether Catholics or PURITANS, faced persecution.

Radicals

The term *radical Reformation* covers a wide range of groups that had little in common with one another. In general, most radical groups believed that the world would end soon and hoped to restore the practices of the earliest Christian churches, including the holding of goods in common. Unlike other Reformation churches, which saw themselves as including every member of a city or territory, from the very dedicated to the nominal believers, radical groups tended to consist of a small number of core believers. Many of these groups rejected infant baptism, earning the name Anabaptists, or "re-baptizers."

The radicals took the principle of "scripture alone" further than the major reformers ever would. While Luther, Calvin, and others argued that scripture was the sole authority, they also believed that it must be studied and interpreted by theological experts. Untrained laypeople were incapable of discovering for themselves the meaning of the scriptures. Many radicals argued that anyone could read and understand the Bible. The diversity of the radical churches only increased when some sects claimed that believers might receive the direct inspiration of the Holy Spirit.

Major radical leaders included Conrad Grebel, Hans Hut, Thomas Müntzer, and Jan Matthijs. The radicals distrusted political and religious elites and often drew their membership from among the poor. The radicals' theological novelties, rejection of political authority, and apparent links to the Peasants' War led both Catholic and Protestant authorities to persecute them. Radical communities existed in Germany, Switzerland, and the Netherlands.

Effects of the Reformation

By 1560 Protestantism was firmly established in much of Europe. England, Scotland, Scandinavia, the Netherlands, many of the cities of the Holy Roman Empire, parts of France, and parts of eastern Europe had adopted one or another of the Protestant faiths. Areas that remained officially Catholic, including France, Spain, and Italy, also saw religious change, as internal reform impulses and the desire to challenge Protestantism led to the Counterreformation.

In Protestant areas the Reformation changed patterns of religious observance. Such traditional practices and beliefs as the veneration of Mary and the saints, the doctrine of purgatory, compulsory fasting, and clerical celibacy were abolished or limited in many European cities and territories. The number of sacraments was reduced from seven to two (or, in some areas, three), and the Catholic administrative structure of priests and bishops was swept away.

What effect did the reformers' messages have on ordinary Christian believers? As a general rule, it appears that most people heard about the reformers from preachers and pamphlets. Their initial response, drawing on a combination of anticlericalism and irritation at Catholic church failings, was often enthusiastic. Such early ardor encouraged the reformers to believe that their efforts were blessed by God and to expect widespread conversions to the new faith. Reformers wrote catechisms to express important beliefs in simple, easily understood ways. They encouraged literacy in order to allow people to read the Bible and come to a more thorough understanding of their faith. Nonetheless, their early hopes were frustrated. In an age of limited literacy, it is unlikely that the reformers' theological ideas, many of which were complex, were readily understood by the peasants and artisans who heard or read (or had read to them) the works of Protestant propagandists.

As the Protestant churches established themselves and came to accommodations with secular authorities, the enthusiasm of the early years died down. Protestantism, rather than representing a challenge to authority, became a new authority. Ministers often found their initial high hopes of a better educated, more pious, more dedicated population frustrated. They complained that they could reach only a minority of true believers, while a larger number of lukewarm adherents showed little interest in or understanding of religion.

Protestant reformers rejected the medieval Catholic ideal of the monastic life. They denied that the celibate life of priests, monks, and nuns was better than that of other people, and they praised family life. Ministers themselves married, and their sons sometimes became ministers. Because Protestants praised married life as a "calling" equal in value to any other, some scholars have suggested that the Reformation raised the status of women. Others have maintained that women's status stayed much the same and that, if anything, the closing of the convents destroyed one of the few careers open to women in the 16th century.

The Reformation had important implications for the settlement of the Western Hemisphere when the colonizing European powers competed with one another in the race to found colonies. The Spanish and Portuguese colonies in Latin America and the French colonies in North America became Catholic, while the English colonies of North America included a range of Protestant churches.

Further reading: Michael G. Baylor, ed. and trans., *The Radical Reformation* (Cambridge, U.K.: Cambridge Uni-

versity Press, 1991); Euan Cameron, *The European Reformation* (Oxford: Clarendon Press, 1991); Eamon Duffy, *The Stripping of the Altars: Traditional Religion in England, c. 1400–c. 1580* (New Haven, Conn.: Yale University Press, 1992); Heiko A. Oberman, *Luther: Man Between God and the Devil* (New Haven, Conn.: Yale University Press, 1989); Steven Ozment, *The Age of Reform, 1250–1550* (New Haven, Conn.: Yale University Press, 1980).

— Martha K. Robinson

religion   See individual entries: Aztecs; Calvin, John; Counterreformation; Foxe's *Book of Martyrs;* Franciscans; Inca; Islam; Jews (Judaism); Luther, Martin; Maya; Puritans; Reconquista; Reformation; Sufism; Trent, Council of.

repartimiento

A system of forced labor used during the early colonial era, the *repartimiento* forced indigenous people to work for Spanish colonial entities a certain percentage of the year.

Translated loosely as "distribution," the *repartimiento* typically meant that indigenous communities in Spanish America had to provide one-seventh of the community's male population to service for those Spaniards, local governments, and industries that had received a grant from the Crown, viceroyalties, or other branches of the colonial government. All males between the ages of 18 and 55 participated within the *repartimiento* system when their term came around. Technically, each individual served only two to four months of labor and then was exempt for a full year, but the system did not always function in this fashion. Communities often received large labor assignments based on inaccurate censuses, and these requirements tended to increase as native populations decreased from abuse, starvation, and the introduction of European DISEASES. As time passed the length of service increased and the break between service requirements decreased. Some people served on local estates, and others were shipped to distant worksites. Any type of labor needed during the early colonial period, such as mining, farming, and ranching, among a host of others, received at least part of its workforce from the *repartimiento*. Many people avoided the *repartimiento* by migrating to those areas that did not have it. This created labor shortages in areas using the *repartimiento* and, in general, destabilized the labor force throughout Spanish America. Most of the work in *repartimientos* was intensive, dangerous, and debilitating. Eventually, wage labor and other forms of work relationships developed to replace the inefficient *repartimiento*.

Further reading: Peter Bakewell, *Miners of the Red Mountains: Indian Labor in Potosi, 1545–1650* (Albuquerque: University of New Mexico Press, 1984); ———, "Mining in Colonial Spanish America," *Cambridge History of Latin America*, vol. 2 (Cambridge, U.K.: Cambridge University Press, 1984), 110–151; Enrique Tandeter, *Coercion and Market: Silver Mining in Colonial Potosi, 1662–1826* (Albuquerque: University of New Mexico Press, 1993).

— Dixie Ray Haggard

Requerimiento

The Requerimiento ("Requirement") was a document that Spanish explorers and conquerors read to Native Americans in order to claim authority over them and their lands (see Documents).

According to the Requerimiento, composed by the Spanish jurist Juan López de Palacios Rubios in 1513, God had given dominion over all people to St. Peter, and this grant of jurisdiction had descended from him to the popes. Because Pope Alexander VI had given authority over the "islands and mainland of the Ocean Sea to the Catholic kings of Spain," the Spanish claimed that they had legitimate power over Indian lands and peoples.

The Requerimiento told Indians that they must submit to Spanish and Catholic authority and warned them that they would face severe penalties if they refused. It commanded Indians to recognize the authority of the Catholic Church and the Spanish monarch. The Indians also had to allow Spanish priests to preach among them. If they refused to submit to these new authorities, the Requerimiento continued, "I will enter forcefully against you, and I will make war everywhere and however I can, and I will subject you to the yoke and obedience of the Church and His Majesty, and I will take your wives and children and I will make them slaves . . . and I will take your goods, and I will do to you all the evil and damages that a lord may do to vassals who do not obey or receive him. And I solemnly declare that the deaths and damages received from such will be your fault and not that of His Majesty, nor mine, nor of the gentlemen who came with me." The Requerimiento allowed the Spanish to claim that any war they took part in against the Indians was a just war, because the Indians were resisting their legitimate authority. However, the Requerimiento did not have to be read in Indian languages, nor were the Spanish required to make sure the Indians understood what they were hearing. As the historian Patricia Seed observed, it might even be "read at full speed from the deck of a ship at night before a daytime raid [or] read to assembled empty huts and trees."

The Requerimiento was controversial in Spain and derided in other European countries. The Spanish Dominican friar BARTOLOMÉ DE LAS CASAS wrote that the Requerimiento was "unjust, impious, scandalous, irrational and absurd" and added that he did not know "whether to laugh or cry" at its demands. The English, French, and Dutch had nothing resembling the Requerimiento in their colonial empires and so also criticized it. SIR WALTER RALEGH wrote, "No Christian prince, under the pretence of Christianity only, and of forcing of men to receive the gospel . . . may attempt the invasion of any free people not under their vassalage; for Christ gave not that power to Christians as Christians."

Further reading: Noble David Cook, "Requerimiento," in *Encyclopedia of Latin American History and Culture*, vol. 4, ed. Barbara A. Tenenbaum (New York: Scribner's, 1996); Lyle N. McAlister, *Spain and Portugal in the New World, 1492–1700* (Minneapolis: University of Minnesota Press, 1984); Anthony Pagden, *Lords of All the World: Ideologies of Empire in Spain, Britain and France, c. 1500–c. 1800* (New Haven, Conn.: Yale University Press, 1995); Patricia Seed, *Ceremonies of Possession in Europe's Conquest of the New World, 1492–1640* (Cambridge, U.K.: Cambridge University Press, 1995).

— Martha K. Robinson

Ricci, Matteo (1552–1610)

A member of the Society of Jesus (see JESUITS) who led the first successful Jesuit mission to China during the Ming Dynasty (1368–1644), Matteo Ricci spent 28 years in China, dying in Beijing as a universally admired and respected scholar, even though the Chinese converts he inspired were later disowned by the church.

Ricci was born in Macerata, Italy, on October 6, 1552. At the age of nine he entered the Jesuit school there and, after seven years of study, became a novice in the Society of Jesus in Rome. IGNATIUS LOYOLA founded the Jesuits in 1540 as part of the COUNTERREFORMATION against the Protestants. Education and scholarship became an important part of their missionary enterprise. Ricci's studies were not completed until May 1577, when he went to Portugal to learn the language, after which the church sent him to the Portuguese trading colony at Goa in India.

The Portuguese led the way in the European rediscovery of China in the early 16th century. Their efforts to establish an overseas empire in South and Southeast Asia centered on the dual pillars of trade and Christianity. Missionary work was frequently the most important part of their enterprise. With the establishment of a small colony at Macao (1555), in southeastern China, the Portuguese attempted to continue this pattern but met with serious difficulties.

China at the time was under the rule of the Ming (1368–1644), who had thrown off the yoke of the foreign Mongols to establish a native Chinese dynasty. As a result,

China's leaders were generally violently antiforeign, convinced of Chinese cultural superiority and determined to keep out unwanted foreign influences. The Chinese allowed the Portuguese to establish themselves at Macao because it was a small, unimportant place far removed from China's commercial, cultural, and governmental centers. Local government officials rebuffed any efforts on the part of the Portuguese to send Catholic missionaries into the interior.

Arriving at Macao in 1582, Matteo Ricci was assigned to join a fellow Jesuit, Michele Ruggieri, in studying to speak, write, and read Chinese. Ricci was by this time a respected scholar possessed of an extremely acute memory. This ability helped him learn the 3,000 to 4,000 Chinese characters he needed to communicate with potential converts. Whereas missionary efforts of the Portuguese in India and the Spanish in America often were accompanied by fire and sword, the Jesuits chose a quieter, more patient path in China. Whether by accident or design, their choices of conscientious scholars capable of communicating in the native language were just the sort of people to impress Chi-

An illustration from a Chinese manuscript of the Jesuit missionary to China, Matteo Ricci, and his first convert *(Hulton/Archive)*

nese officials and gentry, who greatly revered scholarship and learning.

In 1583 Ricci and Ruggieri were invited to reside with the governor of Gwangdong and Gwangxi Provinces in Zhaoqing. Chinese officials remained suspicious of the missionaries, suspecting that invading Portuguese troops might follow behind them, a reasonable fear at the time. As a result, they imposed serious restrictions on Ricci and Ruggieri. In order to reside in the interior, they were forced to adopt Chinese dress and subject themselves to imperial law. At first Ricci chose to wear the robes of a Chinese priest, but after 1594 he exchanged them for scholar's robes, a move that brought him a greater degree of respect and deference, as scholars in China had a much higher reputation than priests.

During his time at Zhaoqing Ricci impressed the Chinese by his diligent study of their language and literature and drew for them a map showing China in relation to the rest of the world that was widely (and illegally) reprinted throughout the nation. He did not attempt to make converts, and after seven years' residence the newly incoming governor forced him to return to Canton. He lived in several other provincial cities and towns, quietly making Chinese converts among the scholar gentry and translating major Chinese scholarly works into Latin and Western works into Chinese.

In 1598 Ricci was allowed to travel to Beijing, but he was unable to gain an audience with the emperor. After spending some time in Nanjing, he finally returned to Beijing in January 1601 and remained there the rest of his life. During his time there he impressed the emperor and his advisers with his knowledge of Western science and philosophy and his interest in Chinese literature and scholarship. He made a number of converts among the Chinese upper classes, but peasants and townsmen did not particularly interest him.

Ricci wrote frequently to Rome asking that an effort be made to send only the most learned and intelligent priests. By the time of his death on May 11, 1610, Ricci was so admired by the imperial court that his burial plot was a personal gift of the emperor. Following the example set by Ricci, a series of highly gifted Jesuit missionaries took up residence in Beijing and managed to maintain a place close to the throne even after the Ming Dynasty had been overthrown by the Manchu Qing (1644–1911).

Further reading: Vincent Cronin, *The Wise Man From the West* (London: R. Hart-Davis, 1955); Jonathan D. Spence, *The Memory Palace of Matteo Ricci* (New York: Penguin Books, 1985); Denis Twitchey and John King Fairbank, eds., *The Cambridge History of China*, 8 vols. (Cambridge, U.K.: Cambridge University Press, 1978).

— Paul Dunscomb

Roanoke

The first English colony in North America, Roanoke proved a failure, and the disappearance of its colonists, sometime between 1587 and 1607, remains a mystery.

In the late 16th century SIR WALTER RALEGH hoped to strengthen England and improve its status by founding colonies in the NEW WORLD. England was a second-rate power, and the English feared the growing wealth and influence of Spain, which had become rich from its American possessions. Ralegh and other promoters of colonial ventures hoped that colonies would provide a Protestant bulwark against Catholic Spain and produce commodities needed by England. Successful colonies might also serve as a new home (or dumping ground) for the increasing number of poor people who seemed to threaten English stability and social order.

In 1584 Queen ELIZABETH I granted Ralegh the exclusive right to set up a colony in North America. He sent two ships, under the command of Philip Amadas and ARTHUR BARLOWE, to find a suitable site for a colony. Ralegh hoped to find a site that was close enough to the West Indies to allow English privateers to use it as a base from which to launch raids on Spanish ships. In July 1585 Amadas and Barlowe reached the islands off the coast of present-day North Carolina. They reported that the land showed great promise and met and traded peacefully with the local Carolina ALGONQUIAN. They returned to England with a favorable report of the land and also brought two Indians with them, MANTEO, a Croatoan of high status, and WANCHESE, a Roanoke Indian. Both learned English and returned to America on a later voyage. Manteo and Wanchese also instructed THOMAS HARRIOT, who would become the great chronicler of the Roanoke colony, in their language.

Having heard the favorable reports of Amadas and Barlowe, Ralegh organized another voyage. This expedition, led by Sir Richard Grenville, arrived at Roanoke in 1585. The colonists included gentlemen leaders; experts in engineering, surveying, and other subjects; and ordinary colonists of the "meaner sort." Among the experts in the new colony were Harriot and JOHN WHITE, a gifted painter. Harriot's book, *A Briefe and True Report of the New Found Land of Virginia* (1590), illustrated with engravings based on White's painting, is a valuable source on the land and people of the region.

Although White and Harriot demonstrated that some of the English sought to understand their Indian neighbors, the colony found itself in trouble from the beginning. Many of the colonists were veterans of Irish and European wars. They were inclined to distrust the Indians and to suspect treachery at every turn. Their belief in English superiority was not matched by self-sufficiency. Instead, the English colonists who derided and distrusted the Indians were also dependent on them for food. When the Indians proved

A Roanoke warrior, in a painting by John White, ca. 1587 *(Hulton/Archive)*

unwilling or unable to feed the colonists indefinitely, tensions increased.

Having practiced brutal warfare in Ireland, the English assumed that the Indians needed to be impressed by their power. Only if the Indians were afraid to attack the colonists, they thought, could there be peace. The colony's commander, Sir Richard Grenville, soon antagonized the Indians. In an early incident, when Indians refused to return a silver cup that he believed they had stolen, he burned an Indian town and destroyed its CORN crop. Grenville soon returned to England, but the new governor, RALPH LANE, did no better. As relations between the Indians and colonists deteriorated, Lane blamed the Indians, claiming that they had conspired against the English. The arrival of the Europeans had indeed affected relations among Indian nations in the area, as some opposed permitting the English to stay while others sought to profit through trade or gain power by alliance with the newcomers. Nonetheless, Harriot suggested that most of the blame for deteriorating relations lay with the English, observing that the colonists were hated because "some of our company towards the end of the year, showed themselves too fierce, in slaying some of the people, in some towns, upon causes that on our part, might easily enough have been borne withall." The year after its founding the colony was already failing. The surviving colonists returned to England with SIR FRANCIS DRAKE in 1586, departing in such a hurry that they left three Englishmen behind.

After the failure of the 1585–86 voyage, Ralegh tried again. The next expedition, in 1587, sought to avoid the mistakes of the earlier voyage. Rather than sending military men, Ralegh sent families and hoped to establish a self-sufficient colony based on agriculture. The new governor, JOHN WHITE, was a veteran of the earlier expedition and thus presumably familiar with the local environment, but this colony faced a serious problem from the beginning. The Indians of the region had already learned that the English were not to be trusted, and so, as the historian Karen Ordahl Kupperman observed, there was "no grace period during which Indians and English would learn about each other."

Despite their earlier actions, the English still had some allies among the native peoples of the region, including Manteo and his people, the Croatoan. But other Indians, including the Roanoke, were hostile toward the colonists. Only six days after this third expedition arrived, Indians killed a colonist, George Howe. Seeking revenge for his death and for the deaths of earlier colonists, Governor White led an attack on a native community, killing at least one Indian. However, the people he attacked were not the ones who had killed Howe, and this unprovoked attack on friendly Indians offered more proof that the English could not be trusted. While the situation remained unresolved, the English fleet was making preparations to return to Europe. In August 1587 White returned to England in the hopes of finding more support for the colony.

Upon his return to England, White and Ralegh began preparing another expedition to strengthen and resupply the colony, but their plans were interrupted. The threat posed by the SPANISH ARMADA was so great that the PRIVY COUNCIL, worried about the defense of the realm, forbade ships that could be used in war to leave England. For three years no English people visited Roanoke. When an expedition led by White finally returned to Roanoke in August 1590, they found the settlement deserted. The colonists had taken some of their belongings and had carved "CRO" on a tree and "CROATOAN" on a post. White therefore believed that they had sought shelter with Manteo's people. Because they had not carved a Maltese cross above the words, a prearranged distress signal, he believed that they were still alive. Storms prevented White from searching further for the colonists, and he decided to winter in the AZORES before attempting to return.

In the end, little was done about the missing colonists for the next 10 years. Ralegh's influence with the queen had declined, and he was also involved in a variety of other ventures that distracted him from the Roanoke colony. When the English finally settled a lasting colony at Jamestown, they tried again to find the missing colonists. In 1612 the secretary of the Jamestown colony reported that the colonists, after leaving Roanoke, had moved north to Chesapeake Bay. There they had lived peacefully among the Indians for 20 years before being killed on the orders of POWHATAN, shortly before the arrival of the Jamestown colonists. Others have speculated that the colonists were absorbed into Indian communities to the west of Roanoke. Their fate remains unknown.

The Roanoke colony faced serious problems from the beginning. Because the English Crown did not support colonies, it was dependent on private financing. Colonies, like Roanoke, that did not make a rapid profit were unattractive to investors and struggled to survive. The colonists did not grow enough food to support themselves and relied too heavily on Indian generosity. Worst of all, early peaceful relations between natives and newcomers degenerated, and violence often flared between one-time trading partners. In the end, the Roanoke colony provided little more than a series of lessons about the causes of colonial failure.

Further reading: David N. Durant, *Ralegh's Lost Colony* (London: Weidenfeld & Nicolson, 1981); Mary C. Fuller, *Voyages in Print: English Travel to America, 1576–1624* (Cambridge, U.K.: Cambridge University Press, 1995); Thomas Harriot, *A Briefe and True Report of the New Found Land of Virginia* (New York: Dover, 1972); Karen Ordahl Kupperman, *Roanoke: The Abandoned Colony* Totowa, N.J.: Rowman & Allanheld, 1984); David Beers Quinn, *Set Fair for Roanoke: Voyages and Colonies, 1584–1606* (Chapel Hill: University of North Carolina Press, 1985).

— Martha K. Robinson

S

Sahagún, Bernardino de (ca. 1499–1590)

Bernardino de Sahagún, a Spanish Franciscan friar (see FRANCISCANS), drew on indigenous informants to compile the Florentine Codex, an account of Aztec culture and the events surrounding the Spanish conquest.

Sahagún was born in Spain but came to NEW SPAIN as a friar and missionary in 1529. He studied Aztec history and culture with the goal of furthering the goal of converting the Indians to Catholicism. He helped found a school in Tlatelolco, where he taught young AZTECS Spanish and Latin and learned NAHUATL from them. By the 1540s he and his Indian assistants, who could read Spanish, Latin, and Nahuatl, began to interview old men who had survived the conquest of 1519–20. They interviewed their informants in Nahuatl, asking the same questions of each of them. Making note of discrepancies, they then conducted follow-up interviews to help settle disputed points. Sahagún was particularly interested in Aztec religion, history, and customs.

The resulting work, the *General History of the Things of New Spain*, took some 30 years to complete. It is known as the Florentine Codex because the most complete manuscript is in Florence, Italy. The final version featured illustrations and parallel columns of text in Spanish and Nahuatl. Its 13 parts, or books, included sections on the Aztec gods and their origins, religious ceremonies, kings and nobles, merchants, philosophy, and the Spanish conquest of MEXICO.

Histories of the conquest of Mexico have often cited the account of the conquest in book 12 of the codex. This account was the first to include the story that the Aztecs believed HERNÁN CORTÉS to be the god QUETZALCOATL. It also emphasized MOCTEZUMA II's fear and vacillation in the face of the Spanish, portraying him as such a weak leader that the Aztec lords turned against him. This version, although often repeated, has been challenged by the historian Inga Clendinnen, who observed that Sahagún's story appeared more than 30 years after the conquest and that his informants were therefore young men when Cortés arrived. These men could provide much information about the Aztec world, but in precontact Tenochtitlán such "young and inconsequential men" would not have had access to Moctezuma. They could not, therefore, have observed Moctezuma's behavior or known what he thought. Despite such difficulties in the text, the Florentine Codex remains a valuable source for students of Aztec history and culture.

Sahagún also wrote other works, including a later account of the conquest, the "Account of the Conquest of New Spain, as the Indian Soldiers who were Present Told It." This work, composed six years after the completion of the Florentine Codex, portrayed Cortés and the Spanish in a more favorable light. Sahagún died in Mexico in 1590.

Further reading: J. Jorge Klor de Alva, H.B. Nicholson, and Eloise Quiñones Keber, eds., *The Work of Bernardino de Sahagún, Pioneer Ethnographer of Sixteenth-Century Aztec Mexico* (Albany, N.Y.: Institute for Mesoamerican Studies, 1988); J. H. Parry, *The Discovery of South America* (London: Paul Elek, 1979); Fray Bernardino de Sahagún, *The War of Conquest: How It Was Waged Here in Mexico,* ed. and trans. Arthur J.O. Anderson and Charles E. Dibble (Salt Lake City: University of Utah Press, 1978); ———, *Florentine Codex: General History of the Things of New Spain,* ed. and trans. Arthur J. O. Anderson and Charles E. Dibble, 13 parts (Salt Lake City: University of Utah Press, 1950–1982); Stuart B. Schwartz, *Victors and Vanquished: Spanish and Nahua Views of the Conquest of Mexico* (Boston: Bedford/St. Martin's Press, 2000).

— Martha K. Robinson

Sahara

The Sahara, the largest desert in the world, covers about 3.3 million square miles, stretching from the Atlantic Ocean to the Red Sea.

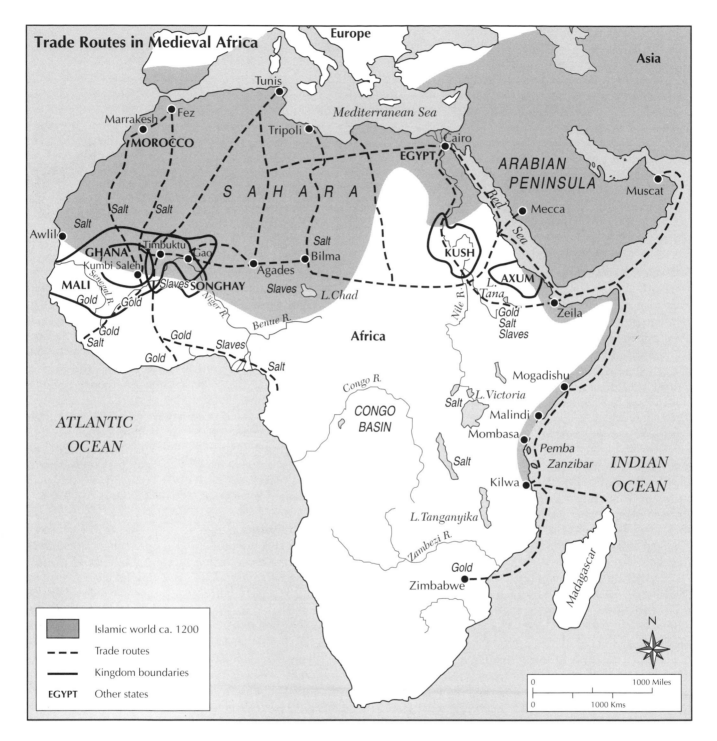

Trade Routes in Medieval Africa

Europe

Tunis

Mediterranean Sea

Asia

Marrakesh Fez

MOROCCO

Tripoli

Cairo

EGYPT

ARABIAN PENINSULA

Muscat

S A H A R A

Mecca

Salt   *Salt*

Salt

Red Sea

KUSH

Awlil

GHANA Timbuktu Gao

Kumbi Saleh

Salt   *Salt*

Bilma

AXUM

L. Tana

Zeila

MALI *Slaves* **SONGHAY**

Agades

Slaves

L. Chad

Gold
Salt
Slaves

Gold   *Gold*

Niger R.

Nile R.

Gold
Salt   *Gold*

Benue R.

Africa

Slaves

Gold

Salt

ATLANTIC OCEAN

Congo R.

Salt

Mogadishu

L. Victoria

CONGO BASIN

Malindi

Salt

Mombasa

Pemba

Zanzibar

INDIAN OCEAN

Kilwa

L. Tanganyika

Zambezi R.

Gold

Zimbabwe

Madagascar

N

	Islamic world ca. 1200
- - -	Trade routes
⸺	Kingdom boundaries
EGYPT	Other states

0		1000 Miles
0		1000 Kms

Over time, the Sahara has functioned as a conduit for trade as well as a barrier to contact between the Mediterranean world and sub-Saharan Africa. Evidence of human activity (rock paintings, artifacts, and tools) in the Sahara dates back more than 10,000 years. The desert has witnessed climatic variations, but it has remained similar to its present conditions for the last 5,000 years. Most of the desert consists of open plains of rock and gravel. Only one-fifth of the Sahara is sand. The boundaries of the desert have expanded in drier periods and contracted in wetter eras.

Today about 2.5 million people live in the Sahara near oases or in the highlands, where the climate is slightly wetter. In the desert people make a living much the same way desert people made a living more than 1,000 years ago: through pastoralism and trade. Regular trade across the Sahara began around the first century, when camels were introduced to the region. The staple goods of the trans-Sahara trade were GOLD, slaves (see SLAVE TRADE), salt, textiles, and weapons. Over the centuries three major routes evolved. One crossed the desert from present,-day Morocco to the ancient Soninke kingdom of GHANA, near the Senegal River. The second crossed from present-day western Algeria to the SONGHAI kingdom near the bend of the NIGER RIVER. The third route crossed from present-day Tripolitania to the kingdom of Kanem, just east of Lake Chad. All three routes were in frequent use by 900 A.D.

In addition to serving as a conduit for trade, the Sahara served as a refuge for political and religious groups. In the 10th and 11th centuries, when Sunni and Shiite Muslims defeated the Ibadi Muslims of the Maghreb, the Ibadi Muslims retreated to the Sahara and formed an independent state in the Fezzan. They have survived as independent communities ever since in Wadi Mzab (Algeria) and Jabal Nafusa (Libya).

In the western portion of the Sahara, the Almoravids, a puritanical and militaristic Muslim sect comprised primarily of Sanhaja Bergers, launched invasions from the desert. In 1078 the Almoravid army sacked Kumbi Salheh, the capital city of Ghana, and took control of the trans-Sahara trade route that ran from Morocco to Ghana. By 1100 the Almoravids controlled territory as far north as Spain and as far south as the kingdom of Ghana. The Almoravid Empire collapsed in the mid-12th century, and most of the Almoravids retreated to the desert. Ghana never fully recovered to its previous level of political and economic power in the western regions.

As European explorers slowly inched their way around the coast of West Africa seeking direct access to the gold fields of the west African kingdoms, trade across the Sahara continued. By 1578 the Portuguese were prepared to launch a major offensive against the Moroccan kingdom in an effort to gain a major foothold in West Africa. The Portuguese suffered a devastating defeat. Inspired by victory, the Moroccans began organizing an assault on the Songhai kingdom across the Sahara. In 1591 they were successful, yet within decades, despite maintaining official power, real control of the desert region reverted to the Tuaregs, the original inhabitants of the Sahara.

In the central region of the Sahara, power changed hands in the 16th century as well. Sultan Idris Aloma of Bornu conquered the old kingdom of Kanem and exerted its control over the desert region and its trade until the 17th century. Then Kel Owey, a Tuareg leader, defeated the Bornu army, giving the Tuareg political control of the central Sahara region until the onset of colonialism.

Further reading: Tony Allan and Andrew Warren, eds., *Deserts: The Encroaching Wilderness: A World Conservation Atlas* (New York: Oxford University Press, 1993); Colin McEvedy, *The Penguin Atlas of African History,* rev. ed. (Harmondsworth, U.K.: Penguin, 1995).

— Tom Niermann

Sandoval, Gonzalo de (ca. 1500–ca. 1528)

One of the highest-ranking officers under HERNÁN CORTÉS, Sandoval played a crucial role in the conquest of the AZTECS before emerging as a successful CONQUISTADOR in his own right.

Sandoval was not even 20 when he joined Cortés's expedition in 1519. Although he was relatively inexperienced, his intelligence, courage, and sharp military mind quickly earned him Cortés's admiration. In fact, Cortés always called him *hijo* ("son") and increasingly came to depend on Sandoval over the next 10 years. Sandoval repaid Cortés with his unswerving loyalty. In 1520, when Cortés had established himself in the Aztecs' capital of TENOCHTITLÁN, he selected Sandoval to command the garrison at VERACRUZ. Cortés correctly suspected that his political enemy, DIEGO DE VELÁZQUEZ, would eventually send troops against him and claim MEXICO for himself. Later that year Sandoval discovered that Velázquez's agent, PÁNFILO DE NARVÁEZ, had landed with the intention of arresting Cortés. Sandoval alerted Cortés of these developments, captured the enemy scouting party, and sent spies to monitor Narváez's movements. Once Cortés arrived on the coast, Sandoval joined with him and defeated Narváez's forces.

Sandoval remained with Cortés, serving as his third in command (under PEDRO DE ALVARADO) and taking an active role in almost every major event of the conquest. On the eve of the Spaniards' disastrous retreat from Tenochtitlán, Cortés sent Sandoval to reconnoiter the causeway to TACUBA, the shortest escape route out of the island city. During the retreat itself Sandoval led the advance column and received several wounds. He waited with Cortés in TLAXCALA while the Spaniards regained their strength. Between 1520 and 1521 Cortés sent Sandoval on a series of expeditions against cities in the Valley of Mexico who were allied to the Aztecs, laying the groundwork for the eventual siege of Tenochtitlán. Also in Tlaxcala, the Spaniards' shipwrights constructed a small fleet of BRIGANTINES to attack Tenochtitlán by water. When finished, Cortés chose Sandoval to lead the armed guard that escorted the fleet overland from Tlaxcala to Lake Texcoco. When the main assault on Tenochtitlán began in 1521, Sandoval first crushed Iztapalapa, the last lakeside city allied with the Aztecs. Then he took command of the northern front, attacking Tenochtitlán along the causeway leading from the city of Tepeyac. Sandoval proved to be one of the Spaniards' most skilled captains, leading his assaults from the front lines. By the time Tenochtitlán fell, the Aztecs had come to respect and fear Sandoval, seeing him as one of their most dangerous foes.

After the Aztecs had been defeated, Cortés sent Sandoval on a series of missions across Mexico. Between 1521 and 1522 Sandoval undertook a major expedition to the area south of Veracruz, pacifying the area around the Coatzacoalcos River and founding the town of Espiritu Santo near the Gulf Coast. In 1523 he crossed over to the Pacific coast, subduing the city of Acapulco and marching northward to Colima, where he founded several towns. Sandoval accompanied Cortés on the harrowing expedition to Honduras from 1524 to 1526. In 1527, as a reward for his efforts, he received a substantial ENCOMIENDA in the TARASCAN territory of Michoacán, although he did not live long enough to enjoy it. Sandoval accompanied Cortés on his triumphant return to Spain in 1528, when he developed a fever. His condition deteriorated quickly, and he stopped to rest in a villa near Palos. Deathly weak, he watched helplessly as his host stole most of his valuables. He lived only long enough to report the theft, dying at age 28. His death was a deep and lasting blow to Cortés, who lost not only his most steadfast ally but a young man he looked upon as his own son.

Further reading: Hernán Cortés, *Letters from Mexico* (New Haven, Conn.: Yale University Press, 1986); Bernal Diaz del Castillo, *The Discovery and Conquest of Mexico* (New York: Da Capo Press, 1996); Peter Gerhard, *A Guide to the Historical Geography of New Spain* (Norman: University of Oklahoma Press, 1993).

— Scott Chamberlain

Sandys, Sir Edwin (1561–1629)

An English parliamentarian, Sandys was also instrumental in the promotion of colonization in Virginia as treasurer of the Virginia Company

Born the second son to the archbishop of York, Sandys was also the older brother of George Sandys, a poet and Virginia colonist. After graduating from Corpus Christi College in 1579, he studied law, traveled, and entered Parliament. Noted early in his governmental career for his support of JAMES I, who knighted Sandys upon his coronation, he later led the parliamentary opposition, although he managed to retain the favor of the king. However, it was in the realm of overseas ventures and colonization efforts where Sandys achieved his real fame.

In 1607 Sandys invested in the newly formed Virginia Company of London, a joint stock company established by a group of affluent merchants and gentry. He later served as the company's treasurer from 1619 to 1624. This period coincided with an upswing in English colonization efforts, but it did not come without a rough beginning. The company's initial efforts at Jamestown bogged down, almost literally, as colonists suffered from typhoid fever, dysentery, malaria, and salt poisoning, all brought on from drinking the water from the muddy James River. In addition, management of the settlement proved disastrous. Negative reports, including one written by George Percy, one of the leaders in the colonization effort, filtered back to England. The company hit a low point around 1616. Undeterred, the Virginia Company circulated propaganda of its own, including the anonymously written *A True Declaration of the Estate of the Colonie in Virginia.*

Sandys is often credited with helping revise the flagging enterprise by becoming the moving force behind a series of reforms in 1618. The reforms paved the way for rapid growth of private plantations, ensured the economic interests of the company as a totality, and encouraged would-be settlers. Before 1618 plantations were few and the colony's population numbered no more than 400 persons. In addition, the colonists endured martial law while lacking commodities other than TOBACCO, a condition Sandys denounced repeatedly.

Sandys, who lobbied for and became the company's treasurer in 1619, macromanaged affairs from abroad, never setting foot in the NEW WORLD. Scouring for colonists from the fringes of society, including vagrant boys and Pilgrims, legend states that Sandys helped establish a veritable flood of colonists after the resumption of emigration in 1618. More recent accounts stress the variety and skills of the settlers he was able to attract, thus demythologizing the legend that associated Sandys with "the sweepings of the London streets." Regardless, the flow of settlers to Jamestown and its environs continued through his tenure as treasurer, arriving at a rate of approximately 1,000 persons per year. Sandys's second major goal—reducing reliance on a single crop—proved elusive, as tobacco became the one safe and profitable return for plantation owners and joint stock investors alike, thus ensuring Virginia's continued existence.

The Virginia Company dissolved in 1624 amid squabbles between Sandys and his rivals, including Sir Thomas Smyth. Despite the dispute, Sandys remained a staunch advocate of English colonial ventures until his death in 1629. Although he is best known for his association with the Virginia Company, Sandys also served a short stint as director of both the EAST INDIA COMPANY and the Somers Island Company.

Further reading: Edmund S. Morgan, "The First American Boom: Virginia 1618–1630," *William and Mary Quarterly,* 3d ser., 28 (1971); Theodore K. Rabb, *Enterprise and Empire: Merchant and Gentry Investment in the Expansion of England 1575–1630* (Cambridge, Mass.: Harvard

University Press, 1967); ———, *Jacobean Gentleman: Sir Edwin Sandys* (Princeton, N.J.: Princeton University Press, 1998); David Ransome, ed., *The Ferrar Papers, 1590–1790* (microform) (West Yorkshire, U.K.: Microform Academic Publishers, 1992).

— Matthew Lindaman

San Martín de Porres   See Porres, St. Martín de

Santa Fe

Santa Fe was the capital of Spanish NEW MEXICO (a territory within the viceroyalty of NEW SPAIN), an isolated frontier settlement that remains the second-oldest European city in what is today the United States of America.

The site of Santa Fe had been inhabited long before the Europeans arrived in the 1500s. The natives lived in pueblos, or multistoried apartment complexes arrayed around a ceremonial plaza. Long before Europeans arrived, the site of Santa Fe was occupied by the Kuapoge pueblo, but it had been more recently built up as the Analco pueblo by the 1540s. Other pueblos lay close to the site, including Quemado Pueblo (Aqua Fria) and Ohke Pueblo. In 1581 Franciscan missionaries from MEXICO began moving into to the region, establishing a network of missions that contained more than 8,000 converts by 1600. In April 1598 the CONQUISTADOR JUAN DE OÑATE arrived, hoping to establish permanent Spanish settlements. Oñate set up a base camp at the site of the Ohke Pueblo, which he renamed San Juan. The region received adequate rainfall and lay on an alluvial flood plain that facilitated agriculture. Within a few years the cramped quarters at San Juan caused the colonists to relocate to the nearby Yúngé Pueblo, which was renamed San Gabriel. Over time population pressure forced some of the colonists to move again. In 1609 Oñate's successor, Don Pedro de Peralta, organized a new settlement called Santa Fe (its official name was La Villa Real de la Santa Fe de San Francisco de Asis), designating it the capital of the colony of New Mexico.

The site of the new Santa Fe offered many attractions for the colonists. It was located at the foot of a mountain range called the Sangre de Cristo along the small Santa Fe River. While much of the surrounding region was rather dry, the site of Santa Fe received a good amount of rain, and the river supplied enough water for daily use and limited irrigation. While there were several settlements in the area, it was not overcrowded, and it allowed for future expansion. Perhaps more important, the site was more defensible than the open site of San Gabriel. Because Santa Fe was the northernmost city of the viceroyalty of New Spain, it needed to be militarily self-reliant. Much of the surrounding countryside was potentially hostile, and native raiders from farther north remained a real threat. If the site was attacked, no reinforcements would arrive for months, if the government bothered to send them at all. Fifty settlers arrived initially, although the population eventually grew to around 200 Spaniards and between 700 and 1,000 natives.

The city of Santa Fe reflected an amalgamation of native and Spanish urban designs. Peralta tried as much as possible to make the new town into a true Spanish city. To this end, he performed the traditional ceremony of foundation as stipulated by royal decree. He also followed the royal edicts of 1573 in determining how the city should be laid out. As a result, much of the city's spatial orientation was Spanish. He established the Spanish town proper on the north bank of the Santa Fe River, forcing natives at the site to build a separate community on the south bank. He followed the guidelines in the establishment of the main plaza, the principal streets, and various lots, paying close attention to the location of the main church, which was located on the east side of the main plaza. He also established a presidio, or fortress, to defend the site, making sure it was adequately armed and supplied. However, despite Peralta's attempt to make his new town as Spanish as possible, Santa Fe had a distinct native feel to it. For one, Spaniards frequently adopted native building materials. They found that adobe was an abundant, cost-effective material that suited the environment of the site. It was cool in the summer but retained heat during the winter. Later governors grumbled that Santa Fe's adobe architecture made it look like a "heathen Timbuktu" built of mud. Moreover, many of the buildings were built in native style, closely resembling the pueblos of the region. This was partially due to the fact that most of the workers erecting the buildings were natives who followed traditional practices. Still, the Spaniards found that the native-style buildings fit well in the environment.

As a frontier town, the citizens of Santa Fe spent most of their energy pacifying the surrounding region. Most of the original settlers were soldiers who were attempting to subdue and control this frontier zone. They were also attempting to relocate natives into Spanish-style towns, hoping that the Spanish environment and Spanish cultural forms would convert Indians to European ways and enable them to become loyal to the king. In fact, the greatest number of inhabitants of Santa Fe were relocated natives, and it seems clear that without them the settlement would have quickly perished. Assisting the military in this attempt to spread Spanish culture was the clergy, who were also based in Santa Fe. The main church in the city served as a religious capital for the region, a sort of headquarters where missionaries met and devised strategies for converting the local populace. They were successful in this aim: By 1630 more than 60,000 natives had converted to Christianity. Besides their religious teachings, many of the missionaries taught natives Spanish as well.

Although Santa Fe was an isolated frontier town, its history was hardly uneventful. The region was raided constantly by the Apache and Navajo. The Spaniards struck back in turn, capturing natives and frequently enslaving them. At times tensions in the area ran quite high, although nothing in the early history of Santa Fe compared to the later Pueblo Revolt of 1680, when natives banded together to drive the Spaniards out of New Mexico.

Further reading: Dora P. Crouch, Daniel J. Garr, and Axel I. Mundigo, *Spanish City Planning in North America* (Cambridge, Mass.: Massachusetts Institute of Technology Press, 1982); Carlos Fernández-Shaw, *The Hispanic Presence in North America from 1492 to Today* (New York: Facts On File, 1991); David J. Weber, *The Spanish Frontier in North America* (New Haven, Conn.: Yale University Press, 1992).

— Scott Chamberlain

São Tomé

Located 180 miles off the western coast of Africa, São Tomé was claimed by Portuguese explorers in the late 15th century and became a testing ground for a type of plantation agriculture that became a model for the agricultural exploitation of the Americas.

São Tomé was a nearly unpopulated island in an archipelago off the western coast of Africa (see also PRÍNCIPE and FERNANDO PO) when the Portuguese explorer Álvaro da Caminha, a member of the Portuguese royal household, landed there in 1476. Caminha initiated large-scale settlement of the island in 1492, although the settlers he attracted were a mixed lot. In 1492 he forcibly resettled several hundred Jewish children aged two through 12 whom the Portuguese authorities had removed from their parents. Many of these parentless children died, but about 600 of them remained on the island in the early 16th century. In addition to children, Caminha imported more than 1,000 slaves and criminals to the island between 1493 and 1500, pairing each male convict with a female slave, presumably to encourage population growth on the island. This policy had a dramatic effect on the ethnic composition of the colony: Within a few decades the majority of São Tomé's population were MESTIZOS, or descendants of one European and one native parent.

SUGAR was São Tomé's main source of profit in its early years as a Portuguese colony. The island's tropical climate made it ideal for growing sugarcane, and planters and their slaves cleared the rain forests that covered the island to provide land for sugar planting. They used the timber to build more ships for Portugal's many seafaring ventures. The sugar economy boomed in the early part of the 16th century, largely due to the fact that the climate made it possible to plant year round and to harvest two full crops. Production jumped from 70 metric tons in 1529 to 2,000 in 1550 and 2,800 in 1570.

São Tomé's other main source of profit was its position as a way station on the transatlantic SLAVE TRADE. In 1500 alone some 5,000 to 6,000 slaves were exported from the African mainland to the island. Some of the men, women, and children stayed on São Tomé, serving as the labor force on one of many sugar plantations, but many were shipped off to the NEW WORLD to replace native Caribbean populations that had been nearly wiped out in the wake of the European conquests.

Portuguese São Tomé fell on hard times in the late 16th century. The development of large-scale sugar production in BRAZIL undercut São Tomé's main source of income. Economic decline was followed by a series of catastrophes. In 1567 a French pirate sacked and burned much of the island. Slaves burned crops and buildings in uprisings in 1574 and 1595. The Dutch rounded off this half century of disasters by attacking the island in 1598–99. By 1615 59 of São Tomé's 72 plantations had been abandoned. The Dutch eventually took over São Tomé for a brief period in the mid-17th century, after which it reverted to Portuguese ownership (although never reaching its former prosperity) until it gained independence in the 1970s.

Further reading: Tony Hodges and Malyn Newitt, *São Tomé and Príncipe: From Plantation Colony to Microstate* (Boulder, Colo.: Westview Press, 1988).

— Marie A. Kelleher

Secotan

The ALGONQUIAN who lived in Secotan (or Secoton), a village near the coast of present-day North Carolina, attracted the attention of JOHN WHITE and THOMAS HARRIOT, whose paintings and descriptions provide a valuable record of 16th-century Algonquian culture.

Secotan culture, like that of other Algonquian peoples in the region, appears to have been hierarchical. Harriot reported on the manners and dress of the "great lords," "chief ladies," and "priests" of the people. The people wore few clothes, usually little more than breechcloths or deerskin aprons or skirts, although they might also wear capes in cold weather. They decorated their bodies with paint and tattoos and wore copper and pearl jewelry.

Secotan, unlike some other villages in the region, was not surrounded by a defensive palisade. The people lived in longhouses that were covered with bark or woven mats. They practiced agriculture, raising CORN, beans, sunflowers, and other crops and supplemented these foods with meat and fish.

John White's painting of Secotan showed the people performing a variety of tasks. Several figures stood outside or walked through the village, while others ate from dishes placed on a mat on the ground. In one of the cornfields, a figure perched on a platform to scare away birds. White also showed two circular areas of ritual significance, both surrounded by carved posts. In the larger circle he painted a ring of dancing figures participating in a religious ceremony.

Harriot and White depicted the people of Secotan and their neighbors sympathetically. They did not portray the Indians as faceless savages, but as individual human beings living in an ordered society. As the historian Karen Ordahl Kupperman observed, "White and Harriot together argued in the most forceful and effective way that the American natives were social beings, possessing all the characteristics necessary to civility: community life and the family structure, hierarchy, and orderliness that made it possible; care for the morrow by cultivating and preserving foods; and all informed by a religious sensibility that honored the human dependence on supernatural forces in the universe."

Further reading: Thomas Harriot, *A Briefe and True Report of the New Found Land of Virginia* (New York: Dover Publications, 1972); Karen Ordahl Kupperman, *Indians and English: Facing Off in Early America* (Ithaca, N.Y.: Cornell University Press, 2000); ———, *Roanoke: The Abandoned Colony* (Totowa, N.J.: Rowman & Allanheld, 1984); David Beers Quinn, *Set Fair for Roanoke: Voyages and Colonies, 1584–1606* (Chapel Hill: University of North Carolina Press, 1985).

— Martha K. Robinson

Seneca

As "guardians of the western door" in the metaphorical longhouse of the IROQUOIS Confederacy, the Seneca (People of the Big Hill) consisted of two main groups occupying two principal villages (along with several smaller ones) at the time of contact by Europeans.

The western band of the Seneca lived around the Genessee and Allegheny Rivers, and the eastern one near Canandaigua Lake in present-day New York State (Livingston and Ontario Counties). Their location put them closest to the western beaver hunting grounds that came to figure so prominently in the 17th-century fur trade. They were also the most populous tribe within the alliance, probably surpassing the combined numbers of the other Iroquois nations (MOHAWK, ONEIDA, ONONDAGA, and CAYUGA).

Despite their numbers, the Seneca held only eight seats (the fewest of any of the Five Nations) in the league's Grand Council. Together with the Onondaga and Mohawk, they represented the "Older Brothers" in this political structure. Nevertheless, their role as protectors of the western flank of Iroquoia from encroachment by whites and their native allies and as guarantors of access to hunting territory pivotal in the fur trade was instrumental in the preservation and power of the confederacy. In fact, the Seneca had helped expand the league's influence by the mid-16th century by moving their villages northward and continued to bargain from a position of strength during most of the colonial period. While they did not escape the changes wrought by contact, including losses to DISEASE and warfare, they held onto cherished ideals and homelands in the face of such adversity and thrived in the area until after the American Revolution.

Further reading: Thomas S. Abler and Elisabeth Tooker, "Seneca," in William Sturtevant, ed., *Handbook of North American Indians*, vol. 15, *Northeast,* vol. ed. Bruce G. Trigger (Washington, D.C.: Smithsonian Institution Press, 1978), 505–517; Marilyn L. Haas, *Seneca and Tuscarora Indians: An Annotated Bibliography* (Hamden, Conn.: Library Professional Publications, 1994); Arthur C. Parker, *History of the Seneca Indians* (Port Washington, N.Y.: I. J. Friedman, 1967); Anthony F. C. Wallace, with the assistance of Sheila C. Steen, *The Death and Rebirth of the Seneca* (New York: Knopf, 1970).

— Eric P. Anderson

Senegambia

Senegambia, the region through which the Senegal and Gambia Rivers flow, is where Saharan and Sudanic history and culture mixed.

Senegambia became a unique meeting ground where peoples of the savanna, desert, and rain forests met and interacted. Among the peoples who lived in Senegambia were the Wolof, Tukolor, Pullo, Manding, Berber, Serer, Susu, Nalu, Diola, Baga, Beafada, Bainuk, and Tenda.

The first governments appeared in the 15th century. Power usually stemmed from control of a river. In the south the KAABU dominated, but they were tributaries to the MALI Empire. In the north along the Senegal River, the Tekrur and Silla maintained control but were later deposed by the Wolof. Senegambian kingdoms operated according to a castelike system that reinforced political hierarchies.

As the Portuguese colonized the Cape Verde Islands in the 15th and 16th centuries, they gradually redirected trade from the interior to the coast. The new Atlantic trade, which focused on GOLD, ivory, and slaves (see SLAVE TRADE), had political consequences. The Kaabu were able to extricate themselves from Mali dominance and became the local dominant power. The Toli Tenegela, by contrast, emigrated and eventually created the Denyankan kingdom that challenged Wolof dominance in the north.

The arrival of Dutch, English, and French traders broke the Portuguese monopoly. The European powers divided the coast into spheres of influence, with trading centers such as Saint Louis, GORÉE ISLAND, Fort James, Cacheu, and Bissau. Slaves soon became the leading export, coming from as far away as the mouth of the NIGER RIVER.

Further reading: G. E. Brooks, Jr., *Yankee Traders, Old Coasters, and African Middlemen* (Brookline, Mass.: Boston University Press, 1970); ———, *Kola Trade and State Building: Upper Guinea Coast and Senegambia, 15th–17th Centuries* (Brookline, Mass.: Boston University Press, 1980); Philip D. Curtin, *Economic Change in Precolonial Africa: Senegambia in the Era of The Slave Trade.* 2 vols. Madison: University of Wisconsin Press, 1975); Charlotte A. Quinn, *Mandingo Kingdoms of the Senegambia: Traditionalism, Islam, and European Expansion* (London: Longman, 1972).

— Tom Niermann

Sepúlveda, Juan Ginés de

A leading humanist of 16th-century Spain, Juan de Sepúlveda argued that the native peoples of the Western Hemisphere were inherently inferior to Europeans.

Sepúlveda was a formidable figure in the intellectual life of Spain. He was a dedicated scholar who had studied Aristotle and other classical authors. Erasmus referred to him as "the Spanish Livy." He is known to have had close contact with several CONQUISTADORES and wealthy landowners in the Americas. More important, he had a number of powerful friends at court, which ensured that his ideas carried enormous weight with the royal government. Today Sepúlveda is primarily remembered for his pivotal debate with BARTOLOMÉ DE LAS CASAS, which took place in 1550. Las Casas, a champion of indigenous rights, had bitterly attacked a number of colonial institutions, particularly the *ENCOMIENDA*, as being destructive not only to the natives, but to the Spanish colonies as a whole. Moreover, he argued that they were abhorrent before God and predicted divine retribution unless they were repealed. Concerned, CHARLES V invited both Las Casas and Sepúlveda to argue their cases before the court in Valladolid.

A popular misconception exists about the nature of this great debate. The two figures did not stand before the court, trading insults and flourishes of rhetoric, but rather addressed the court separately. Sepúlveda spoke first, taking three hours to state his position. He argued that natives were inherently inferior to Europeans and that the Spaniards were justified in conquering them for four reasons. First, because of their idolatry and worship of "demons," the natives had committed mortal sins against God and deserved punishment. Second, the "barbarous" nature of their habits and customs fit into the Aristotelian notion that some humans are born inferior and could thus be enslaved. Third, the most effective way to convert the natives and bring them into civilization was through conquest. Unless the Spaniards used deadly force, he argued, the natives would never willingly give up their religion. Finally, a general conquest of the area would allow the Crown to protect the weaker, less "savage" natives from the depredations of their more violent neighbors. After an adjournment, Las Casas devoted five days to a rebuttal. There was no proclaimed "victor" to the debate, but ultimately the court sided with Las Casas. As a result, many of the laws passed after 1550 reflected a new concern for the plight of the natives, in accordance with Las Casas's arguments.

Sepúlveda's controversial opinions were widely read in Europe, particularly by Spain's enemies in England, France, and the Netherlands. In these areas Sepúlveda was seen as proof that the Spaniards were cruel, vicious, and warlike. These ideas formed one of the cornerstones of the BLACK LEGEND of Spanish cruelty in the Americas.

Further reading: Lewis Hanke, *The Spanish Search for Justice in the Conquest of America* (Philadelphia: University of Pennsylvania Press, 1949); Benjamin Keen, *The Aztec Image in Western Thought* (New Brunswick, N.J.: Rutgers University Press, 1971); Bartolomé de Las Casas, *The Devastation of the Indies: A Brief Account* (Baltimore: Johns Hopkins University Press, 1992).

— Scott Chamberlain

Seville

The capital of the Spanish province of Andalusia, Seville benefited from its monopoly on the Indies trade to become the commercial center of the Spanish Empire during the 16th century.

Seville, the capital of the Spanish province of Andalusia, is located on the banks of the Guadalquivir River in southern Spain. Recaptured from Muslim rulers in the 13th century (see RECONQUISTA), the city continued to bear witness to Arab cultural influence, most dramatically illustrated by the cathedral's spire, which had once been the minaret of Muslim Seville's grand mosque.

While Madrid was the political and administrative center of the Spanish Habsburg empire, Seville was a thriving commercial center that grew to rival Madrid in wealth during Spain's Golden Age. Seville's trade-based economy was one of three distinct economies within

Spanish Iberia: Seville and its hinterlands were oriented toward the NEW WORLD; Castile's wool trade encouraged economic ties with the cloth markets of northern Europe; and the Crown of Aragón, absorbed by CASTILE in the 15th century, maintained its centuries-long mercantile orientation toward the Mediterranean. Seville's star reached its zenith during the final decades of the 16th century and the first decades of the 17th century—not coincidentally the high point of the Indies trade, in which Seville held a shipping monopoly.

An edict of 1503 established the CASA DE CONTRATACIÓN at Seville. The institution operated out of the royal palace of Alcazar as a sort of chamber of commerce, administering colonial shipping between Spain and the Indies, enforcing trade regulations, organizing merchant fleets, training captains and navigators, serving as a tribunal for maritime legal cases, and assuring that the Crown received its one-fifth share of all SILVER from the Americas.

One of the most important regulations that the Casa de Contratación enforced was Seville's monopoly as the port of entry for colonial shipping. Despite the apparent restrictions on foreign involvement in the Indies trade, it was this very trade that made Seville into one of the most cosmopolitan cities in Europe at the time. Foreign merchants and traders, most notably French and Genoans, moved to Spain to capitalize on the wealth generated by the transatlantic trade. Seville's monopoly of trade with the Indies made it the preferred destination for these foreign entrepreneurs. Spanish monarchs had issued edicts banning non-Castilians from trade with Spanish colonies in the Americas, but foreign merchants evaded trade restrictions by hiring locals to fill out the paperwork, thus assuring that the merchant of record was Castilian. Foreign business interests might also act less directly, establishing connections with Spanish "factors," or agents, in Seville in order to buy and sell goods in the lucrative trade with the Americas.

Foreigners contributed to Seville's swelling population. In the course of the 60 years between 1530 and 1590, Seville's population increased by almost 140 percent—an increase all the more noteworthy when viewed in the context of the general population decline of other Castilian towns. In the second half of the 16th century, Seville's population reached a total of 150,000, making Seville 50 percent larger than Madrid and the third-largest city in western Europe at the time, surpassed only by Paris and Naples.

Seville's large foreign population was not the only way in which it differed demographically from the rest of Spain. The *hidalgos*, or poor nobility, so common to most of Castile, were hardly present in Seville. Instead, the upper classes were dominated by aristocratic families who, attracted by the growing wealth of the city, made their primary residences there while living off the wealth generated by large landholdings in the Guadalquivir valley. New wealth lived alongside old as wealthy merchant families strove to ennoble themselves by buying titles and attempting to gain membership in the council of municipal magistrates known as the Twenty-Four. Whether old or new rich, the Sevillian upper classes were famed for their ostentation, and contemporaries remarked upon the opulence of Sevillian houses, dress, and public festivals.

At the opposite end of the socioeconomic spectrum were the peasants of Seville's hinterlands, who also profited from the burgeoning trade economy. The estates of the Guadalquivir valley produced grains, olives, and wine grapes both for the Indies trade and for consumption by the massive urban population. As a result, some Andalusian peasants were able to profit to such an extent that they themselves became owners of substantial tracts of land. Slaves constituted the final piece of Seville's human landscape. Slaves were much more numerous in Andalusia than in other parts of Spain due to the links between the transatlantic slave trade and the Sevillian-dominated Indies trade. Sevillian slaves were usually baptized Christians, sometimes even forming their own pious confraternities.

Seville began to decline in importance during the 17th century as other nations encroached upon the Indies trade, although it remained a significant commercial center until the Bourbon monarchs moved the Casa de Contratación to Cádiz in 1717. Nevertheless, even during its heyday Seville was not without its problems. The city was beset by corruption as officials sought to claim a portion of the city's enormous wealth for themselves. Philip IV rebuked the municipal magistrates in 1621 for neglecting the public welfare for personal gain, and with good reason. Magistrates were often in league with speculators, maintaining high prices; they neglected public sanitation, leading to epidemics; and they did nothing to stem the corruption and bribery that ran rampant in Seville's judicial system.

Further reading: Marcelin Defourneaux, *Daily Life in Spain in the Golden Age* (Stanford, Calif.: Stanford University Press, 1979); J. H. Elliott, *Imperial Spain, 1496–1716* (New York: St. Martin's Press, 1977); John Lynch, *Spain 1516–1598: From Nation State to World Empire* (Oxford: Blackwell, 1992); Ruth Pike, *Aristocrats and Traders: Sevillian Society in the Sixteenth Century* (Ithaca, N.Y.: Cornell University Press, 1972).

— Marie A. Kelleher

Shakespeare, William (1564–1616)

An English playwright and poet, William Shakespeare is often considered the greatest dramatist the world has ever known and the most recognized poet in the English language.

Born the third of eight children to a middling family in Stratford-upon-Avon in 1564, William Shakespeare was the son of John Shakespeare, a glove maker by trade, who owned a small shop and served for a time as Stratford-upon-Avon's elected bailiff, or mayor. Although he faced pecuniary difficulties later in his life, John was able to provide young William with a sound educational background. Scholars believe that by the age of seven, William began attending Stratford's grammar school, where he spent about nine hours a day learning Latin and reading from the classic authors, including Seneca, Ovid, Terence, Cicero, and Virgil. Stratford's lively nature as a market center further stimulated Shakespeare's imagination, exposing him to popular pageants, large fairs, plays, and visitors from afar.

Shakespeare penned at least 37 plays, traditionally divided into the genres of histories, comedies, and tragedies. Containing character types from all walks of life—including kings, generals, shepherds, philosophers, pickpockets, and drunkards—Shakespeare delved into seemingly every type of human nature. With his unique talent for psychological penetration, Shakespeare's characters possess meaning beyond the time and place of his plays. Shakespeare's writings have helped shape the attitudes of millions of people on topics such as romantic love, heroism, and the nature of tragedy.

In addition to his deep understanding of human nature, Shakespeare displayed knowledge in a wide variety of other subjects including, but certainly not limited to, politics, music, law, scripture, hunting, woodcraft, sports, art, and the sea. However, despite these intellectual flourishes, scholars do not believe he had professional experience in any areas outside of theatre. That Shakespeare was interested in politics is apparent from both his historical plays and his many references to contemporary political figures and events. By today's standards he was a political conservative, accepting the power structure and social rankings of his day while displaying unwavering patriotism. Taking the new commercialism and pleasures of the Elizabethan age in stride, he was always careful not to offend Queen ELIZABETH I.

In 1582 Shakespeare married Anne Hathaway. One year later, on May 26, 1583, their first child, Susanna, was baptized. In 1585 Anne gave birth to twins—a girl, Judith, and a boy, Hamnet. From the period of their baptism on February 2, 1585, until 1592, there is little recorded evidence of Shakespeare's whereabouts. Scholars refer to this period as the lost years. By 1592 evidence from a theatrical pamphlet places Shakespeare in London, where he probably began by serving as an apprentice in the city's bustling theatrical life. Scholars are not certain which company or companies Shakespeare joined before 1594. At that time records indicate he was a shareholder in a popular theatrical company known as Lord Chamberlin's Men. In addition, records indicate that by 1594 Shakespeare had produced six plays.

Between 1592 and 1594 many of London's theaters closed down because of continued outbreaks of the PLAGUE. During this time he turned to the medium of poetry as an outlet for his writing talents, penning *Venus and Adonis* and *The Rape of Lucrece.* When the theaters reopened in 1594, Shakespeare devoted his full capacities to London's theater world. In 1597 he wrote the tragedy *Romeo and Juliet,* transforming an old popular story into a tale of "star-cross'd lovers." Between 1598 and 1608 Shakespeare's output was astonishing. During that decade he wrote the classic tragedies—*Hamlet, Othello, King Lear, Macbeth, Antony and Cleopatra,* and *Julius Caesar*—as well as the comedies *Much Ado About Nothing* and *Twelfth Night* and the history *Henry V.* It is possible that no other playwright in the Western world ever had a more productive decade.

In addition to writing plays, Shakespeare participated in the full range of the theatrical experience, including acting, directing, and even owning stock in a number of theater companies. Business records indicate that by the turn of the century he had acquired a comfortable degree of financial success. In 1599 Shakespeare and six associates became owners of the Globe Theatre, a new outdoor venue in the London suburb of Southwark. One of the largest theaters in the London area during the Elizabethan Age, the Globe is believed to have held as many as 3,000 spectators. After purchasing the Globe, his new theater troupe, the King's Men, continued to enjoy unparalleled theatrical success. The company took out a 21-year lease on the Blackfriars Theatre in 1608. Located in a heavily populated area of London known as Blackfriars, the theater served as the company's winter playhouse, while the Globe hosted productions in the summer. In addition, the King's Men made regular appearances at the royal court for both Elizabeth I and her successor, James VI of Scotland, known as JAMES I of England.

During the last eight years of his life, Shakespeare's writing production slowed as he wrote only four plays—*Cymbeline, Henry VIII,* THE TEMPEST, and *The Winter's Tale.* There exists some scholarly dispute concerning which play was his last, *The Tempest* (written about 1610) or *Henry VIII* (written sometime between 1610 and 1613).

Shakespeare's last direct descendent, a granddaughter named Elizabeth, died in 1670, leaving no further heirs. His literary legacy lasted much longer than his family line. As Shakespeare's contemporary, the classical dramatist Ben Jonson, put it, "He was not of an age, but for all time."

Further reading: S. H. Burton, *Shakespeare: Life and Stage* (Edinburgh: 1989); Park Honan, *Shakespeare: A Life* (New York: Oxford University Press, 1998); Emrys Jones, *The Origins of Shakespeare* (Oxford, U.K: Clarendon Press, 1977); John Palmer, *The Political Characters of Shakespeare*

(London, Macmillan 1961); A. L. Rowse, *Shakespeare the Elizabethan* (New York: Putnam, 1977); Robert Shaughnessy, *Representing Shakespeare: England, History, and the RSC* (New York: Harvester Wheatsheaf, 1994).

— Matthew Lindaman

silver

Silver and GOLD mining in NEW SPAIN, along with trade established with East Asia, helped make Spain the richest and most powerful country in the world during the 15th and most of the 16th century, and silver mining remained a cornerstone in the Spanish American economy until the end of the colonial era.

Long before CHRISTOPHER COLUMBUS made his historic discovery, the peoples of the Old World were obsessed with silver. Various coins (known as *grouch* or *grouck*) made of silver circulated in Istanbul and from there outward to the East Indies. Although no silver could be mined in India, silver rupees were in wide circulation by the 16th century. Under the dynasty of the Mings (1368–1644), elite members of Chinese societies traded silver ingots in their transactions, although the value of silver kept it out of the hands of most of the population. Europeans, too, had long come to value silver; they developed elaborate technology for finding silver mines, evident at the famous mine at Croix-de-Lorraine in the Vosges. Such mechanical innovation helped Europeans to increase the rate of silver production by perhaps 500 per cent from 1460 to 1530. Still, no matter how inventive production became, it could not keep up with demand. Hence, Europeans' search for silver became a defining component of the age of expansion.

Desperate to find silver, the Spanish took advantage of indigenous knowledge concerning native mining locations and established settlements near rich silver deposits. Most of the silver-producing areas located before 1600 were situated in the central ANDES MOUNTAINS. In MEXICO the Spanish mined silver in the area stretching from Santa Barbara to Pachuca, including Guanajuato, Sombrerete, and ZACATECAS. The flood of silver and gold taken to Spain during the early colonial era caused inflation in the European economy. Because Spain had a constant flow of specie into its economy during the 16th and 17th centuries, the Spanish fell behind the rest of Europe in creating a domestic manufacturing economy, and this fact contributed to Spain's decline from its position of prestige and power during the late 17th and 18th century.

Most of the laborers used in Spanish silver mines before 1600 were Native Americans. At first, *encomenderos* sent natives assigned to them as part of their ENCOMIENDAs to work the mines. After the 1550s wage labor and drafts provided labor for the silver mines. The Spanish implemented the use of the REPARTIMIENTO to supply draft labor in Mexico. At POTOSÍ in the Andes, the draft was called the *mita,* and it provided more than 10,000 workers for the mines and the processing of ore, although the Spanish also relied on wage laborers to perform the work necessary in the mines.

Once the Spanish began to haul silver to the Old World, it spread everywhere. Mints in Delhi began to produce rupees once shipments of silver began to arrive from New Spain in 1542. The Chinese got silver from Spanish ships sailing west from New Spain toward Manila. As one commentator put it, Chinese merchants "would journey to hell" to get the goods they needed to trade for silver because, as one Chinese aphorism put it, *"plata sa sangre"*—"silver is blood." According to one estimate the Chinese received perhaps 1 million pesos worth of silver each year from New Spain, an extraordinary amount of precious metal that never reached Europe even though the trade enriched the Spanish.

Silver, like other commodities, fluctuated in price. From the 13th century to the mid-16th century its value increased, but by 1550 or so, when a new process of producing silver known as amalgam meant a dramatic expansion in production in the Western Hemisphere, its value slipped and inflation set in. Over time, production spread within the Americas, and silver recovered its value. In the end, one development was obvious: American silver enriched Spain by enabling it to overcome Europe's chronic shortage of specie (hard currency), although the commerce also prompted other nations to increase their efforts to establish colonies and mines in the Western Hemisphere.

Further reading: Peter Bakewell, *Miners of the Red Mountains: Indian Labor in Potosí, 1545–1650* (Albuquerque: University of New Mexico Press, 1984); Fernand Braudel, *The Structures of Everyday Life: Civilization and Capitalism 15th–18th Century,* 3 vols., trans. Siân Reynolds (New York: Harper & Row, 1979); Dennis O. Flynn, *World Silver and Monetary History in the 16th and 17th Centuries* (Aldershot, U.K.: Variorum, 1996); Enrique Tandeter, *Coercion and Market: Silver Mining in Colonial Potosi, 1662–1826* (Albuquerque: University of New Mexico Press, 1993); Immanuel Wallerstein, *The Modern World System I: Capitalist Agriculture and the Origins of the European World Economy in the Sixteenth Century* (San Diego, Calif.: Academic Press/Harcourt Brace Jovanovich, 1974).

— Dixie Ray Haggard

slavery

Ancient in its origins, slavery became of fundamental importance in the early modern Atlantic world when Europeans decided to transport thousands of Africans to the

Western Hemisphere to provide labor, especially for mines and plantation agriculture.

In 1492, the year that CHRISTOPHER COLUMBUS sailed west, slavery was an institution known in perhaps every society in the Atlantic world. Although the nature of slavery and the treatment of slaves varied from one place to another, the institution was based on the idea that certain human beings had a right to own others. In some societies the right to own slaves came to victors in war, who took captives and forced them to perform certain tasks. In other places men, women, and children who were enslaved could be bought and sold, and the commerce in human beings, known as the SLAVE TRADE, frequently led to slaves being forcibly moved far from their homelands. Although some scholars might dispute that slavery existed in many indigenous American nations, even in those societies individuals captured in hostilities often had to perform tasks for their captors. Some of the captives could also become adopted into families and integrated into new communities.

Before the early modern period many Europeans inhabited slave-owning societies. That is, they lived in communities in which individuals possessed slaves—individuals bound into forced labor—but local economies were rarely, if ever, dependent on the labor provided by the slaves. In these societies, those who became enslaved were those who committed certain crimes. For example, someone convicted of violating the English Vagrancy Act of 1547 could be sentenced to a two-year term of servitude. In some places such sentences were less desirable than capital punishment, but the forced labor demanded of a criminal was not the equivalent of slavery as it developed in the Atlantic world. Only in rare instances in Europe was slavery an inherited status that could be passed from parent to child. Further, although a master could control the labor of a convict, he or she could not treat the bound laborer as a piece of property; individuals retained certain basic rights as human beings, notably the right to life. In essence, according to European practice that existed from the age of Aristotle, slaves were subordinate members of families. By the early modern age precedent for such a belief was longstanding. Roman law recognized a *servus* ("slave") as an individual who was legally deficient—unable to be a witness, for example, or execute a will—but still a person.

Slavery existed in Africa long before Europeans began to colonize the continent. The institution thrived in Africa because, as the historian John Thornton has succinctly put it, "slaves were the only form of private, revenue-producing property recognized in African law." Africans were different from Europeans in this sense, because Europeans tended to own land, which became the basis for wealth; laws such as those governing primogeniture and ENTAIL kept land within individual families. Although they did not share Europeans' belief that land could be owned, Africans still held to notions that individuals and families could own property. Thus, slaves became for Africans a form of property that could be used to generate wealth; as Thornton noted, "slaves became the preeminent form of private investment and the manifestation of private wealth—a secure form of reproducing wealth equivalent to landowning in Europe."

Like Europeans, Africans tended to treat slaves as subordinate children. In KONGO, for example, the term *nleke* referred to both a slave and a child. Most slaves, of course, were not children. Men and women became enslaved when they were captured in war. That fact needs to be emphasized because it suggests that those who sold slaves were in the process of selling individuals who tended not to be from the sellers' own communities or cultures. Once enslaved, men and women often performed necessary tasks for elite groups, such as state officials who needed military assistance to advance their goals. Because African empires tended to result from the consolidation of smaller states, slaves bound to serve an empire could be used to suppress internal dissent. Documentary evidence suggests that slave armies were crucial in SUDAN, SONGHAI, Ndongo, and Kongo, among other places. Slavery existed in Muslim societies as well as non-Muslim because ISLAM, like Christianity, accepted slavery as a normal part of social order.

The slave trade began to take on its modern form when Europeans arrived in Africa and sought laborers. The fact that Europeans tended to land in cities where slavery existed and where local elites in all likelihood had their own slaves facilitated the first movements of bound African laborers to Europe, but the existence of slavery within Africa did not, in itself, lead to the slave trade. After all, the supply of slaves in Africa did not create a demand for slave labor in Europe and in European possessions in the Atlantic world. Rather, Europeans who were seeking laborers seized on an already existing institution and transformed it to meet their own interests. In the process the slave trade expanded in Europe when European and African slavers tried to meet growing demand by capturing new groups of potential slaves and sending them into servitude. Thus, the earliest organized transport of slaves from Africa to Europe took place when Portuguese mariners began to purchase near Senegal slaves who were already bound for the SAHARA. DIOGO GOMES's successful negotiations in West Africa led to an expansion of this early trade after 1456. Each year the Portuguese purchased up to 2,500 slaves who would otherwise have remained on the continent. The Portuguese did not take all of these bound laborers to Europe; they often resold the slaves to merchants in the GOLD COAST who had need for their labor and who already inhabited a society where the buying and selling of slaves was commonplace. By the mid-1510s Portuguese colonizers in the Tomistas Islands were importing perhaps 4,500 slaves each year, most of them from Kongo. That trade reflected the fact that Europeans had been gaining slaves not only from West Africa but also from the central parts of the continent as well. By the end of the 15th century, Europeans who wanted to purchase African slaves could do so in Valencia, SEVILLE, and LISBON. A commerce once confined to Africa had become a growing economic concern for Europeans poised to expand their horizons farther west into the Atlantic. However, it should be noted that at least some African states had begun to disassociate themselves from the trade.

From the start Africans and Europeans alike recognized that the Atlantic slave trade represented a new and ominous development. Perhaps it was that recognition that led the rulers of BENIN to halt their active participation in the Atlantic slave trade by 1550, and possibly as early as 1520. Gomes Eannes de Zurara, a courtier to the Portuguese Prince HENRY THE NAVIGATOR, recognized the human consequences of the slave trade when he witnessed a ship landing in Portugal in August 1444. "What heart could be so hard," he later wrote, "as not to be pierced with piteous feeling to see that company? For some kept their heads low, and their faces bathed in tears, looking upon one another. Others stood groaning very dolorously, looking up to the height of heaven, fixing their eyes upon it, crying out loudly, as if asking help from the Father of nature; others struck their faces with the palms of their hands, throwing themselves at full length upon the ground; while others made lamentations in the manner of a dirge, after the custom of their country." He also recognized one of the other defining features of slavery: the fact that slaves were often separated from friends and family members, thereby adding to the horrors they suffered. Prince Henry, for his part, took 46 of the 235 slaves who arrived, the "royal fifth" that was his due.

From the mid-15th century to the end of the century, Europeans purchased African slaves and transported them to the Continent or to European possessions in the Atlantic such as the Portuguese colonies on MADEIRA and the AZORES. By the end of the 15th century slaves could be found not only in the port at Seville, a logical destination, but in thriving Italian cities such as Rome, Florence, Genoa, and VENICE. Although the Portuguese became the most important intermediaries between Africa and Europe, over time slavers arrived in Africa from other European states as well. No country had a monopoly on the slave trade; by the end of the early modern period slaving vessels had emanated from across Europe.

Europeans purchased slaves because they needed their labor. While many Europeans probably would have preferred to employ other Europeans, the booming economy of the 16th-century Atlantic world encouraged colonizers to seek opportunity as quickly as possible. Spanish

colonizers in the Americas did enslave natives and forced others into tributary relationships to satisfy the economic desires of those who owned ENCOMIENDAs. But because the Spanish Crown feared that enslaving Indians represented a conflict with its goal to spread Catholicism among the natives, imperial officials outlawed the enslaving of Native Americans unless the Indians attacked the colonists first. In parts of NEW SPAIN colonists seeking labor at times provoked native peoples to attack, but such efforts had a limited impact on the number of slaves in the Western Hemisphere.

Over time the indigenous peoples of the Americas could not satisfy European colonizers' insatiable desire for labor. Thus, when colonists settled on SUGAR production in the Atlantic islands, Africans became enslaved to perform the back-breaking work of clearing fields, tending crops, and producing molasses. When Native Americans died in the Western Hemisphere as a result of epidemic DISEASES, such as SMALLPOX, which were part of the COLUMBIAN EXCHANGE, Europeans who wanted to mine SILVER turned to African slavers to provide them with the labor they needed. One sign of the rapid development of slavery and the slave trade can be seen in surviving statistics from PERU. The first African slaves arrived in the colony in the early 1560s. By the end of the century slaves in Peru had come from parts of the SENEGAMBIA and Guinea-Bissau region—men and women whose cultures were Biafra, Bran, Berbesi, Jolofo, Mandinga, Nalu, Bañol, Casanga, Fula, and Bioho—but also from other parts of West, central, and South Africa. By the end of the century Portuguese ships had hauled approximately 264,000 Africans into slavery in the Americas, with another 2,000 or so transported by English ships (see the entry on the slave trade for more details). Most went to mines in Spanish America, such as the infamous silver operation at POTOSÍ, which had earlier relied on indigenous slaves drafted through the REPARTIMIENTO system. Eventually the majority worked on plantations producing goods, notably sugar, for European consumers.

The forced migration of thousands of Africans to European colonies in the 16th century represented a decisive stage in the expansion of slavery in the early modern world. When Portuguese slave ships disgorged their human chattel in the Western Hemisphere, they also unleashed a new kind of slavery. Unlike slavery in the Old World, this form of bound labor in the NEW WORLD had distinct racial elements. Europeans might have considered enslaving some members of their own communities, but a specific term of forced labor bore little actual relationship to a system in which individuals captured in war and sold to slavers had to spend the rest of their lives in captivity. African slaves in the Americas did not agree to their captivity, nor did they ever give permission for those enslaving them to claim, as the slavers did, rights to the slaves' children, but in the Western Hemisphere slavery became both racially demarcated and generationally binding. The English, who would later rely on slave labor to produce TOBACCO, rice, and other goods in their southern colonies on the North American mainland, seemed predisposed toward such racial categorizations. Once slavery became a social fact in the Americas, it spread ever further, in the process destroying individual slaves' lives and families, robbing African communities of individuals necessary to sustain them, and forever tainting Europeans who participated in the noxious commerce.

Further reading: Frederick P. Bowser, *The African Slave in Colonial Peru, 1524–1650* (Stanford, Calif.: Stanford University Press, 1974); David Eltis, "Europeans and the Rise and Fall of African Slavery in the Americas: An Interpretation," *American Historical Review* 98 (1993); 1399–1423; ———, *The Rise of African Slavery in the Americas* (Cambridge, U.K.: Cambridge University Press, 2000); Winthrop D. Jordan, *White Over Black: American Attitudes Toward the Negro, 1550–1812* (Chapel Hill: University of North Carolina Press, 1968); John Thornton, *Africa and Africans in the Making of the Atlantic World, 1400–1800* (Cambridge, U.K.: Cambridge University Press, 1992).

slave trade

The shipment of Africans against their will from their communities to outposts scattered across the Atlantic world where those who held them in bondage hoped to use the slaves' labor to produce wealth.

In essence, the slave trade was the mechanism whereby SLAVERY spread outward from Africa during the early modern period. But forced migration of slaves across the Atlantic did not represent the origins of the slave trade. As various scholars have demonstrated, an earlier slave trade had led to the relocation of thousands of Africans to the East long before CHRISTOPHER COLUMBUS ever sailed to the West. Slavery, which existed when scribes wrote both the Old and New Testaments, appeared in the Koran as well; in that sacred text slaveholders learned that they should be willing to offer freedom to the slaves they kept in bondage if the slaves could afford to purchase their liberation. But many Muslims (see ISLAM), like other peoples in the world, nonetheless participated in the slave trade. One historian has estimated that slave traders arranged for the transportation of 4,820,000 slaves across the SAHARA between 650 and 1600. During the 10th and 11th centuries, when this trade hit its peak, perhaps 8,700 slaves left their homelands through this trade each year, although by the 15th century the annual rate had dipped to approximately 4,300 (before rising again, during the 16th century,

to 5,500 per year). These numbers are estimates based on a variety of sources. But whatever the precise figure, there is no doubt that the eastern slave trade took hundreds of thousands of Africans from their communities to new lives. Once enslaved, men might become soldiers, grooms, scholars, clerks, and secretaries; female slaves found themselves as concubines, musicians, cooks, or domestic workers. Although many of the enslaved might have landed in North Africa or southern Europe, others traveled much farther; substantial numbers made it as far as India and China.

Although there had been an internal slave trade within Africa long before Europeans arrived to establish colonies, in addition to the eastern slave trade, the commerce in slaves increased dramatically after the mid-15th century, when Portuguese slavers began to transport Africans to Europe and to offshore European colonies. The Portuguese were able to succeed quickly in the business because they took advantage of the existing African slave trade whereby individuals captured in war were taken against their will to people who were willing to purchase them.

From the time that it began, the slave trade had a devastating effect on individuals, families, and communities. Witnessing the unloading of 235 slaves in the Portuguese port near Lagos in August, 1444, Gomes Eannes de Zurara, an associate of Prince HENRY THE NAVIGATOR, learned that it became necessary "to part fathers from sons, husbands from wives, brothers from brothers. No respect was shown to either friends or relations, but each fell where his lot took him." Wherever slavers hauled their human wares, such desperate scenes invariably followed. He could have added that the capture of large numbers of members of any community had a devastating effect on that settlement's ability to survive, especially if slavers disturbed the sex balance of a town and thereby endangered its ability to stage a demographic recovery from the slave raids.

The Portuguese were the first Europeans to take a sustained interest in the slave trade, and to get their business started they knew they had to provide a range of commercial alternatives to the Africans who controlled the supply of slaves. Thus, when the Portuguese arrived in African ports in the 15th century to purchase human labor, they brought trade goods such as cloth from Flanders and France, German brass goods, Venetian glass, spiced wine from the CANARY ISLANDS, conch shells found in the Canaries, and even goods produced in Africa itself, such as woolen shawls made in Tunis. To get these goods, those in command of slave ships had only to stock up on products in LISBON or some other southern European entrepôt. The horrors of the slave trade, not only the destruction of African communities but also the terrible privations suffered by slaves during the MIDDLE PASSAGE, rested initially on the ability of the Portuguese to offer the wares of countless European artisans to Africans who found them suitable compensation for less fortunate Africans, most of them taken in wars, who were already enslaved. According to one surviving valuation, one HORSE was worth 25 to 30 slaves in SENEGAMBIA in the 1440s. But the Portuguese were not the only Europeans to embrace the opportunities afforded by the sale of human beings. The enterprising English merchant–seaman SIR JOHN HAWKINS became a pioneer of the slave trade for his nation when he made three separate journeys from Africa to the Western Hemisphere in the 1560s, each time hoping to profit from the sale of slaves.

Perhaps the most notable feature of the slave trade was its dramatic expansion over the course of the 16th century. In 1500 slavers exported approximately 5,000 slaves each year from Africa. By 1550 the number had increased to 8,000 annually, and by 1600 the average yearly exports reached 9,500. Of course, the trade took different tolls on different regions. During the 16th century the greatest number of slaves came from Angola,

Portuguese Africa and the Slave Trade

which contributed approximately one-half of all exported slaves in 1500 and whose share increased to more than 65 percent of the total by the mid-17th century. Yet while the share of Angolans rose, those from BENIN decreased after local authorities there moved to ban the trade in the mid-16th century.

The most recent estimates of the slave trade for the period from 1519 to 1600 provide a clear picture of the range of slaves' origins. During those 80 years the largest number of slaves, approximately 221,200, came from West central Africa, with additional slaves from other areas—Senegambia, the GOLD COAST, the Bight of Benin, and the Bight of Biafra, each of which contributed approximately 10,700 humans. With another 2,000 from Sierra Leone, the totals for the period add up to 266,000. Virtually all of these slaves were destined for NEW SPAIN and BRAZIL, suggesting that the Spanish and Portuguese alike recognized the utility of slaves for the colonial economies of the NEW WORLD. By the latter decades of the 17th century, slaves left Africa on ships owned by the English, Dutch, Danes, and French along with those still hauled by the Portuguese.

Despite the ability of slavers to transport humans to new destinations, individual slaves and entire groups often resisted their captors. Recent estimates suggest that as many as 10 percent of all slave ships experienced rebellions, and various kinds of documentary evidence suggest that slaves often decided to take their chances against their captors rather than suffer the continued horrors of being treated like property. The slave trade, then, succeeded in the minds of Europeans, but it could not quell an individual slave's desire to break free.

Further reading: David Eltis, *The Rise of African Slavery in the Americas* (Cambridge, U.K.: Cambridge University Press, 2000); David Eltis, Stephen D. Behrendt, David Richardson, and Herbert S. Klein, *The Trans-Atlantic Slave Trade: A Database on CD-ROM* (Cambridge, U.K.: Cambridge University Press, 1999); Joseph E. Inikori and Stanley L. Engerman, eds., *The Atlantic Slave Trade: Effects on Economies, Societies, and Peoples in Africa, the Americas, and Europe* (Durham, N.C.: Duke University Press, 1992); "New Perspectives on the Transatlantic Slave Trade," special issue of *William and Mary Quarterly*, 3d ser., LVIII (2001), 1–251; William D. Phillips, Jr., "The Old World Background of Slavery in the Americas," in Barbara L. Solow, ed., *Slavery and the Rise of the Atlantic System* (Cambridge, U.K.: Cambridge University Press, 1991), 43–61; Ronald Segal, *Islam's Black Slaves: The Other Black Diaspora* (New York: Farrar, Straus & Giroux, 2001); Hugh Thomas, *The Slave Trade: The History of the Atlantic Slave Trade, 1440–1870* (New York: Simon & Schuster, 1997).

smallpox

A potentially deadly disease that caused so-called virgin soil epidemics to wreak havoc on the populations of the Americas as a result of the COLUMBIAN EXCHANGE.

The extremely infectious DISEASE of smallpox turned out to give Europeans a major (if unintentional) biological advantage in their invasion and colonization of the Western Hemisphere, where American Indian populations had never in recent memory encountered this virus or many other epidemic diseases. Smallpox is communicated through the air, usually entering each host through the respiratory tract. Sufferers can contract the disease not only by breathing infected air exhaled by the victims but also by contact with the fluids from exploding pustules and open sores. The early symptoms of smallpox include headaches and nausea as well as skin eruptions that leave disfiguring scars. In survivors smallpox can also cause blindness and infertility. While many forms of the virus are extremely deadly, it only lives a short time in each host, an average of 12 to 18 days. Death by smallpox takes the form of massive vomiting of blood, either through intestinal or uterine hemorrhage.

In Europe and Africa smallpox was known as a childhood disease in the 15th century. Strains of smallpox could vary greatly in their virulence. In Europe and Africa smallpox was common but not always deadly, and most of the population contracted the disease as children and either died or gained immunities. However, around 1500 the virus in Europe evolved into a strain that killed most of its hosts, and some claimed it was now as deadly as the PLAGUE. This deadly form of smallpox did not come to the Americas for almost two decades. When it did, it arrived either by means of smallpox scabs left in a bale of cloth or from a few infected African slaves from CASTILE who had been born in slavery outside of Africa and thus isolated from contact with a milder form of the disease while children. Smallpox also played an important role in the establishment of the SLAVE TRADE. Most Africans were already immune to the disease as a result of childhood exposure. Based on these early slaves' high survival rate during the smallpox epidemics decimating the indigenous populations of the Americas, Europeans concluded that Africans made a better labor force in reaping the resources of the NEW WORLD.

According to sources from the 16th century, smallpox was one of the first and most deadly European diseases to ravage the indigenous peoples of the Americas, although it is necessary for historians to be cautious in accepting diagnoses of smallpox in the historical records because smallpox is misdiagnosed even today. In addition, smallpox often traveled with other epidemic diseases that could complicate both its diagnosis and its effects. Historians often translate the Spanish word *viruelas*, for example, as "smallpox," but in fact the word means pustule—a skin blister that also occurs in measles, chicken pox, and typhus. Still, because smallpox was a familiar (if usually less devastating) epidemic in European populations, it is likely that, on the whole, most 16th-century Europeans recognized smallpox when they saw it in the indigenous populations of the Americas.

Smallpox accompanied the CONQUISTADORES on their journeys through the Caribbean, South America, and present-day MEXICO and the United States, and the smallpox deaths of Indians in Spanish territories eventually numbered into the millions. In 1518 BARTOLOMÉ DE LAS CASAS wrote of the first major smallpox epidemic to sweep the island of HISPANIOLA. Few Spaniards died, but between one-third and one-half of the local TAINO Indian population perished. Las Casas also blamed the severity of the epidemic on the famine and overwork that the Spaniards forced upon the indigenous peoples. By 1550, as a result of invasion, slavery, and especially smallpox and other diseases, the Taino were extinct.

From the islands smallpox moved quickly to the YUCATÁN PENINSULA. In 1519 HERNÁN CORTÉS and his army inadvertently brought the virus to central Mexico, where it devastated the AZTECS, along with other diseases, including an unidentified one that resulted in massive nosebleeds. After these diseases swept through, the Spaniards laid siege to the Aztec capital for 75 days, after which the weakened population could finally no longer resist the Spanish. As with all of these epidemics, shortage of food and lack of medical care exacerbated the effects of the viruses. A smallpox epidemic is also the major suspect in the devastation of millions of indigenous peoples in the region of the Isthmus of PANAMA. In 1527 smallpox also killed many in the INCA Empire of the Andean highlands in PERU. From 1562 to 1563 the Portuguese in BRAZIL saw approximately 30,000 Indians dying from smallpox in their missions and slave labor camps, while the Portuguese themselves remained relatively unscathed. The Portuguese interpreted their own survival as a sign that they had earned the grace of God, although modern scholars now attribute their health to the acquired immunities they carried in their bloodstreams.

Once introduced, smallpox became the most lethal killer in the Americas. Epidemics continued for generations, forever altering the nature of life in indigenous communities.

Further reading: Alfred W. Crosby, "Conquistador y pestilencia: The First New World Pandemic and the Fall of the Great Indian Empires," in Kenneth F. Kiple and Stephen V. Beck, eds., *Biological Consequences of the European Expansion, 1450–1800, An Expanding World,* vol. 6 (Aldershot, U.K.: Ashgate Publishing, 1997), 91–107; ———, *Germs, Seeds, & Animals: Studies in Ecological History* (London: M. E. Sharpe, 1994); Kenneth F. Kiple and Stephen V. Beck, eds., *Biological Consequences of the European Expansion, 1450–1800, An Expanding World,* vol. 6 (Aldershot, U.K.: Ashgate Publishing, 1997); Sheldon Watts, *Epidemics and History: Disease, Power, and Imperialism* (New Haven, Conn.: Yale University Press, 1997).

— Maril Hazlett

Songhai

The Songhai Empire achieved a dominant position in West Africa after the decline of MALI.

There remains debate about the origins of the Songhai. One tradition claims they descended from the Sorko, fishermen who had migrated from Lake Chad, and the Gow, who were hunters. Another tradition points to Berber migrants who entered the area around the seventh century and laid the foundation for what would become the Songhai Empire. Most historians agree that Songhai origins are sketchy and include the influence of numerous migrant groups to the region of the middle Niger.

The first recognized ruler of what would become the Songhai Empire was King Kossi of GAO. Kossi accepted ISLAM in 1009, which then played an important role in the commerce that developed across the SAHARA. Most historians agree that Kossi probably recognized the economic benefits of converting. Islam also became a unifying factor for the nascent Songhai Empire. Gao became the capital city, and their mixed economy of farming, fishing, herding, and trading provided stability for an increasingly powerful people.

In 1325 the Songhai were forced to pay tribute to Mali. The Mali ruler MANSA MUSA I had stopped at Gao while returning from his famed pilgrimage to MECCA. He demanded that the Songhai submit to his authority and took the Songhai ruler's two sons as hostages, but Songhai's tributary status lasted only about 10 years. Political changes in Mali afforded the hostage brothers an opportunity to betray the new Mali ruler and restore independence to Songhai. Over the next century the Songhai fought off intruders including the TUAREG, the MOSSI, and the Mandingo.

In 1464 Sunni Ali Ber, the 18th ruler in a line of kings established by Kossi, ascended the throne. He was a man of unusual courage and strength of purpose and sympathetic to pagan traditions despite his own Muslim convictions. However, his sympathies stemmed from his interest in consolidating power and loyalty rather than in promoting religious freedom. Sunni Ali became a ruthless ruler who was not particularly well-liked by his own people, although his conquests strengthened his empire and laid the foundation for Songhai's golden age.

Sunni Ali's son took the throne after his father's death in 1492. He lasted only a few months before Mohammad Toure, one of Sunni Ali's generals, usurped the throne with popular support. Mohammad Toure took the title askia and ruled Songhai from 1493 to 528. Under ASKIA MOHAMMAD I's rule, Songhai expanded its borders as far west as Segu and as far northeast as Air. He controlled all of the territory that once belonged to Mali, and he acquired control of the trade routes leading to Egypt, Tunis, and Tripoli. In short, Askia Mohammad created the largest African state in sub-Saharan West Africa. His greatest gift to Songhai was its administrative system. He also encouraged scholarship and commerce. TIMBUKTU and Gao became major centers of learning renowned throughout the Islamic world.

Songhai continued to flourish after Askia Mohammad's reign, but its golden age was near its end. In 1589 El Mansur, the Moroccan ruler, set out to conquer Songhai. At that time no one believed that an army could cross the Sahara, but El Mansur insisted on an attack. He sent 4,000 soldiers with 9,000 transport animals. It took nearly six months for the Moroccan army to cross the desert, and they lost 3,000 men in the process. They met Askia Ishak, the Songhai king, at Tondibi, which was about 25 miles from Gao. The Songhai army numbered more than 25,000 soldiers, but the Moroccans had guns. Despite being outnumbered, the bedraggled Moroccan army defeated Askia Ishak decisively. This defeat marked the beginning of Songhai's decline. Over the next century Songhai fragmented into smaller states and chiefdoms.

Further reading: G. Connah, *African Civilizations: Precolonial Cities and States in Tropical Africa: An Archeological Perspective* (Cambridge, U.K.: Cambridge University Press, 2001); Basil Davidson, *The Lost Cities of Africa* (Boston: Little, Brown, 1970); L. Mair, *African Kingdoms* (Oxford, U.K.: Clarendon Press, 1977).

— Tom Niermann

Soto, Hernando de (ca. 1496–1542)

A CONQUISTADOR who led a contingent of Spanish through the modern-day southeast of the United States on an expedition in which he failed to find great wealth but inadvertently spread infectious DISEASEs to the native peoples of the region.

Hernando de Soto first arrived in the Western Hemisphere in 1514 when he left Spain in the company of Pedro Arias de Ávila, who was on his way to become governor of PANAMA. But Ávila's hope to become governor was thwarted by VASCO NÚÑEZ DE BALBOA, who resisted the newcomer's attempts to supplant him. De Soto witnessed the result of the clash between the two servants of the Spanish king: Ávila had Balboa captured and executed.

Hernando de Soto   *(Library of Congress)*

Over time, de Soto became associated with many of the leading conquistadors of his age. He became a lieutenant to FRANCISCO PIZARRO and joined the expedition in PERU, a venture that led to the ransoming and execution of the INCA king ATAHUALPA. De Soto returned to Spain in 1536 and, like other returning heroes, received royal privileges as a result of his successes in South America. Among his benefits was the position of governor of CUBA.

De Soto left Spain in 1538 and headed once again to the Americas. After provisioning a small army in Cuba, he set sail for present-day FLORIDA, where he arrived in early summer 1539. Over the course of the following months, de Soto and his men often treated local Indians harshly, including the APALACHEE who inhabited the northern part of modern-day Florida (near present-day Tallahassee). In early March 1540 de Soto and his men set off on a journey to the north in search of mineral wealth, including GOLD.

Despite heroic efforts, scholars have never been able to retrace de Soto's exact route through the Southeast. What is certain is that he led his men on a journey that traversed much of modern-day Georgia and relied on various regional rivers to get around. It is possible that they reached as far as the Arkansas River on the farthest northwestern part of their journey and possible that they descended part of the Brazos River in modern-day Texas as well. Archaeological evidence found throughout the Southeast dating roughly to the age of De Soto's *entrada* suggests that he either wandered to countless places or traded with local Native Americans for goods. The four accounts of his journey that survive give differing details, although it is likely that he and his forces traveled through modern-day South Carolina, North Carolina, Tennessee, Alabama, Mississippi, Arkansas, and Louisiana. In 1541 de Soto reached the banks of the Mississippi River

Whatever his precise route, there is little doubt that the Spanish caused enormous problems for the indigenous peoples of the region, including the Choctaw and Mobile, who battled de Soto's forces. During the winter of 1540–41, de Soto and his men often ran into troubles with the indigenous peoples of Chicaza, a community probably located near modern-day Columbus, Mississippi. By the time spring came around, the Chicaza had burned de Soto's encampment and twelve of his men had perished, along with 57 HORSEs and a large number of pigs the Spaniards kept.

Having earned a reputation for cruelty, de Soto himself never managed to complete the journey. On May 21, 1542, after many of his men had died on the journey, he became ill and died near Natchez, Mississippi. His men believed it best to keep his death a secret, perhaps because some of them believed that de Soto had convinced the Indians that he was an immortal; they had also heard stories that Native Americans often desecrated the graves of Spaniards. After they buried him within their compound at night, local natives noticed the grave. This act of discovery terrified de Soto's men, who then dug up his body in the dark of night, filled his burial shroud with sand, and then dumped his body into the Mississippi River. At the time of his death, according to an account of an auction of his goods, he possessed four slaves (two of each sex) along with three horses and 700 hogs.

After wandering for another year, mostly on a venture to the west, the remainder of de Soto's entourage boated down the Mississippi to the sea. They crossed the Gulf of Mexico and eventually reached territory controlled by the Spanish. When they arrived they told tales of a journey that modern scholars estimate stretched over 4,000 miles of the American interior, much of it in dense swampland and thick forests.

An earlier generation of historians celebrated de Soto's achievements and saw him as one of the Spanish colonizers who helped to open North America to European civilization. That notion was based on the idea that de Soto's surviving men spread news about the region when they got to NEW SPAIN. However, recent historical work has suggested that de Soto's men did more than engage in periodic conflicts with Indians. According to surviving documents, it now seems likely that these Spanish spread epidemic diseases, notably SMALLPOX, among the Indians they encountered. An unwitting agent of the COLUMBIAN EXCHANGE, de Soto now appears to historians as yet another misguided Spaniard bent on the acquisition of wealth who never understood the ways in which his own presence in the Americas undermined the indigenous peoples he encountered.

Further reading: Charles Hudson, *Knights of Spain, Warriors of the Sun: Hernando de Soto and the South's Ancient Chiefdoms* (Athens, Ga.: University of Georgia Press, 1997); Angus Konstam, *Historical Atlas of Exploration* (New York: Facts On File, 2000); Anne Ramenovsky, *Vectors of Death: The Archaeology of European Contact* (Albuquerque: University of New Mexico Press, 1987).

Spanish Armada

The brainchild of Spanish King PHILIP II, the Spanish Armada was a fleet of warships that attempted to invade England in 1588.

Animosity between Spain and England escalated during the decade of the 1570s and must be considered amid the political and religious backdrops of the second half of the 16th century. In 1556 CHARLES V, Holy Roman Emperor, abdicated the throne, allowing his son Philip to come into full inheritance. He found himself in command of not only Spain and its American possessions, but also of Sicily, Naples, Burgundy, and the Duchy of Milan. Philip already controlled the Netherlands and was married to English claimant Mary Tudor. In addition to these vast holdings, Philip stood to inherit the throne of Portugal when Sebastian, then king, died. Although already allied to the throne of Spain, the throne of Portugal would cement Spain's already strong military position, especially in the maritime realm, in which the addition of Portugal's fleet would solidify Spain's dominance in the Atlantic sea trade.

A number of events combined to undermine Philip's strong geopolitical position. In 1558 Mary died without leaving Philip, or for that matter England, an heir. The English throne passed to Mary's sister ELIZABETH I, whose long reign upheld Protestantism in a divided country. By political necessity Elizabeth I became Philip's enemy. During the early years of her reign, she concentrated on consolidating her position as the Protestant queen of a nation with a large Catholic minority. Although Philip looked forward to a few years of peace, the revolt of the Netherlands, led by William the Silent, along with the growth of

Huguenot power in France under the direction of HENRY IV, placed Catholicism's most powerful political leader on the defensive.

The destiny of Philip's future plans and potential successes hinged on maintaining control of the English Channel. With the burgeoning seaboard trade of the 16th century, the English Channel became the essential highway for the nations of northern Europe seeking riches in the oceans of the world. Equally important for Philip, control of the channel could be a check on English ambitions.

Slow to enter the world of maritime trade, England's naval power was on the rise during the Elizabethan era. Led by merchant adventurer SIR JOHN HAWKINS and privateer SIR FRANCIS DRAKE, English ambitions on the open seas soon clashed with those of Spain. Engaging in the burgeoning SLAVE TRADE between the coast of Africa and the West Indies, Hawkins's third triangular voyage, in 1568, ended in disaster at San Juan de Ulúa in the West Indies because of Spanish interference. Only one of the English ships was destroyed, and Hawkins, along with Drake, escaped to England. In immediate retribution for the attack, England captured some Spanish treasure ships in the Atlantic. More detrimental to Philip was Drake's new passion to exact vengeance upon the Spanish. Carrying out this goal throughout the decade of the 1570s, Drake struck Spanish vessels on the open seas and pillaged Spanish possessions on the Spanish Main, in PANAMA, and in the West Indies. Historians often refer to his raid of the Spanish controlled West Indies in 1585–86 as the de facto starting point of the war involving the Spanish Armada. In truth, Philip had started plans for an invasion of England years earlier, but it was in January 1586 that he began assembling the armada. More than two years in the making, the armada combined existing Spanish and Portuguese ships, already impressive in number and power, with a new building program. Many in Europe thought of Philip's end result as invincible.

While the English and Spanish each hoped to exert control over much of the Atlantic, technological and technical developments were already changing the nature of naval warfare. Through the middle of the 16th century, most sea battles had been fought at close range, with ships lying next to one another. In 1571 the Spanish, with the help of other Christian forces, defeated the Turkish navy, a power in the Mediterranean Sea, at Lepanto by using galleys propelled by oars, the general type of ship used since Greek and Roman times. However, by then the English Sea Dogs, led by the likes of Drake and Hawkins, were perfecting very different tactics. They began to rely on lowlying and highly maneuverable vessels that could be turned windward so they could pound the enemy's fleet from a distance and thus avoid hand-to-hand combat with the skilled Spanish infantry on the ships.

Departing from LISBON on May 30, 1588, the armada entered the English Channel on July 30, skirmishing in long-range gun battles with English warships over the next few days. Philip's fleet contained 124 vessels of varying sizes carrying 27,000 men and 1,100 guns. The English countered with 197 ships, 16,000 men, and 2,000 guns. Half of the Spanish men were soldiers, while all of the English were seamen. On August 6 the armada anchored at Calais, France. Median Sidonia planned a rendezvous with barges carrying Spanish troops from nearby Dunkerque, a port belonging to the Netherlands at the time, but Dutch gunboats prevented the barges from meeting the armada. Moreover, Drake dislodged the Spanish vessels with fireships—boats filled with combustibles and set afire to drift into the enemy fleet. Attempting to escape the flames, the Spanish ships sailed out to sea. Chaos ensued. Later in the morning 60 English ships attacked an equal number of Spanish ships outside the French port of Gravelines. Employing nimble steerage with a combination of long- and short-range shooting techniques, the English defeated the armada, killing 600 Spanish sailors, wounding 800 more, and taking still others prisoners. The new long-range tactics employed by the English were taken up by other naval powers in the ensuing centuries, replaced only by the advent of steam and armor after 1850, which once again changed the nature of naval warfare.

A mix of anticipation and confusion within the international community characterized the months after the armada fled the English Channel. What remained of the crippled fleet sailed to the North Sea, returning to Spain by sailing northward around the British Isles. Only 67 ships returned to Spain, as heavy winds and storms combined to ground many of the ships off the coast of Ireland. Although rumors passed through France indicating a Spanish victory, the truth of the situation slowly dawned on the Spanish. In their response to the defeat, the Dutch cast a medal depicting the world slipping from the grasp of Philip as larger reverberations echoed across Europe and even the world.

Scholars have long argued that the defeat of the armada was a turning point in Spanish history, although some historians shy away from the phrase "defeat of the Spanish Armada." The Spaniards remained strong enough to keep possession of their established colonies in Central and South America, although they no longer attempted to monopolize America north of FLORIDA. Nor did they expend much effort in defending the Asian empire once controlled by the Portuguese but by then under Spanish control. The English, Dutch, and French took advantage, expanding their influence into the East. In 1600 the English EAST INDIA COMPANY was chartered. The DUTCH EAST INDIA COMPANY (1602) and French East India Company followed.

England, France, and the Netherlands were also able to take advantage on the North American continent. On the immediate horizon the defeat of the armada allowed SIR WALTER RALEGH to send supplies to the 110 colonists who were left behind at ROANOKE, but by the time the English arrived, the colonists had disappeared. Despite the apparent tragedy, the English as well as the French and the Dutch could ply the seas more easily in the years following the demise of the armada.

Further reading: Colin Martin and Geoffrey Parker, *The Spanish Armada* (New York: Norton, 1988); Garrett Mattingly, *The Armada* (Boston: Houghton Mifflin, 1959); Geoffrey Parker, "Why the Armada Failed," *Military History Quarterly* 1 (1988): 18–27; R.A. Stradling, *The Armada of Flanders: Spanish Maritime Policy and European War, 1568–1668*, Cambridge Studies in Early Modern History (Cambridge, U.K., Cambridge University Press, 1992).

— Matthew Lindaman

Spice Islands

A group of islands between southeast Asia and New Guinea, the Spice Islands were the target of European sailors seeking to get to the "Indies" so they could bring back spices that Europeans craved during the early modern period.

From at least the time when medieval crusaders traveled to the Holy Land in search of glory and wealth, Europeans had become accustomed to the spices that travelers brought back to the Continent. By the 15th century the most desirable spices, notably cinnamon and pepper, could be found in a cluster of Pacific islands known collectively as the Spice Islands. These islands had the ideal climate for growing certain types of spices, all of which had great value to Europeans. When the English founded a colony on Run, one of the Bandu Islands, they got nutmeg cheap and resold it back home for, according to one recent estimate, a 32,000 percent profit. Sumatra had substantial supplies of pepper; Ternate, Tidore, and three other small islands contained the world's supply of cloves. As one historian put it, "the cloves, nutmeg, mace, cinnamon, ginger and pepper spawned a new age of revolutionary economics based on credit, the rise of a rudimentary banking system, and ultimately free enterprise." Although such a description exaggerates the significance of the spice trade, it nonetheless reflects the enormous enthusiasm for spices that existed in the 15th and 16th centuries.

In order to break Venetian merchants' control of the spice trade, other Europeans mounted missions to the Indies. The Portuguese got there first, and much of the wealth they earned in the 16th century derived from their privileged position in the business. Diogo Lopes de Sequeira established a route from Goa and Calicut to the Spice Islands in 1509 through the Strait of Malacca. When he arrived in Malacca, he realized that the stories he had heard in India about the wealth to be derived from the spice trade were true. He also found that his ships were not the only foreign vessels in the port; others had come from Arabia, Japan, and China. When conflict between the Portuguese and the local Malaysians erupted, de Sequeira, reinforced by the Portuguese, took control of the city in 1511. His efforts and those of other Portuguese who followed helped Europeans to gain an understanding of the Indies and to master shipping routes through territory on the far side of the world.

Although the Portuguese believed that the TREATY OF TORDESILLAS (see Documents) had given them the right to control the Spice Islands, other Europeans wanted to participate as well. By the early 17th century the English EAST INDIA COMPANY and the DUTCH EAST INDIA COMPANY both aimed to bring back to Europe ships laden with rare and valuable spices. Promoters of overseas expansion and trade such as RICHARD HAKLUYT THE YOUNGER and SAMUEL PURCHAS included reports of ventures to the Spice Islands, thereby giving their readers the political and economic story behind the spices they devoured.

Further reading: Charles Corn, *The Scents of Eden: A History of the Spice Trade* (New York: Kodansha, 1999); Angus Konstam, *Historical Atlas of Exploration, 1492–1600* (New York: Facts On File, 2000); Giles Milton, *Nathaniel's Nutmeg. Or, The True and Incredible Adventures of the Spice Trader Who Changed the Course of History* (New York: Farrar, Straus & Giroux, 1999).

Stade, Hans (Staden) (fl. 1547–1557?)

A German who sought adventure in India, Hans Stade instead traveled from LISBON to BRAZIL, where he was captured by natives and upon his return to Europe published an account of his journey and a description of the society and social mores of the TUPINAMBÁ.

Born in Homburg in Hesse, Stade left Germany for Holland and then Portugal seeking to find work on a ship traveling to the East. When he arrived there in late April 1547, a German innkeeper told him that he had missed his chance, but that it was still possible to travel to Brazil. Stade signed up to be a gunner on a ship whose orders were, as he put it in his account, "to seize such ships as commerced with the white Moors of Barbary" and, if possible, to attack any French vessels if their crews had been trading with Brazil's native peoples. Sixteen months later he returned to Lisbon after having seen the Western Hemisphere and considerable action at sea.

In the spring of 1549 Stade again left Portugal on a vessel bound for America. On the way he saw Portuguese colonies in the Atlantic "rich in sugar" where plantations were tended by slaves (see SLAVERY). When his ship reached Brazil, Stade was captured and then spent an unknown amount of time with the Tupinambá. While with them he paid careful attention, especially since he was convinced that they were preparing to eat him on a number of occasions, something that he knew that cannibals did. However, although Stade did watch his captors consume other victims, he was never eaten. He believed he owed his survival to his faith in his Protestant God, who even at times seemed to work miracles to preserve him. Eventually, a group of French sailors rescued Stade and returned him to Europe.

Sometime after his return, Stade wrote his account. Published in 1557 in Marburg under the title *Warhafftiger Historia and beschreibung einer Landtschaft der Wilden Nacketen Grimmigen Menschenfresser Leuthen in der Newenwelt America*—or, in translation, *Truthful History and Description of a Landscape of Wild, Naked, Cruel Man-Eating People in the New World of America*—Stade's account soon became popular. The first part of the book contained his life story; the second part, far more interesting, consisted of an ethnographic description of the Tupinambá. Throughout the work Stade recognized the hand of the divine, which was especially evident when he kept being spared from death. These references had a specific point. Stade hoped that his book would let "everyone" hear "that Almighty God, now, as much as ever, wonderfully protects and accompanies his believers in Christ among the godless, heathen people[.]" Although the religious references may have appealed to some readers, the popularity of his work might have had something to do with the fact that Stade included a number of illustrations of the Tupinambá in his account, including depictions of their CANNIBALISM.

The success of the book was apparent from its wide circulation. A Flemish translation appeared in 1558, other German editions were published in 1567 and 1593, and a Latin version appeared in 1592; publishers in the 17th, 18th, and 19th centuries also brought out editions of the account, suggesting its almost timeless appeal. Most important, Stade's work fell into the hands of the Flemish engraver THEODOR DE BRY, who used it as the basis for his *America tertia pars*, published with numerous illustrations in 1592. Although de Bry altered many of the illustrations, Stade's observations nonetheless provided the basis for what became perhaps the most famous set of images depicting the Tupinambá in the 16th century. Those images were the ideal complement to Stade's ethnographic description of the Tupinambá.

When the book was first published in Germany in 1557, it contained a preface by Dr. Joh. Drayandi (also known as Zychman) intended to convince readers of the account's accuracy. Because what followed might have seemed incredible, such as the story of Stade's invocation of God's assistance so that rain would not fall on him and two Brazilians while they fished, the preface helped to convince otherwise skeptical readers that Stade was telling the truth despite the fact that travelers often told "unlimited lies" and spread "false and invented stories." Such an assurance of accuracy no doubt kept readers from rejecting the claims of a man whose descriptions of cannibalism were among the most graphic of any published in the 16th century.

Little is known of Stade's life other than the information contained in his account. But the fact of that book's survival is crucial because it provides additional evidence from the descriptions of Brazil and its peoples to that that can be found in the works of JEAN DE LÉRY and ANDRÉ THEVET.

Further reading: Richard F. Burton, trans., *The Captivity of Hans Stade of Hesse, in A.D. 1547–1555, Among the Wild Tribes of Eastern Brazil*, Works Issued by the Hakluyt Society, 1st ser., LI (London: Hakluyt Society, 1874); Hugh Honour, *The New Golden Land: European Images of America from the Discoveries to the Present Time* (New York: Pantheon, 1975).

Sudan

The Sudan, not to be confused with the modern East African nation the Republic of the Sudan, is the geographic region south of the SAHARA that was the home to several important early kingdoms including GHANA, MALI, and SONGHAI.

Originally taken from the Arabic phrase *Bilal as-Sudan*, meaning the "Southern Country" or the "Land of the Blacks," Sudan referred to both a geographical and a cultural region. The dry, hot grasslands of the Sudan lay south of the vast Sahara, separating this ocean of sand from the forested regions bordering the Atlantic Ocean and the Bight of BENIN. Agricultural peoples flourished in the Sudan, cultivating millet, wheat, sorghum, and, by the 16th century, cotton imported from India. In the region's cities, where water was often more plentiful, melons, figs, citrus fruits, and grapes could be found. Millet and sorghum were the staples, each of them particularly suited to the local climatic and soil condition. Intense dry heat occasionally mitigated by seasonal rains, short growing seasons, and relatively poor soils made the cultivation of other grains and cereals untenable. Sorghums were more prevalent in the southern Sudan, where rainfall was heavier, about 25 to 50 inches annually, and millets predominated in the drier, northern region, where less than 25 inches of rain typically fell. Along the river valleys, including that of the NIGER RIVER, rice was an important crop. Farming in the Sudan was a family endeavor and, accordingly, a small one, with most farms ranging from two to eight acres. Irrigation provided some relief from the dry conditions, and wells were common in the savanna, particularly in those areas closest to the desert. Farmers in the Sudan practiced a complex system of agriculture, experimenting with various crops and using crop rotation systems in which certain plots of land would lay fallow, replenishing the soil's nutrients.

Although agriculture was the economic and cultural basis for the majority of those living in the Sudan, the kingdoms that arose there based their power on other, more lucrative resources. GOLD, salt, and SLAVERY formed the foundation of the early Sudanic empires. Indeed, North African traders knew the earliest of these ancient empires, Ghana, as the "land of gold." Ghana and its successor, Mali, traded gold mined from the Bambara and Bure gold fields in the western Sudan for salt mined in and to the north of the Sahara. Control over the trans-Saharan trade route provided these kingdoms with enough wealth and power to become vast empires. Their participation in the trade had an additional result, one with dramatic and important social implications. Through the trans-Saharan trade came ISLAM. Before about 1100 C.E., the people of the Sudan practiced local traditional religions; afterward, beginning with the nobles and elites, the Sudanic empires increasingly adopted Islam as their official religion. Although the general populace of these empires took longer to convert to the new religion, by the mid-15th century Islam became the dominant religion.

The Sudan, with its intermediate location between the Sahara and the forests along the Atlantic, had a unique position in the history of Africa in the early modern period. It served as the gateway between North Africa and the southern empires, and between East and West African kingdoms. As a cultural and geographical region, it served as an important link in the trans-Saharan trade and in the spread of Islam.

Further reading: "A Very Long History," in *West Africa Before Colonization: A History to 1800,* Basil Davidson, (London: Longman, 1998), 1–14; Robert W. July, *Precolonial Africa: An Economic and Social History* (New York: Scribner's, 1975).

— Lisa M. Brady

Sufism

Sufism, a mystical tradition within ISLAM based on a direct and personal communion between the divine and the human, spread from its seventh-century Arabian origins as far as Persia (Iran), Turkey, India, and Africa by the 12th century, gaining influence in North and West Africa by the 15th and 16th centuries.

The term *Sufism* comes from the Arabic word *suf,* meaning wool, and refers to the woolen garments worn by the Muslim mystics. Sufism, with its emphasis on the individual over the communal experience in the practice of Islam, challenged the political, social, and educational institutions that had developed in Islam beginning in the seventh century. Practitioners trace the origins of Sufism to the Prophet Muhammad, taking inspiration from his divine teachings as revealed in the Qur'an. Most Sufists were nomadic, traveling in search of masters who could teach them in the way to spiritual freedom. Although these masters typically were nomadic themselves, by the 13th century Sufism became increasingly institutionalized through the process of establishing schools *(ta'ifa)* based on the method *(tariqa)* of a particular master *(shaykh),* often connected to frontier posts or hotels *(ribat).* Sufism played an essential role in Islamizing Asia and North Africa in the 11th century through the political and religious activity of its adherents, a process documented in the chronicles of the Islamic historians IBN KHALDÛN and IBN BATTUTA. One of the most famous Sufis was Rabi'a al-'Adawiyya, an eighth-century female *shaykh.* Sufism, due to its mystical traditions, allowed women to gain some modicum of power.

By the 13th century Sufism had become a profession, and by the end of that century a new form of power became associated with individual *shaykhs* upon their death. In this tradition a *shaykh* was assumed to have been gifted with spirit, or to hold the power of *baraka,* a gift that was passed on to his or her followers after death. This shift in Sufism from an urban, intellectual movement, as it had become by the 13th century, to a rural, mystical tradition appealed to a more general population, further aiding in the spread of Islam in West Africa. The European experience with Sufi orders began in the 14th century through the work of the Catalonian mystic and scholar Ramon Lull. Much of what was known of Sufism in Europe before this time was learned through translations of Persian classical poetry and occasional travelers' accounts of the "Whirling Dervishes," Sufists known for their ecstatic trance dances.

Sufi orders played an important role in the Maghreb (North Africa) when they resisted Europeans' attempts, particularly those of the Portuguese, to gain a foothold in the region. These orders, associated with the *ribat,* came to be collectively known as MARABOUTs, who waged holy war, or *jihad,* against the invading Europeans. The Marabout movement spread south to west Africa, incorporating local traditions with Islamic tenets, and became an essential means through which Islam was introduced to the area.

Further reading: Mervyn Hiskett, *The Development of Islam in West Africa* (London: Longman, 1984); R. G. Jenkins, "The Evolution of Religious Brotherhoods in North and Northwest Africa, 1523–1900," in John Ralph Willis, ed., *Studies in West African Islamic History: The Cultivators of Islam* (London: Frank Cass, 1979), 40–77;

Annemarie Schimmel, *Mystical Dimensions of Islam* (Chapel Hill: University of North Carolina Press, 1975); J. Spencer Trimingham, *The Sufi Orders in Islam* (Oxford, U.K.: Clarendon Press, 1971).

— Lisa M. Brady

sugar

Arguably the most important foodstuff produced in mass quantities during the early modern period, the European demand for sugar transformed the terrain of islands across the Atlantic Ocean and much of BRAZIL and encouraged those with capital to export bound laborers to produce the crop for distant markets.

At the turn of the first Christian millennium, sugar was a rare commodity, at least for Europeans. Although humans across the planet had consumed sugar (dextrose or glucose) in some form for millennia in fruits as well as the sugar to be found in honey (fructose), sugarcane *(saccharum officinarum)* itself probably originated in the South Pacific, possibly in modern-day Papua New Guinea. The indigenous peoples of Easter Island, the Solomon Islands, and elsewhere include legends about sugarcane in the stories of their origins. References to sugarcane can be found in India possibly as early as 1000 B.C. The ancient Greek historian Herodotus wrote about sugar in the fifth century B.C., and Alexander the Great had some exported from India to Europe in 327 B.C. References to the plant became more common during the first Christian millennium. By A.D. 800 Persians had made improvements to the refining process, and by 1218 a Chinese ambassador to India reported the cultivation of sugarcane, which locals used to make wine. MARCO POLO wrote about sugar in India during the late 13th century, and IBN BATTUTA also mentioned it in his 14th-century chronicle of his travels to the East. By the late 15th century, when VASCO DA GAMA had landed in Calicut, sugarcane cultivation was widespread. Sugarcane had reached China by approximately 1000 B.C. The 16th-century encyclopedist Li-schi-tsching, known as the Chinese Pliny, offered specific details about sugar production and its history in his *Pen-ts'ao-kung-mu*. Cultivation was never guaranteed, of course; mice devastated the Egyptian sugarcane crop in 1174, and caterpillars ate their way through sugarcane in Sicily in 1239.

Europeans acquired sugarcane later than much of the world, but when the crop and the knowledge for producing it spread, they eagerly pursued production. Prince HENRY THE NAVIGATOR arranged for the transportation of sugarcane to MADEIRA in the early 15th century, and the colony's sugar soon reached all of Europe. Extant documents reveal that Madeira sugar reached BRISTOL in 1456, Florence in 1471, and Ulm in 1490. SÃO TOMÉ, first seen by Europeans in 1470, became a major production center for sugar soon after its founding; by 1522 there were 60 sugar factories on the island. Sugar planters extended production to FERNANDO PO soon after.

When the Portuguese crossed the Atlantic Ocean, they believed that they had found an ideal locale for sugar. Although there is no clear evidence for the first production of sugar in Brazil, by 1526 merchants in LISBON were receiving sugar from that Portuguese colony. By the early 1530s sugar had become a staple export, and as a result the colonists who received captaincies often built sugar factories on their holdings. To produce the sugar, the Portuguese soon turned to slave labor (see SLAVERY). The need for slaves to produce sugar was yet another by-product of the COLUMBIAN EXCHANGE: Europeans purchased African laborers because their DISEASES had destroyed the indigenous peoples on many of the islands. By 1584 the slave population in Brazil reached 10,000, primarily as the result of the success of sugar. Those slaves helped boost the colony's annual sugar exports from 2,470 tons in 1560 to 16,300 tons in 1600.

Other Europeans, too, raced to produce sugar. The Spanish established their first sugar works on Palma, in the CANARY ISLANDS, in 1491, although it is possible that they had begun to transport sugar to Gomera, another island in the chain, as early as 1480. CHRISTOPHER COLUMBUS took seed and skilled farmers from Gomera to HISPANIOLA in 1493 (on his second voyage) and thereby began a lucrative export business. Columbus and his chronicler, Pietro Martire d'Anghiera (PETER MARTYR), each claimed that the soil and climate on the island were ideal for sugarcane. Over the course of the 16th century sugar production on Hispaniola expanded, as it did in the Portuguese colonies. In 1589 planters exported 892 tons of sugar from the island, although their output decreased over time; by 1608 sugar factories once capable of producing 2,225 tons were together exporting only 222 tons. A generation later English planters began to produce sugar on Barbados, and they, too, then needed to import slaves to maintain production after the demise of the indigenous population.

Once sugar production took hold, those eager to profit from it transformed once bountiful tropical islands into agricultural factories. By the mid-17th century planters on the English islands in the Caribbean often had to import food to feed themselves and their laborers because they had denuded the islands and eliminated potential sources of nutrition. Because sugar could be processed into various products, such as rum, its markets could not easily be saturated. As a result, sugar became, along with TOBACCO, rice, and wheat, one of the principal crops produced in the Americas shipped to Europeans. The success of the business, at least success for the Europeans who profited from the sale of sugar, was a testament to the farsighted vision of colonial planners such as RICHARD HAKLUYT THE

YOUNGER, who had argued that the Western Hemisphere was an ideal place for the production of agricultural goods to supply European markets. Of course, neither Hakluyt nor any other 16th-century promoter of colonization anticipated the extent of the SLAVE TRADE that would develop to serve the seemingly unquenchable European demand for sugar, nor could they have known that the economics of sugar and slavery enabled European planters to work slaves to death because the profits on sugar were so great that they could purchase more humans to produce the crop.

Further reading: Alfred Crosby, *Ecological Imperialism: The Biological Expansion of Europe, 900–1900* (Cambridge, U.K.: Cambridge University Press, 1986); Alan Davidson, *The Oxford Companion to Food* (New York: Oxford University Press, 1999); Noel Deerr, *The History of Sugar,* 2 vols. (London: Chapman & Hall, 1949); Sidney W. Mintz, *Sweetness and Power: The Place of Sugar in Modern History* (New York: Viking Penguin, 1985).

Suleiman I (Süleyman) (1494–1566)

Ruler of the Ottoman Empire (Turkey) who led his empire to its greatest territorial, scientific, literary, architectural, and artistic heights, known to Europeans as Suleiman the Magnificent and to Turks as Suleiman the Lawgiver.

Born in the Black Sea city of Trabzon on November 6, 1494, little is known about Suleiman's early life. His father, Mehmed II, became governor of the province of Trabzon the year Suleiman was born and used his position as the ruler of the strategic region to position himself for becoming sultan. His mother was probably Hafsa Hatun, a daughter of the khan of the Crimean Tartars named Mengli Gray. As an elite child, Suleiman in all likelihood learned the Qur'an early, as well as Persian and Arabic. His father rose to become sultan by being able to persevere in a bloody struggle for the position. Once Mehmed become sultan, he appointed Suleiman to governor of Istanbul and later of Sarukhan, a post he held at the time his father died and Suleiman become sultan in 1520.

Over the course of his reign, Suleiman organized the internal forces of the Turks and then used his authority to wage military campaigns that added to the empire in Europe and Africa. By the time he died, his empire had expanded as far as Belgrade and Budapest and included such diverse territories as Algiers, Rhodes, and Baghdad. As he informed King Francis I of France in a letter written at Constantinople in 1526, he was "the Sultan of Sultans, Sovereign of Sovereigns, Distributor of Crowns to Monarchs over the whole Surface of the Globe, God's Shadow on Earth, Sultan and Padishah of the White Sea and the Black Sea, of Rumelia and Anatolia, of Karaman and the coun-

tries of Rum, Zulcadir, Diyarbekir, Kurdistan, Azerbaijan, Persia, Damascus, Aleppo, Cairo, Mecca, Medina, Jerusalem and all Arabia, Yemen and many other lands" that he, his family, and his ancestors had "conquered by the force of their arms." When his troops reached as far as Vienna, countless Europeans feared that Christendom itself would not be able to repel the Turks and ISLAM. At the time of his death, the Ottoman Empire was the most powerful in the world. Its lands included perhaps 35 million residents; Istanbul had a population of 700,000, far larger than any European city.

After he died he was entombed in a mausoleum designed by the famed architect Sinan and his memory celebrated by the poet Baki. "The Hungarian unbelievers bowed their heads before his flashing sword! The Franks knew well the cutting edge of his sabre!" Baki wrote. "The sun has come up; will the king of the world not awake from his sleep? Will he not leave his tent like the sky? Our eyes scan the road: no sign comes from the throne, the sanctuary of glory! The colour in his cheeks is faded, he lies with lips dried out, like a pressed rose without sap[.]"

Many Europeans feared Suleiman, but few doubted his abilities or his efforts to support culture and science in Turkey. Under his generous sponsorship the empire witnessed great advances in architecture, ceramics, painting, calligraphy, weaving, and poetry. He supported talented individuals such as Baki and Sinan as well as experts in Muslim law including Ebussuûd and Kemalpaşazade. After he was gone, the Ottoman Empire began its long collapse.

Further reading: André Clot, *Suleiman the Magnificent* (New York: New Amsterdam Books, 1992); Metin Kunt and Christine Woodhead, *Süleyman the Magnificent and His Age: The Ottoman Empire in the Early Modern World* (London: Longman, 1995); Harold Lamb, *Suleiman the Magnificent: Sultan of the East* (Garden City, N.Y.: Doubleday, 1951).

Sundiata Keita (Sundjata or Mari-Djata)
(ca. 1210–ca.1260)

Sundiata's legendary founding of the empire of MALI in the mid-13th century followed a mythical battle between two powerful wizards, Sundiata and Sumanguru.

Griots, traditional keepers of oral history, retell the epic tale of Sundiata's birth and development into the leader of the Mande people. According to legend, Sundiata's mother, Sogolon, took Sundiata with her into voluntary exile shortly after his birth in order to protect him from assassination attempts by his half brother, who had succeeded their father, Nare Maghan, to the throne of the Kangaba kingdom. Crippled at birth, Sundiata miraculously recovered full health by adulthood, giving him the ability to lead the Kangaba into battle against the Sosso (see GHANA) kingdom, which had defeated his half brother and subjected his people. Under Sundiata's leadership, the Kangaba revolt against Sosso domination culminated at a battle at Kirina in 1234. This battle between Sundiata and Sumanguru, leader of the Sosso, was a great contest of magic. Sundiata shot Sumanguru with an arrow affixed with a white feather, which was deadly to Sumanguru's magic, killing him and guaranteeing Sundiata's victory.

Sundiata needed more than a single military victory to gain control, so he cemented his political ties to other Mande clans in the region, bringing them under the protection of the new Mali kingdom. Sundiata established his capital at Niani and extended his empire's territories westward from the upper Senegal Valley toward the Gambia. His kingdom prospered because of a centralized governing structure ruled by the mansa, or king, and because of its connection to and eventual control of trade routes and GOLD fields. Although Sundiata had converted to ISLAM, he reverted to his traditional religion. Islam remained a powerful influence in his kingdom, evidenced by his son Mansa Uli Keita's devout adherence to the Islamic faith. According to the Arab historian IBN KHALDÛN, Sundiata reigned for 25 years and was succeeded by his son Mansa Uli in 1260.

Further reading: Nehemia Levtzion, "The Early Sates of the Western Sudan to 1500," in J. F. Ade Ajayi and Michael Crowder, eds., *History of West Africa,* vol. 1, 3rd. ed. (London: Longman, 1985), 129–166; "The Majesty of Mali," in *West Africa before the Colonial Era: A History to 1850,* Basil Davidson, (London: Longman, 1998), 35–45; D. T. Niane, *Sundiata: An Epic of Old Mali,* trans. G. D. Pickett (London: Longman, 1979); "Sundjata Keita (Mari-Djata)," in Mark R. Lipschutz and R. Kent Rasmussen, *Dictionary of African Historical Biography,* 2nd ed. (Berkeley: University of California Press, 1986), 228–229.

— Lisa M. Brady

T

Tabasco

A major cultural zone of Mesoamerica corresponding roughly to the borders of the modern-day Mexican state of the same name, Tabasco was a peripheral area that occasionally played an important role in the history of ancient MEXICO.

Tabasco lies along the Gulf of Mexico, at the base of the YUCATÁN PENINSULA. It is a low-lying, swampy region, with relatively few mineral resources. Parts of the region receive 120 inches of rain annually. Tabasco forms a fairly narrow bridge between the Mexican highlands and the Yucatán Peninsula, and the area has always been a cultural crossroads. Despite its dearth of resources, the first great civilization of Mesoamerica, the OLMECS, developed both here and in neighboring VERACRUZ. The Olmecs flourished during the preclassic period, from roughly 1800 to 400 B.C. They developed most of the royal rituals, religious traditions, and iconography used by other Mesoamerican civilizations until the arrival of the Spaniards.

During the classic period (A.D. 200–800), Tabasco was inhabited by Putún MAYA. These people developed advanced systems of trade that linked central Mexico with the Maya of the Yucatán and other groups in Central America. The archaeologist Sir Eric Thompson referred to them as the "Phoenicians of the New World." As the great classic cities of central Mexico (TEOTIHUACÁN, MONTE ALBÁN, and CHOLULA) began to decline, these Putún Maya invaded the region. They established a capital at Cholula and spread their culture throughout the Mexican highlands. There is evidence that they had taken power in Monte Albán as well. With the rise of the TOLTECS, the Putún Maya's influence receded back to Tabasco proper.

By the time of the AZTECS' ascent to power in the 1400s, Tabasco had become somewhat of a backwater, with most of the great cultural and political developments taking place elsewhere. Ethnically and linguistically, the area remained strongly Maya, although there were many elements from central Mexico present as well. Commerce had declined somewhat as an important economic activity, and much of the trade that did occur passed through the coast city of Xicallanco, farther to the east in what is now the Mexican state of Campeche. By the time of MOCTEZUMA II, the Aztecs had taken control of much of the Gulf Coast zone, and there is much evidence that Xicallanco itself was under Aztec control. As such, the Aztecs' culture and language made stronger inroads, and some parts of the area spoke the Aztecs' language of NAHUATL until the 20th century.

Tabasco played a fateful role in the Spanish conquest of the early 1500s. In 1519 HERNÁN CORTÉS landed in Potonchán, Tabasco. The Tabascans attacked, but Cortés and his men were victorious and stormed the city. The defeated natives offered gifts of submission to Cortés and told him that far wealthier kingdoms lay to the west. One of his "gifts" was the slave girl MALINCHE, who spoke both Mayan and Nahuatl. Cortés had rescued a Spanish shipwreck survivor, who after eight years in the Yucatán had learned to speak Mayan. Thus, by using Malinche and this Spaniard, Cortés was able to communicate with the native rulers: Malinche translated the Nahuatl into Mayan, and the Spaniard translated the Mayan into Spanish. Eventually, Malinche learned Spanish herself. A shrewd and intelligent woman, Malinche served as Cortés main adviser, explaining the nuances of Aztec ceremony and politics as well as how to use them to his advantage. There is no doubt that she was instrumental in helping Cortés defeat the Aztecs.

After the conquest Tabasco declined in importance. The Gulf Coast's most important cities were outside of Tabasco proper—Veracruz to the north and Campeche to the east. The area was neglected by the Spaniards and remained a predominantly indigenous zone into the 20th century.

Further reading: Michael Coe, *Mexico,* 4th ed. (London: Thames & Hudson, 1994); Hernán Cortés, *Letters from Mexico,* trans. Anthony Pagden (New Haven, Conn.: Yale University Press, 1986).

— Scott Chamberlain

Tacuba (Tlacopan)

A small but historically important city in central MEXICO which served as the junior partner of the Aztec Empire.

The city's origins are somewhat obscure, but by 1400 it had become a wealthy, influential city. Tacuba was located on the shores of Lake Texcoco, directly across from the Aztec city of TENOCHTITLÁN, and had enjoyed stable trade relations with the AZTECS for many years. Both Tenochtitlán, and Tacuba were vassals of the Tepanecs, a powerful kingdom based in the city of Azcapotzalco. Relations between the Tepanecs and the Aztecs became strained, and in 1427 the Aztec king ITZCÓATL rose up in rebellion against his overlords. Unhappy with Tepanec rule and sensing the rising power of their longtime trading partner, residents of the city of Tacuba sided with Tenochtitlán and its ally Texcoco in the war against the king at Azcapotzalco. The three allies were victorious and set up the so-called Triple Alliance to govern their newly conquered territories. This alliance formed the basis of the Aztec Empire, which by 1519 controlled most of Mexico.

Although formally an equal partner in the alliance, Tacuba was clearly its weakest member. For example, Tacuba was allotted one-fifth of the annual tribute taken in by the alliance, while Tenochtitlán and Texcoco each took in two-fifths. Also, its troops were the last to be mobilized and usually were placed away from the main fighting, allowing few chances for earning glory or war booty. During the centralizing reforms of MOCTEZUMA II, Tacuba lost many of the rights and privileges it had formerly enjoyed, becoming little more than a subject city.

Tacuba also played a substantial role in the Spanish conquest. During HERNÁN CORTÉS's disastrous retreat from Tenochtitlán, he fled along the causeway to Tacuba because it was the shortest escape route from the city. In the final siege of Tenochtitlán, Cortés occupied Tacuba and used it as his base to direct military operations against the Aztecs.

Further reading: Peter Gerhard, *A Guide to the Historical Geography of New Spain,* rev. ed. (Norman: University of Oklahoma Press, 1993); Ross Hassig, *Aztec Warfare: Imperial Expansion and Political Control* (Norman: University of Oklahoma Press, 1988); Miguel Leon-Portilla, ed., *The Broken Spears: The Aztec Account of the Conquest of Mexico* (Boston: Beacon Press, 1992).

— Scott Chamberlain

Taino

Arawakan-speaking people organized into autonomous chiefdoms, the Taino inhabited the Greater Antilles and the Leeward Islands of the Lesser Antilles in the Caribbean Sea, and they had the unfortunate circumstance of being the first indigenous group in the Western Hemisphere to suffer the full repercussions of sustained contact with Europeans.

Linguistically related to the Arawakan-speaking natives of Amazonia, the Taino of the Greater Antilles and Leeward Islands lived in hierarchical societies headed by chieftains called CACIQUES. These chiefdoms typically controlled land located along river basins extending from interior mountains to the ocean. This allowed them to maintain control of a variety of resources they needed for survival. The Taino survived on a subsistence diet that consisted of cultivated plants, fish, shellfish, turtles, and birds. They harvested, among other items, peanuts, sweet potatoes, manioc, a wide range of root crops, TOBACCO, and cotton on earth mounds spread equidistant from each other. The Taino used the slash-and-burn technique to clear land for crops and created artificial ponds to husband fish and turtles. They developed pottery of a high quality and slept in hammocks.

Caciques established their positions in Taino society through ownership of a large, seaworthy canoe and prowess in warfare, primarily against the Island CARIB, and in trade with other Taino communities in the Caribbean. These leaders received their choice of food and trade items. They and their families usually lived in villages segregated from the rank and file, who inhabited homes near the fields and rivers.

The Taino played a ball game that had religious significance on rectangular or oval courts surrounded by stones. Around these ball courts they built wooden sanctuaries to worship their pantheon of gods. Sometimes they carved effigies of their gods into the stones that surrounded their ball courts. There existed three variants of Taino culture in the Caribbean: Western Taino, Classic Taino, and Eastern Taino. Classic Taino primarily occupied the islands of HISPANIOLA, PUERTO RICO, and the eastern portion of CUBA, and they tended to be more hierarchically organized than the other two variants. The Western Taino lived in central Cuba and on JAMAICA, and the Eastern Taino inhabited the Leeward Islands of the Lesser Antilles.

The Taino had the misfortune of being the first Native American group to encounter Europeans. These were the people who initially met CHRISTOPHER COLUMBUS on his first voyage to the Americas in 1492. As each island in the Greater Antilles and Leeward Islands of the Lesser Antilles came under the control of the Spanish, its Taino population declined rapidly due to exposure to European DISEASES, malnutrition, overwork, failed rebellions, and outright murder and abuse at the hands of the Spanish. On many islands the Taino population became extinct within 100 years.

Further reading: Mary W. Helms, "The Indians of the Caribbean and Circum-Caribbean at the End of the Fifteenth Century," in *The Cambridge History of Latin America*, vol. 2, ed. Leslie Bethell (Cambridge, U.K.: Cambridge University Press, 1995), 501–545; Peter Hulme, *Colonial Encounters: Europe and the Native Caribbean, 1492–1797* (New York: Methuen, 1986); Irving Rouse, "The Taino," in *Migrations in Prehistory: Inferring Population Movement from Cultural Remains* (New Haven, Conn.: Yale University Press, 1986), 106–156; ———, *The Tainos: Rise and Fall of the People Who Greeted Columbus* (New Haven, Conn.: Yale University Press, 1992).

— Dixie Ray Haggard

Tarascan

A people of pre-Columbian central present-day MEXICO whose territory bordered on the extreme north edge of the Aztec empire.

Tarascan origins are unclear, but they probably arrived in central Mexico from the northwest about the same time as the AZTECS. Like their more famous neighbors to the south, the Tarascan had forged an alliance of three cities—Ihuatzio, Pátzcuaro, and Tzintzuntzan—that were neighbors on the shores of Lake Pátzcuaro. They seem to have been more advanced than their Aztec neighbors in the use of metal for practical, rather than merely ornamental, purposes, and this technological advantage has caused some historians to speculate that had Europeans arrived a century later they would have been confronting a Tarascan empire rather than an Aztec.

The Tarascan military superiority was borne out in at least one instance during the reign of the Aztec great speaker Axayácatl, when the Tarascan served the Aztecs one of their only crushing battlefield defeats. On this occasion the Tarascan had nearly 40,000 troops to the Aztecs' 24,000, and only about 200 of the latter survived. In the end the Aztecs retreated and are not known to have ever attempted another battle with their neighbors to the north.

Further reading: Geoffrey W. Conrad and Arthur A. Demarest, *Religion and Empire: The Dynamics of Aztec and Inca Expansionism* (Cambridge, U.K.: Cambridge University Press, 1984); Nigel Davies, *Aztecs: A History* (Norman: University of Oklahoma Press, 1980).

— Marie A. Kelleher

Téké

An ethnic group in the central region of the modern-day Republic of the Congo, the Téké formed part of the KONGO kingdom but eventually established an independent kingdom in the 17th century.

The Téké migrated to the central plateau in the late 15th century, becoming part of the decentralized kingdom of the Kongo. With the disintegration of the Kongo, the Téké, also called the Anzinka, created the Tio kingdom, ruled by kings called *makoko*. The capital of the Téké administration was Mbe, from where the *makoko* ruled through subchiefs. Contact between the Téké and Europeans began in the mid-17th century with the arrival of Father de Montesarchio, a missionary to the region. The Téké participated in the SLAVE TRADE until the Tio kingdom began to weaken in the late 18th century.

Further reading: "Téké," in F. Scott Bobb, *Historical Dictionary of Democratic Republic of the Congo (Zaire)* (London: Scarecrow Press, 1999), 407–408; "Tio Kingdom," in Bobb, *Historical Dictionary of the Democratic Republic of the Congo*, 411–412; Eric Young, "Téké," in *Africana: The Encyclopedia of the African and African American Experience*, eds. Kwame Anthony Appiah and Henry Louis Gates, Jr. *(New York: Basic* Civitas Books, 1999), 1830.

— Lisa M. Brady

Tempest, The (1611)

A dramatic romance, *The Tempest* represents the last complete composition written by Elizabethan playwright and poet WILLIAM SHAKESPEARE.

First performed at Whitehall on November 1, 1611, *The Tempest* was among the entertainments for the celebration of the betrothal and marriage of JAMES I's daughter, Elizabeth, in the winter of 1612–13. No one source for the play has been discovered. Rather, it appears the author drew a rich confluence of elements from both past and contemporary events. Concerning the latter, Shakespeare was no doubt influenced by the burgeoning English interest in overseas exploration. A storm at sea intensified by St. Elmo's Fire, mutiny, and insurrection on an island, unfamiliar wildlife of a newly discovered world, and an unexpected rescue represent elements within the play culled from contemporary sources. Undoubtedly, Shakespeare had read the recently published "Burmuda Pamphlets," including Sylvester Jordain's *Discovery of the Burmudas*, the Council of Virginia's *True Declaration of the State of the Colonie Virginia with a Confrontation of Such Scandalous Reports as Have Tended to Disgrace of so Worthy an Enterprise,* and a letter by William Strachey, the *True Report of the Wracke*—all written or published in 1610.

It is also quite possible that Shakespeare based the character of Caliban on the description of the Patagonian giants in PETER MARTYR's *Decades*, a tract translated by Englishman RICHARD EDEN in 1555. Shakespeare's use of contemporary materials related to exploration provides a link to the NEW WORLD for *The Tempest*, although he used a deserted Mediterranean island as the setting of his play.

Beyond contemporary source material, scholars have connected *The Tempest* to the Bible, including Paul's arrival on the island of Malta, various Spanish romances, and Virgil's *Aeneid*. Some have argued that the play closely paralleled *Die Schöne Sidea,* a 1605 play by German Jacob Ayrer.

Further reading: Harold Bloom, ed. *William Shakespeare's The Tempest: Modern Critical Interpretations* (New York, Chelsea House 1988); Trevor R. Griffiths, "'This Island's Mine' Caliban and Colonialism," *Yearbook of English Studies* 13 (1983): 159–180; Meredith Anne Skura, "Discourse and the Individual: The Case of Colonialism in the Tempest," *Shakespeare Quarterly* 40 (1989): 60–90; Eugene Wright, "Christopher Columbus, William Shakespeare, and the Brave New World," in Peter Milward, ed., *The Mutual Encounter of East and West, 1492–1992* (Tokyo: Renaissance Institute, 1992).

— Matthew Lindaman

Tenochtitlán

Capital city of the AZTECS, Tenochtitlán was located on an island in Lake Texcoco in the Puebla-Tlaxcala Valley of central MEXICO and conquered by the Spanish CONQUISTADORES under the command of HERNÁN CORTÉS in 1521.

According to most versions of the Aztec origin myth, the god HUITZILOPOCHTLI led his people, originally known as the Mexica, from their home at AZTLÁN into the Puebla-Tlaxcala Valley of central Mexico, currently the location of Mexico City. The Aztecs were newcomers to an already hotly contested territory and thus were forced to found their new home in some of the least desirable territory, on an island and the surrounding swampy ground. They were later able to connect their city, named after Tenoch, one of their early leaders, to the mainland by means of three broad causeways, one north to Tepeyac, one west to Tlacopan, and one south to Coyoacán. These were broken at regular intervals by bridges under which lake traffic could pass spanned by wooden sections removable for defensive purposes.

By the time the Spaniards arrived in 1519, Tenochtitlán had overcome its humble origins. Taken together with its sister city, Tlatelolco, it boasted a population at 200,000, which was about five times the population of LONDON at the time, but size was not the only thing about Tenochtitlán that impressed the Spaniards. BERNAL DÍAZ DEL CASTILLO's description in *The True History of the Conquest of New Spain* was characteristic of the conquistadores' reactions:

> During the morning, we arrived at a broad causeway and continued our march towards Iztapalapa, and when we saw so many cities and villages built in the water and other great towns on dry land and that straight and level causeway going towards Mexico, we were amazed and said that it was like the enchantments they tell of in the legend of Amadis, on account of the great towers and temples and buildings rising from the water, and all built of masonry. And some of our soldiers asked whether the things that we saw were not a dream.

Some of the more well-traveled conquistadores compared Tenochtitlán with VENICE, and with good reason: Its total area of about 20 square miles was laid out on a grid, criss-crossed with canals crowded with canoe traffic, and much of the solid ground was, in fact, CHINAMPAS, or floating islands of soil-covered reed mats upon which the Aztecs planted crops and built dwellings. The *chinampas* were an integral part of the city and may have formed its literal foundations. The first Aztec settlers dug canals in the swampy ground of their new island home, cutting vegetation and piling it up to form their farming plots. They then spread mud from the canal bottoms onto the reed mats to form a fertile soil and anchored the whole complex with willows planted around the perimeter. Some of the residents' dwellings were built right on the *chinampas* and so did indeed rise from the water, but the opulent structures of Díaz's description were not the norm. Residents constructed ordinary houses of mud-plastered reeds with thatch roofs, which were light enough for the *chinampas* to support. More well-heeled residents of the city lived on the island itself in houses made of adobe bricks or masonry, while the highest-ranking officials lived in palatial complexes like those that Díaz described.

The focal point of the city was the temple precinct, the religious and spiritual heart of the Aztec Empire, consisting of a paved area surrounded by the *coatepantli* ("snake wall") and dominated by the Great Pyramid, a huge edifice surmounted with the twin temples of TLÁLOC and Huitzilopochtli. This precinct also contained the ceremonial ball court and the skull rack, upon which sacrificial victims' heads were displayed. The center of the sacred precinct was surrounded by the palaces of the great speaker and members of the Aztec royal line. Four processional avenues leading out from the temple precinct divided the city into four quarters, with the sister city of Tlatelolco functioning as a fifth quarter after the Aztecs subdued and forcibly incorporated it in 1473.

Tenochtitlán, the hub of the extensive Aztec trading network, hosted a market, but it was Tlatelolco, home to many members of the city's merchant class, that boasted the marketplace that was the real commercial heart of the empire. Tlatelolco's market impressed the Spaniards, who described it as being larger than those of Salamanca, Rome, or Constantinople. Every day an average of 60,000 people were engaged in buying and selling goods, ranging from prepared foods to luxury goods made of precious metals or

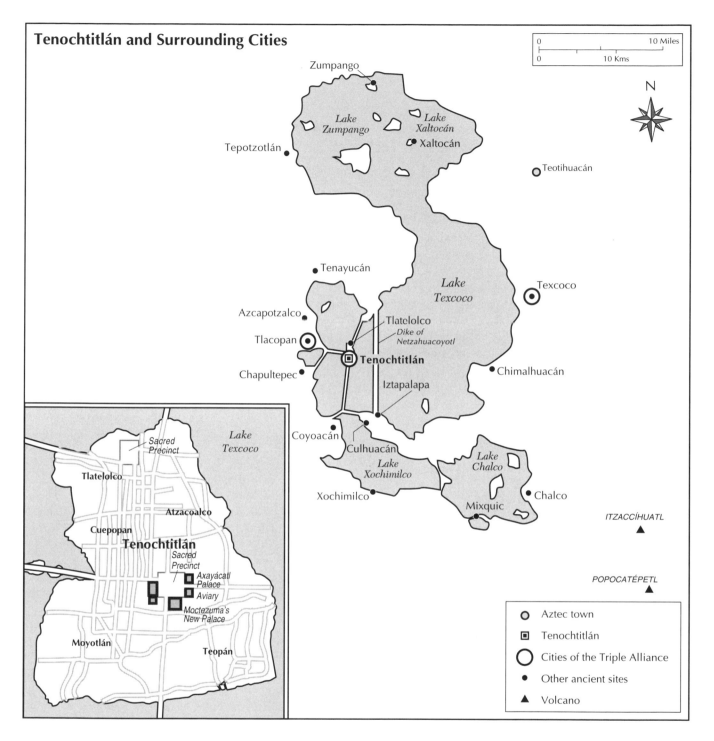

Tenochtitlán and Surrounding Cities

0 — 10 Miles
0 — 10 Kms

N

Zumpango

Lake Zumpango

Lake Xaltocán

Xaltocán

Tepotzotlán

Teotihuacán

Tenayucán

Lake Texcoco

Texcoco

Azcapotzalco

Tlatelolco
Dike of Netzahuacoyotl

Tlacopan

Tenochtitlán

Chapultepec

Chimalhuacán

Iztapalapa

Lake Texcoco

Sacred Precinct

Tlatelolco

Coyoacán

Culhuacán

Lake Xochimilco

Lake Chalco

Atzacoalco

Cuepopan

Tenochtitlán

Sacred Precinct

Axayácatl Palace

Aviary

Moctezuma's New Palace

Xochimilco

Mixquic

Chalco

ITZACCÍHUATL

▲

Moyotlán

Teopán

POPOCATÉPETL

▲

○   Aztec town

▣   Tenochtitlán

◯   Cities of the Triple Alliance

•   Other ancient sites

▲   Volcano

highly prized ornamental feathers. Currency consisted of CACAO beans, cotton cloaks, and, for more expensive items, gold dust–filled quills. The importance of trade and commerce to the Aztec Empire meant that the markets were patrolled by royally appointed inspectors who were to regulate prices and monitor the honesty of transactions.

Thieves caught within the market were punished by being beaten to death on the spot.

While this mercantile activity made Tenochtitlán the economic heart of the empire, it was, in essence, a center of consumption rather than production. The main urban labor force consisted of artisans and other occupational specialists rather than agricultural workers, and although many inhabitants tended small food gardens, these plots were intended to produce only enough to supplement household consumption, which consisted largely of purchased foodstuffs. Fishers, fowlers, and *chinampa* cultivators were able to produce a small supply of locally garnered food, but the city was largely dependent on imports for its sustenance. This would become a critical factor in the Spanish conquest of the city, when the conquistadores were able effectively to cut the city off from its food supply. The combination of hunger and SMALLPOX took its toll on the city during Cortés's four-month siege in 1521, and by the time it was over Tenochtitlán's original population of 200,000 was reduced to an enfeebled 60,000, who surrendered to the invaders.

Further reading: Inga Clendinnen, *Aztecs: An Interpretation* (Cambridge, U.K.: Cambridge University Press, 1991); Michael Coe, *Mexico,* 4th ed. (London: Thames & Hudson, 1994); Bernal Díaz del Castillo, *The True History of the Conquest of New Spain,* trans. A. P. Maudslay (New York: Farrar, Straus & Giroux, 1956); Emily Godbey, "The New World Seen as the Old: The 1524 Map of Tenochtitlán," *Itinerario* 19 (1995): 53–81.

— Marie A. Kelleher

Teotihuacán

The largest, richest, and most powerful city in Mesoamerica until the rise of the AZTECS' capital of TENOCHTITLÁN, Teotihuacán was a city so revered that later generations believed that it was the place where the gods had created the sun and moon.

Unlike many sites in ancient MEXICO, Teotihuacán was never a "lost" city. The area was never fully abandoned, although in Aztec times the only community there was a small squatter settlement taking advantage of the site's steady influx of pilgrims. Teotihuacán was located in the central valley of Mexico, just east of Lake Texcoco. There is no record of what the city was originally called or even what language its inhabitants spoke. The name *Teotihuacán* was given to it by the Aztecs, meaning "The City of the Gods," but by the time the Aztecs explored the site it had been abandoned for almost 800 years. Many of the structures and zones within the city have names given by the Aztecs, although it is not clear whether they reflect ancient memories or were simply colorful labels.

Settled by 1000 B.C., Teotihuacán, along with Cuicuilco, became one of two burgeoning centers within the Valley of Mexico. Both cities developed rapidly and by 300 B.C. had as many as 10,000 people apiece. Shortly thereafter, disaster stuck: A series of volcanic eruptions devastated the agricultural land around Cuicuilco and par-

tially buried the city. With the destruction of its closest rival, Teotihuacán flourished and grew to become an enormous city. There are several reasons for this spectacular growth. First, the lands around Teotihuacán were fertile, facilitating intensive agricultural systems. Second, its residents controlled rich sources of obsidian, a volcanic glass highly valued throughout Mesoamerica. Finally, the city emerged as a great religious center, drawing pilgrims from across the region and exporting cult items and religious paraphernalia. By 100 B.C. there were probably 60,000 people living in the city.

By A.D. 200 Teotihuacán was the largest, most powerful city in the Western Hemisphere. Until 600 its influence stretched throughout Mesoamerica, although the nature of its power remains subject to debate. The city's economic power, based on its near-monopoly of the valuable obsidian trade, almost certainly enabled its rulers to have political power in the region. It also seems clear that the city capitalized on its status as a religious center; many cultures adopted Teotihuacano gods, and cult items manufactured in Teotihuacán spread throughout Mesoamerica. In addition, evidence shows that Teotihuacán was a formidable military power able to attack and conquer cities across a wide area. For example, archaeological evidence shows that the site of Kaminaljuyu in the Guatemalan highlands was closely linked with Teotihuacán. Also, the mighty MAYA city of TIKAL appears to have been defeated by the Teotihuacanos, and a Teotihuacano ruler was set on the throne. There is some evidence that the Maya city of COPÁN in Honduras also was conquered by Teotihuacán. Unfortunately, the archaeological site of Teotihuacán has produced almost no written texts, so it is impossible to reconstruct the nature of these political relationships.

Mysteriously, the city declined and fell shortly after A.D. 600. The reasons for this reversal of fortunes is not entirely clear. After 600 there was a steep decline in the amount of Teotihuacáno goods in other Mesoamerican cities, and it seems that the population declined. There may have been a series of droughts or even civil strife in the city. Lacking written records, scholars have been forced to speculate. Sometime around 700 the city was burned and most of it destroyed. Some survivors continued to occupy the site, although the community there was small and impoverished. Refugees fled to other parts of the central valley, including the city of Azcapotzalco on the western shores of Lake Texcoco and were quickly absorbed into the local societies. The fall of this mighty city did not cause an immediate "Dark Age" in Mexico, for other cultures such as MONTE ALBÁN, CHOLULA, and the Maya continued to thrive for another 200 years. Even in ruins, the city remains impressive, and the Aztecs' awe at its grandeur is readily understandable.

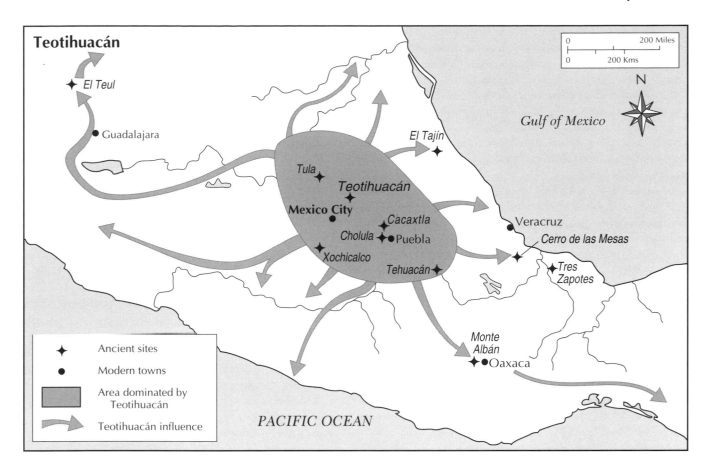

Teotihuacán

Ancient sites

Modern towns

Area dominated by Teotihuacán

Teotihuacán influence

Further reading: Janet Berlo, *Art, Ideology, and the City of Teotihuacán* (Washington, D.C.: Dumbarton Oaks, 1992); Kathleen Berrin and Esther Pasztory, *Teotihuacán: Art from the City of the Gods* (London: Thames & Hudson, 1993); Michael Coe, *Mexico,* 4th ed. (London: Thames & Hudson, 1996); Eduardo Matos Moctezuma, *Teotihuacán: City of the Gods* (New York: Rizzoli, 1990).

— Scott Chamberlain

Tezcatlipoca

A major god of the Aztec pantheon, Tezcatlipoca embodied change through conflict and may have been identified with Christ in the generations after the European conquest of MEXICO.

Tezcatlipoca, a member of the Aztec pantheon, was the omnipotent god of rulers and warriors as well as the patron of magicians and highwaymen. He was believed to be pure spirit and was connected with the gods of the sky and stars, especially those connected with death, illness, and destruction. Known as the bringer of both fortune and disaster, as both creator and destroyer, Tezcatlipoca embodied change through conflict. Because of his varied nature, he was referred to by many epithets. The most common of these were "smoking mirror" and "the sacrificial offering," but one modern scholar has identified no fewer than 360 others, including Titlacuahuan, "he whose slaves we are," Yáotl, "the enemy," and Youalli Ehécatl, "night wind." As Yáotl, the patron of soldiers, he was identified with HUITZILOPOCHTLI (although Yáotl was the warrior of the north of Mictlán, region of death, while Huitzilopochtli ruled in the south, or the region of life). Tezcatlipoca was also sometimes identified with Xiutecuhtli and considered the inventor of fire.

During the month of Tóxcatl (approximately April 23 to May 12), the AZTECS celebrated the principal festival of their year, dedicated to Tezcatlipoca. Each year a young man was selected to embody the god and to serve as the succeeding year's sacrificial victim. Throughout what was to become the last year of his life, he received all sorts of attention and honors and was encouraged to satisfy his every desire. On the day of the festival, he marched in procession to an altar on Lake Texcoco, where he was made to climb the temple steps. During the climb he played on three ceremonial flutes, which he broke in succession. When he reached the top, having broken the final flute, he was sacrificed, just as the new Tezcatlipoca began his procession through the streets of TENOCHTITLÁN.

It was during a celebration associated with this festival that PEDRO DE ALVARADO attacked the Aztecs in the sacred precinct of the Great Pyramid in Tenochtitlán, taking advantage of the fact that HERNÁN CORTÉS had taken his troops to the coast to fight PÁNFILO DE NARVÁEZ, who had challenged his command.

In the religious syncretism that took place after the conquest, indigenous peoples may have identified Tezcatlipoca with Christ, possibly due to the fact that both were associated with sacrificial offerings. One dramatic representation of this tendency exists in Ciudad Hidalgo in Mexico, where one atrial crucifix is adorned with Tezcatlipoca's symbol, an obsidian mirror, surrounded by a crown of thorns in the place in which Jesus' face would normally appear.

Further reading: Inga Clendinnen, *Aztecs: An Interpretation* (Cambridge, U.K.: Cambridge University Press, 1991); Doris Heyden, "Caves, Gods and Myths: Worldview and Planning in Teotihuacan," in *Mesoamerican Sites and World Views*, ed. Elizabeth P. Benson (Washington, D.C.: Dumbarton Oaks, 1981); Mary Miller and Karl Taube, *The Gods and Symbols of Ancient Mexico and the Maya: An Illustrated Dictionary of Mesoamerican Religion* (London: Thames & Hudson, 1993).

— Marie A. Kelleher

Thevet, André (1516?–1592)

Royal cosmographer for the king of France, André Thevet traveled to the Western Hemisphere and produced several works that rank among the most substantial collections of travel accounts in 16th-century Europe.

Born in Angoulême sometime in the early 16th century—scholars disagree whether he was born in 1504 or in the mid-1510s—Thevet received a formal education through the support of a powerful local family, the La Rochefoucaulds, and then became a private secretary to the cardinal of Amboise. In an age when many individuals interested in the Western Hemisphere were Protestants, Thevet remained a Catholic, and his loyalty to the state and its church paid many benefits during his career. He began to travel widely in the 1540s, with journeys to such disparate places as Italy, Switzerland, and Africa. In 1549 he sailed from VENICE to the Levant and stayed four years, touring such cosmopolitan centers as Constantinople, Alexandria, and Athens. Upon his return to France he wrote his first travel book, published under the title *Cosmographie de Levant* in Lyon in 1554.

In 1555 Thevet sailed across the Atlantic and reached BRAZIL, but he became ill and returned to France in late January 1556 after only 10 weeks in the Western Hemisphere. He maintained that he returned to America later on a journey that he claimed took him through the Caribbean, near FLORIDA, and, in his words, "very close to Canada." If he traveled that far north, his expedition would have been especially meaningful to the French, who had long had an interest in lands explored earlier by JACQUES CARTIER. When Thevet returned he published his next significant travel account, *Les Singularitez de la France antarctique,* which appeared in Paris in 1557. The book had a wide following in Europe. SIR WALTER RALEGH even took a copy with him on his later journey to Guinea.

The appearance of *Les Singularitez,* in combination with his earlier account of the Levant, launched Thevet into the highest possible social and political orbits in Paris. After the subsequent publication of other editions of his American travels, including editions published in LONDON in English and in Venice in Italian, Thevet became royal cosmographer to the French court, a position he held under four kings (Henry II, Francis II, Charles IX, and Henry III); he was also *aumônier* ("chaplain") to Catherine de' Medici, the spouse of Henry II and herself a member of one of Italy's richest and most powerful families. In addition, he became an overseer of the king's CABINET OF CURIOSITIES at Fountainebleau. The Catholic Church also offered rewards and positions: abbot of Notre Dame de Masdion in Saintonge and canon of the cathedral of Angoulême in his hometown.

In 1575 he published his masterpiece, *La Cosmographie Universelle,* in two enormous volumes in Paris. In scale it ranked alongside GIOVANNI BATTISTA RAMUSIO's three-volume *Navigationi e Viaggi,* and it gave to a select group of French readers an astonishing glimpse of the world well beyond France. Like other compilers of accounts, Thevet relied heavily on certain authorities, including (not surprisingly) the writings about Florida left by RENÉ DE LAUDONNIÈRE. Among his book's charms were illustrations that accompanied Thevet's description of the Western Hemisphere, including a picture of a ship sailing under a star-filled night sky and another of the *Isle du Rats*—the "Isle of Rats"—where rodents had become so menacing that they seemed to control the island. He even included a description, accompanied by a map, of a wondrous island covered with beautiful birds and bountiful fruit trees—"a second paradise," he called it, and then named it "l'Isle de Thevet" to make sure that he would be forever associated with it. However, although his earlier efforts had received virtually universal praise, the *Cosmographie Universelle* elicited scorn from some readers, including JEAN DE LÉRY who criticized what he believed were Thevet's numerous errors. In the mid-1580s Thevet completed a series of biographical sketches, which he published under the title *Vrais Pourtraicts et vies des hommes illustres—True Portraits and Lives of Illustrious Men—* published in Paris in 1584, and another major geographical work, entitled "Le Grand Insulaire et pilotage d'André Thevet angoumoisin," which remained unpublished during his lifetime. At some point he also put his signature on the cover page of the Codex Mendoza, thereby linking his identity with one of the major written accounts of the indigenous peoples of Mesoamerica and their encounter with the Spanish.

When Thevet died in Paris in November 1592, he left behind a body of work that included not only accounts of his and other travels, but also a preliminary vocabulary list of words used by the indigenous peoples of Canada. Others who followed left behind similar linguistic clues about the early meetings between Europeans and Native Americans. Although such listings have great value, Thevet at the end of his life focused on neither his travels nor his vocabulary but instead on the construction of his own tomb at the Grand Convent of the FRANCISCANS. Having ordered the tomb himself, he apparently spent his last days ensuring that this Parisian grave was suitable for his earthly remains.

Further reading: Frank Lestringant, *Mapping the Renaissance World: The Geographical Imagination in the Age of Discovery* (Berkeley: University of California Press, 1994); Roger B. Schlesinger and Arthur P. Stabler, eds. and trans., *André Thevet's North America: A Sixteenth-Century View* (Kingston, Ontario: McGill-Queen's University Press, 1986).

Tikal

One of the largest, most important of the classic MAYA cities and site of the tallest structure built in the Western Hemisphere before 1492.

Tikal was not among the oldest Maya centers, having been settled only around 800 B.C. By that time many other villages in the region were already flourishing. The city was surrounded by a series of broken hills and swampy basins that may have been lakes in ancient times. It was situated along a series of small rivers and valleys, which helped facilitate trade. The original settlers clustered around what is today called the North Acropolis, which remained the heart of the city until it was abandoned. Many early rulers and high-ranking nobles were buried in this location, and the acropolis seems to be an elaborate system of mortuary temples. During much of the preclassic period (until A.D. 200), Tikal was a subordinate Maya center lying in the shadow of the great city of El Mirador to the north. The decline of El Mirador and the subsequent fragmentation of power allowed Tikal and its rival cities to expand.

Tikal became a great city during the classic era (A.D. 200–900). Much of its political history is now understood thanks to recent breakthroughs in the decipherment of the Maya writing system. Around 200 a new dynasty began under the rulership of Yax Ch'aktel Xok ("First Scaffold Shark"). The ninth ruler of this dynasty, Chak Toh Ich'ak ("Jaguar Claw I"), was one of the most important rulers of his day, ruling from 317 to 378. He built a large palace on the Central Acropolis, which remained essentially unaltered for 400 years. Even when Tikal's enemies invaded the city, the palace was respected and maintained as a holy structure. After his death Tikal fell under the shadow of TEOTIHUACÁN. Texts record that warriors from the city "arrived" and set up a new ruler, who may have been a nobleman from Teotihuacán itself. Tikal briefly adopted Teotihuacáno art, ceremonies, and battle tactics, which it used to subdue several of its neighboring communities. Tikal emerged as a major regional power by 450 but had antagonized many influential cities. In 562 the city of Caracol, aided by Tikal's great rival Kalakmul, defeated Tikal in a bloody war. The city entered a 125-year dormancy.

The ruler Hasaw Chan K'awil ("Heavenly Standard Bearer") acceded to the throne in 682 and restored Tikal's faded glory. He began a large-scale program to restore the monuments defaced by Kalakmul and Caracol and began building a series of magnificent new structures. He inaugurated a new style of architecture, which is evident in most of the surviving buildings in Tikal. The new style featured tall, steep pyramids with narrow bases. At the top of these pyramids was a small temple with an elaborate roof comb designed to give the illusion of added height. The most famous structure at Tikal, Temple I, is the best preserved building in this style and served as the ruler's mortuary temple. Beyond his artistic endeavors, Hasaw was a capable general and led his troops to a crushing victory over Kalakmul. He also maintained two critical alliances with the Maya kingdoms of COPÁN and PALENQUE, thereby creating stability in the region. Under Hasaw's rule Tikal entered a golden age, which continued under his two successors. Hasaw's son built the enormous Temple IV, which at 212 feet stands as the tallest structure built in the ancient Americas. The wealth of royal and noble burials from this time clearly shows that Tikal was at the height of its prosperity. It also reached its greatest size, covering six square miles with approximately 3,000 separate buildings. Population estimates for the city at this time run from 50,000 to 100,000.

After 750 Tikal began its final decline. For generations scholars have debated about why the once flourishing Maya civilization collapsed at the end of the classic period. Decipherment of the Maya writing system has suggested that one strong factor in the decline of Tikal and many other sites was the spread of warfare. Violence escalated after

700, engulfing the whole region. Although powerful, Tikal could not escape the wars' secondary effects: disruption of trade, DISEASE, and famine. The last three rulers of Tikal tried to reach back to the glorious past by adopting the names of illustrious ancestors, including Hasaw Chan K'awil. Grave goods after 700 were less rich, less elaborate, and fewer in number. Those few buildings raised were of inferior material, and the city's rulers could organize the building of only a few public monuments. The last carved date at Tikal was in 869, although the city remained inhabited for many more years. In its final days the community was impoverished and fearful. Several buildings had been destroyed, and it appears that squatters occupied the royal palaces, using one building for a prison stockade. By 950 Tikal was essentially abandoned, although a handful of people lived in the area until around 1200. By the time of the Spanish conquest, the city was all but forgotten and completely overgrown by the jungle.

Tikal has been instrumental in the understanding of the ancient Maya. As one of the largest, wealthiest Maya cities, it has provided archaeologists with a great quantity of material for study. Additionally, Tikal's extensive involvement with other leading centers of the time has contributed to a unified chronology of the Maya area. Still, excavations have uncovered only 10 percent of the city, making it clear that the mysterious ruins have much more to tell.

Further reading: Michael D. Coe, *The Maya*, 6th ed. (London: Thames & Hudson, 1999); William R. Coe, *Tikal: A Handbook of Ancient Maya Ruins* (Philadelphia: University Museum of the University of Pennsylvania, 1967); Peter D. Harrison, *The Lords of Tikal: Rulers of an Ancient City* (London: Thames & Hudson, 1999).

— Scott Chamberlain

Timbuktu

Renowned for its mosques and centers of learning, Timbuktu (Tombouctou) also served as an important commercial center throughout the 16th century.

Founded in the 11th century by TUAREG nomads as a summer camp nine miles from the northwest bend of the NIGER RIVER, Timbuktu gained prominence as a trading center by the 14th century. In 1325 MALI conquered Timbuktu, incorporating the city into its expanding empire. Under the reign of MANSA MUSA I (1307–1337), Timbuktu grew into the region's intellectual and spiritual center with the establishment of several mosques. Mansa Musa brought Andalusian architect and poet Abou-Ishaq Ibrahim Es Saheli to Mali to build Timbuktu's great Dyingerey Ber mosque. The chronicler IBN BATTUTA visited the city in 1353, providing an excellent account of the city and of its

male inhabitants' custom of winding a turban around the head and face, a Tuareg practice called veiling. He also described the relative peace the city enjoyed under the auspices of the Mali Empire. During Mansa Musa's reign Timbuktu's already lucrative position on the trans-Saharan trade routes increased due to better protection against raiders. Copper, salt, sword blades, and, later, Venetian beads (see VENICE) were brought into Timbuktu in exchange for GOLD and slaves (see SLAVERY) from the interior.

Mali controlled Timbuktu and its markets until 1433, when the Tuaregs regained control of the city. In 1468 it became part of the growing SONGHAI Empire, and its importance as a commercial and intellectual center continued to increase. Timbuktu reached its apex during the reign of ASKIA MUHAMMAD I (d. 1538), who took the Songhai throne in 1493. Askia Muhammad was a devout follower of Islam and welcomed the many Islamic scholars who settled in Timbuktu. During Askia Muhammad's reign and throughout the 16th century Islamic scholarship flourished in the city, making it one of the SUDAN's leading intellectual and spiritual centers. Indeed, scholars, especially the Aqit family, made up part of the ruling class of the city.

Although appearing on European maps as early as 1375, Timbuktu came to the wider attention of Europeans in the 1550s through the writings of the Venetian geographer GIOVANNI BATTISTA RAMUSIO, who exhorted its possibilities as a trading center to Italian merchants. He based his recommendations on the descriptions of the kingdoms of West Africa and the Sudan left by the Venetian Ca' da Mosto, who traveled to the Guinea coast in 1455, and by LEO AFRICANUS, the chronicler of the Mali and Songhai Empires in the early 16th century. Leo Africanus described the city and its inhabitants, its government, and its physical environment, providing a valuable source on Timbuktu's history and its connections to the Songhai Empire. Mahmud al-Kati (1468–1593), a Muslim judge and scholar who accompanied Askia Muhammad on his hajj to MECCA (see ISLAM), also chronicled the history of the Sudanic empires of Mali and Songhai. Ibn al-Mukhtar, al-Kati's grandson, completed the *Ta'rikh al-fattash*, which included a history of Timbuktu and biographies of its resident scholars and jurists in the mid-17th century. The most comprehensive contemporary document on the history of Timbuktu remains the *Ta'rikh al-sudan* written by 'Abd al-Rahman ibn' Abd Allah ibn 'Imran al-Sa'di (b. 1594), a native of the city. In the *Ta'rikh al-sudan*, al-Sa'di chronicled the history of the region, detailing the Mali, Songhai, and Moroccan conquests and focusing on Timbuktu, GAO, and DJENNE-DJENO. Al-Sa'di also provided biographies of Timbuktu's scholars and religious leaders.

In 1591 Moroccans, interested in controlling the gold trade, attacked and conquered Timbuktu. Two years later, under the direction of the city's literati, Timbuktu's residents rebelled against the invaders. The next year Mahmud ibn Zargun, the pasha of the region under the Moroccans, deported many of the scholars, including Ahmad Baba (1556–1627), to Marrakech. The Moroccan invasion effectively ended the Songhai Empire as well as Timbuktu's prominence as a center of learning.

Further reading: John O. Hunwick, *Timbuktu and the Songhay Empire: Al-Sa'di's Ta'rikh al-sudan down to 1613 and other Contemporary Documents* (Boston: Brill, 1999); Basil Davidson, "Kingdoms of the Old Sudan," in *The Lost Cities of Africa,* Basil Davidson (Boston: Little, Brown, 1987); "The Majesty of Mali," and "Songhai Achievement," in *West Africa Before the Colonial Era: A History to 1850,* Basil Davidson (London: Longman, 1998); Elias N. Saad, *Social History of Timbuktu: The Role of Muslim Scholars and Notables, 1400–1900* (Cambridge, U.K.: Cambridge University Press, 1983).

— Lisa M. Brady

Timucua

The Timucua Indians, consisting of 25 distinct groups, inhabited present-day north-central and northeast FLORIDA and south-central Georgia at the time of conquest.

Before Europeans arrived the Timucua formed continually shifting alliances and chiefdoms. The eastern Timucuas, living in northeast Florida, cultivated beans, gourds, CORN (maize), marsh elder, squash, sunflower, and TOBACCO. Minimal hunting and gathering supplemented this subsistence. The western Timucua, in north-central Florida and south-central Georgia, did not depend upon horticulture as much as the eastern groups and thus spent more time hunting and gathering. Scholars know a significant amount of information about the Timucua culture from the writings of RENÉ DE LAUDONNIÈRE and the drawings of JACQUES LE MOYNE, two colonists in the French attempt to establish a base in Florida at the mouth of the St. Johns River.

The Spanish *entradas* of PÁNFILIO DE NARVÁEZ and HERNANDO DE SOTO encountered the Timucua in Florida in 1528 and 1539, respectively. By the late 16th century FRANCISCANS began missionizing the Timucua, and these missions developed large farms and ranches with Timucua labor. Modern-day northeast and north-central Florida then became known as the Timucua province. In the early 17th century pandemics (see DISEASE) began to hit the region in successive waves and reduced the population by approximately 80 percent in 100 years. Eventually, other native groups such as the Guale and Apalache migrated, under the direction of the Spanish, to populate the Timucua mission province. Over time the Timucua ceased to exist as an ethnic or cultural identity.

Further reading: John H. Hann, *A History of the Timucua Indians and Missions* (University Press of Florida, 1996); Jerald T. Milanich, *The Timucua* (Cambridge, Mass.: Blackwell, 1996); ———, *Laboring in the Fields of the Lord: Spanish Missions and Southeastern Indians* (Washington, D.C.: Smithsonian Institution Press, 1999); John E. Worth, *The Timucua Chiefdoms of Spanish Florida,* vol. 1, *Assimilation,* (Gainesville: University Press of Florida, 1998); ———, *The Timucuan Chiefdoms of Spanish Florida,* vol. 2, *Resistance and Destruction* (Gainesville: University Press of Florida, 1998).

— Dixie Ray Haggard

Tlacacla (Tlacaélel) (1398–?)

Tlacacla served as *cihuacoatl* under the Aztec great speakers ITZCÓATL and Moctezuma I Ilhuicamina (r. 1440–69) and probably was the driving force behind a number of early reforms of Aztec society and government.

Tlacacla's office of *cihuacoatl* ("woman snake," an aspect of the great mother goddess) made him a secondary ruler in TENOCHTITLÁN, in charge of internal affairs, commanding the army, directing sacrifices, and serving as senior counselor to the great speaker. The *cihuacoatl* could survive changes in administrations with his power intact. Tlacacla himself served through the reigns of two of Itzcóatl's successors, including Motecuhzoma I Ilhuicamina, "the elder," himself Tlacacla's brother. Chronicles report his accomplishments as including the reorganization of civil and religious offices, development of the Aztec educational system (see AZTECS), and the structuring of a strict class system.

The truth of Tlacacla's life and power is difficult to discern because the sources disagree on crucial details. For example, one source treats him as an entirely fictitious character, while another proposes an equally unlikely career beginning with Itzcóatl (r. 1427–40) and ending during the reign of Ahuítzotl (r. 1486–1502). We do know that Tlacacla was the name of the *cihuacoatl* during Motecuhzoma II's reign and that he served until at least 1503. What seems most likely, under the circumstances, is that the Tlacacla who was active during Itzcóatl's reign was the founder of a political dynasty that passed from father to son and that his successors may have had or adopted their patriarch's name.

Many sources portray the first Tlacacla as the power behind the throne, the real ruler during the administrations of Itzcóatl and Motecuhzoma I. He also seems to have been the principal force behind the early diplomacy between Azcapotzalco and Tenochtitlán as well as the later wars between the two powers. He may have also instituted the FLOWERY WARS with other peoples of the region.

Further reading: Geoffrey W. Conrad and Arthur A. Demarest, *Religion and Empire: The Dynamics of Aztec and Inca Expansionism* (Cambridge, U.K.: Cambridge University Press, 1984); Nigel Davies, *The Aztec Empire: The Toltec Resurgence* (Norman: University of Oklahoma Press, 1987).

— Marie A. Kelleher

Tláloc

Tláloc was the Aztec name for an ancient god of rain, earth, and weather phenomena who provided for the AZTECS' agricultural prosperity.

Tláloc, although one of the most prominent members of the Aztec pantheon, was a deity who appeared in nearly all the major belief systems of Mesoamerica. He was worshipped, often under different names, by the OLMECS, Zapotecs, Mixtecs, MAYA, and at TEOTIHUACÁN, where the number of depictions of this god indicate that he may have been that city's principal deity. The Aztecs dedicated one of the twin temples atop the great pyramid in TENOCHTITLÁN to him as well as a special mountain temple just outside the city. Religious continuity or commonality should not, however, imply that beliefs were identical. Aztecs as well as other peoples in the region often altered the nature of foreign gods to suit their own purposes. For example, in Teotihuacán, Tláloc seems to have been a militaristic state god, akin to the Aztec HUITZILOPOCHTLI. By contrast, in the Aztec pantheon he became a peaceful, if capricious, god of rain who could, if he wished, provide for his worshipers' agricultural prosperity, while his older functions as a martial deity were taken over by Huitzilopochtli and his political aspects by TEZCATLIPOCA.

For the Aztecs Tláloc was the god of rain and lightning, whose main purpose was to send enough moisture to nourish the maize crop. Aztecs knew him as "the provider," but he could be generous or miserly. Together with his consort, Chalchiuhtlicue, he ruled over the *tlaloque,* the various spirits of mountains and weather phenomena.

Further reading: Cecelia F. Klein, "Who Was Tlaloc?" *Journal of Latin American Lore* 6 (1980): 155–204; Mary Miller and Karl Taube, *The Gods and Symbols of Ancient Mexico and the Maya: An Illustrated Dictionary of Mesoamerican Religion* (London: Thames & Hudson, 1993); Michael E. Smith, *The Aztecs* (Oxford, U.K.: Blackwell, 1996).

— Marie A. Kelleher

Tlaxcala

A powerful kingdom in MEXICO at the time of the Spanish conquest, Tlaxcala was a fierce rival of the AZTECS and gave crucial military and logistical support to the Spaniards in order to destroy their hated enemy.

Tlaxcala was an unusual state. It was located to the east and south of the Valley of Mexico and was ethnically homogeneous, with all the people being NAHUA who spoke NAHUATL. In this sense they were ethnically indistinct from their neighbors, the Aztecs of TENOCHTITLÁN. But while the latter empire grew to encompass other distinct ethnic groups, the Tlaxcalans did not. The Tlaxcalan "state" was a complex kingdom consisting of four substates. Each component was called an *altepetl,* which had its own traditions, ruling lineage, judicial apparatus, and territory. According to the oral tradition taken down by the Spaniards, the first *altepetl* was Tepeticpac. As the *altepetl* grew, one area split off, becoming the *altepetl* of Ocotelolco. Later, Tizatlan and Quiahuiztlan broke off as well. Each *altepetl* was ruled by a *tlatoani,* or "speaker," who was a member of the royal family. In contrast with European states, the Tlaxcalans rotated power, meaning that the religious duties, taxes, and administrative expenses for the state were the responsibility of one *altepetl* at a time. The *altepetl* fulfilled these duties for a year before they were passed to another *altepetl.* In times of war, each *altepetl* provided companies of troops under a local commander. There was no single capital city for the whole, although each *altepetl* maintained its own capital. The four *tlatoani* generally ruled in conjunction with one another, although there was one who was "first among equals." Originally this honor fell to the *tlatoani* of Tepeticpac, in honor of its position as the original state, but when Ocotelolco became the most powerful *altepetl,* its *tlatoani* assumed this responsibility.

The history of Tlaxcala was closely tied to the history of the central Valley of Mexico. After A.D. 1000 the leading center of the region was the city of CHOLULA, although by the time of the conquest it had lost much of its influence. After 1300 Tlaxcala had expanded its influence and had become one of the leading states of the time, dominating Cholula in turn. It had close ties with the city of Texcoco, which later became one of the founding members of the "Triple Alliance" that formed the Aztec Empire. As time went on the Aztecs and the Tlaxcalans found themselves increasingly at odds. As part of their expansion, the Aztecs systematically attacked a number of Tlaxcalan allies until the kingdom became surrounded by Aztec territory. The two kingdoms then began a slow war of attrition, in which the Aztecs alternately attempted to blockade the state and conquer it outright. In times of peace the two powers initiated the so-called FLOWERY WARS, in which both sides staged mock battles with the sole purpose of taking captives for sacrifice. Through the Aztec blockade Tlaxcala became increasingly impoverished, but its army remained formidable. It seems likely that the Aztecs felt that conquering the area would require great effort and provide few economic benefits.

The role of Tlaxcala in the Spanish conquest of Mexico can hardly be overstated. In September 1519, when HERNÁN CORTÉS and his soldiers first entered the region on his march to Tenochtitlán, the Tlaxcalans took up arms against him. Cortés survived a series of harrowing battles. The difficulties he faced against the Tlaxcalans made him begin to doubt that he would be able to subdue the Aztecs, who had much larger armies. At this crucial juncture, Maxixcatzin, the lord of Ocotelolco, decided to ally with the Spaniards and destroy the hated Aztecs once and for all. He provided several thousand soldiers who functioned as the front line troops in Cortés's forces. Maxixcatzin also provided provisions and guides to help the Spaniards' cause. This alliance survived despite the disastrous Spanish retreat from Tenochtitlán in July 1520. Cortés and his men were again welcomed to Tlaxcala and given shelter, provisions, and more native warriors. This army of native auxiliaries greatly strengthened Cortés's position, helping to offset the great numerical discrepancy between the Spanish and Aztec forces. Using Tlaxcala as a base, Cortés launched attacks on the Aztecs' territory, slowly cutting off the capital from provisions and support troops. In 1521 Cortés began the siege of Tenochtitlán itself, conquering the city in August.

Because of their unwavering support during the conquest, Tlaxcala enjoyed a privileged status after Cortés's victory. While most of central Mexico was divided into ENCOMIENDAs to be given to the CONQUISTADORES, Tlaxcala remained its own province and was declared to be a ward of the Crown. In 1531 a special CORREGIDOR (administrative overseer) was assigned to Tlaxcala and Cholula, and in 1536 the Spaniards founded the new city of Tlaxcala to serve as the area's permanent capital. In the first few years after the conquest, Tlaxcalan auxiliaries accompanied the Spaniards on several conquests in the region. For example, PEDRO DE ALVARADO used them in his conquest of Guatemala, where they received substantial land grants and other favors. War and migration served as a substantial drains on the population of Tlaxcala, whose population fell from 120,000 households in 1520 to 60,000 in 1538. This trend was compounded by a disastrous PLAGUE in 1545, which killed thousands.

Despite its close cooperation with the Spaniards in the conquest, Tlaxcala adapted to Spanish culture rather slowly. Documents from the 1520s to the 1570s were frequently written in Nahuatl, with only an occasional word borrowed from Spanish. The government was still organized along ancient models of rotating power, although Tlaxcalan officials eventually adopted Spanish titles for their positions. Tlaxcalan merchants understood the Spanish concept of money and in principle accepted the need for a money-based economy, but those in local markets resisted using Spanish coins for transactions, preferring to use the traditional barter system or to fix prices in CACAO beans, as they had done before the conquest. The issue of land ownership also demonstrates a slow process of acculturation. Before the conquest most land surrounding a community was held not by individuals, but by the community itself, who parceled it out for individuals to use. As the years progressed, several individuals began to stake claims to the lands they worked, obtaining Spanish titles that could be used in Spanish courts. These attempts were not always successful, and the tension between private and communal ownership of land continued throughout the colonial period.

Tlaxcala's large role in the Spanish conquest ensured that the region was well documented, providing valuable information for historians about native cultures at the time of European contact. Additionally, its wealth of colonial documents has allowed scholars to study the process of acculturation during the first years of Spanish rule.

Further reading: Hernán Cortés, *Letters from Mexico* (New Haven, Conn.: Yale University Press, 1986); Charles Gibson, *Tlaxcala in the Sixteenth Century* (New Haven, Conn.: Yale University Press, 1952); James Lockhart, *The Nahuas After the Conquest* (Stanford, Calif.: Stanford University Press, 1992).

— Scott Chamberlain

tobacco

During the 16th century Europeans believed that tobacco, long used in many indigenous communities in the Americas, was a wonder drug that could cure various bodily ailments.

Before 1492 countless native peoples across the Americas had smoked tobacco, often believing that the plant had sacred properties. As a result, smoking tobacco became a standard part of myriad rituals designed to propitiate the divine forces that governed the world. After Europeans arrived in the Western Hemisphere, they, too, believed that tobacco had special properties, although they tended to emphasize its medicinal and nutritional benefits instead of any connection to the world of spirits. Europeans who traveled to the Americas frequently commented on the value of using tobacco. Some believed that Indians drank the smoke from the burning weed; others were less clear about how users inhaled the product. JEAN DE LÉRY, the Huguenot who spent time among the TUPINAMBÁ of BRAZIL, noted that tobacco had nutritional properties and could cure certain physical ailments, including distilling "the superfluous humors from the brain." The French royal cosmographer ANDRÉ THEVET, who claimed he watched native peoples smoking in Brazil, testified that he could assure his readers that "having tried it, how good it is for purging the heart."

Tobacco, with the first illustration of a cigar, appeared in Martha Loebel's *Stirpium* (Antwerp, 1576)   *(The Granger Collection)*

By the late 16th century Europeans had begun to write systematic catalogs of the flora and fauna they encountered beyond the borders of their continent. Tobacco often took on a prominent role in these treatises. When Dr. NICHOLAS MONARDES, a physician from SEVILLE, published his account of the benefits of certain plants, he paid special attention to tobacco. The plant was, he argued, aesthetically pleasing and would thus be an excellent addition "to adornate Gardens" with its "fairnesse." Monardes enumerated a number of tobacco's alleged benefits, including its ability to cure headaches, uncomfortable intestinal gasses, menstrual cramps, respiratory and bowel problems suffered especially by the elderly and by children, toothaches, worms, and "griefes of the breast." He also claimed that chewing tobacco provided enough nutrition for several days' activities. Although his professions might seem far-fetched to a modern audience skeptical of such claims for any product, 16th-century Europeans were so keen to learn more about tobacco that Monardes's account was published in Spanish, English, Latin, Italian, Flemish, and French. In the years following the publication of Monardes's work, other Europeans, including SIR JOHN HAWKINS and THOMAS HARRIOT, also described how the indigenous peoples of the Americas used tobacco.

Despite its obvious health benefits, some observers became alarmed at the rapidly spreading use of tobacco in Europe. Among the critics was King JAMES I of England, who tried to crack down on the use of tobacco in his realm. However, try as he might to eradicate what he believed was a vice, the "sot weed" could not be removed from the goods that Europeans wanted from the Americas. That fact eventually saved the nascent colony of Jamestown when its existence seemed doubtful in the mid-1610s, and its success came only after English settlers there recognized that the region was ideal for the production of tobacco.

Further reading: Rachel Doggett, ed., *New World of Wonders: European Images of the Americas, 1492–1700* (Seattle: University of Washington Press for the Folger Shakespeare Library, 1992); Anthony Grafton, *New Worlds, Ancient Texts: The Power of Tradition and the Shock of Discovery* (Cambridge, Mass.: Harvard University Press, 1992); Peter C. Mancall, "'Growing by Nature Only': American Plants in Europeans' Imaginations, 1550–1650," *History Now/Te Pae Tawhito O Te Wā* 6:1 (2000), 30–35.

Toltecs

The Toltecs were one of the first great military empires of ancient Mesoamerica, whose exploits were so renowned that even after their decline and fall many Mesoamerican cultures (including the AZTECS) claimed to be their decedents.

It has been difficult to disentangle the truth of the Toltecs from the legendary stories that have surrounded them. By the time of the Spanish conquest of MEXICO, the Toltecs had passed firmly into the realm of legend. The term itself means "The Artificers" in the Aztecs' language of NAHUATL and frequently meant simply "glorious ancestors" rather than a specific group of people. Most of the royal lineages in Mexico claimed a degree of Toltec blood, and the Aztecs believed that their empire was a reconstruction of the lost Toltec kingdom. Moreover, the Aztecs' name for the former Toltec capital, *Tollan* (modern Tula), had come to mean any great metropolis—TENOCHTITLÁN, TEOTIHUACÁN, and CHOLULA were all "Tollans" as well. Scholars were uncertain if the Toltec culture had existed at all until the 1940s, when Wigberto Jiménez Moreno and Jorge Acosta firmly identified Tula, in the modern-day Mexican state of Hidalgo, as the site of the Toltecs' capital. Through careful sifting of the historical documents and archaeological excavations, scholars have been able to develop a basic understanding of Toltec history, culture, and society.

Although most of Toltec history is legendary, the broader patterns do seem to match the archaeological record, suggesting that there is at least a kernel of truth in the stories. It seems likely that the Toltecs began as a group of nomads who wandered the deserts of northern Mexico during the Mesoamericans classic era (A.D. 200–800). They spoke a form of Nahuatl, which was used by most of the people of central Mexico, including the later Aztecs. The decline of Teotihuacán after 600 created a vacuum of power that allowed many groups to flourish. During this period of upheaval, the quasi-legendary ruler Mixcoatl brought the Toltecs into the Valley of Mexico and established the Toltecs as a regional power. Around 800 the Toltecs built a major settlement at Tula, which would become the capital of their realm. In either 935 or 947 Topiltzin, one of the most important leaders in ancient Mexico, was born. He was apparently a high priest of the god QUETZALCOATL (the "Feathered Serpent") and in later stories becomes indistinguishable from the god himself. Under his rule Tula underwent a great transformation, becoming a wealthy, well-ordered metropolis at the core

of a prosperous kingdom. Topiltzin-Quetzalcoatl supposedly developed a cult of peace, eschewing war and sacrifice. A rival cult developed led either by the high priest of the rival god TEZCATLIPOCA or the god himself. The rivalry between these cults festered for many years, and ultimately Tezcatlipoca deceived Topiltzin-Quetzalcoatl with magic, forcing him to humiliate himself. In shame, Topiltzin-Quetzalcoatl fled Tula with his followers in the year 987. Tezcatlipoca and his followers maintained control over the city for the next 200 years. During this time the Toltec kingdom expanded, dominating central Mexico and establishing trade networks that reached from Central America to the American Southwest.

The exiled followers of Topiltzin-Quetzalcoatl did not fade into oblivion. Several stories suggest that they reached the gulf coast, boarded boats, and sailed off, vowing to return. There is some evidence to suggest that this

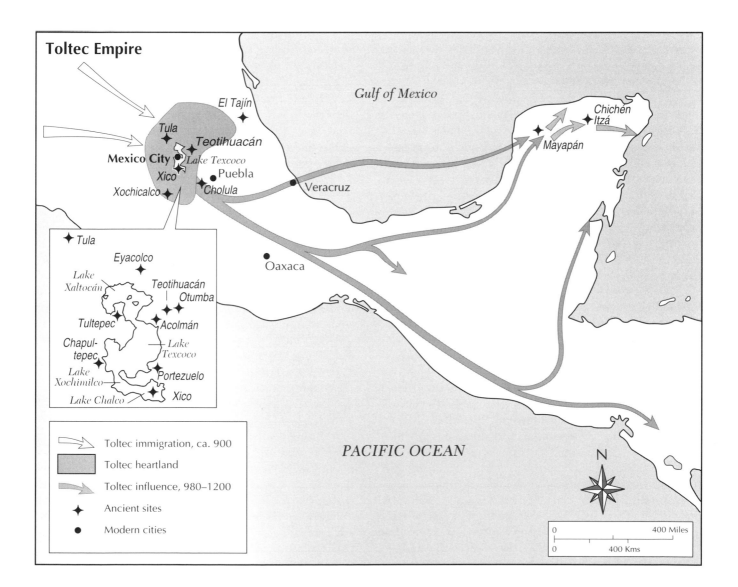

prophecy of return caused the Aztecs to mistake HERNÁN CORTÉS as the god Quetzalcóatl returning again from the east. Regardless of this prophecy, at almost the same time MAYA sources from the YUCATÁN PENINSULA tell of a naval invasion of their territory led by Kukulcán, a Maya name meaning "Feathered Serpent." These invaders set up a kingdom-in-exile based at CHICHÉN ITZÁ whose art, architecture, and iconography bore obvious relation to Toltec designs. These numerous parallels suggest that these mysterious invaders were none other than Toltec refugees from Tula.

The great Toltec empire at Tula survived until the 1150s. During the reign of the last ruler, Huemac, a series of crises weakened the state. A long drought apparently struck the area, bringing famine and disease in its wake. Factional disputes paralyzed the political system. More troublesome were the increased depredations of nomadic groups from the north. These nomads, called the Chichimeca, slowly invaded central Mexico, raiding farms and small towns with hit-and-run tactics. Weakened by internal disputes, the Toltecs were unable to repel the invaders, and the continued raids brought agriculture and trade to a halt. The Chichimeca, emboldened by their successes, began raiding the large cities of the Toltec heartland. In a great climactic battle, the Chichimeca attacked Tula itself and destroyed much of the city. Their capital in ruins, the Toltecs began a series of great migrations. Huemac and a number of followers fled to the city of Chapultepec in the Valley of Mexico. Other groups of refugees fled to Cholula, capturing the city and setting up a minor kingdom there. Some bands continued moving south, establishing new dynasties in the Guatemalan highlands. So widespread was this Toltec diaspora that by 1400 almost every royal lineage claimed some Toltec decent, including the Aztecs.

Tula

The city of Tula was the core of the Toltec state and one of the most important cities of the early postclassic period of Mesoamerica. Tula was located at the northern edge of the central Valley of Mexico in a relatively defensible location. A series of small streams cut through the area, which provided the ancient inhabitants with rich alluvial soil. Before the conquest this land was highly fertile, although overproduction, deforestation, and sheep grazing have left it rather barren today. Tula was strategically located near extensive sources of obsidian, a type of volcanic glass that was used throughout Mesoamerica for knife blades, mirrors, and ceremonial objects. A small community developed in the area around A.D. 700. For the next 250 years there were two important ceremonial zones within the city: Tula Chico and Tula Grande. Sometime before 1000, Tula Chico was suddenly abandoned and remained

an empty area within the densely packed community. It is tempting to see this as archaeological evidence that there were two rival cults within the city and that one was ultimately driven from the city. Whether or not this proves the Topiltzin-Quetzalcoatl story, it is clear that Tula Grande emerged as the uncontested ceremonial core of the city, and it is there that most of the great public buildings were located.

The period between 950 and 1150 marked Tula's greatest era. The city reached its maximum size, covering more than five square miles and housing 30,000 people. Tula did not demonstrate the same level of urban planning as did many other Mesoamerican cities and would not compare with either Teotihuacán or the Aztecs' capital of Tenochtitlán. However, the Toltecs did create a number of impressive works of art and architecture. Centered in the Great Plaza, there were two large pyramids, two large ball courts, a large skull rack, and a series of smaller shrines.

Unfortunately, much of Tula's former splendor is now gone, and modern visitors to the site often express surprise that Tula was ever a great power. The devastation suffered by the city around 1100 suggests that its enemies deliberately toppled temples and defaced monuments. In the years that followed looters repeatedly ransacked the site; even the Aztecs plundered the ruins looking for artifacts. Under these circumstances it seems a minor miracle that anything of interest remains there.

The Toltecs and Militarism

The Toltecs arose as a military power, and all aspects of their culture reflected the importance of their army. The Toltecs were able to create their empire in part because they introduced a number of innovative weapons and tactics that made them almost unbeatable on the field of battle. Earlier most Mesoamerican groups had two divisions within the army: infantry and missile troops. The shock troops did the hand-to-hand fighting, using long-bladed spears or clubs tipped with bits of obsidian; the missile troops used darts propelled by atlatls, or spear throwers. The two divisions depended on each other, with the missile troops protecting the infantry as they advanced while the shock troops protected the missile troops once the main forces engaged each other.

The Toltecs, by contrast, developed a different style of fighting. First, they invented a new type of weapon frequently called a short sword by ethnohistorians. Rather than being a heavy cudgel, it was a light, curved staff shaped like a hockey stick. The outer edge was set with a fine obsidian blade, giving it an incredibly sharp edge; several Spaniards noted that obsidian blades were far sharper than Spanish steel and were fully capable of decapitating a HORSE in a single stroke. This new weapon was light enough that troops could carry it and an atlatl at the same time, laying down their own cover fire and engaging in hand-to-hand combat upon reaching enemy positions. This innovation essentially doubled the size of the Toltecs' army. In addition, the Toltecs had a number of elite troops. These soldiers were members of military orders such as the Coyote Knights and Jaguar Knights. It is unclear what specific functions they carried out on the battlefield, but because membership in these orders was highly restricted—prospective members had to display great courage and prowess on the battlefield—they most likely functioned as special forces.

The combination of these elements indicates that the Toltec military was based not on bloodlines, kinship, or lineage, but was meritocratic in nature. The weapons, constructed and distributed by the state, were standardized. The types of battle formations used by the Toltecs could be successful only with persistent and rigorous training and would not have been successful relying only on a small group of elite warriors. Because the Toltecs had the largest city in central Mexico, they could also field an army significantly larger than their neighbors, who relied on a small corps of elites.

With their powerful military force the Toltecs were able to establish themselves as the dominant power in central Mexico. It is difficult to reconstruct the exact nature of the Toltec state, but it probably resembled the later Aztec Empire. In effect, the Toltecs moved into an area and subdued it by force of arms. Rather than set up direct political control, they left the smaller kingdoms intact, demanding tribute and trade concessions. Moreover, the Toltecs only moved into an area if it was profitable or a relatively easy conquest. They apparently bypassed several large, powerful cities, preferring to encircle and isolate them rather than risk a direct assault. It is probable that as the Toltec state expanded, cities farther away willingly established trade ties with the Toltecs because Tula was the greatest entrepôt in the region. The Toltecs maintained direct political control over the central Valley of Mexico, while the rest of their "empire" was a series of fluctuating relationships with other Mesoamerican centers.

Toltecs and the Arts of Peace

Although militarism was the most important element of Toltec society, they were well accomplished in peaceful pursuits as well. The Toltecs simply did not have the resources to dominate ancient Mesoamerica, so they often relied on trade to supply them with necessities and luxury goods. The city of Tula had a number of specialized artisans who created goods for export. Artisans worked obsidian into blades, cores, and ornaments, and Tula's sculptors and potters produced a variety of ceramics, figurines, and stone tools for export. In return, the city imported luxury goods from across Mesoamerica, including rare glazed ware from the Pacific coast of Guatemala and painted pottery from Honduras. Quartz, amethyst, and cinnabar arrived from the north. Traders from the Pacific brought shells. In recent years evidence has come to light suggesting that there was once a "Turquoise Road" that linked the Toltecs with the American Southwest. In return for the stone, the Toltecs exported tropical parrot feathers (and probably the birds themselves), headdresses, mosaics, and religious objects. Traders also brought elements of Mesoamerican culture, particularly architectural styles and the cult of the feathered serpent.

To ensure that trade goods continued to flow into the city, the Toltecs set up trading colonies in distant lands. Small groups of traders moved into an area and integrated themselves into the local industry. The Toltecs established these colonies throughout Mesoamerica. Because of the number of enclaves and their distance from Tula, most were highly vulnerable to attack. The success of this model suggests that these colonies were not imposed by force, but negotiated with the support of the foreign governments. Further, the Toltec colonists served as brokers to import finished Toltec goods such as obsidian blades, ceramics, and ritual objects.

Toltec arts, somewhat less sophisticated than other cultures', consistently depicted coyotes, jaguars, and eagles, all representing the great military orders. At times human faces protruded from the jaws of these beasts, suggesting that members of these orders dressed in ceremonial costumes (or battle gear) depicting these creatures, much like the Eagle and Jaguar Knights of the Aztecs. Warriors are common in Toltec art, although no depictions of individual rulers or warlords survive. The warriors usually have barrel-shaped headdresses and large butterfly pectorals. One final element common to Toltec art was the feathered serpent, which seems unusual because by all accounts the god and his followers were driven from Tula. In terms of execution, Toltec art was rougher, less elaborate, and more stylized than many other Mesoamerican cultures', which has led some art historians to dismiss their work altogether. Such an assessment is not wholly fair. While Toltec art is hardly graceful, there is a rugged sense of power and strength that effectively conveys their grim, military ethos.

The Toltec Legacy

By 1160 Tula had been destroyed and the Toltecs had scattered. Despite this violent end, the Toltecs loomed large in the Mesoamerican psyche. As a result of political domination, trade colonies, and refugee migrations, most later royal lineages claimed a degree of Toltec blood, suggesting that a direct tie to the Toltecs became crucial for political legitimacy. The decline of the Toltecs disrupted trade, dislocated populations, and destroyed Mesoamerica's political stability. In light of these difficult times, Mesoamericans began to look back to the Toltecs' reign as a golden age of peace and prosperity. Poets and historians claimed that the Toltecs grew cotton in whatever color they wished, built glorious buildings, and refined all the civilized arts. Tula itself became a city of legendary luxury, which partially explains why it was so thoroughly looted. These stories had a tremendous impact on the Aztecs. Upon entering the Valley of Mexico, Aztec rulers went to great lengths to marry into Toltec lineages. They also saw themselves as divinely appointed to restore the Toltecs' greatness. The myth of the Toltecs' glory survived long after their culture had fallen.

Further reading: Michael Coe, *Mexico*, 4th ed. (London: Thames & Hudson, 1994); Nigel Davies, *The Toltecs Until the Fall of Tula* (Norman: University of Oklahoma Press, 1977); ———, *The Toltec Heritage: From the Fall of Tula to the Rise of Tenochtitlán* (Norman: University of Oklahoma Press, 1980); Richard Diehl, *Tula, the Toltec Capital of Ancient Mexico* (London: Thames & Hudson, 1983).

— Scott Chamberlain

T-O maps

Medieval maps portrayed the three known continents, Africa, Asia, and Europe, in a diagram that resembled a capital T within an O.

In a T-O map, following the medieval convention of placing east at the top of maps, the top half represented Asia. Below Asia, Europe filled the bottom left quadrant, and Africa filled the bottom right. The T of the map represented the bodies of water that divided the continents. Africa and Europe, for example, were separated by the Mediterranean. The O, at the outer rim of the map, represented ocean.

The makers of T-O maps apparently did not intend them as depictions of the physical world, and travelers and merchants did not use them as guides. Their significance was religious and symbolic. Such maps usually placed Jerusalem, because of its religious significance to medieval Christians, at the center. They often showed the Garden of Eden, or earthly paradise, at the top of the map, in Asia. Because Europeans believed that all peoples had descended from the three sons of Noah, Shem, Ham, and Japhet, the three continents were often marked with their names.

About 100 examples of T-O maps have survived in various manuscripts. The maps were most common between the ninth and the 13th centuries but survived into the early modern period. The earliest known printed map, a woodcut from 1472, is a T-O map.

Further reading: Valerie I.J. Flint, *The Imaginative Landscape of Christopher Columbus* (Princeton, N.J.: Princeton University Press, 1992); William D. Phillips, Jr., and Carla Rahn Phillips, *The Worlds of Christopher Columbus* (Cambridge, U.K.: Cambridge University Press, 1991); R. V. Tooley, *Maps and Map-Makers* (London: B. T. Batsford, 1987).

— Martha K. Robinson

Tordesillas, Treaty of

The Treaty of Tordesillas of 1494, agreed to by John (João) II of Portugal and FERDINAND AND ISABELLA of Spain, set a boundary between Portuguese and Spanish claims in the NEW WORLD.

After CHRISTOPHER COLUMBUS returned from his first voyage in 1493, many Europeans wondered who should have authority over newfound lands in the western ocean. Because the pope, according to Catholic thought, had spiritual dominion over all peoples of the world, the Spanish monarchs turned to him for a decision. In 1493 Pope ALEXANDER VI issued a series of four bulls, or papal pronouncements, regarding the new lands. Because Pope Alexander was a Spaniard and hoped for support from Ferdinand and Isabella to further his Italian political ambitions, the bulls were favorable to Spain's interests.

The first two bulls granted sovereignty over Columbus's discoveries to CASTILE. The third, *Inter Caetera*, drew a north-south line of demarcation 100 leagues west of the AZORES and Cape Verde Islands. West of this line, all newly found lands were reserved for Spain. The fourth bull extended Spanish claims even further, giving the Spanish lands that might be found in other parts of the world, including lands "in the route of navigation or travel toward the west or south, whether they be in western parts, or in regions of the south and east, and of India[.]" This claim alarmed the Portuguese, who feared that it would infringe on their claims in the East Indies.

John (João) II objected to the terms of these papal decisions, especially the line set out in *Inter Caetera*. He asked that the boundary line be placed farther west, 370 leagues west of the Azores and the Cape Verdes, rather than 100 leagues. It is not clear why John sought this new line. Historians have theorized that the Portuguese may have already known, or at least suspected, that valuable lands might lie on the Portuguese side of the new line. Perhaps the Portuguese feared that the line as drawn in *Inter Caetera* would interfere with their claims to Africa. The most important consequence of the treaty arose in 1500, when the Portuguese explorer PEDRO ALVARES CABRAL reached the coast of BRAZIL. Because a large piece of the Brazilian coastline extended beyond the line of demarcation, the treaty gave Portugal a claim to a large piece of land in the Western Hemisphere.

Treaty of Tordesillas, 1494

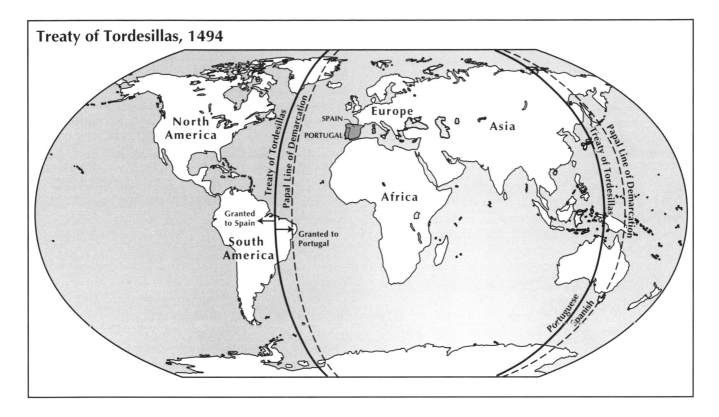

Although the Treaty of Tordesillas, in essence, gave Brazil to the Portuguese and the rest of the Americas to the Spanish, other European powers did not accept the agreement. According to the historian Lyle McAlister, the king of France asked to see "the clause in Adam's will that excluded him from a share in newly discovered lands," while the king of England denied that the pope had any authority to divide the territories of the world.

Further reading: Noble David Cook, "Tordesillas, Treaty of" in *Encyclopedia of Latin American History and Culture*, vol. 5, ed. Barbara A. Tenenbaum (New York: Scribner's, 1996); Felipe Fernández-Armesto, *Columbus* (Oxford, U.K.: Oxford University Press, 1991); Lyle N. McAlister, *Spain and Portugal in the New World, 1492–1700* (Minneapolis: University of Minnesota Press, 1984); J. H. Parry, *The Discovery of South America* (London: Paul Elek, 1979).

— Martha K. Robinson

Toxcatl   See Tezcatlipoca

Trent, Council of (1545–1563)
The Council of Trent, a general council of the Catholic Church called by Pope Paul III, met with three goals: to reunite European Christians, to define a Catholic response to Protestant doctrinal challenges, and to pursue necessary reforms from within the church.

Because of the religious turmoil of the 16th century and the challenges to Catholicism posed by the REFORMATION, clerics had called for a council of the church since the 1520s. Had a council met at such an early date, it is possible that some of the reformers who would later break from the Catholic Church might have participated, but no council met in the 1520s. When the Council of Trent first convened in December 1545, 28 years had passed since MARTIN LUTHER had first protested against the sale of indulgences. The divisions between Catholics and Protestants had become so established that there was no hope of reconciliation.

The council met in three sessions, from 1545 to 1547, 1551 to 1552, and 1562 to 1563. It was attended almost solely by Catholic representatives, most of whom were bishops or theologians. A few Protestant delegates arrived at the second session of the council in 1552, but their presence had no effect. Protestants no longer accepted the authority of a church council to settle disputes, and many Protestants suspected that the council was the work of the Antichrist. The council thus failed in its first goal. It was too late to reunite the Christian churches of Europe.

The council was more active in pursuing its other two goals, but these goals seemed to conflict. The pope wanted a speedy condemnation of what he viewed as Protestant heresies. The Holy Roman Emperor CHARLES V wanted the church to address the abuses that had helped provoke the Reformation. Because these goals were so different, the council proceeded slowly, alternating between theological issues and reform issues.

In its theological statements the Council of Trent clarified and reformulated Catholic positions and attacked Protestant ones. By doing so it drew the lines between the rival faiths more clearly. The council reaffirmed traditional Catholic practices, including the veneration of saints, the use of indulgences, and the celibacy of the clergy. It affirmed the power of the seven sacraments, which most Protestants sought to reduce to two, and restated the Catholic belief in the existence of purgatory.

Among the most important issues discussed by the council was the question of justification—of how human beings can attain salvation. Luther argued that human nature was so distorted by sin that no human actions, or works, had value toward salvation. Human beings could not in any way earn the right to eternal life but must instead rely on faith in God's promise of redemption. The Catholic Church had traditionally rejected the view that any human being could earn salvation, but it held that works had some value toward justification. Salvation came only from the grace of God, but a human being could participate in his or her own redemption by cultivating a disposition to receive grace and voluntarily accepting it from God.

As the council rejected Protestant understandings of justification, it also repudiated Protestant ideas about authority. While Luther and other reformers accepted only the authority of Scripture (sola scriptura), the Council of Trent declared that legitimate authority derived both from scripture and from the traditions of the church, including the rulings of councils and the declarations of popes.

In matters of church reform, the council sought to end some of the abuses to which reformers had objected. Perhaps its most important achievement lay in strengthening the position of bishops within their dioceses. Bishops received greater authority over priests and members of religious orders within their jurisdiction and were commanded to establish schools and seminaries within their territories to promote the training of new priests. Reformers had long objected to bishops who presided over a diocese but lived somewhere else, and bishops were now required to reside within their diocese and to preach regularly.

The Council of Trent was the Catholic Church's answer to the Reformation. It did not promote reconciliation among Christians, nor did it immediately end abuses within the church. However, by clearly distinguishing Catholic beliefs from Protestant and by beginning to reform the church from within, it strengthened the church in an era of continuing religious controversy.

Further reading: Elisabeth G. Gleason, "Catholic Reformation, Counterreformation and Papal Reform in the Sixteenth Century," in *Handbook of European History, 1400–1600: Late Middle Ages, Renaissance and Reformation,* vol. 2, ed. Thomas A. Brady, Jr., Heiko A. Oberman, and James D. Tracy (Leiden, The Netherlands: E. J. Brill, 1995), 317–345; Hans J. Hillerbrand, ed. *The Oxford Encyclopedia of the Reformation* (New York: Oxford University Press, 1996); John C. Olin, *Catholic Reform: From Cardinal Ximenes to the Council of Trent, 1495–1563* (New York: Fordham University Press, 1990); Steven Ozment, *The Age of Reform, 1250–1550* (New Haven, Conn.: Yale University Press, 1980).

— Martha K. Robinson

Tuareg

The Tuareg, an ethnic group of present-day Niger, MALI, Burkina Faso, Algeria, and Libya, participated in the SLAVE TRADE, controlled the trans-Saharan trade route in the 15th century, and dominated much of the territory south of the SAHARA, including the cities of GAO and TIMBUKTU.

Known as the "blue people" because of the color the indigo dye of their clothes left on their skin, the Tuareg were a seminomadic people in the western and southwestern regions of the Sahara and of the Sahel (Arabic for "shore," used to denote the transition zone along the southern edge of the Sahara). They claimed descent from the Berbers of North Africa who migrated south during the Arab invasions of their traditional homeland in the seventh century. The Tuareg formed political confederations, called *kels,* defined by caste hierarchies and clan membership and connected by adherence to ISLAM and their shared Tamacheq language.

The Kel Eway and Kel Gress, among other Tuareg confederations, migrated to the savanna zone of the Sahel, combining pastoralist traditions with trans-Saharan trade and sedentary agricultural practices in efforts to protect themselves from drought. Beginning in the 11th century, the Tuareg raided communities to the south, taking slaves and exacting tribute. Slaves in Tuareg society served the important purpose of maintaining adequate levels of agricultural labor while Tuareg nobles were absent on long trading journeys. By the 15th century Tuareg society consisted of numerous status and caste categories: *iklan,* or slaves; *irewelen,* the descendants of *iklan; imrad,* who payed tribute to the Tuareg, and, finally, the *imageren,* Arabic for "the proud and free," who were fair-skinned nomads of noble descent.

The Tuareg traded most of those captured in slaving raids in order to reduce the captives' chances of escape, but they kept some captives and assimilated them into Tuareg communities. The process of assimilation allowed the slaves to participate not only in agricultural tasks but also to accompany trade caravans. Through marriage and by demonstrating loyalty, slaves could and did achieve social mobility within Tuareg society. Those slaves not kept by the Tuareg became part of the human trade on the trans-Saharan trade routes, which the Tuareg controlled in the 15th century.

The largely nomadic Tuareg faced pressure from more sedentary groups such as the HAUSA as well as from other nomads like the FULANI and attempted to establish a more centralized kingdom during the 15th century. Several Tuareg *kels* united to establish a sultanate in Agadez (in present-day Niger), but no enduring centralized authority structures overcame the long tradition of nomadic life.

Further reading: Elizabeth Heath, "Tuareg," in *Africana: The Encyclopedia of the African and African American Experience,* eds. Kwame Anthony Appiah and Henry Louis Gates, Jr. (New York: Basic *Civitas* Books, 1999), 1891; "The Peoples," in *Cambridge Encyclopedia of Africa,* eds. Roland Oliver and Michael Crowder (Cambridge, U.K.: Cambridge University Press, 1981), 57–86.

— Lisa M. Brady

Tula   See Toltecs

Tupinambá

The Tupinambá, a native people living in present-day BRAZIL, impressed 16th-century Europeans as "noble savages" who went to war for revenge, practiced CANNIBAL-ISM, and yet seemed to lead happy lives.

Three important chroniclers of Tupinambá life were the French Franciscan ANDRÉ THEVET, the French Protestant JEAN DE LÉRY, and a German captive, HANS STADE. The differences between Tupinambá culture and European cultures disturbed visiting Europeans. According to European observers, the Tupinambá did not wear clothes and felt no shame at being naked. Because Europeans believed that human beings were ashamed of their nakedness as a result of humanity's fall in the Garden of Eden, they were surprised to see people who adorned themselves with feathers, paint, and other ornaments but did not wear clothes. Léry, however, who often commented on Tupinambá ways of life in order to criticize European customs, maintained that the nakedness of Tupinambá women "is much less alluring than one might expect" and added that the elaborate and expensive clothing and makeup worn by European women "are beyond comparison the cause of more ills than the ordinary nakedness of the savage women."

European observers also reported that the Tupinambá were warlike and practiced cannibalism. Stade reported that he had barely escaped death at his captors' hands and claimed that he had seen other captives killed and eaten. Léry also described cannibalism but noted that, unlike Europeans, the Tupinambá did not fight over land or to take one anothers' possessions. Instead, they "are impelled by no other passion than that of avenging, each for his side, his own kinsmen and friends who in the past have been seized and eaten. . . ."

In 1550, the city of Rouen staged a tableau to honor Henry II and Catherine de' Medici. This tableau featured Tupinambá (and sailors made up to resemble them) acting out Tupinambá life: hunting, shooting bows and arrows, and resting in hammocks. The scene ended with a simulated attack on the Tupinambá by another Indian group, from which the Tupinambá emerged victorious. Sixteenth-century European illustrators used the image of Tupinambá, with their distinctive headdresses and wooden swords, as allegorical figures representing America.

Further reading: John Hemming, *Red Gold: The Conquest of the Brazilian Indians* (Cambridge, Mass.: Harvard University Press, 1978); Jean de Léry, *History of a Voyage to the Land of Brazil, Otherwise Called America*, intro. and trans. Janet Whatley (Berkeley: University of California Press, 1990); Malcolm Letts, ed. and trans., *Hans Staden: The True History of His Captivity* (London: Routledge & Sons, 1928); J. H. Parry, *The Discovery of South America* (London: Paul Elek, 1979).

— Martha K. Robinson

V

Valdivia, Pedro de (1500–1554)

One of FRANCISCO PIZARRO's best officers in the conquest of PERU, Pedro de Valdivia is best known for leading the conquest of Chile.

Valdivia was born in 1500 in the district of La Savena, Spain. At the age of 19 he entered a military career. He left the service in 1525 and married Marina Ortiz de Gaeta. Growing restless, he left for the Spanish-controlled West Indies in 1535, leaving behind a wife and children whom he would never see again. He quickly established himself among the CONQUISTADORES, but when his hope of gaining riches and glory in Venezuela faded, he welcomed the opportunity to enlist in Diego de Fuenmayor's force of 400 men who were leaving for the Royal Audience of Santo Domingo at the request of Francisco Pizzaro.

In Peru Pedro rose to the rank of quartermaster general in Pizarro's army. For his efforts in the conquest of Peru, he was awarded the valuable La Canela estate along with a lucrative SILVER mine in Porco. Following the conquest of Peru, conquistadores besieged Pizarro with requests to lead expeditions in all directions, although few wanted to head toward Chile, perhaps because Diego de Almagro's recent (and fatal) trip there failed to discover a flourishing civilization, roads, points of communication, or magnificent golden buildings. It was a great surprise to Pizarro when Valdivia requested a commission to explore and subdue Chile.

Overcoming a lack of funds and recruits, Valdivia's expedition embarked from Peru in 1540. He later reflected that potential recruits "fled from it as from the plague." Nevertheless, he managed to muster enough Spanish troops to go along with a contingent of more than 1,000 Indians, who served as porters and camp followers. In his letters Valdivia often referred to the natives as "pieces of service." During battles with Chilean natives, the loss of "pieces" was recorded, if at all, after the loss of horses. Although scholars often portray Valdivia as somewhat less cruel than his fellow conquistadores, his treatment of the natives no doubt hurt him in the end, when his former groom, known as Lautaro, led an ambush that cost Valdivia his life in 1554.

Before his death Valdivia was successful in the founding of a number of towns, including Santiago in 1541. Granted the title of governor of Chile in 1547, he ventured farther to the south, founding Concepción (1550) and Valdivia (1552). To Pedro, town founding was not a haphazard affair. To guide him he possessed a copy of a town-founding guidebook, written by King CHARLES V in 1523. Ostensibly, the conquest of Chile was complete with the founding of Valdivia, but the Spanish encountered continued resistance from the Araucanians that persisted for more than 300 years. Known for their adaptability in the use of weaponry, the Araucanians had perfected the use of a small club (*macanas*), a lasso consisting of a running noose, and pikes, all useful when Lautaro led the ambush that killed Valdivia in 1554. Despite the murder, the Araucanians failed to dispel the Spaniards from their domains, and an epidemic wiped out more than one-third of their population, some 400,000 individuals, between 1554 and 1557.

Further reading: C. R. B. Graham, *Pedro de Valdivia, Conqueror of Chile* (London: W. Heinemann 1926); Arthur Helps, *The Life of Pizarro: With Some Accounts of His Associates in the Conquest of Peru* (London: Bell & Daldy, 1869); H. R. Pocock, *The Conquest of Chile* (New York: Stein & Day, 1967).

— Mathew Lindaman

Velázquez, Diego de (1465?–1524)

Conqueror and governor of CUBA, Diego de Velázquez played a pivotal role in the explorations of the Caribbean basin after 1500, including the sponsorship of HERNÁN CORTÉS's expedition to MEXICO.

Velázquez was a member of the first generation of CONQUISTADORES to arrive in the NEW WORLD. Accompanying CHRISTOPHER COLUMBUS in 1493, he played a critical role in the exploration of the Greater Antilles. In 1511 Velázquez led the expedition that conquered Cuba, becoming its governor shortly thereafter. He divided the natives into ENCOMIENDAs for his friends and supporters, while maintaining the largest grants for himself. Velázquez successfully bred pigs and other livestock on his lands, which he sold to outgoing expeditions at inflated prices. Under his watch colonists discovered substantial deposits of GOLD on the island. Velázquez naturally took a share of the profits for himself. By 1515 he had become enormously wealthy, and Cuba replaced HISPANIOLA as Spain's most valuable colony. During these years Velázquez developed a reputation as an arrogant man of limited capacities who greatly resented his rivals' successes. Worse for the conquistadores, he frequently attempted to take credit for his underlings' feats, robbing them of their hard-earned rewards.

As governor Velázquez used his wealth and position to sponsor further explorations of the Caribbean basin, hoping to augment his own landholdings and political prestige. When the remnants of FRANCISCO HERNÁNDEZ DE CÓRDOBA's expedition recounted tales of the wealthy MAYA cities of the YUCATÁN PENINSULA, Velázquez organized a new party to explore the region under the command of his nephew, JUAN DE GRIJALVA. Grijalva's voyage was a military disaster, but he brought promising reports of both the Yucatán and TABASCO. Encouraged by these reports, Velázquez sent a third and final expedition to the mainland under the leadership of Cortés. Originally Cortés was only to explore and claim lands in Velázquez's name. As the party prepared to leave, Velázquez became convinced (rightly) that Cortés was too ambitious to follow these orders and attempted to remove him from command. Cortés anticipated this move and sailed from Cuba before the governor could stop him.

Velázquez apparently seethed for some months at this open act of rebellion, but he waited until CHARLES V confirmed his governorship of the newly discovered territories of greater Yucatán before he struck back. He then gathered a sizable force of loyal conquistadores to capture Cortés and establish himself as the governor of Mexico. He placed these troops under the command of PÁNFILO DE NARVÁEZ. In Mexico Cortés skillfully brought these troops into his own army by promising them a share of MOCTEZUMA II's treasure. Cortés's subsequent victories against the AZTECS made it difficult for Velázquez to move against him openly, although in 1523 he convinced Cortés's friend and confidant Cristóbal de Olid to break with Cortés and conquer present-day Honduras in Velázquez's name. Cortés left immediately for Honduras in order to deal with this mutiny, and in his absence Velázquez circulated rumors about him and his loyalty to the Crown. Despite his efforts,

Velázquez never achieved the vengeance he so fiercely desired. He died in 1524, one of the wealthiest men in the Americas.

Further reading: Hernán Cortés, *Letters from Mexico* (New Haven, Conn.: Yale University Press, 1986); Bernal Díaz del Castillo, *The Discovery and Conquest of Mexico* (New York: Da Capo Press, 1996); Franklin W. Knight, *The Caribbean: The Genesis of a Fragmented Nationalism* (Oxford, U.K.: Oxford University Press, 1990).

— Scott Chamberlain

Venice

One of the most remarkable cities in the world, where the streets are canals, Venice rose from a group of islands in a lagoon on the edge of the Adriatic Sea to become one of the most vital commercial and artistic centers of Renaissance Europe.

Local myth tells that Venice was founded on Ascension Day in the year 421, although its first residents actually arrived on the islands in the sixth century. Ever since, Venetians have embraced a unique lifestyle. From the start they realized that their existence depended on finding a way to live with the sea—not a sea on its borders but one quite literally all around it. Venetians created their political system, based on the election of the doge (Venetian for duke), in the ninth century, and over time they developed a republican form of government that seemed to them and visitors to be an ideal political system. During the ninth century Venetians also defined their own religious fate when they stole the body of the apostle Mark from Byzantium in 828–29. Although they later misplaced his body, in one of the many miracles that defined Venetian history his body was rediscovered in 1094, an event now celebrated in a mosaic at San Marco, the glorious church that abuts the ducal palace and dominates the Piazza San Marco.

Venetians' connections to the ocean long predated the so-called age of discovery. According to legend, sometime in the medieval era the doge wed the Adriatic, not only in a metaphorical sense but quite literally: He sailed out from the lagoon and into the open water and tossed in a golden ring. The ceremony was reenacted every year on Ascension Day when the doge sailed out to sea in a gilded galley in front of an audience of onlookers.

Venetians used their strategic access to the Adriatic to create the greatest seaborne mercantile domain in southern Europe. Although the republic lacked a substantial territorial base and was thus dependent on other states for an enormous variety of basic goods, including most of its food, enterprising merchants organized commerce that transported the goods of the Levant to the West.

Close ties to East and West led to the spectacular eccentricity of Venice's architecture, (see ART AND ARCHITECTURE), evident in the Church of San Marco. Begun in the mid-11th century, San Marco was built in the shape of a Greek cross crowned by five domes. Local craftsmen spent inordinate time creating and embellishing the ornate interiors, many of them covered by sumptuous mosaics painted with gold leaf, but they paid little attention to its external appearance. By the 13th century or so Venetians, inspired by Romanesque and Gothic architecture, modified the exterior, adding carvings of fishermen, coopers, smiths, masons, and barbers whose talents allowed Venice to boom. The construction next door to the ducal palace signaled the fundamental link between church and state in the republic.

Residents and visitors alike recognized the special features of Venice. In the mid-14th century Petrarch praised the "august city of Venice," which had become "the one home today of liberty, peace and justice, the one refuge of honorable men, the one port to which can repair the storm-tossed, tyrant-hounded craft of men who seek the good life." Material wealth abounded, but Petrarch recognized something more precious: the city's unparalleled "virtue, solidly built on marble but standing more solid on a foundation of civil concord, ringed with salt waters but more secure with the salt of good counsel." The local 16th-century chronicler Marin Sanudo believed that the glories of the city would be perpetual. Venice was, he wrote, "a marvellous thing, which must be seen to be believed[.]" He agreed with those who asserted that "it will last for ever, as appears from this epigram found in the *Supplementum chronicarum:* 'So long as the sea contains dolphins, so long as clear skies contain stars; so long as the moist ground give forth her pleasant fruits; so long as the human race carries on its generations upon the earth, the splendour of the Venetians will be celebrated for all eternity.'"

The modern-day traveler to Venice will notice one of the city's architectural legacies: the desire of the wealthy to build their palaces facing canals. No other city in the world located so many of its finest buildings along canals, nor did craftsmen and architects elsewhere spend so much time constructing façades that were only visible by people in boats or across a lagoon. Venetians spent time and money on their buildings because they realized, as did the residents of other Italian cities, that buildings expressed common beliefs, aspirations, and values. A spectacular and orderly city, especially one constructed in the midst of a lagoon, had to convey to all the world the enormous public spirit of Venetians. What emerged from their efforts was nothing less than a lesson in civics taught by observation: political education absorbed without classes and lectures,

without preaching or priests, even without the explicit attention of the patrician class.

From the late 14th century into the early 15th century, a series of construction projects demonstrated the artistic heights possible during the Renaissance. Local elites, eager to show off their wealth, built one palace after another along the canals. Some of the palaces, such as Cá Dario constructed for the secretary of the senate Giovanni Dario in the late 1480s, sprouted magnificent decoration. Others impressed by their sheer size, such as the palace built for the Loredan family during the first decade of the 16th century and now known as Palazzo Vendramin-Calergi. Owners of these *palazzi* offered public thanks in the form of carved inscriptions to the benevolent authorities who allowed their creation. Within the palaces and inside churches such as San Marco and Madonna dell'Orto, Venice's great painters and artisans created images of lasting power and beauty. As a result, Venice has attracted visitors since the 16th century.

Venice's ascent came from its merchants' ability to organize long-distance commerce, particularly their ability to dominate the trade between the SPICE ISLANDS and Europe. The profits accrued through such commerce allowed Venetian rulers to employ artisans and painters, who transformed their dwellings into ornate urban treasures. As one resident wrote in his diary, "if trade falls off and men live on income little progress will be possible." When a Milanese pilgrim stopped in Venice on his way to Jerusalem in the late 15th century, the signs of mercantile prosperity overwhelmed him. "Something may be said about the quantity of merchandise in the said city, although not nearly the whole truth, because it is inestimable," Pietro Casola wrote in 1494. "Indeed it seems as if all the world flocks there, and that human beings have concentrated there all their force for trading." He found "tapestry, brocades and hangings of every design, carpets of every sort, camlets of every colour and texture, silks of every kind; and so many warehouses full of spices, groceries and drugs, and so much beautiful white wax!"

To its celebrators, Venice was the perfect city. As one local diarist wrote, "whoever lived and stayed there seemed to be in an earthly paradise, without any tumult of war or suspicion of enemies, nor would he look to suffer misfortune or fear any mental perturbation, the city having endured and stood so long, for so many hundreds of years, in peace, quiet, and repose; and whoever wished to live in peace and quiet and expect to go about his business peacefully could not stay or live in a quieter or more peaceful place than the city of Venice[.]"

Despite its marvels, Venice in the 16th century was in crisis. In 1499 the Turks warned a Venetian ambassador that Venice's time had passed. "Until now you have been married to the sea," one informed the emissary; "for the future, that is for us, who are more powerful by sea than you." The barbarians, as the Venetians defined the enemies who surrounded them, could not be kept back. A series of military conquests from 1509 to 1513 reduced the terra ferma that Venetians had managed to gain by the end of the 15th century, and a growing Turkish fleet threatened Venice's control over the seas. Despite an alliance with the Vatican, Spain, and England put together to resist threats from the French, and despite a peace agreement signed between Venice and France in November 1513, Venetians could not retain control over territory they once claimed. By the time the accord was reached, they had lost Padua and much of the rest of their territory. To make matters worse, an earthquake rocked the city on March 26, 1511, a further sign to some locals that they were receiving divine punishment for their material excesses.

Even in its decline Venice remained a vital city in 16th-century Europe. Among the city's residents was GIOVANNI BATTISTA RAMUSIO, the editor of travel accounts whose readers learned about the world beyond the republic's boundaries. Venice was also one of the publishing centers of Europe (see PRINTING PRESS), home to the famous Aldine Press. To the present day, there is no other city like it. Although some fear that the sea from which Venice sprang will ultimately drown it, for the moment, at least, it remains the greatest relic of the Renaissance.

Further reading: Patricia Fortini Brown, *Art and Life in Renaissance Venice* (New York: Abrams, 1997); Frederic C. Lane, *Venice: A Maritime Republic* (Baltimore: Johns Hopkins University Press, 1973); John Julius Norwich, *A History of Venice* (New York: Knopf, 1982); Garry Wills, *Venice, Lion City: The Religion of Empire* (New York: Simon & Schuster, 2001).

Veracruz

The name of the major native cultural zone lying along the Gulf of MEXICO, Veracruz also refers to the first Spanish settlement in Mexico, which became the principal port of the colony of NEW SPAIN.

In ancient times several important native groups developed in the Veracruz area. The earliest and most famous of these were the OLMECS, who flourished between 1700 and 300 B.C. As the first great culture of Mesoamerica, the Olmecs created the iconography, religious rituals, and royal ceremonies that most ancient Mexican cultures used until the arrival of the Spaniards. Other cultures developed in the region after the fall of the Olmecs, including the magnificent El Tajín culture that was contemporary with the classic MAYA. After the classic era, the area increasingly came under the shadow of the great empires of central Mexico, and at the time of the conquest much of the Veracruz region was firmly under the control of the AZTECS.

In 1519 DIEGO DE VELÁZQUEZ, the governor of CUBA, commissioned HERNÁN CORTÉS to explore the coast of Mexico. Concerned about Cortés's arrogant behavior and lavish spending on supplies, he reconsidered his action and moved to remove Cortés from command. Cortés suspected the governor's plans and sailed away before Velázquez could stop him. Realizing he was acting outside of orders and could be tried for treason, Cortés took steps to legitimize his actions as soon as he landed in Mexico. As part of his plan he founded the settlement of La Villa Rica de la Vera Cruz ("The Wealthy Town of the True Cross") in 1519. He meticulously followed the established royal ceremony of foundation, with witnesses swearing to the authenticity of his actions. As founder, he quickly appointed a *CABILDO*, or town council, made up of his own trusted followers and resigned leadership of the community to this body. In response, the *cabildo* appointed Cortés royal captain of the army and commissioned him to explore and conquer Mexico in the name of the king. Although highly suspicious, his actions were entirely legal and provided a veneer of legitimacy to his subsequent actions. After conquering the Aztecs, Cortés moved the site about 20 miles south to a better location (modern-day La Antigua), and in 1598 the Crown ordered the city to relocate once again, to its present location.

The city of Veracruz continued to play an important role during the colonial period. The Crown designated it as the official port of New Spain, meaning that all ships both arriving and departing had to pass through the city. Like other official ports such as Portobelo, Panama City, Acapulco, and Cartagena, Veracruz primarily came to life when the annual treasure fleets gathered, and the collected wealth of New Spain passed through its streets. In other times the threat of raiders and tropical DISEASES kept it from developing into one of the colony's larger cities. In 1567 nine English ships under SIR JOHN HAWKINS sailed into the city's harbor, hoping to sell slaves (see SLAVE TRADE) and contraband. The Spanish fleet trapped and destroyed them, although SIR FRANCIS DRAKE escaped with two ships. Veracruz retained its privileged position within New Spain until 1760, when the Crown allowed ships legally to trade in the colony's other port cities.

Further reading: Lyle N. McAlister, *Spain and Portugal in the New World, 1495–1700* (Minneapolis: University of Minnesota Press, 1984); Michael C. Meyer and William L. Sherman, *The Course of Mexican History* (Oxford, U.K.: Oxford University Press, 1995).

— Scott Chamberlain

Verrazano, Giovanni da (ca. 1485–ca.1528)

Commissioned by the French King Francis I to explore the Atlantic coast of North America, Giovanni da Verrazano in 1525 sailed northward from modern-day South Carolina to a place he called "NORUMBEGA," in the process becoming perhaps the first European to view the coast of present-day New York and Narragansett Bay.

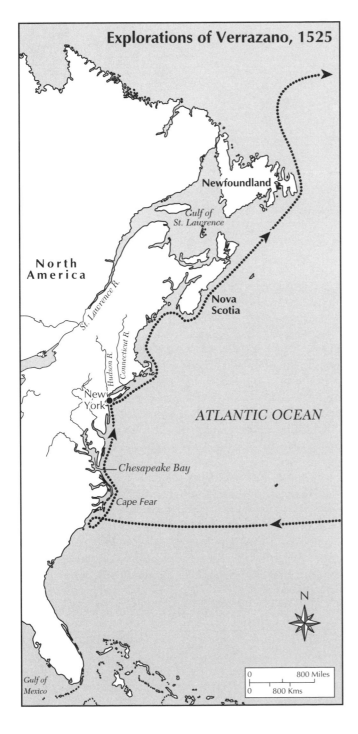

Explorations of Verrazano, 1525

Born in Florence to a wealthy family who possessed estates south of the city, Verrazano received a solid education. Once completed, he moved to Dieppe, France, sometime around 1506. After working on commercial and military ships, he came to the attention of Francis I, who provided four ships to him with orders to explore the North American coastline. Verrazano left France in January 1525. Only two of his ships made it across the Atlantic. The survivors landed at modern-day Cape Fear, North Carolina. After sailing to the south, perhaps as far as modern-day Charleston, South Carolina, he led his ships to the north, passing Chesapeake Bay (which his brother Girolamo labeled the Verrazano Sea on a map of the world), which the explorer believed might lead to the South Sea (the Pacific Ocean). He continued northward on his journey, reaching an area now known as Verrazano Narrows (a channel between Staten Island and Brooklyn, New York) in April 1525. He sailed farther north into Narragansett Bay, where he met local natives who provided assistance to the storm-tossed sailors. By early May he was ready to continue his northward journey. Over the next few weeks his ships followed the coastline until they reached modern-day Maine, where he encountered natives he found unpleasant, and then past the modern-day Maritime Provinces of Canada. In July he sailed back to Dieppe. On his return he described much of what he had seen in positive terms, especially a place he called "Norumbega," which became a fixture on European maps in the 16th century, even though no other explorer managed to figure out exactly where Verrazano had landed.

On a second journey, also sponsored by Francis I, Verrazano sailed to FLORIDA and then southward into the Caribbean. Anchored off one island, possibly Guadeloupe, he led a group onto the shore, where they were killed by local natives and, so some believe, eaten by cannibals.

Further reading: Angus Konstam, *Historical Atlas of Exploration, 1492–1600* (New York: Facts On File, 2000).

Vespucci, Amerigo (1451–1512)

Poet, cosmographer, and banker, Amerigo Vespucci is best known for his voyages from Spain to South America around the turn of the 16th century and for giving his name to two continents.

Born in Florence, Vespucci in his youth was an ambassador to France for Lorenzo de' Medici. In 1492 he traveled to SEVILLE and became involved in the organization of shipping ventures. He had arrived at the right time: After the return of CHRISTOPHER COLUMBUS, Vespucci was able to provision other ships destined for the Western Hemisphere. Eventually, he decided to venture west himself.

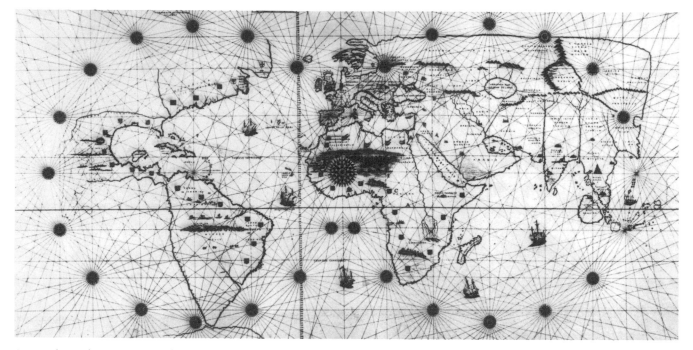

A map drawn by Hieronimus de Verrazano from *Verrazano the Navigator* by J. C. Brevoort *(Hulton/Archive)*

Although he claimed to have made his first transatlantic journey in 1497, more reliable evidence suggests that he sailed to South America for the first time two years later along with Alonso de Ojeda. He arrived near Cape São Roque, on the eastern tip of BRAZIL, and then followed the coast to the northwest for 700 miles. He was, as a result, the first European to lead an extended exploration of the mainland, though PEDRO ÁLVARES CABRAL had, in fact, landed in Brazil earlier but had not yet made it back to Europe to offer his report. On his journey Vespucci crossed the mouths of the AMAZON RIVER and the Orinoco River, the river that would later so entice SIR WALTER RALEGH. When he returned to Spain, he discovered that the Spanish were not particularly interested in his findings, and so he traveled to the court of King Manuel I of Portugal, who welcomed him and the possibility that Vespucci had found territory lying to the east of the line demarcated in the TREATY OF TORDESILLAS and thus part of the world the Vatican believed should be controlled by Portugal.

Vespucci made other trips to Brazil in 1501. On one he explored Darién and made maps of much of what he saw. Upon his return he published his report (see Documents) about what he called a NEW WORLD. In response Martin Waldseemüller, a German cartographer, labeled South America as "the land of Amerigo" on a map. The name stuck, and by the late 1530s Europeans applied the term to the entire Western Hemisphere.

The spread of the PRINTING PRESS meant that news of Vespucci's feats could race across Europe quickly. One edition of his letter to Soderini, published in Strasbourg in 1509, depicted a smiling man and woman chopping up human arms and feet. A broadside published in Augsburg or Nuremburg in 1505 showed a group of Indians at home with plenty of domestic details, such as a mother nursing an infant, a man and a woman kissing, and two men engaged in a serious conversation. The image also included one man eating a human arm and pieces of a human, including the head, suspended from a rope, presumably waiting to be eaten. Such images, based on Vespucci's writing, terrified many Europeans, who feared that all peoples in the Western Hemisphere were cannibals.

Further reading: Hugh Honour, *The New Golden Land: European Images of America from the Discoveries to the Present Time* (New York: Pantheon, 1975); Angus Konstam, *Historical Atlas of Exploration, 1492–1600* (New York: Facts On File, 2000); Clements R. Markham, ed., *The Letters of Amerigo Vespucci and other Documents Illustrative of His Career*, Works Issued by the Hakluyt Society, 1st ser., 90 (London, Hakluyt Society, 1894); Amerigo Vespucci, *Letter to Piero Soderini* [1504], trans. George T. Northup (Princeton, N.J.: Princeton University Press, 1916).

Vikings See Norse

Vinland

The name given by the NORSE to territory in the modern-day Maritime Provinces of Canada, where they arrived around the year 1000 and established a settlement, the first European outpost in the Western Hemisphere.

According to a Norse saga written perhaps 200 years later, sometime around the turn of the first Christian millennium Leif Eriksson, who was himself the son of the famous Norse explorer Erik the Red, set sail from GREENLAND to lands lying farther west. He encountered and named three places: Helluland ("Slab-Land"), Markland ("Forest Land"), and Vinland ("Wineland"). A later Norse explorer named Thorfinn Thordsson Karlsefni and his wife, Gudrid, followed up Leif's efforts and took a small contingent to Vinland in the hope of establishing a colony. Although they had a baby while on their expedition, within a year they returned to Greenland and eventually to Norway before they made a permanent home in ICELAND. In the late 12th century a Norse bishop named Erik Upsi also set sail for Vinland, although no record exists to tell what happened.

In the late 20th century archaeologists working at L'Anse aux Meadows in Newfoundland found evidence of an 11th-century Norse settlement, probably Vinland; others have speculated that Markland was present-day Labrador.

Further reading: Alfred Crosby, *Ecological Imperialism: The Biological Expansion of Europe, 900–1900* (Cambridge, U.K.: Cambridge University Press, 1986); William W. Fitzhugh and Elisabeth I. Ward, eds., *Vikings: The North Atlantic Saga* (Washington, D.C.: Smithsonian Institution Press, 2000); Kirsten Seaver, *The Frozen Echo: Greenland and the Exploration of North America, ca.* A.D. *1000–1500* (Stanford, Calif.: Stanford University Press, 1996); *The Vinland Sagas: The Norse Discovery of America,* trans. Magnus Magnusson and Herman Pálsson (Harmondsworth, U.K.: Penguin, 1965).

Vitoria, Francisco de (ca. 1485–1546)

Francisco de Vitoria, an influential Spanish jurist and professor of theology, argued that the native peoples of the Americas had a legitimate right to the ownership and governance of their own lands.

In 1539 Vitoria entered into a long-standing debate with the publication of his treatise "On the American Indians" ("De Indis"). While most Spaniards accepted the legitimacy of the Spanish conquest of America, some voices, most notably that of the Dominican priest BARTOLOMÉ DE LAS CASAS, condemned the cruelty of the Spanish. In 1511 another Dominican, Anton de Montesinos, warned the Spanish settlers of HISPANIOLA that if they did not stop treating the Indians cruelly, they would be damned to hell. Neither Las Casas nor Montesinos doubted that the Spanish had a legitimate claim to the NEW WORLD, but they believed that the Indians should be treated more fairly.

The mistreatment of the Indians helped sustain a debate in Europe over the justice of the Spanish conquest. In 1510 John Mair, a Scottish theologian teaching in Paris, maintained that the conquest of the Americas was just because the Indians were "natural slaves" who would benefit from European rule. As "natural slaves," the Indians needed Europeans to guide them and introduce them to Christianity. If the natives of the New World had to be conquered before they would accept Christianity, then war against the Indians was just. The Spanish lawyer and adviser to the Crown Juan López de Palacios Rubios also argued that the Spanish conquest of the New World was legitimate. For Palacios Rubios, the Catholic Church had dominion over the entire world. In the TREATY OF TORDESILLAS, Pope ALEXANDER VI had granted authority over the New World to the Spanish. As long as the Indians refused to become Christian, they were in rebellion against the church and could rightfully be subjugated.

Vitoria rejected these arguments. The Indians, he wrote, were rational human beings, not the "natural slaves" that Aristotle had suggested must exist. As rational beings, the Indians had a right to their lands and goods, and the Spanish had no right to take their property or enslave them. Their own rulers, not the Spanish, had legitimate authority over them. Vitoria also maintained that the pope's authority was purely in the spiritual world. Because he lacked power in the temporal world, he could not take the Indians' territories away and give them to one European prince or another. Furthermore, conquest of the Indians could not be justified by the desire to convert them to Christianity. Spanish treatment of the Indians thus far, Vitoria argued, was so cruel as to make the Indians less likely to convert.

The Indians' right to their land was not inviolable, however. Like other Catholics of the day, Vitoria believed that the pope's spiritual (though not temporal) authority extended across the world. The pope, therefore, could declare that only one European power had the right to colonize the New World in the interest of peacefully promoting the conversion of the Indians to Christianity. The Spanish could not compel the Indians to convert, but the Indians had no right to refuse to allow missionaries to travel and preach in their lands. Vitoria also argued that individuals and peoples had a right to trade with one another to their mutual benefit. If the Indians refused to permit missionaries to live among them or did not allow trade, then the Spanish could legitimately make war upon them.

Although Vitoria's arguments did allow for a "just war" to be undertaken against the Indians, their significance lay in his insistence that the Indians were rational human beings with a legitimate claim to their lands and freedoms. The arguments made by Vitoria, Las Casas, and other scholars and theologians helped lead to the Emperor CHARLES V's issuance of the New Laws of 1542. These laws declared that the Indians were vassals of the Crown and defended their rights to self-preservation, property, and justice against Spanish crimes.

Further reading: Suzanne Hiles Burkholder, "Vitoria, Francisco de," in *Encyclopedia of Latin American History and Culture,* vol. 5, ed. Barbara A. Tenenbaum (New York: Scribner's, 1996), 429; Anthony Pagden, *The Fall of Natural Man: The American Indian and the Origins of Comparative Ethnology* (Cambridge, U.K.: Cambridge University Press, 1982); ———, *Lords of All the World: Ideologies of Empire in Spain, Britain and France, c. 1500–c.1800* (New Haven, Conn.: Yale University Press, 1995); "Vitoria on the Justice of Conquest," in *The Conquerors and the Conquered,* vol. 10 *New Iberian World: A Documentary History of the Discovery and Settlement of Latin America to the Early 17th Century,* eds. John H. Parry and Robert G. Keith (New York: Times Books, 1984), 290–323.

— Martha K. Robinson

Waldseemüller, Martin (ca. 1470–ca. 1518–1521)

Martin Waldseemüller, a German artist and cartographer, was the first to use the term *America* to refer to the NEW WORLD.

Waldseemüller was born in Germany but lived in northeastern France. His most important map of the Western Hemisphere, the *Universalis Cosmographia* (1507), was probably commissioned by the duke of Lorraine. This map, almost 10 feet square, was printed from 12 wood blocks and was so popular that 1,000 copies were made, only one of which has survived. The *Universalis Cosmographia* drew on Portuguese and Italian maps and on AMERIGO VESPUCCI's account of his travels (see Documents). Unlike other maps of the day, which portrayed North America as an extension of Asia, on Waldseemüller's map North America appeared as a relatively small but distinct landmass.

In his *Cosmographia Introductio* (1507), Waldseemüller wrote that because Amerigo Vespucci had discovered a fourth continent, it should bear his name. "I do not see," he wrote "why anyone should rightly forbid naming it Amerige—land of Americus, as it were, after its discoverer Americus, a man of acute genius—or America, since both Europe and Asia have received their names from women." Waldseemüller and later cartographers used the term *America* to refer only to South America. Until 1538, when GERHARDUS MERCATOR labeled the northern continent *America*, most cartographers called it *Terra de Cuba, Terra Florida, Terra del Labrador,* or *Parais.*

Waldseemüller also wrote several books and made a globe and a large-scale map of Europe. His works influenced other 16th-century cartographers and were widely imitated.

Further reading: Seymour I. Schwartz and Ralph E. Ehrenberg, *The Mapping of America,* (New York: Abrams, 1980); R. V. Tooley, *Maps and Map-Makers* (London: B. T. Batsford, 1987); Hans Wolff, "Martin Waldseemüller: The Most Important Cosmographer in a Period of Dramatic Scientific Change," in Hans Wolff, ed., *America: Early Maps of the New World* (Munich: Prestel, 1992).

— Martha K. Robinson

Walsingham, Sir Francis (1530?–1590)

An English statesman and diplomat who served for almost two decades as Queen ELIZABETH I's secretary of state.

Early in his career Walsingham left England when Queen MARY I acceded to the throne, remaining abroad until her reign ceased. His five-year sojourn fostered his Protestant zeal and also helped develop his diplomatic career. While abroad he gained information in Spain, Italy, and France, all of it useful when he returned to England when Elizabeth took the throne.

Walsingham became one of the Queen's most trustworthy administrators. His first official task placed him in charge of London's secret service, through which he rooted out nefarious internal and external plots against the monarch. In August 1568, for example, he was able to produce for Lord Burghley (another close ally of the Queen) a list of all persons entering Italy during the previous three months who were hostile toward Elizabeth.

In 1570 Walsingham traveled to Paris on his first officially state-sponsored diplomatic mission. He hoped to establish better relations between England and an increasingly Huguenot influenced France. Rising hostilities between French HUGUENOTS and Catholics, culminating in the St. Bartholomew's Day Massacre, cut Walsingham's efforts short. He returned to England in 1573 with little optimism about future relations between France and England. Upon his return Walsingham became secretary of state, a post he held for the next 17 years. Working with Machiavellian precision both at home and abroad, he trained his attention on Catholic zealots. For his efforts Elizabeth knighted him in 1577.

As part of his foreign policy strategy, Walsingham endorsed maritime ventures and colonial expansion. He corresponded with RALPH LANE, Sir Richard Grenville, and SIR HUMPHREY GILBERT. In addition, he served as a patron to all of England's chief writers on the exploration of the NEW WORLD, including RICHARD HAKLUYT THE YOUNGER. In 1587 Walsingham's spy network supplied him with the numbers of men, characteristics of vessels in commission, and full inventories of HORSES, armor, ammunition, food, and supplies of the heralded SPANISH ARMADA. However, a year later his connections dissolved, leaving him with little information prior to England's upcoming naval confrontation with the armada.

Walsingham died in 1590 after facing pecuniary difficulties toward the end of his life. Living during an age in which the traitor, the conspirator, the spy, the counterspy, and the agent-provocateur appeared within the shadows of the larger backdrop of international diplomacy, he proved the consummate late 16th-century statesman and diplomat.

Further reading: John Bossy, *Giordano Bruno and the Embassy Affair* (New Haven, Conn.: Yale University Press, 1991); Conyers Read, *Mr. Secretary Walsingham and the Policy of Queen Elizabeth* (New York: AMS Press, 1978).

— Matt Lindaman

Wanchese (fl. 1580s)

One of two Indians brought to England from the islands of present-day North Carolina in 1584, Wanchese, a ROANOKE Indian, learned to speak English but rejected the colonists upon returning to America.

Wanchese and MANTEO arrived in England with ARTHUR BARLOWE and Philip Amadas, who had explored the coast of North America in search of a place to build a colony. While in England the two Indians lived with SIR WALTER RALEGH. While Manteo was a man of high status among his people, Wanchese seems to have ranked less high among his, and Manteo likely treated him as an inferior. He may have been sent to England by Wingina, a Roanoke leader, to learn about the English. When he returned to America in 1585, he left the colonists and returned to his own people. He apparently reported that the English were only men and did not have supernatural powers. The colonists, who believed that any reasonable human would acknowledge English superiority, regarded him as something of a traitor for preferring his own people. They also believed that he tried to convince Wingina to conspire against the colony.

Further reading: Thomas Harriot, *A Briefe and True Report of the New Found Land of Virginia* (1590; reprint, New York: Dover Publications, 1972); Karen Ordahl Kupperman, *Indians and English: Facing Off in Early America* (Ithaca, N.Y.: Cornell University Press, 2000); ———,

Roanoke: The Abandoned Colony (Totowa, N.J.: Rowman & Allanheld, 1984); David Beers Quinn, *Set Fair for Roanoke: Voyages and Colonies, 1584–1606* (Chapel Hill: University of North Carolina Press, 1985).

— Martha K. Robinson

werowance

Among the Virginia ALGONQUIAN a *werowance* was a local ruler or leader.

When English settlers arrived in Virginia, they were impressed by the power wielded by POWHATAN. They described Powhatan as the ruler of many villages, exercising his authority over subordinate chiefs called *werowances*. The position of *werowance* was usually inherited through the mother's line, but Powhatan could remove *werowances* at will. Larger communities were governed by *werowances*, smaller ones by "lesser *werowances*." A female leader was known as a *weroansqua*. The number of *werowances* is unknown, but Powhatan may have had authority over some 34 villages.

The word *werowance* has been translated variously as "commander," "he is wise," "he is rich," and "he is of influence." The *werowances* were supported by a system of tribute, including such items as copper, beads, and pearls. In turn, they paid tribute to Powhatan. The extent of the *werowances*' power over the people in their villages is unknown.

Further reading: Frederick W. Gleach, *Powhatan's World and Colonial Virginia: A Conflict of Cultures* (Lincoln: University of Nebraska Press, 1997); Stephen R. Potter, "Early English Effects on Virginia Algonquian Exchange and Tribute in the Tidewater Potomac," in *Powhatan's Mantle: Indians in the Colonial Southeast*, ed. Peter H. Wood, Gregory A. Waselkov, and M. Thomas Hatley (Lincoln: University of Nebraska Press, 1989), 151–172; Helen C. Rountree, *Pocahontas's People: The Powhatan Indians of Virginia Through Four Centuries* (Norman: University of Oklahoma Press, 1990); ———, *The Powhatan Indians of Virginia: Their Traditional Culture* (Norman: University of Oklahoma Press, 1989).

— Martha K. Robinson

White, John (1540?–1606?)

Governor of the short-lived English colony at ROANOKE, John White was best known for his series of watercolor paintings of the Carolina ALGONQUIAN whom the English met in the mid-1580s.

Little is known about the early life of John White. Born in all likelihood at some point between 1540 and 1550, he does not emerge in the historical record until the English attempted colonization of Roanoke. In 1585 SIR WALTER RALEGH chose White to be the official artist on his mission across the Atlantic Ocean. It was an inspired choice. White proved to be an expert companion to the young mathematician THOMAS HARRIOT, whose ethnographic report on the Carolina Algonquian and their world constituted vital information for English colonial planners. If White's orders resembled those of Thomas Bavin, who was the designated artist of SIR HUMPHREY GILBERT's colonizing effort, he would have been instructed to depict everything that was new—each plant, animal, and fish—as well as the people they met and the communities they observed.

White, scholars have universally concluded, was an ideal person for the assignment. His depictions of the Carolina Algonquian provide critical ethnographic information about a people who have since disappeared (at least as a specific cultural group). He drew individual men and women and showed how the Indians prayed, built their villages, grew their crops, and fished with seines and arrows. Brought back to Europe, the Flemish engraver THEODOR DE BRY soon prepared versions of these images that were published in an illustrated edition of Harriot's *Briefe and True Report of the New Found Land of Virginia*, published in London in 1590 under the direction of RICHARD HAKLUYT THE YOUNGER.

White returned to Roanoke in 1587 as Governor of the "Cittie of Raleigh in Virginia." While in LONDON before the venture, he had tried to enlist as many potential colonists as possible, although he managed to attract only 112, a group that included only 17 women and 11 children. After his return to Roanoke in July 1587, he named MANTEO, "Lord of Roanoke and Dasemunkepeuc," and relied on his expertise to help smooth relations between the natives and newcomers. But the settlers wanted more provisions from England, and so White crossed the Atlantic once again, landing in November 1587, eager to tell Ralegh about the needs of the new settlers. Ralegh promised assistance, but when the time came to send out a relief ship the threat of the SPANISH ARMADA suspended any efforts. By the time the English returned to Roanoke, the colonists had disappeared.

Although best known for his paintings of the Carolina Algonquian and their area, White also provided detailed paintings of the fish he encountered in the Atlantic and also rendered copies of other indigenous peoples based on earlier pictures by JACQUES LE MOYNE.

Little evidence exists about what happened to White after his term as governor of Roanoke. It is possible that he was the man referred to when a Brigit White became the administratrix of her brother's estate in 1606, because that John White had been "late of parts beyond the seas."

Further reading: Paul Hulton, *America 1585: The Complete Drawings of John White* (Chapel Hill and London: University of North Carolina Press/British Museum Publications, 1984); ———, *The American Drawings of John White,* 2 vols. (Chapel Hill: University of North Carolina Press, 1964); Karen Ordahl Kupperman, *Roanoke: The Abandoned Colony* (Totowa, N.J.: Rowman & Allanheld, 1984).

witches

Although stories of witches and witchcraft had circulated in Europe for centuries before the early modern period, most witch trials and executions took place in the 16th and 17th centuries, in contrast to Africa and the Americas, where accusations of witchcraft did not lead to widespread public hysteria.

In medieval and early modern Europe belief in magic and witchcraft was almost universal. Local magicians were thought to be able to heal the sick, find lost or stolen property, cast love spells, and otherwise influence things and events by magical means. Popular opinion often regarded these magicians, known in England as "wise women" and "cunning men," as helpful. Witches, on the other hand, were those who used magic to harm others. The ability to use magic was neutral; the difference between cunning folk and witches was thus one of intent.

While popular culture recognized a difference between beneficial and harmful magicians, Catholic and Protestant authorities condemned both the beneficial magic of the cunning folk and the harmful magic of the witches. They argued that any form of supernatural power that did not derive from God must derive from the devil. Both witches and cunning folk deserved punishment for

Protestants and Jews accused of heresy and witchcraft: woodcut, German, 1493

their activities, because their work implied at least a tacit compact with the devil. Witchcraft, therefore, was often prosecuted as a heresy. The witch was hunted because she (or, less often, he) had made a pact with the devil and was thereby a traitor to God. Because of her heresy she deserved to die, whether or not she had used her power to commit evil deeds. This view was expressed by the influential witch-hunting manual of 1486, the *Malleus Malificarum (Hammer of the Witches)*, which was reprinted 14 times from 1487 to 1520.

The extent of witch hunting varied from place to place. The most devastating trials took place in the HOLY ROMAN EMPIRE, where there were probably at least 20,000 executions for witchcraft between 1560 and 1660. One historian estimated that at least 3,229 people were executed for witchcraft in southwestern Germany between 1561 and 1670. German trials were often large, resulting in many executions in one area in a single year. In Ellwangen, for example, about 260 people were executed in 1611–12, while in Wiesensteig 63 people were executed in 1562, and 25 more were killed in 1583. In the Swiss cantons 5,417 people are known to have been executed between 1400 and 1700. Although the largest number of trials took place in the Holy Roman Empire, witches were executed almost everywhere in Europe, from Hungary and ICELAND to France, Scotland, and Italy. In England European ideas of witchcraft as heresy rarely found a receptive audience. When English witches were prosecuted, they were usually accused of causing harm to people, not merely of practicing magic. England seems to have had relatively few witch trials. One historian suggested that fewer than 1,000 people were executed in England for witchcraft in the 16th and 17th centuries.

Certain types of people were more likely to be accused of witchcraft than were others. Approximately 80 percent of accused witches were female. It is not easy to determine why accusations of witchcraft were so commonly levied against women. Contemporaries attributed the great number of female witches to the inherent weakness and foolishness of women, which made them more prone to fall prey to evil. Modern scholars have offered a variety of theories to explain the predominance of women in witch trials. One has suggested that women were often the most dependent people in any community and that their dependence on others made them targets of resentment. Another has argued that the female world of pregnancy, childbirth, and nursing was poorly understood by men of the era, who acted out their suspicions of women's bodies through witch trials. Witch trials often betrayed ongoing social tensions, although why witch hunts sprang up in some areas but not in others remains hard to determine.

Among the most important problems in the study of witchcraft is the difficulty of determining what the accused witches believed they were doing. Some suspects denied their involvement in any kind of magic or claimed that they practiced magic only to help people. Confessions exist, but because they were sometimes extracted by torture, they are unreliable evidence. Some contemporaries of the witch trials maintained that supposed witches often were simply deluded or senile.

The incidence of witchcraft trials declined at different rates across Europe. In general, witch scares developed later but lasted longer in eastern Europe. Trials in western Europe declined in the 17th century. In Hungary and Poland executions for witchcraft continued well into the 18th century. The reasons for the decline of witch hunting remain as mysterious as the earlier causes of widespread accusations and trials.

In other parts of the Atlantic world, accusations of witchcraft were also common. However, in the Americas and Africa there was no similarly documented period when witchcraft was more prominent or when trials and executions took place in large numbers. In these societies individuals in communities feared those they believed were witches, but such fears remained constant and left no major traces in the historical record.

Further reading: Norman Cohn, *Europe's Inner Demons* (London: Sussex University Press, 1975); Christina Larner, *Enemies of God* (Baltimore: Johns Hopkins University Press, 1981); Brian P. Levack, *The Witch-Hunt in Early Modern Europe,* 2nd ed. (New York: Longman, 1994); Alan Macfarlane, *Witchcraft in Tudor and Stuart England* (London: Routledge, 1970); H. C. Erik Midlefort, *Witch-Hunting in Southwestern Germany, 1562–1684* (Stanford Calif.: Stanford University Press, 1972).

— Martha K. Robinson

X

Xicotencatl the Elder (late 15th–early 16th century)
One of the four leaders of the TLAXCALA at the time of the arrival of the Spaniards and a staunch opponent of the foreigners.

Xicotencatl the Elder was one of the four leaders of the Tlaxcala in the early 16th century. He was quite old at the time of the arrival of HERNÁN CORTÉS and was reported to have had some 90 wives and numerous children, among whom was XICOTENCATL THE YOUNGER. The elder Xicotencatl was the only one of the Tlaxcalan co-rulers to oppose the idea of welcoming the Spaniards, for which the others forced him to resign his office. He died shortly thereafter.

Further reading: José Rogelio Alvarez, *Enciclopedia de México,* 4th ed. (Mexico City: Enciclopedia de México, 1998); Stuart B. Schwartz, ed., *Victors and Vanquished: Spanish and Nahua Views of the Conquest of Mexico* (Boston: Bedford/St. Martin's Press, 2000).

— Marie A. Kelleher

Xicotencatl the Younger (ca. 1484–1521)
Tlaxcalan general who led his troops against the Spaniards and their Tlaxcalan allies.

Xicotencatl the Younger (also called Axayacatzin) was the son of XICOTENCATL THE ELDER. A general of TLAXCALA, he was charged with the defense of the frontiers. Like his father, he opposed the admission of the Spanish newcomers to the Puebla-Tlaxcala Valley and led his troops in battle against them beginning in September 1519, until his superiors, who wanted to forge an alliance with the Spaniards against the AZTECS, forced him to withdraw. He deserted with his troops on May 21, 1521, when the Spaniards and their Tlaxcalan allies began the attack on TENOCHTITLÁN. HERNÁN CORTÉS ordered his capture, and he was eventually taken prisoner by Capitan Ojeda in Texcoco and executed by hanging.

Further reading: José Rogelio Alvarez, *Enciclopedia de México,* 4th ed. (Mexico City: Enciclopedia de México, 1998); Stuart B. Schwartz, *Victors and Vanquished: Spanish and Nahua Views of the Conquest of Mexico* (Boston: Bedford/St. Martin's Press, 2000).

— Marie A. Kelleher

Y

Yoruba

A group of peoples in present-day Nigeria, BENIN, and Togo who share language and cultural traditions, some of whose ancestors established the powerful OYO kingdom in the fourteenth century.

Yoruba tradition has several explanations for how the Yoruba originated and how they came to live in Yorubaland. One such tradition credits Oduduwa, son of Olorun, the god of the sky, with founding the holy city Ile-Ife (Ife-Ife) in the eighth century and in so doing creating the Yoruba people. In this account Oduduwa sent his children out from Ile-Ife to settle the surrounding territory, establishing the kingdoms of Owu, Oyo, Benin, Sabe, and Ketu. Another account states that mankind was created at Ile-Ife and then dispersed from there. Other accounts trace Yoruba origins to peoples from the Arabian Peninsula, yet others from the Kush people of the middle Nile. Archaeological evidence suggests that the Yoruba's history as a distinct ethnic group predates the founding of Ile-Ife and that the Yoruba language developed around the NIGER RIVER 3,000 to 4,000 years ago. These Yoruba speakers migrated west to what is now called Yorubaland between the eighth and 11th century. However the Yoruba came into being, they were firmly established in the region by 1000 C.E. and developed unique forms of government and society that distinguished them from their neighbors.

Surrounded by fertile savannah and forest lands, the city of Ife-Ife, the largest precolonial city in West Africa, was the capital of a powerful Yoruba kingdom and remained the most important spiritual and cultural center for the Yoruba peoples even after other Yoruba city-states surpassed its political power. One of these kingdoms was the Oyo, centered at the city of Ile Oyo, which flourished from the 14th through the 19th centuries. The Oyo kingdom's power peaked in the 17th and 18th centuries after they acquired the HORSE through participation in the SLAVE TRADE. Incorporating a cavalry into its military

forces made the Oyo conquest of neighboring kingdoms like DAHOMEY possible.

Yoruba political life centered on and was dominated by towns and cities. The Yoruba tradition of urbanization is centuries old, with the founding of Ife-Ife as the earliest example. Yoruba settlements ranged in size from *abule* (hamlet) and *ileto* (village) to *ilu oloja* (small market towns) and *ilu alade* (large towns). Yoruba kings, or *obas*, who attained their authority through their direct descent from Oduduwa, governed the powerful city-states that developed around densely populated *ilu alade*. The Oyo capital of Ile Oyo was fairly typical of Yoruba "crowned," or capital, cities with its defensive wall and large population. Early in Yoruba history each of the crowned cities and their rulers owed allegiance to the *oni* (chief Yoruba leader) in Ile-Ife spiritually as well as politically. This confederal system gave each state some autonomy while providing a means for keeping the peace within the larger Yoruba system. This system was also seen as an extension of the Yoruba family, with each city state "related" to the others through its connection to the *oni* in Ile-Ife. Only with the rise in the 16th and 17th centuries of the Oyo kingdom, a "junior" member of the family, did the system begin to decline.

Patrilineal family units, in which inheritance, descent, and political status were passed down through the male line, formed the base of the Yoruba's hierarchical culture and society. Although the Yoruba were urbanized, farming remained an essential aspect of their culture and economy. Yoruba men cultivated yams, maize, peanuts, millet, and beans in outlying rural areas and also labored as blacksmiths, woodworkers, and textile weavers. Yoruba women traded these goods at markets and enjoyed increased status, wealth, and independence through their commercial activities.

Further reading: Ari Nave, "Yoruba," in *Africana: The Encyclopedia of the African and African American Experience,* eds. Kwame Anthony Appiah and Henry Louis Gates,

377

Jr. (New York: Basic *Civitas* Books, 1999), 2035–2036; Robin Law, *The Oyo Empire c. 1600–c. 1836: A West African Imperialism in the Era of the Atlantic Slave Trade* (Oxford, U.K.: Clarendon Press, 1977); "The Peoples," in *Cambridge Encyclopedia of Africa,* eds. Roland Oliver and Michael Crowder (Cambridge, U.K.: Cambridge University Press, 1981), 57–86; "The Forest Kingdoms: in the Delta of the Niger and its Peripheries," in *West Africa before the Colonial Era: A History to 1850,* Basil Davidson, (London: Longman, 1998), 109–117.

— Lisa M. Brady

Yucatán Peninsula

A large peninsula in southern MEXICO that was one of most important cultural areas of ancient Mesoamerica and later a frequent battleground for the Spanish colonists and the MAYA.

Geologically, the Yucatán Peninsula is a long, flat table of limestone that juts into the Gulf of Mexico, covering approximately 55,500 square miles. The only significant hills that break the surface are the Puuc Hills in the northwest and the Maya Mountains in Belize. Because there are no mountains to catch moisture-rich clouds from the gulf, most of the Yucatán is dry. Rainfall levels increase toward the south, and the Guatemalan border is considerably wetter than the coast. There are no surface rivers in the Yucatán, although water frequently collects in underground caverns. In some locations the roofs of these caverns have collapsed, exposing underground lakes. Called cenotes, these sources of water were crucial to the Maya of the region, who revered them as portals to the underworld. The great cenote of CHICHÉN ITZÁ was a particularly holy pilgrimage site.

The Yucatán was settled by the Maya by 500 B.C., although it did not rise to prominence until the end of the classic era, roughly A.D. 700. At this time many of the classic-era kingdoms to the south (TIKAL, COPÁN, PALENQUE) had started to decline. In response, the cities of the Yucatán rose to power. Chichén Itzá was the most important of these cities, and by 800 it had established control over much of the northern Yucatán. Chichén Itzá and other Yucatán cities such as Uxmal developed a distinctive style of architecture that differed dramatically from the other Maya cities to the south. These kingdoms did not last, and by 1200 the city of Mayapan conquered and controlled much of the peninsula. This kingdom also fell, and by 1500 the Yucatán had balkanized into a collection of mutually hostile city-states. Although the surviving Maya kingdoms were a shadow of their former glory, the Spanish scouts were still impressed with the architecture and wealth of the Yucatán and quickly made plans to conquer it.

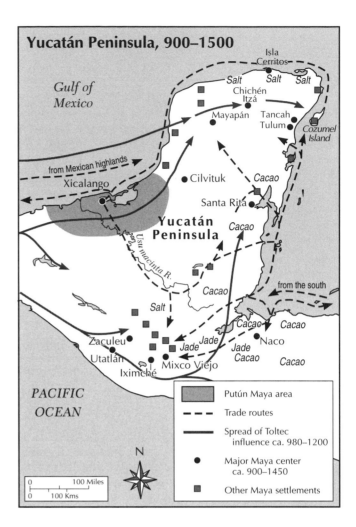

In 1527 the CONQUISTADOR Francisco de Montejo entered the Yucatán. Unlike the conquest of the AZTECS or INCA, the conquest of the Yucatán was a drawn-out, horrible war of attrition. Montejo and his kinsmen had nominally subdued the area by 1547, although the Spanish did not conquer the interior until 1697. The lack of political unity among the Yucatán Maya both aided and hindered the Spanish attempts to subdue the region. On the one hand, petty Maya kings were often more than willing to unite with the Spaniards to attack a more powerful neighbor. The conquistadores found, however, that their alleged allies would quickly change sides, at times while the battles were raging. Also, Maya kingdoms did not stay conquered: Often, they would surrender, wait for the Spanish soldiers to leave, and proclaim their independence all over again. Moreover, the government's attempts to enforce laws or collect tribute often resulted in the Maya abandoning the area and fleeing to the unconquered regions in the interior. The difficulties of governing the Yucatán, coupled with the fact that there were no precious metals, led to a long period of neglect by the royal government. Spanish political control was frequently confined to Mérida (the colonial capital) and a handful of Spanish settlements.

Spanish clerics' attempted spiritual conquest of the Yucatán fared no better. In 1549 the Franciscan missionary Diego de Landa arrived. Because of his zealous efforts to convert the Maya, he became the first bishop of the Yucatán in 1572. De Landa staged mass conversions, burned "heretical" Maya books, constructed churches, and declared that the region had been Christianized. Despite his efforts, the natives continued to worship idols and conduct clandestine ceremonies to the old gods. De Landa resorted to violent purges and INQUISITIONS to combat indigenous apostasy, which led to the death of 157 natives.

His actions shocked both the colonists and the local authorities, who succeeded in having de Landa removed from power. Later missionaries were no more successful in stamping out the natives' religion. Ultimately, the Yucatán remained a semiconquered frontier zone that resisted Spanish influence well into the 20th century.

Further reading: Inga Clendinnen, *Ambivalent Conquests: Maya and Spaniard in Yucatán, 1517–1570* (Cambridge, U.K.: Cambridge University Press, 1987); Michael D. Coe, *The Maya,* 6th ed. (London: Thames & Hudson, 1999); Friar Diego de Landa, *Yucatán Before and After the Conquest* (New York: Dover Publications, 1978).

— Scott Chamberlain

Z

Zacatecas

A city and major SILVER-producing area of northern MEXICO that formed the economic backbone of the Spanish colony of NEW SPAIN until independence.

Spaniards discovered the silver ore near Zacatecas in 1546, a year after the famous silver strikes in POTOSÍ (in modern-day Bolivia). The mines had a difficult beginning. At first the miners attempted to smelt the ore, but Zacatecas was far from large sources of fuel. Additionally, its remote location made it difficult to obtain a steady labor supply. Coercive labor systems, such as those used by the Spanish in Potosí, were only marginally successful in meeting the needs of the silver mines. However, after a few years productivity increased. By the 1550s miners developed an amalgamation process that used mercury to purify the ore. Although more costly than smelting, this process allowed the extraction of a greater quantity of silver from the ore at higher levels of purity. This process increased the overall profitability of the mines, allowing the industry to expand. Silver production from Zacatecas increased throughout the next century, at the same time that production from elsewhere in the empire had begun to decline. In 1670 exports from the mines of Zacatecas surpassed those of PERU for the first time (4 million pesos to 2 million). By 1760 Zacatecas was producing 16 million pesos of silver for the Spanish Crown, making it one of the largest silver-producing areas in the world—a trend that continued until 1810.

The wealth of the Zacatecas mines served as a major pole of development in the colony of New Spain. HACIENDAS sprang up around the mining zones, providing foodstuffs to workers. Small textile factories also developed to serve the local economy. Local silversmiths became highly regarded and provided a wealth of decorative and household items for the colony. An important aspect of the Zacatecas silver mines, in contrast to those in South America, was that there was a slow, constant curve of economic growth. It provided New Spain with a steady income without unduly distorting the economy. Moreover, because the remote location made coerced labor difficult, the mines of Zacatecas relied on wage labor. This provided a more equitable distribution of wealth in the region and had a beneficial effect on the local economy.

Zacatecas remained one of the wealthiest, most developed areas in colonial Mexico until independence. Its rich past remains evident in the many opulent, well-preserved colonial buildings that dot the region.

Further reading: Peter J. Blakewell, *Silver Mining and Society in Colonial Mexico: Zacatecas, 1546–1700* (Cambridge, U.K.: Cambridge University Press, 1971); Louisa Schnell Hoberman, *Mexico's Merchant Elite, 1590–1660: Silver, State, and Society* (Durham, N.C.: Duke University Press, 1991).

— Scott Chamberlain

zambo

Zambos, persons of black and Indian parentage, generally occupied a lowly social status in colonial Latin America.

The high incidence of MESTIZAJE (interracial sexual relations) in 16th-century Latin America led to the development of a complex system of racial classifications used by Spaniards. In addition to *zambo*, other terms used to distinguish among racially mixed persons included *castizo* (mestizo-white mixture), MESTIZO (Indian-white mixture), and *mulatto* (Spanish-black mixture).

Whether slave or free, all blacks in areas settled by the Spanish in the NEW WORLD endured restrictions on their personal autonomy. Although some slaves eventually purchased their freedom from their owners, as freedmen they continued to be treated in ways consistent with their inferior social status by comparison with persons of non-African parentage. In addition to restrictions on a slave's right to travel at night, carry arms, and employ Indians in his service, one law in NEW SPAIN, for example, barred all persons of African descent (slaves, freedmen, mulattoes, and *zambos*) from wearing imported fabrics or dressing in a characteristically Spanish way. Such laws worked to define a social hierarchy with pure-blood Spaniards at the top, Indians someplace in the middle, and blacks at the bottom.

Colonial Spanish society regarded the child of a black slave woman and an Indian male as a slave. However, a child born to an Indian mother and black slave father generally lived among Indians and paid a head tax to the colonial bureaucracy under the same provision that demanded tribute or offerings from members of the indigenous population. Still, all restrictions placed on blacks applied typically to *zambos* as well. Thus, Spanish society denied *zambos* the rights to attend school and to hold religious or political office and banned them from certain industries altogether.

During the early years of conquest and settlement, the ratio of black male slaves to black female slaves was quite considerable. As a result, a sizeable number of black males engaged in sexual relationships with Indian woman. Not surprisingly, as the population of Spanish settlements in the New World grew during the 16th century, so, too, did the number of *zambos* and other mixed-race persons. The Spanish sought to curb this trend by placing sanctions on conjugal relations between blacks and nonblacks even while they accepted marriages between Spaniards and Indians.

Some black slaves, either through revolt or escape, fled from areas of Spanish settlement. Many escapees took refuge in outlying areas and went on to build lives for themselves among indigenous peoples. During the early 16th century the *zambo* descendants of fugitive slaves and members of Manabi and Mantux tribes in present-day Colombia secured themselves as tribal leaders in a settlement they founded, El Portete. Aware that the area represented a haven for fugitive slaves, after several failed efforts the Spanish managed to capture El Portete in 1556. However, through reliance on guerrilla tactics, the *zambo* leaders held onto control until 1598, when they finally acknowledged the Spanish Crown's authority. Despite this, in a real sense they retained much of their autonomy and rule of the area.

Further reading: Irene Diggs, "Color in Colonial Spanish America," *Journal of Negro History* 38:4 (1953): 403–427; Claudio Esteva-Fabregat, *Mestizaje in Ibero-America,* trans. John Wheat (Tucson: University of Arizona Press, 1995); Magnus Mörner, *Race Mixture in the History of Latin America* (Boston: Little, Brown, 1967); Leslie B. Rout, Jr., *The African Experience in Spanish America: 1502 to Present Day* (Cambridge, U.K.: Cambridge University Press, 1976).

— Kimberly Sambol-Tosco

Zumárraga, Juan de (1468–1548)

The first bishop and archbishop of NEW SPAIN, Juan de Zumárraga was instrumental in establishing the agenda and structure of the Catholic Church in Spanish America.

Zumárraga was born in Durango, in the Basque country of Spain, in 1468. He took the vows of the Franciscan order at Valladolid and remained an influential figure in the Spanish church. In 1527, shortly after the conquest of MEXICO, CHARLES V appointed Zumárraga the bishop of New Spain and protector of the Indians. He arrived with members of the first AUDIENCIA of Mexico City in 1528. Upon reaching the colony, he became appalled at the actions the CONQUISTADORES were taking against the natives. He was particularly horrified at the institution of the ENCOMIENDA, feeling that conquistadores were using this institution not to Christianize the natives but rather to exploit them. He was also concerned that the *audiencia* was not actively protecting the natives and was too quick to charge them with the serious crime of heresy. By 1529 he excommunicated the judges of the *audiencia* and sent a strongly worded letter of protest to the king. The king responded by dissolving the *audiencia* and appointing a new panel to take its place.

After 1533 Zumárraga worked diligently to organize the colonial church. He pushed for the church to become active in providing social services, including public health, education, and charity. He established a good working relationship with the first viceroy, ANTONIO DE MENDOZA, and worked with him in establishing the famous College of Santiago in Tlatelolco, a religious school for sons of the native nobility that under BERNARDINO DE SAHAGÚN created such important works as the Florentine Codex. He also founded other schools for both boys and girls as well as hospitals in the capital. Again with Mendoza, he oversaw the foundation of New Spain's first university and brought in the colony's first PRINTING PRESS. With royal support he established the INQUISITION in New Spain, although he was instrumental in removing natives from its jurisdiction. He argued that the natives were "childlike" and should not be responsible for their actions. Of the 131 heresy trials he presided over, only 13 involved natives, and these usually involved cases that contained dangerous political or social overtones. Lamentably, he also presided over the destruction of many native codices, arguing that they were heretical in nature.

Throughout his time in office, Zumárraga worked to create stability and a degree of social justice. He died in 1548, shortly after being raised to the office of archbishop of New Spain.

Further reading: Richard Greenleaf, *Zumárraga and the Mexican Inquisition, 1536–1543* (Washington, D.C.: Academy of Franciscan History, 1961); Michael C. Meyer and William L. Sherman, *The Course of Mexican History* (Oxford, U.K.: Oxford University Press, 1995).

— Scott Chamberlain

Zuni

An indigenous nation inhabiting modern-day western NEW MEXICO whose inhabitants came into contact with Spanish explorers in 1536, the first of a series of encounters characterized by misunderstandings and violence.

Like many of the native peoples of the Southwest of the modern-day United States, the Zuni succeeded by learning how to adapt to an often difficult environment. Their homeland, along a tributary of the Little Colorado River now known as the Zuni River, encompassed both mountains rising to almost 9,000 feet and lowlands. Archaeological evidence at Hawikuh, a community occupied from 1300 to 1680, suggests that Zuni lived in concentrated communities; Hawikuh, for example, had approximately 370 separate rooms and 1,000 graves. Other archaeological evidence suggests that Zuni had become proficient basket makers by approximately A.D. 700 and that families probably inhabited dwellings approximately 10 to 12 feet across clustered in groups, quite likely reflecting the fact that kin groups lived together. Digs at certain sites have revealed storerooms used to preserve CORN, a basic part of the diet of the indigenous peoples of the region, as well as ritual centers (known as kivas) used for extensive periods of time. The material record suggests that the population of the region increased substantially by 1300; some early villages had been abandoned, but others, notably Zuni, grew. Despite extensive archaeological efforts, scholars remain unclear about any clear link between the ancient Zuni habitations and modern-day Zuni, although there seems little doubt that Zuni today are the descendants of people who lived in the region at least 200 to 300 years before the Spanish arrived.

Like all other peoples, the Zuni developed their own religion. It included an indigenous cosmogony based on the relationship between the "Raw People," divine forces that can take anthropomorphic form, and the "Daylight People," human beings, one of whose tasks is to tend to the raw people. Corn, so vital to the Zuni diet, plays a central role in the Zuni traditional religion. It is the duty of the Daylight People to propitiate the Raw People, who manifest themselves in a variety of ways, including corn plants, rainstorms, deer, bears, and kachinas.

Zuni first encountered Europeans in the late 1530s when ÁLVAR NÚÑEZ CABEZA DE VACA arrived in Mexico City (see TENOCHTITLÁN) and reported that he had seen great cities to the north during his long trek across the North American interior. Spanish officials in MEXICO authorized a mission to go north to find the truth of these claims. Although a Franciscan missionary named Marcos de Niza traveled into the region in 1539, he did not venture into the Zuni land after an African slave (see SLAVERY) named Estevan was killed by Zuni on an exploratory venture, a fate quite possibly caused either by misunderstanding or some unknown act of aggression toward the Zuni. In 1540 FRANCISCO CORONADO traveled into the Zuni homeland and battled the Zuni until he could lay claim to Hawikuh in July. From there he continued on his mission to find the mythic Seven Cities of Cíbola, a venture that eventually took him as far east as modern-day Kansas. Although he never found the treasures he believed existed, he returned through the Zuni homeland in 1542 and labeled it Cíbola, a name that stuck. Coronado left a group of indigenous peoples from Mexico with the Zuni in 1542, and they remained there for four decades, or so later Spanish explorers claimed. When those later adventurers arrived in what they called Cíbola in the 1580s, they had better relations with the native peoples than had Marcos or Coronado. Among those later visitors was JUAN DE OÑATE, who traveled there in 1598.

During the early 17th century Spanish clerics turned their attention to the homeland of the Zuni, establishing a mission at Hawikuh in 1629 and a church at Halona (on the site of modern-day Zuni), thereby planting Catholicism in the region, although at the time there was, of course, no way to know how successful this religious import would become among the Zuni, who continue to practice their traditional religion today.

Further reading: Dennis Tedlock, "Zuni Religion and World View," in William C. Sturtevant, gen. ed., *Handbook of North American Indians*, vol. 9, *Southeast*, ed. Alfonso Ortiz (Washington, D.C.: Smithsonian Institution Press, 1979), 499–507; Richard B. Woodbury, "Zuni Prehistory and History to 1850," in *Southwest*, ed., Ortiz, 467–473.

Chronology

★

ca. 11,000 B.C.

The first humans, Paleo-Indians, arrive in the Western Hemisphere from Asia by way of a land bridge over the modern-day Bering Strait; over the next few centuries their descendants spread throughout the Americas.

ca. 4000 B.C.

Native Americans start making pottery.

ca. 3500 B.C.

Native peoples in central Mexico begin to cultivate corn (maize), which becomes the most important food in the Americas.

ca. 3200 B.C.

Peruvian peoples begin to cultivate corn.

ca. 2000 to 1000 B.C.

Indigenous peoples in eastern North America develop agriculture.

ca. 1500 B.C.

The Hopewell mound builders flourish in the southern Ohio region. Emergence of Olmec culture in Mexico.

A.D. ca. 800

Emergence of the Toltecs in Mexico.

A.D. ca. 870

Norse sailors (also known as Vikings) venture westward from modern-day Scandinavia into the North Atlantic and reach Iceland, which becomes the first colony of any European society.

985

The Norse explorer Erik the Red sails from Iceland to Greenland.

1000

The fabled Norse sailor Leif Eriksson travels from Greenland to Vinland; five years later Thorfinn Karlsfeni sails from Iceland to Vinland. Archaeological remains at L'Anse aux Meadows on the northern tip of modern-day Newfoundland reveal that the Norse reached the Western Hemisphere.

1066

Normans invade England; over time the Anglo-Norman population expands westward into Wales and Scotland.

ca. 1100

Anasazi culture flourishes in the Southwest of the modern-day United States. Although the Anasazi dispersed, probably as a result of drought, descendants kept alive certain elements of their culture, including distinctive ceramic styles.

1166

Anglo-Normans cross the Irish Sea and attempt to colonize Ireland; their attempt, and most others that followed, failed to make the native Irish agree to be ruled by the English, although military invasion during the age of Queen Elizabeth I had greater success.

ca. 1339

Madeira begins to appear on European maps, but there are no attempts at colonization until ca. 1425.

ca. 1430

The Portuguese prince Henry the Navigator establishes a library to support navigational studies at Sagres, thereby encouraging Portuguese exploratory efforts.

1432

The Portuguese navigator Gonçalo Cabral, with the authority of Prince Henry the Navigator, lands in the Azores, a discovery that leads to the Portuguese colonization of the island group.

1448

Portuguese slave traders expand their business, sending approximately 700 to 1,000 slaves each year across the Sahara; by the end of the century they were arranging the sale of perhaps 2,500 slaves each year.

1458

The Portuguese explorer Diogo Gomes leads his expedition to the Gulf of Guinea, thereby providing vital information to Europeans about the riches and slaves to be found in West Africa.

1492

Christopher Columbus, sailing west with the support of Ferdinand and Isabella in order to find a shortcut to East Asia, lands in the Bahamas. Initially disappointed that he had not reached his intended destination, Columbus soon realizes that he has found land that no European has ever seen before.

The Spanish complete the Reconquista, driving the Moors out of the Iberian Peninsula. Spanish leaders expel Jews from the realm.

1493

Pope Alexander VI authorizes the papal bull *Inter Caetera* to resolve territorial disputes between Spain and Portugal. That same year a printer in Barcelona publishes the first version of Columbus's account of his discoveries.

1494

Monarchs in Spain and Portugal sign the Treaty of Tordesillas, a pact that gave to Spain rights to all territory west of an imaginary line drawn to the west of the Azores; the Portuguese gained the right to land to the east of the boundary, giving them the privilege (recognized by other Europeans) to colonize current-day Brazil.

1495

Accession of King Manuel I to the throne of Portugal.

1497

John Cabot (Gabota), a Venetian sailing under the authority of the English Crown, leaves Bristol on May 20 and sails westward. By the time he returned to England in 1498, he had reached the northeast coast of North America, thereby giving subsequent English monarchs a claim to land in the Western Hemisphere. Despite his achievements, the English do not mount serious colonizing expeditions to follow on Cabot's success.

Vasco da Gama embarks from Lisbon on a mission to India; after rounding the southern coast of Africa, the Portuguese reach their destination on May 18, 1498.

1498

John Cabot launches a second mission to the west; of his small fleet of five vessels, only one returns to Bristol. Cabot, like countless other sailors during the early modern age, never returns.

1499

Amerigo Vespucci, a commercial adviser to Alonso de Ojeda, arrives near the eastern tip of modern-day Brazil and then travels northwest (along the northeast coast of South America) past the mouths of the Amazon and Orinoco Rivers until he reaches Venezuela before heading into the Caribbean and back to Spain in 1500.

1500

The Portuguese explorer Pedro Álvarez Cabral leaves Lisbon on March 9 bound for India, but in order to gain more favorable winds he travels west into the Atlantic Ocean and eventually lands in present-day Brazil on April 22; he claims the land for the king of Portugal.

1502

Portuguese slavers expand their operations in West Africa.

The first African slaves arrive in Spanish America, representing an expansion of the slave trade across the Atlantic Ocean.

Christopher Columbus makes his fourth and final trip across the Atlantic Ocean.

1504

The Spanish conquistador Hernán Cortés arrives in the Western Hemisphere.

On May 20 Columbus dies in Spain.

ca. 1508

Sebastian Cabot, son of John Cabot, sails to North America to search for the Northwest Passage for the English king Henry VII.

1513

The explorer Juan Ponce de León sails north from Puerto Rico in March and lands in present-day Florida on April 2, thereby becoming the first Spaniard on the North American mainland.

Vasco Núñez de Balboa crosses the Isthmus of Panama and on September 27 becomes the first European to see the Pacific Ocean.

1519

Martin Luther posts his critique of Catholicism on the church at Wittenburg, Germany, thereby launching what became the Protestant Reformation.

The Spanish conquistador Hernán Cortés embarks from Cuba on a journey to the Yucatán Peninsula.

The Portuguese explores Ferdinand Magellan embarks from Sanlúcar de Barrameda with five ships for a journey around the world.

1521

Cortés defeats the Aztec emperor Moctezuma II's forces in Tenochtitlán (modern-day Mexico City) during an assault so devastating that indigenous chroniclers spoke of its horrors for generations.

On April 26 Magellan dies after leading a doomed invasion against Lapu Lapu on Mactan Island, off the coast of Cebu in the Philippines.

1522

The *Victoria*, one of two ships of Magellan's fleet to survive the circumnavigation, arrives at Sanlúcar de Barrameda.

1524

The Italian explorer Giovanni da Verrazano, sailing with the authority of the French king Francis I, crosses the Atlantic and lands in 1525 at modern-day Cape Fear, North Carolina.

1530

Publication in Spain of *De Orbe Novo*, the account of the Italian humanist Peter Martyr based on interviews with Christopher Columbus and other conquistadores returning from the Western Hemisphere.

1532

The Spanish conquistador Francisco Pizarro, after convincing Spanish monarchs to name him captain general of Peru in 1529, conquers the Inca Empire and murders its emperor, Atahualpa.

1533

The English king Henry VIII, seeking a divorce from Catherine of Aragón, forces his nation to break its ties to the Roman Catholic Church; in the aftermath, Henry becomes the head of the church in England as well as the head of state.

1534

The French explorer Jacques Cartier arrives in the Western Hemisphere, the first of his expeditions to the region those in his home country begin to refer to as "New France."

1539

Spanish conquistador Hernando de Soto begins his exploration of the Southwest of the modern-day United States; by the time he finishes his *entrada* in 1541, thousands of indigenous people in the region will have perished, most of them victims of diseases brought by the Europeans.

1540

Spanish conquistador Francisco Coronado arrives in the Southwest of the modern-day United States looking for Cíbola, a fabled city of gold and jewels; he led his men as far east as modern-day Kansas.

1552

Publication in Spain of Bartolomé de Las Casas's *Short Account of the Destruction of the Indies*, a damning critique of the plundering actions of conquistadores that contributes to the decision of the English, a Protestant nation after 1533, to colonize the Western Hemisphere.

1555

Publication in London of an English-language edition of Peter Martyr's *De Orbe Novo*.

ca. 1555

Tobacco arrives in Europe from the Western Hemisphere.

1557

Jacques Cartier dies in St. Malo, France.

1558

Elizabeth I, one of Henry VIII's daughters and an avid supporter of Protestantism, accedes to the English throne; during her long reign she makes the conquest of Ireland, a Catholic island, a crucial part of her foreign policy.

1564

French Huguenots sail across the Atlantic seeking a new homeland; after an abortive attempt to settle at modern-day Port Royal, South Carolina, the migrants establish a colony at Fort Caroline, Florida.

1565

The Spanish force the French out of Fort Caroline and establish a settlement at Saint Augustine, which becomes the longest-settled European city in North America.

1570

Deganawida and Hiawatha establish the Iroquois Confederacy, an alliance of five indigenous nations (Seneca, Oneida, Onondaga, Cayuga, and Mohawk); in the early 18th century the Tuscarora become the sixth nation in the league.

1576

The English explorer Martin Frobisher leaves in search of the Northwest Passage; his venture fails, as did efforts he led in 1578.

1579

The English explorer Sir Francis Drake lands on the coast of California.

1582

Richard Hakluyt the younger publishes *Divers Voyages Touching the Discovery of America and the Ilands Adjacent*, his first serious attempt to encourage English policy makers to establish colonies in the Western Hemisphere.

1583

During an English mission to Newfoundland, the English explorer Sir Humphrey Gilbert and the Hungarian poet Stephen Parmenius drown when their ships sink.

1584

Sir Walter Ralegh, arguably the most significant English adventurer of his age, receives a charter from Queen Elizabeth I to establish colonies in eastern North America.

Richard Hakluyt the younger writes a secret document, known as the "Discourse Concerning Western Planting," which lays out in detail why the English should colonize North America.

Manteo and Wanchese, Carolina Algonquian Indians, travel to England.

1585

Under Sir Walter Ralegh's authority English settlers establish themselves at Roanoke in modern-day North Carolina. Among those who arrive in the colony are the artist John White, who paints memorable images of the Carolina Algonquians he meets there, and Thomas Harriot, who writes about the region in *A Briefe and True History of the Newfound Land of Virginia*, first published in 1588 and then published in four languages in an illustrated version in 1590.

1587

Birth of Virginia Dare, the first English child born in North America.

English colonists arrive in Roanoke with new supplies and take back across the Atlantic some of the first settlers.

1588

The English navy defeats the Spanish Armada in the English Channel.

1590

English colonists, better able to sail across the Atlantic after the defeat of the Spanish Armada, arrive in Roanoke to find it deserted.

1595

Sir Walter Raleigh makes his first visit to Guiana, the area whose allure led him to organize other expeditions to the region.

1598

The governor Juan de Oñate arrives in the Spanish colony of New Mexico; he declares that all indigenous peoples in the region must become subjects of the Spanish monarch (see Requerimiento.) His actions cause long-lasting enmity among the native peoples of the region, whose descendants in 1680 rise up against the Spanish in the most successful indigenous revolt against European colonizers in the early modern age.

1603

Death of Elizabeth I; accession of James I.

1607

The English captain John Smith arrives in Virginia and, along with 143 other men and boys, establishes the colony of Jamestown.

Documents

Privileges and Prerogatives Granted to Columbus, 1492

Francis Newton Thorpe, *The Federal and State Constitutions, Colonial Charters and Other Organic Laws . . .* Vol. 1 (Washington, D.C.: Government Printing Office, 1909), pp. 39–40

PRIVILEGES AND PREROGATIVES GRANTED BY THEIR CATHOLIC MAJESTIES TO CHRISTOPHER COLUMBUS—1492

Ferdinand and Elizabeth, by the Grace of God, King and Queen of *Castile,* of *Leon,* of *Arragon,* of *Sicily,* of *Granada,* of *Toledo,* of *Valencia,* of *Galicia,* of *Majorca,* of *Minorca,* of *Sevil,* of *Sardinia,* of *Jaen,* of *Algarve,* of *Algezira,* of *Gibraltar,* of the *Canary Islands,* Count and Countess of *Barcelona,* Lord and Lady of *Biscay* and *Molina,* Duke and Duchess of *Athens* and *Neopatria,* Count and Countess of *Rousillion* and *Cerdaigne,* Marquess and Marchioness of *Oristan* and *Gociano, &c.*

For as much of you, *Christopher Columbus,* are going by our command, with some of our vessels and men, to discover and subdue some Islands and Continent in the ocean, and it is hoped that by God's assistance, some of the said Islands and Continent in the ocean will be discovered and conquered by your means and conduct, therefore it is but just and reasonable, that since you expose yourself to such danger to serve us, you should be rewarded for it. And we being willing to honour and favour you for the reasons aforesaid: Our will is, that you, *Christopher Columbus,* after discovering and conquering the said Islands and Continent in the said ocean, or any of them, shall be our Admiral of the said Islands and Continent you shall so discover and conquer; and that you be our Admiral, Vice-Roy, and Governour in them, and that for the future, you may call and stile yourself, *D. Christopher Columbus,* and that your sons and suc-

cessors in the said employment, may call themselves Dons, Admirals, Vice-Roys, and Governours of them; and that you may exercise the office of Admiral, with the charge of Vice-Roy and Governour of the said Islands and Continent, which you and your Lieutenants shall conquer, and freely decide all causes, civil and criminal, appertaining to the said employment of Admiral, Vice-Roy, and Governour, as you shall think fit in justice, and as the Admirals of our kingdoms use to do; and that you have power to punish offenders; and you and your Lieutenants exercise the employments of Admiral, Vice-Roy, and Governour, in all things belonging to the said offices, or any of them; and that you enjoy the perquisites and salaries belonging to the said employments, and to each of them, in the same manner as the High Admiral of our kingdom does. And by this our letter, or a copy of it signed by a *Public Notary:* We command Prince *John,* our most dearly beloved Son, the Infants, Dukes, Prelates, Marquesses, Great Masters and Military Orders, Priors, Commendaries, our Counsellors, Judges, and other Officers of Justice whatsoever, belonging to our Household, Courts, and Chancery, and Constables of Castles, Strong Houses, and others; and all Corporations, Bayliffs, Governours, Judges, Commanders, Sea Officers; and the Aldermen, Common Council, Officers, and Good People of all Cities, Lands, and Places in our Kingdoms and Dominions, and in those you shall conquer and subdue, and the captains, masters, mates, and other officers and sailors, our natural subjects now being, or that shall be for the time to come, and any of them, that when you shall have discovered that said Islands and Continent in the ocean; and you, or any that shall have your commission, shall have taken the usual oath in such cases, that they for the future, look upon you as long as you live, and after you, your son and heir, and so from one heir to another forever, as our Admiral on our said Ocean, and as Vice-Roy and Governour of the said Islands and Continent, by you, *Christopher Columbus,* discovered and conquered; and that they treat you and your Lieutenants, by you appointed, for executing the employments of Admiral, Vice-Roy, and Governour, as such in all respects, and give you all the perquisites and other things belonging and appertaining to the said offices; and allow, and cause to be allowed you, all the honours, graces, concessions, prehaminences, prerogatives, immunities, and other things, or any of them which are due to you, by virtue of your commands of Admiral, Vice-roy, and Governour, and to be observed completely, so that nothing be diminished; and that they make no objection to this, or any part of it, nor suffer it to be made; forasmuch as we from this time forward, by this our letter, bestow on you the employments of Admiral, Vice-Roy, and perpetual Governour forever; and we put you into possession of the said offices, and of every of them, and full power to use and exercise them, and to receive the perquisites and salaries belonging to them, or any of them, as was said above. Concerning all which things, if it be requisite, and you shall desire it. We command our Chancellour, Notaries, and other Officers, to pass, seal, and deliver to you, our Letter of Privilege, in such form and legal manner, as you shall require our stand in need of. And that none of them presume to do any thing to the contrary, upon pain of our displeasure, and forfeiture of 30 ducats for each offence. And we command him, who show them this our Letter, that he summon them to appear before us at our Court, where we shall then be, within fifteen days after such summons, under the said penalty. Under which same, we also command any Public Notary whatsoever, that he give to him that shows it him, a certificate under his seal, that we may know how our command is obeyed.

Given at Granada, on the 30th of April, in the year of our Lord, 1492. —

I, the King, I, the Queen.

By their Majesties Command,

John Coloma, Secretary to the King and Queen.

Entered according to order.

Roderick. Doctor. Sebastian Dolona, Francis de Madrid, Councellors.

Registered

Papal Bull Inter Caetera of 1493

Frances G. Davenport, ed., *European Treaties Bearing on the History of the United States and Its Dependencies to 1648* (Washington, D.C.: Carnegie Institution of Washington, 1917–34), pp. 71–78

Alexander, bishop, servant of the servants of God, to the illustrious sovereigns, our very dear son in Christ, Ferdinand, king, and our very dear daughter in Christ, Isabella, queen of Castile, Leon, Aragon, Sicily, and Granada, health and apostolic benediction. Among other works well pleasing to the Divine Majesty and cherished of our heart, this assuredly ranks highest, that in our times

especially the Catholic faith and the Christian religion be exalted and be everywhere increased and spread, that the health of souls be cared for and that barbarous nations be overthrown and brought to the faith itself. Wherefore inasmuch as by the favor of divine clemency, we, though of insufficient merits, have been called to this Holy See of Peter, recognizing that as true Catholic kings and princes, such as we have known you always to be, and as your illustrious deeds already known to almost the whole world declare, you not only eagerly desire but with every effort, zeal, and diligence, without regard to hardships, expenses, dangers, with the shedding even of your blood, are laboring to that end; recognizing also that you have long since dedicated to this purpose your whole soul and all your endeavors—as witnessed in these times with so much glory to the Divine Name in your recovery of the kingdom of Granada from the yoke of the Saracens—we therefore are rightly led, and hold it as our duty, to grant you even of our own accord and in your favor those things whereby with effort each day more hearty you may be enabled for the honor of God himself and the spread of the Christian rule to carry forward your holy and praiseworthy purpose so pleasing to immortal God. We have indeed learned that you, who for a long time had intended to seek out and discover certain islands and mainlands remote and unknown and not hitherto discovered by others, to the end that you might bring to the worship of our Redeemer and the profession of the Catholic faith their residents and inhabitants, having been up to the present time greatly engaged in the siege and recovery of the kingdom itself of Granada were unable to accomplish this holy and praiseworthy purpose; but the said kingdom having at length been regained, as was pleasing to the Lord, you, with the wish to fulfill your desire, chose our beloved son, Christopher Columbus, a man assuredly worthy and of the highest recommendations and fitted for so great an undertaking, whom you furnished with ships and men equipped for like designs, not without the greatest hardships, dangers, and expenses, to make diligent quest for these remote and unknown mainlands and islands through the sea, where hitherto no one had sailed; and they at length, with divine aid and with the utmost diligence sailing in the ocean sea, discovered certain very remote islands and even mainlands that hitherto had not been discovered by others; wherein dwell very many peoples living in peace, and, as reported, going unclothed, and not eating flesh. Moreover, as your aforesaid envoys are of opinion, these very peoples living in the said islands and countries believe in one God, the Creator in heaven, and seem sufficiently disposed to embrace the Catholic faith and be trained in good morals. And it is hoped that, were they instructed, the name of the Savior, our Lord Jesus Christ, would easily be introduced into the said countries and islands. Also, on one of the chief of these aforesaid islands the said Christopher has already caused to be put together and built a fortress fairly equipped, wherein he has stationed as garrison certain Christians, companions of his, who are to make search for other remote and unknown islands and mainlands. In the islands and countries already discovered are found gold, spices, and very many other precious things of divers kinds and qualities. Wherefore, as becomes Catholic kings and princes, after earnest consideration of all matters, especially of the rise and spread of the Catholic faith, as was the fashion of your ancestors, kings of renowned memory, you have purposed with the favor of divine clemency to bring under your sway the said mainlands and islands with their residents and inhabitants and to bring them to the Catholic faith. Hence, heartily commending in the Lord this your holy and praiseworthy purpose, and desirous that it be duly accomplished, and that the name of our Savior be carried into those regions, we exhort you very earnestly in the Lord and by your reception of holy baptism, whereby you are bound to our apostolic commands, and by the bowels of the mercy of our Lord Jesus Christ, enjoin strictly, that inasmuch as with eager zeal for the true faith you design to equip and dispatch this expedition, you purpose also, as is your duty, to lead the peoples dwelling in those islands and countries to embrace the Christian religion; nor at any time let dangers or hardships deter you therefrom, with the stout hope and trust in your hearts that Almighty God will further your undertakings. And, in order that you may enter upon so great an undertaking with greater readiness and heartiness endowed with the benefit of our apostolic favor, we, of our own accord, not at your instance nor the request of anyone else in your regard, but of our own sole largess and certain knowledge and out of the fullness of our apostolic power, by the authority of Almighty God conferred upon us in blessed Peter and of the vicarship of Jesus Christ, which we hold on earth, do by tenor of these presents, should any of said islands have been found by your envoys and captains, give, grant, and assign to you and your heirs and successors, kings of Castile and Leon, forever, together with all their dominions, cities, camps, places, and villages, and all rights, jurisdictions, and appurtenances, all islands and mainlands found and to be found, discovered and to be discovered towards the west and south, by drawing and establishing a line from the Arctic pole, namely the north, to the Antarctic pole, namely the south, no matter whether the said mainlands and islands are found and to be found in the direction of India or towards any other quarter, the said line to be distant one hundred leagues towards the west and south from any of the islands commonly known as the Azores and Cape Verde. With this proviso however that none of the islands and mainlands, found and to be found, discovered and to be discovered, beyond that said line towards the west and south, be in the actual possession of any Christian king or

prince up to the birthday of our Lord Jesus Christ just past from which the present year one thousand four hundred and ninety-three begins. And we make, appoint, and depute you and your said heirs and successors lords of them with full and free power, authority, and jurisdiction of every kind; with this proviso however, that by this our gift, grant, and assignment no right acquired by any Christian prince, who may be in actual possession of said islands and mainlands prior to the said birthday of our Lord Jesus Christ, is hereby to be understood to be withdrawn or taken away. Moreover we command you in virtue of holy obedience that, employing all due diligence in the premises, as you also promise—nor do we doubt your compliance therein in accordance with your loyalty and royal greatness of spirit—you should appoint to the aforesaid mainlands and islands worthy, God-fearing, learned, skilled, and experienced men, in order to instruct the aforesaid inhabitants and residents in the Catholic faith and train them in good morals. Furthermore, under penalty of excommunication *late sententie* to be incurred *ipso facto*, should anyone thus contravene, we strictly forbid all persons of whatsoever rank, even imperial and royal, or of whatsoever estate, degree, order, or condition, to dare, without your special permit or that of your aforesaid heirs and successors, to go for the purpose of trade or any other reason to the islands or mainlands, found and to be found, discovered and to be discovered, towards the west and south, by drawing and establishing a line from the Arctic pole to the Antarctic pole, no matter whether the mainlands and islands, found and to be found, lie in the direction of India or toward any other quarter whatsoever, the said line to be distant one hundred leagues towards the west and south, as is aforesaid, from any of the islands commonly known as the Azores and Cape Verde; apostolic constitutions and ordinances and other decrees whatsoever to the contrary notwithstanding. We trust in Him from whom empires and governments and all good things proceed, that, should you, with the Lord's guidance, pursue this holy and praiseworthy undertaking, in a short while your hardships and endeavors will attain the most felicitous result, to the happiness and glory of all Christendom. But inasmuch as it would be difficult to have these present letters sent to all places where desirable, we wish, and with similar accord and knowledge do decree, that to copies of them, signed by the hand of a public notary commissioned therefore, and sealed with the seal of any ecclesiastical officer or ecclesiastical court, the same respect is to be shown in court and outside as well as anywhere else as would be given to these presents should they thus be exhibited or shown. Let no one, therefore, infringe, or with rash boldness contravene, this our recommendations, exhortation, requisition, gift, grant, assignment, constitution, deputation, decree, mandate, prohibition, and will. Should anyone presume to attempt this, be it known to him that he will incur the wrath of Almighty God and of the blessed apostles Peter and Paul. Given at Rome, at St. Peter's, in the year of the incarnation of our Lord one thousand four hundred and ninety-three, the fourth of May, and the first year of our pontificate. Gratis by order of our most holy lord, the pope. June. For the referendary, A. de Mucciarellis. For J. Bufolinus, A. Santoseverino. L. Podocatharus.

The "Barcelona Letter" of 1493 by Christopher Columbus

Mauricio Obregón, *The Columbus Papers: The Barcelona Letter of 1493, the Landfall Controversy, and the Indian Guides* (New York: Macmillan, 1991), pp. 65–69. Translation of document by Lucia Graves.

SIR: BECAUSE I KNOW you will take pleasure in the great victory that Our Lord has given me in my voyage, I write this letter to inform you of how in twenty days I reached the Indies with the fleet supplied to me by the most illustrious King and Queen, our Sovereigns, and how there I discovered a great many islands inhabited by people without number: and of them all I have taken possession on behalf of Their Highnesses by proclamation and with the royal flag extended, and I was not opposed. I named the first island I found San Salvador, in commemoration of His Divine Majesty, who so wonderfully has created all this the Indians call it Guanaham. The second I named Santa Maria de Concepción; the third Ferrandina; the fourth Isabella, the fifth Juana Island; and so to each a new name.

When I reached Juana I followed its coast westward and found it so large that I thought it might be terra firma, the province of Cathay. I did not discover in this manner any towns or villages along the coast, only small hamlets whose inhabitants I could not speak to because they all fled at our sight, but I continued on that route, not wanting to miss any great city or town. After many leagues there was still no change, and the coast was leading me north, where it was not my wish to go, because winter had set in and I wanted to avoid it and go south; moreover, I had a head wind, so I decided not to wait for better weather and turned back to a large harbor, whence I sent two men inland to find out whether there was a king or any big cities. They walked for three days and discovered an infinite number of little villages and countless people, but no such thing as a government; for which reason they returned.

It was made clear to me, by other Indians whom I had captured earlier, that this entire land was an island; so I followed its coast eastward for one hundred and seven leagues until it came to an end, and from that cape I saw another island to the east, eighteen leagues away, which I later named La Española, and there I went. I sailed eastward along its northern coast, as I had done in Juana, covering 178 long leagues in a straight line. This island and all the other ones are exceedingly grandiose, and this one in the extreme. There are harbors on the coastline that cannot be compared to any others I know in all Christendom, and plenty of good large rivers that are a marvel to see. Its lands are high and have a great many sierras and soaring mountains, unmatched by those of the island of Tenerife, for they are indeed all very beautiful, and of a thousand different shapes, and accessible, and full of all kinds of trees, so tall they seem to touch the sky; I have heard it said, moreover, that these trees never lose their leaves, which I can well believe, for I saw they were as green and beautiful as they are in Spain in the month of May. Some were in blossom, others with fruit, others yet at a different stage, according to variety; and I could hear nightingales and other small birds of a thousand different kinds singing in the month of November, wherever I went. There are six or eight kinds of palm tree which are a wonder to behold on account of their beautiful and unusual shapes, and the same can be said of the other trees, fruits and plants. On this island there are marvelous pine woods and vast fields; and there is honey, and many kinds of birds and a great diversity of fruits. This land also has many mines of metal, and people in uncountable number.

La Española is a marvel. Its sierras and mountains, its lowlands and meadows and its beautiful thick soil, are so apt for planting and sowing, for raising all kinds of cattle and for building towns and villages. As for the seaports here, seeing is believing; and so also the many big rivers of good water, most of which carry gold. The trees, fruits and plants are very different from those of Juana: in this island there are many spices and great mines of gold and other metals.

The people of this island, and of all the other islands I have found or heard about, go naked, men and women alike, just as their mothers bear them, although some women cover one single place with a leaf or with a piece of cotton which they make for this purpose. They have no iron or steel or weapons, nor are they inclined to such things. This is not from lack of vigor or handsome build, but because they are unbelievably fearful. Their only arms are canes, cut when in seed, with a sharp stick attached to the end, but they dare not use them: for it often came to pass that I would send two or three men ashore to some village to talk with its dwellers, and crowds would stream out towards them, but upon seeing our men at close quarters they would turn around and flee, parents not even waiting for their children. This was not because any harm had been done to any of them; on the contrary, in every place I have visited and have been able to talk with the people, I have given them of all I had, such as cloth and many other things, receiving nothing in return; but they are just hopelessly timorous. True it is that once they feel reassured and lose this fear they are then so guileless and generous with what they have that one would not believe it without seeing it. If you ask them for something they have, they never say no; instead, they offer it to you with such love that they would give you their very hearts. Then, whether their gift was of great or little value, they are happy to receive any little trifle in return.

I forbade that they be given such worthless things as pieces of broken bowls, or pieces of broken glass, or lace-tags, although when they could obtain any of these, they considered it the most precious jewel in the world. It happened once that a sailor received the weight of two and a half *castellanos* in gold for a lace-tag; and others, for other things that were worth even less, received even more. For newly coined *blancas* those people would give all they had, even two or three *castellanos'* weight in gold, or a quarter or two of spun cotton. They even accepted broken hoops of wine casks, and like fools gave all they had for them. That seemed wrong to me, so I forbade it and I gave them sundry good things that I brought with me so as to gain their love and, moreover, that they might become Christians, for they are inclined to love and serve Their Highnesses and the whole of the Castilian nation; and they endeavor to gather and give us things which they have in abundance and which are necessary to us. They did not know any sect or idolatry, except that they all believe that power and goodness abide in heaven. Indeed, they believed very firmly that I with these ships and people came from heaven, and with corresponding regard they received me in every place, once they had lost their fear. And this is not because they are ignorant, for they have a very subtle ingeniousness and travel all over those seas, it being a wonder to listen to the good accounts they give of everything, but because they had never before seen people wearing clothes, or ships like ours.

When I arrived in the Indies, I took some of these people by force in the first island I found, so that they might learn our language and give me news of what existed in those parts. And so it happened, for later they understood us and we them, either by speech or by signs: and they have been very useful to us. I am bringing them with me now, and they still think I come from heaven, despite all the conversation they have had with me. These were the first to announce it wherever I went; others would run from house to house and to nearby villages shouting, "Come! Come and see the people from heaven!" Thus they all, men and women, old and young, once their hearts were sure of us, would come out, leaving no one behind, and each bringing something to eat and drink which they gave to us with wondrous good will.

In all these islands there are very many canoes, similar to longboats, some of which are large and others smaller, many being even larger than a longboat of eighteen benches; but not as wide, for they are made of a single piece of timber. A longboat, however, could not keep up with them with oars alone, for they go with incredible speed. With these canoes they travel all over those islands, which are innumerable, and

ply their merchandise. I have seen some of those canoes with 70 or 80 men aboard, and each with his oar.

In all these islands I did not see much diversity in the people's features, or in the customs, or in their language. What is more, they all understand each other, which is a remarkable thing, and for that reason I hope that Their Highnesses will decide on the preaching to them of our Holy Faith, to which they are very well disposed.

I have already related how I traveled 107 leagues along the coast of Juana, following a straight line from west to east. Accordingly, I can say that this island is larger than England and Scotland together: for beyond those 107 leagues there are two provinces on the west side which I have not visited. One of them is called Auan, where people are born with tails. These provinces must be at least fifty or sixty leagues long, or so I understand from the Indians I have with me, who know all these islands.

This other island called Española has a circumference greater than the whole of Spain from Colunya all along the coastline up to Fuenterrabía, in Biscay: for I followed one of its quarters in a straight line from west to east and covered 188 long leagues. This island is to be coveted; and once seen, one would never leave it. Since I have taken possession of all these islands for Their Highnesses, and since they are all richer than I know or can say, I hold them all on behalf of Their Highnesses, who can dispose of them in the same way and just as fully as the very kingdoms of Castile. In Española I have taken possession of a large town, which I have named Villa de Navidad. It is situated in the most convenient spot on the island and in the best district for gold mines and for all kinds of trade with the nearest mainland as well as with the farther one of the Great Khan, where there will be much commerce and gain. In this town I have built fortifications which by now must be entirely completed, and I have left enough men there for the purpose, with arms and artillery and victuals for over a year; also a longboat and a master seaman skilled in all the arts for building more; and I have great friendship with the king of that land, to such a degree that he took pride in calling me his brother and treating me as such. But even if he were to change his mind and act against my men, neither he nor his people know anything about weapons, and go around naked, as I have said: they are the most faint-hearted people in the world, and the few men I have left behind would suffice to destroy the whole of that land. The island offers no danger to their lives as long as they know how to govern it.

In all these islands it seems to me that men are content with one woman, and they give their chief or king up to twenty. Women work more than men, it seems to me, but I have not been able to ascertain whether these people have any private belongings, for I think I saw that what one had was shared by all, especially food.

Until now I have not found any monstrous men in these islands, as many had thought. On the contrary, all these people are very good-looking: they are not black as in Guinea, but have flowing hair, and they do not make their homes in places where the rays of the sun are too strong. Indeed, the sun is very powerful there, being only twenty-six degrees distant from the equator. Where there are high mountains in these islands, it was intensely cold this winter, but they are able to endure it, by habit and with the aid of the many exceeding hot spices which they eat with their food.

So, I have found no monsters nor had any news of any, except from one island, the second one at the entrance to the Indies. It is inhabited by a people who are considered in all the other islands to be extremely fierce, and who eat human flesh. These people have many canoes with which they have the run of all the islands of the Indies; they steal and take all they can. They are no more deformed than the rest, and can only be distinguished from them because they have a habit of keeping their hair long, like women, and use bows and arrows, made of the same canes as the weapons I described earlier, with a stick on the tip instead of iron, which they do not have. They are ferocious when compared to the other islanders, who are cowardly in the extreme; but I am no more afraid of them than of the rest. These are the ones who trade with the women of Matremonio, the first island one reaches on the voyage from Spain to the Indies, and in which there lives not a single man. They are not used to feminine occupations, but carry bows and arrows, likewise made with canes, and they arm and cover themselves with plates of copper, of which they have plenty. I have been assured that there is another island larger than Española where the people are entirely bald. It abounds in gold, and I bring Indians with me from this and the other islands to testify to it.

In conclusion, to speak only of what has been done on this hasty voyage, Their Highnesses can see that I will give them as much gold as they may need, with but a little help from Their Highnesses. Also spices and cotton, as much as Their Highnesses order me to load; and as much mastic as they order loaded, which until now had been found only in Greece on the island of Chios and which the Seignory sell for the asking. They can also have as much aloe as they order loaded, and as many slaves as they order loaded, who will be idolaters. I also think I have found rhubarb and cinnamon, and I will find a thousand other things of substance which the people I have left behind will have discovered. For I have not tarried anywhere when the wind allowed me to sail, except in the Villa de Navidad, which I left secured and well settled. And, truly, I would have done much more if the ships had served me as it would have been reasonable to expect.

This is enough, and Eternal be God our Lord, who grants, to all those who walk in His path, victories over things that appear impossible. And indeed this was a great victory, for even though people may have spoken and written about these lands, all was conjecture, nobody actually having seen them. It amounted to this: that most of those who heard these stories listened, but judged them rather from hearsay than from the least bit of proof. Thus our Redeemer has granted victory in so great a matter to our most Illustrious King and Queen, and to their renowned kingdoms. For which the whole of Christendom should rejoice and make merry, giving solemn thanks to the Holy Trinity, with many a solemn prayer, for all the glory they will receive when so many peoples turn to our Holy Faith; as well as for the temporal benefits, which will bring renewal and gain not only to Spain but to all Christians.

This, in brief, according to the facts. Written on board the caravel, by the islands of Canary, on February 15 of the year 1493.

At your orders. The Admiral *Nema* that came inside the letter:

After this letter was written, being within the seas of Castile, I met with such strong south and southeast winds that I was forced to unload the ships. But today I was driven into this port of Lisbon, an event which was the greatest marvel in the world, and here I have decided to write to Their Highnesses. In all the Indies I have always found the weather to be like that of the month of May. I went there in 33 days and returned in 28, save that these storms have detained me 14 days tossing about the sea. Here all the seamen say that there was never so bad a winter nor such a great loss of ships. Written on the fourteenth day of March.

This letter Columbus sent to the Secretary of the Treasury about the Islands Discovered in the Indies. Contained in another to Their Highnesses.

Patent Granted by King Henry VII to John Cabot and his Sons, March 1496.

> H. P. Biggar, ed., *The Precursors of Jacques Cartier 1497–1534: A Collection of Documents relating to the Early History of the Dominion of Canada* (Ottawa: Government Printing Bureau, 1911) pp. 7–10. Original document housed in the Public Record Office, London.

For John Cabot and his Sons.

The King, to all to whom, etc. Greeting: Be it known and made manifest that we have given and granted as by these presents we give and grant, for us and our heirs, to our well beloved John Cabot, citizen of Venice, and to Lewis, Sebastian and Sancio, sons of the said John, and to the heirs and deputies of them, and of any one of them, full and free authority, faculty and power to sail to all parts, regions and coasts of the eastern, western and northern sea, under our banners, flags and ensigns, with five ships or vessels of whatsoever burden and quality they may be, and with so many and such mariners and men as they may wish to take with them in the said ships, at their own proper costs and charges, to find, discover and investigate whatsoever islands, countries, regions or provinces of heathens and infidels, in whatsoever part of the world placed, which before this time were unknown to all Christians. We have also granted to them and to any of them, and to the heirs and deputies of them and of any one of them, and have given licence to set up our aforesaid banners and ensigns in any town, city, castle, island or mainland whatsoever, newly found by them. And that the before-mentioned John and his sons or their heirs and deputies may conquer, occupy and possess whatsoever such towns, castles, cities and islands by them thus discovered that they may be able to conquer, occupy and possess, as our vassals and governors lieutenants and deputies therein, acquiring for us the dominion, title and jurisdiction of the same towns, castles, cities, islands and mainlands so discovered; in such a way nevertheless that of all the fruits, profits, emoluments, commodities, gains and revenues accruing from this voyage, the said John and sons and their heirs and deputies shall be bound and under obligation for their every voyage, as often as they shall arrive at our port of Bristol, at which they are bound and holden only to arrive, all necessary charges and expenses incurred by them having been deducted, to pay to us, either in goods or money, the fifth part of the whole capital gained, we giving and granting to them and to their heirs and deputies, that they shall be free and exempt from all payment of customs on all and singular the goods and merchandise that they may bring back with them from those places thus newly discovered.

And further we have given and granted to them and to their heirs and deputies, that all mainlands, islands, towns, cities, castles and other places whatsoever discovered by them, however numerous they may happen to be, may not be frequented or visited by any other subjects of ours whatsoever without the licence of the aforesaid John and his sons and of their deputies, on pain of the loss as well of the ships or vessels daring to sail to these places discovered, as of all goods whatsoever. Willing and strictly commanding all and singular our subjects as well by land as by sea, that they shall render good assistance to the aforesaid John and his sons and deputies, and that they shall give them all their favour and help as well in fitting out the ships or vessels as in buying stores and provisions with their money and in providing the other things which they must take with them on the said voyage.

In witness whereof, etc.

Witness ourself at Westminster on the fifth day of March.

By the King himself, etc.

Amerigo Vespucci's "Mondo Nuovo" letter of 1504

George Tyler Northrup, trans. Mundus novus. Letter to Lorenzo Pietro d. Medici. (Princeton, N.J.: Princeton University Press, 1916).

ALBERICUS VESPUCIUS OFFERS HIS BEST COMPLIMENTS TO LORENZO PIETRO DI MEDICI.

On a former occasion I wrote to you at some length concerning my return from those new regions which we found and explored with the fleet, at the cost, and by the command of this Most Serene King of Portugal. And these we may rightly call a new world. Because our ancestors had no knowledge of them, and it will be a matter wholly new to all those who hear about them. For this transcends the view held by our ancients, inasmuch as most of them hold that there is no continent to the south beyond the equator, but only the sea which they named the Atlantic; and if some of them did aver that a continent there was, they denied with abundant argument that it was a habitable land. But that this their opinion is false and utterly opposed to the truth, this my last voyage has made manifest; for in those southern parts I have found a continent more densely peopled and abounding in animals than our Europe or Asia or Africa, and, in addition, a climate milder and more delightful than in any other region known to us, as you shall learn in the following account wherein we shall set succinctly down only capital matters and the things more worthy of comment and memory seen or heard by me in this new world, as will appear below.

On the fourteenth of the month of May, one thousand five hundred and one we set sail from Lisbon under fair sailing conditions, in compliance with the commands of the aforementioned king, with these ships for the purpose of seeking new regions toward the south; and for twenty months we continuously pursued this southern course. The route of this voyage is as follows: Our course was set for the Fortunate Isles, once so called, but which are now termed the Grand Canary Islands; these are in the third climate and on the border of the inhabited west. Thence by sea we skirted the whole African coast and part of Ethiopia as far as the Ethiopic Promontory, so called by Ptolemy, which we now call Cape Verde and the Ethiopians Beseghice. And that region, Mandingha, lies within the torrid zone fourteen degrees north of the equator; it is inhabited by tribes and nations of blacks. Having there recovered our strength and taken on all that our voyage required, we weighed anchor and made sail. And directing our course over the vast ocean toward the Antarctic we for a time bent westward, owing to the wind called Vulturnus; and from the day when we set sail from the said promontory we cruised for the space of two months and three days before any land appeared to us. But what we suffered on that vast expanse of sea, what perils of shipwreck, what discomforts of the body we endured, with what anxiety of mind we toiled, this I leave to the judgment of those who out of rich experience have well learned what it is to seek the uncertain and to attempt discoveries even though ignorant. And that in a word I may briefly narrate all, you must know that of the sixty-seven days of our sailing we had forty-four of constant rain, thunder and lightning—so dark that never did we see sun by day or fair sky by night. By reason of this such fear invaded us that we soon abandoned almost all hope of life. But during these tempests of sea and sky, so numerous and so violent, the Most High was pleased to display before us a continent, new lands. and an unknown world. At sight of these things we were filled with as much joy as anyone can imagine usually falls to the lot of those who have gained refuge from varied calamity and hostile fortune. It was on the seventh day of August, one thousand five hundred and one that we anchored off the shores of those parts, thanking our God with formal ceremonial and with the celebration of a choral mass. We knew that land to be a continent and not an island both because it stretches forth in the form of a very long and unbending coast, and because it is replete with infinite inhabitants. For in it we found innumerable tribes and peoples and species of all manner of wild beasts which are found in our lands and many others never seen by us concerning which it would take long to tell in detail. God's mercy shone upon us much when we landed at that spot, for there had come a shortage of firewood and water, and in a few days we might have ended our lives at sea. To Him be honor, glory, and thanksgiving.

We adopted the plan of following the coast of this continent toward the east and never losing sight of it. We sailed along until at length we reached a bend where the shore made a turn to the south; and from that point where we first touched land to that corner it was about three hundred leagues, in which sailing distance we frequently landed and had friendly relations with those people, as you will hear below. I had forgotten to write you that from the promontory of Cape Verde to the nearest part of that continent is about seven hundred leagues, although I should estimate that we sailed more than eighteen hundred, partly through ignorance of the route and the ship-master's want of knowledge, partly owing to tempests and winds which kept us from the proper course and compelled us to put about frequently. Because, if my companions had not heeded me, who had knowledge of cosmography, there would have been no ship-master, nay not the leader of our expedition himself, who would have known where we were within five hundred leagues. For we were wandering and uncertain in our course, and only the instruments for taking the altitudes of the heavenly bodies showed us our true course

precisely; and these were the quadrant and the astrolabe, which all men have come to know. For this reason they subsequently made me the object of great honor; for I showed them that though a man without practical experience, yet through the teaching of the marine chart for navigators I was more skilled than all the ship-masters of the whole world. For these have no knowledge except of those waters to which they have often sailed. Now, where the said corner of land showed us a southern trend of the coast we agreed to sail beyond it and inquire what there might be in those parts. So we sailed along the coast about six hundred leagues, and often landed and mingled and associated with the natives of those regions, and by them we were received in brotherly fashion; and we would dwell with them too, for fifteen or twenty days continuously, maintaining amicable and hospitable relations, as you shall learn below. Part of this new continent lies in the torrid zone beyond the equator toward the Antarctic pole, for it begins eight degrees beyond the equator. We sailed along this coast until we passed the tropic of Capricorn and found the Antarctic pole fifty degrees higher than that horizon. We advanced to within seventeen and a half degrees of the Antarctic circle, and what I there have seen and learned concerning the nature of those races, their manners, their tractability and the fertility of the soil, the salubrity of the climate, the position of the heavenly bodies in the sky, and especially concerning the fixed stars of the eighth sphere, never seen or studied by our ancestors, these things I shall relate in order.

First then as to the people. We found in those parts such a multitude of people as nobody could enumerate (as we read in the Apocalypse), a race I say gentle and amenable. All of both sexes go about naked, covering no part of their bodies; and just as they spring from their mothers' wombs so they go until death. They have indeed large square-built bodies, well formed and proportioned, and in color verging upon reddish. This I think has come to them, because, going about naked, they are colored by the sun. They have, too, hair plentiful and black. In their gait and when playing their games they are agile and dignified. They are comely, too, of countenance which they nevertheless themselves destroy; for they bore their cheeks, lips, noses and ears. Nor think those holes small or that they have one only. For some I have seen having in a single face seven borings any one of which was capable of holding a plum. They stop up these holes of theirs with blue stones, bits of marble, very beautiful crystals of alabaster, very white bones, and other things artificially prepared according to their customs. But if you could see a thing so unwonted and monstrous, that is to say a man having in his cheeks and lips alone seven stones some of which are a span and a half in length, you would not be without wonder. For I frequently observed and discovered that seven such stones weighed sixteen ounces, aside from the fact that in their ears, each perforated with three holes, they have other stones dangling on rings; and this usage applies to the men alone. For women do not bore their faces, but their ears only. They have another custom, very shameful and beyond all human belief. For their women, being very lustful, cause the private parts of their husbands to swell up to such a huge size that they appear deformed and disgusting; and this is accomplished by a certain device of theirs, the biting of certain poisonous animals. And in consequence of this many lose their organs which break through lack of attention, and they remain eunuchs. They have no cloth either of wool, linen or cotton, since they need it not; neither do they have goods of their own, but all things are held in common. They live together without king, without government, and each is his own master. They marry as many wives as they please; and son cohabits with mother, brother with sister, male cousin with female, and any man with the first woman he meets. They dissolve their marriages as often as they please, and observe no sort of law with respect to them. Beyond the fact that they have no church, no religion and are not idolaters, what more can I say? They live according to nature, and may be called Epicureans rather than Stoics. There are no merchants among their number, nor is there barter. The nations wage war upon one another without art or order. The elders by means of certain harangues of theirs bend the youths to their will and inflame them to wars in which they cruelly kill one another, and those whom they bring home captives from war they preserve, not to spare their lives, but that they may be slain for food; for they eat one another, the victors the vanquished, and among other kinds of meat human flesh is a common article of diet with them. Nay be the more assured of this fact because the father has already been seen to eat children and wife, and I knew a man whom I also spoke to who was reputed to have eaten more than three hundred human bodies. And I likewise remained twenty-seven days in a certain city where I saw salted human flesh suspended from beams between the houses, just as with us it is the custom to hang bacon and pork. I say further: they themselves wonder why we do not eat our enemies and do not use as food their flesh which they say is most savory. Their weapons are bows and arrows, and when they advance to war they cover no part of their bodies for the sake of protection, so like beasts are they in this matter. We endeavored to the extent of our power to dissuade them and persuade them to desist from these depraved customs, and they did promise us that they would leave off. The women as I have said go about naked and are very libidinous; yet they have bodies which are tolerably beautiful and cleanly. Nor are they so unsightly as one perchance might imagine; for, inasmuch as they are plump, their ugliness is the less apparent, which indeed is for the most part concealed by the excellence of their bodily structure. It was to us a matter of astonishment that none was to be seen among them who had a flabby breast, and those who had borne children were not to be distinguished from virgins by the shape and shrinking of the womb; and in the other parts of the body similar things were seen of which in the interest of modesty I make no mention. When they had the opportunity of copulating with Christians, urged by excessive lust, they defiled and prostituted themselves. They live one hundred and fifty years, and rarely fall ill, and if they do fall victims to any disease, they cure themselves with certain roots and herbs. These are the most noteworthy things I know about them.—The climate there was very temperate and good, and as I was able to learn from their accounts, there was never there any pest or epidemic caused by corruption of the air; and unless they die a violent death they live long. This I take to be because the south winds are ever blowing there, and especially that which we call liutus, which is the same to them as the Aquilo is to us. They are zealous in the art of fishing, and that sea is replete and abounding in every kind of fish. They are not hunters. This I deem to be because there are there many sorts of wild animals, and especially lions and bears and innumerable serpents and other horrid and ugly beasts, and also because forests and trees of huge size there extend far and wide; and they dare not, naked and without covering and arms, expose themselves to such hazards.

The land in those parts is very fertile and pleasing, abounding in numerous hills and mountains, boundless valleys and mighty rivers, watered by refreshing springs, and filled with broad, dense and wellnigh impenetrable forests full of every sort of wild animal. Trees grow to immense size without cultivation. Many of these yield fruits delectable to the taste and beneficial to the human body; some indeed do not, and no fruits there are like those of ours. Innumerable species of herbs and roots grow there too, of which they make bread and excellent food. They have, too, many seeds altogether unlike these of ours. They have there no metals of any description except gold, of which those regions have a great plenty, although to be sure we have brought none thence on this our first voyage. This the natives called to our attention, who averred that in the districts remote from the coast there is a great abundance of gold, and by them it is in no respect esteemed or valued. They are rich in pearls as I wrote you before. If I were to seek to recount in detail what things are there and to write concerning the numerous species of animals and the great number of them, it would be a matter all too prolix and vast. And I truly believe that our Pliny did not touch upon a thousandth part of the species of parrots and other birds and the animals, too, which exist in those same regions so diverse as to form and color; because Policletus, the master of painting in all its perfection would have fallen short in depicting them. There all trees are fragrant and they emit each and all gum, oil, or some sort of sap. If the properties of these were known to us, I doubt not but that they would be salutary to the human body. And surely if the terrestrial paradise be in any part of this earth, I esteem that it is not far distant from those parts. Its situation, as I have related, lies toward the south in such a temperate climate that icy winters and fiery summers alike are never there experienced.

The sky and atmosphere are serene during the greater part of the year, and devoid of thick vapors the rains there fall finely, last three or four hours, and vanish like a mist. The sky is adorned with most beautiful constellations and forms among which I noted about twenty stars as bright as we ever saw Venus or Jupiter. I have considered the movements and orbits of these, I have measured their circumferences and diameters by geometric method, and I ascertained that they are of greater magnitude. I saw in that sky three Canopi, two indeed bright, the third dim. The Antarctic pole is not figured with a Great and a Little Bear as this Arctic pole of ours is seen to be, nor is any bright star to be seen near it, and of those which move around it with the shortest circuit there are three which have the form of an orthogonous triangle, the half circumference, the diameter, has nine and a half degrees. Rising with these to the left is seen a white Canopus of extraordinary size which when they reach mid-heaven have this form:

```
         ss
        ssss
        sssss
        ssss
      canopus.
```

After these come two others, the half circumference of which, the diameter, has twelve and a half degrees; and with them is seen another white Canopus. There follow upon these six other most beautiful stars and brightest among all the others of the eighth sphere, which in the upper firmament have a half circumference, a diameter, of thirty-two degrees. With them revolves a black Canopus of huge size. They are seen in the Milky Way and have a form like this when observed on the meridian line:

```
         SS
        SSSSS
       SSSSSS
        SSS
```

I observed many other very beautiful stars, the movements of which I have diligently noted down and have described beautifully with diagrams in a certain little book of mine treating of this my voyage. But at present this Most Serene King has it, which I hope he will restore to me. In that hemisphere I saw things incompatible with the opinions of philosophers. A white rainbow was twice seen about midnight, not only by me but by all the sailors. Likewise we have frequently seen the new moon on that day when it was in conjunction with the sun. Every night in that part of the sky innumerable vapors and glowing meteors fly about.—I said a little while ago respecting that hemisphere that it really cannot properly be spoken of as a complete hemisphere comparing it to ours, yet since it approaches such a form, such may we be permitted to call it.

Therefore, as I have said from Lisbon whence we started, which is thirty-nine and a half degrees distant from the equator, we sailed beyond the equator through fifty degrees, which added together make about ninety degrees, which total inasmuch as it makes the fourth part of a great circle according to the true system of measurement transmitted to us by our ancients, it is evident that we sailed over a fourth part of the world. And by this calculation we who live in Lisbon, thirty-nine and a half degrees north latitude this side of the equator, are with respect to those fifty degrees beyond the same line, south latitude, at an angle of five degrees on a transverse line. And that you may the more clearly understand: A perpendicular line drawn, while we stand upright, from a point in the sky overhead, our zenith, hangs over our head; it comes down upon their side or ribs. Thus comes about that we are on an upright line, but they on a line drawn sidewise. A kind of orthogonal triangle is thus formed, the position of whose upright line we occupy, but they the base; and the hypotenuse is drawn from our zenith to theirs, as is seen in the diagram. And these things I have mentioned are sufficient as regards cosmography.

These have been the more noteworthy things which I have seen in this my last voyage which I call my third chapter. For two other chapters consisted of two other voyages which I made to the west by command of the most Serene King of the Spains, during which I noted down the marvellous works wrought by that sublime creator of all things, our God. I kept a diary of noteworthy things that if sometime I am granted leisure I may bring together these singular and wonderful things and write a book of geography or cosmography, that my memory may live with posterity and that the immense work of almighty God, partly unknown to the ancients, but known to us, may be understood. Accordingly I pray the most merciful God to prolong the days of my life that with His good favor and the salvation of my soul I may carry out in the best possible manner this my will. The accounts of the other two journeys I am preserving in my cabinet and when this Most Serene King restores to me the third, I shall endeavor to regain my country and repose. There I shall be able to consult with experts and to receive from friends the aid and comfort necessary for the completion of this work.

Of you I crave pardon for not having transmitted to you this my last voyage, or rather my last chapter, as I had promised you in my last letter. You have learned the reason when I tell you that I have not yet obtained the principal version from this Most Serene King. I am still privately considering the making of a fourth journey, and of this I am treating; and already I have been promised two ships with their equipment, that I may apply myself to the discovery of new regions to the south along the eastern side following the wind-route called Africus. In which journey I think to perform many things to the glory of God, the advantage of this kingdom, and the honor of my old age; and I await nothing but the consent of this Most Serene King. God grant what is for the best. You shall learn what comes of it.

Jocundus, the translator, is turning this epistle from the Italian into the Latin tongue, that Latinists may know how many wonderful things are daily being discovered, and that the audacity of those who seek to scrutinize heaven and sovereignty and to know more than it is licit to know may be held in check. Inasmuch as ever since that remote time when the world began the vastness of the earth and what therein is contained has been unknown.

Master John Otmar, Vienna, printer, August, 1504.

Requerimiento (The Requirement), 1513

Lewis Hanke, ed. *History of Latin American Civilizations: Sources and Interpretations,* 2nd ed. (Boston: Little, Brown, 1973), pp. 94–95.

On the part of the King, don Fernando, and of doña Juana, his daughter, Queen of Castille and Leon, subduers of the barbarous nations, we their servants notify and make known to you, as best we can, that the Lord our God, Living and Eternal, created the Heaven and the Earth, and one man and one woman, of whom you and I, and all the men of the world, were and are descendants, and all those who came after us. But, on account of the multitude which has sprung from this man and woman in the five thousand years since the world was created, it was necessary that some men should go one way and some another, and that they should be divided into many kingdoms and provinces, for in one alone they could not be sustained.

Of all these nations God our Lord gave charge to one man, called St. Peter, that he should be Lord and Superior of all the men in the world, that all should obey him, and that he should be head of the whole human race, wherever men should live, and under whatever law, sect, or belief they should be; and he gave them the world for his kingdom and jurisdiction.

And he commanded them to place his seat in Rome, as the spot most fitting to rule the world from; but also he permitted him to have his seat in any other part of the world, and to judge and govern all Christians, Moors, Jews, Gentiles, and all other sects. This man was called Pope, as if to say, Admirable Great Father and Governor of men. The men who lived in that time obeyed that St. Peter, and took him for Lord, King, and Superior of the universe; so also have they regarded the others who after him have been elected to the Pontificate, and so it has been continued even until now, and will continue until the end of the world.

One of these Pontiffs, who succeeded that St. Peter as Lord of the world, in the dignity and seat which I have before mentioned, made donation of these isles and Terra-firme to the aforesaid King and Queen and to their successors, our lords, with all that there are in these territories, as is contained in certain writings which passed upon the subject as aforesaid, which you can see if you wish.

So their Highnesses are kings and lords of these islands and the land of Terra-firme by virtue of this donation; and some islands, and indeed almost all those to whom this has been notified, have received and served their Highnesses, as lords and kings, in the way that subjects ought to do, with good will, without any resistance, immediately, without delay, when they were informed of the aforesaid facts. And also they received and obeyed the priests whom their Highnesses sent to preach to them and to teach them our Holy Faith; and all these, of their own free will, without any reward or condition, have become Christians, and are so, and their Highnesses have joyfully and benignantly received them, and also have commanded them to be treated as their subjects and vassals; and you too are held and obliged to do the same. Wherefore as best we can, we ask and require you that you consider what we have said to you, and that you take the time that shall be necessary to understand and deliberate upon it, and that you acknowledge the Church as the Ruler and Superior of the whole world and the high priest called Pope, and in his name the King and Queen doña Juana our lords, in his place, as superiors and lords and kings of these islands and this Terra-firme by virtue of the said donation, and that you consent and give place that these religious fathers should declare and preach to you the aforesaid.

If you do so, you will do well, and that which you are obliged to do to their Highnesses, and we in their name shall receive you in all love and charity, and shall leave you your wives, and your children, and your lands, free without servitude, that you may do with them and with yourselves freely that which you like and think best, and they shall not compel you to turn Christians, unless you yourselves, when informed of the truth, should wish to be converted to our Holy Catholic Faith, as almost all the inhabitants of the rest of the islands have done. And besides this, their Highnesses award you many privileges and exceptions and will grant you many benefits.

But if you do not do this, and wickedly and intentionally delay to do so, I certify to you that, with the help of God, we shall forcibly enter into your country and shall make war against you in all ways and manners that we can, and shall subject you to the yoke and obedience of the Church and of their Highnesses; we shall take you and your wives and your children, and shall make slaves of them, and as such shall sell and dispose of them as their Highnesses may command; and we shall take away your goods, and shall do all the harm and damage that we can, as to vassals who do not obey, and refuse to receive their lord, and resist and contradict him; and we protest that the deaths and losses which shall accrue from this are your fault, and not that of their Highnesses, or ours, nor of these cavaliers who come with us. And that we have said this to you and made this Requirement, we request the notary here present to give us his testimony in writing, and we ask the rest who are present that they should be witnesses of this Requirement.

Excerpt from the *Codex Aubin,* an indigenous account of the Spanish conquest of Tenochtitlán

Miguel Leon-Portilla, ed., *The Broken Spears: The Aztec Account of the Conquest of Mexico* (Boston: Beacon Press, 1962), pp. 80–81.

Motecuhzoma said to La Malinche: "Please ask the god to hear me. It is almost time to celebrate the fiesta of Toxcatl. It will last for only ten days, and we beg his permission to hold it. We merely burn some incense and dance our dances. There will be a little noise because of the music, but that is all."

The Captain said: "Very well, tell him they may hold it." Then he left the city to meet another force of Spaniards who were marching in this direction. Pedro de Alvarado, called The Sun, was in command during his absence.

When the day of the fiesta arrived, Motecuhzoma said to The Sun: "Please hear me, my lord. We beg your permission to begin the fiesta of our god."

The Sun replied: "Let it begin. We shall be here to watch it."

The Aztec captains then called for their elder brothers, who were given this order: "You must celebrate the fiesta as grandly as possible."

The elder brothers replied: "We will dance with all our might."

Then Tecatzin, the chief of the armory, said: "Please remind the lord that he is here, not in Cholula. You know how they trapped the Cholultecas in their patio! They have already caused us enough trouble. We should hide our weapons close at hand!"

But Motecuhzoma said: "Are we at war with them? I tell you, we can trust them."

Tecatzin said: "Very well."

Then the songs and dances began. A young captain wearing a lip plug guided the dancers; he was Cuatlazol, from Tolnahuac.

But the songs had hardly begun when the Christians came out of the palace. They entered the patio and stationed four guards at each entrance. Then they attacked the captain who was guiding the dance. One of the Spaniards struck the idol in the face, and others attacked the three men who were playing the drums. After that there was a general slaughter until the patio was heaped with corpses.

A priest from the Place of the Canefields cried out in a loud voice: "Mexicanos! Who said we are not at war? Who said we could trust them?"

The Mexicans could only fight back with sticks of wood; they were cut to pieces by the swords. Finally the Spaniards retired to the palace where they were lodged.

A narrative relating to Francisco Coronado's explorations of the Southwest, 1540–1542

George P. Hammond and Agapito Rey, eds., *Narratives of the Coronado Expedition, 1540–1542.* Vol 2 (Albuquerque: University of New Mexico Press, 1940), pp. 308–312.

"This is the latest account of Cíbola, and of more than four hundred leagues."

It is more than three hundred leagues from Culiacan to Cíbola, and little of the way is inhabited. There are very few people, the land is sterile, and the roads are wretched. The people go about entirely naked, except the women, who, from the waist down, wear white dressed deerskins which reach to their feet like skirts. Their houses are built of reed mats, and are round and small, a man being hardly able to stand up inside. The place where they are settled and where they have their planted fields has sandy soil. They grow maize, although not much, and beans and calabashes; they also live on game: rabbits, hares, and deer. They do not offer sacrifices. This is true from Culhuacán to Cíbola.

Cíbola is a pueblo of about two hundred houses, which are two, three, four, and five stories high. Their walls are a span thick. The timbers used in their construction are round, as thick as a wrist; the roofs are built of small reeds with the leaves on, on top of which they add well-packed dirt; the walls are built of dirt and mud; the house doors are like the scuttles of ships. The houses are built compact and adjoining one another. In front of them there are some estufas built of adobe, in which the natives shelter themselves from cold in winter, for it is extremely cold; it snows six months of the year.

Some of the people wear cotton and maguey blankets, and dressed deerskins. They wear boots made of these skins that come to above their knees. They also make blankets of hare and rabbit skins, with which they keep warm. The women wear maguey blankets reaching to their feet and wear their clothes tight around the waist. They have their hair rolled above their ears like small wheels. These natives grow maize, beans, and calabashes, which is all they need for subsistence, as they are not very numerous. The land they cultivate is all sandy. The water brackish; the land is very dry. They possess some chickens, although not many. They have no knowledge of fish.

In this province of Cíbola there are seven pueblos within a distance of five leagues. The largest one must have 200 houses; two others have 200, and the rest sixty, fifty, and thirty houses.

It is sixty leagues from Cíbola to the river and province of Tibex [Tiguex]. The first pueblo is forty leagues from Cíbola, and it is called Acuco. This pueblo is situated on the top of a very strong rock. It must contain about 200 houses, built similar to Cíbola, which has a different language. It is twenty leagues from there to the Tiguex River. This river is almost as wide as the one at Seville, although not so deep. It flows through level land; its water is fine; it has some fish; it rises in the north.

The one who makes the foregoing statement saw twelve pueblos within a certain region of the river; others claim to have seen more up the river. Down the river the pueblos are all small, except two which must have about 200 houses. These houses have very strong walls made of mud and sand. The walls are a span thick. The houses are two and three stories high. Their woodwork is like that of the houses of Cíbola. The natives have their estufas as at Cíbola. The land is extremely cold, and the river freezes so hard that laden animals cross over it, and carts could cross also. The natives plant maize, beans, and calabashes, enough for their needs, and they possess some chickens, which they keep to make blankets with their feathers. They grow some cotton, although not much. They wear cotton blankets and shoes of hides as at Cíbola. They are people who know how to defend themselves from their very houses, and they are not inclined to leave them. The land is all sandy.

Four days' journey from the province and river of Tigeux the Spaniards found four pueblos. The first must have thirty houses; the second was a large pueblo destroyed by war; the third had about thirty-five houses, all inhabited. These three pueblos are similar in every respect to those on the river. The fourth is a large pueblo situated between mountains, and called Cíbola. It had some fifty houses with terraces like those of Cíbola, and the walls are of dirt and mud like the Cíbola. The inhabitants have abundant maize, beans, calabashes, and some chickens.

At a distance of four days' travel from this pueblo, the Spaniards came to some land as level as the sea. In these plains there is such a multitude of cattle that they are beyond counting. These cattle are like those of Castile, and some larger. They have small humps on their backs, and are more reddish in color, blending into black. Their hair, over a span long, hangs down between their horns, ears, and chin, and from the neck and shoulders like a mane, and down from the knees. The rest of their bodies is covered with short wool like sheep. Their meat is fine and tender and very fat.

Traveling many days over these plains the Spaniards came to an inhabited rancheria with about two hundred houses. The houses were made of tanned cattle skins, white, and built like pavilions or tents. These Indians live or sustain themselves entirely from the cattle, for they neither grow nor harvest maize. With the skins they build their houses; with the skins they clothe and shoe themselves; from the skins they make ropes and also obtain wool. With the sinews they make thread, with which they sew their clothes and also their tents. From the bones they shape awls. The dung they use for firewood, since there is no other fuel in that land. The bladders they use as jugs and drinking containers. They sustain themselves on their meat, eating it slightly roasted and heated over the dung. Some they eat raw; taking it in their teeth, they pull with one hand, and in the other they hold a large flint knife and cut off mouthfuls. Thus they swallow it, half chewed, like birds. They eat raw fat without warming it. They drink the blood just as it comes out of the cattle. Sometimes they drink it later, raw and cold. They have no other food.

These people have dogs similar to those of this land, except that they are somewhat larger. They load these dogs like beasts of burden and make light packsaddles for them like our packsaddles, cinching them with leather straps. The dogs go about with sores on their backs like pack animals. When the Indians go hunting they load them with provisions. When these Indians move—for they have no permanent residence anywhere, since they follow the cattle to find food—these dogs carry their homes for them. In addition to what they carry on their backs, they carry the poles for the tents, dragging them fastened to their saddles. The load may be from thirty-five to fifty pounds, depending on the dog.

From Cíbola to these plains where the Spaniards came it must be thirty leagues, and perhaps more. The plains extend ahead—we do not know how far. Captain Francisco Vazquez traveled ahead over these plains with thirty mounted men, and Fray Juan de Padilla accompanied him. The rest of the people went back to the settlement by the river to await Francisco Vazquez, for so he had commanded. It is not known whether he has returned.

The land is so level that the men get lost when they draw half a league away. This happened to a man on horseback who got lost and never returned, and also to two horses, with harnesses and bridles, that were never again found. No tracks are left over the places which are traveled. On account of this they must leave land marks of cow dung along the way they follow in order to find their way back, for there are no stones or anything else.

The Venetian, Marco Polo, in chapter xv of his treatise, says that he has seen these same cows, with the same kind of hump. In the same chapter he speaks also of rams the size of horses.

The Venetian, Nicolas, told the Florentine, Micer Pogio, in the second book, toward the end, that in Ethiopia there are oxen with humps like camels, and with horns three cubits long. They throw their horns back over their spine, and one of these horns will hold a pitcher of wine.

In chapter 134, Marco Polo says that in the land of the Tartars, toward the north, there are dogs the size of donkeys, more or or less. They hitch them to a sort of cart and enter very marshy land, a real quagmire, where other animals would not be able to enter without drowning. For this reason they use dogs.

Excerpt from Ambroise Paré, *Des Monstres et Prodiges* (Paris, 1573)

*Janis Pallister, trans. and ed., *Ambroise Paré on Monsters and Marvels* (Chicago: University of Chicago Press, 1982), pp. 38–42.*

Chapter 9: AN EXAMPLE OF MONSTERS THAT ARE CREATED THROUGH THE IMAGINATION

The ancients, who sought out the secrets of Nature (i.e., Aristotle, Hippocrates, Empedocles), have taught of other causes for monstrous children and have referred them to the ardent and obstinate imagination [impression] that the mother might receive at the moment she conceived—through some object, or fantastic dream—of certain nocturnal visions that the man or woman have at the hour of conception. This is even verified by the authority of Moses (Chap. 30 [of Genesis]) when he shows how Jacob deceived his father-in-law Laban and enriched himself with his livestock by having rods barked and putting them in the watering trough, so that when the goats and ewes looked at these rods of various colors, they might form their young spotted in various colors: because the imagination has so much power over seed and reproduction that the stripe and character of them remain [imprinted] on the thing bred.

Whether true or not, Heliodorus (book 10, of his *History of Ethiopia*) writes that Persina, the Queen of Ethiopia, conceived by King Hidustes—both of them being Ethiopians—a daughter who was white and this [occurred] because of the appearance of the beautiful Andromeda that

she summoned up in her imagination, for she had a painting of her before her eyes during the embraces from which she became pregnant.

Damascene, a serious author, attests to having seen a girl as furry as a bear, whom the mother had bred thus deformed and hideous, for having looked too intensely at the image of Saint John [the Baptist] dressed in skins, along with his [own] body hair and beard, which picture was attached to the foot of her bed while she was conceiving.

For a similar reason Hippocrates saved a princess accused of adultery, because she had given birth to a child as black as a Moor, her husband and she both having white skin; which woman was was absolved upon Hippocrates' persuasion that it was [caused by] the portrait of a Moor, similar to the child, which was customarily attached to her bed.

Moreover, one can observe that conies [rabbits] and peacocks who are closed up in white places, through the properties of the pagination, give birth to their white young.

As a result, it is necessary that women—at the hour of conception and when the child is not yet formed (which takes from thirty to thirty-five days for males and forty or forty-two, as Hippocrates says, for females)—not be forced to look at or to imagine monstrous things; but once the formation of the child is complete, even though the woman should look at or imagine monstrous things with intensity, nevertheless the imagination will not then play any role, because no transformation occurs at all, since the child is completely formed.

In Saxony in a village named Stecquer, a monster was born having the four feet of an ox; its eyes, mouth and nose similar to a calf, having on top of its head a red flesh, in a round shape; [and] another behind, similar to a monk's hood, and having its thighs mangled.

In the year 1517, in the parish of Bois-le-Roy, in the Forest of Biere, on the road to Fontainebleau, a child was born having the face of a frog, who was seen and visited by Master Jean Bellanger, a surgeon in the company of the King's Artillery, in the presence of gentlemen from the Court of Harmois: notably the honorable gentleman Jacques Bribon, the king's procurer in said place; and Etienne Lardot, a bourgeois from Melun; and Jean de Vircy, king's notary at Melun; and others. The father's name is Esme Petit and the mother Magdaleine Sarboucat. The aforementioned Bellanger, a man of good wit, wanting to know the cause of the monster, inquired of the father what could have been the cause of it; the latter told him that he figured that his wife having a fever, one of her neighbor ladies advised her, in order to cure her fever, to take a live frog in her hand and hold it until said frog should die. That night she went to bed with her husband, still having said frog in her hand; her husband and she embraced and she conceived; and by the power of her imagination, this monster had thus been produced.

Excerpt from André Thevet, *Cosmographie Universelle* (Paris, 1575).

Roger Schlesinger and Arthur P. Stabler, trans., *André Thevet's North America: A Sixteenth-Century View* (Kingston and Montreal: McGill-Queen's University Press, 1986), pp. 27–45.)

On the Land of Canada and Baccaleos, and on Several Rivers of the Coast of Norumbega

Having left Florida on the left hand, with a great number of isles, islets, gulfs and promontories, you see one of the most beautiful rivers on earth, named by us Norombegue and by the Barbarians *Aggoncy,* and marked as "big river" on some marine maps. Several other beautiful rivers enter into this one, and upon it in the past the French had built a little fort some ten or twelve leagues upstream, which was surrounded by the fresh water which empties into it [the river]: and this place was named Fort Norumbega. Several pilots who think themselves the most knowledgeable of Europe, speaking of pilotage, tried to make me believe that this Norumbegian country was Canada proper. But this is not so, as I told them, since this country is at forty-three degrees and that of Canada at fifty-one degrees and fifty-two degrees. This is what it is to lack experience, mistress of all things.

Before approaching this river an isle surrounded by eight very small islets appears before you, which are near the land of green mountains and the Cape of Isles. From there you continue to sail along the coast to the mouth of the river, whose entry is dangerous because of the great number of large, high rocks, and many reefs; and its mouth is marvelously wide. Some three leagues up the said river a beautiful isle presents itself before you, which has about four leagues circumference, inhabited solely by some fishermen and various kinds of birds. [It is] called by them *Aiayascon* because it has the form of an arm which they call thus. Its length is north and south and it could easily be populated; likewise several other islets which are at some distance, and [one could] make a very fine fortress on it to control the entire coast.

Having set foot on land in the surrounding country, we perceived a large number of people who were coming straight to us from all directions, and in such a multitude that you would have said [that they looked like] a flock of starlings. Those who walked in front were the men, whom they call *Aquehuns;* afterwards the women, whom they call *Peragruastas,* then the *Adegestas,* who are the children; and last were the girls, named *Anias-gestas. All* these people were clothed in pelts (which they call *Rabatatz*) of wild beasts. So observing their appearance and actions, we had some distrust of them and therefore we retired to our ship. However, seeing our fear they raised their hands into the air, signing that we were not to doubt them, and to render us more assured they sent to our ship four of their chiefs who brought us food. In recompense for which we gave them a few cheap trinkets, for which they were as happy as possible.

The following morning I was commissioned with several others to go to them to find out if they would aid us with food, of which we had a great shortage. Having entered the house (which they call *Caneque*) of a certain kinglet whose name was *Peramich,* we saw several dead beasts hanging on the posts of the said house, which they had prepared (as they told us) to send to us. This king gave us a very good welcome, and to show us the good will he bore us he had a good fire made (which they call *Azista*) on which he had meat and fish placed to roast. At this juncture appeared several rogues bringing to the king the heads of six men whom they had taken and massacred in war. This frightened us, fearing that they would do the same to us, so toward evening we stole off to our ship without saying goodbye to our host. At this he was greatly irritated, and so he came to us the next morning accompanied by three of his children, showing a sad countenance because he felt that we had come away discontent. Then he said to us in his language *Cazigno, Cazigno, Casnouy danga addagrin:* which is to say, Come, come ashore my brothers and friends. *Coaguoca Ame Couascon, Kazaconny:* come drink of what we have. *Arcasomioppach, Quenchia dangua ysmay assomaha:* we swear to you by the heaven, the earth, the moon, and the stars: you shall have no more harm than ourselves.

Seeing the good will and attitude of this old man, a score of our men set foot on land, each provided with his arms; and then went with him to his lodge where we were treated with what he had. Meanwhile a great number of people arrived who made over us and offered to do our pleasure, saying that they were our friends. But the climax of this was in the evening when we wished to retire and take leave of the company, giving thanks. This they did not want us to do: the men and the women as well as the children implored us to remain, using these words—*Cazigno aguyda-hoa:* my friends, do not budge from here, you shall sleep with us tonight. However, they harangued and begged in vain; they could not induce us to sleep with them. Rather we retired to our ship, and having remained there five whole days we hoisted anchor and left them with great satisfaction on both sides.

Because of the sandbanks and reefs we made for the open sea. But we had not sailed fifteen leagues out when the east wind was so contrary to us and the sea so swollen that we all thought we would perish. However, finally the tempest blew us some fifty leagues from there to the mouth of the Arnodie river between [the] Juvid river and the Right Cape, where we were forced to anchor and go upriver about half a league to avoid the tempests and storms of the sea.

The people of this country gave us no less of a welcome than the first. To be sure they did not have as much venison, but in fresh and salt water fish they surpassed them, and especially in salmon, which they name *Ondacon*, and in lampreys, which they call *Zistoz*. Of such fish they brought us once a whole boatload full, of which we salted down about half a *muid*, which served us well to complete our voyage. Leaving this river and sailing straight for Baccaleos you cross and sail the sea to the Isle of Thevet, then to the Isles of Sainte Croix, Isles of the Bretons, [Isle] of the Savages, up to the level of Cape Breton, so named because the Bretons discovered that land in the year 1504.

Having designated for you the course to the north, from the point of Florida to that of Baccaleos, which lies at forty-eight degrees thirty minutes of latitude and 327 degrees longitude, there only remains for me to describe the mainland, after having briefly discussed some islands whose approach is dangerous: into which [the mainland] we entered, having been blown there by the winds where we experienced the rigors of the cold which tormented us for more than twenty days. During this time I had the leisure to walk around and seek out what was rare and singular in this country. [It] extends into the sea in the north for a good two hundred leagues.

The neighboring isles are extremely numerous and very large: [for example] those in the gulf between Arcadia and the Promontory called and named by me Angoulesme for my birthplace; those which are near Flora and Paradise; or those which are enclosed in the port of refuge [Refugio]; or those which afterwards extend along the ocean more northwards near those which are called Bonne veueis (which are close to the isle which bears the name of the country of Baccaleos). Some believe that these islands are continental and joined to the mainland because of their great extent: but I, who have seen them in person, I have seen and recognized that there is a good distance and extent of sea from these isles to the mainland. This country is so named because of a large fish named Baccaleos.

Canada is the country which is bordered on the south by the mountains of Florida, on the north by Baccaleos, on the east by the Atlantic Ocean, and to the south again faces the point of Florida and the Isles of Cuba; and the point of Baccaleos extends to the port of refuge [Refugio]. I am sure that the land there [Baccaleos] is even better than that of Canada, and there are very fine rivers which enter one hundred leagues into the middle of the country and are navigable, such as the *Barad*, which word in the Indian language means country. And in my judgment I believe that it would be better to live in this country of Baccaleos, either on the mainland or on the neighboring isles, since the land is not so cold as that of Canada: also the people there are much more approachable and the sea more fertile in fish. Not that I wish to give here a fable, as did a venerable

Spaniard in a little history of the Indies of Peru, where he relates that this sea so swarms with fish that they hinder the course of great ships. You might as well lend credence to this as to what Thomas Porcachi from Arrezzo, an Italian, says in a certain booklet on islands: that what we call the New World (which is properly this coast to Peru [South America]) is the Antarctic country. Poorly considered on his part, seeing as there is more than sixteen hundred leagues distance of coast between them. Also the country of Canada is not the one they call Nurumberg [sic], containing a great extent of mainland which several have tried to explore: but not one has so well succeeded as Jacques Cartier, Breton, one of my best friends, from whom I have obtained bits of information since he has explored the country from one end to the other.

Here before passing on I cannot remain silent about those who play the entrepreneur, and promise mountains of gold to the princes and great lords, proposing the subjection of the barbarians, which would be a good thing to do, and [speak of] the great riches which are to be found in the said countries. But even if all that were true, you have to attend to what I have already said to several of them, that if they were not well-advised, wise, and wily in their enterprises, they would get no more profit out of them than some others have who have lost their lives and their capital in them. Although the kings of Spain and Portugal are friends and allies of our own Sovereign Prince, the sea pilots, sailors, and captains pay no attention to such alliances, or whether there is peace or war on land. So once you leave Europe and go into Africa or in some part of the land of Guinea, the sailors no longer know each other, so that the Spaniard makes a slave of the Portuguese even though their kings may be relatives, neighbors, and good friends. The Frenchman, the Scotsman, and the Englishman scarcely pardon one another in these distant countries. And you cannot blame the princes and princesses, seeing as it is done without their knowledge. I have seen this going on in Africa, chiefly around Cape Verde and the Manicongre River, and on both sides of the Equator, under both tropics, even in Florida and on this northern coast. As for what they try to tell our European princes, that there is on this mainland an abundance of gold, silver, and [precious] stones—this is deceiving them, since most of the riches and treasure which can be got out of Florida, Canada, and Baccaleos is in furs and the cod and whale fishery. I think one could find gold and silver deposits just as well as you might find in France: but what kind of deposits? inferior, and more full of sulphur than of good gold, and which would cost more to doubly refine than any profit you would get out of it. I say the same with regard to gems, which I know from experience.

This country was discovered by our people in the time of the great King François I, regarding which I shall give a brief summary, and I shall speak the least possible number of words that I am able, although I know that few men other than myself have written about it. This country then extends far northwards, and approaches that which is under the Arctic circle, which we call one of the poles or pivots supporting the sphere. Consequently you can imagine how cold the land must be, and yet not uninhabitable. Now Canada is the equivalent of land, and this name came from the first to land there. For when someone asked them what they were looking for in this place, they answered that they were *Segnada Canada,* men seeking land, and since then the name has stuck like a nickname, and also to most of the isles and provinces newly discovered. To the north it extends to the arctic or hyperborean sea. Therefore all this country is included, with Baccaleos and Labrador as well, under the name of Canada. And on the other side there is a mainland called *Campestre de Berge* which extends to the southeast.

In this province to the east lies Cape Lorraine, so named by us, and others call it Cape Breton because it is there that the Bretons, Biscayans, and Normans go and sail, going to the New Land to fish for cod. Near this cape is situated an isle named Heuree to the northeast, four or five leagues in circumference and quite close to the mainland, and another in triangular form named *Carbassa* by the natives and by us Isle of the Virgins. And this land begins at the said cape towards the south, where it lies east-north-east and west-southwest. The majority of it facing Florida is in the form of a half circle, as if looking to the kingdom of Themistitan. The coast of Canada from Cape Lorraine southwards extends into the sea as does Italy into the Adriatic and Ligurian seas, forming a peninsula.

In the region then closest to Florida (which some call French land, and the natives *Norombegue)* the land is quite fertile in various kinds of fruits, as for example mandourles, which is a fruit like a pumpkin, the juice of which is very good and the flesh delicate. The inhabitants of the country are friendly, easy to handle, and pleasant in their conversation. Their range and principal habitat extends westward on the great river of *Hochelaga,* quite close to the promontory called Angoulesme. That is where their king, whom they call in their jargon *Agouhanna,* usually resides, who is quite pleasant to foreigners who come there.

Quite the contrary are those who dwell more inland towards Baccaleos: for they are wicked, deceitful, and cruel, and they mask their faces, not with masks or cloths, but by painting their faces with divers colors, especially with blue and red, so to render themselves more hideous to those who approach them. These men are big and strong and go around clothed in skins, and pluck out all the hair they have on their body except that of the head, which they draw up in a top-knot just like we tie and bind up our horses' tails over here. And they make their laces and bands from the tendons of wild beasts they kill (and so do all their

neighbors, which I had forgotten to tell you). The colors with which they paint their faces are extracted from certain herbs and flowers of which they press out the juice; and so their paints are just as vivid as you would make here with Azure or the finest Lac that they bring you from Oriental countries. They have millet for food and make flour from it. They have melons also, but not as good as ours; and eat much more fish than meat, and especially eels very large and tasty.

If you go farther you will turn towards another great river, which our people have called Chaleur Bay, where there is a great quantity of salmon, larger and meatier than ours. In that country the only trade materials are deer skins, which they call *Aiomesta,* otters, and other furs, for of gold and silver they know little. The inhabitants of this river [Chaleur Bay] usually wage war with those who live on the great *Hochelaga* river, and are different from them in language, customs, and style of life. The Hochelaga ones are those who have been best-known to the French. Indeed our people took two of them [to] King François I, who [later] returned [them] to their own country. [They were] favored and well-treated by all the barbarians who for this reason were more friendly than ever to our people, saying that *Cudragny,* who is their god, was a liar who had told them that their men had been killed by the bearded foreigners. As for the savages who are on the other river [Chaleur Bay], we have not been able to find out what kind of people they are because, having heard that the river got narrower and that it was congealed with ice, Captain Cartier told me that he did not have enough small boats and so put off exploring it for another voyage. As for the other region [the western] and part of Canada, it is situated more than two hundred leagues beyond the Hochelaga River; nevertheless [it was] discovered by our men, although it extends far north and borders the country which is called "unknown."

The country [Canada] is well populated, the inhabitants peaceful and friendly and the most obliging you could see. It was in their country that the French built long ago a fort near a mountain they named Mont Royal, so as to winter there and rest [upon] coming into these lands; plus the fact that the place is in itself pretty. This fort was built [here] because of a fresh-water river, named Stadin which neighbors it, and another of salt water named *Islee* ["full of isles"]. These are not so large as those of Fauve, nor that of Daconie, so named by the barbarians of the country.

As for the great river of Hochelaga, there are very beautiful islands in it, e. g. that of Laisple, which is right at its mouth, and that of Orleans, so named in honor of the late Duke of Orleans. One could easily fortify oneself on these and populate and cultivate them. Our people lived quite well there because the inhabitants of the country brought them more fish than they wanted and also much venison, to which they are accustomed, using the bow and catching the animals with many clever ruses. Among other things they use a kind of rackets, woven and constructed with animal tendons, square, and whose holes are very small like those of a sieve. They are in the proportion of two and a half feet [long] and almost as wide, as the present illustration portrays and represents to you. And they use these, tying them to their feet, as much against cold as to keep them from sinking into the snow when they are hunting wild beasts, and also so as not to slip on the ice. They clothe themselves with pelts cured and prepared in their fashion, in winter the fur side inside against the flesh, and in summer the leather touching their flesh with the fur on the outside.

So to take these animals you will see ten or twelve of them armed and furnished with long staves, like stakes and partisans [truncheons], lances or pikes, some of them twelve, others fifteen feet long, armed at the end not with iron or other metal but with some good bone of a deer or other beast, a good foot long and moreover pointed, and carrying bows and arrows armed in the same manner. Thus provided they go out into the snow all year long, this [snow] being very familiar to them. When hunting deer, wild boars, wild asses, and reindeer in the depths of these snows they prepare their blinks [trail markers] just as our hunters do, so as not to get lost. And sometimes when the stag has come out, whether to feed or otherwise, knowing the route he has taken they make shelters of cedars (which are abundant in this country), and they hide under these green shelters waiting for the stag to come. As soon as the animal approaches they emerge from their ambush and run upon him with their pikes and bows; and with their hue and cries make him lose the beaten path and get into the deep snow up to his belly so that the poor beast cannot get away—partly because of the snow which hinders it and also because by then they usually are hit and mortally wounded by the bows or lances.

After the massacre is over they skin it and cut it into pieces and drag it in its skin to their retreats. These are small villages and tawdry hamlets of a few houses arranged in the form and figure of a semi-circle, which the people call *Canocas,* large and about twenty-five or thirty paces long and ten paces wide with some covered with tree bark others with skins and with reeds. God knows how piercing the cold is in their houses, seeing as how the wind comes in from all sides; and they are so poorly covered and supported that often the pillars and beams either break or give way under the weight of the snow on top, which they call *Camsa,* so that in their sleep they have this dew and refreshment on their covers.

Since all this barbaric people cannot live without this way of doing things, because civilization and literature do not wean them from it, these Canadians, who are the fiercest known people and who have no arts or trades whatever, are always occupied in warring with some of their neighbors. Now those with whom these savages are angry and whom they often fight, are the *Toutaneans, Guadalpes, Chicorins,* and others. These are located along the two great rivers of the *Saguene* [Saguenay] and *Hochelaga,* which are of such marvelous extent that each enters more than four hundred leagues into the land. On them one can navigate [only] some fifty leagues with large vessels because of the rocks which are very numerous; and the savages travel on them from place to place. The natives of Baccaleos, closer to Canada than to anywhere else, are their allies and march with them in war.

The natives say that if you would sail up the said rivers, that *Assomaha,* which is in a few moons (that is how they count and reckon time), you would find masses of gold and silver and a great diversity of peoples. And these two rivers finally join between Florida and the Cape of the Three Brothers, making a crescent as they unite in those regions and flow into the sea, since these regions embrace each other and are neighbors just as are France and Italy. The Hochelaga River, which is the wider, has its first source in the Prat and the Gadate mountains.

Then it makes you a lake—which is at least twenty leagues wide—of fresh water of the rivers named Estendue, which comes from the north, the Corry, Tortimage, and the Passer (named by the first to discover it the Montmorency): all these rivers make a beautiful promontory surrounded by a great number of little islets. This lake bears the name of Angoulesme as does the promontory I have just mentioned, in honor of one of the late royal children, son of the great King François' duke of that city. As for the said Saguene River, the entrance is marvelously beautiful and good too and is to the north. And some twenty leagues from its mouth on the right hand is seen a mountain named Honguade, at the foot of which was built another fort for greater security against the fury of these people.

When therefore it is a question of war in Canada, their great *Agahanna,* which means king or lord, commands each of his people to come to him in such numbers as he specifies and to bring with them their arms and food for their subsistence during the time in which he intends to make war. The king does not pay anyone (since they have no use or knowledge of gold, silver, or other metal proper for money, no more than the other barbarians of all this country from one pole to the other), rather they are obliged to march according to his will. Most of their combats are waged on rivers, in their little [canoes] which are long and narrow made of tree bark, as savages do in many places.

As soon as the assembly and general muster are made they go find the enemy, and know where he is, being informed by their spies. At the hour of the encounter they deploy so skillfully their squadrons and show themselves so clever in either attacking or defending, and making use of ruses and stratagems according to their styles of warring, that it proves that it is nature which makes the good soldier and captain. These people deploy no less than fifteen thousand combatants, fortifying themselves in their lodges and cabins.

Now to fortify themselves without loss of their people they have a lot of faggots, bundles, pieces, and branches of cedar wood, all greased with the fat of the sea-bass and other fish and some poisonous compound. Seeing their enemies, they try to turn themselves against the wind and get their adversaries facing it. And then they set fire to these faggots, from which emerges a smoke so thick, black, and dangerous to smell, from the stench of the materials and the poisons mixed into these faggots, that some are suffocated. And even if they do not die from it, since they are blinded by the smoke, the others who are in the clearness of the daylight without hindrance of the smoke fall on them and make such carnage of them as they wish. Which I have tried to picture for you in the present portrait.

They also have trees which are very tall and large, which they use only for this purpose because they are so poisonous that the mere smell of their smoke will kill a man. If anyone falls asleep under one he feels such a stunning in his head that if he does not take immediate measures he risks losing his life. This tree is called *Hoga Athau,* which means "cold tree." I have seen such trees in Stony Arabia: and the Arabs will not let their horses and camels sleep in the shade of these trees, which they name in their language *Alaos* or *Alhalih,* giving it the name of an almond tree because it has similar leaves. These trees, when the leaves and branches are cut into pieces, produce a certain yellowish milk which they rub on their arrows to make them poisonous. It is this juice which the Canadians use in their wars to kill those whom they wish. They attempted to use this trick against our men when they traveled there, but they were foiled: for our men having been warned about this, and that they planned to set fire to the ships, surprised them before they had time to do it.

I have heard that these poor people had good and just cause to do this because some fools and madmen (more cruel than is the nature of Frenchmen) were killing these savages as a pastime and were cutting off their arms and legs as if they had been no more than tree-trunks or animals. This notwithstanding the fact that these poor people had received them with all kindness, saying to them *Aignah Adagrim Casigno Cazahouquea:* Good day, brother, let us go have a drink together. And then being a bit more familiarized, said to them *azaca, Agaheda:* give us some knives. And so they began to try to prevent the Christians from landing, thinking they would get the same treatment as they had had from these madmen. This people rejoiced exceedingly seeing foreigners: and to attract them to them and have them land, they made a fire for them, which they

name *Agista.* Having cast anchor, you see around you thousands of these poor people, rejoicing at your coming, bringing their little skiffs to the ships, shouting and constantly repeating these words *Cassigno Casnonydanga,* which mean: come into our skiffs, brothers and friends, to see our beautiful country so greatly desired by you. And you must not go trade there except in good numbers since they still remember this outrage, and once offended it is impossible to conciliate them.

But let us come back to our discussion. When these Canadians go into battle they march four by four and utter frightful howls when they approach (just as we have said about the women who are falsely called Amazons) in order to intimidate their enemies. Do not think that they go in disorder, for they have ensigns of branches of birch or other trees, adorned with large plumes of swans and other birds, which are carried by those with the greatest reputation for valiance. Moreover, they use tambourines made of certain skins stretched and laced, like on a frame on which you stretch parchment, which two men on each side carry, and another behind striking this skin with two batons with as much vim as possible. Their flutes are made of the bones of high-striding wild beasts, which they make correspond to the sound of the drum rather skillfully.

Their combats are so furious that once they have attacked each other they must conquer or die or flee; and they do not take prisoners, but kill all those they can. They fight with arrows, with large round clubs, and with [ordinary] clubs. They have shields made of skins and covered with plumes which they use very skillfully when the occasion requires. Some have head-covers difficult to pierce which are made of the skins of the seawolf and of beavers. These Canadians, although they are definitely not cannibals, i.e. eaters of human flesh, still having taken an enemy, they kill him then throw his body to the animals to eat. They skin the face and the head and they set aside these skins out in a circle to dry, then carry it to their houses to show it to their *Aquehum, Peragruasta, Addegesta, Agniagesta,* i.e. the old men, women, children, and girls (for this is what they call them in these lands), by whom they are praised, with glory to their name and family, and they incite them to carry on proposing the examples of their predecessors. They carry their king (having obtained victory over their enemies) seated on the shoulders of two of the biggest and strongest of the troop, which they call *Cabata,* so that everyone can recognize and honor him in the manner that you will see in the present illustration. Now although they are great warriors, still they do not like bloodshed as much as the natives of Peru [South America] and America [Brazil], since the others attack their enemies just for pleasure and to chase them out of their territory. These Canadians do not do so, only making war to avenge a wrong received; otherwise they do not make war on anyone.

The skins from which they make their clothes are of beavers, bears, panthers, foxes, hares, rats, wild asses, reindeer and other beasts, and they prepare the leather with the fur. This has given rise to the statement of some (too simple in my opinion) who say that the savages are hairy. The great Hercules, coming to France, found the people living almost like these savages do today. They in their simplicity on seeing our clothing are astonished and ask what kind of trees they grow on, thinking that wool grows on trees just as cotton grows on little bushes. The men and women have very long black hair which the men wear in a top-knot. The women sometimes have their hair loose on their shoulders, and others bind it like the men without putting any pelt on top of it such as the men do. They dress in deer skin prepared in their way so that not a hair falls out of it, and thus enveloped they cover their whole body with it and fasten it with a belt using three or four turns, having always outside this costume one arm and one breast just like a pilgrim's scarf. These *Peragruasta*, or women, do not go bare-legged but have shoes made of tanned and well-worked leather, enriched with divers colors which they make from herbs and fruits.

These northern peoples are great eaters. That is why in Canada they often suffer famine in the regions which I have described above, since being great gluttons their provisions are soon consumed. Very often the freezes spoil the fruits and roots on which they live. And they cannot fish either, because for three or four months of the year the rivers are frozen with ice, on which they also run just like the Russians and Muscovites on the sea. As for their drink, water suffices when other beverages fail for the lack of plants and fruits.

Excerpt from Jean De Léry, *Histoire d'un voyage faict en la terre du Bresil autrement dite Amerique* (Geneva, 1578).

Jean De Léry, *History of a Voyage to the Land of Brazil*, trans. Janet Whatley (Berkeley: University of California Press, 1992), pp. 15–19, 56–68.

CHAPTER VIII

OF THE NATURAL QUALITIES, STRENGTH, STATURE, NUDITY, DISPOSITION AND ORNAMENTATION OF THE BODY OF THE BRAZILIAN SAVAGES, BOTH MEN AND WOMEN, WHO LIVE IN AMERICA, AND WHOM I FREQUENTED FOR ABOUT A YEAR

Thus far I have recounted both what we saw on the sea on our way to the land of Brazil, and what took place on the Island and Fort of Coligny, where Villegagnon was staying while we were there; I have also described the bay called *Guanabara*. Since I have gone so far into these matters, before reembarking for France I also want to discuss what I have observed concerning the savages' way of life, as well as other singular things, unknown over here, that I have seen in their country.

In the first place then (so that I begin with the chief subject, and take things in order), the savages of America who live in Brazil, called the *Tupinamba*, whom I lived among and came to know for about a year, are not taller, fatter, or smaller in stature than we Europeans are; their bodies are neither monstrous nor prodigious with respect to ours. In fact, they are stronger, more robust and well filled-out, more nimble, less subject to disease; there are almost none among them who are lame, one-eyed, deformed, or disfigured!

Furthermore, although some of them reach the age of a hundred or a hundred twenty years (for they know how to keep track of their ages and count them by moons), few of the elderly among them have white or gray hair. Now this clearly shows not only the benign air and temperature of their country (in which, as I have said elsewhere, there are no frosts or great cold, and the woods, plants, and fields are always greening), but also—for they all truly drink at the Fountain of Youth—the little care or worry that they have for the things of this world. And indeed, as I will later show in more detail, since they do not in any way drink of those murky, pestilential springs, from which flow so many streams of mistrust, avarice, litigation, and squabbles, of envy and ambition, which eat away our bones, suck out our marrow, waste our bodies, and consume our spirits—in short, poison us and kill us off before our due time—nothing of all that torments them, much less dominates or obsesses them.

As for their natural color, considering the hot region where they live, they are not particularly dark, but merely of a tawny shade, like the Spanish or Provencals.

Now this next thing is no less strange than difficult to believe for those who have not seen it: the men, women, and children do not hide any parts of their bodies; what is more, without any sign of bashfulness or shame, they habitually live and go about their affairs as naked as they come out of their mother's womb. And yet, contrary to what some people think, and what others would have one believe, they are by no means covered with hair; in fact, they are not by nature any hairier than we are over here in this country. Furthermore, as soon as the hair begins to grow on any part of the body, even the beard and eyelashes and eyebrows, it is plucked out, either with their fingernails, or, since the arrival of the Christians, with tweezers that the latter have given them—which makes their gaze seem wall-eyed, wandering, and wild. It has been written that the inhabitants of the island of Cumana in Peru do the same. As for our

Tupinamba, they make an exception only of the hair on the head, which on all the males, from their youth onward, is shaved very close from the forehead to the crown, like the tonsure of a monk; behind, in the style of our forefathers or of those who let their hair grow, they have it trimmed on the neck.

To leave nothing out (if that is possible), I will also add this. There are certain grasses in that land with leaves about two fingers wide, which grow slightly curved both around and lengthwise, something like the sheath that covers the ear of the grain that we call "Saracen wheat." I have seen old men (but not all of them, and none of the young men or children) take two leaves of these grasses and arrange them together and bind them with cotton thread around their virile member; sometimes they wrapped it with handkerchiefs and other small pieces of cloth that we gave them. It would seem, on the face of it, that there remains in them some spark of natural shame, if indeed they did this on account of modesty, but, although I have not made closer inquiry, I am still of the opinion that it is rather to hide some infirmity that their old age may cause in that member.

To go on, they have the custom, which begins in the childhood of all the boys, of piercing the lower lip just above the chin; each of them usually wears in the hole a certain well-polished bone, as white as ivory, shaped like one of those little pegs that we play with over here, that we use as tops to spin on a table. The pointed end sticks out about an inch, or two fingers' width, and is held in place by a stop between the gums and the lip; they can remove it and put it back whenever they please. But they only wear this bodkin of white bone during their adolescence; when they are grown, and are called *conomi-ouassou* (that is, big or tall boy), they replace it by mounting in the lip-hole a green stone (a kind of false emerald), also held in place inside by a stop, which appears on the outside to be of the roundness and width of a festoon, with twice its thickness. There are some who wear a stone as long and round as a finger (I brought one such stone back to France). Sometimes when these stones are removed, our Tupinamba amuse themselves by sticking their tongues through that slit in the lip, giving the impression to the onlooker that they have two mouths; I leave you to judge whether it is pleasant to see them do that, and whether that deforms them or not. What is more, I have seen men who, not content with merely wearing these green stones in their lips, also wore them in both cheeks, which they had likewise had pierced for the purpose.

As for the nose: our midwives over here pull on the noses of newborn babies to make them longer and more handsome; however, our Americans, for whom the beauty of their children lies in their being pug-nosed, have the noses of their children pushed in and crushed with the thumb as soon as they come out of their mothers' wombs (just as they do in France with spaniels and other puppies). Someone else has said that there is a certain part of Peru where the Indians have such outlandishly long noses that they set in them emeralds, turquoises, and other white and red stones with gold thread.

Our Brazilians often paint their bodies in motley hues; but it is especially their custom to blacken their thighs and legs so thoroughly with the juice of a certain fruit, which they call *genipap*, that seeing them from a little distance, you would think they had donned the hose of a priest; and this black dye is so indelibly fixed on their skin that even if they go into the water, or wash as much as they please, they cannot remove it for ten or twelve days.

They also have crescent-shaped pendants, more than half a foot long, made of very even-textured bone, white as alabaster, which they name *y-aci*, from their name for the moon; they wear them hung from the neck by a little cord made of cotton thread, swinging flat against the chest.

Similarly, they take innumerable little pieces of a seashell called *vignol*, and polish them for a long time on a piece of sandstone, until they are as thin, round, and smooth as a penny; these they pierce through the center and string onto cotton threads to make necklaces that they call *boüre*, which they like to wear twisted around their necks, as we do over here with gold chains. I think this is what some people call "porcelain shell"; we see many women over here wearing belts of it. When I arrived back in France, I had more than fifteen feet of it, as fine as you might ever see. The savages also make these *boüre* of a certain kind of black wood, which is very well suited to this since it is almost as heavy and shiny as jet.

Our Americans have a great many ordinary hens, which the Portuguese introduced among them and for which they have a use that I will now describe. They pluck the white ones, and after they have boiled the feathers and the down and dyed them red with brazilwood, they cut them up finer than mincemeat (with iron tools since they have acquired them—before that with sharpened stones). Having first rubbed themselves with a certain gum that they keep for this purpose, they cover themselves with these, so that they are feathered all over: their bodies, arms, and legs all bedecked; in this condition they seem to be all downy, like pigeons or other birds newly hatched. It is likely that some observers, who upon their arrival saw these people thus adorned, went back home without any further acquaintance with them, and proceeded to spread the rumor that the savages were covered with hair. But, as I have said above, they are not so in their natural state; that rumor has been based on ignorance and too easily accepted.

In the same vein, someone has written that the people of Cuman anoint themselves with a certain gum or sticky unguent, and then cover themselves with feathers of various colors; they are not unhandsome in such a costume.

As for the head ornaments of our Tupinikin, aside from the tonsure in the front and the hair hanging down in back, which I have mentioned, they bind and arrange wing feathers of rosy or red hues, or other colors, to make adornments for their foreheads somewhat resembling the real or false hair, called "rackets" or "batwings," with which the ladies and young girls of France and of other countries over here have been decorating their heads; you would say that they have acquired this invention from our savages, who call this device *yempenambi.*

They also have pendants in their ears, made from white bone, of almost the same kind as the bodkin that the young boys wear in their pierced lips. Furthermore, they have in their country a bird that they call *toucan,* which (as I will later describe more fully) has a plumage as black as a crow's, except for a patch under the neck, which is about four fingers' width long and three wide, all covered with fine little yellow feathers, edged with red on the bottom. They skin off these patches (which they also call *toucan,* from the name of the bird that bears them), of which they have a large supply; after these are dry, they attach them with a wax that they call *yra-yetic,* one on each side of the face in front of the ears. These yellow plaques, worn on their cheeks, seem like two ornaments of gilded copper on the ends of the bit of a horse's bridle.

If our Brazilians go off to war, or if—as I will recount elsewhere—they ceremonially kill a prisoner in order to eat him, they want to be more gallantly adorned and to look more bold and valiant, and so they put on robes, head-dresses, bracelets, and other ornaments of green, red and blue feathers, and of other various true and natural colors of extreme beauty. When these feathers have been mixed and combined, and neatly bound to each other with very small pieces of cane and cotton thread (there is no feather-worker in France who could handle them better, nor arrange them more skillfully), you would judge that the clothes made of them were of a deep-napped velvet. With the same workmanship they make the ornaments for their wooden swords and clubs, which, decorated and adorned with these feathers so well suited and fashioned to this use, are a marvelous sight.

To finish off their outfitting: they procure from their neighbors great gray-hued ostrich feathers (which shows that there are some of these huge, heavy birds in certain parts of those lands, where, however, not to misrepresent anything, I myself have not seen any). Binding all the quill ends together, with the other ends of the feathers spread out like a little tent, or like a rose, they make a great cluster of plumes that they call *araroye.* They tie this around their hips with a cotton string, the narrow part next to the flesh, and the spread-out feathers facing outward. When

they are rigged out in this you would say (as it has no other purpose) that they were carrying a chicken-coop attached to their buttocks.

I will explain more fully in another place how the greatest warriors among them, in order to show their valor—especially to show how many enemies they have killed, and how many prisoners they have massacred to eat—make incisions in their breast, arms, and thighs; they then rub these slashes with a certain black powder, which makes the scars visible for life, as if they were wearing hose and doublets slit with great gashes in the Swiss fashion.

If it is a question of leaping, drinking and *caouinage* (which is just about their daily occupation), to have—besides their voices and the chants that they customarily use in their dances—something more to arouse their spirits, they gather a certain rather firm-skinned fruit of the size and approximately the shape of a water-chestnut. When these are dried and the pits removed, they put little stones inside them and string several of them together, making leggings that, when tied on, make as much noise as snail shells—indeed, almost as much as the bells we have over here (which they greatly covet).

They have a kind of tree in that region, which bears a fruit as big as an ostrich-egg, and of the same shape. The savages pierce it through the middle (as you see children in France pierce big walnuts to make rattles), then hollow it out and put little round stones into it, or else kernels of their coarse grain (of which I will speak later); they then pass a stick about a foot and a half long through it. In this way they make an instrument that they call a *maraca,* which rattles louder than a pig bladder full of peas, and which our Brazilians usually have in hand. When I discuss their religion, I will tell you the idea they have about this *maraca* and its sound once they have adorned it with beautiful feathers and consecrated it to the use that we will see.

There you have their natural condition, and the accoutrements and ornaments with which our Tupinamba customarily outfit themselves in their country. Besides all that, since we had carried in our ships a great quantity of cloth in red, green, yellow, and other colors, we had coats and multicolored breeches made for them, which we exchanged for food supplies, monkeys, parrots, cotton, long peppers, and other things of their region with which our seamen usually load their ships. Now some, with nothing else on their bodies, would sometimes put on these wide, sailor-style trousers, while others, on the contrary, would leave aside the trousers and put on only the jackets, which came down just to their buttocks. After they had gawked at each other a while and paraded around in these outfits (which gave us our fill of laughing), they would take them off and leave them in their houses until the desire came to don them again; they also did this with the hats and shirts we gave them.

Now that I have fully treated what can be said concerning the exterior of the bodies of the American men and of the male children, if you would picture to yourself a savage according to this description, you may imagine in the first place a naked man, well formed and proportioned in his limbs, with all the hair on his body plucked out; his hair shaved in the fashion I have described; the lips and cheeks slit, with pointed bones or green stones set in them; his ears pierced, with pendants in the holes; his body painted; his thighs and legs blackened with the dye that they make from the *genipap* fruit that I mentioned; and with necklaces made up of innumerable little pieces of the big seashell that they call *vignol.* Thus you will see him as he usually is in his country, and, as far as his natural condition is concerned, such as you will see him portrayed in the following illustration, wearing only his crescent of polished bone on his breast, his stone in the hole in his lip, and, to show his general bearing, his unbent bow and his arrows in his hands. To fill out this plate, we have put near this Tupinamba one of his women, who, in their customary way, is holding her child in a cotton scarf, with the child holding on to her side with both legs. Next to the three is a cotton bed, made like a fishing net, hung in the air, which is how they sleep in their country. There is also the figure of the fruit that they call ananas, which, as I shall describe hereafter, is one of the best produced in this land of Brazil.

For the second contemplation of a savage, remove all the flourishes described above, and after rubbing him with a glutinous gum, cover his whole torso, arms, and legs with little feathers minced fine, like red-dyed down; when you have made him artificially hairy with this fuzzy down, you can imagine what a fine fellow he is.

In the third place, whether he remains in his natural color, or whether he is painted or covered with feathers, attire him again in his garments, headdresses and bracelets so laboriously wrought of these beautiful natural feathers of various colors that I have described to you; when he is thus outfitted, you might say that he is in his full Papal splendor.

For the fourth description, leave him half-naked and half-dressed, in the way I have described him; give him the breeches and jackets of our colored cloth, with one of the sleeves green and the other yellow; you will judge that he no longer needs anything but a fool's bauble.

Finally, if you add to these the instrument called the *maraca* in his hand, the plumed harness that they call *araroye* on his hips, and his rattles made of fruits around his legs, you will then see him (as I will show him again later) equipped as he is when he dances, leaps, drinks, and capers about.

As for the rest of the devices that the savages use to bedeck and adorn their bodies, according to the description that I have just given: you would need several illustrations to represent them well, and even then you could not convey their appearance without adding painting, which would require a separate book. However, beyond what I have already said about them, when I come to speak of their wars and their arms, lacerating their bodies, and putting in their hands their wooden swords (or clubs), and their bows and arrows, I will portray them as more furious.

But for now let us leave a little to one side our Tupinamba in all their magnificence, frolicking and enjoying the good times that they know so well how to have, and see whether their wives and daughters, whom they call *quondam* (and in some parts, since the arrival of the Portuguese, *Maria*) are better adorned and decked out.

First, besides what I said at the beginning of this chapter—that they ordinarily go naked as well as the men—they also share with them the practice of pulling out all body hair, as well as the eyelashes and eyebrows. They do not follow the men's custom regarding the hair of the head: for while the latter, as I have said above, shave their hair in front and clip it in the back, the women not only let it grow long, but also (like the women over here), comb and wash it very carefully; in fact, they tie it up sometimes with a red-dyed cotton string. However, they more often let it hang on their shoulders, and go about wearing it loose.

They differ also from the men in that they do not slit their lips or cheeks, and so they wear no stones in their faces. But as for their ears, they have them pierced in so extreme a fashion for wearing pendants that when they are removed, you could easily pass a finger through the holes; what is more, when they wear pendants made of that big scallop shell called *vignol,* which are white, round, and as long as a medium-sized tallow candle, their ears swing on their shoulders, even over their breasts; if you see them from a little distance, it looks like the ears of a bloodhound hanging down on each side.

As for their faces, this is how they paint them. A neighbor woman or companion, with a little brush in hand, begins a small circle right in the middle of the cheek of the one who is having her face painted; turning the brush all around to trace a scroll or the shape of a snail-shell, she will continue until she has adorned and bedizened the face with various hues of blue, yellow, and red; also (as some shameless women in France likewise do), where the eyelashes and eyebrows have been plucked, she will not neglect to apply a stroke of the brush.

Moreover, they make big bracelets, composed of several pieces of white bone, cut and notched like big fish-scales, which they know how so closely to match and so nicely to join—with wax and a kind of gum mixed together into a glue—that it could not be better done. When the work is finished, it is about a foot and a half long; it could be best compared to the cuff used in playing ball over here. Likewise, they wear the white necklaces (called *boüre* in their language) that I have described above, but they do not wear them hung around the neck, as you have heard that the men do; they simply twist them around their arms. That is why, for the same use, they find so pretty the little beads of glass that they call *mauroubi,* in yellow, blue, green, and other colors, strung like a rosary, which we brought over there in great number for barter. Indeed, whether we went into their villages or they came into our fort, they would offer us fruits or some other commodity from their country in exchange for them, and with their customary flattering speech, they would be after us incessantly, pestering us and saying *"Mair, deagatorem, amabé mauroubi":* that is, "Frenchman, you are good; give me some of your bracelets of glass beads." They would do the same thing to get combs from us, which they call *guap* or *kuap,* mirrors, which they call *aroua,* and all the other goods and merchandise we had that they desired.

But among the things doubly strange and truly marvelous that I observed in these Brazilian women, there is this: although they do not paint their bodies, arms, thighs, and legs as often as the men do, and do not cover themselves with feathers or with anything else that grows in their land, still, although we tried several times to give them dresses and shifts (as I have said we did for the men, who sometimes put them on), it has never been in our power to make them wear clothes: to such a point were they resolved (and I think they have not changed their minds) not to allow anything at all on their bodies. As a pretext to exempt themselves from wearing clothes and to remain always naked, they would cite their custom, which is this: whenever they come upon springs and clear rivers, crouching on the edge or else getting in, they throw water on their heads with both hands, and wash themselves and plunge in with their whole bodies like ducks—on some days more than a dozen times; and they said that it was too much trouble to get undressed so often. Is that not a fine and pertinent excuse? But whatever it may be, you have to accept it, for to contest it further with them would be in vain, and you would gain nothing by it.

This creature delights so much in her nakedness that it was not only the Tupinamba women of the mainland, living in full liberty with their husbands, fathers, and kinsmen, who were so obstinate in refusing to dress themselves in any way at all; even our women prisoners of war, whom we had bought and whom we held as slaves to work in our fort—even they, although we forced clothing on them, would secretly strip off the shifts and other rags, as soon as night had fallen, and would not be content unless, before going to bed, they could promenade naked all around our island. In short, if it had been up to these poor wretches, and if they had not been compelled by great strokes of the whip to dress themselves, they would choose to bear the heat and burning of the sun, even the continual skinning of their arms and shoulders carrying earth and stones, rather than to endure having any clothes on.

And there you have a summary of the customary ornaments, rings, and jewelry of the American women and girls. So, without any other epilogue here, let the reader, by this narration, contemplate them as he will.

When I treat the marriage of the savages, I will recount how their children are equipped from birth. As for the children above the age of three or four years, I especially took great pleasure in watching the little boys, whom they call *conomi-miri;* plump and chubby (much more so than those over here), with their bodkins of white bone in their split lips, the hair shaved in their style, and sometimes with their bodies painted, they never failed to come dancing out in a troop to meet us when they saw us arrive in their villages. They would tag behind us and play up to us, repeating continually in their babble, *"Contoüassat, amabé pinda":* that is, "My friend and my ally, give me some fishhooks." If thereupon we yielded (which I have often done), and tossed ten or twelve of the smallest hooks into the sand and dust, they would rush to pick them up; it was great sport to see this swarm of naked little rascals stamping on the earth and scratching it like rabbits.

During that year or so when I lived in that country, I took such care in observing all of them, great and small, that even now it seems to me that I have them before my eyes, and I will forever have the idea and image of them in my mind. But their gestures and expressions are so completely different from ours, that it is difficult, I confess, to represent them well by writing or by pictures. To have the pleasure of it, then, you will have to go see and visit them in their own country. "Yes," you will say, "but the plank is very long." That is true, and so if you do not have a sure foot and a steady eye, and are afraid of stumbling, do not venture down that path.

We have yet to see more fully, as the matters that I treat present themselves, what their houses are like, and to see their household utensils, their ways of sleeping, and other ways of doing things.

Before closing this chapter, however, I must respond both to those who have written and to those who think that the frequenting of these naked savages, and especially of the women, arouses wanton desire and lust. Here, briefly, is what I have to say on this point. While there is ample cause to judge that, beyond the immodesty of it, seeing these women naked would serve as a predictable enticement to concupiscence; yet, to report what was commonly perceived at the time, this crude nakedness in such a woman is much less alluring than one might expect. And I maintain that the elaborate attire, paint, wigs, curled hair, great ruffs, farthingales' robes upon robes, and all the infinity of trifles with which the women and girls over here disguise themselves and of which they never have enough, are beyond comparison the cause of more ills than the ordinary nakedness of the savage women—whose natural beauty is by no means inferior to that of the others. If decorum allowed me to say more, I make bold to say that I could resolve all the objections to the contrary, and I would give reasons so evident that no one could deny them. Without going into it further, I defer concerning the little that I have said about this to those who have made the voyage to the land of Brazil, and who, like me, have seen both their women and ours.

I do not mean, however, to contradict what the Holy Scripture says about Adam and Eve, who, after their sin, were ashamed when they recognized that they were naked, nor do I wish in any way that this nakedness be approved; indeed, I detest the heretics who have tried in the past to introduce it over here, against the law of nature (which on this particular point is by no means observed among our poor Americans).

But what I have said about these savages is to show that, while we condemn them so austerely for going about shamelessly with their bodies entirely uncovered, we ourselves, in the sumptuous display, superfluity, and excess of our own costume, are hardly more laudable. And, to conclude this point, I would to God that each of us dressed modestly, and more for decency and necessity than for glory and worldliness.

Richard Hakluyt, "A Discourse Concerning Western Planting" (1584)

Reprinted in *The Collections of the Maine Historical Society* (1831–1906), Ser. 2, Vol. 2, pp. 152–61. Some spelling has been modernized.

CHAPTER XX

A BRIEF COLLECTION OF CERTAIN REASONS TO INDUCE HER MAJESTY AND THE STATE TO TAKE IN HAND THE WESTERN VOYAGE AND PLANTINGS THERE.

1. The soil yieldth and may be made to yield all the several commodities of Europe, and of all kingdomes, dominions, and territories that England tradeth with that by trade of merchandise cometh into this realm

2. The passage thither and home is neither to long nor to short but easy and to be made twice in the year. . . .

5. And where England now for certain hundreth years last passed, by the peculiar commodity of wools, and of later years by clothing of the same, hath raised itself from meaner state to greater wealth and much higher honour, mighty and power than before, to the equaling of the princes of the same to the greatst potentates of this part of the world it cometh now so to passe, that by the great endeavour of the increase of the trade of wools in Spain and in the West Indies, now daily more and more multiplying that the wools of England, and the clothe made of the same, will become base, and every day more base then other; which, prudently weighed yet behooveth this realm if it mean not to return to former olde means and baseness but to stand in present and late former honour, glory, and force, and not negligently and sleepingly to slide into beggery, to foresee and to plant at Norumbega or some like place, were it not for any thing else but for the hope of the vent of our wool endraped, the principal and in effect the only enriching continuing natural commodity of this realm. And effectually pursuing that course, we shall not only find on that tract of land, and especially in that firm northward (to whom warm clothe shall be right welcome), an ample vent, but also shall, from the north side of that firm, find out known and unknown islands and dominions replenished with people that may fully vent the abundance of that our commodity, that else will in few years wax of none or of small value by foreign abundance &c.; so as by this enterprise we shall shun the imminent mischief hanging over our heads that else must needs fall upon the realm without breach of peace or sword drawn against this realm by any foreign state; and not offer our ancient riches to scornful neighbors at home, nor sell the same in effect for nothing, as we shall shortly, if presently it be not provided for. . . .

6. This enterprise may stay the Spanish King from flowing over all the face of that waste firm of America, if we seat and plant there in time, in time I say, and we by planting shall [prevent] him from making more short and more safe returns out of the noble ports of the purposed places of our planting, then by any possibility he can from the part of the firm that now his navys by ordinary courses come from, in this that there is no comparison between the ports of the coasts that the King of Spain doth now possess and use and the ports of the coasts that our nation is to possess by planting at Norumbega. . . . And England possessing the purposed place of planting, her Majesty may, by the benefit of the seat having won good and royall havens, have plenty of excellent trees for masts of goodly timber to build ships and to make great navys, of pitch, tar, hemp, and all things incident for a navy royall, and that for no price, and without money or request. How easy a matter may yet be to this realm, swarming at this day with valiant youths, rusting and hurtful by lack of employment, and having good makers of cable and of all sorts of cordage, and the best and most cunning shipwrights of the world, to be lords of all those seas, and to spoil Phillip's Indian navy, and to deprive him of yearly passage of his treasure into Europe, and consequently to abate the pride of Spain and of the suporter of the great

Anti-Christ of Rome and to pull him down in equality to his neighbour princes, and consequently to cut of the common mischiefs that come to all Europe by the peculiar abundance of his Indian treasure, and this without difficulty.

7. . . . this realm shall have by that mean ships of great burden and of great strength for the defense of this realm, and for the defense of that new seat as need shall require, and with all great increase of perfect seamen, which great princes in time of wars want, and which kind of men are neither nourished in few days nor in few years. . .

10. No foreign commodity that comes into England comes without payment of custom once, twice, or thrice, before it come into the realm, and so all foreign commodities become dearer to the subjects of this realm; and by this course to Norumbega foreign princes customs are avoided; and the foreign commodities cheaply purchased, they become cheap to the subjects of England, to the common benefit of the people, and to the saving of great treasure in the realm; whereas now the realm become the poor by the purchasing of foreign commodities in so great a mass at so excessive prices.

11. At the first traffic with the people of those parts, the subjects of this realm for many years shall change many cheap commodities of these parts for things of high valor there not esteemed; and this to the great enriching of the *realm,* if common use fail not.

12. By the great plenty of those regions the merchants and their factors shall lie there cheap, buy and repair their ships cheap, and shall return at pleasure without stay or restraint of foreign prince; whereas upon stays and restraints the merchant raiseth his charge in sale over of his ware; and, buying his wares cheap, he may maintain trade with small stock, and without taking up money upon interest; and so he shall be rich and not subject to many hazards, but shall be able to afford the commodities for cheap prices to all subjects of the realm.

13. By making of ships and by preparing of things for the same, by making of cables and cordage, by planting of vines and olive trees, and by making of wine and oil, by husbandry, and by thousands of things there to be done, infinite numbers of the English nation may be set on work, to the unburdening of the realm with many that now live chargeable to the state at home.

14. If the sea coast serve for making of salt, and the inland for wine, oils, oranges, lemons, figs, &c., and for making of iron, all which with much more is hoped, without sword drawn, we shall cut the comb of the French, of the Spanish, of the Portingal, and of enemies, and of doubtful friends, to the abating of their wealth and force, and to the great saving of the wealth of the realm. . . .

16. Wee shall by planting there enlarge the glory of the gospel, and from England plant sincere religion, and provide a safe and a sure place to receive people from all parts of the world that are forced to flee for the truth of God's word.

17. If frontier wars there chance to arise, and if thereupon we shall fortify, yet will occasion the training up of our youth in the discipline of war, and make a number fit for the service of the wars and for the defense of our people there and at home.

18. The Spaniards govern in the Indies with all pride and tyranny; and like as when people of contrary nature at the sea enter into gallies, where men are tied as slaves, all yell and cry with one voice, *Liberta, liberta,* as desirous of liberty and freedom, so no doubt whensoever the Queen of England, a prince of such clemency, shall seat upon that firm of America, and shall be reported throughout all that tract to use the natural people there with all humanity, curtesy, and freedom, they will yield themselves to her government, and revolt clean from the Spaniard, and specially when they shall understand that she hath a noble navy, and that she aboundeth with a people most valiant for their defense. And her Majesty having Sir Frances Drake and other subjects already in credit with the Symerons, a people or great multitude already revolted from the Spanish government, she may with them and a few hundreths of this nation, trained up in the late wars of France and Flanders, bring great things to pass, and that with great ease; and this brought so about, her Majesty and her subjects may both enjoy the treasure of the mines of gold and silver, and the whole trade and all the gain of the trade of merchandisse, that now passeth thither by the Spaniards only hand, of all the commodities of Europe; which trade of merchandise only were of it self sufficient (without the benefit of the rich mine) to enrich the subjects, and by customs to fill her Majesty's coffers to the full. And if it be high policy to maintain the poor people of this realm in work, I dare affirm that if the poor people of England were five times so many as they be, yet all might be set on work in and by working linen, and such other things of merchandise as the trade into the Indies doth require.

19. The present short trades causeth the mariner to be cast of, and often to be idle, and so by poverty to fall to piracy. But this course to Norumbega being longer, and a continuance of the employment of the mariner, doth keep the mariner from idleness and from necessity; and so it cutteth of the principal actions of piracy, and the rather because no riche pray for them to take cometh directly in their course or any thing near their course.

20. Many men of excellent wits and of divers singular gifts, overthrown by . . . by some folly of youth, that are not able to live in England, may there be raised again, and do their country good service; and many needful uses there may (to great purpose) require the saving of great numbers, that for trifles may otherwise be devoured by the gallows.

21. Many soldiers and servitors, in the end of the wars, that might be hurtful to this *realm,* may there be unladen, to the common profit and quiet of this *realm,* and to our foreign benefit there, as they may be employed.

22. The frye [children] of the wandering beggars of England, that grow up idly, and hurtful and burdenous to this *realm,* may there be unladen, better bred up, and may people waste countries to the home and foreign benefit, and to their own more happy state.

23. If England cry out and affirm, that there is so many in all trades that one cannot live for another, as in all places they doe, this Norumbega (if it be thought so good) offereth the remedy.

Bibliography

Adorno, Rolena, and Pautz, Patrick Charles. *Álvar Núñez Cabeza de Vaca: His Account, His Life, and the Expedition of Pánfilo de Narváez*. 3 vols. Lincoln: University of Nebraska Press, 1999.

Ajayi, J. F. Ade, and Crowder, Michael, eds. *History of West Africa*. 3rd ed. London: Longman, 1985.

Appiah, Kwame Anthony, and Gates, Henry Louis, Jr., eds. *Africana: The Encyclopedia of African and African American Experience*. New York: Basic *Civitas* Books, 1999.

Bethell, Leslie, ed. *Colonial Brazil*. Cambridge, U.K.: Cambridge University Press, 1987.

Boxer, C.R. *The Portuguese Seaborne Empire, 1415–1825*. New York: Knopf: 1969.

Braudel, Fernand. *The Structures of Everyday Life: Civilization and Capitalism, 15th–18th Century*. 3 vols. New York: Harper & Row, 1981.

Braudel, Fernand, and Mollat du Jourdin, Michel, eds. *Le Monde de Jacques Cartier*. Paris: Berger-Levrault, 1984.

Clendinnen, Inga. *Ambivalent Conquests: Maya and Spaniard in Yucatan, 1517–1570*. Cambridge, U.K.: Cambridge University Press, 1987.

———. *Aztecs: An Interpretation*. Cambridge, U.K.: Cambridge University Press, 1991.

Coe, Michael. *Mexico: From the Olmecs to the Aztecs*. 4th ed. London: Thames & Hudson, 1994.

Cook, Noble David. *Born to Die: Disease and New World Conquest, 1492–1650*. Cambridge, U.K.: Cambridge University Press, 1998.

Cortés, Hernán. *Letters from Mexico*, trans. Anthony Pagden. New Haven, Conn.: Yale University Press, 1986.

Crosby, Alfred W. *Ecological Imperialism: The Biological Expansion of Europe, 900–1900*. Cambridge, U.K.: Cambridge University Press, 1986.

Davidson, Basil. *West Africa before the Colonial Era: A History to 1850*. London: Longman, 1998.

Doggett, Rachel, ed. *New World of Wonders: European Images of the Americas, 1492–1700*. Washington, D.C.: Folger Shakespeare Library, 1992.

Durán, Diego. *The History of the Indies of New Spain*, trans. Doris Heyden. Norman: University of Oklahoma Press, 1995.

Elliott, J. H. *The Old World and the New, 1492–1650*. Cambridge, U.K.: Cambridge University Press, 1970.

———. *Spain and Its World, 1500–1700*. New Haven, Conn.: Yale University Press, 1989.

Eltis, David. *The Rise of African Slavery in the Americas*. Cambridge, U.K.: Cambridge University Press, 2000.

Farriss, Nancy M. *Maya Society Under Colonial Rule: The Collective Enterprise of Survival*. Princeton, N.J.: Princeton University Press, 1984.

Fernandez-Armesto, Felipe. *Columbus*. Oxford, U.K.: Oxford University Press, 1991.

Flint, Valerie. *The Imaginary Landscape of Christopher Columbus*. Princeton, N.J.: Princeton University Press, 1992.

Fuentes, Patricia de. *The Conquistadors: First Person Accounts of the Conquest of Mexico*. Norman: University of Oklahoma Press, 1993.

Galloway, Patricia. *Choctaw Genesis, 1500–1700*. Lincoln.: University of Nebraska Press, 1995.

Grafton, Anthony. *New Worlds, Ancient Texts: The Power of Tradition and the Shock of Discovery*. Cambridge, Mass.: Harvard University Press, 1992.

Greenblatt, Stephen. *Marvelous Possessions: The Wonder of the New World*. Chicago: University of Chicago Press, 1991.

Hemming, John. *The Conquest of the Incas*. New York: Harcourt Brace Jovanovich, 1970.

———. *Red Gold: The Conquest of the Brazilian Indians, 1500–1760.* Cambridge, Mass.: Harvard University Press, 1978.

Henderson, John S. *The World of the Ancient Maya,* 2nd ed. Ithaca, N.Y.: Cornell University Press, 1997

Hillerbrand, Hans J., ed. *The Oxford Encyclopedia of the Reformation.* 4 vols. New York: Oxford University Press, 1996.

Hulme, Peter. *Colonial Encounters: Europe and the Native Caribbean, 1492–1797.* London: Methuen, 1986.

Josephy, Alvin M., Jr. *America in 1492: The World of the Indian Peoples Before the Arrival of Columbus.* New York: Knopf, 1992.

Kehoe, Alice Beck. *North American Indians: A Comprehensive Account.* 2nd ed. Englewood Cliffs, N.J.: Prentice Hall, 1992.

Kenseth, Joy, ed. *The Age of the Marvelous.* Hanover, N.H.: Hood Museum of Art/Dartmouth College, 1991.

Konstam, Angus. *Historical Atlas of Exploration, 1492–1600.* New York: Facts On File, 2000.

Kupperman, Karen Ordahl, ed., *America in European Consciousness, 1493–1750.* Chapel Hill: University of North Carolina Press, 1995.

———. *Indians and English: Facing Off in Early America.* Ithaca, N.Y.: Cornell University Press, 2000.

Larner, John. *Marco Polo and the Discovery of the World.* New Haven, Conn.: Yale University Press, 1999.

Las Casas, Bartolomé de. *A Short Account of the Destruction of the Indies,* ed. Anthony Pagden. London: Penguin, 1992.

León-Portilla, Miguel, ed. *The Broken Spears: The Aztec Account of the Conquest of Mexico.* Boston: Beacon Press, 1961.

Levenson, Jay A., ed. *Circa 1492: Art in the Age of Exploration.* Washington, D.C. and New Haven, Conn.: National Gallery of Art/Yale University Press, 1991.

Lockhart, James. *The Nahuas After the Conquest.* Stanford, Calif.: Stanford University Press, 1992.

McAlister, Lyle N. *Spain and Portugal in the New World, 1495–1700.* Minneapolis: University of Minnesota Press, 1984.

Oliver, Roland, and Crowder, Michael, eds. *The Cambridge Encyclopedia of Africa.* Cambridge, U.K.: Cambridge University Press, 1981.

Ozment, Steven. *The Age of Reform, 1250–1550.* New Haven, Conn.: Yale University Press, 1980.

Pagden, Anthony. *European Encounters with the New World.* New Haven, Conn.: Yale University Press, 1993.

Parry, J. H., and Keith, Robert G., eds. *New Iberian World.* 5 vols. New York: Times Books, 1984.

Phillips, William, Jr., and Phillips, Carla Rahn. *The Worlds of Christopher Columbus.* Cambridge, U.K.: Cambridge University Press, 1991.

Pritzker, Barry M. *A Native American Encyclopedia.* New York: Oxford University Press, 2000.

Quinn, David Beers. *Set Fair for Roanoke: Voyages and Colonies, 1584–1606.* Chapel Hill: University of North Carolina Press, 1985.

———, ed. *New American World.* 5 vols. New York: Arno, 1979.

Rouse, Irving. *The Tainos: Rise and Fall of the People Who Greeted Columbus.* New Haven, Conn.: Yale University Press, 1992.

Sacks, David Harris. *The Widening Gate: Bristol and the Atlantic Economy, 1450–1700.* Berkeley: University of California Press, 1991.

Sahagún, Bernardino de. *General History of the Things of New Spain,* trans. Arthur J. O. Anderson and Charles E. Dibble. 13 vols. Santa Fe: School of American Research and University of Utah, 1950–1982.

Schele, Linda, and Miller, Mary Ellen. *The Blood of Kings: Dynasty and Ritual in Maya Art.* New York: George Braziller, 1986.

Schwartz, Stuart B., ed. *Implicit Understandings: Observing, Reporting, and Reflecting on the Encounters Between Europeans and Other Peoples in the Early Modern Era.* Cambridge, U.K.: Cambridge University Press, 1994.

Segal, Ronald. *Islam's Black Slaves: The Other Black Diaspora.* New York: Farrar, Straus & Giroux, 2001.

Shaw, Thurstan, et al., eds. *The Archaeology of Africa: Foods, Metals, and Towns.* London: Routledge, 1993.

Spalding, Karen. *Huarochirí: An Andean Society under Inca and Spanish Rule.* Stanford, Calif.: Stanford University Press, 1984.

Sturtevant, William C., gen. ed. *Handbook of North American Indians.* 14 vols. to date. Washington, D.C.: Smithsonian Institution Press, 1978 –.

Tenenbaum, Barbara A., ed. *Encyclopedia of Latin American History and Culture.* 3 vols. New York: Scribner's, 1996.

Thomas, Hugh. *The Slave Trade: The History of the Atlantic Slave Trade, 1440–1870.* New York: Simon & Schuster, 1997.

Thornton, John. *Africa and Africans in the Making of the Atlantic World, 1400–1800.* 2nd ed. Cambridge, U.K.: Cambridge University Press, 1998.

Trigger, Bruce. *The Children of Aataentsic: A History of the Huron People to 1660.* Montreal: McGill-Queen's University Press, 1976.

Weber, David J. *The Spanish Frontier in North America.* New Haven, Conn.: Yale University Press, 1992.

Williamson, Edwin. *The Penguin History of Latin America.* London: Penguin, 1992.

Index

Boldface page numbers denote extensive treatment of a topic. *Italic* page numbers refer to illustrations; *c* refers to the Chronology; and *m* indicates a map.